The Prentice Hall
Custom Program for CIS

College of Southern Maryland

ITS 1015 The Information Age

PEARSON
Custom
Publishing

PEARSON
Prentice
Hall

Director of Database Publishing: Michael Payne
Executive Marketing Manager: Nathan Wilbur
Operations Manager: Eric M. Kenney
Development Editor: Amy Galvin
Production Manager: Jennifer Berry
Cover Designers: Blair Brown and Kisten Kiley

Cover Art: T/K

This special edition published in cooperation with Pearson Custom Publishing.

Printed in the United States of America.

Please visit our web site at *www.pearsoncustom.com*

Attention bookstores: For permission to return unused stock, call 800-428-4266.

ISBN–13: 9780536761866

ISBN–10: 0536761868

Package ISBN–13: 9780536761873

Package ISBN–10: 0536761876

PEARSON CUSTOM PUBLISHING
501 Boylston Street, Suite 900, Boston, MA 02116
A Pearson Education Company

Attention Students

How to Find Your Student Data Files

Some projects in this book begin from a student data file that has already been started for you. The student data files can be accessed from the enclosed CD-ROM or from the Custom PHIT Web site, www.pearsoncustom.com/customphit/datafiles

Because this is a custom book, student data file names are not always consistent with chapter numbers in your book's Table of Contents. Be sure that any student data file that you use exactly matches the file name cited in the chapter.

Files from the CD-ROM

As specifically directed in each project, navigate to the CD-ROM, and then save and rename the file according to the instructions in the project.

Files from www.pearsoncustom.com/customphit/datafiles

1 Decide where you want to store your student data files.

- If you are storing on the hard drive of your computer or on a network drive, you may want create a folder with an appropriate name on that drive.

- If you are storing on a removable storage device such as a USB flash drive, Zip® disk, or floppy disk, insert the device now.

2 From your Web browser, go to **www.pearsoncustom.com/customphit/datafiles**

3 Select the book that is the source of the files that you need.

4 From the list of the available resources, point to the link for the files you need, and then click the active link.

5 In the displayed dialog box, click the command to **Save** and then click **OK**.

6 In the displayed dialog box, navigate to the location where you decided to store your files—either in a folder on your hard drive or network drive, or on your removable storage device.

7 Click **Save** to begin the downloading process. When complete you can close your browser.

8 As specifically directed in each project, navigate to the location where you have stored the student data files and then save and rename the file according to the instructions in the project.

Contents

1

Why Computers Matter to You:

Becoming Computer Literate

From Chapter 1 of *Technology in Action, Complete*, Fifth Edition, Alan Evans, Kendall Martin, Mary Anne Poatsy. Copyright © 2009 by Pearson Education. Published by Prentice Hall. All rights reserved.

Why Computers Matter to You:

Becoming Computer Literate

1. What does it mean to be "computer literate"?

2. How does being computer literate make you a savvy computer user and consumer?

3. How can becoming computer literate help you in a career?

4. How can becoming computer literate help you understand and take advantage of future technologies?

5. What kinds of challenges do computers bring to a digital society, and how does becoming computer literate help you deal with these challenges?

ACTIVE HELPDESK

This chapter has no Active Helpdesks.

Why Should You Become Computer Literate?

It's safe to say that computers are nearly everywhere in our society. You find them in schools, cars, airports, shopping centers, toys, medical devices, homes, and in many people's pockets. You interact with computers almost every day, sometimes without even knowing it. Whenever you buy something with a credit card, you interact with a computer. And, of course, most of us can't imagine our lives without e-mail. If you don't yet have a home computer and don't feel comfortable using one, you still feel the impact of technology: countless ads for computers, cell phones, digital cameras, and an assortment of Web sites surround us each day. We're constantly reminded of the ways in which computers, the Internet, and technology are integral parts of our lives.

So, just by being a member of our society you already know quite a bit about computers. But why is it important to learn more about computers, becoming what is called computer literate? Being **computer literate** means being familiar enough with computers that you understand their capabilities and limitations, and know how to use them. Being computer literate means more than just knowing about the parts of your computer. The following are some other benefits:

- As a computer-literate individual, you can use your computer more wisely and be a more knowledgeable consumer.

- Computer-literate employees are sought after in most every vocation.

- Becoming computer literate will help you better understand and take advantage of future technologies.

In addition, understanding computers and their ethical, legal, and societal implications will make you a more active and aware participant in society.

Anyone can become computer literate—no matter what your degree of technical expertise. Being computer literate doesn't mean you need to know enough to program a computer or build one yourself. Just as with a car, you should know enough about it to take care of it and to use it effectively, but that doesn't mean you have to know how to build one. You should try to achieve the same familiarity with computers. In this chapter, we'll look at the ways in which computers can affect your life, now and in the future.

Todd
Davidson/Getty
Images/Stock
Illustration Source

SOUND BYTES

- Questions to Ask Before You Buy a Computer
- The History of the Personal Computer

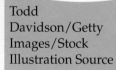

3

Becoming a Savvy Computer User and Consumer

One of the benefits of becoming computer literate is being a savvy computer user and consumer. What does this mean? The following are just a few examples of what it may mean to you:

- **Avoiding hackers and viruses.** Do you know what hackers and viruses are? Both can pose threats to computer security. Being aware of how hackers and viruses operate and knowing the damage they can do to your computer can help you avoid falling prey to them.

- **Protecting your privacy.** You've probably heard of identity theft—you see and hear news stories all the time about people whose "identities" are stolen and whose credit ratings are ruined by "identity thieves." But do you know how to protect yourself from identity theft when you're online?

- **Understanding the *real* risks.** Part of being computer literate means being able to separate the *real* privacy and security risks from things you don't have to worry about. For example, do you know what a cookie is? Do you know whether it poses a privacy risk for you when you're on the Internet? What about a firewall? Do you know what one is? Do you really need one to protect your computer?

- **Using the Internet wisely.** Anyone who has ever searched the Web can attest that finding information and finding *good* information are two different things. People who are computer literate make the Internet a powerful tool and know how to find the information they want effectively. How familiar with the Web are you, and how effective are your searches?

- **Avoiding online annoyances.** If you have an e-mail account, chances are you've received electronic junk mail, or **spam**. How can you avoid being overwhelmed by spam? What about adware and spyware—do you know what they are? Do you know what **software** (the programs that give commands to the computer) you should install on your computer to avoid online annoyances?

- **Being able to maintain, upgrade, and troubleshoot your computer.** Learning how to care for and maintain your computer (see Figure 1) and knowing how to diagnose and fix certain problems can save you a lot of time and hassle. Do you know how to upgrade your computer if you want more memory, for example? Do you know which software and computer settings can help you keep your computer in top shape?

- **Making good purchasing decisions.** Everywhere you go you see ads like the one in Figure 2 for computers and other devices: notebooks (laptops), printers, monitors, cell phones, digital cameras, and personal digital assistants (PDAs). Do you know what all the words in the ads mean? What is RAM? What is a CPU? What are MB, GB, GHz, and cache? How fast do you need your computer to be, and how much memory should you have? Understanding computer "buzz words" and keeping up-to-date with technology will help you better determine which computers and devices match your needs.

FIGURE 1

Being computer literate means that you understand what steps to take to avoid online annoyances and to protect yourself from identity theft.

SOUND BYTE

Questions to Ask Before You Buy a Computer

This Sound Byte will help you consider some important questions you need to ask when you buy a computer, such as whether you should get a notebook or a desktop, or whether you should purchase a new computer or a used or refurbished one.

FIGURE 2

Processor:	Intel® Core 2™ Extreme Quad-Core Processor, 8 MB L2 Cache, 1066 FSB
RAM:	2 GB Dual Channel DDR2 (667 MHz)
Video:	Dual 1GB NVIDIA GeForce 7950 GX2 Dual-GPU Graphics Cards, Quad SLI
Audio:	Creative Labs X-Fi Elite Pro; HDA 7.1 surround channel sound
Network:	Integrated Gigabit Ethernet
Optical Drive:	18x DVD-RW with LightScribe
Storage Drive:	500 GB Serial ATA 3Gb/s (7200 rpm)
Portable Storage:	13 in 1 Media Reader
Physics Accelerator:	Ageia PhysX Card
Ports:	6 USB 2.0 2 IEEE 1394
OS Provided:	Microsoft Windows Vista

NEW!

ViewSonic Corporation

- **Knowing how to integrate the latest technology with your equipment.** Finally, becoming computer literate means knowing which technologies are on the horizon and how to integrate them into your home setup when possible (see Figure 3). Can you connect your notebook to a wireless network? What is "Bluetooth," and does your computer "have" it? Can a device with a USB 2.0 connector be plugged into an old USB 1.0 port? (For that matter, what is a USB port?) How much memory should your cell phone have? Knowing the answers to these and other questions will help you make better purchasing decisions.

Being Prepared for Your Career

Computer careers are on the rise. Regardless of which profession you pursue, if computers are not already in use in that career, they most likely will be soon. **Information technology (IT)** is the set of techniques used in information handling and retrieval of information automatically. IT includes computers, telecommunications, and software deployment. IT careers are on the rise, and the seven fastest-growing occupations are computer related. Even if you are interested in some other career path, by 2010, 70 percent of the U.S. workforce will be using computers at work.

b) Hewlett-Packard Company; c) Handout/MCT/NewsCom; d) Apple/Splash News/NewsCom; f) SanDisk Corporation; g) Linksys Headquarters

FIGURE 3

Can you identify all of these devices? Do you know how to get them all to work well together?

Becoming truly computer literate—understanding the capabilities and limitations of computers and what you can do with them—will undoubtedly help you perform your job more effectively. It also will make you more desirable as an employee and more likely to earn more and grow your career. So, let's begin with a look at how computer systems are used in a wide range of careers. Whether you will become an employee in one of these industries or a user of their services, you will have a great advantage if you understand computer systems.

Computers in Today's World

We all are used to seeing computers at the checkout in stores, at the check-in at an airport, and so on, but there are a number of ways computers are being used that you probably weren't aware of. Before we begin looking at the parts of a computer and how it operates, let's take a look at a whole range of industries and examine how computers are a part of getting work done. Whether you are planning on a career in these fields or will just be a user of these products and services, your life will be affected by the use of computers in:

- Business
- Arts
- Education
- Legal System
- Agriculture
- Sciences

BUSINESS: WORKING IN A DATA MINE

Businesses accumulate a lot of data, but just how do they manage to make sense of all of it? How do they separate the anomalies from the trends? They use a process known as **data mining**, the process of searching huge amounts of data with the hope of finding a pattern. For example, large retailers often study the data gathered from register terminals to determine which products are selling on a given day and in a specific location. This helps managers

figure out how much merchandise they need to order to replace stock that is sold. Managers also use mined data to determine that for a certain product to sell well, they must lower its price—especially if they cut the price at one store and see sales increase, for example. Data mining thus allows retailers to respond to consumer buying patterns.

Did you ever wonder how Amazon.com can suggest purchases that fit your taste? Or how the site automatically displays a list of items people bought after they ordered the camera you just picked out? Data mining can keep track of the purchases customers are making along with their geographic data, past buying history, and lists of items they examined but did not purchase. This can be translated into very specific marketing, immediate and customized to your shopping experience. This is the motivation behind all of the "discount cards" that grocery stores and drug stores offer. In exchange for tracking your personal buying habits, they offer you some kind of special pricing. How much is your private information worth?

RETAIL: LET ME LOOK THAT UP FOR YOU

Wouldn't it be great to have your own shopping assistant working for you at your favorite store? While you look at items on the floor, your assistant could check the latest price, see whether similar items were on sale, and even offer you a better price if you bought it with a related item. If you weren't sure the product was exactly what you wanted, your shopping assistant could show you a video on how to use the product or e-mail the video and a brochure to your home so that you could read about the item at a more convenient time. This great life was once reserved only for the wealthy, but now wireless **PSSs (Personal Shopper Systems)** have arrived at retail stores, making personal shopping assistants available to everyone.

A PSS is a small handheld computer that you can pick up when you enter the store (see Figure 4). As you move about the store, scanning the item's tag or a label, the PSS pulls up the item's current price and any specials the store is offering. The PSS also may alert you to the availability of a

Why Computers Matter to You: Becoming Computer Literate

Marketing receives information on what products you purchased. When combined with information from other shoppers, promotional plans and prices can be adjusted accordingly.

Purchasing information helps Logistics and Fulfillment place orders with wholesalers to ensure the warehouse has adequate stock based on sales.

FIGURE 4

PSSs (Personal Shopper Systems) give a personal touch to each visit. They can offer special discounts based on your purchases, present videos of product information, and coordinate with inventory and checkout system software.

promotional video, or offer a special discount on the item. If you decide to buy, click the appropriate button, and place the item in your basket. If you'd rather think about it a bit more, the system can e-mail information about the product to you. At any time prior to leaving the store, you can check the total amount of your purchases, and the information will be integrated with the self-checkout lanes and with the point-of-sale (POS) software that runs the register. When it is time to leave, simply press the "end of trip" button and pay the total. There's no need to unload and individually scan the items in your shopping cart.

SHIPPING: DATA ON THE GO

Did you know that United Parcel Service (UPS) handles more than 14 million packages *per day*? Just how does the "brown" company ensure that all its customers' packages get from Point A to Point B without ending up forever at Point C? The company uses a sophisticated database and a very efficient package-tracking system that follows the packages as they move around the world.

For UPS, package tracking starts when the sender drops off a package and the company creates a "smart label" for the package (see Figure 5a). In addition to the standard postal bar code and a bar code showing UPS customer numbers, this smart label contains something called a MaxiCode. The MaxiCode is a specially designed scannable sticker that resembles an inkblot and contains all the important information about the package (class of service, destination, etc.). When the package is handled in processing centers, UPS workers scan the MaxiCode using wearable scanners on their wrists (see Figure 5b). These scanners use **Bluetooth technology** (a type of wireless communication) to transmit the scanned data through radio waves to a terminal. This terminal then sends the data across a wireless network, where it is recorded in the UPS database.

To track package delivery, UPS carriers use delivery acquisition devices (see Figure 5c) that feature wireless networking capability, infrared scanners (to scan the smart

FIGURE 5

(a) Package tracking starts at the point of sending by the generation of a smart label for the package. (b) Scanning is accomplished by wearable scanners. (c) Delivery personnel carry delivery acquisition devices that feature wireless networking capability, internal modems, infrared scanners, Global Positioning System (GPS) capabilities, and an electronic pad to capture customer signatures.

a) Photodisc/Getty Images; b) United Parcel Service; c) Symbol Technologies

labels and transmit the information back to the UPS database), and an electronic pad to capture customer signatures. By capturing all of this data and making it available on its Internet database, UPS enables its customers to track their packages. UPS is also able to make informed decisions about staffing and deploying equipment (trucks, airplanes, etc.) based on the volume and type of packages in the system at any given time.

Reprinted by permission

FIGURE 6

Artists like Virginia Twinam Smith display and sell their creations by using custom Web galleries such as Art Show (www.artshow.com).

ARTS: SHALL WE DANCE?

Some art students think that because they're studying art, there is no reason for them to study computers. However, unless you plan on being a "starving artist," you'll probably want to sell your work. To do so, you'll need to advertise to the public and contact art galleries to convince them to purchase or display your work. Wouldn't it be helpful if you knew how to create a Web site like the one shown in Figure 6?

But using computers in the arts goes way beyond using the Internet. The Atlanta Ballet, in conjunction with the Georgia Institute of Technology, is using computers to create virtual dancers and new performances for audiences. As shown in Figure 7, live dancers are wired with sensors that are connected to a computer that captures the dancers' movements. Based on the data it collects, the computer generates a virtual dancer on a screen. The computer operator can easily manipulate this virtual dancer as well as change the dancer's costume with a click of a mouse. This allows the ballet company to create new experiences for the audience by pairing virtual dancers with live dancers.

Of course, not all artwork is created using traditional materials, such as paint and canvas. Many artists today work exclusively with computers. Mastery of software programs such as Adobe Illustrator, Adobe Photoshop, and Flash (formerly

a-b) Stanley Leary/Georgia Tech Communications

Macromedia Flash) are essential to creating digital art.

Other artists are pushing the envelop of creating art with computers even further. For example, through her series *External Measures*, artist Camille Utterback uses a computer to create a work of art that reacts to the presence of—and the absence of—movement of the viewers in the gallery (see Figure 8). When no one is near the art piece, the image paints a small series of dots. However, as onlookers in the gallery move closer to the work, a camera mounted on the ceiling of the art gallery captures the movements and dimensions of the onlookers in the gallery. A computer with specialized software then uses this captured data to create smears of color and patterns of lines that reflect their movements. Because the image itself is created from the current and past movements and sizes of the gallery patrons, the work looks different to each person.

VIDEO GAMING: A LONG WAY FROM PAC-MAN

Revenues from video game sales in the United States are now larger than the movie industry's box office. Computer gaming is now a $10 billion industry in the United States alone and is projected to continue its rapid growth over the next decade. If you're a gamer, you know games must be creative to grab their audience. Large-scale games are impossible to create on your own—you must be part of a team. The good news is that because computer games are best developed for a local market by people native to that market, game development will most likely stay in the United States instead of being **offshored**, or sent to other countries, as many programming jobs have been.

What Can You Do with a Digital Home?

You're probably already using your computer in many different ways to fit your lifestyle. Perhaps you're ripping your CD collection to MP3 files so that you can transfer them from your computer to your iPod. Maybe you're burning a CD of all your favorite songs for a party you're having. But wouldn't it be great if you could manage the music for your party from the iPod iTunes software straight from your computer? And what about that video of your friend's birthday party you shot last week? You've already imported it to your computer, edited it, and added a music track. But when your friends come over for the party this weekend, wouldn't it be fun to be able to show them the video on the TV in the living room instead of having them crowd around your computer monitor?

So when in the future will you do all this? Right now, if you set up a digital home. Setting up a **digital home** means having an appropriate computer and digital devices, which are all connected to a home network. Let's look at the key components you need to have to have a digital home, some of which are shown in Figure 9.

1. **A Computer:** A computer is the nerve center of any digital home, allowing you to interface with all the different digital devices you have connected to the network. For a Windows-based computer (see Figure 10), you should opt for a computer running the current version of Microsoft Windows XP Media Center Edition (MCE) as its operating system. MCE is installed on specially constructed "Media Center" PCs. A typical Media Center PC includes the following components:

   a. **A TV Tuner:** A TV tuner allows your computer to receive television channels from a cable connection and display them on your computer monitor. In fact, you can install more than one TV tuner in your computer (MCE supports up to three tuners), which allows you to receive multiple television channels at the same time.

   b. **Digital Video Recorder Software:** In combination with a TV tuner, digital video recorder software allows you to turn your computer into a digital video recorder (like TiVo). Digital video recorders record TV programs like VCRs, but they use a hard drive (in this case, the computer's hard drive) to store the video instead of a videocassette. If you have multiple TV tuners installed in your computer, you can record several programs onto your computer's hard drive at the same time.

   c. **A Radio Tuner:** A radio tuner allows you to tune into Internet radio stations and record their broadcasts as digital files on your computer.

   d. **DVD and CD Players/Recorder:** To make it easy to transfer your audio or video files from one device to another, DVD and CD players/recorders allow you to record files onto DVDs and CDs instead of your hard drive.

   e. **A Web Browser:** In order to surf the Web and acquire digital content online (at music sites such as iTunes or Napster), your computer needs to have special Web browser software such as Internet Explorer installed.

a) Panasonic Corporation of North America; b) Hewlett-Packard Company; c) Reprinted with permission from Microsoft Corporation. d) Philips Consumer Electronics

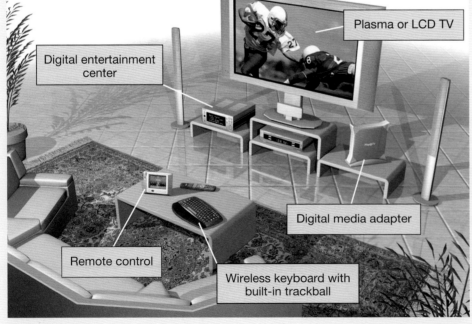

Plasma or LCD TV

Digital entertainment center

Digital media adapter

Remote control

Wireless keyboard with built-in trackball

FIGURE 9

You can create a digital home with only a few devices.

Microsoft Windows Vista Home Premium is an operating system that allows you to manage all your media entertainment from your computer.

f. **A Network Adapter:** A network adapter is a special device that is installed in your computer that allows it to communicate with other devices on a network. For digital devices to communicate with each other, they need to be connected to a network.

g. **Video and Music Players:** This special software (such as iTunes or Windows Media Player) enables you to play back or view digital content on your computer.

2. **A Network (Preferably Wireless):** Unless you're going to view digital and audio files on your computer only, you will need a network to transfer such files easily to other devices (such as televisions) in your home. A wireless network is preferable to a wired network, as it is easier to relocate devices. For example, suppose you rearrange your living room and need to move your TV to the opposite end of the room. If your TV was connected to a wired network, you might have to run a new cable or relocate the existing one. With a wireless network, you'd just move the TV and be done with it.

3. **A Digital TV:** Newer plasma and liquid crystal display (LCD) televisions (see inset, Figure 9) or High-Definition TVs (HDTVs) are an important part of any digital home because they enable you to best show off all your digital entertainment (digital photos, DVDs, and so on). Note that even if you don't have a plasma or LCD television, as long as you bought it within the last five years or so, you can probably use it to display digital content as well. However, televisions are not usually ready to be integrated into a network right out of the box. For this you need a digital media adapter.

4. **A Digital Media Adapter:** A digital media adapter (see inset, Figure 9) allows you to transfer media (such as video, digital photos, or MP3s) from your computer to your other media devices (such as your plasma TV). These devices are also known as media center extenders. Essentially, a digital media adapter allows you to integrate your TV into your home network. The digital media adapter is a device that you connect to your computer network (either wired or wirelessly) and then to your TV through specially designed audiovisual connectors.

5. **A Digital Entertainment Center:** While not a requirement, a digital entertainment center (see inset, Figure 9) is a device that makes your digital system much more manageable as it incorporates the functionality of a DVD player, a CD player/changer, an FM tuner, and a digital video recorder (DVR) all into one device. Instead of having individual devices cluttering up the living room, a digital entertainment center provides a compact solution for managing your digital media.

6. **Remote Controls:** Remote controls that work with your computer, digital media adapters, and digital devices allow you to control the digital devices and access your digital media (such as MP3 files) no matter what device in the house the media is stored on. Such remote controls also allow you to access the Internet directly so that you can download your favorite movies, surf the Web, or even view your e-mail on your TV. Devices such as the iPronto from Philips (see inset, Figure 9) come with software that allows you to program your own custom interface for the remote. You can even program macros that perform multiple commands with the press of a button

With these devices installed, you can get the maximum benefit from your computer and all your digital entertainment devices. When you're in your living room, you can play digital music files stored on your computer (in the den) for the party you're throwing. You can also display the video of your friend's birthday party (downloaded to your computer) on the TV for your friends to see. And when you're in your room, you can watch the latest episode of *CSI* that you recorded on your computer's hard drive, while your sister is simultaneously listening to MP3 files stored on your computer on the TV in the living room. For more information on creating a digital home, check out **www.intel.com/personal/digital-life/home/entertainment.htm**.

You'll need an in-depth knowledge of computers to pursue a career in game programming, or as a gaming artist. Mastering software animation tools such as 3ds Max will enable you to create compelling new worlds and new characters, like the Master Chief of Halo (see Figure 11).

Using powerful tools such as 3ds Max from Autodesk, game developers can create complex worlds and characters to satisfy the most demanding gamer.

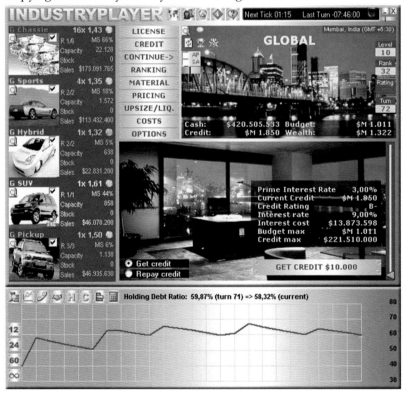

Internet applications have become sophisticated learning resources. IndustryPlayer.com allows students to compete online for domination of a global market while giving instructors the chance to introduce many business concepts.

EDUCATION: TEACHING AND LEARNING

Today's teachers need to be at least as computer savvy as their students. Computers are part of most schools, even preschools. And at many colleges, students are required to have their own computers. Courses are designed to use management software such as Blackboard or WebCT so that students can communicate outside of class, take quizzes online, and find their class materials easily. Teachers must therefore have a working knowledge of computers to integrate computer technology effectively into the classroom.

The Internet has obvious advantages in the classroom as a research tool for students, and effective use of the Internet allows teachers to expose students to places students otherwise could not access. There are simulations and instructional software on the Web that are incredible learning tools. Teachers can employ these to give students a taste of running a global business (see Figure 12) or experience how to dissect a human cadaver.

Many museums have virtual tours on their Web sites that allow students to examine objects in the museum collections. Often, these virtual tours include three-dimensional photos that can be viewed from all angles. So, even if you teach in Topeka, Kansas, you can take your students on a virtual tour of the Smithsonian Institution in Washington, D.C.

But what about when you actually want to take your students to visit museums firsthand? Today, technology is often used to enhance visitors' experiences at museums. New York's Museum of Modern Art, for example, offers PDA tours that provide visitors with additional information about the art they're viewing. By using a **personal digital assistant**, or **PDA** (a small device that enables users to carry digital information), you can listen to music that the artist listened to when he or she was creating the work or look at other works that reflect similar techniques or themes to the one you're viewing (see Figure 13). For more modern artists, you can watch interviews with the artist explaining his or her motivation for the work. You can even use the PDA to contact other members of your group and direct them to specific works you want them to see. Knowing how to use a PDA effectively

Sara Krulwich/The New York Times

FIGURE 13

Multimedia tours using PDAs and wireless technology are now commonplace in museums and galleries. Aside from providing additional contextual material to visitors (such as displaying similar works by other artists), such multimedia tours enable patrons to participate in opinion polls and to send messages to other museum visitors.

may help make a museum tour even more memorable.

Computers in the classroom will become more prevalent as prices continue to fall and parents demand that their children be provided with the necessary computer skills they need to be successful in the workplace. Therefore, as an educator, being computer literate will help you plan constructive computerized lessons for your students and use technology to interact with them.

LAW ENFORCEMENT: PUT DOWN THAT MOUSE—YOU'RE UNDER ARREST!

Today, wearing out shoe leather to solve crimes is far from the only method available to investigators trying to catch criminals. Computers are being used in police cars and crime labs to solve an increasing number of crimes. For example, facial reconstruction systems like the one shown in Figure 14 can turn a skull into a finished digital image of a face, allowing investigators to proceed with identification.

One technique modern detectives are using to solve crimes is to employ computers to search the vast number of databases on the Internet. Proprietary law enforcement databases such as the National Center for the Analysis of Violent Crime (NCAVC) database enable detectives to track a wealth of information about similarities between crimes, trying to detect patterns that may reveal serial crimes. Detectives are also using their knowledge of wireless networking to intercept and read suspects' e-mail messages or chat sessions when they're online, all from the comfort of a car parked outside the suspect's home (where legally permissible).

As detective work goes more high tech, so, too, does crime. To fight such high-tech crime, a law enforcement specialty called computer forensics is growing. **Computer forensics** is the application of computer systems and techniques to gather potential legal evidence. The ability to recover and read deleted or damaged files from a criminal's computer is already providing evidence for trials.

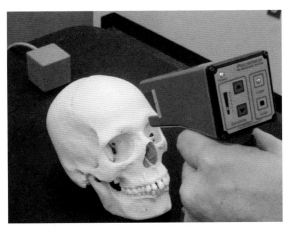

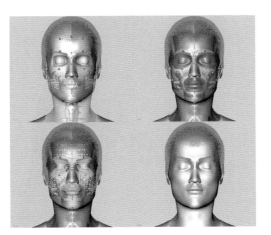

FIGURE 14

(a) The FastScan wand lets forensics teams quickly grab three-dimensional images of skulls and build wire 3D frameworks. (b) Tissue-rendering programs then add layers of muscles, fat, and skin to create faces that can be used to identify victims.

a) Polhemus/Fast Scan; b) HumanCore

Every day, businesses across the world use complicated forecasting models to make predictions about their sales and inventory levels. Thanks to recent technological advancements, law enforcement officials might soon have access to specialized software that can forecast criminal activity, helping police officers to take preventive measures to stop crime.

Don't believe it? Criminologists Jacqueline Cohen and Wilpen Gorr and computer scientist Andreas Olligschlaeger received funding from the U.S. Department of Justice to study police reports from Rochester, New York, and Pittsburgh, Pennsylvania. After entering the data about criminal offenses, precinct staffing, and patrol routes, the two researchers used trend-spotting programs to analyze the data. The result: the program was able to predict criminal activity before it happened an astounding 80 percent of the time. The key to the analysis was identifying and studying leading indicators that trigger crime sprees. Whereas consumer researchers may look at consumer spending patterns and levels of disposable income, criminologists study soft crime statistics such as disorderly conduct and trespassing. Increases in these types of crimes indicate that serious crimes may soon be on the rise. When a trend is identified, patrols in the area can be stepped up to try to head off crimes before they occur. Building, analyzing, and fine-tuning the models will keep law enforcement officials busy for years.

Even something as simple as parking enforcement uses computers today. Smart meters, such as the one shown in Figure 15, are being installed in major cities and can manage up to 10 parking spaces each. When you park in a space, you go to the meter and pay with cash, credit card, or your cell phone. The meter can even send a text message to your cell phone when your time is almost up so you can pay for more. The meter reports revenue and any malfunctions to the parking authority's central computer on a regular basis. Parking officials can access the meter remotely and change parking rates in response to usage patterns, scheduling of special events, or time of day. Parking enforcement officers have special PDAs that communicate wirelessly with the meters to determine when parked cars are in violation. The meters send information (such as the time, date, and location of the violation) to the PDAs, which makes generating tickets quicker and more accurate.

LEGAL SYSTEM: WELCOME TO THE VIRTUAL COURTROOM

In courtrooms today, videos of crimes in progress (often captured by cameras at convenience stores or gas stations) are sometimes shown to the jury to help them understand how the crime unfolded. But what happens if no surveillance camera recorded the crime? Paper diagrams, models, and still photos of the crime scene used to be the only choice for attorneys to illustrate their case. Now there is a much more exciting and lively alternative: computer forensics animations.

Computer forensics animations are extremely detailed (and often lifelike) recreations that have been generated with computers based on forensic evidence, depositions of witnesses, and the opinions of experts. Using sophisticated animation programs, similar to the ones used to cre-

a) Courtesy of Reino International, Ltd.;
b) Reino Parking Systems

FIGURE 15

(a) Smart parking meters, such as the one shown here and made by the Australian company Reino, let you pay with cash, credit card, or cell phone and can send a text message to your phone when your time is almost up. (b) Handheld devices help parking enforcement officers issue tickets faster and record the data from them more accurately.

ate movies such as *Cars*, forensic animators can depict one side's version of how events occurred, allowing the jury to watch it unfold.

Of course, being able to view sophisticated multimedia, televise trials, or record witness testimony for archiving requires modern courtrooms to be wired. Courtrooms such as Florida's Ninth Judicial Circuit Court (see Figure 16) are on the cutting edge, complete with robot-controlled video cameras that pivot to record whoever is speaking on the microphone at the time. Video images can be streamed directly to a Web site for immediate viewing or stored for archival purposes. Meanwhile, the judge has a touch-screen terminal to control the action in the courtroom, including turning on real-time closed-captioning by linking in the court reporter's transcription terminal. Lawyers have access to wireless touch-screen handheld devices that allow them to

access and display evidence they have stored on the courtroom's multimedia systems. Attorneys can also connect their own notebooks to the system, and audio recordings of all proceedings are captured and can be played back immediately.

Outside the courtroom, lawyers and other legal professionals use vast online legal libraries and databases, such as LexisNexis, to research cases and prepare for court.

AGRICULTURE: HIGH-TECH DOWN ON THE FARM

You might think that ranching and farming are low-tech operations that have little use for computers and software. After all, the growing season can't be changed by any computer program! But new technologies are changing life on farms and ranches in many ways.

FIGURE 16

Courtrooms such as Florida's Ninth Judicial Circuit Court are on the cutting edge.

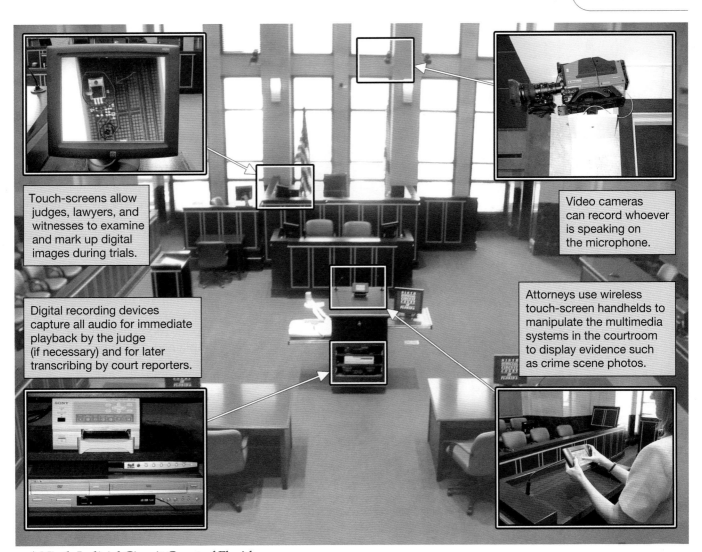

Touch-screens allow judges, lawyers, and witnesses to examine and mark up digital images during trials.

Digital recording devices capture all audio for immediate playback by the judge (if necessary) and for later transcribing by court reporters.

Video cameras can record whoever is speaking on the microphone.

Attorneys use wireless touch-screen handhelds to manipulate the multimedia systems in the courtroom to display evidence such as crime scene photos.

a-e) Ninth Judicial Circuit Court of Florida

Ranchers have many challenges in modern meat production. For example, they must watch for and prevent diseases like hoof and mouth, mad cow, and even an *E. coli* outbreak. The meat you purchase can be introduced to these dangers at many different places in the processing chain—from the ranch to the supermarket.

Fortunately, outbreaks can be managed and minimized with the use of **radio frequency identification tags (RFID tags)**. These RFID tags are small versions of the roadway electronic toll systems used in many states to automate paying tolls as you pass through the toll station. The RFID tag placed on each cow's ear is a very small button. When the cow walks past a panel reader, its location is automatically recorded and tracked in a database.

If a cow is identified as having disease, all of its movements have been recorded. By using the database that stores the RFID information, it is simple to identify exactly which food lots it ate from and which other animals ate from that same food, for example. Using RFID tags, potential crises can be averted, or at least better controlled.

In cranberry bogs, computer technology is being used in some interesting ways. For example, cranberry crops easily can be destroyed by frost. In the past, growers had to race to protect the bogs of berries on cold nights by turning on pumps to force out water to surround the berries and keep them from freezing. Today, growers use a Web-based system that can automatically control the pumps. It analyzes information about the time, the temperature measured near the berries, watering schedules, rainfall, and wind conditions and then automatically turns on and off the pumps around the bog fields as needed.

MEDICINE: FACT OR FICTION?

In movies set in the distant future, humans can sometimes interface with computers just by thinking and looking at a screen or monitor. Until recently, such scenes took place only in movies. But since 2006 companies like Cyberkinetics have been working to understand the human neural interface system. In testing of its software, known as BrainGate, a man suffering from Amyotrophic Lateral Sclerosis, or ALS (also known as Lou Gehrig's Disease), who no longer had any control of muscle movement, is able to control the movement of a robotic arm. The BrainGate software translates his thoughts into commands to the robotic limb. The patient has a tiny array of microelectrodes implanted in his brain (see Figure 17). The computer equipment receiving data from his neural activity identifies the impulses that the brain associates with physical movement (of his arm, for example) and then translates the instructions into commands to the robot. Patient Stephen Heywood explained, "After being paralyzed for so long, it is almost impossible to describe the magical feeling of imagining a motion and having it occur."

In addition to being an integral part of many medical research projects, computers are helping doctors and nurses learn their trades. Training for physicians and nurses can be difficult at best. Often, the best way for medical students to learn is to experience a real emergency situation. The problem is that students are then confined to watching as the emergency unfolds, while trained per-

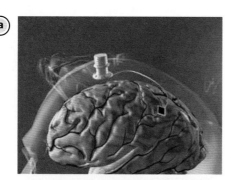
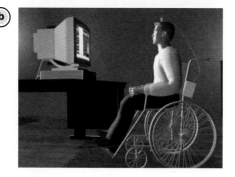

a-b) Courtesy of Cyberkinetics Neurotechnology Systems, Inc.

FIGURE 17

(a) The BrainGate Neural Interface is implanted in the patient's body. A silicon chip studded with microelectrodes is embedded in the brain and is connected to a signal converter, which is in turn connected to a computer (b). The converter sees how neurons fire when the patient thinks certain thoughts and begins to recognize patterns, which are then translated into commands to a robotic arm.

sonnel actually care for patients. Students rarely get to train in real-life situations, and when they do, a certain level of risk is involved.

Medical students are now getting access to better training opportunities thanks to a computer technology called a **patient simulator** (shown in Figure 18). Patient simulators are life-sized mannequins that can speak, breathe, and blink (their eyes respond to external stimuli). They have a pulse and a heartbeat, and they respond just like humans to procedures such as the administration of intravenous drugs.

Medical students can train on patient simulators and experience firsthand how a human would react to their treatments. The best thing about these "patients" is that if they "die," students can restart the computer simulation and try again. Even the U.S. military is using patient simulators to train medics to respond to terrorist attacks that employ chemical and biological agents.

Even more exciting than patient simulators is the work progressing on modeling complete human biological systems. The Physiome Project began as the brainchild of the Bioengineering Institute in Auckland, New Zealand. It now is a global **public domain** effort (not covered by copyright) in which bioengineers are creating realistic computer simulations of all systems and features of the human anatomy. They recently completed a digital re-creation of the human heart and lungs (shown in Figure 19).

Although the current system models a *theoretical* human's lungs, researchers hope to one day use computers to simulate a *specific* person's anatomical systems. With such a system, imaging scans (CTs, MRIs, etc.) of your body and a sample of your DNA would be fed into a computer, which would create an *exact* computer model of your body. This would allow doctors to experiment with different therapies to see how you would react to specific treatments. A great deal of work is still to be done before this treatment becomes a reality, but computer-literate medical professionals will be needed to make it happen.

Surgeons are even using computer-guided robots to perform surgery. Surgeons are often limited by their manual dexterity and can have trouble making small, precise incisions. So how can robots help? Robotic surgery devices can exercise much finer control when making delicate incisions than can

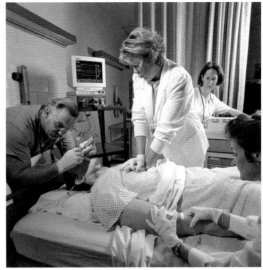

Medical Education Technologies, Inc. (METI)

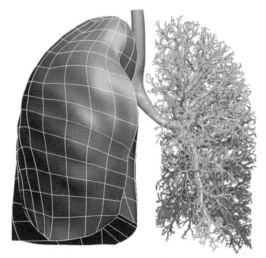

Reprinted by permission of Maryn Tawhai, Physiome Project

a human guiding a scalpel. To use the robots, doctors look into a surgery control device where they manipulate controls that move robotic devices hovering over the patient (see Figure 20). One robot control arm contains a slender imaging rod that allows the doctor to see inside the patient when the rod is inserted into the patient. Doctors can now perform a coronary bypass by making two small incisions in the patient and inserting the imaging rod in one incision and another robotic device with a scalpel into the other. The ability to make small incisions instead of the large ones required by conventional surgery means less trauma and blood loss for the patient. Theoretically, surgeons do not even have to be in the same room as the patient, although this remote method has not yet been

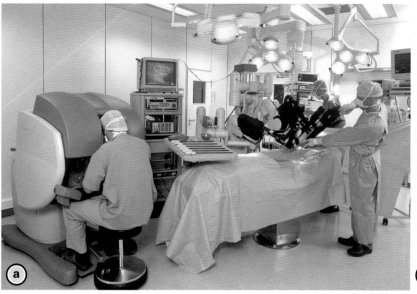

(a)

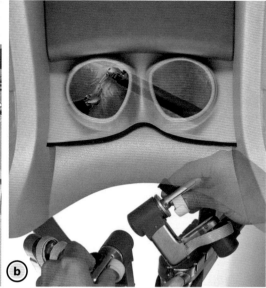

(b)

Surgeons use computer-guided robots, such as the da Vinci Surgical System from Intuitive Surgical, to perform surgery. (a) Here, a doctor looks into the control device where he manipulates controls that move the robotic devices hovering over the patient. (b) This is what surgeons see as they operate on the patient.

Courtesy of Dr. Peter Fromherz/Max Planck Insitute of Biochemistry

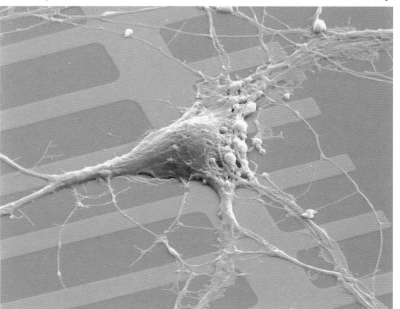

Researchers are experimenting with implantable chips such as this one. Here, we see a nerve cell on a silicon chip. The cell was cultured on the chip until it formed a network with nearby cells. The chip contains a transistor that stimulates the cell above it, which in turn passes the signal to neighboring neurons. Chips such as these could be used to repair nerve damage and restore movement or sensation to parts of the body.

attempted They could be thousands of miles away, controlling the movements of the robotic devices from a control station.

BIOMEDICAL IMPLANTS: THE CHIP WITHIN

When you mention implanting technology into the human body, some people conjure up images of the Terminator, a cybernetic life form from the future that looks human but is mostly machine. The goal of modern-day biomedical chip research is to provide technological solutions to physical problems and to provide a means for positively identifying individuals (see Figure 21).

One potential application of biomedical chip implants is to provide sight to the blind. Macular degeneration and retinitis pigmentosa are two diseases that account for the majority of blindness in developing nations. Both diseases result in damage to the photoreceptors contained in the retina of the eye. (Photoreceptors convert light energy into electrical energy that is transmitted to the brain, allowing us to see.) Researchers are experimenting with chips that contain microscopic solar cells and are implanted in the damaged retina of patients. The idea is to have the chip take over for the damaged photoreceptors and transmit electrical images to the brain. Although these chips have been tested in patients, they have not yet restored anyone's sight. But uses of biomedical chips such as these illustrate the type of medical devices you may "see" in the future.

One type of chip is already being implanted in humans as a means of verifying a person's identity. Called the VeriChip, this "personal ID chip" is about the size of a grain of rice and is implanted underneath the skin. When exposed to radio waves from a scanning device, the chip emits a signal that transmits its unique serial number to the scanner. The scanner then connects to a database that contains the name, address, and medical conditions of the person in whom the chip has been implanted.

Hitachi has a similar device, called the μ- chip (mu-chip), which is smaller than the period at the end of this sentence (see Figure 22). The μ-chip could be easily attached to, or ingested by, a person without his or her knowledge.

The creators of the VeriChip envision it speeding up airport security and being used together with other devices (such as electronic ID cards) to provide tamperproof security measures. If someone stole your credit card, that person couldn't use it if a salesclerk had to verify your identity by scanning a chip in your arm before authorizing a transaction.

Currently, nonimplant versions of identity chips are used in hospitals. Attached with bands to newborn infants the hospital staff can monitor the location of any baby instantly. Elevators and doors are designed to allow only certain people to enter with a specific baby, even if the hospital power is interrupted. Although the use of these tags is becoming more commonplace, it remains to be seen whether the general public will decide that the advantages of having personal identity and medical data quickly available justifies having chips implanted into their bodies.

SIMULATIONS: THE SIMS IS JUST THE BEGINNING

Thanks to a partnership between the National Severe Storms Lab and the National Center for Supercomputing Applications (NCSA), tornado forecasting may be getting more accurate. Scientists have been able to create a model so detailed it takes *nine days* for a supercomputer to generate, even though the computer is executing four billion operations *each second*. Simulations model the structure of

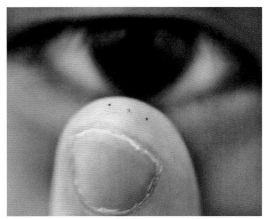

Reuters/Eriko Sugita/Landov LLC

FIGURE 22

No bigger than the period at the end of this sentence, the Hitachi μ-chip can hold digital information, which can then be read when it passes a detector. A triumph of technology or a cause for concern?

solar magnetic flares, which can interfere with broadcasts on Earth (see Figure 23). By studying the data produced by these simulations, forecasters hope to improve their predictions about weather phenomena.

Other technological applications in the sciences are being used on some of the oldest sites on Earth. The ancient site of Pompeii has been under the intense scrutiny of tourists and archaeologists for decades. Sadly, all the foot traffic and exposure to the elements is eroding portions of the ruins. Today scientists are using three-dimensional scanners and imaging software to capture a detailed record of the current condition of the ruins (see Figure 24). The virtual recreation of the ruins is so lifelike that archaeologists can study the ruins on-screen instead of at the actual site. Using the scans

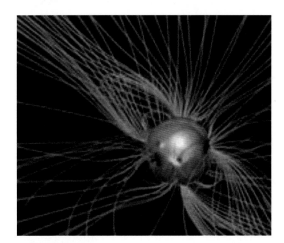

FIGURE 23

A simulation from the University of Michigan shows the structure of the magnetic fields around the sun and how they change in time.

University of Ferrara, Dept. of Architecture-Cy-Ark Foundation of Pompeii

as well as satellite imagery, aerial photography, and other data, scientists will eventually be able to re-create missing portions of the ruins in a virtual model. And scientists won't stop at Pompeii: this method will soon be used to make records of other decaying sites.

SPORTS SCIENCES: COMPUTE YOUR WAY TO A BETTER GAME

Want to be a world-class swimmer or baseball player? Getting an Olympic-caliber coach and training for hours every day are no longer enough. To get that competitive edge, you really need to use a computer.

That's right, computers are now being used to help athletes analyze their performance and improve their game. How does this work? First, video recordings are made of the athlete in action. The video is then transferred into special motion analysis software on a computer. This software measures the exact angles of the athlete's body parts as they progress through ranges of motion, such as the angle of a baseball player's left arm relative to his body as he swings the bat. Minor adjustments can be made on the computer regarding positioning of body parts and the force used in performing various movements. This helps baseball players, for example, enhance their performance by determining what adjustments they should make to hit the ball harder and farther.

BITS AND BYTES

NASA Wants You. . . to Learn

As you read this chapter, hundreds of satellites are orbiting the globe taking wonderfully detailed pictures of Earth. Until recently, these photos weren't available to the general public. However, thanks to NASA (and U.S. taxpayer dollars) and some savvy software developers, an application called World Wind is now making some 10 trillion bytes of imagery available to you. Need a picture of Mount Fuji for your science project or an aerial picture of your house for your PowerPoint presentation? Just download the software from **http://learn.arc.nasa.gov**, and you're ready to go. You'll find several terrific learning applications here as well. Virtual Lab lets you pretend you have your own scanning electron microscope, and What's the Difference takes you on a tour of the planets, complete with information about their composition and atmosphere and fly-throughs. With a few clicks you can have these interactive learning resources that open the world to you.

The United States Olympic Training Center in Colorado makes extensive use of computers in training athletes such as swimmers. The major objective of training swimmers to swim faster is to reduce drag from the water and minimize turbulence (which also can slow down a swimmer). Software has been developed that simulates the way water flows around the parts of a swimmer's body when in motion. Coaches can use the software to experiment with small changes in the position of a swimmer's arms or legs to determine whether turbulence and drag are reduced. The coaches can then train the swimmers to use the new techniques to improve their strokes and speed.

Aren't planning on competing in the next Olympics or playing in the major leagues? How about improving your weekend golf game? Employees in golf shops are now using sophisticated motion capture equipment to improve golfers' swings. To have your golf swing analyzed, golf shop personnel hook you up into shoulder, leg, and hip harnesses containing motion sensors (see Figure 25). As you swing away at a variety of shots (drives, chips, and so on), computers capture information about the motion of your swing, which is then compared to a database of the ideal positions of pro golfers. Trainers then suggest adjustments you can make so that your swing more closely emulates that of successful golfers. Even weekend warriors can benefit from high-tech analysis.

The equipment athletes use is also getting a technology boost. Even in a sport like soccer, where not much equipment is involved, technology is making an impact. Adidas is developing a new soccer ball that contains an integrated circuit chip. When the "Smartball" crosses the goal line, it sends a radio signal to the referee's watch. The ball is not yet approved for World Cup play, but you can expect to see Smartballs showing up in professional soccer matches soon.

NANOTECHNOLOGY: THE NEXT BIG THING IS SMALL

Have you ever heard of nanoscience? Developments in computing, based on the principles of nanoscience, are being touted as the next big wave in computing. Ironically, this realm of science focuses on very small objects. In fact, **nanoscience**

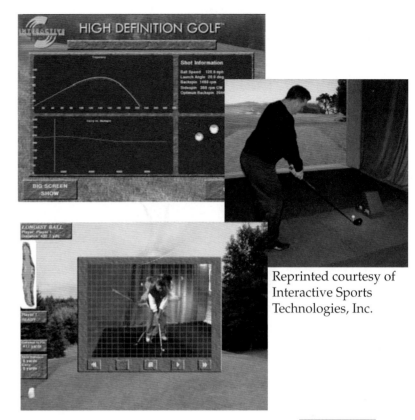

Reprinted courtesy of Interactive Sports Technologies, Inc.

involves the study of molecules and structures (called nanostructures) whose size ranges from 1 to 100 nanometers.

How big is this? The prefix *nano* stands for one-billionth. Therefore, a nanometer is one-billionth of a meter. To put this in perspective, a human hair is approximately 50,000 nanometers wide. Put side by side, 10 hydrogen atoms (the simplest atom) would measure approximately 1 nanometer. Anything smaller than a nanometer is just a stray atom or particle floating around in space. Therefore, nanostructures represent the smallest human-made structures that can be built.

Nanotechnology is the science revolving around the use of nanostructures to build devices on an extremely small scale. Right now, nanoscience is limited to improving existing products such as enhancing fibers used in clothing with coatings so that they repel stains or don't wrinkle (see Figure 26). However, someday scientists hope to use nanostructures to build computing devices too small to be seen by the naked eye. Nanowires, which are extremely small conductors, could be used to create extremely small pathways in computer chips. Developments such as this could lead to computers the size of a pencil eraser that

FIGURE 26

Composed of vaporized gallium nitrate condensed on a silicon wafer, this beautiful grouping of "nanoflowers" is composed of tiny silicon carbide wires. Each "flower" is about one-hundredth the size of a human hair. These "flowers" show a remarkable ability to repel water, which may make them useful for material coatings.

FIGURE 27

This Nanocar was constructed from a single molecule by a team at Rice University. The car can be used to deliver drugs or carry information within computer chips.

will be far more powerful than today's desktop computers.

If you've ever watched *Star Trek*, you know that "nanoprobes" (tiny machines that can be injected into the bloodstream) have already been envisioned. But nanotechnology is a relatively new field (less than 15 years old). Researchers are just beginning to use carbon nanotubes to create devices that deliver medicine and information (see the nanocar in Figure 27). We are still a long way from developing nanoscale machines, and some scientists don't think this will ever be possible. However, researchers are investigating the use of nanostructures to deliver precise doses of drugs on a molecule-by-molecule basis within the human bloodstream. Universities and government laboratories are investing billions of dollars in nanotechnology research every year. If you have an interest in science and engineering, this is the time to pursue an education in nanoscience.

AFFECTIVE COMPUTING: YOU SHOULD SMILE... NOW

Science fiction shows and movies such as *Star Wars* have always been populated with robots that emulate humans, seemingly effortlessly. So, when will we have C-3PO, R2-D2, or the Terminator laughing at our jokes or bringing us our favorite snack when they recognize we're sad? It is a question that pushes us to explore the nature of being human and the nature of machines.

Research is being conducted now to develop computer systems that respond to human affect and emotional expression and to enable computer systems to develop social and emotional skills. **Affective computing** is computing that relates to emotion or deliberately tries to influence emotion. Most computers with which you are familiar can perform calculations and the tasks for which they are programmed much faster than humans, but they fail miserably in reading your expression or modifying their behavior based on your frustration. This wide gap in the computing abilities of computers versus their emotional abilities is the target of research in affective computing.

One project to emerge is the Emotional-Social Prosthesis device (ESP), developed by a group at the MIT Media Lab. The ESP system is targeted at helping people who have autism. Autistic individuals can have very high intelligence but do not easily sense nonverbal cues, such as facial expressions and tone of voice. ESP is a wearable system that isolates the movements and facial expressions of people, interprets what their mood and intention probably are, and communicates this information back to the user. Another project is the creation of computers that can analyze a person's movements, watch their use of the mouse, and interpret the pressure patterns on the chair in which the person is seated. That data is then used to determine the individual's level of attention. The computer could then interrupt the individual who is beginning to lose concentration and refocus him or her on a certain task.

While engineers work to create computers that can understand us emotionally, computer systems are also evolving toward a more human appearance. Teams at the University of Michigan, Ohio State University, and the French Institute of Computer Science Research are working on robots that move in a more human fashion. Their biped (two-legged) robot Rabbit (see Figure 28), which is able to walk, run, and climb stairs, may lead to industrial robots that can tackle new tasks for us.

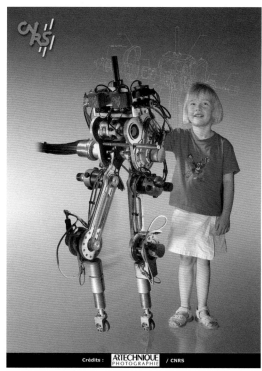

Crédits : ARTECHNIQUE PHOTOGRAPHIE / CNRS

Laboratoire de Automatique de Grenoble/rabbit

FIGURE 28

The Rabbit robot moves on two legs and is remarkably stable. By understanding how to create robots that can walk, hop, and maintain their balance, scientists push into new areas of automation.

Understanding the Challenges Facing a Digital Society

Part of becoming computer literate is also being able to understand and form knowledgeable opinions on the challenges facing a digital society. Although computers offer us a world of opportunities, they also pose ethical, legal, and moral challenges and questions. For example, how do you feel about the following?

SOUND BYTE

The History of the Personal Computer

In this Sound Byte, you will explore the history of the personal computer, including the events that led to the development of today's computers and the people who made them possible.

- Since the tragic events of September 11, 2001, various nationwide surveillance programs have been proposed. Some programs include installing surveillance cameras in public places that could be considered attractive areas to stage terrorist activities. These cameras would be monitored via the Internet, possibly by volunteers. Should the government be allowed to monitor your activities in public places à la George Orwell's famous book *1984* to help keep the country secure?

- Advances in technology in surveillance devices (see Figure 29) are allowing these devices to become smaller and less noticeable. In certain jurisdictions, courts have upheld the rights of employers to install surveillance devices in the workplace (sometimes without needing to notify employees) for the purposes of cutting down on theft and industrial espionage. Do you know if your employer is watching you? Do you think your employer should have this right?

FIGURE 29

With cameras becoming smaller, you could be under surveillance at any time and not even know it. Should the government be allowed to install cameras to monitor sensitive sites for criminal or terrorist activity, or should your privacy be respected?

TBO Technology

AP WorldWide Photos

FIGURE 30

Does downloading music without paying for it hurt anyone? Or is it merely a cost absorbed by huge record companies? What choices do you have to impact the issue?

- Many employees don't know that employers have the right to monitor e-mail and network traffic on the systems they use at work, because those systems are provided at the employer's expense for the sole purpose of allowing employees to do their jobs. Have you visited Web sites that you don't want your employer to know about (such as employment sites as part of a new job search)? Been sending personal e-mail through your company e-mail system? Does your employer know about these activities? Should employers have the right to know?

These are just a few examples of the kind of questions active participants in today's digital society need to be able to think about, discuss, and, at times, take action on. Being computer literate enables you to form *educated* opinions on these issues and to take stands based on accurate information rather than media hype and misinformation. Here are a few other questions you, as a member of our digital society, may be expected to think about and discuss:

- What privacy risks do biomedical chips such as the VeriChip pose? Do the privacy risks of such chips outweigh the potential benefits?
- Should companies be allowed to collect personal data from visitors to their Web site without their permission?
- Should spam be illegal? If so, what penalties should be levied on people who send spam?
- Is it ethical to download music off the Web without paying for it (see Figure 30)? What about copying a friend's software onto your computer?
- What are the risks involved in humans attempting to create computers that can learn and become more human?
- Should we rely solely on computers to provide security for sensitive areas such as nuclear power plants?

As a computer user, you must consider these and other questions to define the boundaries of the digital society in which you live.

ETHICS IN IT

Ethics: Knowledge Is Power—Bridging the Digital Divide

What would your life be like if you had never touched a computer because you simply couldn't afford one? What if there were no computers in your town? If you're like most people in the United States, access to computers is a given. But for many people, access to the opportunities and knowledge computers and the Internet offer is impossible. The discrepancy between the "haves" and "have-nots" with regards to computer technology is commonly referred to as the **digital divide**.

This discrepancy is a growing problem. People with access to computers and the Internet (that is, those who can afford it) are poised to take advantage of the many new developments technology offers, whereas poorer individuals, communities, and school systems that can't afford computer systems and Internet access are being left behind.

For example, in the United States, more teachers are using the Internet to communicate with parents than ever before. E-mail updates on student progress, Web sites with homework postings that allow parents to keep tabs on assignments, and even online parent/teacher conferences are becoming popular. Unwired parents and students are left out of the loop. In the United States, children who do not have access to the Internet and computers won't be prepared for future employment, contributing to the continuing cycle of poverty.

But the digital divide isn't always caused by low income. Terrain can be a factor that inhibits connectivity (see Figure 31). In Nepal's mountainous terrain, even though a village might only be a few miles away "as the crow flies," it might take two days to hike there because of the lack of roads. Volunteers, funded by a generous donor, have installed 12 outdoor access points complete with directional antennas to connect a series of villages to the Internet via a wireless network. The last access

Hugh Sitton/Corbis Zefa Collection

FIGURE 31

Terrain (such as mountains) and remote locations (like the Sahara Desert) can present barriers to conquering the digital divide.

point in the connectivity chain connects to an Internet service provider 22 miles away. The villagers are now able to hold meetings, school classes, and access the Internet without trekking across miles of mountainous terrain. Unfortunately, this solution isn't available throughout Nepal . . . or even throughout some areas of the United States.

So the United States must be the most wired country in the world with the smallest gap in the digital divide, right? Guess again. Although 45.2 percent of American households have broadband connections (either cable or DSL), over 80 percent of South Korean households have high-speed connections. This widespread connectivity is changing the face of Korean society. Government agencies, once known for long lines and mind-numbing paperwork, have installed efficient Web sites to streamline processes. Although we're still in the test-marketing phase of video-on-demand in a few markets in the United States, South Koreans routinely download movies and watch them whenever they want.

What is being done to bridge the digital divide in rural and poor areas of the world? Some organizations are attempting to increase local and global Internet and computer access, whereas community organizations such as libraries and recreation centers are providing free Internet access to the public. Meanwhile, others are sponsoring referendums that increase Internet capacity in schools or are e-mailing their local and state representatives, urging them to back legislation to provide funding for computer equipment in struggling school systems. Others suggest computer users donate their old computers to a charity that refurbishes and distributes them to needy families. To help bridge the digital divide, you can start by supporting such programs and institutions (such as your local library) in your area that are attempting to increase Internet and computer access.

Summary

1. What does it mean to be "computer literate"?

Computer literacy goes way beyond knowing how to use a mouse and send e-mail. If you are computer literate, you understand the capabilities and limitations of computers and know how to use them wisely. Being computer literate also enables you to make informed purchasing decisions, use computers in your career, understand and take advantage of future technologies, and understand the many ethical, legal, and societal implications of technology today.

2. How does being computer literate make you a savvy computer user and consumer?

By understanding how a computer is constructed and how its various parts function, you'll be able to get the most out of your computer. Among other things, you'll be able to avoid hackers, viruses, and Internet headaches; protect your privacy; separate the real risks from those you don't have to worry about; be able to maintain, upgrade, and troubleshoot your computer; and make good purchasing decisions.

3. How can becoming computer literate help you in a career?

As computers become more a part of our daily lives, it is difficult to imagine any career that does not use computers in some fashion. Understanding how to use computers effectively will help you be a more productive and valuable employee, no matter which profession you choose.

4. How can becoming computer literate help you understand and take advantage of future technologies?

The world is changing every day, and many changes are a result of new computer technologies. Understanding how today's computers function should help you utilize technology effectively now. And by understanding computers and how they work today, you can contribute to the technologies of tomorrow.

5. What kinds of challenges do computers bring to a digital society, and how does becoming computer literate help you deal with these challenges?

Although computers offer us a world of opportunities, they also pose ethical, legal, and moral challenges and questions. Being computer literate enables you to form *educated* opinions on these issues and to take stands based on accurate information rather than media hype and misinformation.

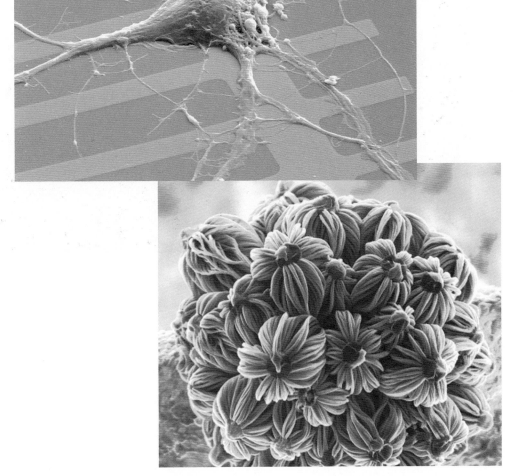

affective computing
Bluetooth technology
computer forensic
computer literate
data mining
digital divide
digital home
information technology (IT)
nanoscience
nanotechnology

offshore
patient simulator
personal digital assistant (PDA)
Personal Shopper System (PSS)
public domain
radio frequency identification tags (RFID tags)
software
spam

Buzz Words

Word Bank

- affective computing
- Bluetooth
- computer forensics
- computer literate
- data mining
- digital divide
- digital home
- information technology (IT)
- nanotechnology
- offshoring
- patient simulator
- personal digital assistant (PDA)
- Personal Shopper System (PSS)
- public domain
- radio frequency identification tags (RFID tags)
- spam

Instructions: Fill in the blanks using the words from the Word Bank above.

Because of the integration of computers into business and society, many fields of study are available now that were unheard of a few years ago. (1) _____, the study of very small computing devices built at the molecular level, will provide major advances in the miniaturization of computing. (2) _____ is already taking criminologists beyond what they could accomplish with conventional investigation techniques. And as the science of (3) _____ advances, computers will perform more and more like human beings in emotion and social cueing.

There are many reasons to know more about computing, or to become (4) _____. It can help you in eliminating unwanted e-mails or (5) _____. You will know how to upgrade your system to the latest standards, like the wireless communication technology (6) _____. More and more aspects of how our homes are run are being coordinated through computers, giving rise to the term (7) _____. You may even find you enjoy computers so much you want to explore careers in (8) _____.

Those who fail to keep up with the knowledge of how to use and maintain computer systems will fall to one side of the gap known as the (9) _____. As an entire country begins to lose computer expertise, jobs leave and are relocated in other, more tech-savvy countries. This shift of work is known as (10) _____.

Becoming Computer Literate

Using the key terms and ideas you learned in this chapter, write a one- or two-paragraph summary for your school advisor so that he or she can use it to explain to students the importance of being computer literate in today's job market. Using the Internet, find examples of careers most people would not expect to use computers and add this to your document to further support this advice.

Self-Test

Instructions: Answer the multiple-choice and true/false questions below for more practice with key terms and concepts from this chapter.

MULTIPLE CHOICE

1. Which of the following is NOT a use of computers in the legal environment?
   a. Creating animations that simulate the crime for use in the courtroom
   b. Tracking criminal behavior patterns
   c. Predicting criminal behavior patterns
   d. Conducting interviews with suspects

2. Art interfaces with technology by
   a. using a computer to generate images that respond to the environment.
   b. having computers suggest appropriate color choices.
   c. using software that completes the plot of a story.
   d. having Web sites that search for prospective clients for artists.

3. Nanotechnology is the science of things on the order of
   a. inches.   c. nanometers.
   b. milometers.   d. nanobytes.

4. Computer systems can NOT be trained to understand
   a. the U.S. tax code.
   b. human emotion.
   c. a good joke.
   d. the perfect golf swing.

5. The most wired country in the world is
   a. Germany.   c. the U. S.
   b. Japan.   d. South Korea.

6. A device that tracks movement is a
   a. PSS.   c. PDA.
   b. RFID tag.   d. patient simulator.

7. Which of the following is NOT a good reason to learn more about computers?
   a. To keep your home system secure
   b. To increase your career options
   c. To learn how to hack into the school's main computer
   d. To make better informed purchasing decisions

8. Infrared scanners cannot
   a. scan packages and detect unusual objects.
   b. be worn on the wrist.
   c. translate a bar code into a computer data file.
   d. be used by shipping companies to track packages.

9. Computer forensics
   a. uses computer technology to gather potential legal evidence.
   b. helps identify the remains of bodies.
   c. investigates a suspect's home computer for evidence.
   d. All of the above

10. Robotic surgery devices help physicians because
   a. they make more accurate incisions.
   b. the doctor does not have to be involved in the actual surgery.
   c. they monitor and make suggestions to the surgeon during the procedure.
   d. if the operation runs into complications, they can suggest creative alternatives.

TRUE/FALSE

___ 1. Computer simulations are used for gaming purposes, but they are not yet accurate enough for criminal investigations.

___ 2. Affective computing is the science that attempts to produce machines that understand and respond to human emotions.

___ 3. Artists use computers for the business side of their work—for example, advertising or record keeping—but they are not useful artistic tools.

___ 4. Ranchers tag their cattle and use computer systems to track and record their movements.

___ 5. In many hospitals, infants are "chipped," or injected with a small, computerized tracking device, so that nurses can monitor their location and keep them safe.

Making the Transition to...
Next Semester

1. Computer Literacy

In your college career, you'll be spending time understanding the requirements of the degree program you choose. At many schools, computer literacy requirements exist, either as incoming requirements (skills students must have before they are admitted) or outgoing requirements (skills students must prove they have before graduating). Does your program require specific computer skills? Which skills are these? Should they be required? How can students efficiently prove that they have these skills?

2. Computing and Education

Think about the schedule of courses you will be taking next semester. How many courses will require you to produce papers in electronic format? How many will require you to use course management software, such as Blackboard or WebCT? Will any course require you to use some specialty software product such as a nutrition monitoring program or a statistics training application? Do any require specialized hardware such as a scanner for your computer?

3. Old Technologies Holding On

What courses and careers have not been impacted by computer technology? Think of three courses that are taught effectively with no use of technology. Think of three careers that do not use computers in a significant way. Research and find the average salary and the rate of growth in these careers.

4. Using Biomedical Implants

If having such a chip implanted meant you would never need to carry cash or a credit card to the bookstore with you because your financial information was encoded on the chip, would you want one? If it could help instructors take attendance automatically in your class by reading your personal information, would that be an acceptable use? Would you consider using such a chip if it could be disabled whenever you wanted it to be or if only individuals you authorized had access to the information?

5. Campus Policing

In this chapter the use of trend-spotting programs to predict criminal activity was discussed. If existing criminal statistics are used to help identify trouble spots (such as wild parties) on your campus and the potential for serious criminal activity, is this the same as profiling? Does your campus police force have the right to take proactive steps to prevent crime based solely on developing trends? Should someone be held accountable if such information is not acted upon and a crime occurs?

Making the Transition to...
The Workplace

1. Computer-Free Workplaces?

In this chapter we listed a number of careers that require computer skills. How are computers used in the profession you are in or plan to enter? Can you think of any careers in which people do not use computers? Can you imagine computers being used in these careers in the future? How?

2. Medical Computing Applications

In their training and work, doctors and nurses rely on computers. What about patients? Does having access to a computer and computer skills help a patient create better health care options? Does having access to a computer help when filing an insurance claim? Does it help with finding the best doctor or hospital for a specific procedure? Explain your answers.

3. Preparing for a Job

An office is looking for help and needs an employee able to manipulate data on Excel spreadsheets, to coordinate the computer file management for the office, and to conduct backups of critical data. How could you prove to the interviewer that you have the skills to handle the job? How could you prove you have the ability to learn the job?

4. Career Outlook

Which career fields are growing the fastest? (Suggestion: Try searching at **www.ask.com.**) What computer skills and knowledge do the top 10 career paths demand? What kinds of continuing training in technology can you imagine would be required as you progress in these careers?

5. IT Careers

Information technology (IT) careers are suited to a wide range of people at different points in their lives.
a. Would an IT career have advantages for a single parent? How?
b. How might an IT career be able to help someone pursue a later career in a nontechnical field?
c. How might an IT career assist someone in completing a college degree?

6. Job Skills Assessment

Frequently, job seekers are asked about their computer literacy when applying for a job.
a. How do you think computer skill levels are determined by employers? How should they be determined?
b. If your interpretation of "expert" doesn't match your prospective employer's definition, does that make you wrong?

Critical Thinking Questions

Instructions: Albert Einstein used "Gedanken experiments," or critical thinking questions, to develop his theory of relativity. Some ideas are best understood by experimenting with them in our own minds. The following critical thinking questions are designed to demand your full attention but require only a comfortable chair—no technology.

1. **Rating Your Computer Literacy**

   This chapter lists a number of ways in which knowing about computers (or becoming computer literate) will help you. How much do you know about computers? What else would you like to know? How do you think learning more about computers will help you in the future?

2. **Data Mining**

   This chapter briefly discusses data mining, a technique companies use to study sales data and gather information from it. Have you heard of data mining before? How might companies like Wal-Mart or Target use data mining to better run their business? Can you think of any privacy risks data mining might pose?

3. **Nanotechnology**

   As you learned in the chapter, nanotechnology is the science revolving around the use of nanostructures to build devices on an extremely small scale. What applications of tiny computers can you think of? How might nanotechnology impact your life?

4. **Biomedical Chips**

   This chapter discusses various uses of biomedical chips. Many biomedical chip implants that will be developed in the future will most likely be aimed at correcting vision loss, hearing loss, or other physical impediments. But chips could also be developed to improve physical or mental capabilities of healthy individuals. For example, chips could be implanted in athletes to make their muscles work better together, thereby allowing them to run faster. Or your memory could be enhanced by providing additional storage capacity for your brain.

   a. Should biomedical implant devices that increase athletic performance be permitted in the Olympics?
   b. What about devices that repair a problem (such as blindness in one eye) but then increase the level of visual acuity in the affected eye so that it is better than normal vision?
   c. Would you be willing to have a chip implanted in your brain to improve your memory?
   d. Would you be willing to have a VeriChip implanted under your skin?

5. **Affective Computing**

   Affective computing is the science that attempts to produce machines that understand and can respond to human emotions and social mores. Do you think humans will ever create a machine that cannot be distinguished from a human being? In your opinion, what are the ethical and moral implications associated with that development?

6. **The World Stage**

   How might access to (or denial of) electronic information improve the education of a country's citizens? Could that affect who the world's next technology power will be? Could it eliminate "Third World" status?

Problem:

People are often overwhelmed by the relentless march of technology. Accessibility of information is changing the way we work, play, and interact with our friends, family, and coworkers. In this Team Time, we consider the future and reflect on how the advent of new technologies will affect our daily lives 10 years in the future.

Task:

Your group has just returned from a trip in a time machine 10 years into the future. Amazing changes have taken place in just a short time. To a large extent, consumer acceptance of technology makes or breaks a new technology. Your mission is to develop a creative marketing strategy to promote the technological changes you observed in the future and accelerate their acceptance.

Process:

Divide the class into three or more teams.

1. With the other members of your team, use the Internet to research up-and-coming technologies (**www.howstuffworks.com** is a good starting point). Prepare a list of innovations that you believe will occur in the next 10 years. Determine how they will be integrated into society and the effect they will have on our culture.

2. Present your group's findings to the class for debate and discussion. Note specifically how the rest of the class reacts to your reports on the innovations. Are they excited? Skeptical? Incredulous? Do they laugh off your ideas, or do they become wildly enthusiastic?

3. Write a marketing strategy paper detailing how you would promote the technological changes that you envision for the future. Also note some barriers for acceptance the technology may have to overcome, as well as any legal or ethical challenges or questions you see the new technology posing.

Conclusion:

The future path of technology is determined by dreamers. If not for innovators such as Edison, Bell, and Einstein, we would not be as advanced a society as we are today. Innovators come from all walks of life, and our creative energies must be exercised to keep them in tune. Don't be afraid to suggest technological advancements that seem outrageous today. In 1966, when the original *Star Trek* series was on television, handheld communicators seemed astounding and beyond our reach. Yet the dreamers who created those communication devices for a science fiction series spawned a multibillion-dollar cell phone industry in the 21st century. The next technological wave may be started in your imagination!

Multimedia

In addition to the review materials presented here, you'll find additional materials featured with the book's multimedia, including the *Technology in Action* Student Resource CD and the Companion Web Site (**www. prenhall.com/techinaction**), which will help reinforce your understanding of the chapter content. These materials include the following:

ACTIVE HELPDESK

In Active Helpdesk calls, you'll assume the role of Helpdesk operator, taking calls about the concepts you've learned in this chapter. You'll apply what you've learned and receive feedback from a supervisor to review and reinforce those concepts. The Active Helpdesk call for this chapter is listed below and can be found on your Student Resource CD:

- This chapter has no Active Helpdesks.

SOUND BYTES

Sound Bytes are dynamic multimedia tutorials that help demystify even the most complex topics. You'll view video clips and animations that illustrate computer concepts, and then apply what you've learned by reviewing with the Sound Byte Labs, which include quizzes and activities specifically tailored to each Sound Byte. The Sound Bytes for this chapter are listed below and can be found on your Student Resource CD:

- Questions to Ask Before You Buy a Computer
- The History of the Personal Computer

COMPANION WEB SITE

The *Technology in Action* Companion Web Site includes a variety of additional materials to help you review and learn more about the topics in this chapter. The resources available at **www.prenhall.com/techinaction** include:

- **Online Study Guide.** Each chapter features an online true/false and multiple-choice quiz. You can take these quizzes, automatically check the results, and e-mail the results to your instructor.
- **Web Research Projects.** Each chapter features a number of Web research projects that ask you to search the Web for information on computer-related careers, milestones in computer history, important people and companies, emerging technologies, and the applications and implications of different technologies.

The History *of* THE PC

Do you ever wonder how big the first personal computer was, or how much the first portable computer weighed? Computers are such an integral part of our lives that we don't often stop to think about how far they've come or where they got their start. But in just 30 years, computers have evolved from expensive, huge machines that only corporations owned to small, powerful devices found in millions of homes. In this Technology in Focus feature, we look at the history of the computer. Along the way, we discuss some developments that helped make the computer powerful and portable, as well as the people who contributed to its development. But first, we start with the story of the personal computer and how it grew to be as integral to our lives as the automobile.

The First Personal Computer: The Altair

Our journey through the history of the personal computer starts in 1975. At that time, most people were unfamiliar with the mainframes and supercomputers that large corporations and the government owned. With price tags exceeding the cost of buildings, and with few if any practical home uses, these monster machines were not appealing or attainable to the vast majority of Americans. But that began to change when the January 1975 cover of *Popular Electronics* announced the debut of the **Altair 8800**, touted as the first personal computer (see Figure 1). For just $395 for a do-it-yourself kit or $498 for a fully assembled unit (about $1,000 in today's dollars), the price was reasonable enough so that computer fanatics could finally own their own computers.

The Altair was a very primitive computer, with just 256 bytes (not *kilo*bytes, just bytes) of memory. It didn't come with a keyboard, nor did it include a monitor or printer. Switches on the front of the machine were used to enter data in unfriendly machine code (strings of 1s and 0s). Flashing lights on the front indicated the results of a program. User-friendly it was not—at least not by today's standards.

Despite its limitations, computer "hackers" (as computer enthusiasts were called then) flocked to the machine. Many who bought the Altair had been taught to program, but until that point had access only to big, clumsy computers. They were often hired by corporations to program "boring" financial, statistical, or engineering programs in a workplace environment. The Altair offered these enthusiasts the opportunity to create their own programs. Within three months, Micro Instrumentation and Telemetry Systems (MITS), the company behind the Altair, received more than 4,000 orders for the machine.

The release of the Altair marked the start of the personal computer (PC) boom. In fact, two men who would play large roles in the devel-

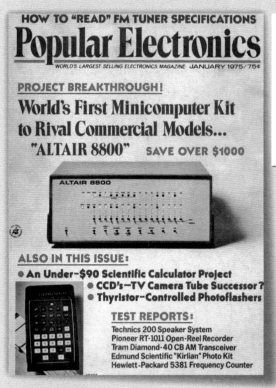

Courtesy of apple2history.org

FIGURE 1

In 1975, the Altair was touted as the "world's first minicomputer" in the January issue of *Popular Electronics*.

opment of the PC were among the first Altair owners. Recent high school grads Bill Gates and Paul Allen were so enamored by this "minicomputer," as these personal computers were called at the time, that they wrote a compiling program (a program that translates user commands into those that the computer can understand) for the Altair. The two friends later convinced its developer, Ed Roberts, to buy their program. This marked the start of a small company called Microsoft. But we'll get to that story later. First, let's see what their future archrivals were up to.

Why Was It Called the "Altair"?

For lack of a better name, the Altair's developers originally called the computer the PE-8, short for Popular Electronics 8-bit. However, Les Soloman, the *Popular Electronics* writer who introduced the Altair, wanted the machine to have a catchier name. The author's daughter, who was watching *Star Trek* at the time, suggested the name Altair (that's where the *Star Trek* crew was traveling that week). The first star of the PC industry was born.

The Apple I and II

Around the time the Altair was released, **Steve Wozniak**, an employee at Hewlett-Packard, was becoming fascinated with the burgeoning personal computer industry and was dabbling with his own computer design. He would bring his computer prototypes to meetings of the Homebrew Computing Club, a group of young computer fans who met to discuss computer ideas in Palo Alto, California. **Steve Jobs**, who was working for computer game manufacturer Atari at the time, liked Wozniak's prototypes and made a few suggestions. Together, the two built a personal computer, later known as the **Apple I**, in Wozniak's garage (see Figures 2 and 3). In that same year, on April 1, 1976, Jobs and Wozniak officially formed the **Apple Computer Company**.

No sooner had the Apple I hit the market than Wozniak was working to improve it. A year later, in 1977, the **Apple II** was born (see Figure 4). The Apple II included a color monitor, sound, and game paddles. Priced around $1,300 (quite a bit of money in those days), it included 4 kilobytes (KB) of random access memory (RAM) as well as an optional floppy disk drive that enabled users to run additional programs. Most of these programs were games. However, for many users, there was a special appeal to the Apple II: the program that made the computer function when the power was first turned on was stored in read-only memory (ROM). Previously, such routine-task programs had to be rewritten every time the computer was turned on. This automation made it possible for the least technical computer enthusiast to write programs.

An instant success, the Apple II would be the most successful in the company's line, outshining even its successor, the **Apple III**, released in 1980. Eventually, the Apple II included a spreadsheet program, word processing, and desktop publishing software. These programs gave personal computers like the Apple functions beyond just gaming and special programming, leading to their increased popularity. We talk more about these advances later. For now, other players were entering the market.

FIGURE 2

Steve Jobs (a) and Steve Wozniak (b) were two computer hobbyists who worked together to form the Apple Computer Company.

FIGURE 3

The first Apple computer, the Apple I, looked like a typewriter in a box. It was one of the first computers to incorporate a keyboard.

Photo courtesy of Apple Computer, Inc.

Original Apple II

FIGURE 4

The Apple II came with the addition of a monitor and an external floppy disk drive.

Photos courtesy of Apple Computer, Inc.

Why Is It Called "Apple"?

Steve Jobs wanted Apple Computer to be the "perfect" computer company. Having recently worked at an apple orchard, Jobs thought of the apple as the "perfect" fruit—it was high in nutrients, came in a nice package, and was not easily damaged. Thus, he and Wozniak decided to name their new computer company Apple.

Enter the Competition

Around the time Apple was experiencing success with its computers, a number of competitors entered the market. The largest among them were Commodore, RadioShack, and IBM. As Figure 5 shows, just years after the introduction of the Altair, the market was filled with personal computers from a variety of manufacturers.

The Commodore PET and TRS-80

Among Apple's strongest competitors were the **Commodore PET 2001**, shown in Figure 6, and Tandy RadioShack's **TRS-80**, shown in Figure 7. Commodore introduced the PET in January 1977. It was featured on the cover of *Popular Science* in October 1977 as the "new $595 home computer." Tandy RadioShack's home computer also garnered immediate popularity. Just one month after its release in 1977, the TRS-80 Model 1 sold approximately 10,000 units. Priced at $599.95, the easy-to-use machine included a monochrome display and 4 KB of memory. Many other manufacturers followed suit over the next decade, launching new desktop products, but none were as successful as the TRS-80 and the Commodore.

FIGURE 5
Personal Computer Development

YEAR	APPLE	IBM	OTHERS
1975			MITS Altair
1976	Apple I		
1977	Apple II		Tandy RadioShack's TRS-80 Commodore PET
1980	Apple III		
1981		IBM PC	Osborne
1983	Lisa		
1984	Macintosh	286-AT	IBM PC clones

©Jerry Mason/Photo Researchers, Inc.

FIGURE 6
The Commodore PET was well received because of its all-in-one design.

©The Computer Museum

FIGURE 7
The TRS-80 hid its circuitry under the keyboard. The computer was nicknamed "trash-80," which was more a play on its initials than a reflection of its capabilities.

The Osborne

The Osborne Company introduced the **Osborne** in April 1981 as the industry's first portable computer (see Figure 8). Although portable, the computer weighed 24.5 pounds, and its screen was just 5 inches wide. In addition to its hefty weight, it came with a hefty price tag of $1,795. Still, the Osborne included 64 KB of memory, two floppy disk drives, and preinstalled software programs (such as word processing and spreadsheet software). The Osborne was an overnight success, with sales quickly reaching 10,000 units per month. However, despite the Osborne's popularity, the release of a successor machine, called the **Executive**, reduced sales of the Osborne significantly, and the Osborne Company eventually closed. Compaq bought the Osborne design and later produced its first portable in 1983.

IBM PCs

By 1980, IBM recognized it needed to get its feet wet in the personal computer market. Up until that point, the company had been a player in the computer industry, but primarily with mainframe computers, which it sold only to large corporations. It had not taken the smaller, personal computer seriously. In August 1981, however, IBM released its first personal computer, appropriately named the **IBM PC**. Because many companies were already familiar with IBM mainframes, they readily adopted the IBM PC. The term *PC* soon became the term used to describe all personal computers.

The IBM PC came with 64 KB of memory, expandable to 256 KB, and started at $1,565. IBM marketed its PC through retail outlets such as Sears and Computerland in order to reach the home market, and it quickly dominated the playing field. In January 1983, *Time* magazine, playing on its annual "man of the year" issue, named the computer "1982 machine of the year" (see Figure 9).

©The Computer Museum

FIGURE 8

The Osborne was introduced as the first portable personal computer. It weighed a whopping 24.5 pounds and contained just 64 KB of memory.

Time Magazine, Copyright Time, Inc.

FIGURE 9

The IBM PC was the first (and only) nonhuman object chosen as "man of the year" (actually, "machine of the year") by *Time* magazine in its January 1983 issue. This designation indicated the impact the PC was having on the general public.

Other Important Advancements

It was not just the *hardware* of the personal computer that was developing during the 1970s and 1980s. At the same time, advances in programming languages and operating systems and the influx of application software were leading to more useful and powerful machines.

The Importance of BASIC

The software industry began in the 1950s with the development of programming languages such as FORTRAN, ALGOL, and COBOL. These languages were used mainly by businesses to create financial, statistical, and engineering programs for corporate enterprises. But the 1964 introduction of **Beginners All-Purpose Symbolic Instruction Code (BASIC)** revolutionized the software industry. BASIC was a programming language that the beginning programming student could easily learn. It thus became enormously popular—and the key language of the PC. In fact, **Bill Gates** and **Paul Allen** (see Figure 10) used BASIC to write the program for the Altair. As we noted earlier, this program led to the creation of **Microsoft**, a company that produced software for the microcomputer.

The Advent of Operating Systems

Because data on the earliest personal computers was stored on audiocassettes (not floppies), many programs were not saved or reused. Rather, programs were rewritten as needed. Then Steve Wozniak developed a floppy disk drive called the **Disk II**, which he introduced in July 1978. With the introduction of the floppy drive, programs could be saved with more efficiency, and operating systems (OSs) developed.

OSs were (and still are) written to coordinate with the specific processor chip that controlled the computer. Apples ran exclusively on a Motorola chip, while PCs (IBMs and so on) ran exclusively on an Intel chip. **Disk Operating System (DOS)**, developed by Wozniak and introduced in December 1977, was the OS that controlled the first Apple computers. The **Control Program for Microcomputers (CP/M)**, developed by Gary Kildall, was the first OS designed for the Intel

©David Wilson/Corbis

FIGURE 10

Bill Gates and Paul Allen are the founders of Microsoft.

8080 chip (the processor for PCs). Intel hired Kildall to write a compiling program for the 8080 chip, but Kildall quickly saw the need for a program that could store computer operating instructions on a floppy disk rather than on a cassette. Intel wasn't interested in buying the CP/M program, but Kildall saw a future for the program and thus founded his own company, Digital Research.

In 1980, when IBM was considering entering the personal computer market, it approached Bill Gates at Microsoft to write an OS program for the IBM PC. Although Gates had written versions of BASIC for different computer systems, he had never written an OS. He therefore recommended IBM investigate the CP/M OS, but no one from Digital Research returned IBM's call. Microsoft reconsidered the opportunity and developed **MS-DOS** for IBM computers. (This was one phone call Digital Research certainly regrets not returning!)

MS-DOS was based on an OS called **Quick and Dirty Operating System (QDOS)** developed by Seattle Computer Products. Microsoft bought the nonexclusive rights to QDOS and distributed it to IBM. Eventually, virtually all personal computers running on the Intel chip used MS-DOS as their OS. Microsoft's reign as one of the dominant players in the PC landscape had begun. Meanwhile, many other software programs were being developed, taking personal computers to the next level of user acceptance.

The Software Application Explosion: VisiCalc and Beyond

Inclusion of floppy disk drives in personal computers not only facilitated the storage of operating systems, but also set off a software application explosion, because the floppy disk was a convenient way to distribute software. Around that same time, in 1978, Harvard Business School student Dan Bricklin recognized the potential for a spreadsheet program that could be used on PCs. He and his friend Bob Frankston (see Figure 11) thus created the program **VisiCalc**. VisiCalc not only became an instant success, it was also one of the

main reasons for the rapid increase in PC sales. Finally, ordinary home users could see how owning a personal computer could benefit their lives. More than 100,000 copies of VisiCalc were sold in its first year.

After VisiCalc, other electronic spreadsheet programs entered the market. **Lotus 1-2-3** came on the market in 1982, and **Microsoft Excel** entered the scene in 1985. These two products became so popular that they eventually put VisiCalc out of business.

Meanwhile, word processing software was gaining a foothold in the PC industry. Up to this point, there were separate, dedicated word-processing machines, and the thought hadn't occurred to anyone to enable the personal computer to do word processing. Personal computers, it was believed, were for computation and data management. However, once **WordStar**, the first word processing application, came out in disk form in 1979 and was available on personal computers, word processing became another important use for the PC. In fact, word processing is now one of the most common PC applications. Competitors such as **Word for MS-DOS** (the precursor to Microsoft Word) and **WordPerfect** soon entered the market. Figure 12 lists some of the important dates in software application development.

Courtesy of Dan Bricklin and Bob Frankston

FIGURE 11
Dan Bricklin and Bob Frankston created VisiCalc, the first business application developed for the personal computer.

FIGURE 12
Software Application Development

YEAR	APPLICATION
1978	**VisiCalc:** First electronic spreadsheet application. **WordStar:** First word processing application.
1980	**WordPerfect:** Thought to be the best word processing software for the PC. WordPerfect was eventually sold to Novell, then later acquired by Corel.
1982	**Lotus 1-2-3:** Added integrated charting, plotting, and database capabilities to spreadsheet software.
1983	**Word for MS-DOS:** Introduced in *PC World* magazine with the first magazine-inserted demo disk.
1985	**Excel:** One of the first spreadsheets to use a graphical user interface. **PageMaker:** First desktop publishing software.

The Graphical User Interface

Another important advancement in personal computers was the introduction of the **graphical user interface (GUI)**, which allowed users to interact with the computer more easily. Until that time, users had to use complicated command- or menu-driven interfaces to interact with the computer. Apple was the first company to take full commercial advantage of the GUI, but competitors were fast on its heels, and soon the GUI became synonymous with personal computers. But who developed the idea of the GUI? You'll probably be surprised to learn that a company known for its photocopiers was the real innovator.

Xerox

In 1972, a few years before Apple had launched its first PC, photocopier manufacturer **Xerox** was hard at work in its Palo Alto Research Center (PARC) designing a personal computer of its own. Named the **Alto** (shown in Figure 13), the computer included a word processor, based on the What You See Is What You Get (WYSIWYG) principle, that was a file management system with directories and folders. It also had a mouse and could connect to a network. None of the other personal computers of the time had any of these features. Still, for a variety of reasons, Xerox never sold the Alto commercially. Several years later, it developed the Star Office System, which was based on the Alto. Despite its convenient features, the Star never became popular, because no one was willing to pay the $17,000 asking price.

The Lisa and the Macintosh

Xerox's ideas were ahead of its time, but many of the ideas of the Alto and Star would soon catch on. In 1983, Apple introduced the **Lisa**, shown in Figure 14. Named after Apple founder Steve Jobs's daughter, the Lisa was the first successful PC brought to market to use a GUI. Legend has it that Jobs had seen the Alto during a visit to PARC in 1979 and was influenced by its GUI. He therefore incorporated a similar user interface into the Lisa, providing features such as windows, drop-down menus, icons, a hierarchical file system with folders and files, and a point-and-click device called a mouse. The only problem with the Lisa was its price. At $9,995 ($20,000 in today's dollars), few buyers were willing to take the plunge.

A year later, in 1984, Apple introduced the **Macintosh**, shown in Figure 15. The Macintosh was everything the Lisa was and then some, and at about a third of the cost. The Macintosh was also the first personal computer to introduce 3.5-inch floppy disks with a hard cover, which were smaller and sturdier than the previous 5.25-inch floppies.

The Internet Boom

The GUI made it easier for users to work on the computer. The Internet provided another reason for consumers to buy computers. Now they could conduct research and communicate with each other in a new and convenient way. In 1993, the Web browser **Mosaic** was introduced. This browser allowed users to view multimedia on the

©The Computer Museum

FIGURE 13
The Alto was the first computer to use a graphical user interface, and it provided the basis for the GUI that Apple used. However, because of marketing problems, the Alto never was sold.

Photo courtesy of Apple Computer, Inc.

FIGURE 14
The Lisa was the first computer to introduce a GUI to the market. Priced too high, it never gained the popularity it deserved.

Photo courtesy of Apple Computer, Inc.

Macintosh in 1984

FIGURE 15
The Macintosh became one of Apple's best-selling computers, incorporating a graphical user interface along with other innovations such as the 3.5-inch floppy disk drive.

Web, causing Internet traffic to increase by nearly 350 percent.

Meanwhile, companies discovered the Internet as a means to do business, and computer sales took off. IBM-compatible PCs became the personal computer system of choice when, in 1995, Microsoft (the predominant software provider to PCs) introduced Internet Explorer, a Web browser that integrated Web functionality into Microsoft Office applications, and **Windows 95**, the first Microsoft OS designed to be principally a GUI OS, although it still was based on the DOS kernel.

About a year earlier, in mid-1994, Jim Clark, founder of the computer company Silicon Graphics Inc., Marc Andreessen, and others from the Mosaic development team developed the commercial Web browser Netscape. Netscape's popularity grew quickly, and it soon became a predominant player in browser software. However, pressures from Microsoft became too strong. In the beginning of 1998, Netscape announced it was moving to the open source market, no longer charging for the product and making the code available to the public.

Making the PC Possible: Early Computers

Since the first Altair was introduced in the 1970s, more than a billion personal computers have been distributed around the globe. Because of the declining prices of computers and the growth of the Internet, it's estimated that a billion more computers will be sold within the next decade. But what made all this possible? The computer is a compilation of parts, all of which are the result of individual inventions. From the earliest days of humankind, we have been looking for a more systematic way to count and calculate. Thus, the evolution of counting machines has led to the development of the computer we know today.

The Pascalene Calculator and the Jacquard Loom

The **Pascalene** was the first accurate mechanical calculator. This machine, created by the French mathematician **Blaise Pascal** in 1642, used revolutions of gears to count by tens, similar to odometers in cars. The Pascalene could be used to add, subtract, multiply, and divide. The basic design of the Pascalene was so sound that it lived on in mechanical calculators for more than 300 years.

Nearly 200 years later, **Joseph Jacquard** revolutionized the fabric industry by creating a machine that automated the weaving of complex patterns. Although not a counting or calculating machine, the **Jacquard Loom** (shown in Figure 16) was significant because it relied on stiff cards with punched holes to automate the process. Much later this process would be adopted as a means to record and read data by using punch cards in computers.

Babbage's Engines

Decades later, in 1834, **Charles Babbage** designed the first automatic calculator, called the **Analytical Engine** (see Figure 17). The machine was actually based on another

FIGURE 16

The Jacquard Loom used holes punched in stiff cards to make complex designs. This technique would later be used in the form of punch cards to control the input and output of data in computers.

machine called the **Difference Engine**, which was a huge steam-powered mechanical calculator Babbage designed to print astronomical tables. Babbage stopped working on the Difference Engine to build the Analytical Engine. Although it was never developed, Babbage's detailed drawings and descriptions of the machine include components similar to those found in today's computers, including the store (RAM) and the mill (central processing unit), as well as input and output devices. This invention gave Charles Babbage the title of the "father of computing."

Meanwhile, Ada Lovelace, the daughter of poet Lord Byron and a student of mathematics (which was unusual for women of that time), was fascinated with Babbage's Engine. She translated an Italian paper on Babbage's machine, and at the request of Babbage added her own extensive notes. Her efforts are thought of as the best description of Babbage's Engines.

The Hollerith Tabulating Machine

In 1890, **Herman Hollerith**, while working for the U.S. Census Bureau, was the first to take Jacquard's punch card concept and apply it to computing. Hollerith developed a machine called the **Hollerith Tabulating Machine** that used punch cards to tabulate census data. Up until that time, census data had been tabulated in a long, laborious process. Hollerith's tabulating machine automatically read data that had been punched onto small punch cards, speeding up the tabulation process. Hollerith's machine became so successful that he left the Census Bureau in 1896 to start the Tabulating Machine Company. His company later changed its name to International Business Machines, or IBM.

The Z1 and Atanasoff-Berry Computer

German inventor **Konrad Zuse** is credited with a number of computing inventions. His first, in 1936, was a mechanical calculator called the **Z1**. The Z1 is thought to be the first computer to include features that are integral to today's systems, including a control unit and separate memory functions, noted as important breakthroughs for future computer design.

©The Computer History Museum

In late 1939, John Atanasoff, a professor at Iowa State University, and his student, Clifford Berry, built the first electrically powered digital computer, called the **Atanasoff-Berry Computer (ABC)**, shown in Figure 18. The computer was the first to use vacuum tubes to store data instead of the mechanical switches used in older computers. Although revolutionary at its time, the machine weighed 700 pounds, contained a mile of wire, and took about 15 seconds for each calculation. (In comparison, today's personal computers can calculate more than 300 billion operations in 15 seconds.) Most important, the ABC was the first to use the binary system. It was also the first to

Courtesy of Ames Laboratory

have memory that repowered itself upon booting. The design of the ABC would end up being central to that of future computers.

The Harvard Mark I

From the late 1930s to the early 1950s, **Howard Aiken** and **Grace Hopper** designed the Mark series of computers at Harvard University. The U.S. Navy used these computers for ballistic and gunnery calculations. Aiken, an electrical engineer and physicist, designed the computer, while Hopper did the programming. The **Harvard Mark I**, finished in 1944, could perform all four arithmetic operations (addition, subtraction, multiplication, and division).

However, many believe Hopper's greatest contribution to computing was the invention of the **compiler**, a program that translates English language instructions into computer language. The team was also responsible for a common computer-related expression. Hopper was the first to "debug" a computer when she removed a moth that had flown into the Harvard Mark I. The moth caused the computer to break down. After that, problems that caused the computer to not run were called "bugs."

The Turing Machine

Meanwhile, in 1936, the British mathematician **Alan Turing** created an abstract computer model that could perform logical operations. The **Turing Machine** was not a real machine but rather a hypothetical model that mathematically defined a mechanical procedure (or algorithm). Additionally, Turing's concept described a process by which the machine could read, write, or erase symbols written on squares of an infinite paper tape. This concept of an infinite tape that could be read, written to, and erased was the precursor to today's RAM.

The ENIAC

The **Electronic Numerical Integrator and Computer (ENIAC)**, shown in Figure 20, was another U.S. government-sponsored machine developed to calculate the settings used for weapons. Created by **John W. Mauchly** and **J. Presper Eckert** at the University of Pennsylvania, it was placed in operation in June 1944. Although the ENIAC is generally thought of as the first successful high-speed electronic digital computer, it was big and clumsy. The ENIAC used nearly 18,000 vacuum tubes and filled approximately 1,800 square feet of floor space. Although inconvenient, the ENIAC served its purpose and remained in use until 1955.

Naval Historical Center

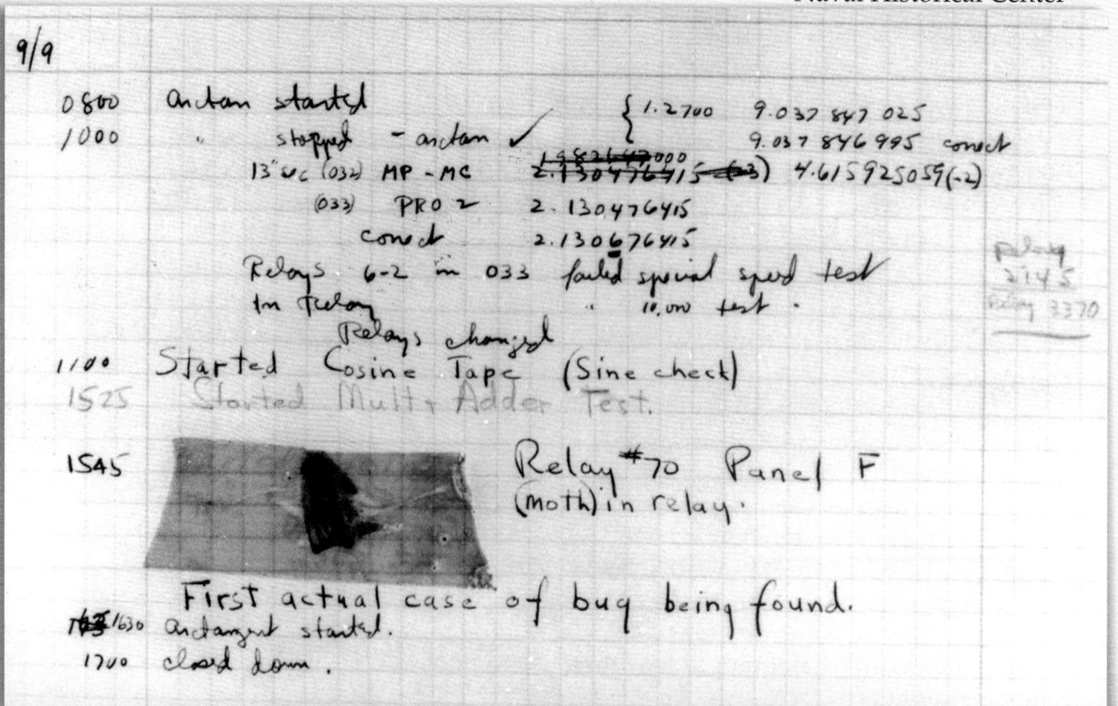

FIGURE 19

Grace Hopper coined the term *computer bug*, referring to a moth that had flown into the Harvard Mark I, causing it to break down.

The UNIVAC

The **Universal Automatic Computer**, or **UNIVAC**, was the first commercially successful electronic digital computer. Completed in June 1951 and owned by the company Remington Rand, the UNIVAC operated on magnetic tape (as opposed to its competitors, which ran on punch cards). The UNIVAC gained notoriety when, in a 1951 publicity stunt, it was used to predict the outcome of the Stevenson-Eisenhower presidential race. By analyzing only 5 percent of the popular vote, the UNIVAC correctly identified Dwight D. Eisenhower as the victor. After that, the UNIVAC soon became a household name. The UNIVAC and computers like it were considered **first-generation computers** and were the last to use vacuum tubes to store data.

©The Computer History Museum

FIGURE 20

The ENIAC took up an entire room and required several people to manipulate it.

Transistors and Beyond

Only a year after the ENIAC was completed, scientists at the Bell Telephone Laboratories in New Jersey invented the **transistor** as a means to store data. The transistor replaced the bulky vacuum tubes of earlier computers and was smaller and more powerful. It was used in almost everything, from radios to phones. Computers that used transistors were referred to as **second-generation computers**. Still, transistors were limited as to how small they could be made.

A few years later, in 1958, **Jack Kilby**, while working at Texas Instruments, invented the world's first **integrated circuit**, a small chip capable of containing thousands of transistors. This consolidation in design enabled computers to become smaller and lighter. The computers in this early integrated circuit generation were considered **third-generation computers**.

Other innovations in the computer industry further refined the computer's speed, accuracy, and efficiency. However, none were as significant as the 1971 introduction by the Intel Corporation of the **microprocessor chip**, a small chip containing millions of

transistors. The microprocessor functions as the central processing unit (CPU), or brains, of the computer. Computers that used a microprocessor chip were called **fourth-generation computers**. Over time, Intel and Motorola became the leading manufacturers of microprocessors. Today, the Intel Itanium 2 chip, shown in Figure 21, is one of Intel's most powerful processors.

As you can see, personal computers have come a long way since the Altair and have a number of inventions and people to thank for their amazing popularity. What will the future bring? If current trends continue, computers will be smaller, lighter, and more powerful. The advancement of wireless technology will also certainly play a big role in the development of the personal computer.

FIGURE 21

The Intel Itanium 2 is one of Intel's most powerful processors.

2

Looking at Computers:

Understanding the Parts

From Chapter 2 of *Technology in Action, Complete*, Fifth Edition, Alan Evans, Kendall Martin, Mary Anne Poatsy. Copyright © 2009 by Pearson Education. Published by Prentice Hall. All rights reserved.

Looking at Computers:

Understanding the Parts

ACTIVE HELPDESK

- Understanding Bits and Bytes
- Using Input Devices
- Using Output Devices

Setting Up Your System

Jillian has just bought a new computer and is setting it up. She spent more than she had planned on a flat-panel monitor, which she places on her small desk. It takes up far less room than her old monitor, which was big and bulky. Next she pulls out her system unit, which she knows is the component to which she'll connect all the other pieces of her system. Although she was tempted to buy the most powerful computer on the market, she bought one that best met her needs and was slightly less expensive. Still, it came with a CD-RW/DVD combo player, a 100-GB hard drive, and what the computer salesperson said was enough memory and power to do almost anything. She sets it on the floor next to her desk and attaches the monitor to it.

Next she pulls out her keyboard. She looked into buying a wireless keyboard, but because her budget was tight, she bought a standard keyboard instead. The box tells her it is a "USB" keyboard, so she finds what looks to be the right port on the back of her system unit and plugs it in. Her mouse also needs a USB port. Finding another USB port, she attaches the mouse there. She's glad that her system has plenty of USB ports and sees there are even several on the front of the system unit. She sets up her speakers next. Although the salesperson told her she'd probably want to upgrade them, she decided to wait until she could afford it. She arranges them on her desk and inserts the speakers into the "speaker out" port on the back of her tower. Last is her printer. She debated over which type of printer to buy but decided to buy an inkjet because she prints a lot of color copies and photos. She finds the right port on her system unit and connects it. She then plugs the power cables of the monitor, speakers, printer, and system unit into the surge protector, which the salesperson told her would protect her devices from power surges. All that's left is to make sure her setup is comfortable, and she's ready to go.

What kind of computer setup do you have? Do you know all the options available and what the different components of your system do? In this chapter, we'll take a look at your computer's basic parts. You'll learn about input devices (such as the mouse and keyboard), output devices (such as monitors and printers), storage devices (such as the hard drive), as well as components inside the computer that help it to function. Finally, you'll learn how to set up your computer so that it's safe from power surges and comfortable to work on.

B2M Productions/Getty
Images-Digital Vision

SOUND BYTES

- Port Tour: How Do I Hook It Up?
- Virtual Computer Tour
- Healthy Computing

Understanding Your Computer

You can see why becoming computer literate is so important. But where do you start? You've no doubt gleaned some knowledge about computers just from being a member of our society. However, although you certainly know what a computer *is*, do you really understand how it works, what all its parts are, and what these parts do? In this section, we'll discuss what a computer does that makes it such a useful machine.

COMPUTERS ARE DATA PROCESSING DEVICES

Strictly defined, a **computer** is a data processing device that performs four major functions:

1. It *gathers* data (or allows users to input data).
2. It *processes* that data into information.
3. It *outputs* data or information.
4. It *stores* data and information.

What is the difference between data and information? People often use the terms *data* and *information* interchangeably. Although in a simple conversation they may mean the same thing, when discussing computers, the distinction between data and information is an important one.

In computer terms, **data** is a representation of a fact or idea. Data can be a number, a word, a picture, or even a recording of sound. For example, the number 6125553297 and the names Derek and Washington are

pieces of data. But how useful are these chunks of data to you? **Information** is data that has been organized or presented in a meaningful fashion. When your computer provides you with a contact listing that indicates Derek Washington can be reached by phone at (612) 555-3297, the data mentioned earlier suddenly becomes useful—that is, it is information.

How do computers interact with data and information? Computers are very good at **processing** (manipulating) data into information. When you first arrived on campus, you probably were directed to a place where you could get an ID card. You most likely provided a clerk with personal data (such as your name and address) that was entered into a computer. The clerk then took your picture with a digital camera (collecting more data). This information was then processed appropriately so that it could be printed on your ID card (see Figure 1). This organized output of data on your ID card is useful information. Finally, the information was probably stored as digital data on the computer for later use.

BITS AND BYTES: THE LANGUAGE OF COMPUTERS

How do computers process data into information? Unlike humans, computers work exclusively with numbers (not words). In order to process data into information, computers need to work in a language they understand. This language, called **binary language**, consists of just two digits: 0 and 1. Everything a computer does (such as process data or print a report) is broken down into a series of 0s and 1s. Each 0 and 1 is a **binary digit**, or **bit** for short. Eight

Computers process data into information.

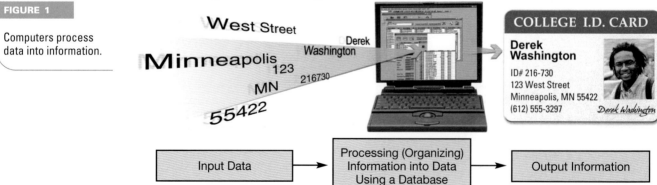

Input Data → Processing (Organizing) Information into Data Using a Database → Output Information

binary digits (or bits) combine to create one **byte**. In computers, each letter of the alphabet, each number, and each special character (such as the @ sign) consists of a unique combination of eight bits, or a string of eight 0s and 1s. So, for example, in binary (computer) language, the letter K is represented as 01001011. This equals eight bits, or one byte.

What else can bits and bytes be used for? You've probably heard the terms *kilobyte (KB)* and *megabyte (MB)* before. Not only are bits and bytes used as the language that tells the computer what to do, they are also what the computer uses to represent the data and information it inputs and outputs. Word-processing files, digital pictures, and even software programs are all represented inside a computer as a series of bits and bytes. These files and applications can be quite large, containing many millions of bytes. To make it easier to measure the size of these files, we need larger units of measure than a byte. Kilobytes, megabytes, and gigabytes are therefore simply amounts of bytes. As shown in Figure 2, a **kilobyte (KB)** is approximately 1,000 bytes, a **megabyte (MB)** is about a million bytes, and a **gigabyte (GB)** is about a billion bytes. As our information processing needs have grown, so too have our storage needs. Today, some computers can store up to a petabyte of data—that's more than one quadrillion bytes!

How does your computer process bits and bytes? Your computer uses a combination of hardware and software to process data into information and enable you to complete tasks (such as writing a letter or playing a game). An anonymous person once said that hardware is any part of a computer that you can kick when it doesn't work properly. A more formal definition of hardware is any part of the computer you can physically touch. However, a computer needs more than just hardware to work: it also needs some form of software. Think of a book without words or a CD without music. Without words or music, these two common items are just shells that hold nothing. Similarly, a computer without software is a shell full of hardware components that can't do anything. **Software** is the set of computer programs that enables the hardware to perform different tasks. There are two broad categories of software: application software and system software.

When you think of software, you are most likely thinking of application software. **Application software** is the set of programs you use on a computer to help you carry out tasks. If you've ever typed a document, created a spreadsheet, or edited a digital photo, for example, you've used a form of application software.

System software is the set of programs that enables your computer's hardware devices and application software to work together. The most common type of system software is

ACTIVE HELPDESK

Understanding Bits and Bytes

In this Active Helpdesk call, you'll play the role of a helpdesk staffer, fielding calls about the difference between data and information and what bits and bytes are and how they are measured.

FIGURE 2 How Much Is a Byte?

Name	Abbreviation	Number of Bytes	Relative Size
Byte	B	1 byte	Can hold one character of data.
Kilobyte	KB	1,024 bytes	Can hold 1,024 characters or about half of a double-spaced typewritten page.
Megabyte	MB	1,048,576 bytes	A floppy disk holds approximately 1.4 MB of data, or approximately 768 pages of typed text.
Gigabyte	GB	1,073,741,824 bytes	Approximately 786,432 pages of text. Since 500 sheets of paper is approximately 2 inches, this represents a stack of paper 262 feet high.
Terabyte	TB	1,099,511,627,776 bytes	This represents a stack of typewritten pages almost 51 miles high.
Petabyte	PB	1,125,899,906,842,624 bytes	The stack of pages is now 52,000 miles high, or about one-fourth the distance from the earth to the moon.

the **operating system (OS)**, the program that controls the way in which your computer system functions. It manages the hardware of the computer system, such as the monitor and the printer. The operating system also provides a means by which users can interact with the computer. For the rest of this chapter, we'll explore hardware.

Your Computer's Hardware

Considering the amount of amazing things computers can do, they are really quite simple machines. A basic computer system is made up of software and hardware. In this chapter, we look more closely at your computer's **hardware**, the parts you can actually touch (see Figure 3). Hardware components of a computer consist of the **system unit**, the box that contains the central electronic components of the computer, and **peripheral devices**, those devices such as monitors and printers that are connected to the computer. Other devices, such as routers, help a computer communicate with other computers to facilitate sharing documents and other resources. Together the system unit and peripheral devices perform four main functions: they enable the computer to *input* data, *process* that data, and *output* and *store* the data and information. We begin our exploration of hardware by taking a look at your computer's input devices.

Input Devices

An **input device** enables you to enter data (text, images, and sounds) and instructions (user responses and commands) into the computer. The most common input devices are the **keyboard** and the **mouse**. You use keyboards to enter typed data and commands, whereas you use the mouse to enter

FIGURE 3

Each part of the computer serves a special function.

user responses and commands. There are other input devices as well: microphones input sounds, whereas scanners and digital cameras input nondigital text and digital images, respectively. Styluses (devices that look like skinny pens but have no ink) and electronic pens are also becoming quite popular and are often used in conjunction with graphics tablets that can translate a user's handwriting into digital input.

KEYBOARDS

Aren't all keyboards the same? Most desktop and notebook computers come with a standard keyboard, which uses the **QWERTY keyboard** layout (see Figure 4a). This layout gets its name from the first six letters in the top-left row of alphabetic keys on the keyboard. Over the years, there has been some debate over what is the best layout for keyboards. The QWERTY layout was originally designed for typewriters and was meant to slow typists to prevent typewriter keys from jamming. Today, the QWERTY layout is considered inefficient because it slows typing speeds. Now that technology can keep up with faster typing, other keyboard layouts are being considered.

The **Dvorak keyboard** is the leading alternative keyboard, although it is not nearly as common as the QWERTY. The Dvorak keyboard puts the most commonly used letters in the English language on "home keys," the keys in the middle row of the keyboard (see Figure 4b). The Dvorak keyboard's design reduces the distance your fingers travel for most keystrokes, increasing typing speed. Although alternative layout keyboards have not caught on with most users, they are very popular with gamers. Keyboards such as the DX1 from Ergodex (see Figure 4c) allow placement of the keys in any position on the keyboard tray, and the keys can be programmed to perform specific tasks. This makes it easy for gamers to configure a keyboard in the most desirable way for each game they play.

Because users are demanding more portability out of their computing devices, recent development efforts have focused on reducing the size and weight of keyboards. The virtual laser keyboard (see Figure 5) is a

Ergodex

Martin Meissner/AP Wide World Photos

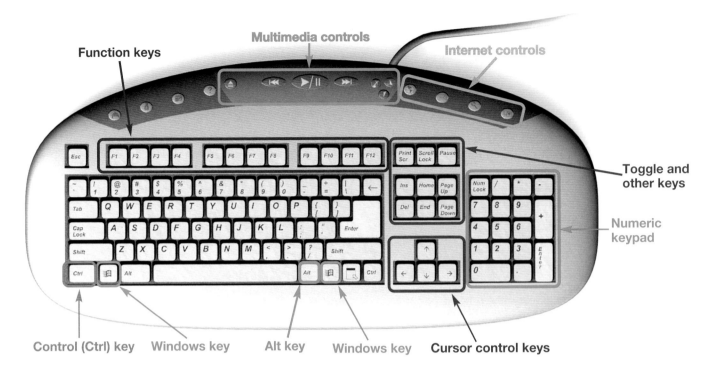

Function keys

Multimedia controls

Internet controls

Toggle and other keys

Numeric keypad

Control (Ctrl) key　**Windows key**　**Alt key**　**Windows key**　**Cursor control keys**

device that is about the size of a cellular phone. It projects the image of a keyboard on any surface, and sensors detect the motion of your fingers as you "type" on a desk. Data is transmitted via Bluetooth technology. **Bluetooth** is a wireless transmission standard that facilitates the connection among electronic computing devices such as cell phones, PDAs, and computers to peripheral devices such as keyboards and headsets.

How can I use my keyboard most efficiently? All keyboards have the standard set of alpha and numeric keys that you regularly use when typing. As shown in Figure 6, other keys on a keyboard also have special functions. Knowing how to use these special keys will help you improve your efficiency:

- The **numeric keypad** allows you to enter numbers quickly.

- **Function keys** act as shortcut keys you press to perform special tasks. They are sometimes referred to as the "F" keys because they start with the letter *F* followed by a number. Each software application has its own set of tasks assigned to the function keys, although some are more universal. For example, the F1 key is usually the Help key in software applications. However, function keys sometimes perform different actions

in different software packages. For instance, the F2 key moves text or graphics in Microsoft Word but allows editing of the active cell in Microsoft Excel.

- The **Control (Ctrl) key** is used in combination with other keys to perform shortcuts and special tasks. For example, holding down the Control (Ctrl) key while pressing the B key adds bold formatting to selected text. Similarly, you use the **Alt key** with other keys for additional shortcuts and special tasks. (On Macs, the Control or Ctrl key is the Apple key or Command key, whereas the Alt key is the Option key.)

- The **Windows key** is specific to the Windows operating system. Used alone, it brings up the Start menu; however, it's used most often in combination with other keys as shortcuts (which produce different results in different versions of Windows). For example, pressing the Windows key plus the M key minimizes all Windows in Windows Vista.

Some keyboards (such as the one shown in Figure 6) also include multimedia and Internet keys or buttons that enable you to open a Web browser, view e-mail, access Help features, or control your CD/DVD player. Unlike the other keys on a standard keyboard, these buttons are not always in the same position on every keyboard, but the symbols on top of the buttons generally help you determine their function. For hard-core gamers, gaming companies are now selling **gaming keyboards** that are optimized for playing specific video games. These keyboards contain special keys that perform special functions (such as changing the weapon being used by a character) so that with one key press, game play speeds up, allowing players to react quicker to difficult challenges within the game.

Another set of controls on standard keyboards are the **cursor control keys** that move your **cursor** (the flashing I symbol on the monitor that indicates where the next character will be inserted). The cursor control keys also are known as arrow keys because they are represented by arrows on standard keyboards. The arrow keys move the cursor one space at a time in a document, either up, down, left, or right.

Above the arrow keys, usually you'll find keys that move the cursor up or down one full page or to the beginning (Home) or end (End) of a line of text. The Delete (Del) key allows you to delete characters, whereas the Insert key allows you to insert or overwrite characters within a document. The Insert key is a **toggle key** because its function changes each time you press it: when toggled on, the Insert key inserts new text within a line of existing text. When toggled off, the Insert key replaces (or overwrites) existing characters with new characters as you type. Other toggle keys include the Num Lock key and the Caps Lock key, which toggle between an on/off state.

Are keyboards different on notebooks (laptops)? Notebook computers are portable computers that are powered by batteries and have keyboards, monitors, and other devices integrated into a single compact case. To save space and weight, notebook keyboards are more compact than standard keyboards and therefore have fewer keys. Still, a lot of the notebook keys have alternate functions so that you can get the same capabilities from the limited keys as you do from the special keys on standard keyboards. For example, many notebook keyboards do not have separate numeric keys. Instead, the letter keys function as number keys when they are pressed in combination with another key (every notebook will be different). The keys you use as numeric keys on notebooks have number notations on them so you can tell which keys to use (see Figure 7).

BITS AND BYTES

Keeping Your Keyboard Clean

To keep your computer running at its best, it's important that you occasionally clean your keyboard.

To do so, follow these steps:

1. Turn off your computer. Disconnect the keyboard from your system.
2. Turn the keyboard upside down and *gently* shake out any loose debris. You may want to spray hard-to-reach places with compressed air (sold in cans and found in most computer stores) or use a vacuum device made especially for computers. Don't use your home vacuum because the suction is too strong and may damage your keyboard.
3. Wipe the keys with a cloth or cotton swab lightly dampened with a diluted solution of dishwashing liquid and water or rubbing alcohol and water. Don't spray or pour cleaning solution directly onto the keyboard. Make sure you hold the keyboard upside down or at an angle to prevent drips from running into the circuitry.

Hewlett-Packard Company

Keys function as number keys when pressed with another key

FIGURE 7

Notebook keyboards are more compact than traditional desktop keyboards and usually don't include extra keys such as the numeric keypad. However, on many notebooks, certain letter keys can function as number keys.

What about keyboards for PDAs and Tablet PCs? Generally, you enter data and commands into a personal digital assistant (PDA) by using a **stylus**, a pen-shaped device that you use by tapping or writing on the PDA's touch-sensitive screen. Tablet PCs, as shown in Figure 8, are similar to notebook PCs but also feature a touch-sensitive screen and handwriting recognition software. Tablet PCs also allow user input via a stylus. However, all tablets and some PDAs have built-in keyboards that allow you to type text just as you would with a normal keyboard. If your PDA doesn't include a built-in keyboard, you can buy keyboards that attach to the PDA or use a virtual laser keyboard.

Are all conventional keyboards connected to the computer via wires? Although most desktop PCs ship with wired keyboards, wireless keyboards are available. These keyboards are powered by batteries and send data to the computer using a form of wireless technology. Infrared wireless keyboards communicate with the computer using infrared light waves (similar to how a remote control communicates with a TV). The computer receives the infrared light signals through a special infrared port. The disadvantage of infrared keyboards is that you need to point the keyboard directly at the infrared port on the computer for it to work. Other wireless keyboards use radio frequency signals to transmit data, and many adhere to the Bluetooth standard.

What are the best wireless keyboards? The best wireless keyboards send data to the computer using radio frequency (RF). These keyboards contain a radio transmitter that sends out radio wave signals. These signals are received either by a small receiving device that sits on your desk and is plugged into the back of the computer where the keyboard would normally plug in, or in the case of Bluetooth-compatible computers, by a receiving device contained in the system unit. Unlike infrared technology, RF technology doesn't require that you point the keyboard at the receiver for it to work. RF keyboards used on home computers can be placed as far as 6 to 30 feet from the computer, depending on their quality.

FIGURE 8

The stylus is the tablet PC's primary input device. You use it by tapping or writing on the tablet's touch-sensitive screen.

BITS AND BYTES

Keystroke Shortcuts

You may know that you can combine certain keystrokes to take short cuts within the Windows operating system. The following are a few of the most helpful shortcuts to make more efficient use of your time. For more shortcuts for Windows-based PCs, visit **http://support. microsoft.com**. For a list of shortcuts for Macs, see **www. apple.com/support**.

Text Formatting	File Management	Cut/Copy/Paste	Windows Controls
CTRL+B Applies (or removes) **bold** formatting to selected text	**CTRL+O** Opens the Open dialog box	**CTRL+X** Cuts (removes) selected text from document	Alt+F4 Closes the current window
CTRL+I Applies (or removes) *italic* formatting to selected text	**CTRL+N** Opens a new document	**CTRL+C** Copies selected text	**Ctrl+Esc** Opens the Start menu
	CTRL+S Saves a document	**CTRL+V** Pastes selected text (previously cut or copied)	**Windows Key + F1** Opens Windows Help
CTRL+U Applies (or removes) underlining to selected text	**CTRL+P** Opens the Print dialog box		**Windows Key + F** Opens the Search (Find Files) dialog box

(Bluetooth devices have a much shorter range.) RF keyboards used in business conference rooms or auditoriums can be placed as far as 100 feet away from the computer, but they are far more expensive than traditional wired keyboards.

MICE AND OTHER POINTING DEVICES

What kinds of mice are there? The mouse you're probably most familiar with is the optical mouse (see Figure 9a). An **optical mouse** uses an internal sensor or laser to detect the mouse's movement. The sensor sends signals to the computer, telling it where to move the pointer on the screen. Optical mice are often preferable to other types of mice because they have very few moving parts, which lessens the chances that dirt will interfere with the mechanisms or that parts will break down. Although optical mice are most common now, you may still use a mouse at home or in school that has a rollerball on the bottom, which moves when you drag the mouse across a mousepad. The movement of the rollerball controls the movement of your cursor that appears on the screen.

Mice also have two or three buttons that enable you to execute commands and open shortcut menus. (Mice for Macs sometimes have only one button.) Most new mice have additional programmable buttons and wheels that let you quickly scroll through documents or Web pages.

Do mice still need mousepads? Optical mice will work on any surface without a mousepad, but some people still use a pad to protect their furniture from being marred as the mouse moves. Trackball mice also don't require mousepads. A **trackball mouse** (see Figure 9b) is basically a traditional mouse that has been turned on its back. The rollerball sits on top or on the side of the mouse and you move the ball with your fingers, allowing the mouse to remain stationary. A trackball mouse doesn't demand much wrist motion, so it's considered better for the wrist than an optical mouse.

Are there wireless mice? Just as there are wireless keyboards, there are wireless mice, both optical and trackball. Wireless mice are similar to wireless keyboards in that they use batteries and send data to the computer by radio or light waves. If you also have an RF wireless keyboard, your RF wireless mouse and keyboard usually can share the same RF receiver.

What about mice for notebooks? Most notebooks do not come with mice. Instead, they have integrated pointing devices such as a **touchpad**. A touchpad is a small, touch-sensitive area at the base of the keyboard. To use the touchpad, you simply move your finger across the pad. Some touchpads are also sensitive to taps, interpreting them as mouse-button clicks. Other notebooks incorporate a **trackpoint device**, a small, joystick-like nub that allows you to move the cursor with the tip of your finger. Figures 10a and 10b show some of the mouse options you'll find in notebooks.

Many people still prefer to use a traditional external mouse with their notebooks. Small, compact devices like the MoGo Mouse (see Figure 10c) are designed for portability. The MoGo Mouse fits into a peripheral slot on the side of a notebook; this slot serves to store the mouse, protect it, and charge its batteries all at the same time.

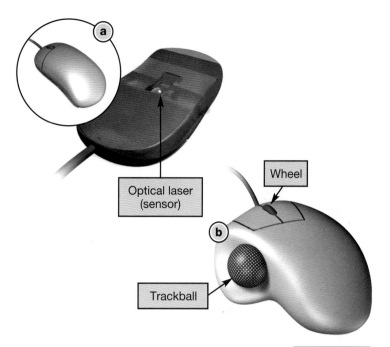

Optical laser (sensor)

Wheel

Trackball

FIGURE 9

(a) An optical mouse has an optical laser (or sensor) on the bottom that detects its movement. (b) A trackball mouse turns the traditional mouse on its back, allowing you to control the rollerball with your fingers.

ACTIVE HELPDESK

Using Input Devices

In this Active Helpdesk call, you'll play the role of a Helpdesk staffer, fielding calls about different input devices, such as the different mice and keyboards on the market, what wireless input options are available, and how to best use these devices.

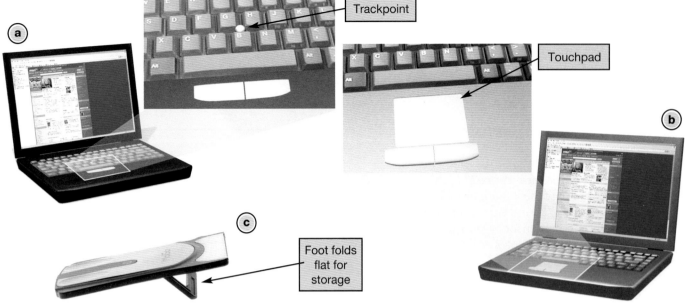

Trackpoint

Touchpad

Foot folds
flat for
storage

Newton Peripherals, LLC

The MoGo Mouse is wireless and uses Bluetooth technology to transmit data to the notebook.

What else can I do with my mouse? Manufacturers of mice are constantly releasing new models that allow you to perform ever more useful tasks with a few clicks of the mouse. For example, on new mouse models, Microsoft and Logitech now provide features such as these:

- **Instant Viewer.** Shrinks all windows currently open to thumbnail-size images so that you can see everything open on your desktop at a glance.

- **Magnifier.** Pulls up a magnification box that you can drag around the screen to enhance viewing of hard-to-read images (see Figure 11).

- **Customizable buttons.** Provides extra buttons on the mouse that can be programmed to perform the functions that you use most often to help you speed through tasks.

- **Web Search.** Allows you to quickly highlight a word or phrase and then press the search button (on the mouse) to start a Web search.

So check out the features of new mice as they come on the market to see if you can benefit from the purchase of a new mouse.

Are game controls considered mice? Game controls (such as joysticks, game pads, and steering wheels) are not mice per se, but they are considered input devices because they send data to the computer. Game pads, similar to the devices used on gaming consoles (such as the Xbox 360 and the PlayStation), are available for computers. Game pads have buttons and miniature pointing devices that provide input to the computer. Force-feedback joysticks and steering wheels deliver data in both directions: they translate your movements to the computer and translate its responses as forces on your hands, creating a richer simulated experience. If you like to move around a lot while you play games, you can purchase wireless game controllers at most computer stores. Portable gaming devices such as the Nintendo DS feature touch-sensitive screens that use a stylus (or finger) for input.

Window provides magnified view

FIGURE 11

The magnifier is a new mouse feature that provides access to a window that can be dragged around the screen to provide instant magnification of images or text.

What other types of input devices are available? Tablet PCs were developed primarily because many people find it easier to write than type input into a computer. But tablet PCs are expensive compared to conventional notebooks. An alternative is a digital pen like the EPOS Digital Pen (see Figure 12). This pen works in conjunction with a flash drive (a portable electronic storage device that connects to a port on a computer). You can write with the pen on any conventional paper, and your writing is captured and then wirelessly transmitted and stored in the flash drive. When the flash drive is connected to a computer, you can use software to translate your writing into digital text.

IMAGE INPUT

How can I input digital images into my computer? Digital cameras, camcorders, and webcams are the most common devices for capturing pictures and video, and are all considered input devices. Digital cameras and camcorders are usually used in remote settings (away from the computer) to capture images for later downloading to the computer. These devices are either connected to the computer by a data cable or transmit data wirelessly. Windows automatically recognizes these devices when they are connected to the computer and makes the input of the digital data to the computer very easy.

Webcams (see Figure 13) are small cameras that usually sit on top of your computer monitor (connected to the computer by a cable) or are built into your notebook computer. Although some webcams are able to capture still images, they are used mostly for transferring live video directly to your computer. Webcams make it possible to transmit live video over the Web and are often used to facilitate videoconferencing or calls made with video phones. Videoconferencing technology allows a person sitting at a computer equipped with a personal video camera (webcam) and a microphone to transmit video and audio across the Internet (or other communications medium).

SOUND INPUT

Why would I want to input sound to my computer? Equipping your computer to accept sound input opens up a variety of possibilities. You can conduct audio confer-

Flash drive

When you write on regular paper with the pen, digital information is transmitted wirelessly to the flash drive.

FIGURE 12

The EPOS digital pen captures writing and stores it in a flash drive for later transfer to a computer. No typing required!

ences with work colleagues, chat with friends or family over the Internet instead of using a phone, record podcasts, and more. Inputting sound to your computer requires equipping it with a **microphone** or **mic**, a device that allows you to capture sound waves (such as your voice) and transfer them to digital format on your computer. Many notebook computers come with built-in microphones, and some desktop computers come with inexpensive microphones. If you don't have a microphone or you aren't getting the quality you need from your existing microphone, you probably need to shop for one.

What types of microphones are available for my computer? Most microphones that are sold to be used with computers are **magnetically shielded microphones**, also known as computer microphones. The microphone plugs into a port on the sound card in your computer, so make sure you select a microphone that has the correct connector to fit your available sound input port.

Microphones come in two basic types, depending on how they are configured to pick up sound. **Unidirectional microphones** pick up sound from only one direction. These are best used for recording podcasts with a single voice or making phone calls over the Internet with only one person on your end of the call. **Omnidirectional microphones** pick up sounds from all directions at once. These mics are best for recording more than one voice, such as during a conference call when you need to pick up the voices of multiple speakers.

What's the best microphone to have? This answer depends on what you are using the microphone to do. Close-talk

FIGURE 13

Webcams, usually placed on top of your monitor, enable you to bring live video streams into your computer to facilitate video chats or conferences with your friends or coworkers.

Logitech Inc.

Headset and desktop microphones offer convenient, inexpensive, hands-free voice input.

microphones (see Figure 14a), which are usually attached to a headset, are useful in situations such as using speech-recognition software, videoconferencing, or making telephone calls. With a microphone attached to a headset, your hands are free to perform other tasks while you speak (such as making notes or referring to paper documents). All computers participating in a videoconference need to have a microphone and speakers installed so that participants can speak to and hear one another.

In **speech-recognition systems**, you operate your computer through a microphone, telling it to perform specific commands (such as to open a file) or to translate your spoken words into data input. Speech recognition has yet to truly catch on, but its popularity is growing. In fact, it's included in the software applications found in Office 2007.

Handheld microphones (which often have a base attached) are convenient for recording podcasts or in other situations where you might need your hands to be free. Clip-on (or lavaliere) microphones are useful in situations where you are presenting at a meeting and need to keep your hands free for other activities (such as writing on a white board) or wander around the room. Many of these microphones are wireless.

Are expensive microphones worth the money? Microphone quality varies widely. For personal use, an inexpensive microphone is probably sufficient. However, if you plan to create professional products and sell them to others, you'll most likely need a more expensive professional recording studio microphone. Music stores and other stores that sell equipment for outfitting recording studios are usually good places to obtain advice on high-quality microphones.

INPUT DEVICES FOR PHYSICALLY CHALLENGED INDIVIDUALS

What input devices are available for people with disabilities? Individuals with physical challenges often use comput-

ers, but sometimes they need special input devices to access them. For visually impaired users, voice recognition is an obvious option. For those users whose visual limitations are less severe, keyboards with larger keys are available. On-screen keyboards also can make input easier for some individuals. These keyboards are displayed as graphics on the computer screen and represent a standard keyboard layout. Keys are pressed with the use of a pointing device or by using a touch-screen monitor.

People with motor control issues may have difficulty with pointing devices. To aid such users, special trackballs are available that are manipulated easily with one finger and are attachable to almost any surface (such as a workstation or wheelchair). When arm motion is severely restrained, head-mounted pointing devices can be used. Generally, these involve a camera mounted on the computer monitor and a device attached to the head (often installed in a hat). When the user moves his or her head, the camera detects the movement that controls the cursor on the screen. In this case, mouse clicks are controlled by a switch that can be manipulated by the user's hands or feet or even by using an instrument that fits into the mouth and senses the user blowing into it.

Output Devices

Output devices enable you to send processed data out of your computer. This can take the form of text, pictures (graphics), sounds (audio), and video. One common output device is a **monitor** (sometimes referred to as a **display screen**), which displays text, graphics, and video as *soft copies* (copies you can see only on-screen). Another common output device is the **printer**, which creates tangible or hard copies (copies you can touch) of text and graphics. Speakers and earphones (or ear buds) are obviously the output devices for sound.

MONITORS

What are the different types of monitors? There are two basic types of monitors: CRTs and LCDs. If your monitor looks like a traditional television set, it has a picture tube device called a **cathode-ray tube (CRT)**

Ethics: What Is Ethical Computing?

If you were asked to cite an example of unethical behavior while using a computer, you probably wouldn't have trouble providing an answer. You've probably heard news stories about crimes conducted using computers, such as people unleashing viruses or committing identity theft. You may have read about students who were prosecuted at a neighboring university for illegally sharing copywrited material such as videos. Both of these are examples of unethical behavior while using a computer. But if you were asked what constitutes ethical behavior while using a computer, could you provide an answer just as quickly?

Loosely defined, ethics is a system of moral principles, rules, and accepted standards of conduct. So what are the accepted standards of conduct when using computers? The Computer Ethics Institute developed the Ten Commandments of Computer Ethics, which is widely cited as a benchmark for companies that are developing computer usage and compliance policies for employees. Our Ethical Computing Guidelines listed below are based the Computer Ethics Institute's work:

Ethical Computing Guidelines

1. Avoid causing harm to others when using computers.
2. Do not interfere with other people's efforts at accomplishing work with computers.
3. Resist the temptation to snoop in other people's computer files.
4. Do not use computers to commit theft.
5. Agree not to use computers to promote lies.
6. Do not use software (or make illegal copies for others) without paying the creator for it.

7. Avoid using other people's computer resources without appropriate authorization or proper compensation.
8. Do not claim other people's intellectual output as your own.
9. Consider the social consequences of the products of your computer labor.
10. Only use computers in ways that show consideration and respect for others.

The United States has enacted laws that support some of these guidelines, such as Number 6—the breaking of which would violate copyright laws. Or Number 4, which is covered by numerous federal and state larceny laws. Other guidelines, however, require more subtle interpretation as to their unethical nature because there are no laws designed to enforce them.

Consider the seventh guideline against using unauthorized resources, for example. The college you attend probably provides computer resources for you to complete coursework. However, just because you are provided with a computer and access to the Internet doesn't necessarily mean it is ethical for you to run a business on eBay in between classes or on the weekends in the college library. Although it might not be technically illegal, you are tying up computer resources that could be used by other students for the intended purpose of learning and completing coursework (which, of course, also violates guidelines 2 and 10).

Throughout the chapters in this book, we'll touch on many topics related to these guidelines. So keep them in mind as you study, and think about how they relate to the actions you take as you use computers in your life.

---

like the one shown in Figure 15a. If your monitor is flat, such as those found in notebooks, it's using **liquid crystal display (LCD)** technology (see Figure 15b), similar to that used in digital watches. LCD monitors (also called **flat-panel monitors**) are lighter and more energy efficient than CRT monitors, making them perfect for portable computers such as notebooks. The sleek style of LCD monitors also makes them a favorite for users with small workspaces.

Which monitor type is most popular? By far, LCD monitors are the most popular. In fact, CRT monitors can be diffi-

cult to find even if you want to buy one as they are fast becoming legacy technology. **Legacy technology** is comprised of computing devices or peripherals that use techniques, parts, and methods from an earlier time that are no longer popular. Although legacy technology may still be functional, it is quickly being replaced by newer technological advances. This doesn't mean that if you have a CRT monitor that is functioning well you should throw it away and buy an LCD monitor. But when your CRT monitor begins to fail, you will most likely want to consider replacing it with newer technology.

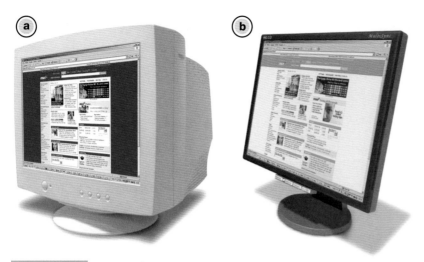

FIGURE 15

(a) CRT monitors are big and bulky and look like television sets. (b) LCDs (flat-panel monitors) save precious desktop space and weigh considerably less than CRT monitors.

Key Monitor Features

How do monitors work? Monitor screens are grids made up of millions of **pixels**, or tiny dots (see Figure 16). Simply put, illuminated pixels are what create the images you see on your monitor. There are three pixel colors: red, blue, and green. LCD monitors are made of two (or more) sheets of material filled with a liquid crystal solution. A fluorescent panel at the back of the LCD monitor generates light waves. When electric current passes

through the liquid crystal solution, the crystals move around, either blocking the fluorescent light or letting the light shine through. This blocking or passing of light by the crystals causes images to be formed on the screen. In CRT monitors, pixels are illuminated by an electron beam that passes back and forth across the back of the screen very quickly so that the pixels appear to glow continuously. The various combinations of red, blue, and green make up the components of color we see on our monitors.

What factors affect the quality of an LCD monitor? The most important factor to consider when choosing an LCD monitor is resolution. The clearness or sharpness of the image—its **resolution**—is controlled by the number of pixels displayed on the screen. The higher the resolution, the sharper and clearer the image will be. Monitor resolution is listed as a number of pixels. A high-end monitor may have a native (or maximum) resolution of 1,600 x 1,200, meaning it contains 1,600 vertical columns with 1,200 pixels in each column. Note that you can adjust a monitor's resolution either to make the screen display larger (reducing the resolution) or to fit more on your screen (increasing the resolution). You cannot increase the resolution of an LCD monitor beyond its native resolution. Generally, you should select a monitor with the highest resolution available for the screen size (measured in inches).

You'll generally find two types of LCD monitors on the market: **passive-matrix displays** and **active-matrix displays**. Less expensive LCD monitors use passive-matrix displays, whereas more expensive monitors use active-matrix displays. Passive-matrix technology uses an electrical current passed through the liquid crystal solution to charge groups of pixels, either in a row or a column. This causes the screen to brighten with each pass of electrical current and subsequently fade. With active-matrix displays, each pixel is charged individually, as needed. The result is that an active-matrix display produces a clearer, brighter image with better viewing angles. As the price of active-matrix displays continues to drop, passive-matrix displays will soon become a thing of the past.

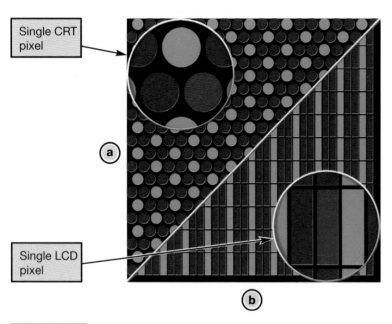

Single CRT pixel

Single LCD pixel

FIGURE 16

A pixel, short for picture element, is one dot. CRT pixels (a) are round, whereas LCD pixels (b) are rectangular and are laid out in a matrix. There are three pixel colors: red, blue, and green. Millions of pixels make up an image, and color is created by various shades and combinations of these pixels.

Other factors to consider when judging the quality of an LCD monitor are as follows:

- **Viewing angle.** An LCD's viewing angle, which is measured in degrees, tells how far you can move to the side of (or above or below) the monitor before the image quality degrades to unacceptable levels. For monitors that measure 17 inches or more, a viewing angle of at least 150 degrees is usually recommended.
- **Contrast ratio.** This is a measure of the difference in light intensity between the brightest white and the darkest black colors that the monitor can produce. If the contrast ratio is too low, colors tend to fade when you adjust the brightness to a high or low setting. A contrast ratio of between 400:1 and 600:1 is preferable.
- **Brightness.** Measured as candelas per square meter (cd/m2) or nits, brightness is a measure of the greatest amount of light showing when the monitor is displaying pure white. A brightness level of 250cd/m2 or greater is recommended.
- **Response time.** This is the measurement (in milliseconds) of the time it takes for a pixel to change color. The lower the response time, the smoother moving images will appear on the monitor. A low response time is important when using a monitor to play a game or display full-motion video (such as movies or television).

LCD VERSUS CRT

Why did LCD monitors become so much more popular than CRT monitors? LCD monitors are much smaller than CRT monitors and therefore take up far less space on a desktop. LCD monitors are also generally brighter than CRT monitors and use different refresh methods for their pixels, which causes less eyestrain. Another advantage is that LCD monitors use significantly less energy and emit less electromagnetic radiation, making them more environmentally friendly. And finally, LCD monitors weigh less, making them the obvious choice for mobile devices.

CRT monitors used to offer a wider range of resolutions than LCD monitors and produced better clarity and color accuracy. However, the newest LCD monitors have closed the gap with the old CRTs in all of

BITS AND BYTES

Cleaning Your Monitor

Have you ever noticed how quickly your monitor attracts dust? It's important to keep your monitor clean because dust buildup can act like insulation, keeping heat in and causing the electronic components to wear out much faster. To clean your monitor, follow these steps:

1. Turn off the monitor and make sure it is unplugged from the electrical power outlet.
2. For a CRT monitor, wipe the monitor's surface using a sheet of fabric softener or a soft cloth dampened with window cleaner or water. Never spray anything directly onto the monitor. (Check your monitor's user manual to see if there are cleaning products you should avoid using.) For an LCD (flat-panel) monitor, use a 50/50 solution of rubbing alcohol and water on a soft cloth and wipe the screen surface gently.
3. In addition to the screen, wipe away the dust from around the case.

Finally, don't place anything on top of the monitor because the items may block air from cooling it, and avoid placing magnets (including your speaker system's subwoofer) anywhere near the monitor because they can interfere with the mechanisms inside the monitor.

these areas and are now considered excellent substitutes for CRT monitors by most users.

Because of their different technologies, you can see more with an LCD screen than you can with the same-size CRT monitor. For example, there are 17 inches of viewable area on a 17-inch LCD monitor but only 15 inches of viewable area on a 17-inch CRT monitor.

What features of monitors can help physically challenged individuals? If a monitor (or display in a notebook or PDA) accepts input from a user touching the screen, then the monitor also doubles as an input device. Although these monitors, known as **touch-screen monitors**, are available for home computers, they are uncommon. However, people with limited motor control that prevents them from typing quickly and accurately are often greatly assisted by the installation of a touch-screen monitor. In fact, people with significant paralysis often use a stylus (sometimes held in their mouth) in conjunction with a touch-screen monitor to virtually eliminate the need for a keyboard.

Hasbro/Tiger Electronics/Litzky Public Relations

FIGURE 17

Inexpensive projectors such as the Zoombox are showing up more frequently in the home.

Individuals with impaired vision can reduce the resolution of a monitor, which causes the images on the screen (like icons and text) to appear larger. Windows and many other software applications have magnification features that can further enhance viewing.

How do I show output to a large group of people? Crowding large groups of people around your computer just isn't practical. **Data projectors** are devices that are used to project images from your computer onto a wall or viewing screen. Data projectors are commonly used in business and education in conference rooms and classrooms. These projectors are becoming smaller and lighter, making them ideal for businesspeople who have to make presentations at client locations. The price of these projectors has been falling significantly in recent years, making them a good option for use in the home. Projectors like the Zoombox Entertainment Project from Hasbro (see Figure 17) can not only project a 60-inch image on a screen (or wall) but also can play CDs and DVDs with the built-in DVD combo drive and speakers—all for less than $300.

ACTIVE HELPDESK

Using Output Devices

In this Active Helpdesk call, you'll play the role of a Helpdesk staffer, fielding calls about different output devices, including the differences between LCD and CRT monitor technologies and between inkjet and laser printers and the advantages and disadvantages of each.

PRINTERS

What are the different types of printers? There are two primary categories of printers: impact and nonimpact. **Impact printers** have tiny hammer-like keys that strike the paper through an inked ribbon, thus making a mark on the paper. The most common impact printer is the dot-matrix printer. In contrast, **nonimpact printers** spray ink or use laser beams to transfer marks onto the paper. The most common nonimpact printers are inkjet printers and laser printers. Such nonimpact printers have replaced dot-matrix printers almost entirely. They tend to be less expensive, quieter, and faster, and they offer better print quality. The only place you may still see a dot-matrix printer is at a company (like a car rental agency) that still uses them to print multipart forms. Dot-matrix printers are truly legacy technology.

What are the advantages of inkjet printers? Compared with dot-matrix printers, **inkjet printers** (see Figure 18) are quieter, faster, and offer higher-quality printouts. In addition, even high-quality printers are affordable. Inkjet printers work by spraying tiny drops of ink onto paper. The key advantage is that inkjets print acceptable quality color images cost effectively. In fact, when using the right paper, higher-end inkjet printers print images that look like professional-quality photos. Because of their high quality and low price, inkjet printers are still the most popular printer for color printing.

Cherry Blossom Bonsai

FIGURE 18

Inkjet printers are popular among home users, especially with the rise of digital photography. Many inkjet printers are optimized for printing photos from digital cameras.

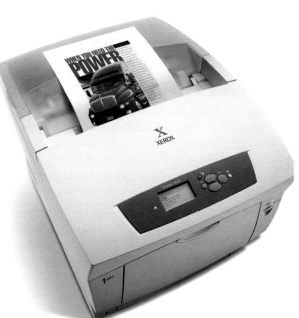

Courtesy Xerox Corporation

Modern portable printers feature Bluetooth connectivity, allowing them to be used with mobile devices such as notebooks, tablets, PDAs, and smartphones.

Paper exits here

NewsCom

Laser printers print quickly and offer high-quality printouts. Models that print color at prices affordable enough for personal use or a small business are becoming more common.

Why would I want a laser printer? **Laser printers** are often preferred for their quick and quiet production and high-quality printouts (see Figure 19). Because they print quickly, laser printers are often used in schools and offices where multiple computers share one printer. Although more expensive to buy than inkjet printers, over the long run, for high-volume printing, laser printers are more economical than inkjets (they cost less per printed black-and-white page) when you include the price of ink and special paper in the overall cost. Recently, the prices of color laser printers have fallen dramatically, making them very price competitive with high-end inkjet printers.

What kind of printer could I use for my notebook? Although any printer that is suitable for your desktop is appropriate to use with your notebook, you may want to consider a portable printer for added mobility and flexibility (see Figure 20). Portable printers (including many inkjet printers) often are compact enough to fit in a briefcase, are lightweight, and sometimes run on battery power instead of AC current.

Are there wireless printers? Infrared-compatible or wireless printers allow you to print from your handheld device, notebook, or camera. Most of these printers work using Bluetooth technology.

Are there any other types of specialty printers? A **multifunction printer**, or an all-in-one printer, is a device that combines the functions of a printer, scanner, copier, and fax into one machine. Popular for their space-saving convenience, all-in-one printers can be either inkjet or laser-based. **Plotters** are large printers used to produce oversize pictures that require precise continuous lines to be drawn, such as maps, images (see Figure 21), or architectural plans. Plotters use a computer-controlled pen that provides a greater level of precision than the

Plotters are large printers used to print oversize images, maps, or architectural plans.

Hewlett-Packard Company

series of dots that laser or inkjet printers are capable of making.

Thermal printers, such as the one shown in Figure 22, are another kind of specialty printer. These printers work either by melting wax-based ink onto ordinary paper (in a process called thermal wax transfer printing) or by burning dots onto specially coated paper (in a process called direct thermal printing). They are used in stores to print receipts and in airports for electronic ticketing, among other places. Thermal printers are also emerging as a popular technology for mobile and portable printing, for example, in conjunction with PDAs and similar devices. These are the printers car rental agencies use to give you an instant receipt when you drop off your rental car. Many models feature wireless infrared technology for complete portability.

FIGURE 22

Thermal printers are ideal for mobile computing because they are compact and lightweight, and require no ink cartridges. Here you see a PDA set into a thermal printer.

Choosing a Printer

How do I select the best printer? Web sites such as **www.printerdb.com/ColorPrinter. html** provide excellent tips on selecting a printer appropriate for your needs. You should conduct research before buying a printer, and be sure to consider these factors when making your choice:

- **Speed.** A printer's speed determines how many pages it can print per minute (called *pages per minute*, or *ppm*). The speed of inkjet printers has improved over the years so that many inkjet printers now print as fast as laser printers. Printing speeds vary by model and range from 8 to 30 ppm for both laser and inkjet printers. Text documents printed in black and white print faster than documents printed in color.

- **Resolution.** A printer's resolution (or printed image clarity) is measured in *dots per inch (dpi)*, or the number of dots of ink in a one-inch line. The higher the dpi, the greater the level of detail and quality of the image. You'll sometimes see dpi represented as a horizontal number multiplied by a vertical number, such as 600×600, but you may also see the same resolution simply stated as 600 dpi. For general-purpose printing, 300 dpi is sufficient. If you're going to print photos, 1,200 dpi is better. The dpi for professional photo-quality printers is twice that.

- **Color output.** If you're using an inkjet printer to print color images, buy a four-color (cyan, magenta, yellow, and black) or six-color printer (four-color plus light cyan and light magenta) for the highest-quality output. Some printers come with a single ink cartridge for all colors; others have two ink cartridges, one for black and one for color. The best setup is to have individual ink cartridges for each color so you can replace only the specific color cartridge that is empty. Color laser printers have four separate toner cartridges (black, cyan, magenta, and yellow), and the toner is blended in various quantities to produce the entire printer spectrum.

BITS AND BYTES

Does It Matter What Paper I Print On?

The quality of your printer is only part of what controls the quality of a printed image. The paper you use and the printer settings that control the amount of ink used are equally important. If you're printing text-only documents for personal use, using low-cost paper is fine. You also may want to consider selecting "Draft" mode in your printer setting to conserve ink. However, if you're printing documents for more formal use, such as résumés, you may want to adjust your print settings to "Normal" or "Best" and choose a higher-quality paper. Paper quality is determined by the paper's weight, whiteness, and brightness.

The *weight* of paper is measured in pounds, with 20 pounds being standard. A heavier paper may be best for projects such as brochures, but be sure to check that your printer can handle the added thickness. It is a matter of personal preference as to the degree of paper whiteness. Generally, the whiter the paper, the brighter colors appear. However, in some more formal printings such as résumés, you may want to use a creamier color. The brightness of paper usually varies from 85 to 94. The higher the number, the brighter the paper and the easier it is to read printed text. Opacity is especially important if you're printing on both sides of the paper, because it determines the amount of ink that shows through or is concealed from the opposite side of the paper.

If you're printing photos, paper quality can have a big impact on the results. Photo paper is more expensive than regular paper and comes in a variety of textures ranging from matte to high gloss. For a photo-lab look, high-gloss paper is the best choice. Semigloss (often referred to as satin) is good for portraits, while a matte surface is often used for black-and-white printing.

DIG DEEPER

How Inkjet and Laser Printers Work

Ever wonder how a printer knows what to print and how it puts ink in just the right places? Most inkjet printers use drop-on-demand technology in which the ink is "demanded" and then "dropped" onto the paper. Two separate processes use drop-on-demand technology: thermal bubble, used by Hewlett-Packard and Canon, and piezoelectric, used by Epson. The difference between the two processes is how the ink is heated within the print cartridge reservoir (the chamber inside the printer that holds the ink).

In the thermal bubble process, the ink is heated in such a way that it expands (like a bubble) and leaves the cartridge reservoir through a small opening, or nozzle. Figure 23 shows the general process for thermal bubble.

In the piezoelectric process, each ink nozzle contains a crystal at the back of the ink reservoir that receives an electrical charge, causing the ink to vibrate and drop out of the nozzle.

Laser printers use a completely different process. Inside a laser printer is a big metal cylinder (or drum) that is charged with static electricity. When you ask the printer to print something, it sends signals to the laser in the laser printer, telling it to "uncharge" selected spots on the charged cylinder, corresponding to the document you wish to print. Toner, a fine powder that is used in place of liquid ink, is attracted to only those areas on the drum that are not charged. (These uncharged areas are the characters and images you want to print.) The toner is then transferred to the paper as it feeds through the printer. Finally, the toner is melted onto the paper. All unused toner is swept away before the next job starts the process all over again.

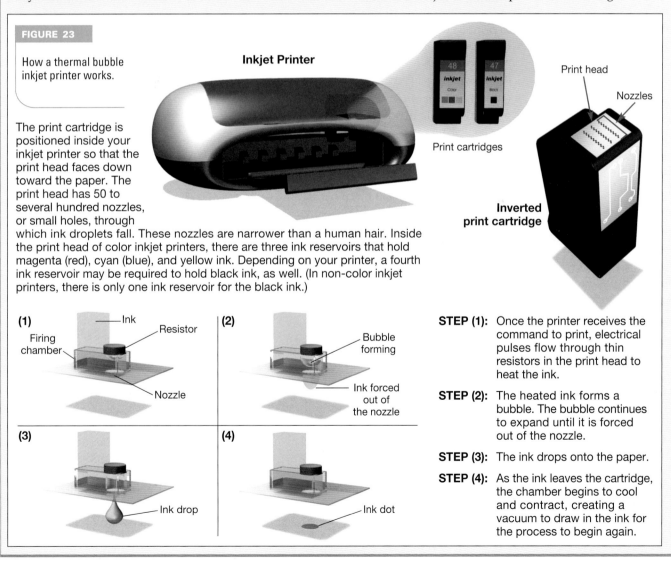

FIGURE 23

How a thermal bubble inkjet printer works.

Inkjet Printer

Print cartridges

Print head

Nozzles

Inverted print cartridge

The print cartridge is positioned inside your inkjet printer so that the print head faces down toward the paper. The print head has 50 to several hundred nozzles, or small holes, through which ink droplets fall. These nozzles are narrower than a human hair. Inside the print head of color inkjet printers, there are three ink reservoirs that hold magenta (red), cyan (blue), and yellow ink. Depending on your printer, a fourth ink reservoir may be required to hold black ink, as well. (In non-color inkjet printers, there is only one ink reservoir for the black ink.)

(1)
Firing chamber — Ink — Resistor — Nozzle

(2)
Bubble forming — Ink forced out of the nozzle

(3)
Ink drop

(4)
Ink dot

STEP (1): Once the printer receives the command to print, electrical pulses flow through thin resistors in the print head to heat the ink.

STEP (2): The heated ink forms a bubble. The bubble continues to expand until it is forced out of the nozzle.

STEP (3): The ink drops onto the paper.

STEP (4): As the ink leaves the cartridge, the chamber begins to cool and contract, creating a vacuum to draw in the ink for the process to begin again.

- **Memory.** Printers need memory in order to print. Inkjet printers run slowly if they don't have enough memory. If you plan to print small text-only documents on an inkjet printer, 1 to 2 megabytes (MB) of memory should be enough. You need about 4 MB of memory if you expect to print large text-only documents and 8 MB if you print graphics-heavy files. Unlike inkjet printers, laser printers won't print at all without sufficient memory. To ensure your laser printer meets your printing needs, buy one with 16 MB of memory. Some printers allow you to add more memory later.

- **Use and cost of the printer.** If you will be printing mostly black-and-white, text-based documents or will be sharing your printer with others, a black-and-white laser printer is best because of its printing speed and overall economies for volume printing. If you're planning to print color photos and graphics, an inkjet printer or color laser printer is a must, even though the cost per page will be higher.

- **Cost of consumables.** You should carefully investigate the cost of consumables (such as printer cartridges and paper) for any printer you are considering purchasing. Often, the cost of inkjet cartridges can exceed the cost of the actual printer when purchased on sale. Check reviews in consumer magazines (such as *PC Magazine* or *Consumer Reports*) to help you evaluate the overall cost of producing documents with a particular printer.

SOUND OUTPUT

What are the output devices for sound? As noted earlier, most computers include inexpensive **speakers** as an output device for sound. These speakers are sufficient to play the standard audio clips you find on the Web and usually enable you to participate in videoconferencing or phone calls made over the Internet. However, if you plan to digitally edit audio files or are particular about how your music sounds, you may want to upgrade to a more sophisticated speaker system, such as one that includes **subwoofers** (special speakers that produce only low bass sounds) and **surround-sound capability** (speaker systems set up in such a way that they surround you with sound). And wireless speaker systems are available now to help you avoid cluttering up your rooms with speaker wire!.

If you work in close proximity to other employees or are traveling with a notebook, you may need to use headphones (or ear buds) for your sound output to avoid distracting other people. Headphones will plug into the same jack on the computer that speakers are connected to, so using them with a computer is easy. Studies of users of MP3 players have shown that hearing might be damaged by excessive volume, especially when using ear buds because they fit into the ear canals. Therefore, you should exercise caution when using these devices.

The System Unit

We just looked at the components of your computer that you use to input and output data. But where does the processing take place and where is the data stored? The system unit is the box that contains the central electronic components of the computer, including the computer's processor (its brain), its memory, and the many circuit boards that help the computer function. You'll also find the power source and all the storage devices (CD/DVD drive and hard drive) here.

BITS AND BYTES

Maintaining Your Printer

In general, printers require very little maintenance. Occasionally, it's a good idea to wipe the case of the printer with a damp cloth to free it from accumulated dust. However, do not wipe away any ink residue that has accumulated inside the printer. If you are experiencing streaking or blank areas on your printed paper, your print head nozzles may be clogged. To fix this, run the printer's cleaning cycle. (Check your printer's manual for instructions, because every printer is different.) If this doesn't work, you may want to use a cleaning sheet to brush the print head clean. These sheets often come with printers or with reams of photo paper. If you still have a problem, try a cleaning cartridge. Cleaning cartridges contain a special fluid that scrubs the print head. Such cartridges can be found where most ink cartridges are sold (just make sure you buy one that is compatible with your printer).

Dell, Inc.

Apple Computer, Inc.

Which is the best system unit style? Most system units on desktop computers are tower configurations, which typically stand vertically (see Figure 24a). Some creatively designed desktop system units, such as the Apple iMac (see Figure 24b), house not just the computer's processor and memory, but its monitor as well. Although the all-in-ones like the iMac take up less desktop space, tower configurations make it easier for you to expand your computer. This is because most tower configurations have empty areas that allow you to install additional storage drives, such as an additional DVD or CD drive that didn't come with your system.

ON THE FRONT PANEL

What's on the front panel of my computer? No matter whether you choose a desktop or tower design, the front panel of your computer provides you with access to power controls and the storage devices on your computer. Figure 25 shows the front panel of a typical system. Although your system might be slightly different, chances are it includes many of the same features.

Power Controls

What's the best way to turn my computer on and off? Your system has a power-on button on the front panel. (You may also find power-on buttons on some keyboards.) Although you use this button to turn on your system, you *don't* want to use it to turn off (or power off) your system. Modern operating systems want control over the shutdown procedure, so you turn off the power by clicking on a shutdown icon on the desktop, not by pushing the main power button.

If you do shut off the power using the main power button without shutting down your operating system first, nothing on your system will be permanently damaged. However, some files and applications may not close properly, so the operating system may need to do some extra work the next time you start your computer.

Should I turn off my computer every time I'm done using it? Some people say you should leave your computer on at all times. They argue that turning your computer on and off throughout the day subjects its components to stress as the heating

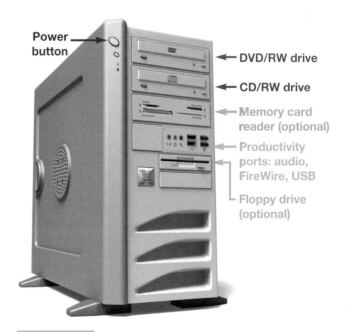

Power button

DVD/RW drive

CD/RW drive

Memory card reader (optional)

Productivity ports: audio, FireWire, USB

Floppy drive (optional)

and cooling process forces the components to expand and contract repeatedly. Other people say you should shut down your computer when you're not using it. They claim that you'll end up wasting money on electricity to keep the computer running all the time. However, modern operating systems include power-management settings that allow the most power-hungry components of the system (the hard drive and monitor) to shut down after a short idle period.

If you use the computer sporadically throughout the day, it may be best to keep it on while you're apt to use it and power it down when you're sure you won't be using it for long periods. However, if you use your computer only for a little while each day; you'll be paying electricity charges during long periods of nonuse. If you're truly concerned about the stresses incurred from powering on and off your computer, you may want to buy a warranty with the computer.

Can I "rest" my computer without turning it off completely? As mentioned earlier, your computer has power-management settings that help it conserve energy. In Windows Vista, the two main methods of power management are Sleep and Hibernate. When your computer enters **Sleep mode**, all the documents, applications, and data you were using are in RAM (memory) where they are quickly accessible upon starting to use your computer again (in Windows XP this was called Standby).

Hibernation is another power-saving mode that stores your data in memory and saves it to your computer's hard disk. In either mode, the computer then enters a state of greatly reduced power consumption to save energy. But a big advantage to using Hibernate is that if there is a power failure while your computer is conserving power, your information is protected from loss, because it is saved on the hard drive. To put your computer to sleep (or hibernate), open the Start menu and click the power button. To wake up your computer, tap a key on the keyboard or move the mouse; in a few seconds, the computer resumes with exactly the same programs running and documents displayed as when you put the computer to sleep.

In Windows Vista, you can change what happens when you press the power button on the Start menu. By accessing the Power Options screen (see Figure 26), you can decide if you want your computer to sleep or hibernate when you click the power button.

What's the restart option in Windows for? If you're using Windows Vista, you have the option to *restart* the computer when you click the right arrow button next to the lock button on the Start menu (see Figure 27). Restarting the system while it's powered on is called a **warm boot**. You might need to perform a warm boot if the operating system or other software application stops responding or if you have installed new programs. It takes less time to perform a warm boot than to power down completely and then restart all of your hardware.

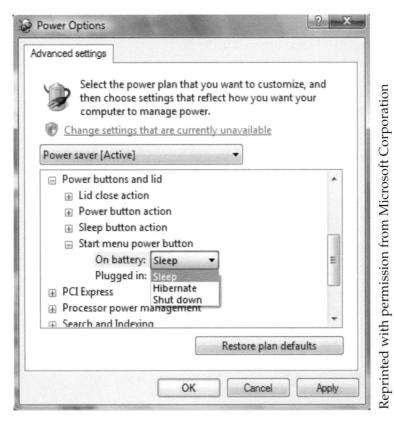

Reprinted with permission from Microsoft Corporation

FIGURE 26

Using the Sleep and Hibernation settings is not only good for the environment, but it is also good for your wallet. Windows Vista allows you to control the sleep and hibernation settings for a variety of operations.

>Open Power Options by left-clicking the **Start** button, clicking **Control Panel**, and then clicking **Power Options**. On the **Select a power plan** page, click **Change plan settings** under the selected plan. On the **Change settings for the plan** page, click **Change advanced power settings**. On the **Advanced settings** tab, expand **Power buttons and lid**, expand **Start menu power button**, click **On battery** or **Plugged in** (or both), click the arrow, and then click **Sleep**, **Hibernate**, or **Shut Down**.

Starting your computer when it has been completely powered down, such as first thing in the morning, is a **cold boot**. With the power management options of Windows Vista, however, you really need to shut down your computer completely only when you need to repair or install hardware in the system unit or move the system unit to another location.

Drive Bays: Your Access to Storage Devices

What else is on the front panel? Besides the power button, the other features that can be seen at the front of your system unit are **drive bays**. These bays are special shelves reserved for storage devices, those devices that hold your data and applications when the power is shut off. There are two kinds of drive bays:

1. Internal drive bays cannot be seen or accessed from outside the system unit. Generally, internal drive bays are reserved for internal **hard disk drives** (or just hard drives). An internal **hard drive** usually holds all permanently stored programs and data.

2. External drive bays can be seen and accessed from outside the system unit. External drive bays house CD and DVD drives, for example. Empty external drive bays are covered by a faceplate.

By looking at the front panel of your system unit, you can tell which devices have been installed, and often how many bays remain available for expansion.

What kind of data is saved on the internal hard disk drive? The hard disk drive is your computer's primary device for permanent storage of software and documents. The **hard disk drive** is a **nonvolatile storage** device, meaning it holds the data and instructions your computer needs permanently, even after the computer is turned off. Today's internal hard drives, with capacities of up to 750 GB, can hold more data than would fit in the books in your neighborhood library.

Originally, all hard disk drives were installed inside the system unit with all the other drive bays (see Figure 28a). However, unlike the other drive bays, you can't access an internal hard disk drive from the outside of the system unit, making it a form of nonportable permanent storage. Today, external hard drives are readily available.

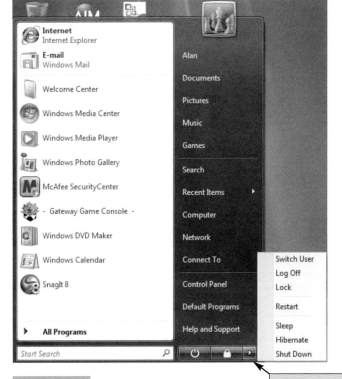

Reprinted with permission from Microsoft Corporation

Right arrow button

FIGURE 27

When you select the right arrow button from the Start menu in Windows Vista, you are presented with several options. For a warm boot, choose Restart. To power down the computer completely, choose Shut Down. You can also put your computer into a lower power mode by selecting Sleep or Hibernate.

>Click the Start menu button in the taskbar and then click the right arrow button to access your options.

Seagate Technology, Inc.

FIGURE 28

(a) Internal hard drives usually hold all the data and instructions that the computer needs, even after the power is turned off. Although the photo here shows an open internal hard disk drive, the drives are actually enclosed within the system unit in a hermetically sealed protective case to prevent contamination. In fact, a smoke or dust particle is enough to crash a hard drive. (b) External hard drives reside outside the system unit and are connected via cables, usually through a USB or Firewire data port. Because they are portable, they can easily be used for backing up multiple computers.

Courtesy Western
Digital Corporation

FIGURE 29

(a) Classic style flash drives are about the size of your thumb and can hold up to 8 GB of data (or more).
(b) Now available are larger versions of flash drives that can hold 16 GB of data (or more).

External hard drives (see Figure 28b) are essentially internal hard drives that have been made portable by enclosing them in a protective case, enabling them to easily connect to computers via cables, and by making them small and lightweight. External hard drives are usually connected to your computer with a data transfer cable. They are often used to back up (make a copy of) data that is contained on the internal hard drive in case a problem develops with the internal hard drive and data needs to be recovered.

What kinds of external drive bays do most PCs have? On the front panel, you'll see one or two bays for other storage devices such as CD drives. **CD-ROM drives** read CDs, whereas **CD-RW drives** can both read from and write (record) data to CDs. Some computers may also come with a separate **DVD drive**, which allows them to play DVDs and CDs, or a **DVD-RW drive**, which allows them to both read and write DVDs. DVDs are the same size and shape as CDs but can hold more than 25 times as much data. DVD-RW drives are especially useful if you're creating digital movies. Today, many computers come with a "combo" CD-RW/DVD drive, a device that can read and write CDs and play DVDs.

Blu-ray is the latest incarnation of optical storage to hit the market. While a dual-layered DVD can store about 9.8 gigabytes (GB) of information, this isn't enough to hold movies in the high-definition (HD) digital format that has become so popular. Blu-ray discs, which are very similar in size and shape to DVDs, can hold up to 50 GB of data. This is enough to hold approximately 4.5 hours of high-definition video.

You may occasionally see a PC that still has a bay for a **floppy disk drive**, which reads and writes to easily transportable floppy disks that hold a limited amount of data. Some computers also feature a **Zip disk drive**, which resembles a floppy disk drive but has a slightly wider opening. Zip disks work just like standard floppies but can carry much more data. These storage devices are fast becoming legacy technologies and are no longer found on new computers.

Flash drives, sometimes referred to as jump drives, USB drives, or thumb drives, are the new alternative to storing portable data (see Figure 29). These devices originally were about the size of your thumb, but now they vary in size and can hold upwards of 12 GB of data. Flash drives conveniently plug into universal serial bus (USB) ports.

Several manufacturers now also include slots on the front of the system unit in which you can insert portable **flash memory cards** such as Memory Sticks and CompactFlash cards. Many notebooks also include slots for flash memory cards. Flash memory cards let you transfer digital data between your computer and devices such as digital cameras, PDAs, smartphones, video cameras, and printers. Although incredibly small—some are just the size of a postage stamp—these memory cards have capacities that match or exceed that of a CD.

Figure 30 shows the storage capacities of the various portable storage media used in your computer's drive bays. As you learned earlier in this chapter, storage capacity is measured in bytes.

Ports

What are the ports on the front of my computer for? Ports are the place on the system unit where peripheral devices attach to the computer so that data can be exchanged between them and the operating system. Traditionally, ports have been located on the back of the system unit. However, in many new computer models, some commonly used ports are placed on the front of the computer for easier access when connecting portable devices such as digital cameras, MP3 players, and PDAs to the computer.

ON THE BACK

Are there still ports on the back of my system unit? Yes, even more ports are located on the back of your system unit, and often they duplicate ports that are provided on the front. Peripheral devices, such as monitors, printers, keyboards, and mice, connect to the system unit through ports. Because peripheral devices exchange data with the computer in various ways, a number of different ports have been created to accommodate these devices (see Figure 31) on the back of desktop systems. Notebooks have a similar selection of ports (see Figure

FIGURE 30 **Storage Media Capacities**

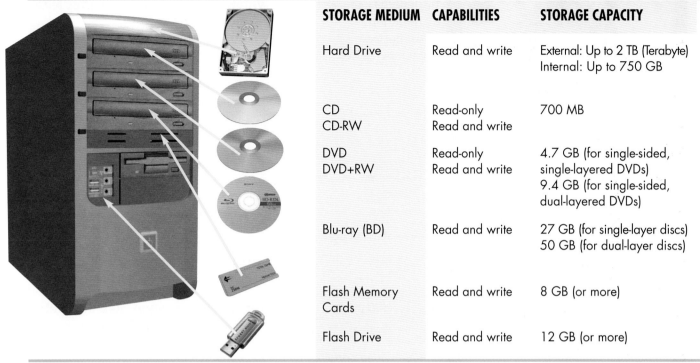

STORAGE MEDIUM	CAPABILITIES	STORAGE CAPACITY
Hard Drive	Read and write	External: Up to 2 TB (Terabyte) Internal: Up to 750 GB
CD CD-RW	Read-only Read and write	700 MB
DVD DVD+RW	Read-only Read and write	4.7 GB (for single-sided, single-layered DVDs) 9.4 GB (for single-sided, dual-layered DVDs)
Blu-ray (BD)	Read and write	27 GB (for single-layer discs) 50 GB (for dual-layer discs)
Flash Memory Cards	Read and write	8 GB (or more)
Flash Drive	Read and write	12 GB (or more)

d) Sony Electronics, Inc./NewsCom; e) SanDisk Corporation f) Lexar/USB drive

32). The ports on the back of the system unit are usually used for devices that stay attached to the computer at all times (such as a printer) while ports on the front are used for convenient connection of portable devices (digital cameras). Serial ports and parallel ports have long been used to connect input and output devices to the computer but are fast becoming legacy technology. Traditional **serial ports** send data one bit (or piece of data) at a time and are often used to connect modems (devices used to transmit data over telecommunications lines) to the computer. Sending data one bit at a time is a slow way to communicate. Data sent over serial ports is transferred at a speed of 115 kilobits per second (Kbps), or 115,000 bits per second. A **parallel port** sends data between devices in *groups* of bits at speeds of 500 Kbps and is therefore much faster than a traditional serial port. Parallel ports were often used to connect printers to computers, but USB ports are now vastly more popular.

Universal serial bus (USB) ports are now the most popular ports used to connect input and output devices to the computer. This is mainly because of their ability to transfer data quickly. **USB 2.0** ports transfer data at 480 Mbps and are approximately 40 times faster than the original USB port. USB

BITS AND BYTES

Getting a New Car? Consider One with Bluetooth!

Many cell phone users have Bluetooth headsets to use their phone hands-free. So why shouldn't you enjoy the same convenience in your car? Many manufacturers (such as Toyota, Nissan, and Audi) offer Bluetooth systems as options for their cars. So forget bulky, ugly docking stations for your mobile phone. If your phone and car are Bluetooth enabled, just hop in and use your phone in the hands-free mode with no wired connections to worry about. Microphones and control panels for the systems are usually mounted in the dash. And car manufacturers are beefing up the memory for the Bluetooth systems that are in their cars with more memory to hold information such as your mobile phone address book or the contents of your PDA. With many states passing laws prohibiting cell phone use in cars except in a hands-free mode, Bluetooth might be a necessary car option in your future.

ports can connect a wide variety of peripherals to the computer, including keyboards, printers, mice, smartphones, and digital cameras. Because most peripheral devices today offer USB connectivity, given two equal computers, you should consider

The System Unit

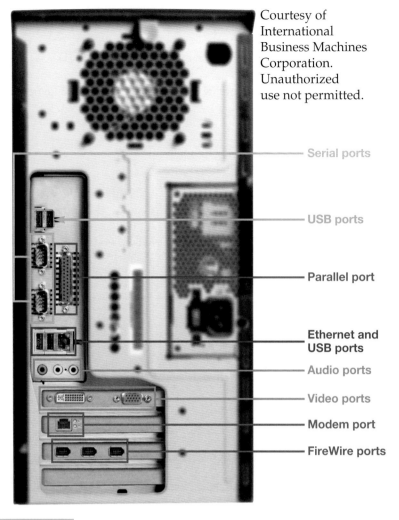

Courtesy of International Business Machines Corporation. Unauthorized use not permitted.

Serial ports

USB ports

Parallel port

Ethernet and USB ports

Audio ports

Video ports

Modem port

FireWire ports

The back of your computer probably has many or all of these ports, although they may not be in the same places. There are several different ports because many devices exchange data with the computer in various ways. Color coding helps identify the correct device to connect to each port.

purchasing the computer with the greater number of USB ports.

Which ports help me connect with other computers and the Internet? Another set of ports on your computer helps you communicate with other computers. Called **connectivity ports**, these ports give you access to networks and the Internet and enable your computer to function as a fax machine. To find connectivity ports, look for a port that resembles a standard phone jack but is slightly larger. This port is called an **Ethernet port**. This port transfers data at speeds up to 1000 Mbps. You use it to connect your computer to a DSL/cable modem or a network. Many computers still feature a second connectivity port that will accept a standard phoneline connector. This jack is the **modem port**. It uses a traditional telephone signal to connect to the Internet over a standard phone line.

Besides ports, what else can help me make connections? Many computers (especially notebooks) and other devices, such as smartphones, printers, and keyboards, feature built-in wireless connectivity devices. If your computer is equipped with technologies such as Bluetooth or wireless Ethernet (a way of transmitting Internet or network connection data), you can connect to other devices that have these technologies without using traditional ports and cables.

What are the fastest ports available? Interfaces such as **FireWire 400** (or **IEEE 1394**) and the latest **FireWire 800** are the fastest ports available. The FireWire 400 interface moves data at 400 Mbps, while the newer FireWire 800 doubles the rate to 800 Mbps. Devices such as external hard drives, digital video cameras, MP3 players, and digital media players all benefit from the speedy data transfer of FireWire.

Notebooks have many of the ports you find on desktop computers.

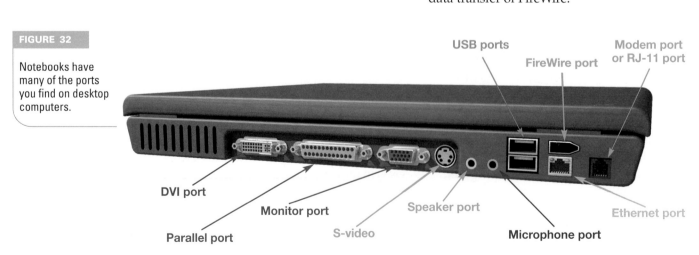

USB ports

FireWire port

Modem port or RJ-11 port

DVI port

Monitor port

Parallel port

S-video

Speaker port

Microphone port

Ethernet port

Looking at Computers: Understanding the Parts

What are the other ports on the back? Other ports on the back of the computer include the audio and video ports. The VGA (video graphics array) monitor port is the standard port to which monitors (both CRT and LCD) connect. Audio ports or jacks are where you connect headphones, microphones, and speakers to the computer.

INSIDE THE SYSTEM UNIT

What's inside the system unit? Figure 33 shows the layout common to many system units. As you can see, the **power supply** is housed inside the system unit to regulate the wall voltage to the voltages required by computer chips. Inside the system unit, you'll also find many printed circuit boards, which are flat, thin boards made of material that won't conduct electricity. On top of this material, thin copper lines are traced, allowing designers to connect a set of computer chips.

The various circuit boards have specific functions that augment the computer's basic functions. Some provide connections to other devices, so these are usually referred to as **expansion cards** (or **adapter cards**). Typical expansion cards found in the system unit are the sound card and video card. A **sound card**

provides a connection for the speakers and microphone, while a **video card** provides a connection for the monitor. Other expansion cards provide a means for network and Internet connections such as the **modem card**, which provides the computer with a connection to the Internet via a traditional phone line, and a **network interface card (NIC)**, which enables your computer to connect with other computers or to a cable modem to facilitate a high-speed Internet connection.

On the bottom or side of the system unit, you'll find the largest printed circuit board, called the **motherboard**. The motherboard is named such because all of the other boards (video cards, sound cards, and so on) connect to it to receive power and to communicate—therefore, it's the "mother" of all boards.

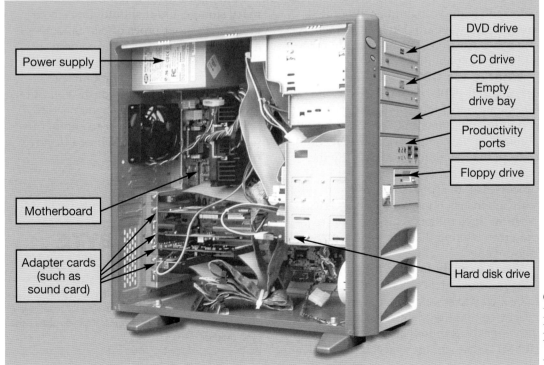

FIGURE 33

Inside the System Unit

Power supply

Motherboard

Adapter cards (such as sound card)

DVD drive

CD drive

Empty drive bay

Productivity ports

Floppy drive

Hard disk drive

Courtesy of International Business Machines Corporation. Unauthorized use not permitted.

The System Unit

77

FIGURE 34

A motherboard contains the CPU, the memory (RAM) cards, and slots available for expansion cards.

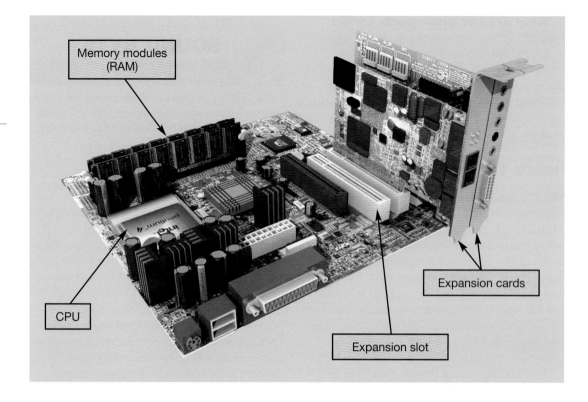

Memory modules (RAM)

CPU

Expansion cards

Expansion slot

What's on the motherboard? The motherboard contains the set of chips that powers the system, including the central processing unit (CPU). The motherboard also houses the chips that provide the short-term memory for the computer as well as a set of slots available for expansion cards (see Figure 34). Many low-end computer models have motherboards with video and sound capabilities integrated into the motherboard. High-end models still use expansion cards to provide video and sound capabilities.

What is the CPU? The **central processing unit (CPU, or processor)** is the largest and most important chip in the computer. It is sometimes referred to as the "brains" of the computer because it controls all the functions performed by the computer's other components and processes all the commands issued to it by software instructions. Modern CPUs can perform three billion tasks a second without error, making them extremely powerful components.

What exactly is RAM? Because the CPU processes data so rapidly, there needs to be a way to store data and commands nearby so that they can be fed to the CPU very quickly. **Random access memory (RAM)** is that storage space. If you look at

a motherboard, you'll see RAM as a series of small cards (called memory cards or memory modules) plugged into slots on the motherboard. The CPU can request the contents of RAM, which can be located, opened, and delivered to the CPU for processing in a few billionths of a second (or nanoseconds).

Sometimes RAM is referred to as primary storage, but it should not be confused with other types of permanent storage devices. Because all the contents of RAM are erased when you turn off the computer, RAM is the temporaryor **volatile storage** location for the computer. To save data permanently, you need to save it to the hard drive or to another permanent storage device such as a floppy disk, CD, or flash drive.

SOUND BYTE

Virtual Computer Tour

In this Sound Byte, you'll take a video tour of the inside of a system unit. From opening the cover to locating the power supply, CPU, and memory, you'll become more familiar with what's inside your computer.

Opening Your System Unit

Many people use a computer for years without ever needing to open their system unit. But there are two reasons you might want or need to do so: to replace a defective expansion card or device or to upgrade your computer. If your hard drive or CD-ROM drive fails, with a bit of guidance, you can open the system unit yourself and replace the drive yourself. Adding more memory or adding a DVD-RW drive are upgrade procedures that you can do safely at home. However, it's important that you follow the device's specific installation instructions. These instructions will detail any safety procedures you'll need to observe, such as unplugging the computer and grounding yourself to avoid static electricity

discharge, which can damage internal components. It's also important to check with the manufacturer of your system to see if opening the case will void the system's warranty.

Does my computer need anything else to function? If you have other digital devices in your house (such as computers, a TiVo, or gaming consoles) that need to be connected to the Internet, you probably need to set up a home computer network. A network is a combination of hardware and software that facilitates the sharing of information between computing devices. Therefore, your computer may require additional networking hardware such as a router and cables.

Does the system unit contain any other kinds of memory besides RAM? In addition to RAM, the motherboard also contains a form of memory called **read-only memory (ROM)**. ROM holds all the instructions the computer needs to start up. Unlike data stored in RAM, which is volatile storage, the instructions stored in ROM are permanent, making ROM a nonvolatile storage location. As is the case with the hard disk drive, this means it does not get erased when the power is turned off.

Setting It All Up

It's important that you understand not only your computer's components and how they work together, but also how to set up these components safely. *Merriam-Webster's Dictionary* defines **ergonomics** as "an applied science concerned with designing and arranging things people use so that the people and things interact most efficiently and safely." In terms of computing, ergonomics refers to how you set up your computer and other equipment to minimize your risk of injury or discomfort.

Why is ergonomics important? Workplace injuries related to musculoskeletal disorders occur frequently in the United States. Approximately 375,500

workers experienced such disorders in 2005 (the latest year for which data is available), and these disorders required an average of 9 days off from work as reported by the United States Department of Labor Bureau of Labor Statistics (**www.bls.gov/news.release/osh2.toc.htm**). This resulted in businesses incurring billions of dollars of direct costs (sick pay, medical costs) and even more indirect costs (lost productivity, overtime, value of employee time involved in the accident, cost of recordkeeping and investigation, etc.). Avoiding workplace injuries is not only good for employees, but it is very financially favorable for businesses, too.

How can I avoid injuries when I'm working at my computer? The following are some guidelines that can help you avoid discomfort, eyestrain, or injuries while you're working at your computer:

• **Position your monitor correctly.** Studies suggest it's best to place your monitor at least 25 inches from your eyes. You may need to decrease the screen resolution to make text and images more readable at that distance. Also, experts recommend the monitor be positioned either at eye level or so that it is at an angle 15 to 20 degrees below your line of sight.

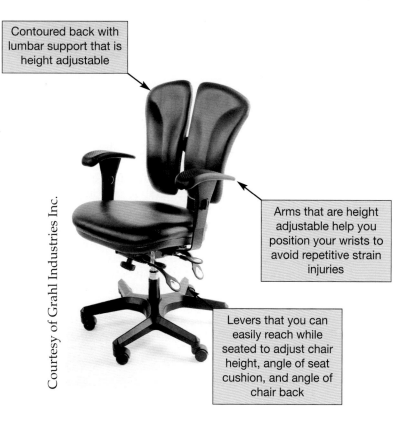

Contoured back with lumbar support that is height adjustable

Arms that are height adjustable help you position your wrists to avoid repetitive strain injuries

Levers that you can easily reach while seated to adjust chair height, angle of seat cushion, and angle of chair back

Courtesy of Grahl Industries Inc.

FIGURE 35

Look for these key features when selecting an ergonomic chair.

Datadesk Technologies

Courtesy of Kensington Technology Group

FIGURE 36

(a) Ergonomic keyboards that curve and contain built-in wrist rests help you maintain proper hand position to minimize strain on your wrists. (b) Ergonomic pointing devices replace conventional mice to reduce stress on the wrist and fingers.

• **Purchase an adjustable chair** (see Figure 35). Adjust the height of your chair so that your feet touch the floor. (You may need to use a footrest to get the right position.) Back support needs to be adjustable so that you can position it to support your lumbar (lower back) region. You should also be able to move the seat or adjust the back so that you can sit without exerting pressure on your knees. If your chair doesn't adjust, placing a pillow behind your back can provide the same support.

• **Assume a proper position while typing.** A repetitive strain injury (RSI) is a painful condition caused by repetitive or awkward movements of a part of the body. Improperly positioned keyboards are one of the leading causes of RSIs in computer users. Your wrists should be flat (unbent) with respect to the keyboard and your forearms parallel to the floor. You can either adjust the height of your chair or install a height-adjustable keyboard tray to ensure a proper position. Specially designed ergonomic keyboards like the ones shown in Figure 36 can help you achieve the proper position of your wrists.

• **Take breaks from computer tasks.** Remaining in the same position for long periods of time increases stress on your body. Shift your position in your chair and stretch your hands and fingers periodically. Likewise, staring at the screen for long periods of time can lead to eyestrain, so rest your eyes by periodically taking them off the screen and focusing them on an object at least 20 feet away.

• **Ensure the lighting is adequate.** Assuring proper lighting in your work area is a good way to minimize eyestrain. To do so,

SOUND BYTE

Healthy Computing

In this Sound Byte, you'll see how to set up your workspace in an ergonomically correct way. You'll learn the proper location of the monitor, keyboard, and mouse, as well as ergonomic features to look for when choosing the most appropriate chair.

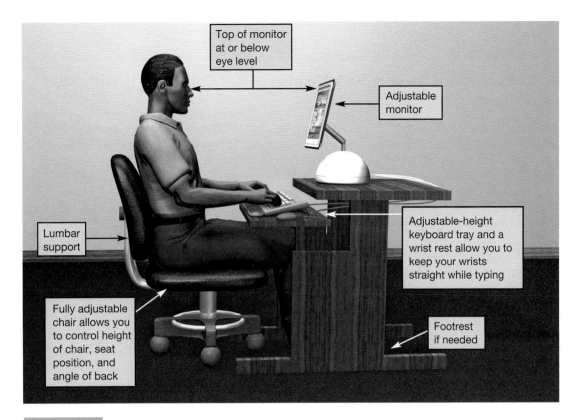

Top of monitor
at or below
eye level

Adjustable
monitor

Lumbar
support

Adjustable-height
keyboard tray and a
wrist rest allow you to
keep your wrists
straight while typing

Fully adjustable
chair allows you
to control height
of chair, seat
position, and
angle of back

Footrest
if needed

FIGURE 37

Achieving comfort and a proper typing position is the way to avoid repetitive strain injuries and other aches and pains while working at a computer. To achieve this, obtain equipment that boasts as many adjustments as possible. Every person is a different shape and size, requiring each workspace to be individually tailored. In addition, look for ergonomically designed peripheral devices such as keyboards, wrist rests, and antiglare screens to facilitate a safe working environment.

eliminate any sources of direct glare (light shining directly into your eyes) or reflected glare (light shining off the computer screen) and ensure there is enough light to read comfortably. If you still can't eliminate glare from your computer screen, you can purchase an antiglare screen to place over your mon-

itor. Look for ones that are polarized or have a purplish optical coating for the greatest relief.

Figure 37 illustrates how you should arrange your monitor, chair, body, and keyboard to avoid injury or discomfort while you're working on your computer.

TRENDS IN IT

Emerging Technologies: Tomorrow's Display—You Can Take It with You!

Today, LCD monitors dominate the desktop PC and notebook markets. Lighter and less bulky than previous monitors, they can be easily moved and take up less space on a desk. LCD technology has improved significantly over the past three years, and now monitors are sporting increased viewing angles, higher resolutions, and faster pixel response time, which makes full-motion video (critical for gamers) appear very smooth.

Despite these advances, LCDs can still be improved and are expected to continue to be the predominant display device in the next few years. Here are a few technologies that sources like *PC Magazine* feel will take LCD displays to the next level.

Flexible Screens

The most promising displays currently under development are organic light-emitting displays (OLEDs).

These displays, currently used in digital cameras, use organic compounds that produce light when exposed to an electric current. OLEDs tend to use less power than other flat-screen technologies, making them ideal for portable battery-operated devices. However, most research is being geared toward flexible OLEDs (FOLEDs). Unlike LCDs and CRTs, which use rigid surfaces such as glass, FOLED screens would be designed on lightweight, inexpensive, flexible material such as transparent plastics or metal foils. As shown in Figure 38, the computer screen of the future might roll up into an easily transported cylinder the size of a pen!

FOLEDs would allow advertising to progress to a new dimension. Screens could be hung where posters are hung now (such as on billboards). And wireless transmission of data to these screens would allow advertisers to display easily updatable full-motion

FIGURE 38

Universal Display Corporation

With FOLED technology, you'll be able to unroll a computer screen wherever you need it from a container the size of a pen. The prototype shown is currently being developed by Universal Display Corporation (**www.universaldisplay.com**) and should be available within a few years.

images. Combining transparency and flexibility would also allow these displays to be mounted on windshields or eyeglasses.

Another promising new technology is transparent thin-film transistors (TFTs). These transistors contain a mixture of zinc and tin oxides, instead of the traditional silicon, and the coolest thing about them is that they are transparent, flexible, and extremely heat resistant! Imagine a computer chip crammed with transistors but totally clear. Because they are clear, TFTs could eventually find their way into heads-up displays on car windshields or in stores as advertising on plate-glass windows.

There are some obstacles to be overcome before these types of screens will be widely available. In OLEDs and FOLEDs, the compounds that create blue hues age faster than the ones that produce reds and greens. This makes it difficult to maintain balanced colors over time. And the compounds used to form the OLEDs can be contaminated by exposure to water vapor or oxygen. The TFT technology is so new that it will probably be at least a decade before this technology appears in the consumer market. However, because of ongoing research, you can be sure that in your lifetime flexible displays will be popping up everywhere.

Wearable Screens

Who needs a screen when you can just wear one? With the rise of the iPod and other portable devices that play digital video, users are demanding larger viewing areas. Although a larger screen is often incompatible with the main design features of portable devices (lightweight and long battery life), wearable virtual displays offer a solution. Personal media viewer displays such as the myvu, shown in Figure 39, are available now (**www.myvu.com**). Eventually, when the technology advances sufficiently, you might purchase conventional eyeglasses with displays built right in. Wearable displays might eventually replace heavier screens on notebooks, desktops, and even PDAs.

"Bistable" Screens

Your computer screen constantly changes its images when you are surfing the Internet or playing a game. Because PDA and cell phone screens don't necessarily change that often, something called a "bistable" display,

currently used in retail stores for pricing signs, may one day be used in these devices. A bistable display has the ability to retain its image even when the power is turned off. In addition, bistable displays are lighter than LCD displays and reduce overall power consumption, resulting in longer battery life—research by Motorola indicates up to 600 times longer life! As the market for portable devices, such as smartphones, continues to explode, you can expect to see bistable technologies emerging in mobile computer screens.

Myvu Corporation

A prototype developed by MicroOptical Corporation features a microdisplay embedded in a pair of glasses. To users, it appears as though the display is projected right in front of them. Within a few years, you'll be able to buy a microdisplay when you buy glasses.

Summary

1. What exactly is a computer, and what are its four main functions?

Computers are devices that process data. They help organize, sort, and categorize data to turn it into information. The computer's four major functions are (1) to gather data (or allow users to input data); (2) to process that data (perform calculations or some other manipulation of the data); (3) to output data or information (display information in a form suitable for the user); and (4) to store data and information for later use.

2. What is the difference between data and information?

Data is a representation of a fact or idea. The number 3 and the words *televisions* or *Sony* are pieces of data. Information is data that has been organized or presented in a meaningful fashion. An inventory list that indicates that "3 Sony televisions" are in stock is processed information. It allows a retail clerk to answer a customer query about the availability of merchandise. Information is more powerful than raw data.

3. What are bits and bytes, and how are they measured?

To process data into information, computers need to work in a language they understand. This language, called binary language, consists of two numbers: 0 and 1. Each 0 and 1 is a binary digit, or bit. Eight bits create one byte. In computers, each letter of the alphabet, each number, and each special character consists of a unique combination of eight bits (one byte), or a string of eight 0s and 1s. For describing large amounts of storage capacity, the terms *kilobyte* (approximately 1,000 bytes), *megabyte* (approximately one million bytes), and *gigabyte* (approximately one billion bytes) are used.

4. What devices do you use to get data into the computer?

An input device enables you to enter data (text, images, and sounds) and instructions (user responses and commands) into a computer. You use keyboards to enter typed data and commands, whereas you use the mouse to enter user responses and commands. Keyboards are distinguished by the layout of the keys as well as the special keys found on the keyboard. The most common keyboard is the QWERTY keyboard. The Dvorak keyboard is a leader in alternative keyboards. The Dvorak keyboard puts the most commonly used letters in the English language on "home keys," which are the keys in the middle row of the keyboard. Keyboards that feature keys that can be rearranged and reprogrammed are popular with gamers.

Notebook keyboards are more compact and have fewer keys than standard keyboards. Still, many notebook keys have alternate functions so that you can get the same capabilities from the limited number of keys as you do from the special keys on standard keyboards. PDAs use a stylus instead of a keyboard.

Most computers come with wired optical mice, but other options include trackball mice and wireless mice. An optical mouse uses an internal sensor or laser to control the mouse's movement. In a trackball mouse, a rollerball sits on top or on the side of the mouse so that you can move the ball with your fingers. Wireless mice use batteries and send data to the computer via radio or light waves.

Notebooks incorporate the mouse into the keyboard area. Notebook mice include trackpoints and touchpads. Microphones are the devices used to input sounds, whereas scanners and digital cameras input nondigital text and images.

5. What devices do you use to get information out of the computer?

Output devices enable you to send processed data out of your computer. This can take the form of text, pictures, sounds, and video. Monitors display soft copies of text, graphics, and video, while printers create hard copies of text and graphics. LCDs are the most popular type of monitor. Also called flat panel monitors, they take up less space and are lighter and more energy efficient than older CRT monitors (which look like TV sets), making them perfect for portable computers. Today's

LCD monitors support high-screen resolutions, have wider viewing angles and feature fast response pixel time so full-motion video appears smooth.

There are two primary categories of printers: impact and nonimpact. Impact printers have hammer-like keys that strike the paper through an inked ribbon. Nonimpact printers spray ink or use laser beams to transfer marks on the paper. The most common nonimpact printers are inkjet printers and laser printers. Specialty printers are also available. These include multifunction printers, plotters, and thermal printers. When choosing a printer, you should be aware of factors such as speed, resolution, color output, memory, and cost.

Speakers are the output devices for sound. Most computers include speakers. However, you may want to upgrade to a more sophisticated speaker system, such as one that includes subwoofers and surround-sound.

6. What's on the front of your system unit?

The system unit is a box that contains the central electronic components of a computer. On the front of the system unit, you'll find the power source as well as access to the storage devices in your computer. Most PCs include one or two bays for storage devices such as CD drives and DVD drives. Zip drives and floppy disk drives are becoming legacy technologies and are not found on new computers. Most computers include access to USB and other ports on the front panel, and some manufacturers now also include slots on the front of the system unit into which you can insert portable flash memory cards such as Memory Sticks and CompactFlash cards.

7. What's on the back of your system unit?

On the back of the system unit or notebook, you'll find a wide variety of ports that allow you to hook up peripheral devices (such as your monitor and keyboard) to your system. The most common ports found on the back of the system unit are USB and connectivity (networking) ports. Serial ports and parallel ports are legacy technology now. The most popular port for connecting devices is the USB port. USB 2.0 ports transfer data at 480 Mbps, which is much faster than the parallel and serial ports they displaced. Firewire 400 and 800 ports provide even faster data transfer at approximately 400 and 800 Mbps, respectively.

Connectivity ports give you access to networks and the Internet and enable your computer to function as a fax machine. Connectivity ports include Ethernet ports and modem ports.

8. What's inside your system unit?

The system unit contains the main electronic components of the computer. The motherboard, the main circuit board of the system, contains a computer's central processing unit (CPU), which coordinates the functions of all other devices on the computer. RAM, the computer's volatile memory, is also located on the motherboard. RAM is where all the data and instructions are held while the computer is running. ROM, a permanent type of memory, is responsible for housing instructions to help start up a computer. The hard drive (the permanent storage location) and other storage devices (CD and DVD drives) are also located inside the system unit, as are expansion cards (such as sound, video, modem, and network interface cards) that help a computer perform special functions.

9. How do you set up your computer to avoid strain and injury?

Ergonomics refers to how you arrange your computer and equipment to minimize your risk of injury or discomfort. This includes positioning your monitor correctly, buying an adjustable chair that ensures you have good posture while using the computer, assuming a proper position while typing, and making sure the lighting is adequate. Other good practices include taking frequent breaks as well as using other specially designed equipment such as ergonomic keyboards.

Key Terms

active-matrix display
Alt key
application software
binary digit (bit)
binary language
Blu-ray
Bluetooth
brightness
byte
cathode-ray tube (CRT)
CD-ROM drive
CD-RW drive
central processing unit (CPU,
    or processor)
cold boot
computer
connectivity port
contrast ratio
Control key (Ctrl key)
cursor
cursor control keys
data
data projector
drive bay
DVD drive
DVD-RW drive
Dvorak keyboard
ergonomics
Ethernet port
expansion card (adapter card)
external hard drive
FireWire 400 (IEEE 1394)
FireWire 800
flash drive
flash memory card
flat-panel monitor
floppy disk drive
function keys
gaming keyboard
gigabyte (GB)
hard disk drive (hard drive)
hardware
hibernation
impact printer
information
inkjet printer
input device
keyboard
kilobyte (KB)
laser printer
legacy technology
liquid crystal display (LCD)
magnetically shielded microphone
megabyte (MB)
microphone (mic)

modem card
modem port
monitor (display screen)
motherboard
mouse
multifunction printer
network interface card (NIC)
nonimpact printer
nonvolatile storage
notebook computer
numeric keypad
omnidirectional microphone
operating system (OS)52
optical mouse
output device
parallel port
passive-matrix display
peripheral device
pixel
plotter
port
power supply
printer
processing
QWERTY keyboard
random access memory (RAM)
read-only memory (ROM)
resolution
response time
serial port
Sleep mode
software
sound card
speaker
speech-recognition system
stylus
subwoofer
surround-sound capability
system software
system unit
thermal printer
toggle key
touch-screen monitor
touchpad
trackball mouse
trackpoint device
unidirectional microphone
universal serial bus (USB) port
USB 2.0
video card
viewing angle
volatile storage
warm boot
webcam
Windows key
Zip disk drive

Buzz Words

Word Bank

- CPU
- CRT
- Dvorak
- ergonomics
- FireWire
- inkjet printer
- laser printer
- LCD
- microphone
- monitor
- mouse
- optical
- QWERTY
- RAM
- ROM
- speakers
- system unit
- USB

Instructions: Fill in the blanks using the words from the Word Bank above.

Austin had been getting a sore back and stiff arms when he sat at his desk, so he redesigned the (1) _____ of his computer setup. He placed the (2) _____ so that it was 25 inches from his eyes, and he bought an adjustable chair. He also decided to improve his equipment in other ways. His (3) _____ was old, so he replaced it with a(n) (4) _____ mouse that didn't need a mousepad. To plug in the mouse, he used a(n) (5) _____ port on the back of his (6) _____ . He considered buying an alternative keyboard to replace the (7) _____ keyboard he got with his computer, but he didn't know much about alternative keyboards like the (8) _____ keyboard, so he decided to wait.

Because he often printed flyers for his band, Austin decided to buy a printer that could print text-based pages quickly. Although he decided to keep his (9) _____ to print photos, he decided to buy a new (10) _____ to print his flyers faster. While looking at printers, Austin also noticed (11) _____ monitors that would take up less space on his desk than the (12) _____ monitor he had. Unfortunately, he couldn't afford to buy a new monitor. However, he decided he could afford new (13) _____ because the ones that came with his computer didn't have subwoofers. He also bought a professional (14) _____ a while back for use with his band. Finally, knowing his system could use more memory, Austin checked out prices for additional (15) _____ .

Becoming Computer Literate

Your parents live a day's drive from your school and have just called asking you for help in setting up their new computer.

Instructions: Because you can't help them in person, prepare a setup guide for your parents as either a Word document or slide presentation. Your setup guide should have all the components of a computer system illustrated and defined. In addition, you should describe with illustrations and words the various ports your parents will need to use to attach various peripheral devices to the system unit. You may use the Internet for information, device pictures, and illustrations, but remember to credit all sources at the end of your guide.

Instructions: Answer the multiple-choice and true/false questions below for more practice with key terms and concepts from this chapter.

MULTIPLE CHOICE

1. Which devices below are considered input devices?
   a. Keyboard and mouse
   b. Scanner and printer
   c. Hard drive and speakers
   d. Microphone and CD-ROM drive

2. Which of the following is NOT one of the four major functions of a computer?
   a. Output
   b. Storage
   c. Processing
   d. Calculation

3. Which of the following is NOT an output device?
   a. Printer
   b. Monitor
   c. Hard drive
   d. Speakers

4. The resolution of a monitor is governed by the
   a. size of the screen.
   b. cost of the monitor.
   c. number of pixels on the screen.
   d. contrast of the pixels on the screen.

5. All of the following are important to consider when buying an LCD monitor EXCEPT
   a. brightness.
   b. pixel swap rate.
   c. viewing angle.
   d. resolution.

6. Restarting the system after it has been completely powered off is called
   a. a warm boot.
   b. a standby start.

   c. hibernation.
   d. a cold boot.

7. An Ethernet port is used for connecting your computer to
   a. a network.
   b. a printer.
   c. a monitor.
   d. a digital camera.

8. Which of the following devices is considered the "brains" of the computer?
   a. Read–only memory
   b. Central processing unit
   c. Random access memory
   d. Motherboard

9. Which of the following statements about hard disks is TRUE?
   a. Hard disks are always installed inside the system unit of a computer.
   b. Hard disks are considered volatile storage devices.
   c. With the rise of flash drives, hard disks are becoming legacy technology.
   d. Hard disks are considered non-volatile storage devices.

10. Why is an ergonomically correct setup for your computer system essential?
   a. Reduces eyestrain
   b. Prevents repetitive strain injuries
   c. Complies with federal laws
   d. a & b
   e. b & c
   f. a & c
   g. All of the above
   h. None of the above

TRUE/FALSE

____ 1. The terms *data* and *information* can be used interchangeably.

____ 2. ROM is volatile storage that is located on the motherboard.

____ 3. The CPU is located on the expansion board.

____ 4. USB ports are the most popular port used for connecting peripherals to a computer.

____ 5. Keeping your wrists flat while typing at a computer will help prevent repetitive strain injuries.

Making the Transition to...
Next Semester

1. Choosing the Best Keyboard

Once you become more familiar with software products such as Microsoft Office, you may want to migrate to a customized keyboard design. Although keyboards have similar setups, some keyboards provide special keys and buttons to support different users. For example, some keyboards are designed specifically for multimedia use, Internet use, and gaming use use. Which one is best for you?

a. Examine the various keyboard setups at the Microsoft Web site (**www.microsoft.com/hardware/mouseandkeyboard/default.mspx**). Which keyboard would best suit your needs and why? What features would be most useful to you? How would you evaluate the additional costs versus the benefits?

b. What advantages would a wireless keyboard give you? How much do wireless keyboards cost? What price would you be willing to pay to go wireless?

c. When would you need a keyboard for your portable computing devices (such as a smartphone or PDA)? What is the current price for a portable folding keyboard? Would the virtual keyboard described in the chapter be a better choice for you? Explain your answers.

2. Choosing the Best Mouse

On the Web, research the different kinds of mice available and list their special features, functions, and costs. Of these mice, which do you think would be most useful to you? Why?

3. Pricing Computer Upgrades

On the Internet, investigate the following:

a. How much would it cost to add a Blu-ray drive to your computer? Does your system have an extra drive bay to install a Blu-ray drive?

b. How much would it cost to buy new 21-inch LCD monitors? What kind of monitor would be best to play games, view DVDs, or play back recorded TV shows?

c. How much do various computer speaker systems cost? What speakers would be best to listen to CDs? What speakers would be useful when playing games?

d. Do you know whether your current sound card and video card support the new devices? How could you find this out?

4. Exploring Scanners

One input device you did not explore in the text is a scanner. Conduct the following research on the Web to find out about scanners:

a. What are the different kinds of scanners on the market?

b. What qualities do good scanners have?

c. How much do scanners cost?

d. Create a table comparing all the specifications listed earlier for several different scanners. Highlight the scanner you would be most interested in purchasing.

5. Keyboard Shortcuts

Knowing and using keyboard shortcuts can save you a lot of time while you are doing your work or homework. Research and compile a list of keyboard shortcuts for the following software:

a. Microsoft Windows Vista

b. Apple OS X

c. Microsoft Word 2007

Making the Transition to... the Workplace

1. **Desktop Versus Notebook**

   There are two main types of computers in the workplace: desktop computers with separate system units and monitors, and notebook computers that are portable and have the monitors, keyboards and the system unit all contained within a single case. If you were being interviewed for a job, what types of questions would you need to ask your prospective boss about the job to determine whether you needed a desktop or a notebook computer?

2. **What System Will You Use?**

   When you arrive at a new position for a company, you'll most likely be provided with a computer. Based on the career you are in now or are planning to pursue, answer the following questions:

   a. What kind of computer system would you most like to use (PC, Mac, desktop configuration, notebook, PDA, and so on)?

   b. If you were required to use a type of computer you had never used before (say a Mac instead of a PC), how would you go about learning to use the new computer?

   c. What kind of keyboard, mouse, monitor, and printer would you like to have?

   d. Would you need any additional input or output devices to perform your job?

3. **What Hardware Will You Use?**

   What types of computer hardware would make your work life more efficient? What adjustments would you need to make on your current system to accommodate those hardware devices? (For example, does your computer have the right kind of port or enough ports to support additional hardware devices?)

4. **Choosing the Best Printer**

   You are looking for a new printer for your home business. You have always had an inkjet printer, but now that the costs for color laser printers are dropping, you're considering buying a color laser printer. However, you're still unsure because they're more expensive than inkjet printers, although you've heard that there is an overall cost savings with laser printers when the cost of toner/ink and paper is taken into consideration.

   a. Using the Internet, investigate the merits of different inkjet and color laser printers. Narrow in on one printer in each category and note the initial cost of each.

   b. Research the cost of ink/toner for each printer. Calculate the cost of ink/toner supplies for each printer, assuming you will print 5,000 color pages per year. How much will it cost per page of printing, not including the initial cost of the printer itself?

   c. Investigate the multipurpose printers that also have faxing, scanning, and copying capabilities. How much more expensive are they than a traditional inkjet or laser printer? Are there any drawbacks to these multipurpose machines? Do they perform each function as well as their stand-alone counterparts? Can you print in color on these machines?

   d. Based on your research, which printer would be the most economical?

5. **Office Ergonomics**

   Your boss has designated you as the "ergonomics coordinator" for the department. She has asked you to design a flyer to be posted around the office informing your coworkers of the proper computer setup as well as the potential risks if such precautions are avoided. Create an ergonomics flyer, making sure it fits on an 8.5 x 11 piece of paper.

Looking at Computers: Understanding the Parts

Critical Thinking Questions

Instructions: Albert Einstein used "Gedanken experiments," or critical thinking questions, to develop his theory of relativity. Some ideas are best understood by experimenting with them in our own minds. The following critical thinking questions are designed to demand your full attention but require only a comfortable chair—no technology.

1. **Keyboard of the Future**

   What do you think the keyboard of the future will look like? What capabilities will it have that keyboards currently don't have? Will it have ports? cables? special communications capabilities?

2. **Mouse of the Future**

   What do you think the mouse (or other pointing device) of the future will look like? What sorts of improvements on the traditional mouse can you imagine? Do you think there will ever be a day when we won't need mice and keyboards to use our computers?

3. **Storage Devices of the Future**

   How do you think storage devices will change in the future? Will increased storage capacity and decreased size affect the ways in which we use computers? Will we need storage devices in the future, or will we access all of our data via the Internet?

4. **Computers Decreasing Productivity?**

   Can you think of any situations in which computers actually decrease productivity? Why? Should we always expect computers to increase our productivity? What do you think the impact of using computers would be:

   a. in a third-grade classroom?
   b. in a manager's office for a large chain supermarket?
   c. for a retired couple who purchases their first computer?

5. **"Smart" Homes**

   The Smart Medical Home project of the University of Rochester's Center for Future Health is researching how to use technology to monitor many aspects of your health. The Smart Medical Home is the creation of a cross-disciplinary group of scientists and engineers from the college, the Medical Center, and the university's Center for Future Health. This particular "smart home" includes a sophisticated computer system that helps keep track of items such as eyeglasses or keys, and the kitchen is equipped with a new kind of packaging to signal the presence of dangerous bacteria in food. Spaces between ordinary walls are stuffed with gadgetry, including banks of powerful computers.

   a. What abilities should a smart home have to safeguard and improve the quality of your life?
   b. Could there be potential hazards of a smart home?

6. **Toy or Computer?**

   When do you think a toy becomes a computer? The Microsoft Xbox 360 has a hard disk drive, a processor with three cores, internal RAM, and wireless capability. Apple iPods also have hard disk drives (or flash memory and a processor). Are these devices computers or toys? What capabilities do you think the next generation gaming consoles and iPods should have?

Problem:

There are two major classes of computer systems in the marketplace today: PCs and Apple computers. Many people have chosen one camp with an almost religious fervor. In this exercise, each team will explore the trade-offs between a PC and an Apple computer and defend their allegiance to one system or the other.

Task:

Split your class into two teams:

Team A is a group of PC diehards. They believe these computers perform as well as Apple systems and cost less, providing better value.

Team B is a group of hard-working, Apple-loving software developers. They believe there are no systems as user-friendly and reliable as those made by Apple.

Look at the following list of settings for computer labs. Each team should decide why their particular system would be the best choice in each of these settings.

1. An elementary school considering incorporating more technology into the classroom
2. A small accounting firm expanding into new offices
3. A video production company considering producing digital video
4. A computer system for a home office for an aspiring author

Process:

1. Form the two teams. Think about what your goals are and what information and resources you need to tackle this project.
2. Research and then discuss the components of each system you are recommending. Are any components better suited for each particular need? Consider all the input, output, processing, and storage devices. Are any special devices or peripherals required?
3. Write a summary position paper. For each of the four settings, support your system recommendation for

   Team A A PC computer system

   Team B An Apple system

Conclusion:

There are a number of competing designs for computer systems. Being aware of the options in the marketplace and knowing how to analyze the trade-offs in different designs allows you to become a better consumer as well as a better computer user.

Multimedia

In addition to the review materials presented here, you'll find more materials featured with the book's multimedia, including the *Technology in Action* Student Resource CD and the Companion Web site (**www. prenhall.com/techinaction**), which will help reinforce your understanding of the chapter content. These materials include the following:

ACTIVE HELPDESK

In Active Helpdesk calls, you'll assume the role of Helpdesk operator, taking calls about the concepts you've learned in this chapter. You'll apply what you've learned and receive feedback from a supervisor to review and reinforce those concepts. The Active Helpdesk calls for this chapter are listed below and can be found on your Student Resource CD:

- Understanding Bits and Bytes
- Using Input Devices
- Using Output Devices

SOUND BYTES

Sound Bytes are dynamic multimedia tutorials that help demystify even the most complex topics. You'll view video clips and animations that illustrate computer concepts, and then apply what you've learned by reviewing with the Sound Byte Labs, which include quizzes and activities specifically tailored to each Sound Byte. The Sound Bytes for this chapter are listed below and can be found on your Student Resource CD:

- Port Tour: How Do I Hook It Up?
- Virtual Computer Tour
- Healthy Computing

COMPANION WEB SITE

The *Technology in Action* Companion Web Site includes a variety of additional materials to help you review and learn more about the topics in this chapter. The resources available at **www.prenhall.com/techinaction** include:

- **Online Study Guide.** Each chapter features an online true/false and multiple-choice quiz. You can take these quizzes, automatically check the results, and e-mail the results to your instructor.
- **Web Research Projects.** Each chapter features a number of Web research projects that ask you to search the Web for information on computer-related careers, milestones in computer history, important people and companies, emerging technologies, and the applications and implications of different technologies.

3
Using the Internet:
Making the Most of the Web's Resources

From Chapter 3 of *Technology in Action, Complete*, Fifth Edition, Alan Evans, Kendall Martin, Mary Anne Poatsy. Copyright © 2009 by Pearson Education. Published by Prentice Hall. All rights reserved.

Using the Internet:

Making the Most of the Web's Resources

ACTIVE HELPDESK

- Staying Secure on the Internet
- Getting Around the Web
- Using Subject Directories and Search Engines
- Connecting to the Internet

Interacting with the Internet

It's 10:00 P.M. as Max sits down to begin his online coursework. Although it's been a long day, he likes taking online courses because they let him finish his degree and still keep his full-time job. While downloading the assignment file from the course Web site, he opens his Instant Messenger (IM) account to see if any of his friends are online. Seeing his friend Tom is logged on, he chats with him for a while. Like many of his friends, Max has become a fan of IM. He uses it more than he does e-mail. It's more like talking.

As his file finishes downloading, he visits ESPN.com to check out the score of the Red Sox game. He then goes to his favorite search engine, Google, and starts researching the topic he plans to write about for his class. As he conducts his searches, he experiments with some Web search techniques he learned about in his online class. He's amazed at how much information he can find when he searches the Web, yet surprised about how hard it is to find truly useful information. To make his presentation more interesting, Max uses Google's video search feature to find clips he can use. Max reflects on how glad he is that he finally ditched his slow dial-up connection for a faster Internet connection. Downloading files and searching the Internet, playing videos, and chatting with his friends is so much quicker with a broadband connection.

Finally, Max checks his e-mail and finds the usual spam as well as a message from the student loan office reminding him that his payment is due. Max decides he'd better make this payment before he forgets. He accesses his bank's Web site from his Favorites list. With a few more clicks, he transfers enough money from his savings account to his checking account to cover his payment, which he then makes online.

Does this level of Internet interaction sound at all like yours? Most likely you use the Internet as much as you do your television, maybe even more. But do you really know how to get the most out of your Internet experience and which connection option is best for you?

In this chapter, you'll learn what you should know about the Internet in order to use it to your best advantage. We'll look at the activities that you use the Internet for most often, such as communication technologies (e-mail, IM, Weblogs, podcasts, and the like), multimedia experiences, and doing business over the Web. Next, we'll discuss problems that you may encounter by using the Internet and the Web, and how they might be managed. We'll then discuss how you can navigate and search the Web effectively so that your time spent on the Internet is useful. Finally, we'll discuss how the Internet works, including options you have for connecting to the Internet, how data travels across this big network, as well as the history and future of the Internet as we know it today.

Courtesy of Corbis

SOUND BYTES

- Blogging
- Creating a Web-Based E-mail Account
- The Best Utilities for Your Computer

- Welcome to the Web
- Finding Information on the Web
- Connecting to the Internet

The Internet

You've no doubt been on the Internet countless times. According to the Nielsen Net Ratings, by the end of 2006, nearly 70 percent of homes in the United States were connected to the Internet. But what exactly *is* the Internet? The **Internet** is the largest computer network in the world, actually a network of networks, connecting billions of computer users. Although 20 countries represent the majority of computer users, some reports estimate that nearly 150 countries have some form of connection to the Internet! Communication is the primary reason people use the Internet, but when Internet users are not communicating, they also spend the majority of their online time shopping, searching for information, and just browsing the Internet for fun.

Communicating Through the Internet: E-Mail and Other Technologies

E-mail is fast becoming the primary means of communication in the 21st century. However, e-mail is not the only form of Internet-based communication. You can use instant messaging, Weblogs, podcasts, chat rooms, newsgroups, and more for communicating via the Internet. You can even talk over the phone through the Internet! Like any other means of communication, you need to know how to use these tools efficiently to get the most out of them.

INSTANT MESSAGING

How does instant messaging work?

Instant messaging (IM) services are programs that enable you to communicate in real time with others who also are online (see Figure 1). AOL's AIM and its newest instant messenger service, Triton, are some of the most popular instant messaging services. ICQ, Yahoo!, Google, and MSN also host popular instant messaging services. ZangoMessenger and Messenger City are other IM services that allow users of all the popular IMs to talk to each other regardless of the service they are using.

When you use IM, you set up a list of contacts, often called a **buddy list**. To communicate with someone from your buddy list, that person must be online at the same time as you are. When someone is trying to communicate with you when you're online, you are notified and can then accept or reject the communication. Some programs, such as Yahoo! and AOL's Triton, offer stealth settings so that you can appear offline to certain buddies. If you want to chat, or communicate, with more than one person, you can hold simultaneous individual conversations, or if you all want to talk together, you can create custom IM chat rooms. Many IM services, such as AOL AIM or MSN Messenger, offer chat services so you can talk to your buddies if you have a microphone and speakers. A video camera will help you see them as you chat.

AIM is a registered trademark of AOL, LLC. ©AOL LLC. Used with permission

FIGURE 1

Instant messaging services such as AOL Instant Messenger enable you to have real-time online conversations with friends and family.

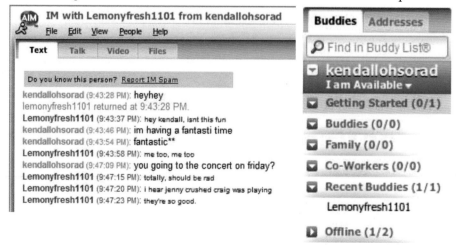

Using the Internet: Making the Most of the Web's Resources

PODCASTS

What is a podcast? A **podcast** is a clip of audio or video content that is broadcast over the Internet using compressed files, such as MP3s. This content might include radio shows, audio books, magazines, and even educational programs (see Figure 2). Typically, you must subscribe to be able to access the most current version of the online content, which is delivered to your computer automatically so that you can listen to the content when you want. You can use a media player, such as RealPlayer or Windows Media Player on your computer, or you can transfer the content from your computer to a portable media device, such as an iPod.

How do podcasts work? Podcasts are possible because of RSS technology. RSS 2.0 (Really Simple Syndication) is an XML-based format that allows frequent updates of content on the World Wide Web. Web content can be formatted in such a way that aggregators (programs that search for new Web content) can find them and download only the new content to your computer. Some aggregators work with Atom, another specification, to distribute new Web content.

Where can I find podcasts? Podcasts can be found all over the Web. Most newspapers, TV news, and radio sites offer podcasts of their programs. But the content doesn't have to be news-related. The television network ABC, for example, offers podcasts of some of its most popular TV shows, such as Grey's Anatomy and Lost, and audible.com enables you to download entire books so that you can enjoy them anywhere: in the gym, in the car, on the train, or while riding the bus to work. Many schools are beginning to recognize this format as a means to supply students with course content updates, and instructors are creating podcasts of their lectures.

Sites such as iTunes (**www.itunes.com**), Podcast Alley (**www.podcastalley.com**), and Podcast.net (**www.podcast.net**) are great directories of podcasts, organized by genre, to help you easily locate podcasts of most interest to you. If there is a particular topic for which you'd like to hear a podcast, Podscope (**www.podscope.com**) and Podzinger (**www.podzinger.com**) are podcast-specific search engines that search podcasts for specific words or phrases and then display the results with audio clips. YouTube is also becoming a popular source of podcasts.

FIGURE 2

Podcasts are available in a wide variety of topics and content. Web sites like **www.podcast.net** allow you to add your own podcast to their directory.

Do I need anything special to get and listen to podcasts? In addition to a computer and an Internet connection, you need to install an aggregator and have a media player. **Aggregators** are software programs that go out and grab the latest update of Web material according to your specifications. Aggregators are available for all the major operating systems, as well as for some mobile devices, such as smart phones and PDAs. Podcast directories, such as iTunes and Podcast Alley, are also aggregators that work with both Windows and Macintosh platforms. If you want to listen to a podcast on your computer, you'll need a media player, such as QuickTime, RealPlayer, or Windows Media Player. If you want to listen to your podcasts while on the go, then you'll need a mobile device such as an MP3 player, PMP, smartphone, or PDA device that plays MP3 files. If you want to enjoy a video podcast, you will need to make sure your mobile device can play video files as well.

Can I create my own podcast? The ability to create audio content that can be delivered to the Web and then listened to by people all over the world is very simple, turning the average person into a radio broadcaster overnight. Although high-end equipment always will produce more sophisticated output, you really need only very basic equipment to make your own podcast.

To record the content, at the minimum you need a computer with a microphone. If you want to make a video podcast, you also need a Web camera (webcam) or video camera. Then, additional software may be

needed to edit the digital audio and video content. Sound-editing software, such as the freeware program Audacity, can be used to record and later edit audio files. After the podcast content has been recorded and edited, it needs to be exported to MP3 format. Fortunately, Audacity has the capability to export files into MP3 format. The last step involves creating an RSS file and then uploading the content to the Web.

WEBLOGS (BLOGS) AND VIDEO LOGS (VLOGS)

What is a blog? **Weblogs** (or **blogs**) are personal logs, or journal entries, that are posted on the Web. The beauty of blogs is that they are simple to create, manage, and read. Although different types of blogs exist, there are some basic similarities. First, blogs are arranged as a listing of entries on a single page, with the most recent blog (entry) appearing on the top of the list. Second, blogs are public. Everyone who has a Web browser and access to the Internet can read a blog. Finally, blogs are searchable, making them user friendly.

What do people write in blogs? Many people use blogs as a sort of personal scrapbook. Whenever the urge strikes, they just write a stream-of-conscious flow of thoughts or a report of their daily activities. Many blogs, however, focus on a particular topic. For example, **www.rottentomatoes.com** is a blog site that contains reviews and opinions about movies, and **www.gizmodo.com** is a blog site that devotes itself to discussing techno-gadgets (see Figure 3).

How do I create a blog? It is easy to write and maintain a blog, and you'll find many Web sites that provide the necessary tools for you to create your own blog. Two sites that offer blog hosting for free are **www.blogger.com** and **www.livejournal.com**. For a relatively small fee, you can add other features to your blog, such as pictures or subpages. Another alternative is to host your blog yourself. Hosting your own blog requires that you have an IP address (like 64.202.163.148) and a URL, such as **www.pandoblog.com** in order for people to access it online.

What is a video blog? The traditional form of Weblogs are primarily text based but may also include images and audio.

BITS AND BYTES

Can Blogging Get You in Trouble?

The news is full of stories of bloggers getting fired from their jobs, and in some instances, even imprisoned, because of the content of their blogs. Generally, the content may include negative discussion about the blogger's job, employer, or colleagues, or perhaps inappropriate content about the blogger. Blogs, because they are on the Internet, can be found and read by anyone, including bosses, potential employers, friends, relatives, neighbors, and colleagues. Therefore, illegal and socially unacceptable content should not be included in blogs. Bloggers who post negative or inappropriate content should be prepared for potential consequences.

GIZMODO

Gizmodo, the gadget guide. So much in love with shiny new toys, it's unnatural.

view by category

TIPS@GIZMODO.COM

TOP STORIES : Helios X3000 Upscaling Network DVD/DivX Player Hands-On | LG DN19 IH Upconverting DVD/DivX Player Hands-On | CES 2007: Gizmodo Jumps All Over It | Tokyo Found: Porn Shots of Japanese Cellphones

SEARCH

« || next »

THU JAN 04 2007

SanDisk Unveils 32GB Drop-In Replacement Drive for Notebooks

SSD UATA 5000 1.8"

SanDisk

SanDisk is looking to replace that spinning, power-hungry hard drive in your laptop with a 1.8-inch solid state 32GB flash drive. The company says its cool-running SSD Ultra ATA 5000 1.8" drive is a drop-in replacement for those old-fashioned mechanical hard disks. It packs the performance, too, with a 62MB-per-second read speed while using less than half the battery power of conventional discs.

Its most impressive spec is its random read rate of 7300 inputs and outputs per

COMMENTS

elvindeath says:

Wow. I must have missed this tech ... first I've heard of a primary flash drive. Sounds intriguing. Of course, I've still got boxes of 5.25" floppies from my old Apple][, so I'm a little nostlagic about my drive technology.

/Remebers laying out $750 for a 10 megabyte hard drive back in the day for an old 8008 IBM PC and wondering if I'd ever need to buy storage again. lol.

01/04/07 09:07 AM

strider_mt2k says:

As long as the reliability is there and they can get the things up a little more in capacity it sounds like it'll be a great upgrade for an existing notebook.

It'll mean lower-end notebooks that fell short of tasks because of lower RPM HDs might now be up to those tasks after all.

01/04/07 09:09 AM

TheCapt says:

OK, I won't 10 of these, 'cept 100GB, in a RAID for my desktop! Highspeed, quiet and environmentally friendly... ok, I only care about two of those.

01/04/07 09:24 AM

Reprinted by permission

Video logs (vlogs) are personal journals that use video as the primary content in addition to text, images, and audio. Vlogs quickly are becoming a very popular means of personal expression. Software such as Vlog It! (**www.seriousmagic.com**) makes adding video content to your blog easy. Video logs have become so popular that Google has added a Video search engine to its list of features (see Figure 4).

WEBCASTS

What's a webcast? A **webcast** is the broadcast of audio or video content over the Internet. Unlike podcasts, webcasts are not updated automatically. Instead, the most current content must be located manually by the user and then downloaded. Webcasts use streaming media technology to facilitate the viewing and downloading process of large audio and video files. Webcasts can include noninteractive content, such as a simulcast of a radio or TV broadcast, but, more recently, webcasts have initiated interactive responses from the viewing or listening audience. For example, the webcast of the Democratic National Convention in 2004 gave potential voters the ability to interact with and ask questions of politicians, convention delegates, and media personalities. Webcasts also

are used in the corporate world to broadcast annual meetings and in the educational arena to transmit seminars.

WIKIS

What are wikis? Unlike traditional Web content, which the site viewer cannot change, a **wiki** is a type of Web site that allows anyone visiting the site to change its content by adding, removing, or editing the content. The popular collaborative online encyclopedia Wikipedia (**www.wikipedia.org**) uses wiki technology. The intent of using wiki technology with an online encyclopedia is that the content is updated continually and kept accurate by the many expert eyes that view the content.

How accurate is Web content that anyone can change? In late 2005, Wikipedia content was measured for accuracy in its scientific content and was found to be as accurate as the Encyclopedia Britannica. Nonetheless, the free and easy access to edit pages also can lead to improper manipulation, which results in tighter access controls. To thwart malicious editing of the wiki content, for example, users who want editing privileges are required to register. These same collaborative efforts also extend to user manuals.

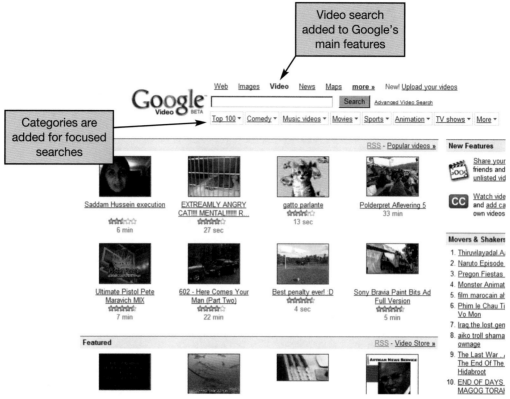

Google, Inc.

wikiHow (**www.wikihow.org**) is an online project that is using both wikis and the collaborative process to build a large, online how-to manual. Blender (**www.blender3d.org**), an open-source software application for 3D modeling, uses mediawiki, a more feature-rich wiki implementation product, to provide users with documentation, help on game development and 3D modeling, and tutorials for Blender software.

Are wikis used for anything other than encyclopedias and manuals? Wikis provide an excellent source for collaborative writing, both in and out of the classroom. Wiki technology is currently incorporated in Blackboard, a popular online course management software application, to encourage collaborative learning in online courses. Tag You're It (**www.tagyoureit.org**) is a collaborative writing community dedicated to creating stories online.

Like blogs, wikis also can be used to express thoughts and opinions about certain topics. Unlike blogs, however, wikis can be edited and therefore maintain a more "common" opinion, rather than the direct expressed opinion of the initial individual writer. Chicago Living Arts (**www.chicagowikiarts.org**) is experimenting with wiki pages as a means for people to

contribute and collaborate on Chicago cultural arts through an evolving collection of writings.

VOICE OVER INTERNET PROTOCOL (VOIP)

How is VoIP different from regular telephone service? VoIP is a form of voice-based Internet communication that turns a standard Internet connection into a means to place phone calls, including long-distance phone calls. Traditional telephone communications use analog voice data and telephone connections. VoIP uses technology similar to that used in e-mail to send your voice data digitally over the Internet.

What do I need to use VoIP? For the simplest and least costly VoIP service, you need speakers, a microphone, an Internet connection, and a VoIP provider. Depending on the VoIP provider you choose, you also may need to install software or a special adapter. For example, Skype (**www.skype.com**) requires that both the person placing the call and the person receiving the call have its free software installed on their computers. An alternative VoIP service, such as Vonage (**www.vonage.com**), lets you use your own telephone (instead of the speakers and microphone system) by connecting your phone to a special adapter that the company provides. A third alternative is to buy a special IP phone that connects to your broadband Internet connection (cable or DSL) or a USB port on your computer. New to join the market are WiFi IP phones, which will allow you to place calls from any WiFi hotspot location.

E-MAIL

Why did e-mail catch on so quickly? **E-mail** (short for **electronic mail**) is a written message that is sent and received over electronic communication systems. The messages can be formatted and enhanced with graphics as well as include other files as attachments. E-mail has quickly caught on as the primary method of electronic communication because it's fast and convenient and reduces the costs of postage and long-distance phone calls. In addition, with e-mail, the sender and receiver don't have to be available at the same time in order to communicate. Because of these and other reasons, more than 90 percent of Americans who access the Internet claim that their main online activity is sending and receiving e-mail.

E-mail is not meant for every type of communication, however. Because it is not the most secure form of transmission, e-mail should not be used to send personal or sensitive information such as banking numbers or social security numbers that could lead to identity theft. Similarly, employers have access to your e-mail sent from your workplace, so caution should be taken when putting negative or controversial content in an e-mail. It could just come back to haunt you.

What do I need to send and receive e-mail? All you need to send and receive e-mail is a computer, an Internet connection, and an e-mail account. Each of these components, however, entails additional considerations. Although it's most common to send and receive e-mail from your computer, today many e-mail messages are exchanged between cell phones, PDAs, and notebooks. An Internet connection can be wired or wireless, and an e-mail account may or may not be Web-based.

What is the difference between e-mail accounts? To read, send, and organize your e-mail, you use some sort of

e-mail client. **E-mail clients**, such as Microsoft Outlook, are software programs running on your computer that access your Internet service provider's (ISP's) server. However, with these e-mail clients, you are able to view your e-mail only from the computer on which the client program is installed, which can be less than convenient if you travel or want to view your e-mail when you're away from that computer.

Today, many ISPs offer the services of a Web-based e-mail client so that users can look at their e-mail directly from the Web. Web-based e-mail uses the Internet as the client; therefore, you can access a Web-based e-mail account from any computer that has access to the Web—no special client software is needed. Free e-mail accounts such as Yahoo!, Hotmail, or Gmail use Web-based e-mail clients. If you use a broadband connection, such as cable or DSL, your broadband provider will provide you with a Web-based e-mail account. Some e-mail clients, such as AOL, offer both client and Web access to e-mail. Even if you have a Web-based e-mail client, you still can choose to use an e-mail client program such as Outlook. These programs offer organizational features that most Web-based e-mail clients do not.

What are the advantages of a Web-based e-mail account? Unlike client-based e-mail, which is accessible only from the computer on which it is installed, if you have a Web-based e-mail account, your e-mail is accessible from any computer as long as you have access to the Internet. A secondary Web-based e-mail account also provides you with a more permanent e-mail address. Your other e-mail accounts and addresses may change when you switch ISPs or change employers, so having a permanent e-mail address is important.

Why would I need a client-based e-mail program? Many people have more than one e-mail account. You may have a personal account, a work account, and an account you use when filling out forms on the Internet. One of the benefits of using a client-based e-mail program such as Microsoft Outlook is that you can download your e-mail from many different e-mail accounts so that it all can be accessed in one location. In addition, client e-mail programs offer several features to help you manage and organize your e-mail and coordinate e-mail with your calendar, tasks, and contact

SOUND BYTE

Creating a Web-Based E-mail Account

In this Sound Byte, you'll see a step-by-step demonstration that explains how to create a free Yahoo! Web-based e-mail account. You'll also learn the options available with such accounts.

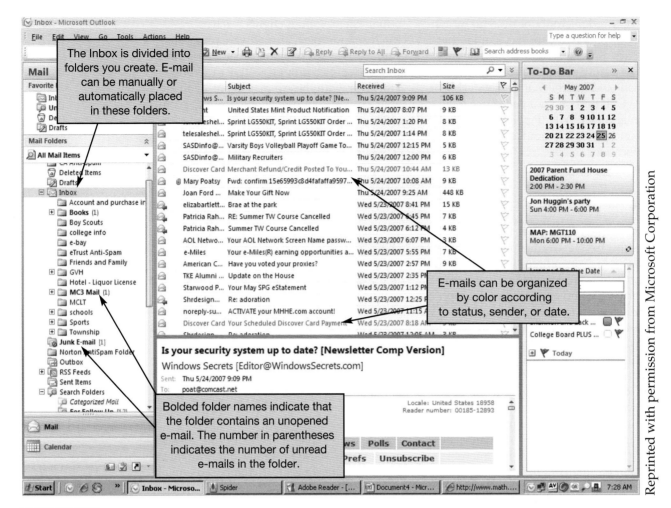

The Inbox is divided into folders you create. E-mail can be manually or automatically placed in these folders.

E-mails can be organized by color according to status, sender, or date.

Bolded folder names indicate that the folder contains an unopened e-mail. The number in parentheses indicates the number of unread e-mails in the folder.

FIGURE 5

You can organize your e-mail by color coding it and assigning messages to specific folders. In addition, you can automatically filter out unwanted e-mail and sort the remaining e-mail into topic-specific folders.

lists. As you can see in Figure 5, you can choose to organize your e-mail by task, sender, or priority using color codes, or you can distribute your messages to designated folders within your inbox.

GROUP COMMUNICATION

What kinds of online group communication exist? There are many ways you can interact with a wide variety of people online. Some forms are real time, or synchronous, and others are asynchronous. Figure 6 describes the various ways in which you can communicate with a group of people online.

Do dangers exist in group communications? When you use group communications, you generally need to register and sign in with a username and password. It's best not to disclose your identity but rather to "hide" behind a username, thus protecting your privacy. On the other hand, the people you are chatting with are also hiding their identities. Some chatters use this veil of privacy to cover

dishonest intentions. Undoubtedly, you have heard stories of individuals, especially young teenagers, being deceived (and sometimes harmed) by someone they've met in a chat room. A number of Web sites, such as **www.chatdanger.com**, try to protect vulnerable people such as children from malicious online users (see Figure 7).

Are there special ways to behave with group communication? General rules of etiquette (often referred to as **netiquette**) exist across chat rooms and other online forums, including obvious standards of behavior such as introducing yourself when you enter the room and specifically addressing the person you are talking to. Chat room users also are expected to refrain from swearing, name calling, and using explicit or prejudiced language and are not allowed to harass other participants. In addition, chat room users cannot post the same text repeatedly with the intent to disrupt the chat. (This behavior is called flooding.) Similarly, as in e-mail, users shouldn't type in all capital letters, because this is interpreted as shouting.

FIGURE 6 **Ways to Communicate Online with Groups**

Internet Social Network **myspace.com** **facebook.com**	**Social Networks** are online personal networks where individuals are invited or allowed to join. Social networks allow a group of individuals to create personal profiles, exchange information, and find others with similar interests.
Multiplayer Online Game Services **xbox.com/live** **worldofwarcraft.com** **guildwars.com**	There are many **Multiplayer Online Games** in which play occurs among hundreds or thousands of other players over the Internet, in a persistent or ever-on game environment. In some games, you can interact with other players around the world in a meaningful context by trading, chatting, or playing cooperative or combative mini-games.
Chat Rooms **icq.com/icqchat**	**Chat Rooms** are a form of synchronous communication in which online conversations occur in real time and are visible to everyone in the chat room. Usually, chat rooms are organized around a specific theme or topic.
Newsgroups **groups.google.com** **tile.net/news**	A **newsgroup** is similar to a discussion group or forum in which people create threads, or conversations. In a thread, a newsgroup member will post messages and read and reply to messages from other members of the newsgroup.
Listserv **tile.net/lists**	**Listservs** are electronic mailing lists of e-mail addresses of people who are interested in a certain topic or an area of interest. They are used to share information with a group of individuals who share a common interest.

Reprinted courtesty of Childnet International

Web Entertainment: Multimedia and Beyond

Internet radio, MP3 music files, streaming video, and interactive gaming are all part of a growing entertainment world available over the Internet. What makes the Web appealing to many people is its enriched multimedia content. **Multimedia** is anything that involves one or more forms of media in addition to text.

Many types of multimedia are used on the Web. Graphics (drawings, charts, and photos) are the most basic form of multimedia on the Web. Audio files are what give sound to the Web—the clips of music you hear when you visit certain Web sites, MP3 files that you download, or live broadcasts you can listen to through Internet radio. Video files on the Web range from the simple (such

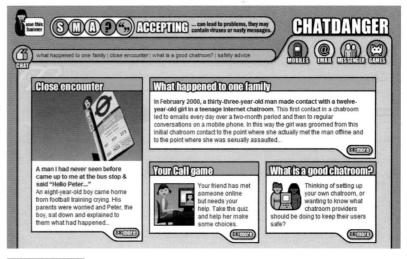

FIGURE 7

The site **www.chatdanger.com** is produced by Childnet International, a nonprofit organization working to help make the Internet safe for children. It provides a lot of good safety advice for using chat rooms, mobile phones, e-mail, instant messenger programs, and games.

Social Networking

Networking has long been a means of creating links between you and your friends—and their friends and acquaintances. Traditionally, networking has been helpful in the business community for the purposes of finding and filling open job positions. The Internet, with its speedy connections and instantaneous means of communications, is facilitating such networking. For example, the site LinkedIn (**www.linkedin.com**) is a professional network through which members can find potential clients, business opportunities, jobs, or job candidates. Like a true business network, LinkedIn helps you meet other professionals through the people you know.

The Internet also is promoting a different kind of networking among the younger, nonprofessional population. Social networking Web sites, such as Facebook, MySpace, and Friendster (see Figure 8), have gained in popularity among high school and college students. They are becoming increasingly popular

among preteens as well. The growth has been explosive. MySpace membership, for example, has topped 78 million members and registers about 250,000 new members each day. It is fast becoming the most frequently visited Web site, toppling Yahoo! and Google from the list.

What's the attraction? **Social networking** sites, such as MySpace, are an easy place for members to hang out, meet new people, and share common interests. They also provide a way for members to communicate with their friends by voice, chat, instant message, videoconference, and blogs, so members don't need separate communication accounts.

MySpace, for example, is simple to set up, and it's free of charge. Members quickly can create personalized profiles in which they include their own photographs and personal information and create a circle of friends by linking to friends' profiles or by inviting others to join their network.

FIGURE 8

Social networking sites are popular places for students to meet and make new friends.

as short video clips) to the complex (such as hour-long live concerts). In addition to movies, you can watch live or prerecorded television broadcasts, movie trailers, and sporting events. In early 2006, Disney, owner of American Broadcasting Company (ABC), began putting prime-time television shows on the Internet to be viewed for free.

What is streaming audio and video? Because of the large file sizes of media content, watching video files such as movies or TV shows, or listening to live audio

broadcasting, is possible because of streaming media. **Streaming audio** continuously feeds an audio file to your browser so you avoid having to wait for the entire file to download completely before listening to it. Likewise, **streaming video** continuously feeds a video file to your browser so that you can watch large files as they download instead of first having to download the files completely.

Do I need anything besides a browser to view or hear multimedia on the Web? Without any additional soft-

Although most members congregate on these sites without a problem, the sites are susceptible to attacks by nefarious individuals, so users should take precautions to avoid interactions with cyberbullies, con artists, and other predators. Cyberbullies are just like real-life bullies. They pick on the weak or vulnerable just as in real life, only they use the Internet to do it. This type of behavior tends to occur among children or young adults. Some sites encourage members to "rate" other members based on their profile or photos. Although often harmless, such behavior can leave users subject to bullying, harassment, or ridicule.

Another risk associated with social networking sites occurs when users reveal too much personal information. In an effort to find other members with similar interests, members of social networking sites often include information such as age, school, and club affiliations (and sometimes home addresses, banking information, or even social security numbers) that make it easy to steal a person's identity or track down someone in an "offline" environment. Identity thieves constantly are searching social networking sites for new victims. Or, under the guise of a member with similar interests, con artists may ply people with phishing, e-mail messages, or bogus product offers in an attempt to defraud them.

Sexual predators who also are operating online are a problem, especially if users of social networking sites reveal information that can help pinpoint their location in the "real world." Accounts of predators targeting minors through these sites create concern among parents, educators, and public officials. In response, some of the more popular social networking sites have instituted tighter security measures to protect their members from strangers. MySpace, for example, has hired a former federal prosecutor as its first chief security officer.

His security initiatives include efforts to have MySpace staff members view all photos uploaded to the site to catch any occurrences of pornography, and the introduction of technology security measures to allow children aged 14 to 16 to shield their information from strangers. Other initiatives are being explored. Examples include the limiting of keyword searches to prevent predators and others from searching profiles based on broad terms, such as "cheerleader" or "10-year-old boys"; making it easier for parents and children to remove profiles; and ultimately, limiting profiles to clients over 18 (although the site is restricted now to those 14 and older, many younger members lie about their age).

Although these initiatives are a good step, the question is whether these are enough to protect today's youth from the unfortunate perils of online communication. Ultimately, the first line of defense in the battle of Internet safety is the parents. Most experts agree that parents must get involved in their children's online activities. This might be easier said than done, because many students have access to computers outside the home, and despite the best efforts of any parent, a child might do something he or she knows is not right simply out of curiosity or peer pressure. The other defense is to make the security measures strong enough to keep predators away, but not so restrictive as to drive away the users to a less restrictive Web site where the predators will follow. Therefore, all the major players (Web site administrators, school officials, and parents) must actively participate in promoting and employing Internet safety measures. Web sites such as WiredSafety (**www.wiredsafety.org**) provide help and education to Internet and mobile device users of all ages. These sites are a good place to start for more information on protecting children and adults in online activities.

ware, most graphics on the Web will appear in your browser when you visit a site. However, to view and hear some multimedia files on the Web, such as podcasts, videos on YouTube, and MP3 files, you might need a special software program called a **plug-in** (or **player**). Figure 9 lists the most popular plug-ins.

If you've purchased your computer within the past several years, you'll find plug-ins already installed with your browser. For those plug-ins you don't have,

the Web site requiring the plug-in usually displays a message on the screen that includes links to a site where you can download the plug-in free of charge. For example, to use streaming audio on a Web site, your browser might send you to **www.adobe.com**, where you can download Shockwave Player.

Do I need to update players and plug-ins? Like most technological resources, improvements and upgrades are available for players and plug-ins. Most plug-ins and players will alert you to check

FIGURE 9 **Popular Plug-Ins/Players and Their Uses**

	Plug-In/Player Name	Where You Can Get the Plug-In/Player	What the Plug-In/Player Does
	Adobe Reader	**www.adobe.com**	Lets you view and print Portable Document Format (PDF) files
	Authorware Player	**www.adobe.com**	Helps you view animations
	Flash Player	**www.adobe.com**	Lets you play animation and other graphics files
	QuickTimePlayer	**www.apple.com**	Lets you play MP3 animation, music, Musical Instrument Digital Interface (MIDI), audio, and video files
	RealPlayer	**www.real.com**	Lets you play streaming audio, video, animations, and multimedia presentations
	Shockwave Player	**www.adobe.com**	Lets you play interactive games, multimedia, graphics, and streaming audio and video on the Web
	Windows Media Player	**www.microsoft.com**	Lets you play MP3 and WAV files, listen to music files and live audio, and view movies and live video broadcasts on the Web

for and download upgrades when they are available. It is best to keep the players and plug-ins as current as possible so that you get the full effects of the multimedia running with these players.

Are there any risks with using plug-ins? When a browser requires a plug-in to display particular Web content, it usually automatically accesses the plug-in, generally without asking you for consent to start the plug-in. This automatic access can present security risks. To minimize such risks, update your plug-ins and browser software frequently so that you will have the most up-to-date remedies against identified security flaws.

Is there any way to get multimedia Web content to load faster? When you're on the Internet, your browser keeps track of the Web sites you've visited so that it can load them faster the next time you visit them. This cache (or temporary storage place) of the HTML text pages, images, and video files from recently visited Web sites can make your Internet surfing more efficient, but it also can congest your hard drive. To keep your system running efficiently, delete your temporary Internet cache periodically. All popular Web browsers have an option to clear the Internet cache manually, and most have a setting to allow you to automatically clear the cache every time you exit the browser.

BITS AND BYTES

Travel Without the Cost

If you can't afford the time or money to get to visit places like the Colosseum in Rome or the Louvre in Paris, check out **www.fullscreenqtvr.com**. Full-screen QTVR is a collaborative effort that uses the QuickTime plug-in, panoramic photography, and virtual reality technology to display high-quality, full-screen photographic virtual reality exploration on the Internet.

Conducting Business over the Internet: E-Commerce

E-commerce, or **electronic commerce**, is the business of conducting business online for purposes ranging from fund-raising to advertising to selling products. A good example of an e-commerce business (or e-business) is **www.dell.com**. The company's online presence offers customers a convenient way to shop for computer systems. Its success is due to creative marketing, an expanding product line, and reliable customer service and product delivery—all hallmarks of traditional businesses as well. Traditional stores that have an online presence are referred to as click-and-brick businesses. These stores, such as Best Buy (**www.bestbuy.com**) and Target (**www.target.com**), are able to provide a variety of services on Web sites. Customers can visit their sites to check the availability of items or to get store locations and directions. Some click and bricks allow online purchases and in-store pickup and returns.

A significant portion of e-commerce consists of **business-to-consumer (B2C)** transactions—transactions that take place between businesses and consumers, such as the purchases consumers make at online stores. There is also a **business-to-business (B2B)** portion of e-commerce; this consists of businesses buying and selling goods and services to other businesses, such as Omaha Paper Company (**www.omahapaper.com**), which distributes paper products to other companies. Finally, the **consumer-to-consumer (C2C)** portion of e-commerce consists of consumers selling to each other through online auction sites such as eBay.

What are the most popular e-commerce activities? Approximately $100 billion each year is spent on goods purchased over the Internet. At a growth rate of 25 percent a year, some experts predict that Internet sales will make up 25 to 30 percent of all retail sales by 2012. So, what is everyone buying online? Consumers buy books, music and videos, movie and event tickets, and toys and games more often online than in retail stores. Travel items, such as plane tickets, hotel reservations, and rental car reservations are frequently made online. With more lenient return policies, online retail sales of clothing and shoes also have increased. Auction sites such as eBay, together with payment exchange services such as PayPal, are becoming the online equivalent to the weekend yard sale and have dramatically increased in popularity.

But e-commerce encompasses more than just shopping opportunities. Today, anything you can do inside your bank you can do online, and more than 25 percent of U.S. households do some form of online banking (another form of B2C). Most people use online services to check their account balances, and checking stock and mutual fund performances is also popular. Credit card companies also allow you to view your credit card statement, brokerage houses allow you to conduct investment activities online, and banks allow you to pay your bills online (although some companies charge a fee for this service).

E-COMMERCE SAFEGUARDS

Just how safe are online transactions? When you buy something over the Web, you most likely use a credit card; therefore, the exchange of money is done directly between you and a bank. Because online shopping eliminates a sales clerk or other human intermediary from the transaction, it can actually be safer than traditional retail shopping. Still, because users are told to be wary of online transactions and because the integrity of online transactions is the backbone of e-commerce, businesses must have some form of security certification to give their customers a level of comfort. Businesses hire security companies such as VeriSign to certify that their online transactions are secure. Thus, if the Web site displays the VeriSign seal, you can usually trust that the information you submit to the site is protected.

Another indication that a Web site is secure is the appearance of a small icon of a closed padlock (IE, Netscape, and Firefox) or the VeriSign seal on the status bar at the bottom of the screen, as shown in Figure 10. In addition, the beginning of the URL of the site will change from http:// to https://, with the s standing for "secure."

How else can I shop safely online? To ensure that your online shopping experience is a safe one, follow these guidelines:

Shop at well-known, reputable sites. If you aren't familiar with a site, investigate

ACTIVE HELPDESK

Staying Secure on the Internet

In this Active Helpdesk call, you'll learn about e-commerce and what e-commerce safeguards protect you when you're online as well as what cookies are and what risks they pose.

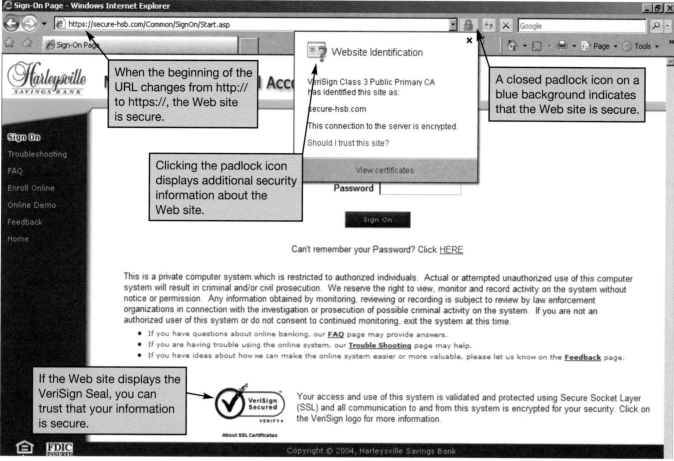

When the beginning of the URL changes from http:// to https://, the Web site is secure.

A closed padlock icon on a blue background indicates that the Web site is secure.

Clicking the padlock icon displays additional security information about the Web site.

If the Web site displays the VeriSign Seal, you can trust that your information is secure.

Website Identification

VeriSign Class 3 Public Primary CA has identified this site as:

secure-hsb.com

This connection to the server is encrypted.

Should I trust this site?

View certificates

FIGURE 10

The VeriSign seal, a closed padlock icon in the browser status bar, and https in the URL are indications that the site is secure.

it with the Better Business Bureau (**www.bbb.org**) or at **www.bizrate.com** or **www.webassured.com**. When you place an order, print a copy of the order and make sure you receive a confirmation number. Make sure the company has a phone number and street address in addition to a Web site. Always pay by credit card. The U.S. federal consumer credit card protection laws protect credit card purchases. If possible, restrict the use of one credit card for Internet purchases only. Check the return policy. Print a copy and save it. If the site disappears overnight, this information may help you in filing a dispute or reporting a problem to a site such as the Better Business Bureau.

Managing Online Annoyances

Surfing the Web, sending and receiving e-mail, and chatting online have become a common part of most of our lives. Unfortunately, the Web has become fertile ground for people who want to advertise

their products, track our Web browsing, or even con people out of personal information. In this section, we'll look at ways in which you can manage, if not avoid, these and other online headaches.

SPAM

How can I best avoid spam? Companies that send out **spam**—unwanted or junk e-mail—find your e-mail address either from a list they purchase or with software that looks for e-mail addresses on the Internet. (Unsolicited instant messages are known as spam.) If you've used your e-mail address to purchase anything online or to open an online account, or if you've participated in a newsgroup or a chat room, your e-mail address eventually will appear on one of the lists spammers get.

One way to avoid spam in your primary account is to create a free Web-based e-mail address that you use only when you fill out forms on the Web. For example, both Hotmail and Yahoo! allow you to set up free e-mail accounts. If your free Web-based e-mail account is saturated with spam, you can abandon that account with little inconvenience. It's much harder to abandon your primary e-mail address.

Another way to avoid spam is to filter it. A **spam filter** is an option you can select in your e-mail account that places known or suspected spam messages into a folder other than your inbox. Most Web-based e-mail services, such as Hotmail and Yahoo!, offer spam filters (see Figure 11). Since the release of Outlook 2003, Outlook has featured a spam filter, but if you still are using a previous version of Outlook to manage your e-mail, then you need to obtain special spam filtering software and install it on your computer. Programs that provide some control over spam include MailWasher Pro, Spam Alarm, and SpamButcher, all of which can be obtained at **www.download.com**.

How do spam filters work? Spam filters and filtering software can catch up to 95 percent of spam. They work by checking incoming e-mail subject headers and sending addresses against databases of known spam. Spam filters also check your e-mail for frequently used spam patterns and keywords (such as "for free" and "over 21"). E-mail that the filter identifies as spam does not go into your inbox but rather to a folder set up for spam. Because spam filters aren't perfect, you should check the spam folder rather than just delete its contents because legitimate e-mail might end up there by mistake.

How else can I prevent spam? There are several additional ways you can prevent spam:

1. Before registering on a Web site, read its privacy policy to see how it uses your e-mail address. Don't give the site permission to pass on your e-mail address to third parties.

2. Don't reply to spam to remove yourself from the spam list. By replying, you are confirming that your e-mail address is active. Instead of stopping spam, you may receive more.

3. Subscribe to an e-mail forwarding service such as **www.emailias.com** or **www.sneakemail.com**.

4. These services screen your e-mail messages, forwarding only those messages you designate as being okay to accept.

COOKIES

What are cookies? Cookies are small text files that some Web sites automatically store on your computer's hard drive when you visit the site. When you log on to a Web site that uses cookies, a cookie file assigns an ID number to your computer. The unique ID is intended to make your return visit to a Web site more efficient and better geared to your interests. The next time you log on to that site, the site marks your visit and keeps track of it in its database.

What do Web sites do with cookie information? Cookies provide Web sites with information about your browsing

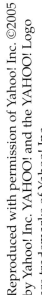

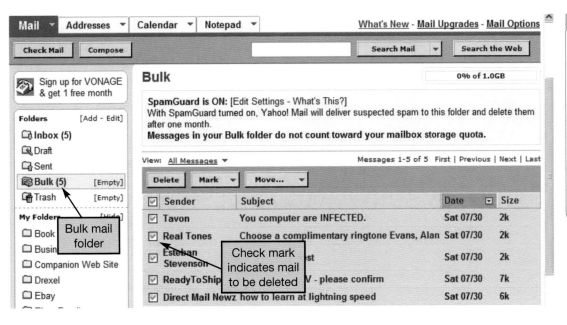

Reproduced with permission of Yahoo! Inc. ©2005 by Yahoo! Inc. YAHOO! and the YAHOO! Logo are trademarks of Yahoo! Inc.

FIGURE 11

In Yahoo! Mail, turning on the SpamGuard feature alerts the Yahoo! Mail server to screen your incoming mail for obvious or suspected spam. This mail is then directed into a folder called "Bulk" where you can review the mail (to ensure it is really spam) and delete it.

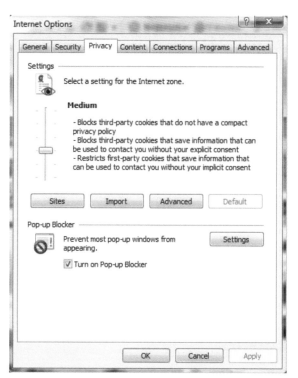

©2007 Dell Inc. All Rights Reserved

habits, such as the ads you've opened, the products you've looked at, and the time and duration of your visits. Cookies also remember personal information you enter into Web site forms, such as your credit card information, name, mailing address, and phone number. Companies use this information to determine the traffic flowing through their Web site and the effectiveness of their marketing strategy and Web site placement. By tracking which pages you view, how long you stay on the site, and how many times you come back to the site, cookies enable companies to identify different users' preferences.

Can companies get my personal information when I visit their sites? Cookies do not go through your hard drive in search of personal information such as passwords or financial data. The only personal information a cookie obtains is the information you supply when you fill out forms online.

Do privacy risks exist with cookies? Some sites sell the personal information their cookies collect to Web advertisers that are building huge databases of consumer preferences and habits, collecting personal and business information such as credit card numbers, phone numbers, credit reports, and the like. The ultimate concern is that advertisers will use this information indiscriminately, thus infiltrating your privacy.

Should I delete cookies from my hard drive then? Because cookies pose no security threat (it is virtually impossible to hide a virus or malicious software program in a cookie), take up little room on your hard drive, and offer you small conveniences on return visits to Web sites, there is no great reason to delete them. Deleting your cookie files could also cost you the inconvenience of reentering data you have already entered into Web site forms. However, if you're uncomfortable with the accessibility of your personal information, you can periodically delete cookies or configure your browser to block certain types of cookies, as shown in Figure 12. Software programs such as Cookie Pal (**www.kburra.com**) also exist to help monitor cookies for you.

ADWARE

What is adware? Adware are software programs that download on your computer when you install or use other software, such as a freeware program, game, or utility. Adware is considered a legitimate (though sometimes annoying) means of generating revenue for those developers who do not charge for their software. Generally, adware enables sponsored advertisements to appear in a section of your browser window or as a pop-up ad box.

BITS AND BYTES

Configure a Firewall Before Going Online

As soon as you connect to the Internet, you are susceptible to unwanted communications to and from your PC. You may wish to install a firewall to help filter traffic entering or leaving your PC. Routers used to share Internet connections in a home network can act as a firewall, but some users prefer additional protection from dedicated firewall software applications. Individual software programs such as McAfee Firewall Plus or Norton Personal Firewall offer specific protection, or you can find firewall protection included in Internet security and utility suites such as McAfee Internet Security Suite and Norton Internet Security. However, the Windows firewall included with Windows Vista provides adequate protection from the majority of problems. When you use the Connection Wizard to create a new Internet connection or enter the Security Center from the Control Panel, you have the opportunity to enable the Windows Firewall.

How do I get rid of pop-up windows? **Pop-up windows** are the billboards of the Internet. These windows pop up when you install freeware programs or enter Web sites. They often offer "useful" information or tout products. Although some sites use pop-ups to increase the functionality of their site (your account balance may pop up at your bank's Web site, for example), many pop-ups are just plain annoying.

Fortunately, there are ways to reduce or eliminate pop-ups. Firefox, Safari, and Internet Explorer 7 have pop-up blockers built into their browsers (see Figure 13).

Some of the more popular search engines (Google, Yahoo!, and MSN) provide toolbars that, when installed in your Web browser, allow you to access the search engine directly from a toolbar in the Web browser. In addition to the immediate convenience, these toolbars also contain pop-up blockers. Generally, between the new pop-up provisions in your browser and your search engine toolbar, additional protection is unnecessary. However, if you feel you need more protection, you can install anti-pop-up software. Two free anti-

pop-up programs are Pop-Up Stopper Companion and Super Ad Blocker, both of which are available at **www.download.com**.

SPYWARE

What is spyware? Some adware programs are more intrusive. Without your knowledge, they transmit information about you, such as your Internet surfing habits, to the owner of the adware program so that the information can be used for marketing purposes. In these instances, such adware becomes more malicious in intent and can be considered spyware. **Spyware** is an unwanted piggyback program that downloads with the software you want to install from the Internet and runs in the background of your system. Many spyware programs use cookies to collect information, whereas others work like Trojan horses (which are disguised as more benign programs, such as games, but are really malicious programs) or act as keystroke loggers (which monitor keystrokes with the intent of stealing passwords, login ids, or credit card information).

a) © 2006 Lavasoft. All Rights Reserved.

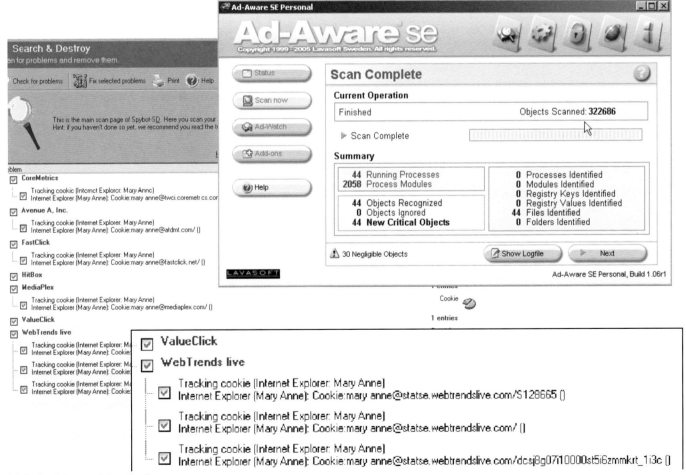

b) Safer-Networking Ltd.

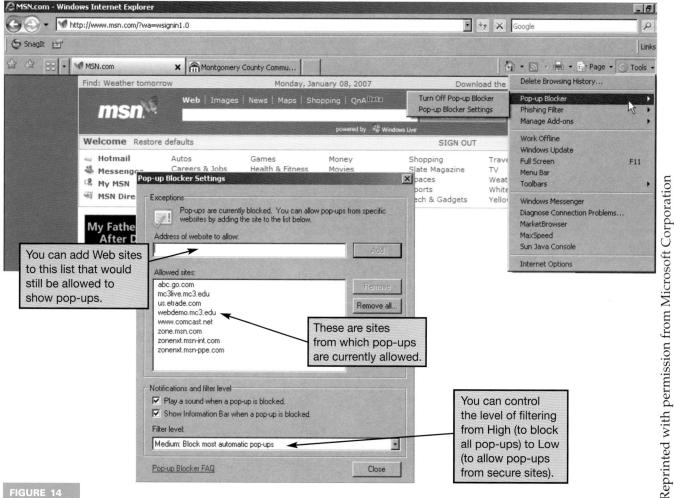

You can add Web sites to this list that would still be allowed to show pop-ups.

These are sites from which pop-ups are currently allowed.

You can control the level of filtering from High (to block all pop-ups) to Low (to allow pop-ups from secure sites).

Reprinted with permission from Microsoft Corporation

FIGURE 14

Internet Explorer 7 has pop-up controls built into the browser. You can toggle the blocker on and off, as well as selectively control specific sites by adding them to the Allowed sites box in the Pop-up Blocker Settings box.

> Pop-up Blocker is found in the Tools menu on the Internet Explorer 7 toolbar.

Can I prevent spyware? Most antivirus software doesn't detect spyware or prevent spyware cookies from being placed on your hard drive. However, you can obtain spyware removal software and run it on your computer to delete unwanted spyware. Because new spyware is created all the time, you should update your spyware removal software regularly. Windows Vista comes with a program called Windows Defender, which scans your system for spyware and other potentially unwanted software. Ad-Aware and Spybot–Search & Destroy (both available for free at **www.download.com**) and eTrust PestPatrol (available at **www.pestpatrol.com**) are programs that are easy to install and update. Figure 14 shows an example of Ad-Aware and Spybot in action.

MALWARE

What is malware? Although it's annoying, adware renders no harm to your computer. **Malware**, on the other hand, is software that has a malicious intent (hence the prefix "mal"). Spyware, described earlier, is a form of malware. Some other types of malware come in the form of viruses, worms, and Trojan horses and can be thought of as electronic vandalism or pranks. The intent of such malware is to render the system temporarily or permanently useless (with a flood of e-mail messages, for example) or to penetrate a computer system completely.

PHISHING AND INTERNET HOAXES

What is phishing? One of the more recent scams involving the Internet is **phishing** (pronounced "fishing"). Phishing lures Internet users into revealing personal information such as credit card or social security numbers or other sensitive information that could lead to identity theft. The scammers send e-mail messages that look like they are from a legitimate business the recipient deals with, such as an online bank. The e-mail states that the recipient needs to update or confirm his or her account information, and provides a link that, when clicked, sends the recipient to a Web site. The site looks like a legitimate site but is really a fraudulent copy the scammer has created. Once the e-mail recipient confirms his or her personal information, the scammers capture it and can begin using it.

How can I avoid being caught by phishing scams? The best way to avoid falling for such scams is to avoid replying directly to any e-mail asking you for personal information. Similarly, do not click on a link in an e-mail to go to a Web site. Instead, type the Web site address yourself in the browser. Check with the company asking for the information and only give the information if you are certain it is needed—and then only over the phone. Never give personal information over the Internet unless you know the site is a secure one. Look for the closed padlock, https, or a certification seal, such as VeriSign, to indicate that the site is secure. Firefox 2 and Internet Explorer 7 have phishing filters built in, so each time you access a Web site, the phishing filter checks for the site's legitimacy and warns you of possible Web forgeries.

What is an Internet hoax? Internet **hoaxes** contain information that is untrue. Hoax e-mail messages may request that you send money to cover medical costs for an impoverished and sick child or ask you to pass on bogus information, such as how to avoid a virus. Chain e-mail letters also are considered a form of Internet hoax.

Why are hoaxes so bad? The sheer number of e-mail messages generated by hoaxes can cost millions in lost opportunity costs caused by time spent reading, discarding, or resending the message, and they can clog up the Internet system. If you receive an e-mail you think might be a hoax, don't pass it on. First determine whether it is a hoax by visiting the U.S. Department of Energy's Hoaxbusters site at **http://hoaxbusters.ciac.org**.

Navigating the Web: Web Browsers

None of the activities for which we use the Web could happen without an important software application: a Web browser. A **Web browser**, or **browser**, is software installed on your computer system that allows you to locate, view, and navigate the Web. The most common browsers in use today are Microsoft's **Internet Explorer (IE)** and Mozilla's Firefox. Most browsers being used today are graphical browsers, meaning they can display pictures (graphics) in addition to text and other forms of multimedia, such as sound and video.

What new features do browsers offer? The latest version of Internet Explorer, IE7, has a much more streamlined approach than its predecessors. The browser's toolbars provide convenient navigation and Web page management tools. The newest features include tabbed browsing and quick tabs. Quick tabs shows thumbnail images of all open Web pages in open tabs (see Figure 15). The browser also includes a built-in search box in which you can designate your preferred default search engine. Tools for printing, page formatting, and

FIGURE 15

The newest features of Internet Explorer 7 (IE7) include tabbed browsing and quick tabs. IE7 has also abbreviated the display of the navigation tools to a simple toolbar and built a Google search engine right into the browser.

Reprinted with permission from Microsoft Corporation

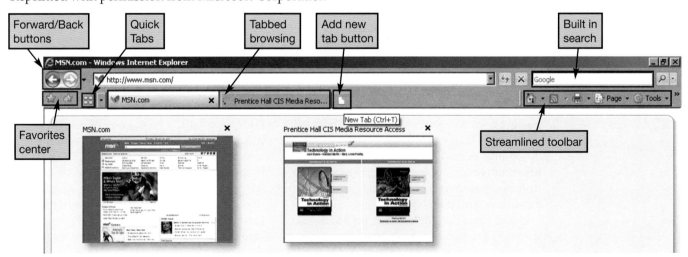

security settings are allocated to a special toolbar. Whether you are like most surfers using Internet Explorer or are using another Web browser, you will find similar toolbar navigation features on each of the browsers.

Most of the popular Web browsers, including IE7, have tabbed browsing. With tabbed browsing, Web pages are loaded in "tabs" within the same browser window (see Figure 15). Rather than having to switch among Web pages on several open windows, you can flip between the tabs in one window. You can even open several Favorites from one folder and choose to display them as tabs. You may also save groups of tabs as a Favorites group, if there are always several you like to open together at the same time.

What other Web browsers are there? Internet Explorer (IE) has enjoyed predominant market share, but recently other browsers have also become very popular.

Firefox, a free browser from Mozilla, was the first to have tabbed browsing. Other handy features found in Firefox are spell checking for e-mail, blogs, and other Web postings; session restore that brings back all your active Web pages if the system shuts down unexpectedly; and Live Titles, which fits nicely on the toolbar and brings you updated summaries of the most important information on a Web page.

Safari is the default browser for Macs. Like IE7 and Firefox, Safari has tabbed browsing, a

built-in search engine feature, spell-checking capabilities, and a pop-up blocker.

Opera (**www.opera.com**) is a browser that has a small but dedicated following. Opera's advantage, similar to Firefox, is that it can preserve your surf sessions: When you launch Opera, it loads and opens all the Web sites you had open when you last used it.

Camino (**www.caminobrowser.org**) is a new browser developed by Mozilla for the Mac OS X platform. This browser offers an efficient and secure browsing experience with the look and feel of a Mac OS X application.

Getting Around the Web: URLs, Hyperlinks, and Other Tools

Unlike text in a book or a Microsoft Word document, which is linear (meaning you read it from top to bottom, left to right, one page after another), the Web is anything but linear. As its name implies, the Web is a series of connected paths, or links, that connect you to different **Web sites**, or locations on the Web. You gain initial access to a particular Web site by typing its unique address, or **Uniform Resource Locator** (**URL**, pronounced "you-are-ell"), in your browser. For example, the URL of the Web site for *Popular Science* magazine is **http://www.popsci.com**. By typing in this URL for *Popular Science* magazine, you connect to the **home page**, or main page, of the Web site. Once you are in the home page, you can move all around the site by clicking specially formatted pieces of text called hyperlinks. Let's look at these and other navigation tools in more detail.

URLS

What do all the parts of the URL mean? As noted earlier, a URL is a Web site's address. And like a regular street address, a URL is composed of several parts that help identify the Web document for which it stands, as shown in Figure 16. The first part of the URL indicates the set of rules (or **protocol**) used to retrieve the specified document. The protocol is generally followed by a colon, two forward slashes, *www* (indicating World Wide Web), and then the

domain name. (Sometimes, the domain name is also thought to include the *www*.)

What's the protocol? For the most part, URLs begin with http, which is short for the **HyperText Transfer Protocol (HTTP)**. The protocol allows files to be transferred from a Web server so that you can see them on your computer by using a browser.

Another common protocol used to transfer files over the Internet is **File Transfer Protocol (FTP)**. FTP is used to upload and download files from one computer to another. FTP files use an FTP file server, whereas HTTP files use a Web server. In order to connect to most FTP servers, you need a user ID and a password. FTP addresses, like e-mail or URLs, identify one location on the Web. They can have several formats, such as **ftp://ftp.frognet.net** or **ftp://ourcompany.com**. To upload and download files from FTP sites, you can use a Web browser (such as Internet Explorer) or file transfer software, such as WS_FTP, Fetch, or CuteFTP.

What's in a domain name Domain names consist of two parts. The first part identifies who the site's **host** is. For example, in the URL **www.berkeley.edu**, *berkeley.edu* is the domain name and *berkeley* is the host. The suffix in the domain name after the dot (such as .com or .edu) is called the **top-level domain (TLD)**. This suffix indicates the kind of organization to which the host belongs. Figure 17 lists the top-level domains that are currently approved and in use.

Each country in the world has its own TLD. These are two-letter designations such as .za for South Africa and .us for the United States. Within a country-specific domain, further subdivisions can be made for regions or states. For instance, the .us domain contains subdomains for each state, using the two-letter abbreviation of the state. For example, the URL for Pennsylvania's Web site is **www.state.pa.us**.

What's the information after the domain name that I sometimes see? When the URL is only the domain name (such as **www.nytimes.com**), you are requesting a site's home page. However, at times, a forward slash and additional text follow the domain name, such as **www.nytimes.com/pages/cartoons**. The information after the slash indicates a particular file or **path** (or **subdirectory**) within the Web site. In this example, you would connect to the cartoon pages in the *New York Times* site.

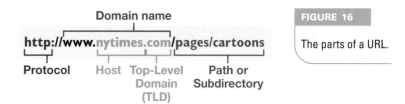

FIGURE 16

The parts of a URL.

FIGURE 17 Current Top-Level Domains and Their Authorized Users

Domain Name	Who Can Use the Domain Name
.aero	Members of the air transport industry
.biz	Businesses
.com	Originally for commercial sites, can be used by anyone now
.coop	Cooperative associations
.edu	Degree-granting institutions
.gov	United States government
.info	Information service providers
.jobs	Posting and recruiting job opportunities
.mil	United States military
.museum	Museums
.name	Individuals
.net	Originally for networking organizations, is no longer restricted
.org	Organizations (often nonprofits)
.pro	Credentialed professionals
.travel	Travel-related services
.uk	United Kingdom country code
.us	United States country code

Note: For a full listing of country codes, refer to **www.norid.no/domenenavnbaser/domreg.html**.

HYPERLINKS AND BEYOND

What's the best way to get around in a Web site? As mentioned earlier, once you've reached a Web site, you can jump from one location, or Web page, to another within the same Web site or to another Web site altogether by clicking on specially coded text called **hyperlinks**, shown in Figure 18. Generally, text that operates as a hyperlink appears in a different color (often blue) and is underlined. Sometimes images also act as hyperlinks. When you pass your cursor over a hyperlinked image, the cursor changes to a

The TV Domain Name

Two-letter domains are reserved for countries worldwide. The domain .tv is the domain for the little Pacific island country of Tuvalu. The domain name is popular as well as economically valuable because it is an abbreviation of the word "television." In the late 1990s, Tuvalu began selling the right to use the ".tv" Internet domain name as a means of generating revenue for the country. The domain is currently operated by The .tv Corporation, a VeriSign company.

hand with a finger pointing upward. To access the hyperlink, you simply click the image.

To retrace your steps, some sites also provide a **breadcrumb list**—a list of pages within a Web site you've visited that usually appears at the top of a page. Figure 18 shows an example of a breadcrumb list. Breadcrumbs get their name from the Hansel and Gretel fairy tale in which the children dropped breadcrumbs on the trail to find their way back out of the forest. By clicking on earlier links in a breadcrumb list, you can retrace your steps back to the page on which you first started.

To get back to your original location or visit a Web page you viewed previously, you use the browser's Back and Forward buttons (see Figure 18). If you want to back up more than one page, click the down arrow next to the Back button to access a list of most recently visited Web sites. By selecting any one of these sites in the list, you can return to that page without having to navigate through other Web sites and Web pages you've visited.

The **History list** on your browser's toolbar is also a handy feature. The History list shows all the Web sites and pages that you've visited over a certain period of time. These Web sites are organized according to date and can go back as far as three weeks. To access the history list on IE7, click the down arrow next to the navigation arrows. The history button is the alarm clock icon on the Firefox toolbar.

FAVORITES AND BOOKMARKS

What's the best way to mark a site so I can return to it later? If you want an easy way to return to a specific Web page without always having to remember to type in the address, you can use your browser's **Favorites** or **Bookmark** feature, as shown in Figure 19. (Internet Explorer and Safari call this feature Favorites; Firefox calls the same feature a Bookmark.) This feature places a marker of the site's URL in an easily retriev-

FIGURE 18

When you click on a hyperlink, you jump from one location in a Web site to another. When you click on the links in a breadcrumb list, you can navigate your way back through a Web site.

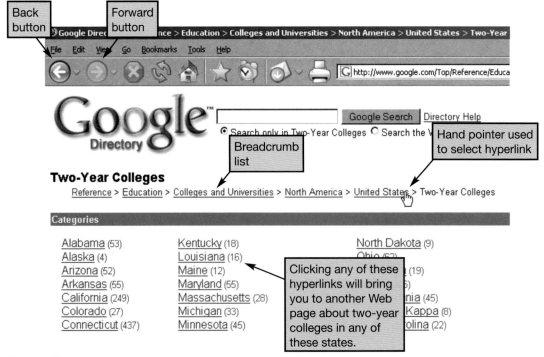

Google, Inc.

Favorites center

Fandango, Microsoft

able list in your browser's toolbar. To organize the sites into categories, most browsers also offer tools to create folders. Most browsers also provide features to export the list of bookmarks to another computer, or to another browser. To access your Bookmarks and Favorites from any computer, anywhere, you can use MyBookmarks (**www.mybookmarks.com**), a free Internet service that stores your Bookmarks and Favorites online.

To bookmark a Web page in IE7, on the toolbar bar, click the Add to Favorites button. You may change the name of the bookmark and designate a folder.

What are live bookmarks? Live bookmarks, found in the Firefox browser, add the technology of RSS (Really Simple Syndication) feeds to bookmarking. Because the Web is constantly changing, the site you bookmarked last week may subsequently change and add new content. Traditionally, you would notice the change only the next time you visited the site. With live bookmarks, the content comes to you. Instead of constantly checking your favorite Web pages for new content, a **live bookmark** delivers updates to you as soon as they become available. Live bookmarks are useful if you are interested in the most up-to-date news stories, sports scores, or stock prices.

Searching the Web: Search Engines and Subject Directories

The Internet, with its billions of Web pages, offers its visitors access to masses of information on virtually any topic. To quickly narrow down the massive quantity to something more useful, there are two main tools you can use to find information on the Web. The first tool is a **search engine**, which is a set of programs that searches the Web for specific words (or **keywords**) you wish to

query (or look for) and then returns a list of the Web sites on which those keywords are found. Popular search engines include Google and AlltheWeb. Second, you also can search the Web using a **subject directory**, which is a structured outline of Web sites organized by topics and subtopics. Librarians' Internet Index (**www.lii.org**) is a subject directory, and popular search engines such as Google and Yahoo! also feature directories. Figure 20 lists popular search engines and subject directories and their URLs.

BITS AND BYTES

Folksonomy and Tagging

While bookmarks and favorites are great to quickly locate those sites you use the most, they are accessible to you only when you are on your own computer. A newer development in the Web is the addition of sites such as del.icio.us and digg.com, which allow you to put your bookmarks on the Web so that they are available to you anywhere and on any computer. In addition to the convenience of access, these sites also allow you to provide your own key words, called tags, so that you can categorize your favorite Web sites.

FIGURE 19

Using the IE Favorites feature makes returning to an often-used or hard-to-find Web page much easier.

ETHICS IN IT

Ethics: What Can You Borrow from the Internet?

You've no doubt heard of *plagiarism*—claiming another person's words as your own. And you've probably heard the term *copyright violation*, especially if you've been following the music industry's battle to keep "free" music off the Web. But what constitutes plagiarism, and what constitutes copyright violation? And what can you borrow from the Web? Consider these scenarios:

- You find a political cartoon that would be terrific in a PowerPoint presentation you're creating for your civics class. You copy it into your presentation.
- Your hobby is cooking. You design a Web site that includes videos of you preparing recipes, as well as the recipes themselves. Some of these recipes you take from your favorite cookbooks; others you get from friends. You don't cite your sources, nor do you obtain permission from the originators of the recipes you post to your Web site.
- You're pressed for time and need to do research for a paper due tomorrow. You find information on an obscure Web site and copy it into your paper without documenting the source.
- You download a song from the Internet and incorporate it into a PowerPoint presentation for a school project. Because you figure everyone knows the song, you don't credit it in your sources.

Which of the preceding scenarios represent copyright violations? Which represent plagiarism? The distinctions between these scenarios are narrow in some cases, but it's important to understand the differences.

As noted earlier, plagiarism occurs when you use someone else's ideas or words and represent them as your own. In today's computer society, it's easy to copy information from the Internet and paste it into a Word document, change a few words, and call it your own. To avoid plagiarism, use quotation marks around all words you borrow directly and credit your sources for any ideas you paraphrase or borrow. Avoiding plagiarism means properly crediting *all* information you obtain from the Internet, including words, ideas, graphics, data, and audio and video clips.

Copyright violation is more serious because it is punishable by law. The law assumes that all original work including text, graphics, software, multimedia, audio or video clips, and even ideas is copyrighted, regardless of whether the work displays the copyright symbol (©). Copyright violation occurs when you use another person's material for your own personal *economic* benefit, or when you take away from the economic benefit of the originator. Don't assume that by citing a source you're abiding by copyright laws. In most cases, you need to seek *and receive* written permission from the copyright holder. There are exceptions to this rule. For example, there is no copyright on government documents; therefore, you can download and reproduce material from NASA, for example, without violating copyright laws. The British Broadcasting Corporation (BBC) is also beginning to digitize and make available its archives of material to the public without copyright restrictions.

Teachers and students receive special consideration regarding copyright violations. This special consideration falls under a provision called academic fair use. As long as the material is being used for educational purposes only, limited copying and distribution is allowed. For example, an instructor can make copies of a newspaper article and distribute it to her class, or a student can include a cartoon in a PowerPoint presentation without seeking permission from the artist. However, to avoid plagiarism in these situations, you still must credit your sources of information. So, do you now know which of the four scenarios above are plagiarism or copyright violations?

1. You are not in violation because the use of the cartoon is for educational purposes and falls under the academic fair use provision. You must still credit the source, however.
2. If your Web site is for your economic benefit, you would be in violation of copyright laws because no credit was given for the recipes, and you are presenting them as your own.
3. You are guilty of plagiarism because you copied from another source and implied it was your own work.
4. Again, because it is for a school project, you are not in violation because of the academic fair use provision. However, it's always important to document your sources.

FIGURE 20 Popular Search Engines and Subject Directories

Search Tools on the Internet

AlltheWeb	**www.alltheweb.com**	Keyword search engine
AltaVista	**www.altavista.com**	Keyword search engine
Dogpile	**www.dogpile.com**	Meta search engine that searches Google, Yahoo!, MSN Search, and Ask
Excite	**www.excite.com**	Portal with keyword search capabilities
Google	**www.google.com**	Keyword search engine Directory feature
Complete-Planet	**www.completeplanet.com**	Deep Web Directory; searches databases not normally searched by regular search engines
LookSmart	**www.looksmart.com**	Keyword search engine and subject directory search engine
Open Directory Project	**www.dmoz.org**	Subject directory with keyword search capabilities
InfoMine	**http://infomine.ucr.edu**	Subject directory of academic resources with keyword search engine capabilities
Yahoo!	**www.yahoo.com**	Subject directory and keyword search engine with portal content

Note: For a complete list of search engines, go to **www.high-search-engine-ranking.com.**

SEARCH ENGINES

How do search engines work? Search engines have three parts. The first part is a program called a **spider**. The spider constantly collects data on the Web, following links in Web sites and reading Web pages. Spiders get their name because they crawl over the Web using multiple "legs" to visit many sites simultaneously. As the spider collects data, the second part of the search engine, an indexer program, organizes the data into a large database. When you use a search engine, you interact with the third part: the search engine software. This software searches the indexed data, pulling out relevant information according to your search. The resulting list appears in your Web browser as a list of **hits,** or sites that match your search.

Why don't I get the same results from all search engines? Each search engine uses a unique formula, or algorithm, to formulate the search and create the resulting index of related sites. In addition, search engines differ in how they rank the search results. Most search engines rank their results based on the frequency of the appearance of your queried keywords in Web sites as well as the location of those words in the sites. Thus, sites that include the keywords in their URL or site name most likely appear at the top of the hit list. After that, results vary because of differences in each engine's proprietary formula, as shown in Figure 21.

In addition, search engines differ as to which sites they search. For instance, Google and AlltheWeb search nearly the entire Web, whereas specialty search engines search only sites that are specifically relevant to the particular specialty subject. Specialty search engines exist for almost every industry or interest. For example, **www.dailystocks.com** is a search engine used primarily by investors that searches for corporate information to help them make educated decisions. Search

FIGURE 21

Google and AlltheWeb are popular search engines. Although they have many similarities, the search results pages are different because the underlying formulas that are used to search the Web are different.

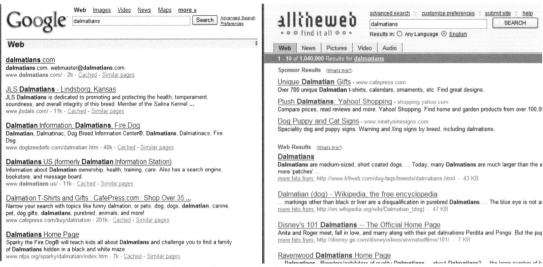

a) Google, Inc.; b) ©Reproduced with the permission of Overture Services, Inc. All rights reserved

Engine Watch (**www.searchenginewatch.com**) has a list of many specialty search engines organized by industry. If you can't decide which search engine is best, you may want to try a **meta search engine**, such as Dogpile (**www.dogpile.com**). Meta search engines search other search engines rather than individual Web sites.

Can I use a search engine to search for images and videos on the Web? With the increasing popularity of multimedia, search engines such as Google, AlltheWeb, and Yahoo! have capabilities to search the Web for digital images and audio and video files. YouTube is one of many sites that have gained recent popularity because of its wealth of video content. In addition to the amusing videos that are captured in popular news, YouTube contains instructional and informational videos.

SUBJECT DIRECTORIES

How can I use a subject directory to find information on the Web? As mentioned earlier, a subject directory is a guide to the Internet organized by topics and subtopics. Yahoo! was one of the original subject directories, and although it still has a subject directory, it now has a search engine feature. Google, which started as a search engine, also has added a subject directory feature. With a subject directory, you do not use keywords to search the Web. Instead, after selecting the main subject from the directory, you narrow your search by successively clicking on subfolders that match your search until you have reached the appropri-

ate information. For example, to find previews on newly released movies in Google's subject directory, you would click on the main category of Arts, select the subcategory Movies, select the further subcategory Previews, and then open one of the listed Web sites.

Can I find the same information with a subject directory as I can with a search engine? Most subject directories started as commercial- and consumer-oriented rather than academic- or research-based directories. The main categories in Google's subject directory, for example, include Computers, Shopping, Recreation, and Sports. Even within categories such as Reference, you find consumer-oriented subcategories such as Phone Numbers and Quotations. Many Web sites that began strictly as subject directories, such as Yahoo! and MSN, are now part of a larger Web site that focuses on offering its visitors a variety of information, such as the weather, news, sports, and shopping guides. This type of Web site is referred to as a **portal**.

When should I use a subject directory instead of a traditional search engine? Directory searches are great for finding information on general topics (such as sports and hobbies) rather than narrowing in on a specific or unusual piece of information. For example, conducting a search on the keyword hobbies on a search engine does not provide a convenient list of hobbies, as does a subject directory. And although most directories tend to be commercially oriented, there are academic and professional directories that use subject experts to select and annotate sites.

SOUND BYTE

Finding Information on the Web

In this Sound Byte, you'll learn how and when to use search engines and subject directories. Through guided tours, you'll learn effective search techniques, including how to use Boolean operators and meta search engines.

Using the Internet: Making the Most of the Web's Resources

These directories are created specifically to facilitate the research process. The Librarians' Internet Index (**www.lii.org**), in Figure 22, for example, is an academic directory whose index lists librarian-selected Web sites that have little if any commercially sponsored content.

EVALUATING WEB SITES

How can I make sure the Web site is appropriate to use for research?

When you're using the Internet for research, you shouldn't assume that everything you find is accurate and appropriate to use. Before you use an Internet resource, ask yourself the following questions:

1. Who is the author of the article or the sponsor of the site? If the author is well known or the site is published by a reputable news source (such as the *New York Times*), you can feel more confident using it as a source than if you are unable to locate information about the author or do not know who sponsors the site. (*Note*: Some sites include a page with information about the author or the site's sponsor.)

2. For what audience is the site intended? Ensure that the content, tone, and style of the site match your needs. You probably wouldn't want to use information from a site geared toward teens if you're writing for adults, or use a site that has a casual style and tone for serious research.

3. Is the site biased? The purpose of many Web sites is to sell you a product or service, or to persuade rather than inform. These sites, though useful in some situations, present a biased point of view. Look for sites that offer several sets of facts or consider opinions from several sources.

ACTIVE HELPDESK

Using Subject Directories and Search Engines

In this Active Helpdesk call, you'll play the role of a Helpdesk staffer, fielding calls about how to search the Internet using search engines and subject directories, and how to use Boolean operators to search the Web more effectively.

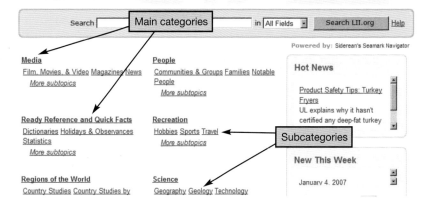

FIGURE 22

Subject directories are best for searches that are more general, or just for browsing within a topic. Some academic subject directories, such as www.lii.org, are annotated by experts.

BITS AND BYTES

Citing Web Site Sources

After you've evaluated a Web site and determined it to be a credible source of information, you will need to list the source in the Works Cited section of your paper. There are formal guidelines as to how to cite Web content, but unlike books and periodicals, the standards are still being developed. At a minimum, the following components should be included in the citation: author, title of document and/or publication, date of publication and/or last revision, complete URL, and date accessed. Following are examples of Web citations for MLA and APA for an article found in BusinessWeek online:

Example of MLA style
MacMillian, Douglas. "Hybrids Cost-Efficient Over Long Haul." *BusinessWeek*. 09 January 2007. 12 February 2007. **http://www.businessweek.com/autos/content/jan2007/bw20070108_774581.htm**

Example of APA style
MacMillian, D. (January 9, 2007). Hybrids Cost-Efficient Over Long Haul. *BusinessWeek*. Retrieved February 12, 2007, from **http://www.businessweek.com/autos/content/jan2007/bw20070108_774581.htm**.

For further assistance, go to **www.citationmachine.net**, which is an interactive tool designed to output the proper MLA or APA citation format with information you provide in an online form.

Refining Your Web Searches: Boolean Operators

When you conduct Web searches, you often receive a list of hits that includes thousands—even millions—of Web pages that have no relevance to the topic you're trying to search. **Boolean operators** are words you can use to refine your searches, making them more effective. These words—AND, NOT, and OR—describe the relationships between keywords in a search. Figure 23 shows examples of these operators being used as well as the results the searches would produce.

Narrowing and Expanding Searches

Using the Boolean operators AND, NOT, and OR alone or in combinations in your keyword searches can help to expand or limit your search results, as shown in Figure 21. The Boolean AND operator helps you narrow (or limit) the results of your search. When you use the AND operator to join two keywords, the search engine returns only those documents that include both keywords (not just one).

You can also narrow your search by using the NOT operator. When you use the NOT operator to join two keywords, the search engine doesn't show the results of any pages containing the word following NOT. Be aware, however, that when you use the NOT operator, you may eliminate documents that contain the unwanted keyword but that also contain important information that may have been useful to you. Note that some search engines also let you use the plus sign (+) and minus sign (−) instead of the words AND and NOT, respectively.

The OR operator expands a keyword search so that the search results include either or both keywords. Boolean OR searches are particularly helpful if there are a variety of synonymous keywords you could use in your search.

Other Helpful Search Strategies

Combining search terms produces more specific results. To do so, however, you must use parentheses to add order to your search. For example, if you are looking for tutorials or lessons to better use the program Microsoft Excel, you can search for (*Tutorials OR Lessons) AND Excel*. Similarly, if you want to know

FIGURE 23 Using Boolean Operators

Operator	Example	Results
AND	Car AND Ford	Only those documents that contain both the words **Car** AND **Ford**. Most search engines assume that the word AND is used as a default.
NOT	Car NOT Ford	Only those documents that contain the word **Car** but do NOT also contain the word **Ford**. This is the most restrictive of all searches and will return the smallest number of documents.
OR	Car OR Ford	All documents that contain either the word **Car** OR the word **Ford** OR **both** words. This results in the greatest number of documents.
Combinations	(Car AND Ford) NOT Gerald	Will give you all the documents referring to **Cars** and **Fords**, but no documents relating to the 38th U.S. president, Gerald Ford.
Quotation Marks	"Lord of the Rings"	Will return only those documents that contain the string of words "Lord of the Rings" in that exact order. Without the quotation marks, you would get documents containing any of those words.
Wildcard*	Psych*	Stands in place of a series of letters. Good for those searches when you are searching for a term that can have several different endings, such as psychology or psychiatry, and you want to research all of them.
Wildcard%	Goldsm%th	Stands in place of a single letter. Good to use when there are different spellings of the same word, such as Goldsmith and Goldsmyth.

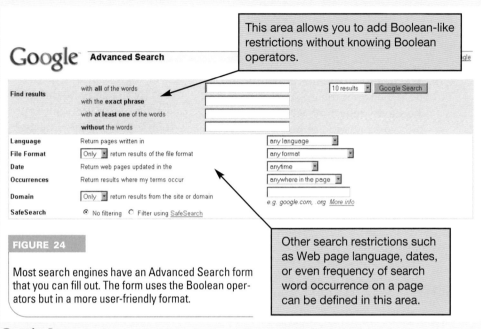

This area allows you to add Boolean-like restrictions without knowing Boolean operators.

Other search restrictions such as Web page language, dates, or even frequency of search word occurrence on a page can be defined in this area.

FIGURE 24

Most search engines have an Advanced Search form that you can fill out. The form uses the Boolean operators but in a more user-friendly format.

Google, Inc.

how to better use the entire Microsoft Office suite with the exception of Access, you can search for *(Tutorials OR Lessons) AND (Office NOT Access)*.

To search for an exact phrase, place quotation marks around your keywords. The search engine will look for only those Web sites that contain the words in that exact order. For example, if you want information on the movie *Lord of the Rings* and you type these words without quotation marks, your search results will contain pages that include any of the words *Lord*, *of*, *the*, and *Rings*, although not necessarily in that order. Typing *"Lord of the Rings"* in quotes guarantees search results will include this exact phrase.

Some search engines let you use an asterisk (*) to replace a series of letters and a percent sign (%) to replace a single letter in a word. These symbols, called **wildcards**, are helpful when you're searching for a keyword but are unsure of its spelling, or if a word can be

spelled in different ways or may contain different endings. For example, if you're doing a genealogy project and are searching for the name *Goldsmith*, you might want to use *Goldsm%th* to take into consideration alternative spellings of the name (such as Goldsmyth). Similarly, if you're searching for sites related to psychiatry and psychology and you type *psych**, the search results will include all pages containing the words *psychology, psychiatry, psychedelic*, and so on.

Using Boolean search techniques can make your Internet research a lot more efficient. With the simple addition of a few words, you can narrow your search results to a more manageable and more meaningful list. Meanwhile, most search engines offer an Advanced Search page that provides the same type of strategies in a well-organized form (see Figure 24).

4. Is the information in the site current? Material can last a long time on the Web. Some research projects (such as historical accounts) depend on older records. However, if you're writing about cutting-edge technologies, you need to look for the most recent sources. Therefore, look for a date on information to make sure it is current.

5. Are the links available and appropriate? Check out the links provided on the site to determine whether they are still working and appropriate for your needs. Don't assume that the links provided are the only additional sources of information. Investigate other sites on your topic as well.

The answers to these questions will help you decide whether you should consider a Web site to be a good source of information.

Internet Basics

The Internet is such an integral part of our lives that it's hard to imagine life without it. Looking forward, our ability to use and interact with the Internet and the World Wide Web will converge even more with our daily lives. Therefore, it's important to understand how the Internet works and the choices available for connecting to it.

THE INTERNET'S CLIENTS AND SERVERS

How does the Internet work?
Computers connected to the Internet communicate (or "talk") to each other like we do when we ask a question and get an answer. Thus, a computer connected to the Internet acts in one of two ways: it is a **client**, a computer that asks for data, or a **server**, a computer that receives the request and returns the data to the client. Because the Internet uses clients and servers, it is referred to as a **client/server network**.

How do computers talk to each other? Suppose you want to access the Web to check out snow conditions at your favorite ski area. As Figure 25 illustrates, when you type the Web site address of the ski area in your Web browser, your computer acts as a client computer because you are asking for data from the ski area's Web site. Your browser's request for this data travels along several pathways, similar to interstate highways. The largest and fastest pathway is the main artery of the Internet, called the **Internet backbone**, to which all intermediary pathways connect. All data traffic flows along the backbone and then on to smaller pathways until it reaches its destination, which is the server computer for the ski area's Web site. The server computer returns the requested data to your computer by using the most expedient pathway system (which may be different from the pathway the request took). Your Web browser then interprets the data and displays it on your monitor.

How does the data get sent to the correct computer? Each time you connect to the Internet, your computer is assigned a unique identification number. This number, called an **Internet Protocol (IP) address**, is a set of four numbers separated by dots, such as 123.45.245.91. IP addresses are the means by which all computers connected to the Internet identify each other. Similarly, each Web site is assigned an IP address that uniquely identifies it. However, because the long strings of numbers that make up IP addresses are difficult for humans to remember, Web sites are given text versions of their IP addresses. So, the ski area Web site mentioned earlier may have an IP address of 66.117.154.119 and a text name of **www.skislope.com**. When you type **www.skislope.com** into your browser window, your computer (with its own unique IP address) looks for the ski area's IP address (66.117.154.119). Data is exchanged between the ski area's server computer and your computer using these unique IP addresses.

Connecting to the Internet

To take advantage of the resources the Internet offers, you need a means to connect your computer to it. Home users have several connection options available. Originally, the only means to connect to the Internet was with a **dial-up connection**. With dial-up connections, you connect to the Internet using a standard telephone line. However, other connection options, collectively called **broadband connections**, offer faster means to connect to the Internet. Broadband connections include cable, satellite, and DSL. Broadband connections are

Using the Internet: Making the Most of the Web's Resources

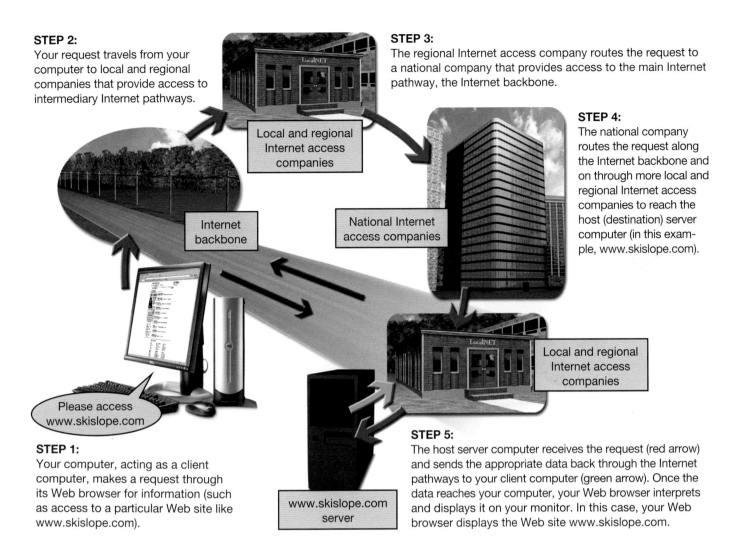

STEP 2:
Your request travels from your computer to local and regional companies that provide access to intermediary Internet pathways.

Local and regional Internet access companies

STEP 3:
The regional Internet access company routes the request to a national company that provides access to the main Internet pathway, the Internet backbone.

STEP 4:
The national company routes the request along the Internet backbone and on through more local and regional Internet access companies to reach the host (destination) server computer (in this example, www.skislope.com).

Internet backbone

National Internet access companies

Local and regional Internet access companies

Please access www.skislope.com

STEP 1:
Your computer, acting as a client computer, makes a request through its Web browser for information (such as access to a particular Web site like www.skislope.com).

www.skislope.com server

STEP 5:
The host server computer receives the request (red arrow) and sends the appropriate data back through the Internet pathways to your client computer (green arrow). Once the data reaches your computer, your Web browser interprets and displays it on your monitor. In this case, your Web browser displays the Web site www.skislope.com.

FIGURE 25

How the Internet's client/server network works.

quickly becoming the preferred method of connecting to the Internet. By the end of 2006, nearly 205 million people, worldwide, connected to the Internet via broadband.

BROADBAND CONNECTIONS

What broadband options do I have? The two leading broadband home Internet connection technologies are DSL, which uses a standard phone line to connect your computer to the Internet, and cable, which uses your television's cable service provider to connect to the Internet. Some users, especially those located in rural areas, connect to the Internet by satellite.

Why would I choose a broadband connection? A cable Internet connection has slightly better speed than a DSL connection and DSL is faster than satellite, but any broadband connection is much faster than dial-up. The capabilities of the Web are designed assuming that the majority of

Internet users are accessing the Internet via some form of broadband connection. No matter which broadband connection you choose, the quality of your Web experience will be greatly enhanced with a broadband connection. Depending on the area in which you live, you might just not have a choice as to the type of broadband connection that is available to you. Check with your local cable TV provider, phone company, and satellite TV providers to determine what broadband options are available where you live and what the transfer rates are in your area. It might also be good to check with your neighbors to see what kind of broadband connections they are using. Speeds vary by neighborhood, sometimes exceeding advertised rates, so it's always good to check actual experiences.

Cable
If I have cable TV, do I have access to cable Internet? Although both cable TV and a **cable Internet connection** use coaxial

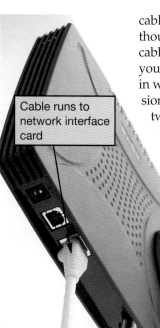

Cable runs to network interface card

FIGURE 26

A cable Internet connection. To gain cable Internet access, you need a cable modem. This modem connects to a network interface card located inside your computer's system unit.

cable, they are separate services. In fact, even though you may have cable TV in your home, cable Internet service may not be available in your area. Coaxial cable is a one-way service in which the cable company feeds your television programming signals. In order to bring two-way Internet connections to homes, cable companies must upgrade their networks for two-way data transmission capabilities and with fiber-optic lines, which transmit data at close to the speed of light along glass or plastic fibers or wires. Because data sent through fiber-optic lines is transmitted at the speed of light, transmission speeds are much faster than are those along other conventional copper wire technologies.

What do I need to hook up to cable Internet?
Cable Internet connection requires a **cable modem**, as shown in Figure 26. Generally, the modem is located somewhere near your computer. The cable modem is then connected to an expansion (or adapter) card called a **network interface card (NIC)**, located inside your system unit. The cable modem works to translate the cable signal into digital data and back again. Because the cable TV signal and Internet data can share the same line, you can watch cable TV and be on the Internet at the same time.

Are there any disadvantages to cable Internet?
Because you share your cable Internet connection with your neighbors, you may experience periodic decreases in connection speeds during peak usage times. Although cable Internet connection speeds are still faster than the dial-up alternative, your ultimate speed depends on how many other users are trying to transmit data at the same time as you are.

DSL

How does DSL work? Similar to a dial-up connection, **DSL** (short for **Digital Subscriber Line**) uses telephone lines to connect to the Internet. However, unlike dial-up, DSL allows phone and data transmission to share the same line, thus eliminating the need for an additional phone line. Phone lines are made of twisted copper wires known as twisted-pair wiring. Think of this twisted copper wiring as a

three-lane highway with only one lane being used to carry voice data. DSL uses the remaining two lanes to send and receive data separately, at much higher frequencies. Thus, although it uses a standard phone line, a DSL connection is much faster than a dial-up connection.

Can anyone with a phone line have DSL? Just because you have a traditional phone line in your house doesn't mean that you have access to DSL service. Your local phone company must have special DSL technology to offer you the service. Although more phone companies are acquiring DSL technology, many areas in the United States, especially rural ones, still do not have DSL service available.

What special equipment do I need for DSL service? You need a special DSL modem like the one shown in Figure 27. A **DSL modem** is a device that connects the computer data to the DSL line and then separates the types of signals into voice and data signals so that they can travel in the right "lane" on the twisted-pair wiring. Voice data is sent at the lower speed, while digital data is sent at data transfer rates ranging from 500 Kbps to 1.5 megabits per second (Mbps), which is 1,500 Kbps. Sometimes a DSL filter is required in DSL installations. Filters are necessary to reduce interference caused when the DSL equipment shares the same lines as the standard phone line. If a filter is required, the phone line is fit into the filter, and the filter plugs into the phone wall jack. As with cable, your computer will need a network interface card.

Are there different types of DSL service? The more typical DSL transmissions download (or receive) data from the Internet faster than they upload (or send) data. Such transmissions are referred to as Asymmetrical Digital Subscriber Line (ADSL). Other DSL transmissions, called Symmetrical Digital Subscriber Line (SDSL), upload and download data at the same speed. If you upload data to the Internet often (if you design and update your own Web site, for example), you may want to investigate the range of sending-speed capabilities of your DSL connection, or check to see if your DSL provider offers SDSL service.

Another type of DSL service is Fiber Optic Service (FiOS). One of the main benefits of FiOS is its speed. Verizon claims that speeds delivered over FiOS lines can reach 30 megabits a second. This is a huge improvement over current DSL lines, which deliver data at up to 1.5 Mbps. The higher speeds achieved with FiOS lines can enable users to download full-length movies in just a handful of minutes.

What are the advantages of DSL?
With data transfer rates that reach 1.5 Mbps, DSL beats the slow speeds of dial-up by a great deal, and with DSL service, you can connect to the Internet without tying up your phone line. In addition, unlike cable and satellite, DSL service does not share the line with other network users in your area. In times of peak Internet usage, DSL speed is not affected, whereas cable and satellite hookups often experience reduced speeds during busy times. Because you are not sharing a line with DSL as you are with cable, some people maintain that DSL is less subject to denial of service attacks, service theft, and the like. In addition, bad weather does not affect DSL service as it can with satellite, and DSL service is less susceptible to the radio frequency interference that hinders cable.

Are there drawbacks to DSL? As mentioned earlier, DSL service is not available in all areas. If you do have access to DSL service, the quality and effectiveness of your service depend on your proximity to a phone company central office (CO). A CO is the place where a receiving DSL modem is located. Data is sent through your DSL modem to the DSL modem at the CO. For the DSL service to work correctly, you must be within approximately three miles of a CO because the signal quality and speed weaken drastically at distances beyond 18,000 feet. A simple call to your local phone company can determine your proximity to a CO and whether DSL service is available. You can also find out whether DSL is available in your area by checking **www.dsl.com** or **www.getconnected.com**.

Fiber-Optic Internet

What is fiber-optic Internet? Fiber-optic lines are strands of optically pure glass as thin as a human hair. They are arranged in bundles called optical cables and are used to transmit data via light signals over long distances. **Fiber-optic Internet** transmits data by sending light through optical fibers. Because light travels so quickly, this technology can bring an enormous amount of data to your home at super fast speeds. When the data reaches your house, it's converted to electrical

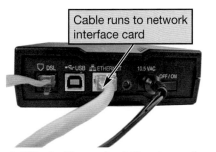

Cable runs to network interface card

a) ©Paolo Florendo / Courtesy of www.istockphoto.com

©Sam Lee / Courtesy of www.istockphoto.com

pulses that transmit digital signals your computer can "read."

What are the advantages of fiber-optic Internet? The biggest advantage to fiber-optic Internet is its speed. Most providers offer several packages of varying speed and costs. Similar to cable and traditional DSL, fiber-optic Internet is available bundled with TV and phone services.

Are there disadvantages to fiber-optic Internet? Right now, for the fastest transmission speeds, cost might be the main disadvantage. For data transmission speeds of 30 Mbps, the cost is approximately $150/year. Also, because fiber-optic lines must be laid in place before service is available, the service is available only in select areas. The first town to go fiber optic was Keller, Texas, in 2004. Since then, fiber optic has become available to parts of many east and west coast areas.

Satellite

What is satellite all about? Satellite Internet is another way to connect to the Internet. Most people choose satellite Internet when other high-speed options are unavailable. To take advantage of satellite Internet, you need a satellite dish, which is placed outside your home and connected to your computer with coaxial cable, the same type of cable used for cable TV. Data from your computer is transmitted between your personal satellite dish and the satellite company's receiving satellite dish by a satellite that orbits the Earth.

What are the advantages of satellite Internet connections? Because several major telecommunications companies maintain satellites in orbit above the equator, almost anyone in the United States can receive satellite service. This makes it a particularly popular choice for those who live in rural areas where neither cable nor DSL service is available.

Are there any drawbacks to satellite? Unfortunately, limitations to this service do apply. Because it takes longer for data to be transferred with satellite broadband than with cable or DSL, this type of connection is not best for some Internet uses such as online gaming or online securities trading. In addition, because download transmissions are not "wired," but rather are sent as radio waves, the strength and reliability of the signal are more vulnerable to interference. Last, if you live in North America, your satellite dish must face south for the best line of sight to the satellites circling the Earth's equator. If high buildings, mountains, or other tall objects obstruct your southern exposure, your signal may be blocked. Unfavorable weather conditions also can block or interfere with the satellite transmission signal.

DIAL-UP CONNECTIONS

How does a dial-up connection work?

A dial-up connection is the least costly method of connecting to the Internet, needing only a standard phone line and a modem. A **dial-up modem** is a device that converts (modulates) the digital signals the computer understands to the analog signals that can travel over phone lines. In turn, the computer on the other end also must have a modem to translate (demodulate) the received analog signal back to a digital signal that the receiving computer can understand.

Although external modems do exist, modern desktop computers generally come with internal modems built into the system unit. Notebooks (laptops) today usually have internal modems, but if not, small credit card-sized devices called **PC cards** (sometimes called **PCMCIA cards**) can be inserted into a special slot on the notebook.

What are the advantages of a dial-up Internet connection?

A dial-up connection is the least costly way to connect to the Internet. Although slower than broadband connections, dial-up connections, with today's 56K modems, are often fine for casual Internet users who do not need a very fast connection.

What are the disadvantages of dial-up?

In a word: speed. Dial-up modems have a maximum data transfer rate of 56 kilobits per second. Even at 56 Kbps, moving through the Internet with a dial-up connection can be a slow and frustrating experience. Web pages can take a long time to load, especially if they contain multimedia, which is the norm for most Web pages today. Similarly, if you visit many Web sites at the same time or receive or send large files through e-mail, you'll find that a dial-up connection is very slow. Another disadvantage of dial-up is that when you're on the Internet, you tie up your phone line if you don't have a separate line.

CHOOSING THE RIGHT INTERNET CONNECTION OPTION

How do I choose which Internet connection option is best for me?

Dial-up is no longer the most common means of Internet connection. In 2006, 68 percent of all U.S. households connected to the Internet used some form of broadband connection. If you are thinking about making the switch to broadband, you might not have the luxury of a choice between services. Many areas will have access to only one type of service. If you live in a rural area, satellite may be your only option. But, if you live in an area where you have a choice between cable, DSL, or satellite, then cable or DSL should generally be your first choice for high-speed Internet access because both services are overall better options than satellite.

One factor to consider in choosing the right Internet connection is speed. **Data transfer rate** is the measurement of how fast data travels between computers. It is also informally referred to as connection speed. For example, dial-up modems have a maximum data transfer rate of 56 kilobits per second (Kbps, usually referred to as 56K). A kilobit is 1,000 bits, normally used to represent the amount of data that is transferred in a second between two telecommunication points. Satellite Internet is about 10 times faster than dial-up, but is still significantly slower than DSL and cable. While DSL is catching up, cable wins out over DSL for speed. The availability of fiber-optic Internet through DSL providers increases download rates to as high as 30 Mbps.

Finally, you may also need to consider which other services you want bundled into your payment, such as phone or TV. The table in Figure 28 compares several features of cable and DSL to help you with your decision.

FIGURE 28 Comparing Cable and DSL Internet Connection Options

	DSL	Cable Modem
Maximum Upload Speeds	Average speeds of 1.5 Mbps, with a maximum of 6+ Mbps.	Average speeds of 3 Mbps, with a maximum of 12+ Mbps.
Pros	Lets you surf the Net and talk on the same phone line	Speeds are not dependent on distance from central office.
	Fiber-optic services continue rolling out fastest download speeds.	Sometimes cheaper than DSL, especially when bundled with TV service.
Cons	Speed drops as you get further from phone company central office.	Line shared with others in neighborhood; speeds may vary.
	Not every phone line will work; no easy way to find out if yours will.	May require professional installation if cable not already present.

Note: The data transfer rates listed in this table are approximations. As technologies improve, so too do data transfer rates.

Finding an Internet Service Provider

After you have chosen the method by which you'll connect to the Internet, you need a way to access the Internet. **Internet service providers (ISPs)** are national, regional, or local companies that connect individuals, groups, and other companies to the Internet. EarthLink, for example, is a well-known national ISP.

As mentioned earlier, the Internet is a network of networks, and the central component of the Internet network is the Internet backbone. The Internet backbone is the main pathway of high-speed communications lines through which all Internet traffic flows. Large communications companies, such as AT&T, Qwest, and Sprint, are backbone providers that control access to the main lines of the Internet backbone. These backbone providers supply Internet access to ISPs, which, in turn, supply access to other users.

Where do I find an ISP? If you have a broadband connection, your broadband provider is your ISP. If you're accessing the Internet from a dial-up connection, you need to determine which ISPs are available in your area. Look in the phone book, check ads in the newspaper, or ask friends which ISP they use. In addition, you can go to sites such as **www.thelist.com** or **www.all-free-isp.com** for listings of national and regional ISPs.

The Origin of the Internet

Why was the Internet created? To understand why the Internet was created, you need to understand what was happening in the early 1960s in the United States. In the midst of the Cold War with Russia, military leaders and civilians alike were concerned about a Russian nuclear or conventional attack on the United States. Meanwhile, the U.S. armed forces were becoming increasingly dependent on computers to coordinate and plan their activities. For the U.S. armed forces to operate efficiently, computer systems located in various parts of the country needed to have a reliable means of communication—one that could not be disrupted easily. Thus, the U.S. government funded much of the early research into the Internet.

At the same time, researchers also hoped the Internet would address the problems involved with getting different computers to communicate with each other. Although computers had been networked since the early 1960s, there was no reliable way to connect computers from different manufacturers because these computers used different proprietary methods of communication. What was lacking was a common communications method that all computers could use, regardless of the differences in their individual designs. The Internet was

created to respond to these two concerns: to establish a secure form of military communications and to create a means by which all computers could communicate.

Who invented the Internet? The modern Internet evolved from an early "internetworking" project called the Advanced Research Projects Agency Network (ARPANET). Funded by the U.S. government for the military in the late 1960s, ARPANET began as a four-node network involving UCLA, Stanford Research Institute, the University of California at Santa Barbara, and the University of Utah in Salt Lake City. The first real communication occurred in late 1969 between the computer at Stanford and the computer at UCLA. Although the system crashed after the third letter was transmitted, it was the beginning of a revolution that has grown into millions of computers connected to the Internet today. Although many people participated in the creation of the ARPANET, two men who worked on the project, Vinton Cerf and Robert Kahn, are generally acknowledged as the "fathers" of the Internet. They earned this honor because they were primarily responsible for developing the communications protocols (or standards) in the 1970s that are still in use on the Internet today.

THE WEB VERSUS THE INTERNET

So are the Web and the Internet the same thing? Because the **World Wide Web** (**WWW** or the **Web**) is what we use the most, we sometimes think of the "Net" and the "Web" as being interchangeable. However, the Web is the means we use to access information over the Internet. What distinguishes the Web from the rest of the Internet is its use of

- Common communication protocols (such as TCP/IP) and special languages (such as the HyperText Markup Language, or HTML). These protocols enable different computers to talk to each other and display information in compatible formats.
- Special links (called hyperlinks) that enable users to jump from one place to another on the Web.

Other ways to disseminate information over the Internet include communications systems, such as e-mail, and information exchange technologies, such as File Transfer Protocol (FTP).

Did the same people who invented the Internet invent the Web? The Web was invented many years after the original Internet. In 1989, Tim Berners-Lee, a physicist at the European Organization for Nuclear Research (CERN), wanted a method for linking his research documents so that other researchers could access them. In conjunction with Robert Cailliau, Berners-Lee developed the basic architecture of the Web and created the first Web browser. The original browser could handle only text and was usable only on computers running the NeXT operating system (a commercially unsuccessful OS), which limited its usage. So, Berners-Lee put out a call to the Internet community to assist with development of browsers for other platforms.

In 1993, the National Center for Supercomputing Applications (NCSA) released the Mosaic browser for use on the Macintosh and Windows operating systems. Mosaic could display graphics as well as text. As the popularity of this browser grew, Marc Andreessen, the leader of the Mosaic development team, formed a company called Mosaic Communications Corporation (later renamed Netscape Communications) with Jim Clark. Within six months, many of the developers from the original Mosaic project at the NCSA were working for this new company, which released the Netscape browser (Netscape Navigator 1.0) in December 1994. This new browser featured improvements in usability over Mosaic and quickly became the dominant Web browser. The launch of Netscape heralded the beginning of the Web's monumental growth.

How much has the Internet grown? There was explosive growth of the Internet in the early to mid 1990s as shown in Figure 29. By 1997, nearly the entire world had access to an Internet connection.

Because of that availability, as well as the increasing capabilities of hardware and software, the amount of growth of Web sites has also increased exponentially. In December 1990, the first Web domain was hosted on the Web. Four years later, approximately 10,000 sites were online, and by June 1996, a whopping 252,000 Web site domains were hosted. In November 2006, over 100 million Web sites were online!

The Future of the Internet

What does the future have in store for the Internet? Certainly, the Internet

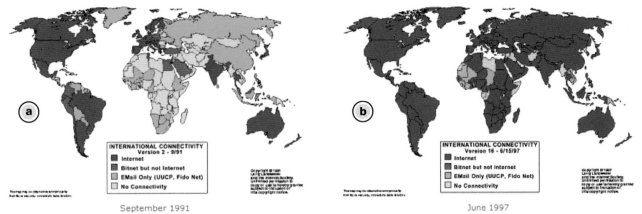

September 1991

June 1997

of the future will have more bandwidth and offer increased services. One thing is certain: because of the prevalence of wireless technologies, the Internet will be more accessible, and we will become more dependent on it. With the increase of commerce and communication activities dominating the Internet, the concern is that there will be no bandwidth left for one of the Internet's original purposes: exchange of scientific and academic research. Two major projects currently under way in the United States to develop advanced technologies for the Internet are the Large Scale Networking (LSN) program and Internet2.

What are the Large Scale Networking and Internet2 programs?

Out of a project titled the Next Generation Internet (which ended in 2002), the U.S. government created the **Large Scale Networking (LSN)** program. LSN's aim is to fund the research and development of cutting-edge networking and wireless technologies and to increase the speed of networks.

The **Internet2** is an ongoing project sponsored by more than 200 universities (supported by government and industry partners) to develop new Internet technologies and disseminate them as rapidly as possible to the rest of the Internet community. The Internet2 backbone supports extremely high-speed communications (up to 9.6 gigabits per second, or Gbps) and provides an excellent testing area for new data transmission technologies. It is hoped that the Internet2 will solve the major problem plaguing the current Internet: lack of bandwidth. Once the Internet2 is fully integrated with the current Internet, greater volumes of information should flow more smoothly.

How else will the Internet become a more integral part of our lives?

As this chapter explained, the Internet is already an integral part of our lives. It is the way we communicate, shop, research, entertain, and express ourselves. Many of the tools on the Web that have been described in this chapter, such as social networking sites, wikis, podcasts, and user content databases such as YouTube and Flikr, are part of a new wave of Web-based services that emphasize online collaboration and sharing among users. These and more services have been collectively referred to as **Web 2.0**. The future Internet will continue to evolve with more Web-based applications driven by user input, interaction, and content.

In the future, you can expect to use the Internet to assist you with many day-to-day tasks that you now do manually. No longer will PCs and mobile devices be our primary access to the Internet. We can already see the convergence of the Internet with the telephone, television, and gaming devices. As other less obvious Internet-enabled devices become popular and more accessible to the common consumer, our lives will become more Internet dependent. For example, Internet-enabled appliances and household systems are now available that allow your home virtually to run itself. Today, there are refrigerators that can monitor their contents and go online to order more diet soda when they detect that the supply is getting low. Meanwhile, Internet heating and cooling systems can monitor weather forecasts and order fuel deliveries when supplies run low or bad weather is expected. These appliances will become more widespread as the price of equipment drops. The uses for the Internet are limited only by our imaginations and the current constraints of technology. At some point, the Internet will no longer be a place we "go" to, but truly an integral part of our lives.

FIGURE 29

(a) In 1991, only a few regions of the world were connected to the Internet. (b) Within six years, nearly the entire world had Internet connectivity.

ACTIVE HELPDESK

Connecting to the Internet

In this Active Helpdesk call, you'll play the role of a Helpdesk staffer, fielding calls about various options for connecting to the Internet and how to choose an Internet service provider.

Summary

1. **How can I communicate through the Internet with IM, Weblogs, podcasts, VoIP, Webcasts, wikis, e-mail, chat, newsgroups, and listservs?**

   Communication was one of the reasons the Internet was developed and is one of the primary uses of the Internet today. E-mail allows users to communicate electronically without the parties involved being available at the same time, while chat rooms are public areas on the Web where different people communicate. Weblogs are journal entries posted to the Web that are generally organized by a topic or area of interest and that are publicly available. Instant messaging enables you to communicate in real time with friends who are also online. Listservs are electronic mailings to groups of people, and newsgroups are online discussion forums in which people post messages and read and reply to messages from other newsgroup members. Both listservs and newsgroups are organized by topic or areas of interest. Listservs are private, whereas newsgroups are public.

2. **What are the various kinds of multimedia files found on the Web, and what software do I need to use them?**

   The Web is appealing because of its enriched multimedia content. Multimedia is anything that involves one or more forms of media in addition to text, including graphics, audio, and video clips. Sometimes you need a special software program called a plug-in (or player) to view and hear multimedia files. Plug-ins are often installed in new computers or are offered free of charge at manufacturers' Web sites.

3. **What is e-commerce, and what e-commerce safeguards protect me when I'm online?**

   E-commerce is the business of conducting business online. E-commerce includes transactions between businesses (B2B), between consumers (C2C), and between businesses and consumers (B2C). Because more business than ever before is conducted online, numerous safeguards have been put in place to ensure transactions are protected.

4. **How do I manage online annoyances like spam, cookies, adware, spyware, malware, phishing, and Internet hoaxes?**

   The Web is filled with annoyances such as spam, pop-ups, cookies, spyware, and scams such as phishing that make surfing the Web frustrating and sometimes dangerous. Software tools help to prevent or reduce spam, adware, and spyware, while exercising caution can prevent serious harm being done due to phishing and other Internet scams and hoaxes.

5. **What is a Web browser?**

   Once you're connected to the Internet, in order to locate, navigate to, and view Web pages, you need special software called a Web browser installed on your system. The most common Web browsers are Microsoft Internet Explorer, Firefox, and Safari.

6. **What is a URL, and what are its parts?**

   You gain access to a Web site by typing in its address, or Uniform Resource Locator (URL). A URL is composed of several parts, including the protocol, the host, the top-level domain, and, occasionally, paths (or subdirectories).

7. **How can I use hyperlinks and other tools to get around the Web?**

   One unique aspect of the Web is that you can jump from place to place by clicking on specially formatted pieces of text called hyperlinks. You can also use tools such as Back and Forward buttons, History lists, breadcrumb lists, and Favorites or Bookmarks to navigate the Web.

8. **How do I search the Internet using search engines and subject directories?**

   A search engine is a set of programs that searches the Web for specific keywords you wish to query and then returns a list of the Web sites on which those keywords are found. A subject directory is a structured outline of Web sites organized by topic and subtopic.

9. What are Boolean operators, and how do they help me search the Web more effectively?

Sometimes, search engines return lists with thousands or millions of hits. Boolean operators are words (AND, NOT, and OR) you can use to refine your searches, making them more effective.

10. How do I evaluate a Web site?

Not all Web sites are equal, and some are better sources for research than others. To evaluate whether it is appropriate to use a Web site as a resource, determine whether the author of the site is reputable and whether the site is intended for your particular needs. In addition, make sure that the site content is not biased, the information in the site is current, and all the links on the site are available and appropriate.

11. How does data travel on the Internet?

A computer connected to the Internet acts either as a client, a computer that asks for information, or a server, a computer that receives the request and returns the information to the client. Data travels between clients and servers along a system of communication lines, or pathways. The largest and fastest of these pathways is the Internet backbone. To ensure that data is sent to the correct computer along the pathways, IP addresses (unique ID numbers) are assigned to all computers connected to the Internet.

12. What are my options for connecting to the Internet?

Home users have many options for connecting to the Internet. A dial-up connection, in which you connect to the Internet using a standard phone line, was at one time the standard way to connect to the Internet. Now, other connection options, called broadband connections, are faster and will soon make dial-up a legacy connection technology. Broadband connections include cable, DSL, and satellite. Fiber-optic Internet is being deployed in select areas around the country and will become a standard of Internet delivery in the near future.

13. How do I choose an Internet service provider?

Internet service providers (ISPs) are national, regional, or local companies that connect individuals, groups, and other companies to the Internet. Factors to consider in choosing an ISP include cost, quality of service, and availability.

14. What is the origin of the Internet?

The Internet is the largest computer network in the world, connecting millions of computers. Government and military officials developed the Internet as a reliable means of communications in the event of war. Eventually, scientists and educators used the Internet to exchange research. Today, we use the Internet and the Web (which is a part of the Internet) to shop, research, communicate, and entertain ourselves.

15. What will the Internet of the future look like?

The Internet of the future will have higher bandwidth and will be able to provide additional services as a result of projects such as the Large Scale Networking (LSN) program and Internet2. Design enhancements to the Internet will engage more of our senses, including smell and taste. The Internet will become more ingrained into our daily lives as Internet-enabled appliances and household systems will provide more remote-control features for our homes.

Key Terms

adware
aggregator
Bookmark
Boolean operator
breadcrumb list
broadband connection
buddy list
business-to-business (B2B)
business-to-consumer (B2C)
cable Internet connection
cable modem
chat room
client
client/server network
consumer-to-consumer (C2C)
cookie
data transfer rate
dial-up connection
dial-up modem
Digital Subscriber Line (DSL)
domain name
DSL modem
e-commerce (electronic commerce)
e-mail (electronic mail)
e-mail client
Favorites
fiber-optic Internet
File Transfer Protocol (FTP)
History list
hit
home page
host
hyperlink
HyperText Transfer Protocol (HTTP)
instant messaging (IM)
Internet
Internet2
Internet backbone
Internet Explorer (IE)
Internet hoax
Internet Protocol (IP) address
Internet service provider (ISP)

keyword
Large Scale Networking (LSN)
listserv
live bookmark
malware
meta search engine
multimedia
multiplayer online game
netiquette
network interface card (NIC)
newsgroup
path (subdirectory)
PC card (PCMCIA card)
phishing
plug-in (or player)
podcast
pop-up window
portal
protocol
satellite Internet
search engine
server
social networking
spam
spam filter
spider
spyware
streaming audio
streaming video
subject directory
top-level domain (TLD)
Uniform Resource Locator (URL)
video logs (vlogs or video blog)
VoIP (Voice over Internet Protocol)
webcast
Web 2.0
Weblog (blog)
Web browser (browser)
Web site
wiki
wildcard
World Wide Web (WWW or the Web)

Using the Internet: Making the Most of the Web's Resources

Buzz Words

Word Bank

- AOL
- bookmark
- breadcrumb list
- browser
- buddy list
- cable modem

- cookie(s)
- dial-up
- DSL
- hyperlink
- instant messaging
- keyword

- Internet service provider
- satellite
- search engine
- spam
- subject directory
- URLs

Instructions: Fill in the blanks using the words from the Word Bank above.

The day finally arrived when Juan no longer was a victim of slow Internet access through a traditional (1) _____ connection. He could finally hook up to the Internet through his new high-speed (2) _____. He had been investigating broadband access for a while and thought that connecting through his existing phone lines with (3) _____ would be convenient. Unfortunately, it was not available in his area. Where Juan lives, a clear southern exposure does not exist, so he did not even entertain the idea of a (4) _____ connection. Juan was looking forward to the speedy access provided by the cable company, his new (5) _____, but he was faced with the need to change his e-mail from (6) _____, his old ISP, because he didn't want to pay for duplicate services. Although he needed to change his e-mail address, he was glad he didn't have to give up instant messaging, because his (7) _____ of online contacts had grown to be quite extensive. With the new speed of his broadband connection, Juan especially liked being able to quickly scan the Internet with his preferred (8) _____ Firefox.

Juan clicked on his list of favorite Web sites and found the movie review site he had saved as a (9) _____ the day before. He prefers to use this browser feature rather than entering in the (10) _____ of the sites he visits often. Juan navigated through the site, clicking on the (11) _____ that took him immediately to the page he was most interested in. Finding the movie he wanted to see, Juan ordered tickets online. The account information he input during an earlier visit to the site automatically appeared. In this case, Juan is glad that Web sites use (12) _____ to capture such information.

Then, using the (13) _____ at the top of the Web site, he traced his steps back to his starting point. Juan next typed in the address for Google, his preferred (14) _____, and typed the (15) _____ to begin his search for a good restaurant in the area.

Becoming Computer Literate

Using keywords from the chapter, write a letter to your local cable company imploring it to bring cable modem service to your neighborhood. In the letter, include your dissatisfaction with dial-up as well as your opinion on why cable is better than DSL (which is currently being offered in your neighborhood) and satellite. Also include the activities on the Internet you think people in the community could benefit from by using high-speed cable access.

Self-Test

Instructions: Answer the multiple-choice and true/false questions below for more practice with key terms and concepts from this chapter.

MULTIPLE CHOICE

1. Which one of the following statements is NOT true about instant messaging?
   a. It is a popular form of communication.
   b. You communicate in real time.
   c. Only two people can IM at the same time.
   d. Like e-mail, IM is not good for private conversations.

2. When shopping online, which of the following does NOT indicate that you have a secure connection displays?
   a. A closed padlock icon in the status bar.
   b. The URL begins with *https*.
   c. The word "secure" in the title bar.
   d. The VeriSign seal on the Web page.

3. With a podcast, you can
   a. subscribe to video and audio content.
   b. have the most recent content "delivered" automatically.
   c. play the video and audio content on an MP3 player.
   d. All of the above.

4. An online journal or chronological postings of thoughts and opinions is a(n)
   a. podcast.   c. blog.
   b. wiki.   d. IM chat.

5. Which of the following is annoying, but really doesn't render any harm to your computer?
   a. Adware   c. Sneakware
   b. Spyware   d. Malware

6. One scam that lures Internet users into revealing personal information is
   a. malware.   c. spam.
   b. phishing.   d. Internet hoax.

7. When searching the Internet, which of the following is true?
   a. It doesn't matter which search engine you use; they all provide the same results.
   b. A subject directory is best to use when you can provide keywords.
   c. Boolean operators and advanced search pages will help to narrow your results.
   d. Search engines are best to use when you need to narrow the search by specific topics.

8. In a Web address **http://www.irs.gov**, the .gov would be considered the
   a. URL.
   b. top-level domain.
   c. protocol.
   d. Web address.

9. Which of the following provides the fastest broadband Internet connection by transmitting data at the speed of light?
   a. Cable   c. Fiber optics
   b. DSL   d. Satellite

10. The primary disadvantage to DSL Internet access is the quality and effectiveness of the service
    a. are affected by the number of users on the same DSL line at any time.
    b. depend on your proximity to a phone company central office.
    c. can be affected by adverse weather conditions.
    d. depend on the Internet service provider you select.

TRUE/FALSE

_____ 1. The Web and the Internet are interchangeable terms.

_____ 2. DSL service is not affected by the number of users on the line at the same time.

_____ 3. Google, because it generates the most search results of any of the search engines, is called a meta search engine.

_____ 4. You can get computer viruses from cookies, so you should not allow them and/or should delete them often.

_____ 5. Most of the world's population has access to an Internet connection.

Making the Transition to...
Next Semester

1. Online Support Facilities

Your school most likely has many online support facilities. Do you know what they are? Go to your school's Web site and search for online support.

a. Is online tutoring available?
b. Can you reserve a book from the library online?
c. Can you register for classes online?
d. Can you take classes online?
e. Can you buy books online?

2. Plagiarism Policies

Does your school have a plagiarism policy?

a. Search your school's Web site to find the school's plagiarism policy. What does it say?
b. How well do you paraphrase? Find some Web sites that help test or evaluate your paraphrasing skills.

3. Advanced Web Searches

Using search engines effectively is an important tool. Some search engines help you with Boolean-type searches using advanced search forms. Choose your favorite search engine and select the Advanced Search option. (If your favorite search engine does not have an advanced search feature, try Yahoo! or Google.)

a. Conduct a search for inexpensive vacation spots for spring break using Boolean search terms. Record your results along with your search queries.
b. Conduct the same search but use the advanced search form with your favorite search engine. Were the results the same? If there were any differences, what were they? Which was the best search method to use in this case, and why?

4. Free Speech Online

Jeanne was suspended from school for several days because her posts on MySpace about her teacher and a few of her classmates were "vulgar" and "derogatory." Tom was expelled from his school because the picture he posted of himself was in violation of his school's code of conduct. Similarly, Bill, a local employer, changed his mind about a job offer to a recent graduate after seeing the questionable content on the candidate's Facebook.com page.

a. Should a person be penalized for his or her content on any Web site?
b. Is the issue denial of free speech or prudent actions to improper behavior?

5. Using Web 2.0 in Education

Social networking sites, blogs, wikis, and file-sharing sites commonly are referred to as Web 2.0, the "second generation" of the Internet. These sites offer opportunities for collaboration, creativity, and enterprise. Describe how Web 2.0 sites such as Wikipedia, YouTube, and Digg might change how you learn and manage information.

Making the Transition to... the Workplace

1. Online Résumé Resources

Using a search engine, locate several Web resources that offer assistance in writing a résumé. For example, the University of Minnesota (**http://www1.umn.edu/ohr/careerdev/resources/resume**) has a résumé tutor that guides you as you write your résumé.

a. What other Web sites can you find that help you write a résumé?
b. Do they all offer the same services and have the same features?

2. Online Cover Letter Resources

Your résumé will need to be accompanied by a cover letter. Research Web sites that offer advice for and samples of cover letters.

a. Which Web sites do you feel offer the best advice on how to write a cover letter? Which style cover letter works best for you?
b. What do the Web sites say you should include in your cover letter, and why?

3. Evaluating Web Content

You have noticed that your coworkers are using the Internet to conduct research. However, they are not careful to check the validity of the Web sites they find before using the information.

a. Research the Internet for Web site evaluation guidelines. Print out your sources and findings.
b. Using the material from Step (a), create a scorecard or set of guidelines that will help others determine whether a Web site is reliable.

4. Internet Connection Option

Now that you've graduated, you are planning to move into your first apartment and leave behind the comforts of broadband access of the residence halls. Evaluate the Internet options available in your area.

a. Create a table that includes information on cable Internet, DSL, and satellite broadband service providers, as well as dial-up ISPs. The table should include the name of the provider, the cost of the service, the upload and download transfer rates, and the installation costs (service and parts). Also include whether a Web-based e-mail account will be available. Include the URL of each ISP or broadband service provider's Web site.
b. Based on the table you create, write a brief paragraph describing which service you would choose and why.

5. Internet Connection Speed

You would like to know how fast your Internet connection speed is. Your coworker in the Information Technology (IT) department recommended the following sites for you to check out: **www.testmyspeed.com**, **www.bandwidthplace.com**, and **www.pcpitstop.com**.

a. Choose one of the recommended sites and test your connection speed. How is the test conducted? What is used to measure the connection speed?
b. List reasons you would be interested in measuring your Internet connection speed.

6. E-Mail Privacy

Take a moment to think about this statement: An e-mail is no more private than a postcard.

a. Search the Internet for resources that can help you support and oppose the preceding statement. Print out sources for both sides of the argument.
b. Write a paragraph that summarizes your position.

Using the Internet: Making the Most of the Web's Resources

Critical Thinking Questions

Instructions: Albert Einstein used "Gedanken experiments," or critical thinking questions, to develop his theory of relativity. Some ideas are best understood by experimenting with them in our own minds. The following critical thinking questions are designed to demand your full attention but require only a comfortable chair—no technology.

1. **Internet and Society**

   The Internet was initially created in part to enable scientists and educators to share information quickly and efficiently. The advantages the Internet brings to our lives are evident, but does Internet access also cause problems?

   a. What advantages and disadvantages does the Internet bring to your life?
   b. What positive and negative effects has the Internet had on our society as a whole?
   c. Some people argue that conducting searches on the Internet provides answers but does not inspire thoughtful research. What do you think?
   d. Should use of the Internet be banned, or at least limited, for research projects in schools? Why or why not?

2. **File-Swapping Ethics**

   The unprecedented rise of Napster, the original file-swapping site, came to a quick halt because of accusations of copyright infringements. However, downloading free music from the Internet still occurs.

   a. What's your opinion on having the ability to download free music files of your choice? Do you think the musicians who oppose online music sharing make valid points?
   b. Discuss the differences you see between sharing music files online and sharing CDs with your friends.
   c. The current price to buy a song online is about $1. Is this a fair price? If not, what price would you consider to be fair?

3. **The Power of Google**

   Google is the largest and most popular search engine on the Internet today. Because of its size and popularity, some people claim that Google has enormous power to influence a Web user's search experience solely by its Web site ranking processes. What do you think about this potential power? How could it be used in negative or harmful ways?

   a. Some Web sites pay search engines to list them near the top of the results pages. These sponsors therefore get priority placement. What do you think of this policy?
   b. What effect (if any) do you think that Google has on Web site development? For example, do you think Web site developers intentionally include frequently searched words in their pages so that they will appear in more hits lists?
   c. When you "google" someone, you type their name in the Google search box to see what comes up. What privacy concerns do you think such "googling" could present? Have you ever "googled" yourself or your friends?

4. **Charging for E-Mail?**

   Should there be a charge placed on sending e-mail or on having IM conversations? What would be an appropriate charge? If a charge was placed on e-mail and IM conversations, what would happen to their use?

5. **Internet and Politics**

   What role has and will the Internet play in political campaigns? Do you see the day when voting will happen through the Internet? Why or why not?

Team Time Comparing Internet Search Methods

Problem:

With millions of sites on the Internet, finding useful information can be a daunting—at times, impossible—task. However, there are methods to make searching easier, some of which have been discussed in this chapter. In this Team Time, each team will search for specific items or pieces of information on the Internet and compare search methodologies.

Task:

Split your group into three or more teams depending on class size. Each group will search for the same items.

Search Items:

1. What was America's first penny candy to be individually wrapped?

2. At which fraternity at which college was the movie Animal House based?

3. What were the previous names for the American League baseball team the Los Angeles Angels of Anahein?

4. What is the cheapest price to purchase a copy of the latest version of Microsoft Office Professional?

5. What are Kingda Ka and Son of Beast, and what do they have in common?

Process:

1. Teams are positioned at computers connected to the Internet.

2. Each team is given the list of search items. Each team should use a different search strategy from the following list: (1) use only a subject directory, (2) use only a search engine, or (3) use only the Advanced Search feature of a search engine. If more teams are allowed, you could also add a team that only uses a meta search engine. Other than these restrictions, teams can use whichever search strategies they feel will best reach the desired goal with the most accuracy in the least amount of time.

3. Print the results from each search page. Teams compare printouts and notes to determine which search methods worked best for each item.

Conclusion:

Were subject directories better than search engines for certain searches? Which methods were used to narrow down choices? How were final answers determined?

Multimedia

In addition to the review materials presented here, you'll find additional materials featured with the book's multimedia, including the Technology in Action Student Resource CD and the Companion Web site (**www.prenhall.com/techinaction**), which will help reinforce your understanding of the chapter content. These materials include the following:

ACTIVE HELPDESK

In Active Helpdesk calls, you'll assume the role of Helpdesk operator, taking calls about the concepts you've learned in this chapter. You'll apply what you've learned and receive feedback from a supervisor to review and reinforce those concepts. The Active Helpdesk calls for this chapter are as follows and can be found on your Student Resource CD:

- Staying Secure on the Internet
- Getting Around the Web
- Using Subject Directories and Search Engines
- Connecting to the Internet

SOUND BYTES

Sound Bytes are dynamic multimedia tutorials that help demystify even the most complex topics. You'll view video clips and animations that illustrate computer concepts, and then apply what you've learned by reviewing with the Sound Byte Labs, which include quizzes and activities specifically tailored to each Sound Byte. The Sound Bytes for this chapter are as follows and can be found on your Student Resource CD:

- Blogging
- Creating a Web-Based E-mail Account
- The Best Utilities for Your Computer
- Welcome to the Web
- Finding Information on the Web
- Connecting to the Internet

COMPANION WEB SITE

The Technology in Action Companion Web Site includes a variety of additional materials to help you review and learn more about the topics in this chapter. The resources available at **www.prenhall.com/techinaction** include:

- **Online Study Guide.** Each chapter features an online true/false and multiple-choice quiz. You can take these quizzes, automatically check the results, and e-mail the results to your instructor.

- **Web Research Projects.** Each chapter features a number of Web research projects that ask you to search the Web for information on computer-related careers, milestones in computer history, important people and companies, emerging technologies, and the applications and implications of different technologies.

TECHNOLOGY IN FOCUS

Computer Abuse

Security

iStock Photo International

Information Technology

ethics

In this Technology in Focus, we explore what ethics are, how your personal ethics develop, and how your personal ethics fit into the world around you. We'll also examine how technology and ethics affect each other and how technology can be used to support ethical conduct. Finally, we'll examine several key issues in technology ethics today, including the areas of social justice, intellectual property rights, privacy, Internet commerce, free speech and computer abuse.

Gambling

Censorship

People speak of ethics, and the lack of ethics, casually all the time, but the ethical choices individuals make is an extremely serious matter and can have a far-reaching impact. It is important to have a very clear idea of what ethics are, what your personal ethics are, and how personal ethics fit into the world at large.

ETHICS IN COMPUTING

You just bought a new notebook computer. You know you can go to BitTorrent or Limewire to download the latest Spiderman movie and its soundtrack. You also probably know this is unethical. Although pirating music and videos is a valid example of unethical behavior, it has been overused as an illustration of the ethical challenges of technology. There is a vast range of ethical issues surrounding technology (as shown in **Figure 1**), several of which we will discuss in this section.

WHAT IS ETHICS?

Ethics is the study of the general nature of morals and of the specific moral choices made by individuals. Morals involve conforming to established or accepted ideas of right and wrong (as generally dictated by society) and are usually black and white. Ethics usually involves subtle distinctions such as fairness and equity; ethical values are the guidelines you use to make decisions each day. For example, the person in front of you at Starbucks drops a dollar on the floor and doesn't notice it. Do you tell him about it, or do you pick up the dollar and use it to pay for your coffee?

Doesn't everyone have the same basic ethics? There are many systems of ethical conduct. On one extreme is moral relativism, a theory that holds that there is no universal moral truth and that instead there are only beliefs, perspectives, and values. Everyone has his or her own ideas of right and wrong, and so who are we to judge anyone

else? Another ethical philosophy is situational ethics, which states that decision making should be based on the circumstances of a particular situation and not on fixed laws.

Many other ethical systems have been proposed over time, some of which are defined by religious traditions. For example, the expression "Judeo-Christian ethics" refers to the common set of basic values shared across both Jewish and Christian religious traditions. These include behaviors such as respecting property and relationships, honoring one's parents, and being kind to others.

Don't some people behave with no ethics at all? Although many valid systems of ethical conduct exist, it is still true that sometimes people act in a manner that violates the beliefs they hold or the beliefs of the ethical system they say they follow. Unethical behavior can be defined as not conforming to a set of approved standards of social or professional behavior. For instance, using your phone to text message your friend during an exam is prohibited by most college rules of student conduct. This behavior is different from amoral behavior, when a person has no sense of right and wrong and no interest in the moral consequences of their actions.

PERSONAL ETHICS

What are personal ethics? Every day you say certain things and take specific actions, and at each point you are making decisions based on some criteria. It may be that you are trying to care for the people around you or you are trying to eliminate a source of pain or anger in your life. Or your words and actions may be driven by a combination of criteria. As you choose your words and actions, you are following a set of personal ethics, a checklist of personal decisions you have compiled to organize your life. Some people have a clear, well-defined set of principles they follow. Others' ethics are inconsistent or are applied differently in similar situations.

It can be challenging to adhere to your own ethical system if the consequences of your decisions today might lead to an unhappy result for you in the short term!

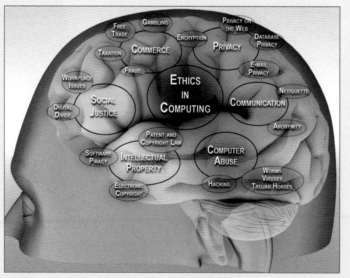

FIGURE 1

Ethics in computing covers a wide range of areas, not just privacy and security.

For instance, in order to get the job of your dreams, should you exaggerate a bit on your résumé and say you've already finished your college degree, even though you are still one credit short? Is this lying? Is such behavior justified in this setting? After all, you do intend to finish that last credit, and you would work really hard for this company if you were hired. If you tell the truth and state that you haven't finished college yet, you might be passed over for the position. Making this choice is an ethical decision (see **Figure 2**).

How do a person's ethics develop? Many elements contribute to your ethical development (see **Figure 3**). Naturally, your family has a major impact in establishing the values you cherish in your own life, and these might include a cultural bias toward certain moral positions. Your religious affiliation is another major influence in your ethical life, as most religions have established specific codes of ethical conduct. How these sets of ethics interact with the values of the larger culture is often challenging. Issues such as abortion, the death penalty, or war all force confrontations between personal ethical systems and the larger society's established legal ethical system.

©Anton Seleznev/Courtesy of www.istockphoto.com

FIGURE 2

It would be nice if there were signposts to ethical conduct, but the issues are complex.

As you mature, your life experiences also affect your personal ethics. Does the behavior you see around you make sense within the ethical principles your family, your church, or your first-grade teacher taught you? Has your experience led you to abandon some ethical rules while adopting others? Have you modified how and when you apply these laws of conduct, depending on what is at stake?

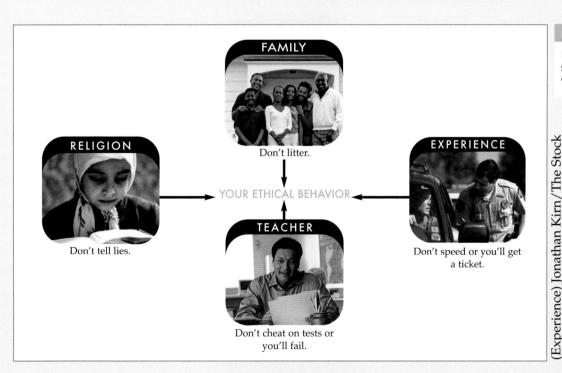

FAMILY
Don't litter.

RELIGION
Don't tell lies.

YOUR ETHICAL BEHAVIOR

EXPERIENCE
Don't speed or you'll get a ticket.

TEACHER
Don't cheat on tests or you'll fail.

FIGURE 3

Many different forces shape your ethical world view.

TECHNOLOGY IN FOCUS: INFORMATION TECHNOLOGY ETHICS

FIGURE 4

The field of positive psychology shows that living and working ethically impacts your happiness.

Cheating
Stealing
Selfish
Lying

Generosity
Honesty
Trust

What if I'm not sure what my personal ethics are? When you have a very clear and firm idea of what values are most important to you, it may be easier to handle situations in your professional and your personal life that demand ethical action. Follow these steps to help define your personal ethics:

1. **Describe yourself**. Write down a description of who you are based on how others view you. Would a friend describe you as honest or helpful or kind?
2. **List your beliefs**. Make a list of all the beliefs that influence your decision making. For example, would you be okay with working as a research assistant in a lab that infected dogs with diseases to use them for medical research? How important is it to you that you never speak a lie? Consider whether your answers to each of these questions are "flexible." Are there situations where your answers might change (say, if a friend was ill or in danger)?
3. **Identify external influences**. Consider the places you work and live and how you relate to the people you see during the day. Are there things that you would like to change about these relationships that would involve listing them in a code of ethics?
4. **Consider "why."** After writing down your beliefs, think about why you believe them. Have you accepted them without investigation, or do they stand up to the test of real-world experiences in your life?

Which of these values are worthy of short-term sacrifice in order to uphold your beliefs?
5. **Prepare a statement of values**. It can be useful to distill what you have written into a short list. By having a well-defined statement of the values you hold most important in your own life that you can refer to in times of challenge, it will be easier for you to make ethical decisions.

Are there tangible benefits to ethical living? Society has established its own set of rules of conduct as laws. Ignoring or being inconsistent in following these principles can surely have an immediate impact! Whether it is complying with a law that affects the way your business is run or with a law that impacts your personal life (don't exceed the speed limit or you'll receive a fine), decision-making principles that work with society's legal boundaries can make your life much simpler!

More and more research is showing the health benefits of ethical living. When your day-to-day decisions are in conflict with the values you consider most important as a human being, you often develop stress and anger. Constant conflict between what you value and what actions you are forced to take can lead to a variety of mental and physical damages.

Perhaps even happiness itself is a result of living ethically (see **Figure 4**). " Positive psychology" is a new focus in the field of psychology. This field, pioneered by Dr. Martin

FIGURE 5

Courtesy Images.com

Seligman of the University of Pennsylvania, works to discover the causes of happiness instead of addressing the treatment of mental dysfunctions. Dr. Seligman's research has shown that, by identifying your personal strengths and values and by aligning your life so that you can apply them every day, you can experience an increase in happiness (and a decrease in depression) equivalent to the effects of antidepressant medication and therapy. So, finding a way to identify and then apply your ethics and values to your daily life has an impact on your health and happiness.

PERSONAL ETHICS IN THE WORLD VIEW

How do my personal ethics fit into the world at large? All of your actions, words, and even thoughts are controlled by your personal ideas of right and wrong. But do your ethics shift when you go to work? Your responsibility at work is to follow the ethics that the owner has established for the business. Although each person at your workplace may be trying to follow the corporate ethical guidelines, each person will follow them differently based on their personal ethics. Person A may feel it is acceptable to tell white lies to get his project more fund-

ing, while Person B might believe that telling the truth at all times is the only and best way she can foster teamwork and cooperation to get a project completed. But overall, when dealing in a business environment, your ethics are guided by the ethical principles that are defined by the business owner or management.

How do employers affect personal ethics? Should your boss have control (or even input) about your conduct outside of the office? Do behavior, integrity, and honesty off the job relate to job performance? They might. But even if they don't, your actions could reflect poorly on your employer from your employer's perspective. Consider Ellen Simonetti, who was fired by Delta Airlines for blogging. Even though Ms. Simonetti never mentioned Delta Airlines by name on her blog (Queen of the Sky: Diary of a Dysfunctional Flight Attendant), Delta Airlines objected to photos that she posted of herself and fellow flight attendants in their Delta uniforms. Delta Airlines felt that the photos were inappropriate and portrayed negative images of Delta Airlines employees. So although your ethics might dictate one mode of behavior, you need to consider how your actions might be viewed by your employer (see **Figure 5**).

TECHNOLOGY AND ETHICS: HOW ONE AFFECTS THE OTHER

Technology is all around us and affects almost every aspect of our daily lives. Because technology moves faster than rules can be formulated to govern it, how technology is used is left up to the individual with the guidance of their personal ethics. In both good and bad ways, technology affects our community life, family life, work environment, education, and medical research, to name only a few areas of our lives.

Technology constantly challenges our ethics as individuals and as a society. In the rest of this Technology in Focus feature, we will explore the different relationships between technology and ethics. Specifically, we present different viewpoints of situations with regard to social justice, intellectual property (fair use), privacy, e-commerce (online gambling), electronic communication issues (free speech), and computer abuse (protection versus access) in which ethics and technology impact each other.

Ethical considerations are never black and white. They are complex, and reasonable people can have different valid views. We present alternative viewpoints of situations in which ethics and technology impact each other for you to consider and discuss. The table shown in Figure 6 summarizes these issues.

USING COMPUTERS TO SUPPORT ETHICAL CONDUCT

Although there are many opportunities to use computers and the Internet unethically, many more ways are available to use technology to support ethical conduct.

Many charitable organizations use the Internet for fund raising. When hurricane Katrina struck, the Red Cross (see **Figure 7**) and other charities supporting relief efforts used their Web pages to enable donors to quickly, easily, and securely make contributions to aid hurricane victims. Using technology to garner contributions enabled charities to quickly raise in excess of $2.6 billion for relief efforts.

When you spot unethical behavior at your company, you need a fast, secure way to report it to the appropriate members of management. The Sarbanes-Oxley Act of 2002 requires companies to provide mechanisms for employees and third parties to report complaints, including ethics violations. And these mechanisms are required to provide the employees with anonymity.

FIGURE 6		
Ethics in Computing		
Topic	**Ethical Discussion**	**Debate Issue**
Social justice	Can technology be used to benefit everyone?	Does technology provide economic opportunity for all?
Intellectual property	What is fair about fair use?	What kind of fair use standards are beneficial?
Privacy	Is personal privacy a casualty of the modern age?	Should personal privacy be protected?
E-commerce	Is online gambling a problem?	Should online gambling be banned or regulated?
Electronic communication	When does big business limit free speech?	Did Google make the right choice in China?
Computer abuse	Does restricting online information protect children?	Is filtering or monitoring software helpful?

FIGURE 7

Most major charities facilitate donations through the Internet.

Many businesses are using their Web sites to allow whistleblowers to report wrongdoing anonymously, replacing their previous e-mail and telephone hotline systems that did not shield the employee from being identified. With an electronic system, it is easier for a company to sort and classify complaints and designate them for appropriate action.

Electronic systems such as Intranets and e-mail are also excellent mechanisms for informing employees about ethics policies. Storing ethics guidelines electronically on a company Intranet ensures that employees have access to information whenever they need it. And by using e-mail, new policies or changes to existing policies can be quickly and efficiently communicated to employees.

Throughout your life, you will encounter many ethical challenges relating to information technology. Your personal ethics—combined with the ethical guidelines your company provides and the general ethical environment of society—will guide your decisions.

For further information on ethics, check out the following Web sites:

www.ethics.csc.ncsu.edu

www.ethicscenter.net

www.business-ethics.com

or www.business-ethics.org

Social Justice

Can Technology Be Used to Benefit Everyone?

SUMMARY OF THE ISSUE

Does our society have a responsibility to use technology to help achieve social justice? Freeman Dyson, an American physicist and mathematician, has sparked discussion about this issue by saying that science is concentrating too much on "making toys for the rich" instead of addressing the necessities of the poor. One has the promise of great financial reward in creating an even smaller cellular phone, but one has little incentive to find solar energy solutions to help struggling rural communities. Dyson proposes that three technologies could be applied to turn poor rural areas into sources of wealth: solar energy, genetic engineering, and Internet access (see **Figure 8**).

Solar energy is available virtually anywhere in the world and could become cheap enough to compete with oil. The spiraling price of oil, due primarily to increased worldwide demand, has created a barrier against elevating poor rural communities above the poverty level.

Through genetic engineering it might be possible to design new plants (or modify existing plants) to achieve novel things such as converting sunlight into fuel efficiently. If plants could be engineered to make them more efficient sources of energy or provide other qualities in demand (such as being better sources of protein and fiber when consumed), rural residents would be able to produce items with high market demand and would have greater opportunities to increase their standard of living.

The Internet can help businesses and farms in remote areas become part of the modern economy. Currently, it is difficult for rural farmers in Third World countries to determine the best place to take their crops to market. By consulting the Internet, however, they could obtain price quotes for markets within their reach and determine which ones would provide the best prices for their crops.

QUESTIONS TO THINK ABOUT AND RESEARCH

1. Are the types of technology Dyson suggests plausible or out of the reach of current scientific methods?

2. Would Dyson's suggested use of technology help people or spark social revolution?

3. What impact would a widespread distribution of solar-powered cell phones have on a country that lacks the infrastructure for telephone and electrical wires? Has any country ever experienced such a leap in technology in a short period of time?

4. Dyson was a winner of the Templeton Prize in 2000. What kind of award is the Templeton, and what was the basis for Dyson's selection?

Technology Provides Economic Opportunity for All

The advocates of Dyson's position maintain that a lack of technology or resources is not what keeps the majority of the world's population in poverty. Instead, they would argue that it is a lack of commitment and focus on the problem of social justice that allows poverty to continue.

1. If we all share a conviction that gross inequities in wealth are unacceptable, we have the technology and resources to eliminate poverty.

2. Technology can improve the quality of life of poor countries (and poor people in rich countries) if scientists and business leaders join together.

3. Technology can be an ethical force to humanize us, giving us the ability to deeply impact the lives of all. Francis Bacon, the 17th century English philosopher, once wrote that science can "endow the human family with new mercies."

Technology Doesn't Provide Economic Opportunity for All

Dyson's critics maintain that his suggestions on using technology for social change are impractical and cannot be achieved with the current resources. They even feel his plan might be dangerous inasmuch as it may have unforeseen scientific and political results.

1. No one can solve the problems of poverty. The proof is that it has never been done.

2. The problem of poverty is not an issue for technologists. It should be addressed by religious leaders, education experts, and politicians.

3. Genetic engineering may hold the promise of great benefits, but it should not be explored because of the potential risks.

4. Any move away from an oil-centered energy plan threatens the stability of the world economies.

(Cell phone) Courtesy of www.istockphoto.com

(Solar panel) istockphoto.com

FIGURE 8

Should technology focus on "toys for the rich" or the needs of the poor?

Intellectual Property

What is Fair about Fair Use?

SUMMARY OF THE ISSUE

Intellectual property (such as music, writing, and art) is protected through copyright law. This means that creative works such as songs, video productions, television programs, and written manuscripts cannot be reproduced without the permission of the creator and usually not without payment to the copyright owner (see **Figure 9**).

Historically, the policy of "fair use" has allowed a range of exceptions to this copyright provision. Fair use is based on the belief that the public is entitled to freely use portions of copyrighted materials for certain purposes. If you wish to criticize a novelist, for example, under fair use, you have the freedom to quote a portion of the novelist's work without asking permission. Without this provision, copyright owners could prevent any negative comments about their work. Fair use decisions are guided by four criteria:

- What is the purpose of the "fair use" of the work (for example, is it a for-profit use or an educational use)?
- What is the nature of the proposed work (for example, will it be a published document or an unpublished product)?
- How much of the copyrighted material is being used?
- What is the effect of the "fair use" of the material (for example, would it decrease the number of copies of the original that would be sold)?

In this age of easy digital media creation and distribution, however, the interpretation of fair use is being questioned. For example, Kevin Ryan is facing off against Dr. Seuss Enterprises. He created a set of songs that imitated the style of Bob Dylan singing such Seuss classics as *Green Eggs and Ham* and *The Cat in the Hat*. He posted the MP3 files to a Web site, and soon bloggers found the songs and publicized them widely. A cease-and-desist letter from Dr. Seuss Enterprises for alleged copyright violations was issued quickly, and Ryan now has to decide what legal course he'll follow. So in today's fast-paced digital world, the question of the proper role of the fair use exclusion in copyright law may have to be reconsidered.

QUESTIONS TO THINK ABOUT AND RESEARCH

1. How should the four factors of fair use be interpreted in the age of electronic media distribution?

2. Can an online music reviewer post a song's audio in order to illustrate his criticism of the artist's album? Does that infringe on the artist's right to earn income from her work?

3. Should a documentary film maker be allowed to pull pieces of television interviews and organize them in a way that criticizes the person featured?

4. Should a parody of the original be allowed to quote or play sections of the original work? By its nature, a parody can be negative or mocking in tone. Does this invite too much criticism when made publicly available on the Internet?

POINT

Liberal Fair Use Standards Are Beneficial

Artists and critics will be silenced if they are forced to fear legal action every time they use a portion of copyrighted material. The aggressive—and expensive—style of enforcement that copyright holders now use limits the free expression of ideas that is a cornerstone of most democratic societies.

1. Allowing an open interpretation of fair use encourages a wide dissemination of information.

2. Creative work and open criticism together allow the flourishing of the most democratic, free society. If copyright owners can shut down the use of any part of their works, they have too much control of the creative process of others.

3. Although the existing laws on fair use worked well in the past, they cannot cope with the widespread dissemination of information that is possible with the modern Internet.

COUNTERPOINT

Strict Fair Use Standards Are Beneficial

Guidelines for what defines fair use already exist. Because these guidelines have worked well to protect the interests of both the creators and users/critics, there is no need to modify them.

1. The existing laws on fair use have worked well for print media and do not need to be modified because of modern electronic distribution techniques.

2. The copyright holders are within their rights to be as aggressive as they wish in enforcing control of their own work. They should be allowed to set whatever licensing fee they wish. The artists or critics can still use the material but must be able to pay the licensing fee set.

GRANTLAND®

I GOT IT OFF THE INTERNET, WHY?

DID YOU GET PERMISSION FROM THE AUTHOR?

NO,

WHY SHOULD I? ALL I DID WAS TO DOWNLOAD IT.

YOU CALL IT "DOWNLOADING", OUR ETHICS POLICY CALLS IT ELECTRONIC SHOPLIFTING.

FIGURE 9

The issues of intellectual property have become critical as all the media we produce become digital.

Privacy

Is Personal Privacy a Casualty of the Modern Age?

SUMMARY OF THE ISSUE

Privacy, like respect for others and being treated with dignity, is a basic human right. But what exactly is privacy? Simply stated, privacy is the right to be left alone to do as one pleases. The idea of privacy is often associated with hiding something (a behavior, a relationship, or a secret). But privacy really means not being required to explain your behavior to others. With the advent of the digital society, however, is there any such thing as personal privacy (see **Figure 10**)? Like Hansel and Gretel, we leave a veritable trail of electronic breadcrumbs almost everywhere we go.

Debit and credit cards are fast replacing cash, and they leave records of our purchases at merchants and transactions at the bank. E-mail is fast replacing snail mail, so now your correspondence (and your secrets) may live on indefinitely in Web servers around the world. Have you visited a Web site lately? Chances are, the owner of that site kept track of what you looked at while you were visiting their site.

Can't we just modify our behavior to protect our privacy? We could, but a recent survey by the Ponemon Institute revealed that only about 7 percent of Americans are willing to change their behavior to protect privacy. Many people freely give up personal information (such as their name, address, and phone number) to obtain buyer loyalty cards that qualify them for discounts at supermarkets and pharmacies. And to obtain a discount on tolls and speed up their trips, many people sign up for electronic toll passes (which are actually RFID devices) that can be used to track where you were at a specific point in time. Information gathered by these programs could then be used against you in a divorce case to prove you were a bad parent because you were routinely out in your car at 2 a.m. on school nights or because you bought mostly junk food at the supermarket. Although many Americans say they are concerned about a loss of privacy, few moves have been made in the United States to preserve privacy rights.

QUESTIONS TO THINK ABOUT AND RESEARCH

1. Is privacy protected by the U.S. Constitution? If it isn't currently protected, would you be willing to join a group that was working toward a constitutional amendment on privacy?

2. Which is more important to you: protecting the United States from potential terrorists by surrendering some personal privacy or keeping all of your personal privacy rights?

3. Should U.S. citizens have the right to access personal information collected about them by companies and make corrections if the information is erroneous? How would you manage such a process if you ran a company that collected this information?

POINT

Protect Personal Privacy

The advocates for protecting privacy in the United States argue that the right to privacy is a basic human right that should be afforded to everyone. As long as individuals aren't hurting anyone or breaking any laws, people should be entitled to do what they want without fear of being monitored.

1. If I'm not doing anything wrong, then you have no reason to watch me.

2. If the government is collecting information by watching citizens, it might misuse or lose control of the data.

3. By allowing the government to determine what behaviors are right and wrong, we open ourselves to uncertainty because the government may arbitrarily change the definition of which behaviors are unacceptable.

4. Requiring national ID cards is reminiscent of the former Nazi or Soviet regimes.

5. Implementing privacy controls (such as national ID cards) is extremely expensive and a waste of taxpayer funds.

COUNTERPOINT

Reduced Privacy Is a Fact of Modern Life

Advocates for stronger monitoring of private citizens usually cite national security concerns and the prevention of terrorist activities. Inconveniencing ordinary people who are doing nothing wrong is just a price that must be paid to ensure that society is free from malicious acts by a few malcontents.

1. If you aren't doing anything wrong, you don't have anything to hide.

2. Electronic enhancements to identification documents are essential in the digital world we live in so that government agencies can more efficiently exchange information to enhance detection of suspected terrorists.

3. Laws protect citizens from being abused or taken advantage of by overzealous government officials who are involved in monitoring activities.

4. It is not possible to put a price on freedom or security; therefore, projects like a national ID system are worth the cost of implementation.

Courtesy of www.istockphoto.com

FIGURE 10

Is personal privacy possible any longer?

Commerce

Should Online Gambling Be Banned or Regulated?

SUMMARY OF THE ISSUE

Internet gambling is currently a multibillion-dollar industry. The industry generated approximately $12 billion in revenues in 2005 from an estimated 1,800 Internet gambling sites worldwide. Americans alone increased their Internet gambling activity from $1.5 billion in 2001 to $6 billion in 2005. With wireless Internet connectivity increasingly available, online gambling via cell phones will make online gambling even more accessible. The basic online gambling activities are predominantly sports betting, casino games, the lottery, and poker (see **Figure 11**).

Internet gambling is already illegal in the United States. Legislation was passed in October 2006 to reinforce the prohibition of online gambling; yet it remains a viable and growing industry worldwide. Since there are no boundaries to the Internet and Internet activity, restrictive legislation cannot ban the user (the gambler) or the provider (the online casino, which is based outside the boundaries of the United States), but rather seeks punitive damages against those who promote the activity—namely, the financial intermediaries: banks and credit card companies—thereby making it more difficult for an online Internet casino to operate. The debate remains whether such activity should continue to be banned altogether or whether it should be allowed to operate legally but under the regulated environment of the U.S. government.

Internet gambling's characteristics are unique, and advocates of both sides of this issue acknowledge the obvious concerns of online gambling. Online gambling, unlike gambling done in brick-and-mortar facilities, encourages gamblers to play 24 hours a day from home and facilitates addictive gambling. Betting with a credit card can undercut a player's perception of the value of cash, further leading to gambling addiction, bankruptcy, and crime. In addition, children may play without sufficient age verification.

QUESTIONS TO THINK ABOUT AND RESEARCH

1. How big an industry is online gambling?

2. In what ways can Internet gambling businesses be used to facilitate other illegal activities?

3. How might the prohibition of online gambling be compared to the prohibition of alcohol in the United States in the 1920s?

4. Why is online gambling legalized in other countries, and how do those countries handle concerns voiced by opponents to legalized online gambling in America?

POINT

Ban Online Gambling

The advocates for continuing the ban on online gambling in the United States argue that thorough and extensive enforcement of the current prohibition would stop online gambling and hence eliminate the source of the problems.

1. Internet gambling is too easily accessible to minors and compulsive gamblers (brick-and-mortar casinos provide restrictions that help control access to minors and compulsive/addictive gamblers).

2. Offshore Internet gambling facilities could be used to support criminal activities such as illegal money laundering and identity theft.

3. Unlike physical gambling facilities, it is difficult to put controls in place to ensure that the operations are "honest"—for example, odds being unfairly tweaked in the favor of the "house" or money being collected from players but winnings never paid out.

4. Online gambling facilitates the hiding of gambling addiction from family members, thereby adding to the potential financial burden on families and society (through loss of jobs, homes, and marriages).

COUNTERPOINT

Legalize Online Gambling

Advocates for legalizing online gambling in the United States argue that legalizing it will bring it out of the underworld and place stricter controls on the industry. Enforced governmental regulations placed on current onsite gambling facilities could be applied to online sites and eliminate the source of the problems.

1. Current multibillion public online gambling companies exist outside the United States. Increased regulatory action would bring to light the legitimate organizations that can and do protect consumers, restrict access by minors, and protect those lured into gambling addiction. Enhanced regulation would make the illegitimate operations more difficult to operate.

2. Online gambling is "transparent"—every transaction is logged and available for scrutiny.

3. Regulation would standardize the industry and bring in tax revenues to the U.S. government.

4. Online gambling is regulated in 64 countries, including the United Kingdom.

5. Prohibiting online gambling would send it underground and leave the vulnerable unprotected.

6. It's much easier to regulate online activity than prohibit it.

FIGURE 11

Online access to gambling makes it convenient. But how do you stop children from gambling in this environment?

Communication

When Does Big Business Limit Free Speech?

SUMMARY OF THE ISSUE

In early 2006, Google conceded to Beijing's demands that it self-censor its search engine. Google was following in the footsteps of other large U.S. high-tech companies that had previously collaborated with the Chinese government in suppressing dissent in return for access to the booming Chinese Internet market. Corporate America's definition of the price it is willing to pay to obtain Chinese business has stirred up a vigorous controversy. Google justified its decision by stating that when a company decides to do business, it must operate within the rules of that market.

Chinese policies include the following:

- Filters that block objectionable foreign Web sites
- Regulations that ban what the Chinese government considers subversive and pornographic content
- Requirement that the Internet service providers enforce government censorship

How big is the Chinese Internet market? More than 137 million people in China are online, representing about 10 percent of the Chinese population. In comparison, 211 million people in the United States are online, representing 90 percent of the U.S. population. Thus, there is much room for expansion of Chinese access to the Internet. In fact, by 2009, Chinese e-commerce is expected to be a $390.9 billion market—at that point, China would have more Internet users than the United States. Google and others decided to give in to the government demands because otherwise they would lose out on a huge market. History has shown that many businesses will put monetary gain (for shareholders) over protecting basic human rights, such as free speech (see **Figure 12**).

QUESTIONS TO THINK ABOUT AND RESEARCH

1. Does the presence of U.S. tech companies in China contribute to the overall expansion of access to information in China?

2. What kind of parallels can be drawn to the U.S. corporate response to apartheid in South Africa in the 1970s?

3. Can U.S. government action help by pressing U.S. concerns on censorship during talks with foreign governments?

POINT

Google Acted Unethically

Those who have protested Google's actions are those who fight for human rights at any level. They feel that Google's compliant behavior only condones China's censorship policies and continues to thwart the effort to promote human rights initiatives in China.

1. Google sacrificed free speech for business. This action violates human rights, international law, and corporate ethics.

2. Cooperating with China violates human rights.

3. If international businesses can't stand up to China, then how will China ever have the incentive to change?

4. Most other rights hang on the community's ability to have open discussions. Preventing that from happening is a serious assault on human rights.

5. If the policy were to make children work or to kill women, would the companies choose not to comply? Are human rights and the freedom of speech any different?

COUNTERPOINT

Google's Actions Were Justified

The advocates of Google's actions tend to be other businesses and those with large economic interests that can relate to Google's business predicament. They feel that Google acted in accordance with "doing business" and should abide by the laws of the local governments.

1. Companies are free to pursue profits as long as they follow the country's laws.

2. Withdrawing from China would further restrict speech.

3. Google's presence, as muted as it is, continues to advance the slow progress the Chinese government is making toward democracy. U.S. companies can ethically stay in China if they make an effort to improve human rights there. U.S. companies operating in China should agree on guidelines that respect human rights.

Courtesy of www.istockphoto.com

FIGURE 12

As globalization brings us all in closer contact, how will our ethics and values come into conflict with others?

Computer Abuse

Does Restricting Online Information Protect Children?

SUMMARY OF THE ISSUE

Computer abuse is loosely defined as using a computer or the Internet to harm another individual. By providing anonymity, the Internet facilitates such unsavory activities as:

- The ability of sexual predators to contact potential victims
- The distribution of pornography
- Cyberbullying (harassing individuals through electronic means)
- Phishing, or tricking individuals out of sensitive information
- The dissemination of hate speech

Although computer abuse is a threat to everyone, children are especially vulnerable because they tend to use technology more than adults, are more trusting than many adults, and may lack the real-life experience to identify malicious intent or behavior. No one argues that protecting children from harm is not a laudable goal, but the question is how best to accomplish it. Laws restricting the Internet's content have largely failed when they are overturned by courts on the grounds that they violate free speech. Therefore, controlling access to objectionable material has been the avenue pursued.

Content-filtering software is designed to block objectionable content from view and is usually designed for shielding children (see **Figure 13**). But problems have arisen as public institutions such as schools and libraries have installed filtering software to protect children. When objectionable material is blocked, the free speech rights of the individual are affected—not by preventing them from exercising their right of free speech but rather by infringing upon their rights of free access to information. The courts have usually viewed access to information as a First Amendment (free speech) issue.

Filtering software presents a problem when it is unable to discriminate between information that should be blocked and information that is not objectionable but rather informational. Blocking software has blocked informational sites, such as the Safer Sex Page; groups supporting gay rights; sites with information about breast cancer; and even the home pages of politicians such as former Representative Richard (Dick) Armey (R, Texas). Furthermore, designers of objectionable Web sites (such as pornography sites) are often clever enough to disguise their objectionable content so that it fools the filters. The public has raised a huge outcry, demanding that publicly funded institutions must protect children from objectionable content. So what is the best way to satisfy this demand if filtering isn't the answer?

QUESTIONS TO THINK ABOUT AND RESEARCH

1. Does your school use filtering software in computer labs on campus? Do you think your school should restrict objectionable content if it receives public funds?

2. Who should decide what types of sites should be blocked by filtering software? Educators? Librarians? Software programmers? The government?

3. If you have children (or when you have children in the future), will you install filtering software on computers in your home?

4. What alternatives to filtering software would be effective in protecting children from objectionable content?

POINT

Monitoring Software Protects Children

Most advocates of filtering software in publicly funded institutions cite the need to protect minors from material deemed objectionable by accepted public standards.

1. Since laws have proven ineffective, filtering software is the only way to protect children from objectionable material, such as pornography or violence.

2. Parents need to be assured that publicly funded institutions, such as schools and libraries, are "safe havens" where their children will not be allowed to access objectionable material.

3. Publicly funded institutions have a right to uphold the moral standards of the public.

4. Filtering Internet content is a logical extension of the existing library screening process, whereby librarians decide what books to put on the shelves.

COUNTERPOINT

Monitoring Software Restricts Access to Information

Opponents of filtering software cite the First Amendment, which guarantees free speech and hence free access to information.

1. Filtering software routinely blocks Web sites with informational content as opposed to objectionable material.

2. Filtering software is akin to censorship, which violates the First Amendment.

3. Filtering software is not 100 percent reliable and fails to screen out a lot of objectionable material.

4. Filtering widens the "digital divide" by adversely affecting the poor. Wealthier individuals tend to have Internet access in their homes and are less affected by filters in public institutions.

5. Educating children about using the Internet carefully and responsibly will be more effective in the long run than filtering software.

FIGURE 13

Net Nanny content filtering software allows parents to exercise control over what their children can view.

4

Application Software:

Programs That Let You Work and Play

From Chapter 4 of *Technology in Action, Complete*, Fifth Edition, Alan Evans, Kendall Martin, Mary Anne Poatsy. Copyright © 2009 by Pearson Education. Published by Prentice Hall. All rights reserved.

Application Software:

Programs That Let You Work and Play

Objectives

After reading this chapter, you should be able to answer the following questions:

1. What's the difference between application software and system software?

2. What kinds of applications are included in productivity software I might use at home?

3. What are the different types of multimedia software?

4. What are the different types of entertainment software?

5. What is reference software?

6. What are the different types of drawing software?

7. What kinds of software do small and large businesses use?

8. Where can I go for help when I have a problem with my software?

9. How can I purchase software or get it for free?

10. How do I install, uninstall, and open software?

ACTIVE HELPDESK

- Choosing Software
- Buying and Installing Software

Using Application Software

Finals are this week. Jenna sits down to tackle the last project for her computer literacy class, a research assignment on "simulation" software. She's a fan of *The Sims* software games and is researching how different professions are using simulation software to train workers. Her instructor said students could use any format for the project, so Jenna decides to do a PowerPoint presentation. With the Insert Slides from the Outline feature, she transfers the outline she has already prepared in Word to PowerPoint slides. Using that as the basis for her presentation, she adds visual interest to the slides with photographs and other illustrations, being careful to include references to her sources.

With the presentation complete, she burns it onto a CD and then checks off the project as "complete" in the tasks list in Outlook. While in Outlook, Jenna turns to her calendar to check out tomorrow's activities and answers a few e-mail messages that have accumulated in her Inbox. Last, she makes a note to balance her checkbook and to record her income and expenses from last month. Because she records all her banking transactions in the financial planning application Quicken, balancing her checkbook against the bank's records and monitoring her budget is a breeze. Later, she will download the information into TurboTax, a tax-preparation software program, so that she can do her taxes herself. She has saved a lot of money by doing her own taxes, and the programs were simple to learn.

Before going to dinner, Jenna quickly checks into Blackboard, the course management software program her online class uses to manage assignments, homework, and discussions. Not seeing anything new to do, Jenna relaxes by playing a bit of *The Sims*.

How often do you use software, and what kinds of software are you familiar with? Do you know what software programs are on the market and what their most important features are? In this chapter, you'll learn about the kinds of software you can use to perform a variety of tasks, from simple word processing to digital image editing—at home, school, and work. We'll then discuss how you can buy software, what the different versions of software mean, and how you can legally get software for free off the Web. Finally, we'll look at how you can install and uninstall software safely on your system.

©Digital Art/Corbis AX010966
Microsoft Corporation

SOUND BYTES

- Creating Web Queries with Excel
- Using Speech-Recognition Software
- Enhancing Photos with Image-Editing Software

The Nuts and Bolts of Software

A computer without software is like a sandwich with no filling. Although the computer hardware is obviously critical, a computer system does nothing without software. What is software? Technically speaking, the term **software** refers to a set of instructions that tells the computer what to do. These instruction sets, also called **programs**, provide a means for us to interact with and use the computer, all without specialized computer programming skills. Your computer has two basic types of software:

- **System software** helps run the computer and coordinates instructions between application software and the computer's hardware devices. System software includes the operating system and utility programs (programs in the operating system that help manage system resources).

- **Application software** is what you use to do tasks at home, school, and work. You can do a multitude of things with application software, such as writing letters, sending e-mail, balancing a budget, creating presentations, editing photos, and taking an online course, to name a few.

Figure 1 shows the various types of application software available. In this chapter, we look at all of these types in detail, starting with productivity software.

More Productivity at Home

One reason to have a computer is to make it easier to tackle the tasks you have in your day-to-day life. Productivity software is all about helping you do that, making it easier to keep your budget, send letters, or keep track of the kids' school events. It's safe to say you already regularly use some form of productivity software. **Productivity software** includes programs that enable you to perform various tasks generally required in home, school, and business. This category includes word-processing, spreadsheet, presentation, database, and personal information manager (PIM) programs.

WORD-PROCESSING SOFTWARE

What is the best software to use to create general documents? Most students use **word-processing software** to create and edit documents such as research papers, letters, and résumés. Microsoft Word and Corel WordPerfect are popular word-processing programs. Writer, a word-processing program from the OpenOffice.org suite (OpenOffice), is gaining in popularity because it's available as a free download

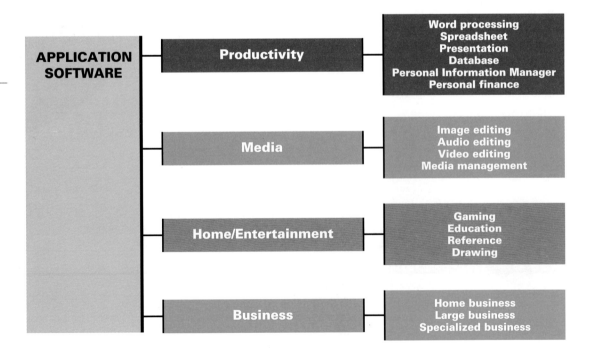

FIGURE 1

Organization of Application Software

APPLICATION SOFTWARE

Productivity — Word processing, Spreadsheet, Presentation, Database, Personal Information Manager, Personal finance

Media — Image editing, Audio editing, Video editing, Media management

Home/Entertainment — Gaming, Education, Reference, Drawing

Business — Home business, Large business, Specialized business

Application Software: Programs That Let You Work and Play

from the Internet. Writer has many of the same features as its higher-priced Word and WordPerfect competitors, making it a great choice for the cost-conscious.

Because of its general usefulness, word-processing software is the most widely used software application. Word-processing software has a key advantage over its ancestral counterpart, the typewriter: You can make revisions and corrections without having to retype an entire document. You quickly and easily can insert, delete, and move pieces of text. Similarly, you can remove and insert text from one document into another seamlessly.

How do I control the way my documents look? Another advantage of word-processing software is that you can easily format, or change the appearance of, your document. As a result, you can produce professional-looking documents without having to send them to a professional printer. With formatting options, you can change fonts, font styles, and sizes; add colors to text; adjust margins; add borders to portions of text or entire pages; insert bulleted and numbered lists; and organize your text into columns. You also can insert pic-

tures from your own files or from a gallery of images called clip art that is included with the software. Using formatting tools, you also can enhance the look of your document by creating an interesting background or by adding a "theme" of coordinated colors and styles throughout your document. Figure 2 shows an example of some of the formatting options.

What special tools do word-processing programs have? You're probably familiar with the basic tools of word-processing software. Most applications come with some form of spelling/grammar checker and a thesaurus, for example. Another popular tool is the search and replace tool, which allows you to search for text in your document and automatically replace it with other text.

The average user is unaware of many interesting word-processing software tools. For example, did you know that you could translate words or phrases to another language or automatically correct your spelling as you type? You also can automatically summarize key points in a text document. Writer, the word-processing program in the OpenOffice suite, has many of the same

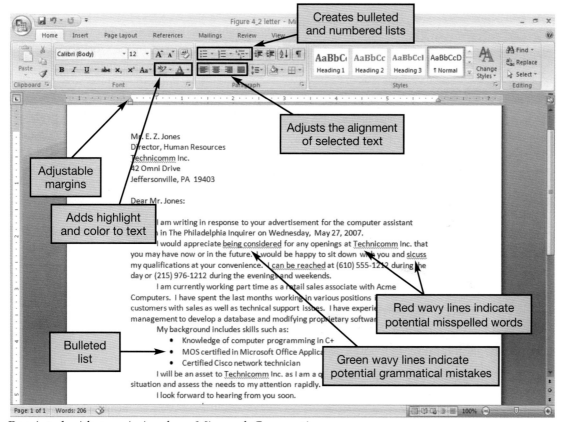

FIGURE 2

Nearly every word-processing software application has basic features to help you make your document look professionally formatted and to ensure that words are spelled correctly and used grammatically.

BITS AND BYTES

What's the Difference Between Save and Save As?

Imagine you're working on a Word document. Before you leave for class, you (1) save the document to your hard drive for the first time. Later, you open the file to add some finishing touches. When you're done, you (2) save the file again. The next day, you (3) save the file to a flash drive. Finally, your friend asks for the file in a different format so she can read it in an older version of the program, and you have to (4) save it yet again. In these four situations, when do you use the Save command and when do you use Save As?

When you save a file for the first time (situation 1), you use Save As to give the file a name and designate where it should be located. (When you save a file for the first time, the Save command automatically brings you to the Save As dialog box.) When you already have saved the file and are saving changes to it (situation 2), you use the Save command. However, if you want to change the name or location of a file that you saved previously (situation 3), you use the Save As command. The Save As command also allows you to select from a list of different file types, so it is the command to use when you need to change file types (situation 4). The following table illustrates these four options.

When to Use	Save As	Save
Saving a file for the first time	X	X
Saving changes to contents of an existing file, but not to filename or location		X
Saving changes to filename and/or location	X	
Saving to a different file type	X	

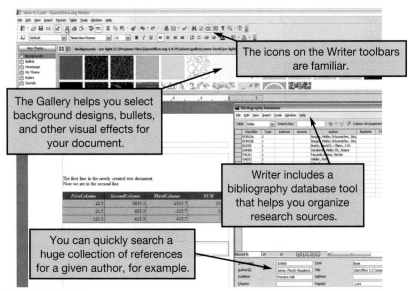

The Gallery helps you select background designs, bullets, and other visual effects for your document.

The icons on the Writer toolbars are familiar.

Writer includes a bibliography database tool that helps you organize research sources.

You can quickly search a huge collection of references for a given author, for example.

FIGURE 3 Reprinted with permission from Microsoft Corporation

Writer, the word-processing program in the OpenOffice suite, has many of the same features as Word and WordPerfect as well as some unique ones.

tools you're used to seeing in Microsoft Word and Corel WordPerfect, as well as some unique ones (see Figure 3).

SPREADSHEET SOFTWARE

Why would I need to use spreadsheet software? Spreadsheet software, such as Microsoft Excel or Lotus 1-2-3, enables you to do calculations and numerical analyses easily. You can use spreadsheet software to track your expenses and to create a simple budget. You also can use spreadsheet software to determine how much you should be paying on your student loans, car loan, or credit card bills each month. You know you should pay more than the minimum payment to spend less on interest, but how much more should you pay and for which loan? Spreadsheet software can help you easily evaluate different scenarios, such as planning the best payment strategy.

How do I use spreadsheet software? The basic element in a spreadsheet program is the worksheet, which is a grid consisting of columns and rows. As shown in Figure 4, the columns and rows form individual boxes called cells. Each cell can be identified according to its column and row position. For example, a cell in column A, row 1, is referred to as cell A1. There are several types of data you can enter into a cell:

- *Labels* are descriptive text that identifies the components of the worksheet.
- *Values* are numeric data either typed in directly or entered by the program as a result of a calculation.
- *Formulas* are equations that you build yourself using addition, subtraction, multiplication, and division, as well as values and cell references. For example, in Figure 4, you would type the formula =B8-B22 to calculate net income for September.
- *Functions* are formulas that are pre-programmed into the spreadsheet software. Functions help you with calculations ranging from the simple (such as adding groups of numbers) to the complex (such as determining monthly loan payments), without your needing to know the exact formula. So, in Figure 4, to calculate your average earned income in September, you could use the built-in AVERAGE function, which would look like this: =AVERAGE(B4:B7).

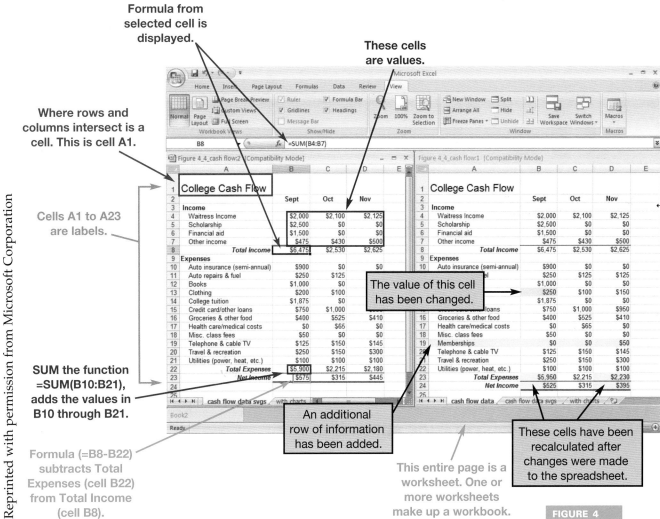

Formula from selected cell is displayed.

These cells are values.

Where rows and columns intersect is a cell. This is cell A1.

Cells A1 to A23 are labels.

SUM the function =SUM(B10:B21), adds the values in B10 through B21.

Formula (=B8-B22) subtracts Total Expenses (cell B22) from Total Income (cell B8).

The value of this cell has been changed.

An additional row of information has been added.

These cells have been recalculated after changes were made to the spreadsheet.

This entire page is a worksheet. One or more worksheets make up a workbook.

FIGURE 4

Spreadsheet software enables you to calculate and manipulate numerical data easily with the use of built-in formulas and other features.

The primary benefit of spreadsheet software is its ability to recalculate all functions and formulas in the spreadsheet automatically when values for some of the inputs are changed. For example, in Figure 4, you can insert an additional row (Memberships) and change a value (September clothing expense), and then recalculate the results for Total Expenses and Net Income without having to redo the worksheet from scratch.

Because automatic recalculation enables you to see immediately the effects that different options have on your spreadsheet, you can quickly test different assumptions in the same analysis. This is called a "what-if" analysis. Look again at Figure 4 and ask, "What if I add $50 to my clothing budget? What impact will such an increase have on my budget?" By adding another $100 to tuition, as shown in the budget in Figure 4, you will automatically know the impact a tuition increase will have on your expenses and net income.

What kinds of graphs and charts can I create with spreadsheet software? Sometimes it's easier to see the meaning of numbers when they are shown in a graphical format, or a chart. As shown in Figure 5, most spreadsheet applications allow you to create a variety of charts, including basic column charts, pie charts, and line charts—with or without three-dimensional (3-D) effects. In addition to these basic charts, you can use stock charts (for investment analysis) and scatter charts (for statistical analysis), as well as create custom charts.

Are spreadsheets used for anything besides financial analysis? There are so many powerful mathematical functions built into spreadsheet programs that they can be used for serious numerical analyses or simulation. For example, an Excel spreadsheet could be designed to compute the output voltage at a point in an electrical circuit or to simulate

SOUND BYTE

Creating Web Queries with Excel

In this Sound Byte, you'll learn what Excel Web queries are, as well as how to use them effectively.

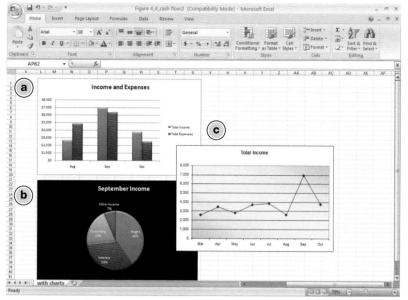

Reprinted with permission from Microsoft Corporation

FIGURE 5

(a) Column charts show comparisons. (b) Pie charts show how parts contribute to the whole. (c) Line charts show trends over time.

customer arrival and wait times. In these settings, spreadsheet programs can often solve problems that formerly required custom programming.

PRESENTATION SOFTWARE

What software do I use to create presentations?

You've probably sat through presentations during which the speaker's dialogue is displayed in slides projected on a screen. These presentations can be very basic outlines, containing only a few words and simple graphics, or elaborate multimedia presentations with animated text, graphic objects, and colorful backgrounds. You use **presentation software** such as Microsoft PowerPoint or OpenOffice Impress, shown in Figure 6, to create these types of dynamic slide shows. Because these applications are so simple to use, you can produce high-quality presentations without a lot of training.

How do I create a presentation?

Using the basic features included in presentation software, creating a slide show is very simple. To arrange text and graphics on your slides easily, you can choose from a variety of slide layouts. These layouts give you the option of using a single or double column of bulleted text, various combinations of bulleted text, and other content such as clip art, graphs, photos, and even video clips.

You also can lend a theme to your presentation by choosing from different design templates. You can use animation effects to

control how and when text and other objects enter and exit each slide. Similarly, slide transitions add different effects as you move from one slide to the next during the presentation.

DATABASE SOFTWARE

How can I use database software?

Database software, such as Oracle, Corel Paradox, and Microsoft Access, is basically a complex electronic filing system. As mentioned earlier, spreadsheet applications include many database features and are easy to use for simple database tasks such as sorting, filtering, and organizing data. However, you need to use a more robust, full-featured database application to manage larger and more complicated groups of data that contain more than one table or to group, sort, and retrieve data and to generate reports.

Traditional databases are organized into fields, records, and tables, as shown in Figure 7. A field is a data category such as "First Name," "Last Name," or "Street Address." A record is a collection of related fields, such as "Douglas Seaver, Printing Solutions, 7700 First Avenue, Topeka, KS, (888) 968-2678." A table groups related records, such as "Sales Contacts."

How do you benefit when businesses use database software?

Companies such as FedEx and UPS let customers search their online databases for tracking numbers, allowing customers to get instant information on the status of their packages. Other businesses use databases to keep track of clients, invoices, or personnel information. Often that information is available to a home computer user. For example, at Amazon.com you can use the company's Web site to access the entire history of all the purchases you have ever made.

PERSONAL INFORMATION MANAGER (PIM) SOFTWARE

Which applications should I use to manage my time, contact lists, and tasks?

Most productivity software suites contain some form of **personal information manager (PIM) software**, such as Microsoft Outlook or Lotus Organizer. These programs strive to replace the management tools found on a traditional desk, such as a calendar, address book, notepad, and to-do list. Some

Application Software: Programs That Let You Work and Play

There are several programs that allow you to create presentation materials: (a) Microsoft Office PowerPoint 2007, (b) OpenOffice Impress, and (c) Zoho.com's Show.

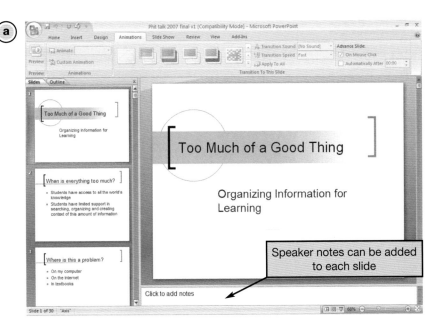

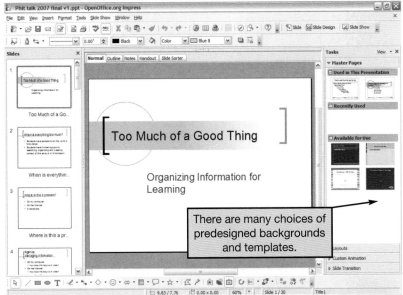

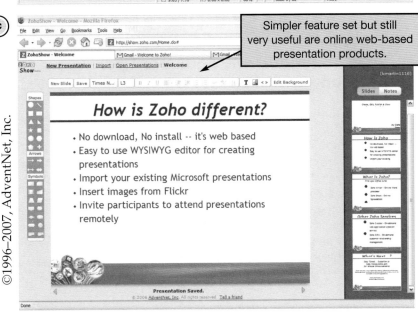

PIMs contain e-mail management features so that you can not only receive and send e-mail messages, but also organize them into various folders, prioritize them, and coordinate them with other activities in your calendar (see Figure 8 on the next page).

If you share a common network at home or at work and are using the same PIM software as others on the network, you can use a PIM program to check people's availability before scheduling meeting times. Whether coordinating a team project or a family event, you can create and electronically assign tasks to group members by using a PIM. You can even track each person's progress to ensure that the tasks are finished on time.

PRODUCTIVITY SOFTWARE TOOLS

What tools can help me work more efficiently with productivity software?
Whether you are working on a word-processing document, spreadsheet, database, or slide presentation, you can make use of several tools to increase your efficiency:

- **Wizards** are step-by-step guides that walk you through the necessary steps to complete a complicated task. At each step, the wizard asks you questions. Based on your responses, the wizard helps you complete that portion of the task. Many productivity software applications include wizards. For example, you can easily create charts in Excel using the Excel Chart Wizard.

- **Templates** are forms included in many productivity applications that provide the basic structure for a particular kind of document, spreadsheet, or presentation. Templates can include specific page layout designs, special formatting and styles relevant to that particular document, as well as automated tasks (macros). Typical templates allow you to lay out a professional-looking résumé, to structure a home budget, or to communicate the results of a project in a presentation.

a-b) Reprinted with permission from Microsoft Corporation

FIGURE 7

In databases, similar information is organized by main topic into tables and grouped into categories called fields. Each individual row of data is called a record. Some databases have multiple tables that "relate" to each other through common fields.

This entire group of records represents the SalesContacts table

The category FirstName is a field

All the information for Douglas Seaver represents one record

Reprinted with permission from Microsoft Corporation

FIGURE 8

The Outlook Today feature in Microsoft Outlook includes common PIM features, such as a summary of your appointments, a list of your tasks, and the number of new e-mail messages you have.

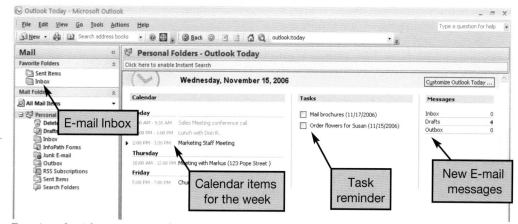

E-mail Inbox

Calendar items for the week

Task reminder

New E-mail messages

Reprinted with permission from Microsoft Corporation

BITS AND BYTES

Productivity Software Tips and Tricks

Looking for tips on how to make better use of your productivity software? A number of Web sites send subscribers daily e-mails full of tips, tricks, and shortcuts to their favorite software programs. Nerdy Books (**www.nerdybooks.com**), for example, sends a free tip each day to the e-mail accounts of its subscribers. Nerdy Books also has a free *Who Knew?* blog and a free podcast full of software tips. Dummies eTips (**http://etips.dummies.com**), based on the *For Dummies* series of help books, offers subscribers tips on a variety of topics, including productivity software applications. Most of these services are free, although some require that you subscribe to an ancillary product.

- **Macros** are small programs that group a series of commands to run as a single command. Macros are best used to automate a routine task or a complex series of commands that must be run frequently. For example, a teacher may write a macro to sort the grades in her grade book automatically in descending order and to highlight those grades that are below a C average. Every time she adds the results of an assignment or test, she can set up the macro to run through those series of steps automatically.

INTEGRATED SOFTWARE APPLICATIONS VERSUS SOFTWARE SUITES

Are there different ways to buy productivity software? You can buy productivity software as individual programs, as

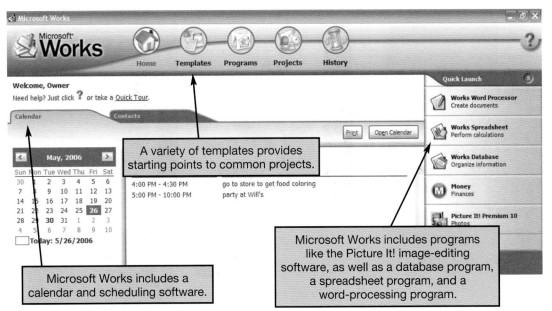

A variety of templates provides starting points to common projects.

Microsoft Works includes a calendar and scheduling software.

Microsoft Works includes programs like the Picture It! image-editing software, as well as a database program, a spreadsheet program, and a word-processing program.

FIGURE 9

Although an integrated software application such as Microsoft Works is one program, it contains the most commonly used features of several individual productivity software applications. Integrated software applications also often contain a number of templates and wizards.

integrated software applications, or as a suite of software applications.

Integrated Software Applications

What's an integrated software application? An **integrated software application** is a single software program that incorporates the most commonly used tools of many productivity software programs into one integrated stand-alone program. Note that integrated software applications are not substitutes for the full suite of applications they replace. Generally, because they don't include many of the more complex features of the individual productivity software applications, they can be thought of as "software lite." To have access to the full range of functionality of word-processing and spreadsheet software, for example, you should purchase the individual applications or a suite that includes each of these applications.

Microsoft Works is an example of an integrated software application. Figure 9 shows the Task Launcher for Microsoft Works. The Task Launcher is the first window that opens when you launch Microsoft Works. This integrated software application includes word-processing, spreadsheet, and database features, as well as templates, a calendar, an encyclopedia, and map features.

Why would I use an integrated software application instead of individual, stand-alone programs? Integrated software applications are perfect if you don't need the more advanced fea-

tures found in the individual productivity software applications. Like stand-alone applications, integrated software programs provide templates for frequently developed documents such as résumés and invoices. Integrated software programs also are less expensive than their full-featured counterparts. If you find your needs go beyond the limited capabilities of an integrated program, you might want to consider buying those individual programs that meet your particular requirements, or you may want to consider buying a software suite.

Software Suites

What's a software suite? A **software suite** is a group of software programs that have been bundled as a package. You can buy software suites for many different categories of applications, including productivity, graphics, and virus protection. Microsoft Office is just one example of the many types of software suites on the market today (see Figure 10). You also can buy different versions of the same suite, the difference being the combination of software applications included in each version.

Which software applications do productivity software suites contain? Most productivity software suites contain the same basic software programs, such as word-processing, spreadsheet, presentation, and PIM software. The Standard edition of the Microsoft Office 2007 suite bundles the word-processing program Microsoft Word, the spreadsheet program

f) V-Com

Excel, the presentation program PowerPoint, and the PIM program Outlook. However, depending on the version and manufacturer, some suites also include other programs, such as database programs and desktop publishing software. When you are shopping for software, it can be difficult to figure out which bundle is the right one for your needs. For example, Microsoft Office 2007 is bundled in eight different ways; four of these are described in the table in Figure 11. Be sure to carefully research the bundling options for software you are buying.

What are the most popular productivity software suites? There are three primary developers of productivity software suites: Microsoft, Corel, and Lotus. Microsoft and Corel offer different packages with different combinations of software applications, whereas Lotus offers only SmartSuite.

Why would I buy a software suite instead of individual programs? Most people buy software suites because suites are cheaper than buying each program individually. In addition, because the pro-

grams bundled in a software suite come from the same developer, they work well together (that is, they provide for better integration) and share common features, toolbars, and menus. For example, say you use Google Docs as your word-processing software application, and the stand-alone spreadsheet program Microsoft Excel. The toolbars and menus will all have different names and different organization, and the feature sets and names will be different. This could be a problem if you are working with other people and trying to communicate with them about how you are designing your work.

SOUND BYTE

Using Speech-Recognition Software

In this Sound Byte, you'll see a demonstration of the speech-recognition software included with Microsoft Office 2007 and Windows Vista. You'll also learn how to access and train speech-recognition software so that you can create and edit documents without typing.

Application Software: Programs That Let You Work and Play

FIGURE 11 **A Sampling of Microsoft Office Suites**

	Word Processing, Spreadsheet, Presentation	Database	PIM	Desktop Publishing	Note Taking	Other (Info Path, Groove)
Microsoft Office 2007	Word, Excel, PowerPoint	Access	Outlook	Publisher	One Note	
	X	X	X	X	X	X
Professional 2007	X	X	X	X		
Standard 2007	X		X			
Home and Student 2007	X				X	

PERSONAL FINANCIAL SOFTWARE

What software can I use to prepare my taxes? Everyone has to face doing their taxes, and having the right computer software can make this burden much simpler and keep it completely under your control. **Tax-preparation software** such as Intuit TurboTax and H&R Block TaxCut enable you to prepare your state and federal taxes on your own rather than having to hire a professional. Both programs offer a complete set of tax forms and instructions, as well as videos that contain expert advice on how to complete each form. In addition, error-checking features are built into the programs to catch mistakes. TurboTax also can run a check for audit alerts, file your return electronically, and offer guidance on financial planning to help effectively plan and manage your financial resources for the following year (see Figure 12). Remember, however, that the tax code changes annually so you must purchase the current tax year's version of the software each year.

What software can I use to help keep track of my finances? Financial **planning software** helps you manage your daily finances. Intuit Quicken and Microsoft Money are popular examples. These programs include electronic checkbook registers

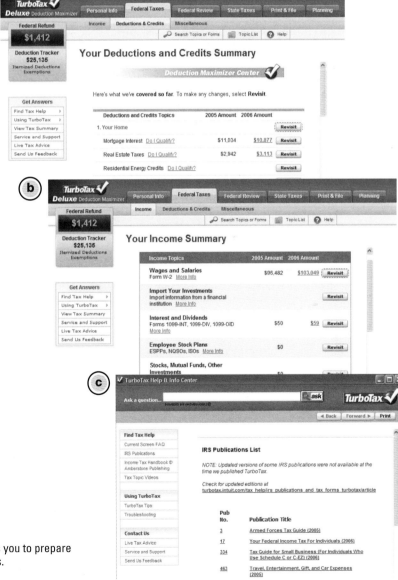

FIGURE 12

Tax-preparation software, such as Intuit TurboTax, enables you to prepare and file your taxes by using a guided, step-by-step process.

Speech-Recognition Software

Microsoft has incorporated speech-recognition software into its latest operating system, Windows Vista. **Speech-recognition software**, or **voice-recognition software**, translates your spoken words into typed text. You can dictate documents and e-mail messages; use voice commands to start and switch between applications, and control the operating system; and even fill out forms on the Web. Speech-recognition software is available in different languages, so Chinese, Japanese, or Spanish commands work just as well as English. Accuracy levels of 95 to 99 percent can be achieved in quiet environments with a quality microphone.

After starting speech recognition (from the Control Panel on the Start menu), the speech-recognition toolbar appears and indicates whether or not the computer is "listening" for voice input. Just click the microphone icon to make the computer listen to or ignore voice input. Figure 13 shows how you can use Vista's speech-recognition to instruct the software to run commands within an application. If you aren't sure what speech commands are available, just say "What can I say?" to display the speech reference card.

How does speech-recognition software work?

It's a complicated process. As you speak, the software divides each second of your speech into 100 individual samples, or sounds. It then compares these individual sounds with a database (called a codebook) containing samples of every sound a human being can make. When a match is made, your voice sound is given a number that corresponds to the number of the similar sound in the database.

After your voice sounds are assigned values, these values are matched with another database containing phonemes for the language being spoken. A phoneme is the smallest phonetic unit that distinguishes one word from another. For example, "b" and "m" are both phonemes that distinguish the words *bad* and *mad* from each other in the English language. A typical language such as English is comprised of thousands of different phonemes. And because of differences in pronunciation, some phonemes may actually have several different corresponding matching sounds.

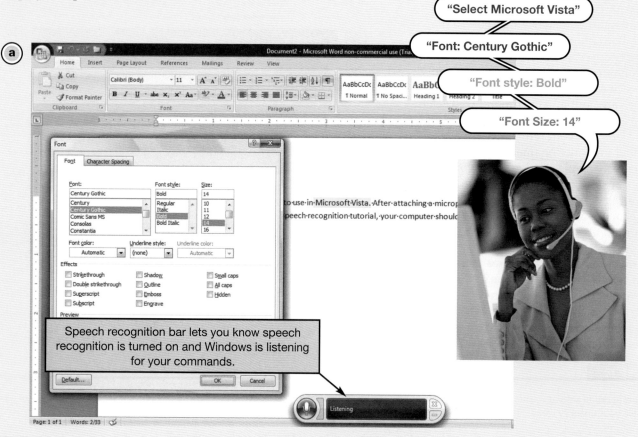

"Select Microsoft Vista"

"Font: Century Gothic"

"Font style: Bold"

"Font Size: 14"

Speech recognition bar lets you know speech recognition is turned on and Windows is listening for your commands.

Once all the sounds are assigned to phonemes, word and phrase construction can begin. The phonemes are matched against a word list that contains transcriptions of all known words in a particular language. Because pronunciation can vary (for example, *the* can be pronounced so that it rhymes with *duh* or *see*), the word list must contain alternative pronunciations for many words. Each phoneme is worked on separately; the phonemes are then chained together to form words that are contained in the word list. Because a variety of sounds can be put together to form many different words, the software analyzes all the possible values and picks the one value that it determines has the best probability of correctly matching your spoken word. The word is then displayed on the screen or is acted upon by the computer as a command.

Why are there problems with speech-recognition software? We don't always speak every word the same way, and accents and regional dialects result in great variations in pronunciations. Therefore, speech recognition is not perfect and requires training. Training entails getting the computer to recognize your particular way of speaking, a process that involves reading prepared text into the computer so the phoneme database can be adjusted to your specific speech patterns.

Another approach to improve speech inconsistencies is to restrict the word list to a few keywords or phrases and then have the computer guess the probability that a certain phrase is being said. This is how cell phones that respond to voice commands work. The phone doesn't really figure out that you said "call home" by breaking down the phonemes. It just determines how likely it is that you said "call home" as opposed to "call office." This cuts down on the processing power needed and reduces the chance of mistakes. However, it also restricts the words you can use to achieve the desired results.

Though not perfect, speech-recognition software programs can be of invaluable service for individuals who can't type very well or who have physical limitations that prevent them from using a keyboard or mouse. For those whose careers depend on a lot of typing, using speech-recognition software reduces the chances of their incurring debilitating repetitive strain injuries. In addition, because most people can speak faster than they can write or type, speech-recognition software can help individuals work more efficiently. It also can help you to be productive during generally nonproductive times. For example, you can dictate into a digital recording device while doing other things such as driving, then later download the digital file to your computer and let the program type up your words for you.

Speech recognition should continue to be a hot topic for research over the next decade. Aside from the obvious benefits to persons with disabilities, many people are enamored with the idea of talking to their computers!

©Michael Keller/Corbis/photo

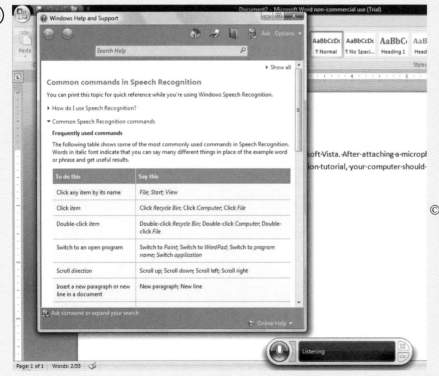

FIGURE 13

(a) Speech-recognition software allows you to create documents, with simple voice commands. (b) Forget what speech command to use? Just say "What can I say?" to display the speech reference card.

BITS AND BYTES

Looking for a Free or More Affordable Productivity Suite?

If you're looking for a more affordable software alternative to the big three (Microsoft Office, Corel WordPerfect Office, and Lotus SmartSuite), you may want to consider downloading the free open-source productivity suite OpenOffice, or for a reasonable fee, Sun Microsystems StarOffice 8 may be worth a try. **Open-source software** is program code made publicly available for free, with very few restrictions. It can be copied, distributed, or changed without the stringent copyright protections of software products you purchase. Compared to Microsoft Office, you won't find all the features you're used to seeing, but OpenOffice and StarOffice offer most of the features required by the average user. And if you use OpenOffice and

StarOffice, you can easily read, write, and edit files created in other applications, although you may lose some formatting when migrating to StarOffice and OpenOffice. Similarly, users of other productivity suites can open files created in StarOffice and OpenOffice. Functionally, OpenOffice and StarOffice are very similar.

One thing to keep in mind when you choose a free or low-cost software product is support: OpenOffice is an open-source product, so there is no formal support like that found in products you buy. Instead, OpenOffice is supported from its community users across Web sites and newsgroups. StarOffice, on the other hand, is supported by Sun Microsystems.

FIGURE 14

When you write checks using your personal financial planning software, your transactions are entered automatically into an electronic checkbook.

and automatic bill payment tools, as shown in Figure 14. With these features, you can print checks from your computer or pay recurring monthly payments, such as rent or student loans, with automatically scheduled online payments. The software automatically records all transactions, including online payments, in your checkbook register. In addition, you can assign categories to each transaction and then

use these categories to analyze your spending patterns. You even can set up a budget and review your spending habits.

Financial planning software applications also coordinate with tax-preparation software. Quicken, for example, integrates seamlessly with TurboTax, so you never have to go through your checkbook and bills to find tax deductions, tax-related income,

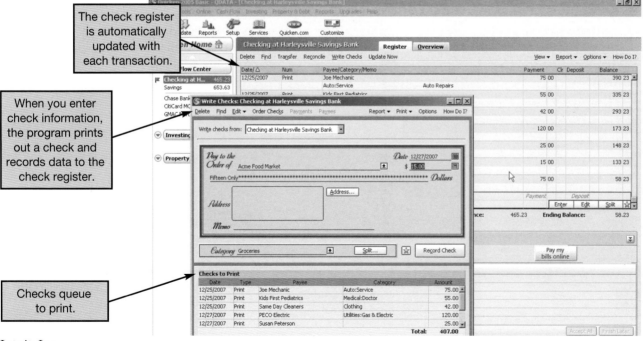

Intuit, Inc.

or expenses. Many banks and credit card companies also offer online services that download a detailed monthly statement into Quicken or Money. Quicken even offers a credit card. All of your purchases are organized into categories and are downloaded automatically to your Quicken file to further streamline your financial planning and recordkeeping. You also can purchase a Pocket PC version of Quicken to install on your personal digital assistant (PDA) so that your financial records are always at your fingertips.

More Media at Home

From movies and television to music and photography, the entertainment world is becoming all digital. Your computer can help you create, organize, and modify digital images, songs, and movies, if you have the right software. **Multimedia software** includes image, video, and audio editing software, animation software, and other specialty software required to produce computer games, animations, and movies. In this section, we look at a number of popular types of multimedia software, shown in Figure 15.

DIGITAL IMAGE-EDITING SOFTWARE

What can I do with a digital image that I can't do with a photograph? Once the image information is in a digital format (the image is taken with a digital camera or scanned), you can use it easily with all your other software. With the digital file, it is simple to store a picture of each person in your Outlook contacts list or add an image you captured into a newsletter you are writing.

Products like Microsoft Photo Story or Google's Picasa, both free downloads, make it easy for you to use your collection of digital images in new ways. In Photo Story, you can add text, music, and camera movement to create full-featured slide shows that will let you use your images. Using Picasa, you can create a poster from an image or several different styles of collages.

What software do I use to edit my photos? As its name implies, **image-editing**

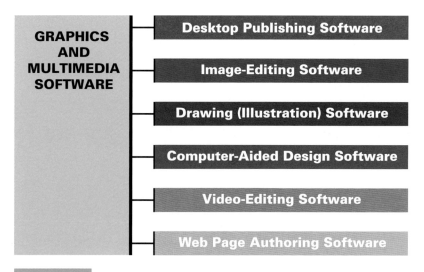

FIGURE 15

There are many varieties of graphics and multimedia software.

software (sometimes called **photo-editing software**) enables you to edit photographs and other images. Image-editing software includes tools for basic modifications to digital images such as removing red-eye, modifying contrast, sharpness, and color casts, or removing scratches or rips from scanned images of old photos. Many of these software packages now also include an extensive set of painting tools such as brushes, pens, and artistic-type mediums (paints, pastels, oils) that allow you to create realistic-looking images as well. Often graphic designers use digital photos and images as a basis for their design and then modify these images within image-editing software to create their final product.

Adobe Photoshop CS3 and Corel Paint Shop Pro are full-featured image-editing software applications. They each offer sophisticated tools such as those for layering images (placing pictures on top of each other) and masking images (hiding parts of layers to create effects such as collages). See Figure 16. Designers use these more sophisticated tools to create the enhanced digital images used commercially in logos, advertisements, and on book and CD covers.

Can a nonprofessional use image-editing software? Image-editing programs such as ArcSoft PhotoStudio, Microsoft Digital Image, and Roxio PhotoSuite are programs geared toward the casual home user. With these applications, you can perform the most

improve the color balance of an image, touch up an image (by removing red-eye, for example), add creative effects to an image, or group images together to create montages. If you later decide to upgrade to the professional Adobe Photoshop CS3, you will already be familiar with the user interface.

DIGITAL AUDIO SOFTWARE

Why would I have digital audio files on my computer? Best-selling novels, newspapers, and radio shows all can be purchased as audio files from sellers such as Audible, Inc. (**www.audible.com**). There are also huge numbers of free sources of audio files through the phenomenon of podcasting, which is the distribution of audio files, such as radio shows or music videos over the Internet. These audio files are delivered to your machine free with the release of each edition with your subscription. You may also choose to digitize (or rip) your CD collection to store on your computer. So you may quickly have several gigabytes of audio files on your hard drive!

Why are MP3 files so popular? MP3 is a type of audio compression format that reduces the file size of traditional digital audio files so that more files will take up less storage capacity. For example, a typical CD stores between 10 and 15 songs in uncompressed format, but with files in MP3 format, the same CD can store between 100 and 180. The smaller file size not only lets you store and play music in less space, but also distributes it quickly and easily over the Internet. You can find hundreds of digital audio software applications that allow you to copy (or rip), play, edit, and organize MP3 files, as well as to record and distribute your own music online. Most digital audio software programs support one of the following functions, whereas others, such as iTunes, incorporate many of these capabilities into one multifunctional program:

- **MP3 recording:** Allows you to record directly from streaming audio and other software or microphone sources to MP3 format.

- **CD ripping:** Allows you to encode CDs to the MP3 format.

- **CD burning:** Allows you to create your own CDs from your MP3 collection.

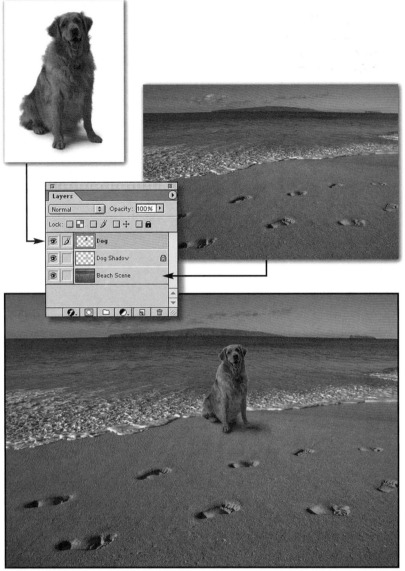

PayPal

With some image-editing software, you can take two individual pictures and combine them into one picture.

common image-editing tasks, such as taking out red-eye, and cropping and resizing pictures. These programs enable you to add creative effects such as borders and frames. Some include templates in which you can insert your favorite pictures into preformatted calendar pages or greeting cards. They may also have photo fantasy images that let you paste a face from your digital image onto the body of a professional athlete or other famous person.

If you want to use a program that offers you more than basic features but that is still easy to use, Adobe Photoshop Elements is a good starting point for the novice (see Figure 17). With this program, you can

- **Encoding and decoding/format conversion:** Encoders are programs that convert files to MP3 format at varying levels of quality. Most ripping software has encoders built in to convert the files directly into MP3 format. Decoding/format conversion programs allow you to convert MP3 files to other digital audio formats, such as WAV (short for WAVE form audio format), WMA (Windows Media Audio), or AIFF (Audio Interchange File Format).

Can I edit audio files? Audio editing software includes tools that make editing your audio files as easy as editing your text files. Software such as the open-source Audacity (**http://audacity.sourceforge.net**) or Sony Sound Forge (**www.sonymediasoftware.com**) enables you to perform basic editing tasks, such as cutting dead-air space from the beginning or end of the song or cutting a portion from the middle. You also can add special sound effects, such as echo or bass boost, or remove static or hiss from your MP3 files. Both of these applications support recording sound files from a microphone or any source you can connect through the input line of the sound card.

Image-editing software like Adobe Photoshop Elements enables you to easily create (a) calendars, (b) greeting cards and postcards, (c) slide shows, and (d) more from your digital photos.

DIGITAL VIDEO-EDITING SOFTWARE

What kind of software do I need to edit my digital videos? With the boom of digital camcorders and the improved graphics capabilities on home computers, many people are experimenting with **digital video-editing software**. Several video-editing software applications are available, at a wide range of prices and capabilities. Although the most expensive products (such as Adobe Premiere Pro 2.0) offer the widest range of special effects and tools, some moderately priced video-editing programs have enough features to keep the casual user happy. Microsoft Movie Maker and Apple iMovie HD have intuitive drag-and-drop features that make it simple to create professional-quality movies with little or no training (see Figure 18). If Microsoft Movie Maker meets your needs, you'll be happy to know you can download it for free from the Microsoft Web site. Other software developers offer free trial versions for you to try so that you can decide whether the product meets your needs before purchasing it.

Does video-editing software support all kinds of video files? Video files come in a number of formats. Many of the affordable video-editing software packages support only a few types of video files. For example, one application may support Windows Media Player video files, whereas another may support Apple QuickTime or RealPlayer video files instead. Fortunately, software boxes list which types of video files the software supports. You should buy the least expensive application with the greatest number of supported file formats.

SOUND BYTE

Enhancing Photos with Image-Editing Software

In this Sound Byte, you'll learn tips and tricks on how to best use image-editing software. You'll learn how to remove the red-eye from photos and incorporate borders, frames, and other enhancements to produce professional effects.

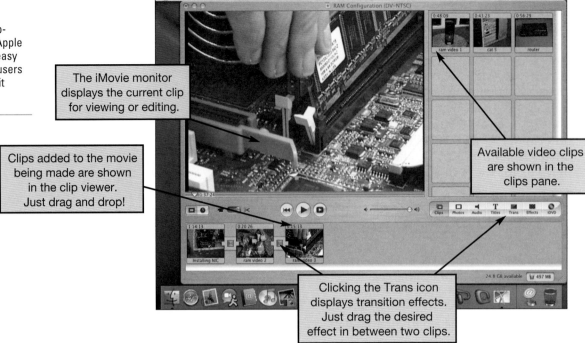

The iMovie monitor displays the current clip for viewing or editing.

Clips added to the movie being made are shown in the clip viewer. Just drag and drop!

Available video clips are shown in the clips pane.

Clicking the Trans icon displays transition effects. Just drag the desired effect in between two clips.

iStock Photo International

MEDIA MANAGEMENT SOFTWARE

How do I manage the audio, video, and image files on my system? Many people add hundreds or even thousands of files to their systems by purchasing music and downloading images and video. Your hard disk drive is a convenient place to store all your music and images, but only if you can find what you're looking for!

Software such as Windows Media Player, Nullsoft Winamp, or Apple iTunes allows you to organize audio and video files so that you can sort, filter, and search your music collection by artist, album, or category (see Figure 19). Using these programs, you can manage individual tracks, generate playlists, and even export the files to a database or spreadsheet application for further manipulation. Then you can burn the songs to a CD, and the program will print liner notes that you can place inside the CD case.

To organize your stored image files into albums, you can use programs such as ArcSoft PhotoStudio or Google's Picasa. With these programs, you can label and rate every shot, write a caption to describe each image, and add annotations to parts of the image. Picasa also helps you send the image to your friends, your mobile devices, or your blog! Picasa will automatically resize a huge 5-megapixel image to a more manage-

able size for e-mail, attach it to your outgoing message, and send it. It allows you to transfer images directly to your blog or to mobile devices, such as an iPod or PDA.

More Fun at Home

Entertainment software is, as its name implies, designed to provide users with thrills, chills, and all-out fun! Computer games make up the vast majority of entertainment software. These digital games began with Pong, Pac-Man, and Donkey Kong and have evolved to include many different categories, including action, driving, puzzle, role-playing, card-playing, sports, strategy, and simulation games. Entertainment software also includes other types of computer applications, such as **virtual reality programs**, which turn artificial environments into a realistic experience.

GAMING SOFTWARE

Do I need special equipment to run entertainment software? As with any computer software, you need to make sure your system has enough processing power, memory (RAM), and hard disk capacity to run the program. Because games often push the limit of sound and video quality, you

FIGURE 19

Software programs such as iTunes help you manage all the MP3 files on your computer. You can sort, filter, and search your collection by artist, album, or category, as well as create playlists.

Album covers flow by in a smooth display

Smart playlists can select a list of songs from library on specific criteria

Reprinted by permission of Apple Computer, Inc.

need to ensure your system has the appropriate sound cards, video cards, speakers, monitor, and CD or DVD drives as well.

Some software may require a special controller to play the game. In the gaming console world, games such as Steel Battalion and Guitar Hero actually are sold with their own specialized controllers (see Figure 20). These controllers can be adapted to your PC as well. Complex simulation programs can benefit from configurable, wireless controllers such as the Cyborg Evo (see Figure 20).

How do I tell what computer games are appropriate for a certain user? The **Entertainment Software Rating Board (ESRB)** is a self-regulatory body established in 1994 by the Entertainment Software Association (**www.esrb.org**). The ESRB rating system helps consumers choose the computer and video games that are right for their families by providing information about game content so that they can make informed purchase decisions. ESRB ratings have two parts: rating symbols suggest age appropriateness, and content descriptors indicate elements in a game that may have triggered a particular rating or may be of interest or concern. It's important to check both the rating symbol (on the front of the game box) and the content descriptors (on the back of the game box). The rating symbols currently in use by the Entertainment

Software Ratings Board (ESRB) are listed here:

- **EC (Early Childhood):** For ages 3 and older.
- **E (Everyone):** For ages 6 and older.
- **E 10+ (EVERYONE 10+):** For ages 10 and older.

Saitek Industries

FIGURE 20

Computer joysticks can be specialized. (a) This Saitek x52 is a fully integrated PC flight control system for flight simulation games. (b) The Cyborg EVO controller is wireless. Buttons can be programmed to map to specific game commands.

- **T (Teen):** For ages 13 and older.
- **M (Mature):** For persons ages 17 and older.
- **AO (Adults Only):** For adults.

Can I make video games? Now that video games represent an industry with revenue of more than 10 billion dollars each year, designing and creating video games is emerging as a desirable career opportunity. Professionally created video games involve artistic storytelling and design, as well as sophisticated programming. Major production houses, such as Electronic Arts, use software applications that are not easily available to the casual home enthusiast. However, you can use the editors and game engines available for games such as EverQuest, Oblivion, and Unreal Tournament to create custom levels and characters, and extend the game.

If you want to try your hand at creating your own video games, multimedia software applications such as Macromedia Flash (owned by Adobe Systems Incorporated) and RPG MAKER XP provide the tools you need to explore game design and creation. The program GameMaker (**www.gamemaker.nl**) is a free product that allows you to build a game with no programming at all, instead dragging and dropping key elements of the game into place. Alice (**www.alice.org**) is another free environment to check out. It lets you easily create 3-D animations and simple games and will soon have the actual Sims characters included!

EDUCATIONAL SOFTWARE

What kinds of educational software applications are there? Although a multitude of educational software products are geared toward the younger set, software developers have by no means ignored adult markets. In addition to all the products relating to the younger audience, there are software products that teach users new skills such as typing, languages, cooking, or playing the guitar. Test preparation software is popular for students taking the SAT, GMAT, LSAT, or MCAT exams.

Popular programs are also available to help students during lectures, organizing their notes and maintaining the notes and recordings they create from lectures. For example, Microsoft OneNote allows students with tablet PCs to write their notes directly onto the tablet, using it as an electronic notebook. Pieces of text can be easily moved around the page, Web links can be quickly integrated, and audio or video recordings of lectures can be added with one click. Students can search for a term across the full set of notebooks they have created during this term, helping to find connecting ideas from course to course.

What types of programs are available to train you to use software or special machines? Many programs provide tutorial-like training for popular computer software applications. These programs use illustrated step-by-step instructions to guide users through unfamiliar skills. Some training programs, known as simulation training programs, are used in a realistic environment, where the learning takes place. Such simulation training programs include commercial and military flight training, surgical instrument training, and machine operation training. Often these simulators can be delivered locally on CD/DVD or over the Internet.

One benefit of these simulated training programs is that they safely allow users to experience potentially dangerous situations, such as flying a helicopter during high winds. Consequently, users of these training programs are more likely to take risks and learn from their mistakes—something they could not afford to do in real-life situations. Simulated training programs also help to prevent costly errors. Should something go awry, the only cost of the error is restarting the simulation program.

Do I need special software to take courses online? As long as you have a compatible Web browser, online classes will be accessible to you. Depending on the content and course materials, however, you may need a password or special plug-ins to view certain videos or demos.

Taking classes over the Internet is rapidly becoming a popular method of learning because it offers greater schedule flexibility for busy students. Although some courses are run from an individually developed Web site, many online courses are run through **course management software** programs such as Blackboard, Moodle, and WebCT. These programs provide traditional classroom tools, such as calendars and grade books, over the Internet (see Figure 21). Special areas are available for students and

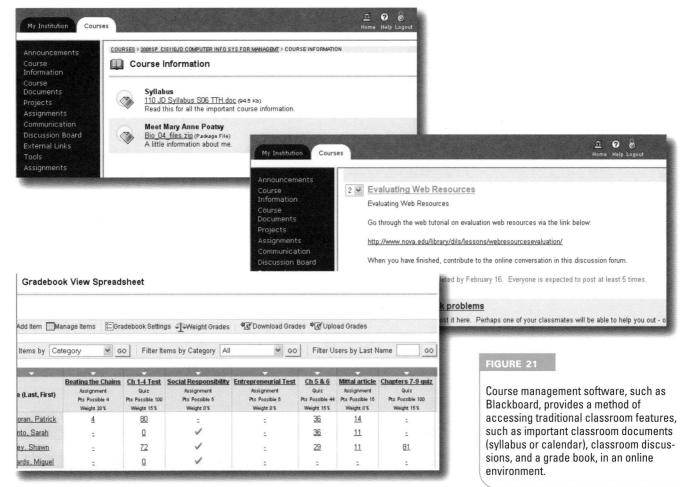

FIGURE 21

Course management software, such as Blackboard, provides a method of accessing traditional classroom features, such as important classroom documents (syllabus or calendar), classroom discussions, and a grade book, in an online environment.

professors to exchange ideas and information, including the use of chat rooms and discussion forums, and sending e-mail messages. Other areas are available for posting assignments, lectures, and other pertinent class information.

REFERENCE SOFTWARE

How can I use software to research information? Encyclopedias are no longer those massive sets of books in the library. Now you can find full sets of encyclopedias on CDs or DVDs. In addition to containing all the information found in traditional paper encyclopedias, electronic encyclopedias, a type of reference software, include multimedia content such as interactive maps, and video and audio clips. When researching famous sports figures, for example, you not only can read about Jackie Robinson, but you also can view a video of Robinson in play. World Book, Britannica, and Grolier all offer their encyclopedias on CD/DVD. Many traditional encyclopedias have online components, as well. Encarta, for example, can be found on the Web at **encarta.msn.com**.

What other types of reference software are available? As with all other categories of software, reference software is a growing field. In addition to the traditional atlases, dictionaries, and thesauri available on CD, many other types of reference software are available. The American Sign Language dictionary is available on DVD and includes video clips that show finger spelling and the modeling of each gesture. Medical and legal reference software is available for basic information you previously would have had to pay a professional to obtain. For example, medical references, such as Franklin Physicians' Desk Reference, enable you to access information on Food and Drug Administration (FDA)-approved drugs, whereas legal references, such as Family Lawyer, provide standard legal forms.

BITS AND BYTES

How to Open the Unknown

Normally, when you double-click a file icon on your desktop, the program that knows how to read the selected file is automatically run. For example, when you double-click a *.doc file, MS Word starts and displays the file. Sometimes, however, a pop-up appears with the message "Unknown File Type." Or a document may open with a program other than the one you wanted to open it with. To assign a program to a file type or to change the program opening that type of file, follow these instructions.

1. Click the Start button, and then click Search.
2. Use the search and navigation tools in this folder to locate the file you want to change (you can search for all .doc files by searching for *.doc). Right-click on a file of the correct type, and then, depending on the type of file, either click Open With or point to Open With, and then click Choose Default Program.
3. Click the program that you want to use to open this type of file. A list of programs installed on your computer will be provided.
4. Although you can choose to open individual files with a certain program, normally you would select the "Always use the selected program to open this kind of file" check box, and then click OK.
5. When you double-click that type of file in the future, the file will open in the program you selected.

DRAWING SOFTWARE

What kind of software should I use for simple illustrations? Drawing software (or **illustration software**) programs let you create or edit two-dimensional, line-based drawings. You use drawing software to create technical diagrams or original nonphotographic drawings, animations, and illustrations using standard drawing and painting tools such as pens, pencils, and paintbrushes. You also can drag geometric objects from a toolbar onto the canvas area to create images and use paint bucket, eyedropper, and spray can tools to add color and special effects to the drawings.

ACTIVE HELPDESK
Choosing Software

In this Active Helpdesk call, you'll play the role of a Helpdesk staffer, fielding calls about the different kinds of multimedia software, educational and reference software, and entertainment software.

Are there different types of drawing software? Drawing software is used in both creative and technical drawings. Software applications such as Adobe Illustrator include tools that let you create professional-quality creative and technical illustrations. The Illustrator tools help you to create complex designs, such as muscle structures in the human body, and use special effects, such as charcoal sketches. Its warping tool allows you to bend, stretch, and twist portions of your image or text. Because of its many tools and features, Illustrator is one of the preferred drawing software programs of most graphic artists.

Microsoft Visio is a program used to create technical drawings, maps, basic block diagrams, networking and engineering flowcharts, and project schedules. Visio uses project-related templates with special objects that you drag onto a canvas. For example, by using the Visio floor template and dragging furniture and other interior objects onto it, you can create an interior design like the one shown in Figure 22. Visio also provides mind-mapping templates that help you organize your thoughts and ideas.

Business Software

A number of software packages are designed to organize and help with the day-to-day operations of a typical business. If you ever begin to run a business from your own home, or even if you are just a user of large business products and services, it is helpful to know what functions business software can perform.

HOME BUSINESS SOFTWARE

With the amount of power available in a typical home computer, you have more opportunities than ever to run a business from your home. No matter what service or product you are providing, there are common types of software you'll want to consider. Accounting software will help manage the flow of money, and desktop publishing and Web page creation tools will help you market and grow your new enterprise.

What programs are good for people with small businesses? If you have a small business or a hobby that produces income, you know the importance of keeping good records and tracking your

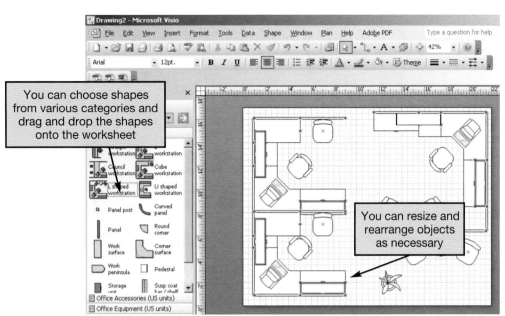

FIGURE 22

The drawing program Visio lets you create different types of diagrams easily with drag-and-drop options.

You can choose shapes from various categories and drag and drop the shapes onto the worksheet

You can resize and rearrange objects as necessary

Reprinted with permission from Microsoft Corporation

expenses and income. **Accounting software** helps small-business owners manage their finances more efficiently by providing tools for tracking accounts receivable and accounts payable. In addition, these applications also offer inventory management plus payroll and billing tools. Examples of accounting software applications include Intuit QuickBooks and Peachtree from Sage Accounting. Both programs include templates for invoices, statements, and financial reports so that small-business owners can create common forms and reports.

What software can I use to lay out and design newsletters and other publications? Desktop publishing (DTP) software allows you to incorporate and arrange graphics and text in your documents in creative ways. Although many word-processing applications allow you to use some of the features that are hallmarks of desktop publishing, specialized desktop publishing software, such as QuarkXPress and Adobe InDesign, allows professionals to design books and other publications with complex layouts (see Figure 23).

What tools do desktop publishing programs include? Desktop publishing programs offer a variety of tools with which you can format text and graphics. With text formatting tools, you easily can change the font, size, and style of your text, as well as arrange text on the page in different columns, shapes, and patterns. You also can import files into your docu-

ments from other sources, including elements from other software programs (such as a chart from Excel or text from Word), or image files. You can readily manipulate graphics with tools that can crop, flip, or rotate images or modify the image's color, shape, and size. Desktop publishing programs also include features that allow you to publish to the Web.

What software do I use to create a Web page? Web page authoring software allows even the novice to design

BITS AND BYTES

Need a Way to Share Files? Try PDF

Say you've created a file in Microsoft Excel, but the person to whom you want to send it doesn't have Excel, or any spreadsheet software, installed on his computer. Or say your sister owns a Mac and you own a PC. You constantly are running into file-sharing problems. What do you do in these situations? One solution is to create a PDF file. Portable Document Format (PDF) is a file format you can create with Adobe Acrobat. This program transforms any file, regardless of its application or platform, into a document that can be shared, viewed, and printed by anyone who has Adobe Reader. If you are using Microsoft Word 2007, OpenOffice Writer, or Corel WordPerfect, you can create PDF files easily. Adobe Reader, the program you need to read all PDF files, is a free download available at **www.adobe.com**.

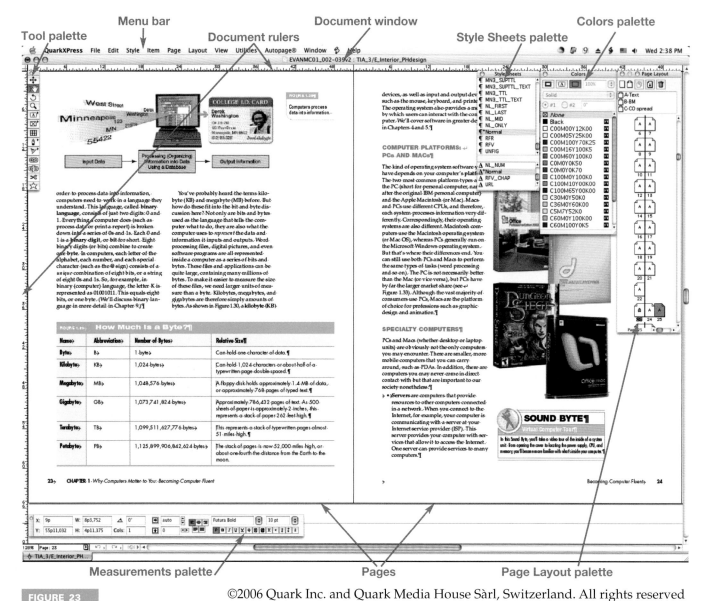

FIGURE 23

Major publishing houses use professional desktop publishing programs such as QuarkXPress to lay out the pages of textbooks.

interesting and interactive Web pages, without knowing any HyperText Markup Language (HTML) code. Web page authoring applications often include wizards, templates, and reference materials to help you easily complete most Web page authoring tasks. More experienced users can take advantage of the advanced features included in this software, including features that enable you to add headlines and weather information, stock tickers, and maps to make your Web content current, interactive, and interesting. Microsoft Office SharePoint Designer 2007 and Adobe Dreamweaver (formerly Macromedia

Dreamweaver) are two of the leading programs to which both professionals and casual Web page designers turn.

Are there other ways to create Web pages? If you need to produce only the occasional Web page and do not need a separate Web page authoring program, you'll find that many software applications include features that enable you to convert your document easily into a Web page. For example, in some Microsoft Office applications, you can choose to save the file as a Web page, and the application will automatically convert the file to a Web-compatible format.

Large-Business Software

What financial and business-related software do bigger businesses use?

As indicated earlier, some business software is task-specific and used across a variety of industries. This type of software includes programs such as Palo Alto Software's Business Plan Pro and Marketing Plan Pro, which help businesses write strategic and development plans.

Another good example of general business software is **project management software**, such as Microsoft Project. Such software helps project managers easily create and modify project management scheduling charts like the one shown in Figure 24. Charts like these help project managers plan and track specific project tasks, as well as coordinate personnel resources.

What other kinds of software do businesses often use?

Mapping programs such as DeLorme Street Atlas USA and Microsoft Streets & Trips are perfect for businesses that require employees to travel frequently. These programs provide street maps and written directions to locations nationwide, and you can customize the maps so that they include landmarks and other handy traveling sites such as airports, hotels, and restaurants.

These programs often are available in versions for PDAs and for cars and work in conjunction with a Global Positioning System (GPS) device to help you navigate your way around. Mapping programs are essential for sales representatives or delivery-intensive businesses but also are useful for nonprofessionals traveling to unfamiliar locations.

Businesses also use **customer relationship management (CRM) software** to store sales and client-contact information in one central database. Sales professionals use CRM programs to get in touch and follow up with their clients. These programs also include tools that enable businesses to assign quotas and to create reports and charts to document and analyze actual and projected sales data. CRM programs coordinate well with PIM software such as Outlook and can be set up to work with PDAs. GoldMine Corporate Edition from FrontRange Solutions is an example of a CRM program.

CRM software deals directly with the customer. Other software products, such as

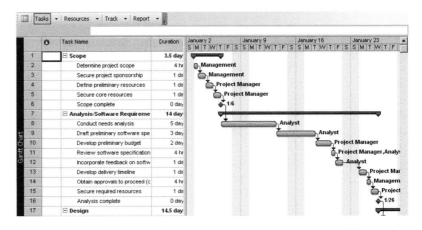

Reprinted with permission from Microsoft Corporation

FIGURE 24

A Gantt chart in Microsoft Project provides project managers with a visual tool for assigning personnel and scheduling and managing tasks.

Enterprise Resource Planning (ERP) systems, are used to control many "back-office" operations and processing functions such as billing, production, inventory management, and human resources management. ERP systems are implemented by third-party vendors and matched directly to the specific needs of a company.

SPECIALIZED BUSINESS SOFTWARE

What kinds of specialized business software are there?

Some software applications are tailored to the needs of a particular company or industry. Such software designed for a specific industry is called **vertical market software** . For example, the construction industry uses software such as Intuit Master Builder, which features estimating tools to help construction companies bid on jobs. It also integrates project management functions and accounting systems that are unique to the construction industry.

Other examples of vertical market software include property management software for real estate professionals; ambulance scheduling and dispatching software for emergency assistance organizations; and library automation software for cataloging, circulation, inventory, online catalog searching, and custom report printing at libraries.

In addition to these specific business software applications that companies can buy off the shelf, programs often are custom

Emerging Technologies: Is It Real or Is It Virtual?

Software can take us beyond what is familiar to alternate realities. Virtual reality uses software to allow people to interact with a simulated environment. The applications of virtual reality, beyond familiar video games, are almost endless. Three-dimensional environments created by computers are getting better and better at helping people experience new things, or experience familiar things in new ways (see Figure 25).

Overcoming fear is a growing application for virtual reality programs. Dentists, for instance, are trying virtual reality headsets for their patients to help reduce their anxiety about getting their teeth cared for. And fear of flying can be treated with virtual reality therapy. Gradual exposure to takeoff and landing in a virtual environment allows would-be travelers to face their phobias and prepare to take the next step into a real flight. Fears of heights, spiders, thunderstorms, and even public speaking (which is many people's greatest fear) have been treated with virtual reality therapy.

Virtual reality programs provide the opportunity for people with disabilities to practice maneuvering wheelchairs or to become familiar with public transportation before venturing into a new city or town. Surgeons can practice difficult procedures on a virtual patient without risk. And therapy for burn patients that incorporates

virtual reality seems to ease pain more when used with medication than medication alone. While being treated, patients wear virtual reality goggles and immerse themselves in a world apart from their pain. Psychologists say that patients are so absorbed in the virtual reality experience that they are not as aware of their pain.

You won't lose any weight or get in shape in a virtual gym. But you can get instant coaching feedback and see a replay of your performance. And you can do it without getting hurt, which is a big advantage for coaches in risky sports, such as football and skiing. Swiss Olympic skier Simon Ammann used a virtual reality program to compare his jumps wearing two different pairs of skis to determine which was best. He and his coach believe the change in skis that resulted from the experiment was a factor in his gold-medal performance at the 2002 Winter Olympics.

Of course, if you'd rather travel, you can always use the virtual reality program created at UCLA to explore the world of ancient Rome in A.D. 400, through simulations of 22 temples, courts, and monuments. The ancient cityscape is loaded into a supercomputer with a special spherical screen that fills the viewer's field of vision. Not only can you see the monuments, but you also can move around them and even levitate for a closer look. See you there!

VirtuSphere, Inc.

FIGURE 25

The VirtuSphere was developed by scientists at the University of Washington's Human Interface Technology Laboratory (HITLab). Virtual Reality training simulations are appearing in many different fields.

developed to address the specific needs of a particular company. These custom applications are referred to as **proprietary software** because they are owned and controlled by the company that uses them.

What software is used to make 3-D models? Computer-aided design (CAD) programs are a form of 3-D modeling that engineers use to create automated designs, technical drawings, and model visualizations. Specialized CAD software like Autodesk's AutoCAD is used in areas such as architecture, automotive, aerospace, and medical engineering.

With CAD software, architects can build virtual models of their plans and readily visualize all aspects of design prior to actual construction. Engineers use CAD software to design everything from factory components to bridges. The 3-D nature of these programs allows engineers to rotate their models and make adjustments to their designs where necessary, thus eliminating costly building errors.

CAD software also is being used in conjunction with GPS devices for accurate placement of fiber-optic networks around the country. The medical engineering community uses CAD to create anatomically accurate solid models of the human anatomy to develop medical implants quickly and accurately. The list of CAD applications keeps growing as more and more industries realize the benefits CAD can bring to their product development and manufacturing processes.

Many graphics, animation, video, and gaming systems use an application from AutoDesk, called 3D Studio Max, to create 3-D models with complex textures and lighting models. A 30-day free trial version of the software is available at **www.autodesk.com**. 3D Studio Max is a complex and rich program. A slightly simpler package is the open-source program Blender, available free of charge at **www.blender.org**.

Getting Help with Software

If you need help while you work with software, you can access several different resources to find answers to your questions. For general help or information about the product, many Web sites offer **frequently**

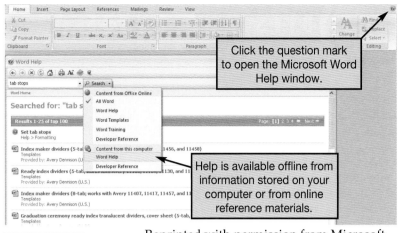

FIGURE 26

Reprinted with permission from Microsoft Corporation

Microsoft Office gives you tips on tasks you're working on or answers specific questions you have using online and offline resources.

asked questions (FAQs) for answers to the most common questions.

Some programs also offer online help and support. Sometimes online help is comparable to a user's manual. However, many times, online help also allows you to chat (using the Internet) with a member of an online support team. Some applications are context-sensitive and offer help based on what task you're doing or ScreenTips to explain where your cursor is resting.

In Microsoft Office applications, on the far, top right of the screen, you'll find a question mark icon. This takes you to the main Help interface. **Integrated help** means that the documentation for the product is built directly into the software so that you won't need to keep track of bulky manuals. You can type your question, search for a term, or browse the Help topics (see Figure 26). Like many software packages, Microsoft Office offers help documentation, which is installed locally on your machine, and online help resources, which are updated continually.

Finally, there is the Help menu on the menu bar of most applications. You can use help to choose to search an index or content outline to find out the nature of almost any feature of a Microsoft application.

Where do I go for tutorials and training on an application? If you need help learning how to use a product, sometimes the product's developer offers online tutorials or program tours that show you how to use the software features. Often, you

can find good tutorials simply by searching the Internet. **PCShowandTell.com**, for example, includes more than 40,000 multimedia help files and is accessible for a small annual fee. **Webnests.com**, an online company dedicated to online hosting products, offers free tutorials for many software applications.

Buying Software

These days, you no longer need to go to a computer supply store to buy software. You can find software in almost any retail environment. In addition, you can purchase software online, through catalogs, or at auctions.

PREINSTALLED SOFTWARE

What application software comes with my computer? Virtually every new computer comes with some form of application software, although the applications depend on the hardware manufacturer and computer model. You usually can count on your computer having some form of productivity software preinstalled, such as Microsoft Works or Corel WordPerfect Office.

Multimedia-enriched computers also may offer graphics software or a productivity suite that includes Web page authoring software. Many new computers also include some form of software that is useful to the home user, such as image-editing software or financial planning software.

If you know you'll need a particular type of software not offered as standard on your new computer, you may want to see if the computer manufacturer has a special offer that will allow you to add that particular software at a reduced price. Sometimes, initially buying software through the hardware manufacturer is less expensive than buying software on the retail market, but this is not always the case, so do some comparative pricing before you buy.

WEB-BASED APPLICATION SOFTWARE

Does all application software require installation on my computer? Most application software you acquire, whether by purchasing a CD or DVD at a retail store or by downloading the software from a Web site, requires the software to be installed on your computer prior to use. However, Web-based application software is growing in popularity. **Web-based application software** is a program hosted on a Web site and does not require a large installation on your computer. In some cases, a Web application will add nothing at all to your system; sometimes a small plug-in or control software module will be quickly downloaded.

Many Web sites offer no-charge Web-based applications, such as the mapping software Mapquest (**www.mapquest.com**) and Yahoo! Maps (**www.maps.yahoo.com**) that allow you to generate driving directions from point to point.

Other Web sites charge a fee to use their application software. TurboTax Online (**www.turbotax.com**) is a version of the popular tax-preparation software that you can access online to prepare your tax returns. Aside from saving the hassle of software installation on your computer, TurboTax Online also stores your information in a secure location so that you can retrieve it anytime.

More and more of your software needs might be met by some of the emerging Web-based providers. Sites like **zoho.com**, **ThinkFree.com**, and **docs.google.com** offer Web-based applications that cover a range of word-processing, presentation, project management, and spreadsheet needs. These products are run from software stored completely on the Web server instead of your hard drive. They are typically free of charge. They are a reflection of a movement toward a new software distribution model. Perhaps we will see the day that software is available online and rented for the period of time you need access to it.

The features of these programs are generally a subset of what the installed versions offer, but they do offer other advantages. Google Docs, for example, is a free application for word processing. You can invite people to share your files and work together in real time, watching as others make changes to the document. As long as you have a Web browser, you can access your files, which are stored securely online. Google also provides a spreadsheet application that provides many of the capabilities of Excel. While neither of these free applications is as full featured as the products from Microsoft, they each can read and export to many different file formats, and can be used together with other packages. The trend toward Web-based applications is interesting to watch.

DISCOUNTED SOFTWARE

Is it possible to buy software at a discount? Software manufacturers understand that students and educators often need to use software for a short period of time because of a specific class or project. In addition, software developers want to encourage you to learn with their product, hoping you'll become a long-term user of their software. Therefore, if you're a student or an educator, you can purchase software that is no different from regularly priced software at prices that are sometimes substantially less than general consumer prices. (Figure 11 shows what applications are included in the academic versions of productivity software suites.)

Sometimes, campus computer stores or college bookstores also offer discounted prices to students and faculty who possess a valid ID. Online software suppliers such as Journey Education Marketing (**www.journeyed.com**), CampusTech, Inc. (**www.campustech.com**), and Academic Superstore (**www.academicsuperstore.com**)

also offer the same software applications available in the store to students at reduced prices. You also can find software through mail-order companies. Check out Google Catalogs (**http://catalogs.google.com**) for an extensive listing of companies that offer software by mail order.

Can I buy used software? Often, you can buy software through online auction sites such as eBay. If you do so, you need to ensure that you are buying licensed (legal) copies. Computer shows that display state-of-the-art computer equipment are generally good sources for software. However, here, too, you must exert a bit of caution to make sure you are buying licensed copies and not pirated versions.

Can I buy software directly from the Internet? As with many other retail products, you can buy and download software applications directly from many developers and retail store Web sites. You also can use the Internet to buy software that is custom developed to your specific needs. Companies such as Ascentix Corporation (**www.ascentix.com**) act as intermediaries between you (the software user) and a software developer. With custom-developed software, the developer tweaks open-source software code to meet your particular needs.

Microsoft .NET program (**www.microsoft. com/net**) offers software over the Internet for all devices—not just computers—that have a connection to the Internet. Therefore, you can download software specifically for your PDA or wireless phone by using .NET. In addition, if you have a Microsoft .NET account (available free of charge at the Microsoft Web site), you can connect to any other .NET-connected device.

FREEWARE AND SHAREWARE

Can I get software for free legally? **Freeware** is any copyrighted software that you can use for free. Plenty of freeware exists on the Web, ranging from games and screen savers to business, educational, graphics, home and hobby, and system utility software programs. To find free software, type freeware in your search engine. One good source of freeware offering a large variety of programs is Freeware Home (**www.freewarehome.com**).

Although they do not charge a fee, some developers release free software and request that you mail them a postcard or send them an e-mail message to thank them for their time in developing the software and to give them your opinion of it. Such programs are called postcardware and e-mailware, respectively.

Another option is to search for an open-source program to fit your needs. Open-source programs are free to use on the condition that any changes you make to improve the source code also must be distributed for free. SourceForge.net (**http://sourceforge.net**) is an excellent site to begin your hunt for a group that may already have built a solution that will work for you!

Can I try out new software before it is really released? Some software developers offer **beta versions** of their software free of charge. Beta versions are software applications that are still under development. By distributing free beta versions, developers hope users will report errors or bugs they find in the program. This helps the developers correct any errors before they launch the software on the market at retail prices.

Is it still freeware if I'm asked to pay for the program after using it for a while? One model for distributing software is to allow users to test software first (run it for a limited time, free of charge). Large corporations do this by offering free trial software products. These are fully functional packages, but they expire if not purchased within a certain timeframe. Small software developers also use this kind of distribution. This is

referred to as **shareware**. Shareware software is distributed freely, but with certain conditions. Sometimes the software is released on a trial basis only and must be registered after a certain period of time; in other cases, no support is available unless the software is registered. In some cases, direct payment to the author is required. Shareware is not freeware. If you use the software after the initial trial period is over, you will be breaking the software license agreement.

Software developers put out shareware programs to get their products into users' hands without the added expense and hassle of marketing and advertising. Therefore, quite a few great programs are available as shareware, and they can compete handily with programs on retail shelves. For example, TechSmith Corporation (**www.techsmith.com**) offers screen capture and desktop recording software applications, such as SnagIt Screen Capture and Sharing and Camtasia Studio Screen Recording and Presentation, as shareware. You can try these products for free for a 30-day period, after which you must purchase the software to continue using it. For a listing of other shareware programs, visit the CNET Download.com (**www.download.com**), as shown in Figure 27, or the CNET Shareware.com (**www.shareware.com**) Web sites.

Can shareware programmers make me pay for the shareware once I have it? The whole concept of shareware assumes that users will behave ethically and abide by the license agreement. However, to protect themselves, many developers have incorporated code

FIGURE 27

Download.com is a useful site for finding freeware applications. The site provides product reviews, hardware requirements, and details of the limitations of the free version of the software.

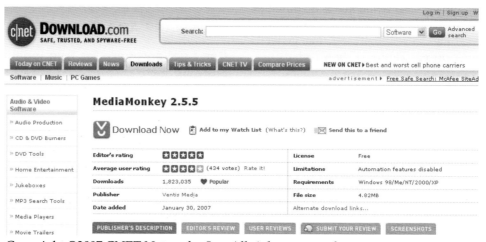

Application Software: Programs That Let You Work and Play

into the program to stop it from working completely, or to alter the output slightly, after the trial period expires.

Are there risks associated with installing or downloading from the Internet beta versions, freeware, and shareware? Not all files available as shareware and freeware will work on your computer. You easily can crash your system and may even need to reinstall your operating system as a result of loading a freeware or shareware program that was not written for your computer's operating system.

Of course, by their very nature, beta products are most likely not bug-free, so you always run the risk of something going awry with your system. Unless you're willing to deal with potential problems, it may be best to wait until the last beta version is released. By that time, most of the serious bugs have been worked out.

As a matter of precaution, you should be comfortable with the reliability of the software developer before downloading a freeware, shareware, or beta version of software. If it's a reliable developer whose software you are already familiar with, you can be more certain that a serious bug or virus is not hiding in the software. However, downloading software from an unknown source could potentially put your system at risk for contracting a virus.

A good practice to establish before installing any software on your system is to use the Windows Vista operating system's Restore feature and create a *restore point*. That way, if anything goes wrong during installation, you can restore your system back to how it was before you started. Also, make sure that your virus protection software is up-to-date.

SOFTWARE VERSIONS AND SYSTEMS REQUIREMENTS

What do the numbers after software names indicate? Software developers change their software programs to repair problems (or bugs) or to add new or upgraded features. Generally, they keep the software program's name but add a number to it to indicate that it is a different version. Originally, developers used num-

BITS AND BYTES

Keeping Your Software Up-to-Date

Bugs in software occur all the time. Software developers are constantly testing their product, even after releasing the software to the retail market, and users report errors they find. In today's environment where security is a large concern, companies test their products for vulnerabilities against hackers and other malicious users. Once a fix or patch to a bug or vulnerability is created, most software developers will put the repair in downloadable form on the Internet, available at no charge. You should check periodically for any software updates or service packs to ensure your software is up-to-date. For your convenience, many products have an automatic update feature that downloads and installs updates automatically.

bers only to indicate different software versions (major upgrades) and releases (minor upgrades). Today, however, software developers also use years (such as Microsoft Office 2007) and letters (such as WordPerfect Office X3) to represent version upgrades.

When is it worth it to buy a newer version? Although software developers suggest otherwise, there is no need to rush out and buy the latest version of a software program every time one is released. Depending on the software, some upgrades are not significantly different from the previous version to make it cost-effective for you to buy the newest version. Unless the upgrade adds features that are important to you, you may be better off waiting to upgrade every other release. You also should consider how frequently you use the software to justify an upgrade and whether your current system can handle the new system requirements of the upgraded version.

If I have an older version of software and someone sends me files from a newer version, can I still open them? Software vendors recognize that people work on different versions of the same software. Vendors therefore make the newest version *backward compatible*, meaning the newest software can recognize (open) files created with older versions. However, many software programs are not *forward compatible*, meaning that older versions cannot recognize files created on newer versions.

How do I know whether the software I buy will work on my computer? Every software program has a set of **system requirements** that specify the minimum recommended standards for the operating system, processor, primary memory (RAM), and hard drive capacity. Sometimes there are other specifications for the video card, monitor, CD drive, and other peripherals. These requirements generally are printed on the software packaging or are available at the publisher's Web site. Before installing software on your computer, ensure your system setup meets the minimum requirements by having sufficient storage, memory capacity, and processing capabilities.

Installing/Uninstalling and Opening Software

Before you use your software, you must permanently place it, or install it, on your system. The installation process is slightly different depending on whether you've purchased the software from a retail outlet and have an installation CD or whether you are downloading it from the Internet. Deleting, or uninstalling, software from your system requires certain precautions to ensure you remove all associated programs from your system.

How do I install software? When you purchase software, the program files may come on a CD. For most programs being installed on a PC, an installation wizard automatically opens when you insert the CD, as shown in Figure 28. By following the steps indicated by the wizard, you can install the software application on your system. If for some reason the wizard doesn't open automatically, the best way to install the software is to go to the Programs and Features icon located in the Control Panel on the Start menu. This feature locates and launches the installation wizard.

How is the installation process different for software I download off the Web? When you download software from the Internet, you do not get an installation CD. Instead, everything you need to install and run the downloaded program is contained in one file that has been compressed (or *zipped*) to make the downloading process quicker. For the most part, these downloaded files unzip, or decompress, themselves and automatically start, or *launch*, the setup program. During the installation and setup process, these programs select or create the folder on your computer's hard drive in which most of the program files will be saved. Usually, you also can select a different location if you desire. Either way, note the name and location of the files, because you may need to access them later.

What do I do if the downloaded program doesn't install by itself? Some programs you download do not automatically install and run on your computer. Although the compressed files

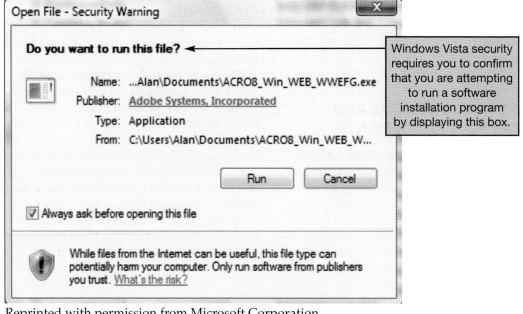

Installation wizards guide you through the installation process and generally appear automatically when you install new software.

Windows Vista security requires you to confirm that you are attempting to run a software installation program by displaying this box.

Reprinted with permission from Microsoft Corporation

Application Software: Programs That Let You Work and Play

Ethics: Can I Borrow Software That I Don't Own?

Most people don't understand that, unlike other items they purchase, software applications they buy don't belong to them. The only thing they're actually purchasing is a license that gives them the right to use the software for their own purposes as the *only* user of that copy. The application is not theirs to lend or copy for installation on other computers, even if it's another one of their own.

Software licenses are agreements between you, the user, and the software developer. You accept this agreement prior to installing the software on your machine. It is a legal contract that outlines the acceptable uses of the program and any actions that violate the agreement. Generally, the agreement will state who the ultimate owner of the software is, under what circumstances copies of the software can be made, or whether the software can be installed on any other machine. Finally, the license agreements will state what, if any, warranty comes with the software.

A computer user who copies an application onto more than one computer, if the license agreement does not permit this, is participating in **software piracy**. Historically, the most common way software has been pirated among computer users has been when they supplement each other's software library by borrowing CDs and installing the borrowed software on their own computers. Larger-scale illegal duplication and distribution by counterfeiters also is quite common. The Internet also provides a means of illegally copying and distributing pirated software.

Is it really a big deal to copy a program or two? As reported by the Business Software Alliance, 40 percent of all software is pirated. Not only is pirating software unethical and illegal, the practice also has financial impacts on all software application consumers. The reduced dollars from pirated software lessen the amount of money available for further software research and development while increasing the up-front cost to legitimate consumers.

To determine whether you have a pirated copy of software installed on your computer at work or at home, you can download a free copy of GASP (a suite of programs designed to help identify and track licensed and unlicensed software and other files) from the Business Software Alliance Web site (**www.bsa.org/usa**). There is a similar program available at the Microsoft Web site (**www.microsoft.com/piracy**). These programs check the serial numbers for the software installed on your computer against software manufacturer databases of official licensed copies and known fraudulent copies. Any suspicious software installations are flagged for your attention.

As of yet, there's no such thing as an official software police, but software piracy is so rampant that the U.S. government is taking steps to stop piracy worldwide. Efforts to stop groups that reproduce, modify, and distribute counterfeit software over the Internet are in full force. Software manufacturers also are becoming more aggressive in programming mechanisms into software to prevent repeated installations. For instance, with many Microsoft products, installation requires the activation of the serial number of your software with a database maintained at Microsoft. This is different from the traditional "registration," which enrolled you voluntarily and allowed you to be notified of product updates, for example. Activation is required, and failure to activate your serial number or attempting to activate a serial number that has been used previously results in the software going into a "reduced functionality mode" after the 50th time you use it. So without activation, you would not be able to save documents in Office—a strong motivator to let Microsoft watch how many times you install the software you purchased!

may unzip automatically as part of the download process, the setup program may not run without some help from you. In this case, you need to locate the files on the hard drive (this is why you must remember the location of the files) and find the program that is controlling the installation (sometimes named setup.exe or install.exe). Files ending with the .exe extension are executable files, or applications. All other files in the folder are support, help, and data files. Once the setup program begins, you will be prompted with the necessary actions to complete the installation.

What's the difference between a custom installation and a full installation? One of the first steps in the installation wizard is deciding between a full installation and a custom installation. A **full installation** will copy all the files and pro-

grams from the distribution CD to the computer's hard drive. By selecting **custom installation**, you can decide which features you want installed on the hard drive. Installing only the features you know you want allows you to save space on your hard drive.

Can I just delete a program to uninstall it? A software application contains many different files, such as library files, help files, and other text files, in addition to the main file you use to run the program. By deleting only the main file, or simply deleting the icon on your desktop, you are not ridding your system of all the pieces of the program. In addition, some applications make changes to a variety of settings, and none of these are restored if you just delete the desktop icon or remove the main file.

Reprinted with permission from Microsoft Corporation

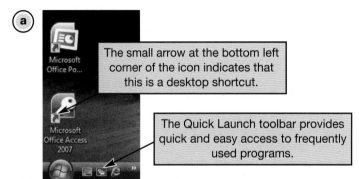

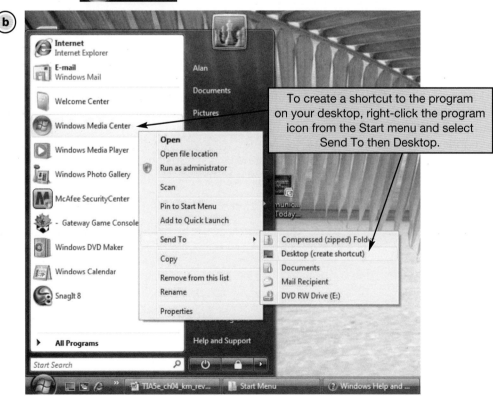

FIGURE 29

To quickly access an application you use often, you can place a shortcut in (a) the Quick Launch toolbar or (b) on your desktop.

Application Software: Programs That Let You Work and Play

Sometimes, programs have an Uninstall Program icon in the main program folder on the Start menu. Using this icon will run the proper cleanup to clear out all of the files associated with the application as well as restore any settings that have been changed. If you can't locate the uninstall program for your particular software application, click the Start menu, click Control Panel, and then click Programs and Features. This will give you a list of software applications installed on your system, from which you choose the software application you would like to uninstall.

Is there a best way to open an application? The simplest way to open an application is by clicking its icon in the All Programs list found on the Start menu. Every program that you install on your system is listed on the Start menu. However, if you find you use only a few programs most often, you can place a shortcut to that program either on the Quick Launch toolbar on the taskbar or on your desktop. To place a program in the Quick Launch toolbar on the taskbar, right-

ACTIVE HELPDESK

Buying and Installing Software

In this Active Helpdesk call, you'll play the role of a Helpdesk staffer, fielding calls about how to best purchase software or get it for free, how to install and uninstall software, and where you can go for help when you have a problem with your software.

click the program icon on your desktop or right-click the program name on the Start menu. From the shortcut menu that is displayed, select Add to Quick Launch to place an icon for this program on the Quick Launch toolbar (see Figure 29a).

To create a shortcut on the desktop, right-click the icon of the desired program and click Send To, and then select Desktop (see Figure 29b). This places the shortcut icon directly on the Desktop. You can identify a shortcut icon by the little black arrow in the lower-left corner of the icon, as shown in Figure 29a.

Summary

1. What's the difference between application software and system software?

System software is the software that helps run the computer and coordinates instructions between application software and the computer's hardware devices. System software includes the operating system and utility programs. Application software is the software you use to do everyday tasks at home, school, and work. Application software is productivity software, such as word-processing and finance programs; media software, such as those used for image editing; home/entertainment, such as games or educational programs; and business software.

2. What kinds of applications are included in productivity software I might use at home?

Productivity software programs include word-processing, spreadsheet, presentation, personal information manager (PIM), and database programs. You use word-processing software to create and edit written documents. Spreadsheet software enables you to do calculations and numerical and what-if analyses easily. Presentation software enables you to create slide presentations. Personal information manager (PIM) software helps keep you organized by putting a calendar, address book, notepad, and to-do lists within your computer. Database programs are electronic filing systems that allow you to filter, sort, and retrieve data easily. Individuals can also use software to help with business-like tasks such as preparing taxes or managing personal finances.

3. What are the different types of multimedia software?

Multimedia software includes digital image, video- and audio-editing software, animation software, and other specialty software required to produce computer games. A wide variety of software programs is used to play, copy, record, edit, and organize MP3 files. Modern users have so many audio, video, and image files that there are a number of software solutions for organizing and distributing these types of files.

4. What are the different types of entertainment software?

Beyond the games that most of us are familiar with, entertainment software includes virtual reality programs that use special equipment to make users feel as though they are actually experiencing the program in a realistic 3-D environment.

5. What is reference software?

Software applications that act as sources for reference materials, such as the standard atlases, dictionaries, and thesauri, are referred to collectively as reference software. A lot of reference software on the market incorporates complex multimedia.

6. What are the different types of drawing software?

Drawing software lets you create and edit line-based drawings to produce both imaginative and technical illustrations. Floor plans, animations, and mind-maps are some of the types of images that can be created.

7. What kinds of software do small and large businesses use?

Many businesses, including home businesses, use general business software, such as Business Plan Pro and Marketing Plan Pro, to help them with tasks common to most businesses. In addition, businesses may use specialized business software (or vertical market software) that is designed for their specific industry.

8. Where can I go for help when I have a problem with my software?

Most software programs have a Help menu built into the program with which you can search through an index or subject directory to find answers. Some programs group those most commonly asked questions in a single frequently asked questions (FAQ) document. In addition, vast resources of free or fee-based help and training are available on the Internet or at booksellers.

9. How can I purchase software or get it for free?

Almost every new computer system comes with some form of software to help you accomplish basic tasks. All other software you need to purchase unless it is freeware or open-source code, which you can download from the Internet for free. You can also find special software called shareware that lets you run it free of charge for a test period. Although you can find software in almost any store, as a student you can purchase the same software at a reduced price with an academic discount.

10. How do I install, uninstall, and open software?

When installing and uninstalling software, it's best to use the specific Add/Remove Program feature that comes with the operating system. Most programs are installed using an installation wizard that steps you through the installation. Other software programs may require you to activate the setup program, which will begin the installation wizard. Using the Add/Remove Programs feature when uninstalling a program will help you ensure that all ancillary program files are removed from your computer.

accounting software

application software

audio editing software

beta version

computer-aided design (CAD)

course management software

custom installation

customer relationship management (CRM) software

database software

desktop publishing (DTP) software

digital video-editing software

drawing software (illustration software)

Enterprise Resource Planning (ERP) system

entertainment software

Entertainment Software Rating Board (ESRB)

financial planning software

freeware

frequently asked questions (FAQ)

full installation

image-editing software (photo-editing software)

integrated help

integrated software application

macros

mapping program

multimedia software

open-source software

personal information manager (PIM) software

presentation software

productivity software

program

project management software

proprietary software

shareware

software

software licenses

software piracy

software suite

speech-recognition software (voice-recognition software)

spreadsheet software

system requirements

system software

tax-preparation software

template

vertical market software

virtual reality program

Web-based application software

Web page authoring software

wizards

word-processing software

Buzz Words

Word Bank

- application software
- beta version
- freeware
- illustration software
- image-editing software
- integrated help

- integrated software
- productivity software
- shareware
- software piracy
- software suite
- speech-recognition software

- spreadsheet
- system requirements
- system software
- templates
- wizards
- word processing

Instructions: Fill in the blanks using the words from the Word Bank above.

Roxanne is so psyched! Her aunt is upgrading to a newer computer and is giving Roxanne her old one. Roxanne has just enrolled in college and knows she's going to need at least a(n) (1) _____ program to help her write papers and a(n) (2) _____ program to help her keep track of expenses while at school. Because both of these software applications are part of a larger group of applications called (3) _____ , she knows she can buy them as a group. She's been told that it's cheaper to buy them as a(n) (4) _____ than to buy them individually. Because she knows she'll need the stable, tested versions of the software, she cannot get by using a(n) (5) _____ of the program.

Because she's not a great typist, Roxanne is interested in (6) _____ that will convert her dictated words into typed text. As a graduation present, Roxanne received a new digital camera. She needs to install the (7) _____ that came with her camera to edit and manage her digital pictures. Although she's used the software a couple of times on her parents' computer, she is still glad for the (8) _____ feature to assist her with specific feature questions and the (9) _____ that provide step-by-step guides to help her do things.

Roxanne especially likes the decorative preformatted (10) _____ she can use to insert pictures and make them seem professional. She also knows of some (11) _____ games she can download without cost from the Internet and other (12) _____ programs that she could try but eventually pay for. There are some really useful utility programs she found under the category of (13) _____ programs that she can download for no charge and would like to install and try out. It's tempting for her to borrow software from her friends, but she knows that it's considered (14) _____ . She also knows that before installing any of the programs she must check the (15) _____ to determine if the software is compatible with her system as well as whether the system has enough resources to support the software.

Becoming Computer Literate

Using key terms from this chapter, write a letter to one of your friends or relatives about which software applications he or she may need to work more productively. Also include which software application(s) that individual may need to modify, review, and store the pictures taken with a digital camera he or she just purchased.

Self-Test

MULTIPLE CHOICE

Instructions: Answer the multiple-choice and true/false questions below for more practice with key terms and concepts from this chapter.

1. Application software
   a. is another name for system software.
   b. helps maintain the resources of the computer.
   c. includes products like MS Office, tax software, and video editing packages.
   d. Both A and C.

2. Which of the following is an example of a software suite?
   a. Microsoft SharePoint
   b. Google Docs
   c. WordPerfect Office X3
   d. None of the above is an example.

3. A Web-based software program is a(n)
   a. stand-alone program developed to work exclusively for one company.
   b. application designed specifically for a Web-based business or industry.
   c. program that helps you design Web pages.
   d. application that does not need to be installed but is run directly from the Web.

4. Productivity software suites are often
   a. sold as individual programs only.
   b. meant only for business purposes.
   c. sold in specific collections, which reduces the price.
   d. not available in open source format.

5. The type of software you would use to help you with coordinating many people on a single project is
   a. database.   c. project management.
   b. spreadsheet.   d. system.

6. What software is the best for creating a newsletter?
   a. Word-processing software
   b. Desktop publishing software
   c. Computer-aided design software
   d. Media management software

7. ESRB is responsible for providing
   a. licensing of entertainment software.
   b. educational software standards.
   c. ratings for game software.
   d. resolution of complaints about software products.

8. Which of the following is true?
   a. MP3 files contain audio data.
   b. MP3 files are the only recognized format for digital audio.
   c. Windows Media player is able to organize large collections of audio files.
   d. Only A and C are true.

9. A good practice before installing any software on your system is to
   a. check the hard drive to make sure there is space for the new program.
   b. create a restore point, if you are using Windows Vista.
   c. read the documentation that came with the program.
   d. All of the above are good practices.

10. Once you install a shareware software program, you can
   a. install it on only one computer.
   b. install it on all computers in your home.
   c. lend it to your friends as long as they are using it for academic purposes only.
   d. use the software legally until the trial period expires.

TRUE/FALSE

____ 1. Microsoft SharePoint is a bundled package of word-processing, spreadsheet, database, and presentation software applications.

____ 2. Open-source software such as Audacity is used to organize video files.

____ 3. The best way to delete a program from your system is to delete the shortcut on the desktop.

____ 4. Freeware software is a form of open-source software.

____ 5. Web-application software runs from any computer without any installation from CD.

Application Software: Programs That Let You Work and Play

Making the Transition to...
Next Semester

1. Installing Software

You have just spent $285 on a software package. You have a desktop computer that you use at home and a notebook that you use only at work.

a. Are you allowed to install the software on both computers? Should you be allowed to do that?

b. What if you wanted to install the software on two computers that you own and use exclusively at home?

c. Can you install the software on two computers if you use only one computer at a time?

d. Are you allowed to install the software package on your computer and also on a friend's computer if she is interested in buying her own copy but wanted to test it first?

2. Software Training

You are most likely familiar with many software applications. Undoubtedly, you will use many more applications before your course work is done. Make two lists. In one list, itemize by category the software applications you are already familiar with. In the other list, identify at least three other software applications you think you may need, or would want to try, in the future. Research the types of on-campus or online training or help features that may be offered for those programs you have on your second list.

3. Upgrading Software

You are trying to decide whether you want to upgrade some software that you used this past semester. How do the following items weigh into your decision to upgrade the software or not?

a. The cost of the upgrade

b. The length of time the upgrade has been available

c. Hardware requirements

d. Features of the upgrade versus the stability of your current system

4. Choices, Choices

You have many options of software available for doing word processing. Describe the decision process you would use to select between a free Web-based word-processing application, an open source word-processing application, and a standard packaged software application if you are:

a. Traveling abroad for a semester, visiting 15 different cities, and will not be carrying a notebook with you.

b. Staying at home for the term and compiling a capstone report using several hundred researched sources of information.

c. Working with three people from other colleges on a joint paper that will be presented at a conference at the end of the term.

5. Choosing the Best Software

This past semester you spent a lot of time doodling and created a comic strip character that all your friends love. You've decided to start releasing a small newsletter, including some articles and a few comics each week. Which software applications would be the best fit for the following tasks:

a. Designing and laying out the newsletter

b. Creating the text articles

c. Creating the comic strip

After the first five issues, it is clearly a smash. You decide to expand it into a zine, an Internet-delivered magazine. Now which software applications are important to you for the same tasks?

Making the Transition to... the Workplace

1. **Surveying the Competition**

   You are asked to develop a departmental report that analyzes the key competitors in your market. You will need to:

   a. Identify the major competitors in your market.
   b. Gather information on their companies, their sales, and the features of their products.
   c. Organize your data so it can be easily sorted and filtered.
   d. Analyze the trends in the marketplace and predict future direction of growth.
   e. Create a final report and presentation to deliver to the department heads.

   Identify what software products you would use to complete each of these tasks. How would you use them, and how would they work together to support your efforts.

2. **Integrating Applications**

   Some software applications work well together and some do not. Certainly, all of the applications within a given suite such as Microsoft Office are well integrated. Give an example of a business office need that would benefit from the following:

   a. Integrating Excel with Word
   b. Integrating Access with Excel
   c. Integrating Access with Word

3. **Choosing the Best Software for the Job**

   For each of the following positions, describe the set of software applications you would expect to encounter if you were:

   a. A photographer opening a new business to sell your own photography
   b. An administrative assistant to a college president
   c. A graphic designer at a large publishing house
   d. A director in charge of publicity for a new summer camp for children
   e. A presenter to elementary students discussing your year living abroad
   f. A Web page designer for a small not-for-profit organization
   g. A construction site manager
   h. A person in the career you are pursuing

4. **The Right Productivity Suite**

   You are asked to research the cost and use of productivity software for your small company. Right now, the company has been using Microsoft Works, but the need to expand to a full-fledged productivity suite is evident. Research the major productivity suites on the market. Look at cost, the ability to exchange files between customers and other employees easily (for example, does file type make a difference?), and the various features within each version of software. Explore the major developers' products as outlined in Figure 1 as well as the open-source option OpenOffice and a set of Web-based packages. Which productivity suite would you recommend? Be specific in your recommendation.

Critical Thinking Questions

Instructions: Albert Einstein used "Gedanken experiments," or critical thinking questions, to develop his theory of relativity. Some ideas are best understood by experimenting with them in our own minds. The following critical thinking questions are designed to demand your full attention but require only a comfortable chair—no technology.

1. **Software Ethics 1**

   The cost of new software applications can be prohibitively high. You need to do a project for school that requires the use of a software application you don't own, but your roommate has a copy that her dad gave her from his work. She is letting you install it on your machine.

   a. Is it okay for you to borrow this software?
   b. Would it be okay if you uninstalled the application after you were finished using it?
   c. Would it be okay if the software was on the school's network and you could copy it from there?

2. **Software Ethics 2**

   Currently, there is no true system to check for illegal installations of software programs. What kind of program or system do you think could be developed to do this type of checking? Who would pay to develop, run, and maintain the program: the developers or the software users?

3. **Media Management**

   Less than a decade ago, home users had no media files on their computer systems. Today, many users have a library of music, a collection of digitized movies, personal photo collections, and even a large set of recorded television shows. Examine three different software packages on the market today for managing these materials. What features do they need to make the PC the primary entertainment device for a home? What would make users move their PC from the office into the living room?

4. **Software and Microcredit**

   The 2006 Nobel Peace Prize was awarded to Muhammad Yunus, who created the Grameen Bank. This bank makes very small loans to the poor of Bangladesh, without requiring collateral. Often these loans are less than $200 but allow women to begin small businesses and climb out of poverty. How has software made the Grameen Bank productive and able to serve almost 7 million borrowers? What other ways could software make a difference to the struggling peoples of the world?

5. **Software for the Hearing and Visually Impaired**

   The World Wide Web Consortium (W3C) currently has an initiative to ensure that all Web pages are accessible to everyone, including those with visual and hearing impairments. Currently, software such as the freeware program Watchfire WebXACT (**http://webxact.watchfire.com**) can test Web pages to determine whether alternatives to auditory and visual Web content are available, such as closed captioning for auditory files and auditory files for visual content. WebXACT generates a report that identifies and prioritizes Web site areas that do not meet the guidelines.

   a. Can you think of any other unique uses of software that might make the world a better place for those with visual and hearing impairments?
   b. Pick a favorite Web site and see how it checks out using the WebXACT software. What changes would be necessary for that Web site to conform to W3C standards?
   c. How might recommendations made by the W3C also benefit people without physical limitations?

Problem:

Gizmos, Inc. is a start-up company in the business of designing, building, and selling the latest gizmos. You have been hired as director of information systems. As such, one of your responsibilities is to ensure that all necessary software applications are purchased and installed on the company's server.

Task:

Split your class into as many groups of four or five as possible. Each group is to perform the same activity and present and compare results with each other at the end of the project.

Process:

1. Identify a team leader who will coordinate the project and record and present results.

2. Each team is to identify the various kinds of software that Gizmos, Inc. needs. Ensure that all activities and departments of the company have software to meet their needs. Consider software employees will need for a number of tasks: software they can use to design the gizmos, productivity software they may need, and software the sales reps will need to help keep track of their clients. Also consider software that human resources personnel can use to keep track of employee data and that software product managers can use to track projects. In addition, think of other software that might be useful to Gizmos, Inc.

3. Create a detailed and organized list of required software applications. If possible, include licensing fees, assuming the company has 50 users.

Conclusion:

Software applications help us do the simplest and most complex tasks every day. It's important to understand how dependent we are becoming on computers and technology. Compare your results with those of other team members. Were there software applications that you didn't think about that other members did? How expensive is it to ensure that even the smallest company has all the software required to carry out daily activities?

Multimedia

In addition to the review materials presented here, you'll find additional materials featured with the book's multimedia, including the *Technology in Action* Student Resource CD and the Companion Web site (**www.prenhall.com/techinaction**), which will help reinforce your understanding of the chapter content. These materials include the following:

ACTIVE HELPDESK

In Active Helpdesk calls, you'll assume the role of Helpdesk operator, taking calls about the concepts you've learned in this chapter. You'll apply what you've learned and receive feedback from a supervisor to review and reinforce those concepts. The Active Helpdesk calls for this chapter are listed below and can be found on your Student Resource CD:

- Choosing Software
- Buying and Installing Software

SOUND BYTES

Sound Bytes are dynamic multimedia tutorials that help demystify even the most complex topics. You'll view video clips and animations that illustrate computer concepts, and then apply what you've learned by reviewing with the Sound Byte Labs, which include quizzes and activities specifically tailored to each Sound Byte. The Sound Bytes for this chapter are listed below and can be found on your Student Resource CD:

- Creating Web Queries with Excel
- Using Speech-Recognition Software
- Enhancing Photos with Image-Editing Software

COMPANION WEB SITE

The Technology in Action Companion Web site includes a variety of additional materials to help you review and learn more about the topics in this chapter. The resources available at **www.prenhall.com/techinaction** include:

- **Online Study Guide.** Each chapter features an online true/false and multiple-choice quiz. You can take these quizzes, automatically check the results, and e-mail the results to your instructor.
- **Web Research Projects.** Each chapter features a number of Web research projects that ask you to search the Web for information on computer-related careers, milestones in computer history, important people and companies, emerging technologies, and the applications and implications of different technologies.

5

Using System Software:

The Operating System, Utility Programs, and File Management

Using System Software:

The Operating System, Utility Programs, and File Management

ACTIVE HELPDESK

- Managing Hardware and Peripheral Devices: The OS
- Starting the Computer: The Boot Process
- Organizing Your Computer: File Management
- Using Utility Programs

Working with System Software

Franklin begins his workday as he does every morning, powering on his computer and watching it boot up. Once he sees the welcoming image of his desktop, he opens Microsoft Outlook to check his e-mail, Internet Explorer to access his company's Web site, and Microsoft Word to bring up the proposal he needs to finish. As he reads his e-mail, a warning pops up alerting him that one message may contain a file with a virus. He deletes the file without opening it, glad that his antivirus software had been automatically updated yesterday.

Using Windows Explorer, Franklin searches for a proposal he worked on last year. Fortunately, he knows where to look because he has been creating folders for his projects and diligently saving his files in their proper folder. He learned the hard way that keeping his files organized in folders is worth the effort it takes to create them. Last year, his desktop was a complete mess. He was constantly losing time trying to find files because he couldn't remember where he saved them, and he gave them names he easily forgot. His organized folders now make finding his files a snap.

Later, at the end of the workday, Franklin has one more thing to do. Recently, his computer has been running sluggishly, so he is hoping to improve its performance. Last night, he ran Disk Cleanup, a utility program that removes unneeded files from the hard drive, as well as Error-checking, a utility program that checks for disk errors. Although he had seen an improvement in his computer's performance, he decides to use Disk Defragmenter to defrag his hard drive, hoping it will give him more space and allow his system to work more efficiently. As he's leaving work, Franklin hears the clicking of the hard drive as the defrag utility goes to work.

Can you take advantage of the features in your operating system as much as Franklin has? In this chapter, you'll learn all about system software and how vital it is to your computer. We'll start by examining the operating system (OS), looking at the different operating systems on the market as well as the tasks the OS manages. We'll then look at how you can use the OS to keep your files and folders organized so that you can use your computer more efficiently. Finally, we'll look at the many utility programs included as system software on your computer. Using these utility programs, you'll be better able to take care of your system and extend its life.

© Picture Quest

SOUND BYTES

- Customizing Windows Vista
- File Management
- File Compression

- Hard Disk Anatomy Interactive
- Letting Your Computer Clean Up After Itself

215

System Software Basics

There are two basic types of software on your computer: application software and system software. **Application software** is the software you use to do everyday tasks at home and at work. It includes programs such as Microsoft Word and Excel. **System software** is the set of software programs that helps run the computer and coordinates instructions between application software and the computer's hardware devices. From the moment you turn on your computer to the time you shut it down, you are interacting with system software.

System software consists of two primary types of programs: the operating system and utility programs. The **operating system (OS)** is a group of programs that controls how your computer system functions. The OS manages the computer's hardware, including the processor (also called the central processing unit, or CPU), memory, and storage devices, as well as peripheral devices such as the monitor and printer. The operating system also provides a consistent means for software applications to work with the CPU. In addition, it is responsible for the management, scheduling, and interaction of tasks as well as system maintenance. Your first interaction with the OS is the user interface, the features of the program that allow the user to communicate with the computer system.

System software also includes **utility programs**. These are small programs that perform many of the general housekeeping tasks for the computer, such as system maintenance and file compression.

Do all computers have operating systems? Every computer, from the smallest notebook to the largest supercomputer, has an operating system. Even tiny personal digital assistants (PDAs) as well as some appliances have operating systems. The role of the OS is critical; the computer cannot operate without it. As explained more fully in the later section "What the Operating System Does," the operating system coordinates the flow of data and information through the computer system by coordinating the hardware, software, user interface, processor, and the system's memory. But first, let's look at the types of operating systems and what kinds of computers they are used with.

Operating System Categories

Although most computer users can name only a few operating systems, many exist. As Figure 1 illustrates, these operating systems can be classified into four categories, depending on the number of users they service and the tasks they perform. Some operating systems coordinate resources for many users on a network (multiuser operating system), whereas other operating systems, such as those found in some household appliances and car engines, don't require the intervention of any users at all (real-time operating system). Some operating systems are available commercially, for personal and business use (single-user, multitask operating system), whereas others are proprietary systems developed specifically for the devices they manage (single-user, single-task operating system).

REAL-TIME OPERATING SYSTEMS

Do machines with built-in computers need an operating system? Machinery that is required to perform a repetitive series of specific tasks in an exact amount of time requires a **real-time operating system (RTOS)**. This type of operating system is a program with a specific purpose and must guarantee certain response times for particular computing tasks; otherwise the machine's application is useless. Devices that must perform regimented tasks or record precise results, such as measurement instruments found in the scientific, defense, and aerospace industries, require real-time operating systems. Some examples include digital storage oscilloscopes, as well as the Mars Exploration Rovers *Spirit* and *Opportunity*, and the Mars Reconnaissance Orbiter.

Real-time operating systems are also found in many types of robotic equipment. Television stations use robotic cameras with real-time operating systems that glide within a suspended cable system to record sports events from many angles. You also encounter real-time operating systems in devices you use in your everyday life, such as fuel-injection systems in car engines, video game consoles, and many home appliances (see Figure 2).

FIGURE 1 **Operating System Categories**

Category of Operating System	Examples of Operating System Software	Examples of Devices Using the Operating System
Real-Time Operating System (RTOS)	Nucleus RTOS is one of the few commercially available programs. Noncommercially available programs include QNX Neutrino and Lynx.	Scientific instruments Automation and control machinery Video games
Single-User, Single-Task Operating System	Palm OS Pocket PC (Windows CE) Windows Mobile 2003 MS-DOS Symbian OS Linux	PDAs Embedded computers in cell phones, cameras, appliances, and toys
Single-User, Multitask Operating System	Windows family (Vista, 2003, XP, 2000, Me, 98, NT) Mac OS X Linux	Personal desktop computers Notebooks
Multiuser Operating System	Novell NetWare Windows Server 2003 OS/2 Windows XP Windows Vista Linux	Networks (both home and business) Mainframes Supercomputers

Real-time operating systems require minimal user interaction. The programs are written specifically to the needs of the devices and their functions. Therefore, there are no commercially available standard RTOS software programs.

SINGLE-USER OPERATING SYSTEMS

What type of operating system controls my personal computer? Because your computer, whether it's a desktop, notebook (laptop), or even a tablet PC, can handle only one person working on it at a time but can perform a variety of tasks simultaneously, it uses a **single-user, multitask operating system**. The Microsoft Windows operating systems and the Macintosh operating system (Mac OS) are most commonly used as single-user multitask operating systems. (Note, however, that the newer versions, such as Windows XP and Windows Vista, have networking capabilities, so technically they also can be considered multiuser operating systems.) We will discuss the features of single-user, multitask operating systems in more detail in the next section of this chapter.

a) iRobot Corporation/Robotic vacuum "Roomba";
b) ©Henry Adams/Corbis car pick up; c) NASA/space shuttle;
d) White Box Robotics/robot

FIGURE 2

Devices such as the space shuttle, cars, and robots use real-time operating systems.

Usually, when you buy a desktop or notebook computer, its operating system software is already installed on the computer's hard disk so that you can just turn on the computer and start using it immediately. Sometimes you may need to install the OS yourself if you change or upgrade to a different version, or you might reinstall it in the case of a system problem.

Does the same kind of operating system also control my PDA? All computers on which one user is performing just one task at a time require a **single-user, single-task operating system**. PDAs currently can perform only one task at a time by a single user, so they require single-user, single-task operating system software such as Palm OS.

Microsoft's Windows Mobile is an application that includes both operating system software (Windows CE) and application components bundled specifically for PDAs (see Figure 3). Besides the address book, date book, memo pad, and to-do list that are standard with Windows Mobile, the bundled Pocket PC software also includes versions of Word, Excel, Outlook, and Internet Explorer that are designed specifically for PDAs.

Palm OS is another operating system found in many personal digital assistant devices. Palm OS includes an address book, clock, notepad, sync capability, memo viewer, and security software. Palm OS, unlike Windows Mobile, does not include any other applications, such as productivity software. The BlackBerry PDAs, manufactured by Research In Motion (RIM), feature their own proprietary operating system. The

unique feature of this OS is the always-on wireless capability.

Cell phones also use a single-user, single-task operating system that not only manages the functions of the phone but also provides other functionality, such as built-in phone directories, games, and calculators. Symbian OS is the leading OS software for mobile phones or smartphones.

Are there any other single-user, single-task operating systems? Another example of a single-user, single-task operating system is **Microsoft Disk Operating System (MS-DOS)**. MS-DOS (or DOS) was the first widely installed operating system in personal computers. Compared to the operating systems we are familiar with today, DOS was a highly user-"unfriendly" OS. To use it, you needed to type specific commands. For example, to copy a file named "letter" from the hard drive to a floppy disk, you would type the following command after the C prompt:

        C:\>copy letter.txt A:

Although DOS is used infrequently today as a primary operating system, information technology (IT) professionals still use it to edit and repair system files and programs.

MULTIUSER OPERATING SYSTEMS

What kind of operating system do networks use? A **multiuser operating system** (also known as a **network operating system**) enables more than one user to access the computer system at one time by efficiently handling and prioritizing all the requests from multiple users. Networks (groups of computers connected to each other for the purposes of communicating and sharing resources) require a multiuser operating system because many users access the server computer at the same time and share resources such as printers. A network operating system is installed on the server and manages all user requests, ensuring they do not interfere with each other. For example, on a network on which users share a printer, the printer can produce only one document at a time. The OS is therefore responsible for managing all the printer requests and making sure they are processed one at a time.

Although PDAs use a single-user, single-task operating system in which only one user can perform one task at a time, the operating system has a similar look to that of a traditional desktop operating system.

Motorola, Inc.

Examples of network operating systems include Linux, UNIX, Novell NetWare, and Windows Server. Windows XP and Vista also can be considered network OSs because they enable users to create a home network without needing to install a different operating system.

What other kinds of computers require a multiuser operating system? Large corporations with hundreds or thousands of employees often use powerful computers known as mainframes. These computers are responsible for storing, managing, and simultaneously processing data from all users. Mainframe operating systems fall into the multiuser category. Examples include UNIX and IBM's OS/2 and z/OS.

Supercomputers also use multiuser operating systems. Scientists and engineers use supercomputers to solve complex problems or to perform massive computations. Some supercomputers are single computers with multiple processors, whereas others consist of multiple computers that work together.

Desktop and Notebook Operating Systems

As mentioned earlier, desktop computers (and notebooks) use multitask operating systems, of which there are several available, including Windows, Linux, and Mac OS. The type of processor in the computer determines which operating system a particular desktop computer uses. The combination of operating system and processor is referred to as a computer's **platform**.

For example, Microsoft Windows operating systems are designed to coordinate with a series of processors from Intel Corporation and AMD (Advanced Micro Devices) that share the same or similar sets of instructions. However, up until recently, Apple Macintosh operating systems worked primarily with processors from the Motorola Corporation and IBM designed specifically for Apple computers. Now, Apple is making Intel-based Macs. Still, the two operating systems (Windows and Mac OS) are not interchangeable. If you attempt to load a Windows OS on a

Mac, for example, the Mac processor would *not* understand the operating system and would not function properly. Most application software is also platform dependent. However, the use of the Intel chip in Apple computers may change this proprietary relationship. In addition, Mac OS X Leopard provides a variety of features and technologies that enable Macs and PCs running Windows to work seamlessly together. Macs and PCs can easily share files, the same network, and even the same peripherals, such as printers, scanners, and cameras.

MICROSOFT WINDOWS

What is the difference between the various Windows operating systems? With each new version of its operating system, Microsoft continues to make improvements. Figure 4 outlines the features and benefits of each version of Windows Vista, the newest operating system from Microsoft. What was once only a single-user, single-task operating system is now a powerful multiuser operating system. Over time, Windows improvements have concentrated on increasing user functionality and friendliness, improving Internet capabilities, and enhancing file privacy and security. Unlike the versions of Windows XP that centered around features (such as Windows XP Tablet PC Edition, Windows XP Media Center Edition, Windows XP Home Edition, and Windows XP Professional), Windows Vista comes in a number of versions to accommodate the user: the home user (Home Basic, Home Premium), the business user (Business and Enterprise), or the combination user (Ultimate).

MAC OS

How is Mac OS different from Windows? Although the Apple **Mac OS** and the Windows operating systems are not compatible, they are very similar in terms of functionality. In 1984, Mac OS became the first commercially available operating system to incorporate a Graphical User Interface (GUI) with its user-friendly point-and-click technology in an affordable computer. Both operating systems now have similar window

FIGURE 4 **Windows Vista**

Versions	Description	Windows XP Comparable Version
Windows Vista Home Basic	This version is for low-level, budget home users who do not require advanced media support.	Windows XP Home Edition
Windows Vista Home Premium	This version combines the media features of Windows XP Media Center Edition with the Windows XP Home Edition to support advanced home media uses such as HDTV and DVD authoring.	Windows XP Home Edition with features from Windows XP Media Center Edition
Windows Vista Business	As its name implies, this version is aimed at the business market. Similar to Windows XP Professional, this version has added support for networking capabilities. This product comes bundled with a new version of Internet Information Services (IIS), one of the most widely used Web servers for corporate Web sites.	Windows XP Professional
Windows Vista Enterprise	This edition is aimed at the enterprise segment of the business market and is not available through retail stores or OEMs (Original Equipment Manufacturers). It comes with Microsoft Virtual PC, which enables it to run on any platform, and has a multilingual user interface.	
Windows Vista Ultimate	This is the "ultimate" operating system for high-end PC users, gamers, multimedia professionals, and PC enthusiasts. Vista Ultimate comes with RSS (Really Simple Syndication) support for easy access to podcasts and weblogs, a game performance tweaker, DVD ripping capabilities, and other online capabilities for downloading media.	

work areas on the desktop that house individual applications and support users working in more than one application at a time (see Figure 5).

Despite their similarities, there are many subtle and not-so-subtle differences that have created loyal fans of each product. Macs have long been recognized for their superior graphics display and processing capabilities. Users also attest to Mac's greater system reliability and better document recovery. Despite these advantages, fewer software applications are available for the Mac platform, and Mac systems tend to be a bit more expensive than Windows-based PCs.

The most recent version of the Mac operating system, Mac OS X Leopard, is based on the UNIX operating system. Mac OS X includes a streamlined user interface with a Dock for the most commonly used programs and a Dashboard with widgets, or mini-applications, for quick access to up-to-the-minute information such as stock prices or flight tracking.

LINUX

What is Linux? Linux is an open-source operating system. The Linux operating system uses a Linux kernel (the key code to an operating system), and the rest of the code is from the GNU (pronounced "gunoo") Project and other sources. Linux is designed for use on personal computers and as a network operating system. An **open-source program** is one that is freely available for developers to use or modify as they wish. Linux began in 1991 as a part-time project by a Finnish university student named Linus Torvalds, who wanted to create a free operating system to run on his home computer. He posted his operating system program code to the Web for others to use and modify. It has since been tweaked by scores of programmers as part of the Free Software Foundation GNU Project.

Today, Linux is gaining a reputation as a stable operating system that is not subject to crashes and failures. Because the code is open and available to anyone, Linux is quickly tweaked to meet virtually any new operating system need. For example, when Palm PDAs emerged, the Linux OS was promptly modified to run on this new device. Similarly, only a few weeks were necessary to get the Linux OS ready for the new Intel Xeon processor, a feat unheard of in proprietary operating system development. Some Linux-based operating systems have been modified to run iPods and gaming systems. Linux is also gaining popularity among computer manufacturers, which have begun to ship it with some of their latest PCs.

Where can I buy Linux? You can download the open-source versions of Linux for free off the Internet. However, several versions of Linux are more proprietary in nature. These versions come with support and other products that are not generally associated with the open-source Linux. Red Hat has been packaging and selling versions of Linux since 1994 and is probably the most well-known Linux distributor. Red Hat Enterprise Linux 5 (RHEL) is the current version on the market. Other Linux distributors include Mandriva, Suse, Debian GNU/Linux, and Gentoo Linux. For a full listing and explanation of all Linux distributors, visit **www.distrowatch.com**.

Operating Systems for Servers and Mainframes

What operating system is best for computers that handle multiple users and multiple tasks? As mentioned in the beginning of the chapter, there are several different types of operating systems. So far, we've described operating systems for single-user, single-task computers (cell phones and PDAs) and single-user, multitask computers (notebooks and desktops). Larger computers, known as mainframes and servers, need a different type of operating system that supports multiple users requesting multiple tasks simultaneously. **Servers** are computers on a network that manage network resources, and

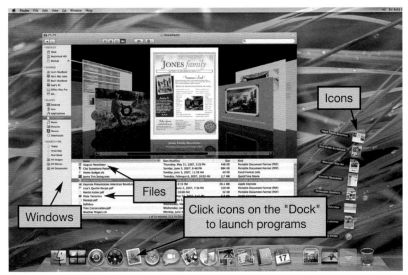

Apple Computer Inc.

mainframes are very large computers that handle the requests of hundreds or thousands of users simultaneously. Mainframe computers run operating systems developed by IBM and Unisys. The most common operating systems that run large servers and networks are Windows Server and UNIX. Since the release of Windows 2000 (Windows NT), home users have had an operating system that could support a small network—multiple users, multiple tasks—which have allowed home and small-business users to create small networks.

What is UNIX? UNIX is a multiuser, multitask operating system used primarily with mainframes as a network operating system, although it is also often found on PCs. Originally conceived in 1969 by Ken Thompson and Dennis Ritchie of AT&T's Bell Labs, the UNIX code was initially not proprietary—in other words, no company like Microsoft or Apple owned it. Rather, any programmer was allowed to use the code and modify it to meet his or her needs. Later, AT&T licensed the UNIX source code to the Santa Cruz Operation (SCO) Group. UNIX is a brand that belongs to the company The Open Group, but any vendor that meets testing requirements and pays a fee can use the UNIX name. Individual vendors then modify the UNIX code to run specifically on their hardware. HP/UX from Hewlett-Packard, Solaris from Sun, and AIX from IBM are some of the UNIX systems currently available in the marketplace.

FIGURE 5

The most recent version of the Mac operating system, Leopard, is based on the UNIX operating system. Although not compatible with each other, Windows OS and the Mac OS have many similar features.

TRENDS IN IT

Emerging Technologies: Open Source Software: Why Isn't Everyone Using Linux

Proprietary software, such as Microsoft Windows and Mac OS, is developed by corporations and sold for profit. This means that the **source code**, the actual lines of instructional code that make the program work, is not accessible to the general public. Without being able to access the source code, it's difficult to modify the software or see exactly how the program author constructed various parts of the system.

Restricting access to the source code protects companies from having their programming ideas stolen and prevents customers from using modified versions of the software. This benefits the companies that create the software because their software code can be pirated (or stolen). However, in the late 1980s, computer specialists became concerned over the fact that large software companies (such as Microsoft) were controlling a large portion of market share and driving out competitors. They also felt that proprietary software was too expensive and contained too many bugs (errors).

These people felt that software should be developed without a profit motive and distributed with its source code free for all to see. The theory was that if many computer specialists examined, improved, and changed the source code, a more full-featured, bug-free product would result. Hence, the open-source movement was born.

Open-source software is freely distributed (no royalties accrue to the creators), contains the source code, and can in turn be redistributed freely to others. Most open-source products are created by teams of programmers and are modified (updated) by hundreds of other programmers around the world. You can download open-source products for free off the Internet. Linux is probably the most widely recognized name in open-source software, but other products such as MySQL (a database program) and OpenOffice.org (a suite of productivity applications) are also gaining in popularity.

So, if an operating system such as Linux is free, why does Windows (which you must pay for) have such a huge market share? Corporations and individuals have grown accustomed to one thing that proprietary software makers can provide: technical support. It is almost impossible to provide technical support for open-source software because it can be freely modified, and there is no one specific developer to take responsibility for technical support (see Figure 6). Therefore, corporations have been reluctant to install open-source software extensively because of the cost of the internal staff of programmers that must support it.

Companies such as Red Hat have been combating this problem. The company provides a warranty and technical support for its version of Linux (which Red Hat programmers modified from the original source code). Packaging open-source software in this manner has made its use much more attractive to businesses. Today, many Web servers are hosted on computers running Linux.

So, when will free versions of Linux (or another open-source operating system) be the dominant OS on home computers? The answer is maybe never. Most casual computer users won't feel comfortable without technical support; therefore, any open-source products for home use would need to be marketed the way Red Hat markets Linux. Also, many open-source products are not easy to maintain.

However, companies such as Linspire (**www.linspire.com**) are making easy-to-use visual interfaces that work with the Linux operating system. If one of these companies can develop an easy-to-use product and has the marketing clout to challenge Microsoft, you may see more open-source software deployed in the home computer market in the future.

FIGURE 6

Companies like Linspire provide free Linux software, but a lack of technical support scares many companies away from wide-scale adoption.

What the Operating System Does

As shown in Figure 7, the operating system is like a traffic cop that coordinates the flow of data and information through the computer system. In doing so, the OS performs several specific functions:

- It provides a way for the user to interact with the computer.
- It manages the processor, or central processing unit (CPU).
- It manages the memory and storage.
- It manages the computer system's hardware and peripheral devices.
- It provides a consistent means for software applications to work with the CPU.

In this section, we look at each of these functions in detail.

THE USER INTERFACE

How does the operating system control how I interact with my computer? The operating system provides a **user interface** that enables you to interact with the computer. As noted earlier, the first personal computers had a DOS operating system with a command-driven interface, as shown in Figure 8a. A **command-driven interface** is one in which you enter commands to communicate with the computer system. The commands were not always easy to understand; as a result, the interface proved to be too complicated for the average user. Therefore, PCs were used primarily in business and by professional computer operators.

The command-driven interface was later improved by incorporating a menu-driven interface, as shown in Figure 8b. A **menu-driven interface** is one in which you choose a command from menus displayed on the

Manages the computer system's hardware and peripheral devices

Provides a way for the user to interact with the computer

The Operating System

Manages the processor

Manages the memory and storage

Provides a consistent means for software applications to work with the CPU

Reprinted by permission of Cherry Blossom Bonsai

FIGURE 8

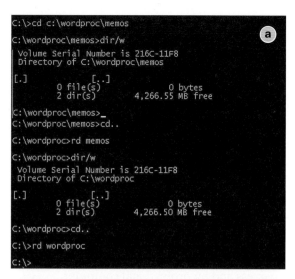

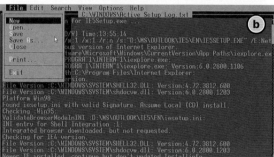

screen. Menu-driven interfaces eliminated the need to know every command because you could select most of the commonly used commands from a menu. However, they were still not easy enough for most people to use.

What kind of interface do operating systems use today? Most current personal computer operating systems, such as Mac OS and Microsoft Windows, use a **graphical user interface**, or **GUI** (pronounced "gooey"). Unlike the command- and menu-driven interfaces used earlier, GUIs display graphics and use the point-and-click technology of the mouse and cursor, making them much more user friendly. As illustrated in Figure 9, a GUI uses **windows** (rectangular boxes that contain programs displayed on the screen), **menus** (lists of commands that appear on the screen), and **icons** (pictures that represent an object such as a software application or a file or folder). Because users no longer have to enter commands to interact with the computer, GUIs are a big reason desktop computers are now such popular tools.

Unlike Windows or Mac OS, Linux does not have a single, default GUI interface.

Instead, users are free to choose among many commercially available or free interfaces, such as GNOME, KDE, and Motif, each of which provides a different look and feel. For example, GNOME (pronounced "gah-NOHM") actually allows you to select which desktop appearance (Windows or Mac) you'd like your system to display. This means that if you're using Linux for the first time, you don't have to learn a new interface: you just use the one you're most comfortable with already.

PROCESSOR MANAGEMENT

Why does the operating system need to manage the processor? When you use your computer, you are usually asking it to perform several tasks at once. For example, you might be printing a Word document, waiting for a file to download from the Internet, listening to a CD from your CD drive, and working on a PowerPoint presentation, all at the same time—or at least what *appears* to be at the same time. Although the processor is the powerful brains of the computer, processing all of its instructions and performing all of its calculations, it needs the operating system to arrange for the execution of all these activities in a systematic way to give the appearance that everything is happening simultaneously.

To do so, the operating system assigns a slice of its time to each activity requiring the processor's attention. The OS must then switch between different processes thousands of times a second to make it appear that everything is happening seamlessly. Otherwise, you wouldn't be able to listen to a CD and print at the same time without experiencing delays in the process. When the operating system allows you to perform more than one task at a time, it is said to be **multitasking**.

How exactly does the operating system coordinate all the activities? When you type and print a document in Word while also listening to a CD, for example, many different devices in the computer system are involved, including your keyboard, mouse, CD drive, and printer. Every keystroke, every mouse click, and each signal to the printer and from the CD drive creates an action, or **event,** in the respective device (keyboard, mouse, CD

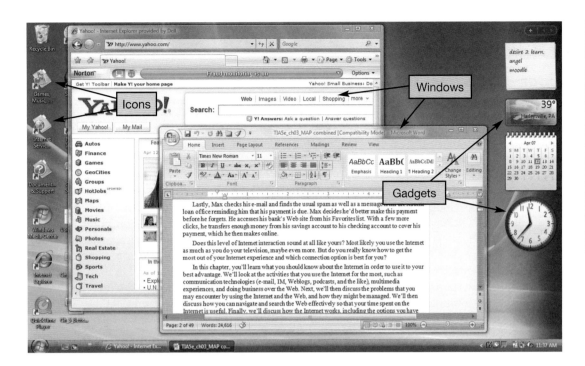

FIGURE 9

Today's operating systems coordinate a user's experience through a graphical user interface (GUI). GUIs are more user friendly than command- and menu-driven interfaces because they include features such as icons, windows, and other helpful graphical programs known as gadgets.

drive, or printer) to which the operating system responds.

Sometimes these events occur sequentially (such as when you type characters one at a time), but other events require two or more devices working simultaneously (such as the printer printing while you continue to type and listen to a CD at the same time). Although it *looks* as though the keyboard, CD drive, and printer are working at the same time, in effect, the operating system switches back and forth between processes, controlling the timing of events the processor works on.

For example, assume you are typing and you want to print another document. When you tell your computer to print your document, the printer generates a unique signal called an **interrupt** that tells the operating system that it is in need of immediate attention. Every device has its own type of interrupt, which is associated with an interrupt handler, a special numerical code that prioritizes the requests. These requests are placed in the interrupt table in the computer's primary memory (or random access memory, RAM). The operating system processes the task assigned a higher priority before processing a task that has been assigned a lower priority. This is called **preemptive multitasking**.

In our example, the operating system pauses the CPU from its typing activity and from the CD activity when it receives the interrupt from the printer and puts a "memo" in a special location in RAM called a stack. The memo is a reminder of where the CPU was before it left off so that it can work on the printer request. The CPU then retrieves the printer request from the interrupt table and begins to process it. On completion of the printer request, the CPU goes back to the stack, retrieves the memo it placed about the keystroke or CD activity, and returns to that task until it is interrupted again.

What happens if there is more than one document waiting to be printed? The operating system also coordinates multiple activities for peripheral devices such as printers. When the processor receives a request to send information to the printer, it first checks with the operating system to ensure that the printer is not already in use. If it is in use, the OS puts the request in another temporary storage area in RAM called the buffer. It will wait in the buffer until the **spooler**, a program that helps coordinate all print jobs currently being sent to the printer, indicates the printer is available. If more than one print job is waiting, a line, or queue, is formed so that the printer can process the requests in order.

Ethics: Sugar—The Sweet OS for the $100 Laptop

The Internet is a fantastic tool, but only if you can access it. In an effort to give children of developing countries a better opportunity to "learn, share, and create," the One Laptop Per Child (OLPC) initiative was founded by Nicholas Negroponte and other faculty from MIT Media Lab, in conjunction with partners such as Google, AMD, and News Corporation. The mission of OLPC (**www.laptop.org**) is to ensure that all school-aged children in lesser developed communities receive their own personal computer so that they are no longer excluded from the educational, economic, and entertainment benefits that computers can provide. This ambitious project to develop and distribute a $100 (current expected cost now closer to $200) notebook computer would provide access to electronic textbooks and other learning aids—and eventually the Internet. Currently, the project has expanded to include a wide variety of professionals from academia, business, the arts, and technology.

The notebook itself is revolutionary in design (see Figure 10). The notebook, called the XO, is small and has a comfortable, child-sized, built-in handle. It also has a tablet-like monitor that can twist to turn the notebook into an e-book, or electronic book, which is critical in areas where books are hard to come by. The outside of the notebook is rugged and child-friendly. In addition, it is power efficient—running on less than one-tenth of the power a standard notebook requires. Because access to electricity is minimal in many of the target areas for the project, the notebook is also self-powered by a pull-string, which is easy for the children to use.

At the core of the project is the operating system—Sugar—which completely rethinks the computer user interface. Credit goes to the developers, who really thought about how the users of the notebook would interact with the device. The operating system is based on open-source code components from Red Hat's Fedora Core 6 version of the Linux operating system. The OLPC notebooks will most likely be the first computer that many of these children have used. Because children have no idea of what to do with the machine and may not have anyone to tell them, the user interface was designed to be as intuitive as possible. Although the computer and its software are still works in

progress, there are some basic concepts that are fundamental to its design and functionality.

The operating system focuses on activities rather than applications. When the machine powers up, the first image is that of the XO man (an O on top of an X) in the middle of a circle surrounded by icons that represent home, friends, and neighborhood. The computer includes a built-in microphone and webcam for children to create their own multimedia. For example, the multimedia tool allows children to add music to their drawings. Other activities include browsing the Internet, chatting, text editing, and playing games. At the core of each activity is the ability to collaborate, which facilitates the community learning experience. To further enhance collaboration, the notebooks are all interconnected in a wireless mesh network, providing the potential for every activity to be a networked activity. Browsing, for example, would no longer be an isolated, individual activity; it could also be a collaborative group experience (see Figure 11a). Wireless capabilities also help to extend the community beyond the physical borders. These computers make it possibile for a child in Africa, for exam-

Fuse Project

FIGURE 10

The revolutionary design of the XO notebook is rugged yet child friendly. The XO can be easily converted from a traditional notebook to an e-book. It is extremely power efficient but can also be self-powered.

ple, to connect with another child in Europe.

In addition, the operating system uses a journaling technique for file management (see Figure 11b). The file system records what the child has done (rather than just what the student has saved), reading more as a scrapbook of the student's interactions with the computer as well as with peers. The journal can be tagged, searched, and sorted in a variety of ways).

Another general concept behind the operating system is that children learn through doing, so the software puts an emphasis on tools for exploring and expressing, as well as learning by helping each other. Because Sugar is built on an open-source platform, it also encourages students to explore how it works and to modify the code to meet their individual preferences.

The OLPC is not the only organization interested in increasing the reach of technology to those in less-developed nations. Intel has gone forward with its own program and produced the Classmate PC. While the Classmate PC is more closely aligned with a traditional Windows-based PC—running on either Windows or the open-source OS Mandravia, it offers some of the same user-friendly hardware features of the XO machine. Some reviewers and followers of both projects have offered the opinion that the Classmate PC is better suited for the older student user while the XO laptop is geared toward a younger, less sophisticated user. With so many children waiting to be exposed to technology and to a more fun and intuitive learning process, there is most likely room in the market for both machines.

FIGURE 11

(a) The user is sharing a browsing experience with several others. (b) The journaling file management system chronicles what the student saves as well as the student's interaction with the machine and with others.

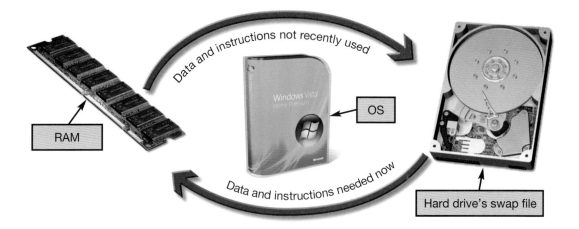

FIGURE 12

Virtual memory borrows excess storage capacity from the hard drive when there is not enough capacity in RAM.

RAM

OS

Data and instructions not recently used

Data and instructions needed now

Hard drive's swap file

MEMORY AND STORAGE MANAGEMENT

Why does the operating system have to manage the computer's memory?

As the operating system coordinates the activities of the processor, it uses RAM as a temporary storage area for instructions and data the processor needs. The processor then accesses these instructions and data from RAM when it is ready to process them. The OS is therefore responsible for coordinating the space allocations in RAM to ensure that there is enough space for all the waiting instructions and data. It then clears the items from RAM when the processor no longer needs them.

Can my system ever run out of RAM space?

RAM has limited capacity. As you add and upgrade your software applications and usage of the computer system, you will likely find that the amount of RAM you once found to be quite sufficient is no longer enough. The average computer system has anywhere from 512 megabytes (MB) to 4 gigabytes (GB) of memory in RAM. A system with 1 or 2 GB of RAM may be sufficient if you're running several applications at the same time. If you're running Windows Vista, however, the minimum requirement just to run the minimum capabilities of the operating system alone is 1 GB, and if you want to incorporate the Aero capabilities of Windows Vista, it's recommended that your system have at least 2 GB of RAM. Those systems with 512 MB or less will only be able to run Windows Vista Basic, and even without Windows Visual Basic, such systems may be challenged by limited RAM resources, especially with graphic intensive programs such as Adobe Photoshop, many gaming applications, and even the new version of Microsoft Office. Like most users, over time, you will expand how you use your computer by adding new software and new peripherals, so it's best to consider adding as much RAM as you can afford to your system.

What happens if my computer runs out of RAM?

When there isn't enough RAM for the operating system to store the required data and instructions, the operating system borrows room from the more spacious hard drive. This process of optimizing RAM storage by borrowing hard drive space is called **virtual memory**. As shown in Figure 12, when more RAM is needed, the operating system swaps out from RAM the data or instructions that have not been recently used and moves them to a temporary storage area on the hard drive called the **swap file** (or **page file**). If the data or instructions in the swap file are needed later, the operating system swaps them back into active RAM and replaces them in the hard drive's swap file with less active data or instructions. This process of swapping is known as **paging**.

Can I ever run out of virtual memory?

Only a portion of the hard drive is allocated to virtual memory. You can manually change this setting to increase the amount of hard drive space allocated, but eventually your computer system will become sluggish as it is forced to page more and more often. This condition of excessive paging is called **thrashing**. The solution to this problem is to increase the amount of RAM in your system so that it will not be necessary for it to send data and instructions to virtual memory.

How does the operating system manage storage? If it weren't for the operating system, the files and applications you save to the hard drive and other storage locations would be an unorganized mess. Fortunately, the OS has a file management system that keeps track of the name and location of each file you save and the programs you install. We will talk more about file management later in the chapter.

HARDWARE AND PERIPHERAL DEVICE MANAGEMENT

How does the operating system manage the hardware and peripheral devices? Each device attached to your computer comes with a special program called a **device driver** that facilitates the communication between the hardware device and the operating system. Because the OS must be able to communicate with every device in the computer system, the device driver translates the specialized commands of the device to commands that the operating system can understand, and vice versa. Thus, devices will not function without the proper device driver, because the OS would not know how to communicate with them.

Do I always need a driver? Today, most devices such as flash drives, mice, keyboards, and many digital cameras come with the driver already installed in Windows. The devices whose drivers are included in Windows are called **Plug and Play (PnP)**. Plug and Play is not a driver. Instead, it is a software and hardware standard that Microsoft created with the Windows 95 operating system. This standard is designed to facilitate the installation of a new piece of hardware in personal computers by including the driver the device needs to run into the OS. Because the OS includes this software, incorporating a new device into your computer system seems automatic. Plug and Play enables users to plug in their new device to a port on the system unit, turn on the computer, and immediately play, or use, the device. The OS automatically recognizes the device and its driver without any further user manipulations to the system.

What happens if the device is not Plug and Play? Some devices, such as many types of printers, are not Plug and Play. Similarly, many older devices also may not be Plug and Play. When you install a non-Plug and Play device, you will be prompted to

insert the driver that was provided with the device. If you obtain a non-Plug and Play device secondhand and did not receive the device driver, or if you are required to update the device driver, you can often download the necessary driver from the manufacturer's Web site. You can also check out Web sites such as **www.driverzone.com** or **www.driverguide.com** to locate drivers.

Can I damage my system by installing a device driver? Occasionally, when you install a driver, your system may become unstable (that is, programs may stop responding, certain actions may cause a crash, or the device or the entire system may stop working). Although this is not common, it can happen. Fortunately, Windows Vista has a Roll Back Driver feature that reinstalls the old driver and remedies the problem (see Figure 13).

SOFTWARE APPLICATION COORDINATION

How does the operating system help software applications run on the computer? Software applications feed the

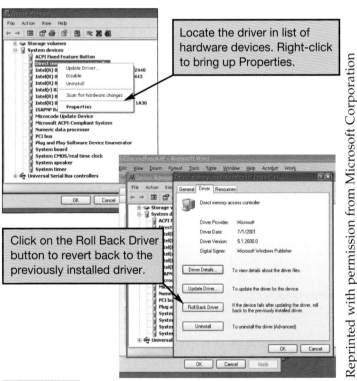

Locate the driver in list of hardware devices. Right-click to bring up Properties.

Click on the Roll Back Driver button to revert back to the previously installed driver.

Reprinted with permission from Microsoft Corporation

FIGURE 13

If you think a recent driver update may be making your computer unstable, you can use the Roll Back Driver feature (accessible through the System icon in the Control Panel) to get rid of the new driver and replace it with the last one that worked. However, Roll Back Driver permits only one level of rollback and does not work for printer drivers.

CPU the instructions it needs to process data. These instructions take the form of computer code. Every software application, no matter what its type or manufacturer, needs to interact with the CPU. For programs to work with the CPU, they must contain code that the CPU recognizes. Rather than having the same blocks of code for similar procedures in each software application, the operating system includes the blocks of code that software applications need to interact with it. These blocks of code are called **application programming interfaces (APIs)**. Microsoft DirectX, for example, is a group of multimedia APIs built into the Windows operating system that improves graphics and sounds when you're playing games or watching video on your PC.

To create programs that can communicate with the operating system, software programmers need only *refer* to the API code blocks in their individual application programs, rather than including the entire code in the application itself. Not only do APIs avoid redundancies in software code, but they also make it easier for software developers to respond to changes in the operating system.

Large software developers such as Microsoft have many software applications under their corporate umbrella and use the same APIs in all or most of their software applications. Because APIs coordinate with the operating system, all applications that have incorporated these APIs have common interfaces such as similar toolbars and menus. Therefore, many features of the software applications have the same look. An added benefit to this system is that applications sharing these same formats also can easily exchange data between different programs. As such, it's easy to create a chart in Microsoft Excel from data in Microsoft Access and incorporate the finished chart into a Microsoft Word document.

BITS AND BYTES

A Web-Based Operating System

Now that broadband Internet access is becoming the norm rather than the exception, the concept of a more universal operating system, called a Web-based OS, is being discussed and some prototype sites are in their infancy. So what is a Web-based operating system? Actually, the terms Web-based operating environment or portable desktop might be more accurate. Nonetheless, the concept behind this movement is to make the Web the primary application interface through which users can view content, manage data, and use various services (calendars, e-mail, and picture sharing and storage) on their local machine and on the Web without noticing any difference.

Currently, we can use applications that have been installed on a specific computer only. A Web-based operating environment would allow users access to applications and content via the Web, regardless of the machines they are using. This means business travelers would not need to lug their notebooks everywhere they went; instead they would need only to find a computer that had Internet access and they would be able to work on documents, see their calendar, read their e-mail, and so on. All of their settings and preferences (yes, even a customized desktop image), as well as working documents, could be stored in an individual Web-based account for them to access anywhere and on any machine at any time. Because security measures have not been completely worked out, it's advisable that Web-based accounts not be used to manipulate personal or proprietary data and information. For more information, or to begin your own account, check out the Web sites of the current Web-based OS innovators, including eyeOS (**www.eyeos.org**), GoGUI (**www.gogui.com**), and YouOS (**www.youos.com**).

The Boot Process: Starting Your Computer

Although it only takes a minute or two, a lot of things happen very quickly between the time you turn on the computer and when it is ready for you to start using it. As you learned earlier, all data and instructions (including the operating system) are stored in RAM while your computer is on. When you turn off your computer, RAM is wiped clean of all its data (including the OS). So, how does the computer know what to do when you turn it on if there is nothing in RAM? It runs through a special process, called the **boot process** (or start-up process), to load the operating system into RAM. The term *boot*, from *bootstrap loader* (a small program used to start a larger program), alludes to the straps of leather, called *bootstraps*, that men used in former times to help them pull on their boots. The use of bootstraps in this way created the expression to "pull oneself up by the bootstraps."

What are the steps involved in the boot process? The boot process, illustrated in Figure 14, consists of four basic steps:

1. The basic input/output system (BIOS) is activated by powering on the CPU.

2. The BIOS checks that all attached devices are in place (called a power-on self-test, or POST).

3. The operating system is loaded into RAM.

4. Configuration and customization settings are checked.

As the computer goes through the boot process in Windows operating systems, indicator lights on the keyboard and disk drives will illuminate and the system will emit various beeps. If you have a version of Windows earlier than XP, text will scroll down the screen as well. When you boot up on a PC with Windows Vista or a Mac, you won't hear any beeps or see any keyboard lights illuminate. Instead, a welcome screen will appear, indicating the progress of the start-up process. Once the boot process has completed these steps, it is ready to accept commands and data. Let's look at each of these steps in more detail.

STEP 1: ACTIVATING BIOS

What's the first thing that happens after I turn on my computer? In the first step of the boot process, the CPU activates the **basic input/output system (BIOS)**. BIOS (pronounced "bye-OSE") is a program that manages the data between the operating system and all the input and output devices attached to the system, hence its name. BIOS is also responsible for loading the OS from its permanent location on the hard drive into RAM.

BIOS itself is stored on a special read-only memory (ROM) chip on the motherboard. Unlike data stored in RAM, data stored in ROM is permanent and does not get erased when the power is turned off.

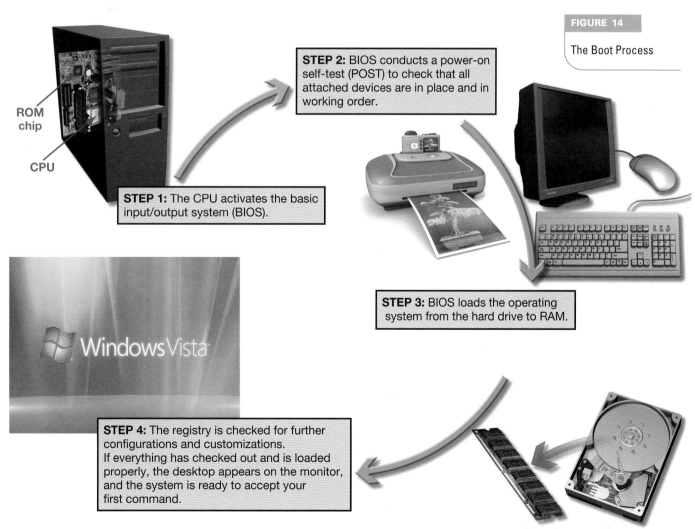

FIGURE 14

The Boot Process

ROM chip

CPU

STEP 1: The CPU activates the basic input/output system (BIOS).

STEP 2: BIOS conducts a power-on self-test (POST) to check that all attached devices are in place and in working order.

STEP 3: BIOS loads the operating system from the hard drive to RAM.

STEP 4: The registry is checked for further configurations and customizations. If everything has checked out and is loaded properly, the desktop appears on the monitor, and the system is ready to accept your first command.

Reprinted by permission of Cherry Blossom Bonsai

STEP 2: PERFORMING THE POWER-ON SELF-TEST

How does the computer determine whether the hardware is working properly? The first job BIOS performs is to ensure that essential peripheral devices are attached and operational. This process is called the **power-on self-test**, or **POST**. The POST consists of a test on the video card and video memory, a BIOS identification process, and a memory test to ensure memory chips are working properly.

The BIOS compares the results of the POST with the various hardware configurations that are permanently stored in CMOS (pronounced "see-moss"). CMOS, which stands for complementary metal-oxide semiconductor, is a special kind of memory that uses almost no power. A little battery provides enough power so that its contents will not be lost after the computer is turned off. CMOS contains information about the system's memory, types of disk drives, and other essential input and output hardware compo-

nents. If the results of the POST compare favorably to the hardware configurations stored in CMOS, the boot process continues. If new hardware has been installed, this will cause the POST to disagree with the hardware configurations in CMOS, and you will be alerted that new hardware has been detected.

STEP 3: LOADING THE OPERATING SYSTEM

How does the operating system get loaded into RAM? When the previous steps are successfully completed, BIOS goes through a preconfigured list of devices in its search for the drive that contains the **system files**, the main files of the operating system. When it is located, the operating system loads from its permanent storage location on the hard drive to RAM.

Once the system files are loaded into RAM, the **kernel** (or **supervisor program**) is loaded. The kernel is the essential component of the operating system. It is responsible for managing the processor and all other components of the computer system. Because it stays in RAM the entire time your computer is powered on, the kernel is called memory resident. Other parts of the OS that are less critical stay on the hard drive and are copied over to RAM on an as-needed basis so that the entire RAM is not taken up. These programs are called nonresident. Once the kernel is loaded, the operating system takes over control of the computer's functions.

STEP 4: CHECKING FURTHER CONFIGURATIONS AND CUSTOMIZATIONS

When are the other components and configurations of the system checked? CMOS checks the configuration of memory and essential peripherals in the beginning of the boot process. In this last phase of the boot process, the operating system checks the registry for the configuration of other system components. The **registry** contains all the different configurations (settings) used by the OS and by other applications. It contains the customized settings you put into place, such as mouse speed and the display settings for your monitor and desktop, as well as instructions as to which programs should be loaded first.

BITS AND BYTES

What Do I Do When My Computer Freezes?

At some point in time, we have all experienced our computers freezing up—nothing seems to respond to a mouse click or tap on any keyboard key. What to do? Try following these steps:

1. Press the Ctrl + Alt + Delete keys at the same time to access the Task Manager. On the Applications tab, close the application that is listed as *Not Responding*.
2. If the nonresponding application will not close from the Task Manager, press Ctrl + Alt + Delete again to restart the computer. Restarting the computer is called a "soft" or "warm" boot. You might also try using the Start menu and choosing Restart.
3. If the computer will not restart from the Task Manager or from the Start menu, then press the power button one time to try to reset the computer (older computers may have a separate Restart button).
4. If the computer still won't restart, press and hold down the Power button until the power is completely turned off. You may have to hold down the power button for several seconds.
5. Leave the computer turned off for a minute or so to allow all the internal components to shut down completely. Then turn the computer on again. (Powering the computer on from an off position is called a "cold" or "hard" boot.)

Why do I sometimes need to enter a password at the end of the boot process? In a networked environment, such as that found at most colleges, the operating system services many users. To determine whether a user is authorized to use the system (that is, whether a user is a paying student or college employee), authorized users are given a login name and password. The verification of your login name and password at the end of the boot process is called **authentication**. The authentication process blocks unauthorized users from entering the system.

You also may need to insert a password following the boot process to log in to your user account on your computer. The newest version of the Windows operating system, Windows Vista, is a multiuser system. Even in a home environment, all users with access to a Windows Vista computer (such as family members or roommates) can have their own user accounts. Users can set up a password to protect their account from being accessed by another user without permission.

How do I know if the boot process is successful? The entire boot process takes only a minute or two to complete. If the entire system is checked out and loaded properly, the process completes by displaying the desktop. The computer system is now ready to accept your first command.

HANDLING ERRORS IN THE BOOT PROCESS

What should I do if my computer doesn't boot properly? Sometimes problems occur during the boot process. Fortunately, you have several options for correcting the situation. If you have recently installed new software or a new hardware device, try uninstalling it. (Make sure you use the Add or Remove Programs feature in the Control Panel to remove the software.) If the problem no longer occurs when rebooting, you have determined the cause of the problem. You can then reinstall the device or software. If the problem does not go away, the first option is to restart your computer in Safe mode.

What is Safe mode? Sometimes Windows does not boot properly, and you

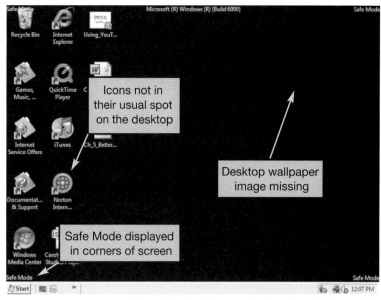

Reprinted with permission from Microsoft Corporation

If there is an error in the boot process, your system might boot into Safe mode. Safe mode offers limited—but enough—functionality so you can perform diagnostic testing.

end up with a screen with the words *Safe Mode* in the corners, as shown in Figure 15. (Alternatively, you can boot directly into Safe mode by pressing the F8 key during the boot process.) **Safe mode** is a special diagnostic mode designed for troubleshooting errors. When in Safe mode, only the essential devices of the system (such as the mouse, keyboard, and monitor) function. Even the regular graphics device driver will not be activated in Safe mode. Instead, the system runs in the most basic graphics mode, resulting in a neutral screen, eliminating any desktop images and nonessential icons. While in Safe mode, you can use the **Device Manager**, a feature in the operating system that lets you view and change the properties of all devices attached to your computer. Safe mode boots Microsoft Windows with only the necessary original Microsoft Windows drivers to boot.

If Windows detects a problem in the boot process, it will add Last Known Good Configuration to the Windows Advanced Options Menu (found also by pressing the F8 key during the boot process). **Last Known Good Configuration** is a feature in Windows XP and Vista. Every time your computer boots successfully, a configuration

of the boot process is saved. When you choose to boot with the Last Known Good Configuration, the operating system starts your computer by using the registry information that was saved during the last shutdown. Using Safe mode and Last Known Good Configuration are the two most widely used methods of booting into Windows when you're unable to do so with your current configuration.

Finally, if all other attempts to reboot fail, try a system restore. **System Restore** can be used to roll back to a past configuration. Because it doesn't restore any personal data files, you can be assured that your personal data will stay intact, meaning the files will match the files the last time you changed them, regardless of system restore. A system restore point is made every day you use your computer. You also can create a custom restore point if needed.

What should I do if my keyboard or other device doesn't work after I boot my computer? Sometimes during the boot process, BIOS skips a device (such as a keyboard) or improperly identifies it. You won't hear any beeps or see any error messages when this happens. Your only indication that this sort of problem has occurred is that the

device won't respond after the system has been booted. When that happens, you can generally resolve the problem by rebooting. If the problem persists, you may want to check the operating system's Web site for any patches (or software fixes) that may resolve the issue. If there are no patches or the problem persists, you may want to get technical assistance.

The Desktop and Windows Features

The **desktop** is the first interaction you have with the operating system and the first image you see on your monitor. As its name implies, your computer's desktop puts at your fingertips all of the elements necessary for a productive work session that are typically found on or near the top of a traditional desk, such as files and folders.

What are the main features of the desktop? The very nature of a desktop is that it enables you to customize it to meet your individual needs. As such, the desktop on your computer may be different from the desktop on your friend's computer. However, most desktops share common features, some of which are illustrated in Figure 16.

FIGURE 16

The Windows desktop puts the most commonly used features of the operating system at your fingertips.

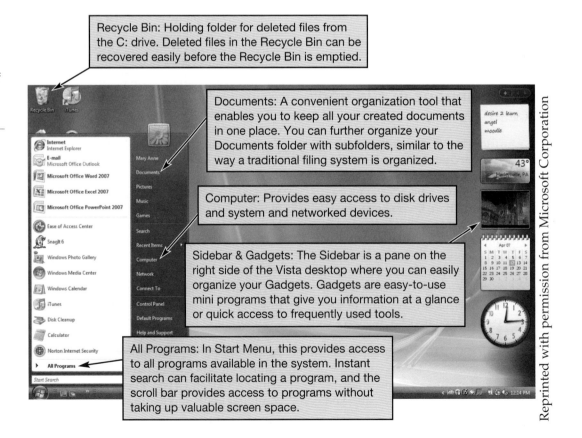

Recycle Bin: Holding folder for deleted files from the C: drive. Deleted files in the Recycle Bin can be recovered easily before the Recycle Bin is emptied.

Documents: A convenient organization tool that enables you to keep all your created documents in one place. You can further organize your Documents folder with subfolders, similar to the way a traditional filing system is organized.

Computer: Provides easy access to disk drives and system and networked devices.

Sidebar & Gadgets: The Sidebar is a pane on the right side of the Vista desktop where you can easily organize your Gadgets. Gadgets are easy-to-use mini programs that give you information at a glance or quick access to frequently used tools.

All Programs: In Start Menu, this provides access to all programs available in the system. Instant search can facilitate locating a program, and the scroll bar provides access to programs without taking up valuable screen space.

Reprinted with permission from Microsoft Corporation

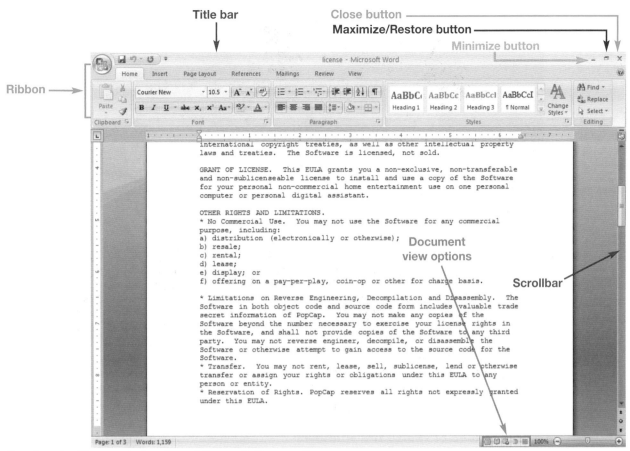

Title bar

Close button

Maximize/Restore button

Minimize button

Ribbon

Document view options

Scrollbar

Reprinted with permission from Microsoft Corporation

Windows Vista includes new features called the Sidebar and Gadgets. The **Sidebar** is a pane on the right side of the desktop that organizes gadgets for easy access. **Gadgets** can be any items you refer to frequently, including weather information, calendar items, calculators, games, photo albums, and more.

What are common features of a window? As noted earlier, one feature introduced by the graphical user interface is *windows* (with a lowercase *w*), the rectangular panes on your computer screen that display applications running on your system. Windows provide for a flexible, user-friendly, multitasking environment. Figure 17 illustrates some of the features of windows, including **toolbars** or **ribbons** (groups of icons collected for easy access) and **scrollbars** (bars that appear at the side or bottom of the screen that control which part of the information is displayed on the screen). Using the Minimize, Maximize and Restore, and Close buttons, you can open, close, and resize windows.

How can I see more than one window on my desktop at a time? You can easily arrange the windows on a desktop by tiling them, which means arranging separate windows so that they sit next to each other either horizontally or vertically. You also can arrange windows by cascading them so that they overlap one another, or you can simply resize two open windows so that they appear on the screen at the same time.

Tiling windows makes accessing two or more active windows more convenient. To untile the windows, or to bring a window back to its full size, click the Restore button in the top right corner of the window.

Windows Vista offers two more ways to navigate through open windows. Windows **Flip** allows you to scroll through open windows by using Alt+Tab. Although the Alt+Tab feature was available in Windows XP, Vista's improvements include live thumbnail images of the open windows instead of an icon and file name, which appeared in Windows XP. Windows Vista **Flip 3D** lets you "flip" through open

Tiling windows is a great way to see two windows at the same time. Vista's new Flip 3D gives you the ability to move through live images of open windows. You can also arrange windows in more traditional cascade, stacked, or side-by-side arrangements by right-clicking an empty space on the taskbar.

Reprinted with permission from Microsoft Corporation

windows in a stack by using the scroll wheel on your mouse. The open windows appear in a 3D configuration, as shown in Figure 18.

Can I move or resize the windows once they are tiled? Regardless of whether the windows are tiled, you can resize and move them around the desktop. You can reposition windows on the desktop by pointing to the title bar at the top of the window with your cursor and, when holding down the left mouse button, drag them to a different location. To resize a window, place your cursor on any side or corner of a window until it changes to a double-headed arrow [$\updownarrow$]. You can then left-click and drag the window to the new desired size.

Organizing Your Computer: File Management

So far you have learned that the operating system is responsible for managing the processor, memory, storage, and devices, and that it provides a mechanism for applications and users to interact with the computer system. An additional function of an operating system is to enable **file management**, which entails providing organizational structure to the computer's contents. The OS allows you to organize the contents of your computer in a hierarchical struc-

ture of **directories** that includes files, folders, and drives. In this section, we discuss how you can use this hierarchical structure to create a more organized and efficient computer.

ORGANIZING YOUR FILES

What exactly is a file? Technically, a **file** is a collection of related pieces of information stored together for easy reference. A file in an operating system is a collection of program instructions or data stored and treated as a single unit. Files can be generated from an application, such as a Word document or Excel spreadsheet. In addition, files can represent an entire application, a Web page, a set of sounds, or an image. Files are stored on the hard drive, a flash drive, or another storage medium for permanent storage. As the number of files you save increases, it is important to keep them organized in **folders**, or collections of files.

How does the operating system organize files? Windows organizes the contents of the computer in a hierarchical structure with drives, folders, subfolders, and files. The hard drive, represented as the C drive, is where you permanently store most of your files. Other storage devices on your computer are also represented by letters. The A drive has traditionally been reserved for the floppy drive. Any additional drives (flash, CD, or DVD drives) installed on your computer are represented by other letters (D, E, F, or another letter designation).

How is the hard drive organized? The C drive, or hard drive, is like a large filing cabinet in which all files are stored. As such, the C drive is the top of the filing structure of the computer system and is referred to as the **root directory**. All other folders and files are organized within the root directory. There are areas in the root directory that the operating system has filled with folders holding special OS files. The programs within these files help run the computer and generally shouldn't be touched. The Windows Vista operating system also creates other folders, such as Documents, Pictures, and Music (My Documents, My Pictures, and My Music in Windows XP); which are available for you to begin to store and organize your text, image, and audio files, respectively.

How can I easily locate and see the contents of my computer? If you use a Windows PC, Windows Vista **Explorers** are the main tool for finding, viewing, and managing the contents of your computer by showing the location and contents of every drive, folder, and file. In Windows Vista, Explorers are dialog boxes that consistently appear when you open any folder. As illustrated in Figure 19, Explorers is divided into two panes, or sections.

The navigation pane on the left pane shows the contents of your computer in a traditional hierarchical tree structure and also the new Search Folders. It displays all the drives of the system, as well as other commonly accessed areas such as the Desktop and the Documents folder. There are shortcut folders that take you to Documents, Pictures, or Music Explorers. The Searches link lets you see all the Search Folders on your PC. A Search Folder organizes your files logically, without physically rearranging the files to expedite searches of a particular file type. For example, if you have picture files stored not only in the Pictures folder, but also in other folders, it might take you a while to find a particular picture file you need. By clicking on the Picture Search folder, all of the picture files, no matter where they are stored on your computer, will appear in the Picture Search folder.

How should I organize my files? Creating folders is the key to organizing your files, because folders keep related documents together. Again, think of your computer as a big filing cabinet to which you can add many separate filing drawers, or subfolders. Those drawers, or subfolders, have the capacity to hold even more folders, which can hold other folders or individual files. For example, you might create one folder called Classes to hold all of your class work. Inside the Classes folder, you could create folders for each of your classes (such as Intro to Computers, Bio 101, and British Literature). Inside each of those folders, you could create subfolders for each

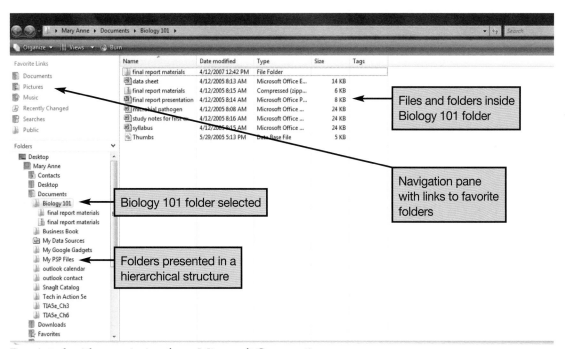

FIGURE 19

Windows Explorer lets you see the contents of your computer.

>Right-click the Start button and choose Explore.

Files and folders inside Biology 101 folder

Navigation pane with links to favorite folders

Biology 101 folder selected

Folders presented in a hierarchical structure

FIGURE 20

Details view enables you to sort and list your files in a variety of ways to enable quick access to the correct file.

>To access Details view, click View from the Command Bar at the top of the folder dialog box.

Reprinted with permission from Microsoft Corporation

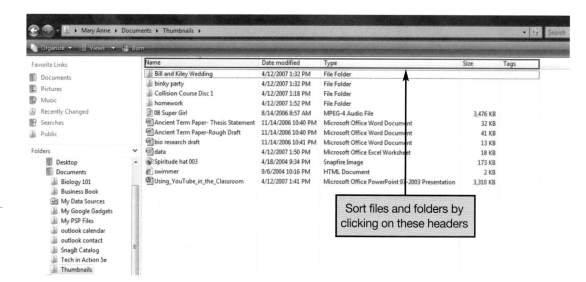

Sort files and folders by clicking on these headers

class's assignments, completed homework, research, notes, and so on.

Grouping related files into folders makes it easier for you to identify and find files. Which would be easier, going to the Bio 101 folder to find a file or searching through the 143 individual files in Documents hoping to find the right one? Grouping files in a folder also allows you to move them more efficiently, so you can quickly transfer critical files needing frequent backup to a CD, for instance.

VIEWING AND SORTING FILES AND FOLDERS

Are there different ways I can view and sort my files and folders? A new feature in Windows Vista is Live Icons. Live Icons allows you to preview the actual contents of a specific file or folder without actually opening the file. Live Icons can be displayed in a variety of views, which are discussed in more detail below.

- **Tiles view** displays files and folders as icons in list form. Each icon includes the filename, the application associated with

SOUND BYTE

File Management

In this Sound Byte, you'll examine the features of file management and maintenance. You'll learn the various methods of creating folders, how to turn a group of unorganized files into an organized system of folders, and how to maintain your file system.

the file, and the file size. The display information is customizable. The Tiles view also displays picture dimensions, a handy feature for Web-page developers.

- **Details view** is the most interactive view. Files and folders are displayed in list form, and the additional file information is displayed in columns alongside the filename. You can sort and display the contents of the folder by any of the column headings, so you may sort the contents alphabetically by filename or type, or hierarchically by date last modified or by file size (see Figure 20).

- **List view** is another display of even smaller icons and filenames. This is a good view if you have a lot of content in the folder and need to see most or all of it at once.

- **Small and Medium Icon views** also display files and folders as icons in list form, but the icons are either a small or medium size and include no other file information than the filename. However, additional file information is displayed in a ScreenTip (the text that appears when you place your cursor over the file icon).

- **Large Icon view**, illustrated in Figure 21, replaces the Thumbnails view in Windows XP. Large Icon view shows the contents of folders as small images. There is also **Extra Large Icon view**, which shows folder contents and other icons as even larger images. Large and Extra Large icon views are the best to use if your folder contains picture files.

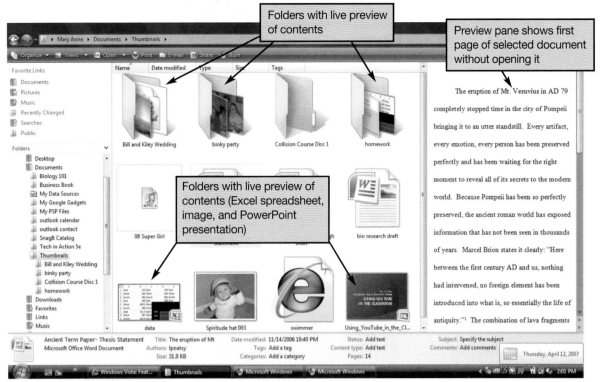

Reprinted with permission from Microsoft Corporation

Folders with live preview of contents

Preview pane shows first page of selected document without opening it

Folders with live preview of contents (Excel spreadsheet, image, and PowerPoint presentation)

FIGURE 21

In Windows Vista, Large icons is an especially good way to display folders containing different files. Live Icons display a thumbnail image of actual contents, making it easier to find a given item. The preview pane on the right enables you to see the first page of your document without first opening it.

>To access Large Icon view, from the command bar in any folder dialog box, click View, and then select Large Icon view. You may also use the scalable feature to adjust the size of the icons.

For those folders that contain collections of MP3 files, you can download the cover of the CD or an image of the artist to display on any folder to further identify that collection

What's the best way to search for a file? You've no doubt saved a file and forgotten where you saved it, or you have downloaded a file from the Internet and are not sure where it was saved. What's the quickest way to find a file? Looking through every file stored on your computer could take hours, even with a well-organized file management system. Fortunately, Windows Vista includes Instant Search, found on the Start menu, that searches through your hard drive or other storage device (CD or flash drive) to locate files that match criteria you provide. Your search can be based on a part of the filename or just a word or phrase in the file. You can also narrow your search by providing information about the type of file, which application was used to create the file, or even how long ago the file was saved. (Mac OS Leopard has a similar feature called Spotlight, known as Sherlock in earlier versions.) Instant Search can also find e-mails based on your criteria. Instant Search is also found in Explorer boxes to search the content of each Explorer.

NAMING FILES

Are there special rules I have to follow when I name files? Files have names just like people. The first part of a file, or the **filename**, is similar to our first names and is generally the name you assign to the file when you save it. For example, "bioreport" may be the name you assign a report you have completed for a biology class.

In a Windows application, following the filename and after the dot (.) comes an **extension**, or **file type**. Like our last name, this extension identifies what kind of family of files the file belongs to or which application should be used to read the file. For example, if "bioreport" is a document created in Works, it has a .wks extension and is named bioreport.wks. If the bioreport file is a Word 2003 document, it has a .doc extension and is named bioreport.doc. If the file is created in Word 2007, then the file extension is .docx and is named bioreport.docx. All Word, Excel, and PowerPoint files created in the 2007 version, will have an "x" at the end of the traditional three-letter extension. Figure 22 lists some common file extensions and the types of documents they indicate.

FIGURE 22 **Filename Extensions**

Extension	Type of Document	Application that Uses the Extension
.doc	Word-processing document	Microsoft Word 2003
.docx	Word-processing document	Microsoft Word 2007
.wks	Word-processing document	Microsoft Works word processing
.wpd	Word-processing document	Corel WordPerfect
.xls	Spreadsheet	Microsoft Excel
.slr	Spreadsheet	Microsoft Works spreadsheet
.mdb	Database	Microsoft Access
.ppt	PowerPoint presentation	Microsoft PowerPoint
.pdf	Portable Document Format	Adobe Acrobat or Adobe Reader
.rtf	Text	Any program that can read text documents
.txt	Text	Any program that can read text documents
.htm or .html	Web page	HyperText Markup Language
.bmp	Bitmap image	Windows
.zip	Compressed file	WinZip

Do I need to know the extensions of all files to save them? As shown in Figure 23, when you save a file created in a Windows operating system, you do not need to add the extension to the filename; it is added automatically for you. Mac and Linux operating systems do not require file extensions. This is because the information as to the type of application the computer should use to open the file is stored inside the file itself. However, if you're using these operating systems and will be sending files to

FIGURE 23

When you save a file in Windows Vista, (a) you can first select in what format you would like the file to be saved, and then (b) type the filename in the Save As dialog box.

>The Save As features are displayed by selecting the Office button and then selecting Save As.

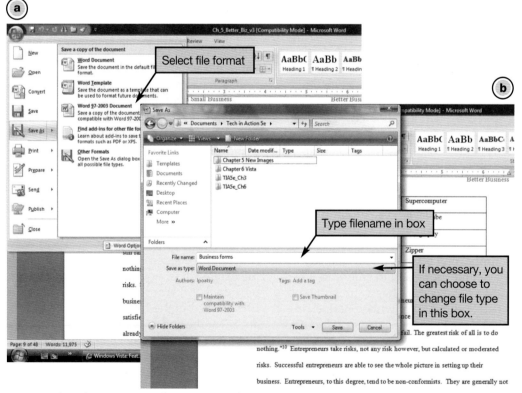

Reprinted with Permission from Microsoft Corporation

FIGURE 24 **File Naming Conventions**

	Mac OS	**Windows**
File and folder name length	Up to 255 characters*	Up to 255 characters
Case sensitive?	Yes	No
Forbidden characters	Colon (:)	" / \ * ? < > | :
File extensions needed?	No	Yes
Path separator	Colon (:)	\

*Note: Although Mac OS X supports filenames with up to 255 characters, many applications running on OS X still support only a maximum of 31-character filenames.

Windows users, you should add an extension to your filename so that Windows can more easily open your files. Because files saved as Office 2007 files cannot be opened with any previous version of the application, when using any Office 2007 application, you can choose to save the file in either a 2007 format or a 2003 or earlier format.

Are there things I shouldn't do when naming my file? Each operating system has its own naming conventions, or rules, which are listed in Figure 24. Beyond those conventions, it's important that you name your files so that you can easily identify them. A filename like research.doc may be descriptive to you if you're only working on one research paper. However, if you create other research reports later and need to identify the contents of these files quickly, you'll soon wish you had been more descriptive. Giving your files more descriptive names, such as bioresearch.doc or, better yet, bio101research.doc, is a good idea.

Keep in mind, however, that every file in the same folder or storage device (hard disk, CD, and so on) must be *uniquely* identified. Therefore, files may share the same filename (such as *bioreport*.doc or *bioreport*.xls), or they may share the same extension (bioreport.*xls* or budget.*xls*); however, no two files stored on the same device and folder can share *both* the same filename *and* the same extension.

How can I tell where my files are saved? When you save a file for the first time, you give the file a name and designate where you want to save it. For easy reference, the operating system includes default folders where files are saved unless you specify otherwise. In Windows Vista, the default folders are "Documents" for files, "Downloads" for files downloaded from the Internet, "Music" for audio files, "Pictures" for graphic files, and "Videos" for video files. Although you can create your own folders, these default folders are the beginning of a well-organized system.

You can determine the location of a file by its **file path**. The file path starts with the drive in which the file is located, and includes all folders, subfolders (if any), the filename, and extension. For example, if you were saving a picture of Emily Brontë for a term paper for an English Comp course, the file path might be C:\ My Documents\ Spring 2009\ English Comp\ Term Paper\ Illustrations\ EBronte.jpg.

As shown in Figure 25, the C indicates the drive on which the file is stored (in this case, the hard drive), and My Documents is the file's primary folder. Spring 2009, English Comp, Term Paper, and Illustrations are successive subfolders within the My Documents main folder. Last is the filename, EBronte, separated from the file extension (in this case, .jpg) by a period. Notice that in between the drive, primary folder, subfolders, and filename are backslash characters (\ ). These backslash characters, used by Windows and DOS, are referred to as **path separators**. Mac files use a colon (:), whereas UNIX and Linux files use the forward slash (/) as the path separator.

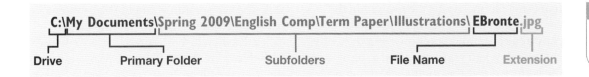

C:\My Documents\Spring 2009\English Comp\Term Paper\Illustrations\ EBronte.jpg

Drive | Primary Folder | Subfolders | File Name | Extension

FIGURE 25

Understanding File Paths

A File Type for Everyone

Imagine you are sending an e-mail to a diverse group of individuals. You are not sure what word-processing software each of them uses, but you assume that there will be a mix of people who use Word, WordPerfect, and even Writer. How can you be sure that everyone will be able to open the attachment regardless of the program installed on his or her computer? Save the file in Rich Text Format (.rtf) or Text (.txt) format. Both file formats can be read by any word-processing program, although some formatting may be lost when saving as a Text (.txt) format. To save files as RTF or Text files, simply change the file type when saving your file. In Microsoft Word, for example, you can change the file type in the Save As dialog box shown in Figure 26.

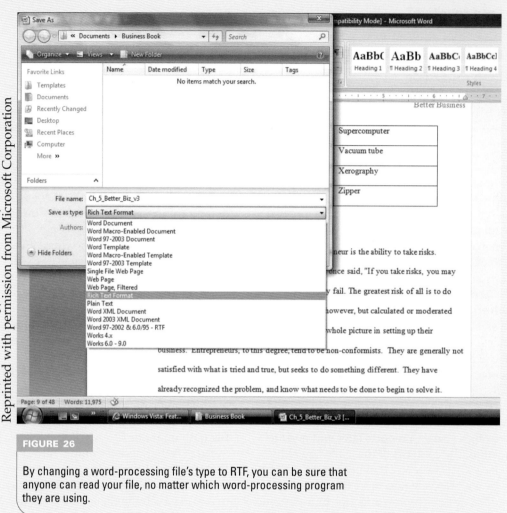

Reprinted with permission from Microsoft Corporation

FIGURE 26

By changing a word-processing file's type to RTF, you can be sure that anyone can read your file, no matter which word-processing program they are using.

WORKING WITH FILES

How can I move and copy files? Once you've located your file with Windows Explorer, you can perform many other file management actions, such as opening, copying, moving, renaming, and deleting files. You open a file by double-clicking the file from its storage location. Based on the file extension, the operating system then determines which application needs to be loaded to open the requested file and opens the file within the correct application automatically. You can copy a file to another location using the Copy command. When you copy a file, a duplicate file is created and the original file remains in its original location. To move a file from one location to another, you use the Move command. When you move a file, the original file is deleted from its original location.

Where do deleted files go? The **Recycle Bin** is a folder on the desktop, where files deleted *from the hard drive* reside until you permanently purge them from your system. Unfortunately, files deleted from other drives, such as the CD, flash drive, or network drive, do not go to the Recycle Bin but are deleted from the system immediately. (Mac systems have something similar to the Recycle Bin, called Trash, which is represented by a wastebasket icon. To delete files on a Mac, you simply drag the file to Trash on the Dock.)

How do I permanently delete files from my system? Files in the Recycle Bin or Trash are being held only until they are permanently deleted. To delete your files from the Recycle Bin permanently, select Empty the Recycle Bin after right-clicking the desktop icon. On Macs, select Empty Trash from the Finder menu in OS X, or from the Special menu in earlier versions.

Is it possible to retrieve a file that I've accidentally deleted? The benefit of the Recycle Bin is that you can restore the files you place there—as long as you've not emptied the Recycle Bin. To restore a file, open the Recycle Bin, locate and select the file, and select Restore. Take note that once the Recycle Bin has been emptied, deleted files are not easily retrievable, although it's not impossible to get them back with the right software.

Utility Programs

You have learned that the operating system is the single most essential piece of software in your computer system because it coordinates all the system's activities and provides a means by which other software applications and users can interact with the system. However, there is another set of programs included in system software. Utility programs are small applications that perform special functions. Some utility programs help manage system resources (such as disk defragmenter utilities, or defrag utilities), others help make your time and work on the computer more pleasant (such as screen savers), and still others improve efficiency (such as file compression utilities).

Some of these utility programs are incorporated into the operating system. For example, Windows Vista has its own firewall and file compression utility. Other utility programs, such as antivirus and security programs, have become so large and require such frequent updating that they are sold as stand-alone off-the-shelf programs in stores or as Web-based services available for an annual fee. Sometimes utility programs, such as Norton SystemWorks, are offered as software suites, bundled with other useful maintenance and performance-boosting utilities. Still other utilities, like Lavasoft's Ad-Aware, are offered as freeware or shareware programs and are available as downloads from the Web. Figure 27 illustrates

some of the various types of utility programs available within the Windows operating system as well as those available as off-the-shelf programs in stores. In general, the basic utilities designed to manage and tune the computer hardware are incorporated in the operating system. The off-the-shelf utility programs typically offer more features, or an easier user interface, for backup, security, diagnostic, or recovery functions.

In this section, we explore many of the utility programs you'll find installed on a Windows operating system. Unless otherwise noted, you can find these utilities in the Control Panel or on the Start menu by selecting Programs, Accessories, and then System Tools. (We also take a brief look at some Mac utilities.)

DISPLAY UTILITIES

How can I change the appearance of my desktop? The Display icon, found in Appearance and Themes in the Control Panel, has all the features required to change the appearance of your desktop, providing different options for the desktop background, screen savers, windows colors, font sizes, and screen resolution. Although Windows comes with many different background themes and screen saver options pre-installed, hundreds of downloadable options are available on the Web. Just search for "backgrounds" or "screen savers" on your

Windows Utility Program	Off-the-Shelf (Stand-Alone) Windows Utility Program	Function
File Management		
Add/Remove Programs		Properly installs and uninstalls software
Windows Explorer File Compression	WinZip	Reduces file size
Windows System Maintenance and Diagnostics		
Backup	Norton Ghost	Backs up important information
Disk Cleanup		Removes unnecessary files from hard drive
Disk Defragmenter	Norton SystemWorks	Arranges files on hard drive in sequential order
Error-checking (previously ScanDisk)		Checks hard drive for unnecessary or damaged files
System Restore	FarStone RestoreIT!	Restores system to a previously stable state
Task Manager		Displays performance measures for processes; provides information on programs and processes running on computer
Task Scheduler		Schedules programs to run automatically at prescribed times

favorite search engine to customize your desktop. Another way to access the background and screen saver options and all display utilities is to right-click an empty space on your desktop and choose Properties from the shortcut menu.

Do I really need to use a screen saver? Screen savers are animated images that appear on a computer monitor when no user activity has been sensed for a certain time. Originally, screen savers were used to prevent burn-in, the result of an image being burned into the phosphor inside the monitor's cathode-ray tube when the same image was left on the monitor for long periods of time. In the early CRT monitors, when the cursor was left blinking in the same spot for hours, burn-in was a concern. However, today's CRT display technology has changed; thus, burn-in is unlikely. Screen savers are now used almost exclusively for decoration.

You can control how long your computer sits idle before the screen saver starts. For example, if you don't want people looking at what's on your screen when you leave your computer unexpectedly for a time, you may want to program your screen saver to run after only a minute or two of inactivity. (Right-click on the Windows desktop to access Display Properties and click the Screen Saver tab.) However, if you find that you let your computer sit inactive for a while but need to look at the screen image (while you study or read a document or spreadsheet, for example), you may want to extend the period of inactivity.

Can I make the display on my LCD monitor clearer? If you use a notebook computer or have a flat-panel liquid crystal display (LCD) monitor, you may be interested in the Clear Type feature Windows Vista offers. Clear Type is a default setting

BITS AND BYTES

Putting Pictures on Your Desktop

You can have most any picture displayed as your desktop background with only a few clicks of your mouse. If you have a digital photograph or an image that you want displayed as your desktop background, simply right-click the image, select Set as Desktop Background, and you're done. Your image will appear immediately as the desktop background. With Mac OS X, you choose System Preferences, then Desktop & Screen Saver, and then the Desktop tab. Locate and select the image you want to use and the background changes immediately. Windows Vista offers a Gadget called Slide Show that displays a thumbnail-sized slide show of a group of images.

that smoothes the edges of screen fonts to make text easier to read. Note that Clear Type is not very effective with cathode-ray tube (CRT) monitors, so if you're working with a Vista-based system that still has a CRT monitor, you might want to turn off this feature.

THE ADD OR REMOVE PROGRAMS UTILITY

What is the correct way to add new programs to the system? These days, when you install a new program to your system, the program automatically runs a wizard (a step-by-step guide) that walks you through the installation process. If a wizard does not start automatically, however, you should go to the Add or Remove Programs folder in the Control Panel. This prompts the operating system to look for the setup program of the new software and starts the installation wizard.

What is the correct way to remove unwanted programs from my system? Some people think that deleting a program from the Program Files folder on the C drive is the best way to remove a program from the system. However, most programs include support files such as a help file, dictionaries, and graphics files that are not located in the main program folder found in Program Files. Depending on the supporting file's function, support files can be scattered throughout various folders within the system. You would normally miss these files by just deleting the main program file from the system. By selecting the Windows uninstaller utility, Add or Remove Programs, found in the Control Panel, you not only delete the main program file, but you delete all supporting files as well.

FILE COMPRESSION UTILITIES

What is file compression? A **file compression utility** is a program that takes out redundancies in a file to reduce the file size. File compression is helpful because it makes a large file more compact, making it easier and faster to send over the Internet, upload to a Web page, or save onto a disk. As shown in Figure 28, Windows Vista has built-in compression (or zip) file support. There are also several stand-alone freeware and shareware programs, such as WinZip (for Windows) and StuffIt (for Windows or Mac), that you can obtain to compress your files.

How does file compression work? Compression programs look for repeated patterns of letters and replace these patterns with a shorter placeholder. The repeated

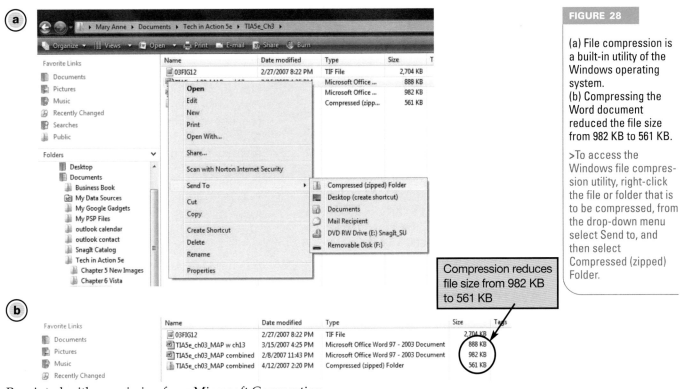

FIGURE 28

(a) File compression is a built-in utility of the Windows operating system.
(b) Compressing the Word document reduced the file size from 982 KB to 561 KB.

>To access the Windows file compression utility, right-click the file or folder that is to be compressed, from the drop-down menu select Send to, and then select Compressed (zipped) Folder.

Reprinted with permission from Microsoft Corporation

patterns and the associated placeholder are cataloged and stored temporarily in a separate file, called the dictionary. For example, in the following sentence, you can easily see the repeated patterns of letters:

The rain in Spain falls mainly on the plain.

Although this example contains obvious repeated patterns (**ain** and **the**), in a large document, the repeated patterns may be more complex. The compression program's algorithm (a set of instructions designed to complete a solution in a step-by-step manner) therefore runs through the file several times to determine the optimal repeated patterns to obtain the greatest compression.

How effective are file compression programs? The effectiveness of file compression—that is, how much a file's size is reduced—depends on several factors, including the type and size of the individual file and the compression method used. Current compression programs can reduce text files by as much as 50 percent. However, some files such as PDF files already contain a form of compression and therefore it is not necessary to compress further. Other file types, especially some graphics and audio formats, have gone through a compression process that reduces file size by permanently discarding data. For example, image files such as Joint Photographic Experts Group (JPEG), Graphics Interchange Format (GIF), and Portable Network Graphics (PNG) files discard small variations in colors that the human eye may not pick up. Likewise, MP3 files permanently discard sounds that the human ear cannot hear. These graphic and audio files do not need further compression.

How do I decompress a file I've compressed? When you want to restore the file to its original state, you need to decompress the file so that the pieces of file that the compression process temporarily removed are restored to the document. Generally, the same program you used to compress the file has the capability to decompress the file as well (see Figure 29).

SYSTEM MAINTENANCE UTILITIES

Are there any utilities that make my system work faster? Disk Cleanup is a Windows utility that cleans unnecessary files

from your hard drive. These include files that have accumulated in the Recycle Bin as well as temporary files, which are files created by Windows to store data temporarily when a program is running. Windows usually deletes these temporary files when you exit the program, but sometimes it forgets or doesn't have time if your system freezes up or incurs a problem preventing you from properly exiting a program. Disk Cleanup, found in System Tools in the Accessories folder in the Start Menu, also removes temporary Internet files (Web pages stored on your hard drive for quick viewing) as well as offline Web pages (pages are stored on your computer so you can view them without being connected to the Internet). If not deleted periodically, these unnecessary files can deter efficient operating performance.

How can I control which files Disk Cleanup deletes? When you run Disk Cleanup, the program scans your hard drive to determine which folders have files that can be deleted and calculates the amount of hard drive space that would be freed by doing so. You check off which type of files you would like to delete, as shown in Figure 30.

What else can I do if my system runs slowly? Over time, as you add and delete information in a file, the file pieces are saved in scattered locations on the hard disk. Locating all the pieces of the file takes extra time, making the operating system less efficient. **Disk defragmenter** regroups related pieces of files on the hard disk, allowing the OS to work more efficiently. You can find the Windows Disk Defragmenter utility under System Tools in the Accessories folder of the Start menu. Using the Windows Disk Defragmenter Analyzer feature, you should check several times a year to determine whether your drive needs to be defragmented. Unfortunately, Macs do not have a defrag utility built into the system because the thought is that the file system used by Mac OS X is so efficient that defragging the hard drive is unnecessary. Still, for those users who feel the need to defrag their Mac, iDefrag is an external program that can be purchased from Coriolis Systems.

How do I diagnose potential errors or damage on my storage devices? Error-checking, once known as ScanDisk, is a Windows utility that checks for lost files and fragments as well as physical errors on your hard drive. Lost files and fragments of files occur as you save, resave, move, delete,

SOUND BYTE

File Compression

In this Sound Byte, you'll learn about the advantages of file compression and how to use Windows Vista to compress and decompress files. If you own an earlier operating system, this Sound Byte will teach you how to find and install file compression shareware software programs.

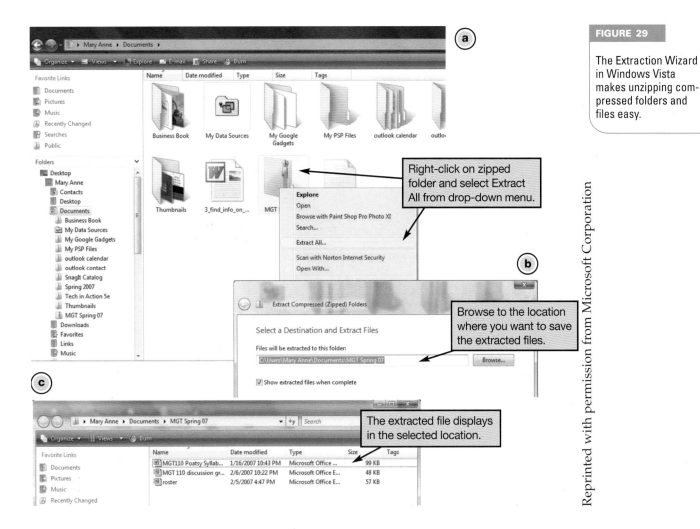

FIGURE 29

The Extraction Wizard in Windows Vista makes unzipping compressed folders and files easy.

Right-click on zipped folder and select Extract All from drop-down menu.

Browse to the location where you want to save the extracted files.

The extracted file displays in the selected location.

and copy files on your hard drive. Sometimes the system becomes confused, leaving references on the **file allocation table** or **FAT** (an index of all sector numbers in a table) to files that no longer exist or have been moved. Physical errors on the hard drive occur when the mechanism that reads the hard drive's data (which is stored as 1s or 0s) can no longer determine whether the area holds a 1 or a 0. These areas are called bad sectors. Sometimes Error-checking can recover the lost data, but more often it deletes the files that are taking up space unnecessarily. Error-checking also makes a note of any bad sectors so that the system will not use them again to store data.

Where can I find Error-checking? In Windows XP and Vista, the Error-checking utility can be found in Disk Properties. In earlier versions of a Windows operating system, Error-checking can be found in System Tools. To locate Error-checking in Windows Vista or XP, after clicking Computer from the Start menu, right-click the disk you want to

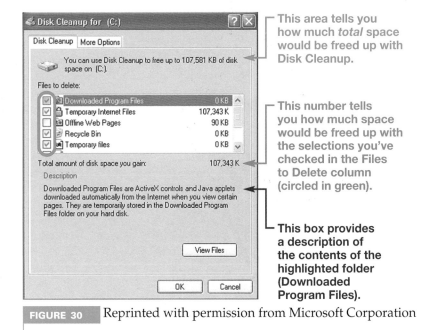

This area tells you how much *total* space would be freed up with Disk Cleanup.

This number tells you how much space would be freed up with the selections you've checked in the Files to Delete column (circled in green).

This box provides a description of the contents of the highlighted folder (Downloaded Program Files).

FIGURE 30 Reprinted with permission from Microsoft Corporation

Using Disk Cleanup will help free space on your hard drive.

>Disk Cleanup is accessed by clicking Start, All Programs, Accessories, and then System Tools.

How Disk Defragmenter Utilities Work

To understand how disk defragmenter utilities work, you must first understand the basics of how a hard disk drive stores files. A hard disk drive is composed of several platters, or round thin plates of metal, that are covered with a special magnetic coating that records the data. The platters are about 3.5 inches in diameter and are stacked onto a spindle. There are usually two or three platters in any hard disk drive, with data being stored on one or both sides. Data is recorded on hard disks in concentric circles, called **tracks**, which are further broken down into pie-shaped wedges called **sectors** (see Figure 31). The data is further identified by clusters, which are the smallest segments within the sectors.

When you want to save (or write) a file, the bits that make up your file are recorded onto one or more clusters of the drive. To keep track of which clusters hold which files, the drive also stores an index of all sector numbers in a table. To save a file, the computer will look in the table for clusters that are not already being used and will then record the file information on those clusters. When you open (or read) a file, the computer searches through the table for the clusters that hold the desired file and reads that file. Similarly, when you delete a file, you are actually not deleting the file itself, but rather the reference in the table to the file.

So, how does a disk become fragmented? When only part of an older file is deleted, the deleted section of the file creates a gap in the sector of the disk where the data was originally stored. In the same way, when new information is added to an older file, there may not be space to save the new information sequentially near where the

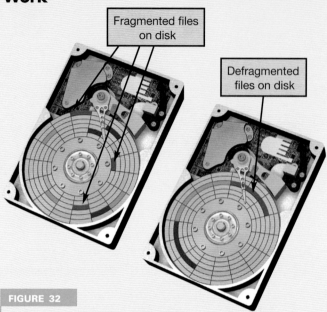

FIGURE 32

Over time, as files are saved, deleted, and modified, the fragments of information for various files fall out of sequential order on the hard disk and the disk becomes fragmented. Defragmenting the hard drive arranges file fragments so that they are located next to each other. This makes the hard drive run more efficiently.

file was originally saved. In that case, the system writes the added part of the file to the next available location on the disk, and a reference is made in the table as to the location of this file fragment. Over time, as files are saved, deleted, and modified, the bits of information for various files fall out of sequential order and the disk becomes fragmented.

Disk fragmentation is a problem because when a disk is fragmented, the operating system is not as efficient. It takes longer to locate a whole file because more of the disk must be searched for the various pieces, greatly slowing down the performance of your computer.

How can you make the files line up more efficiently on the disk? At this stage, the disk defragmenter utility enters the picture. The defragmenter tool takes the hard drive through a defragmentation process in which pieces of files that are scattered over the disk are placed together and arranged sequentially on the hard disk. Also, any unused portions of clusters that were too small in which to save data before are grouped, increasing the available storage space on the disk. Figure 32 shows before and after shots of a fragmented disk having gone through the defragmentation process.

For more about hard disks and defragmenting, be sure to check out the Sound Byte "Hard Disk Anatomy Interactive."

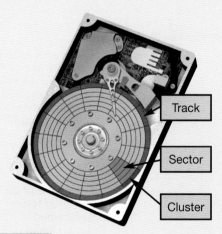

FIGURE 31

On a hard disk platter, data is recorded onto tracks, which are further broken down into sectors and clusters.

diagnose, select Properties, select Tools, and select Check Now. On Macs, you can use the Disk Utility to test and repair disks. You will find Disk Utility in the Utilities folder in the Applications folder on your hard drive.

How can I check on a program that has stopped running? If a program on your system has stopped working, you can use the Windows **Task Manager utility** to check on the program or to exit the nonresponsive program. Although you can access Task Manager from the Control Panel, it is more easily accessible by pressing the Ctrl+Alt+Del keys on your keyboard at the same time, or by right-clicking an empty space on the taskbar at the bottom of your screen. The Applications tab of Task Manager lists all programs that you are using and indicates whether they are working properly (running) or have stopped improperly (not responding). You can terminate programs that are not responding by clicking the End Task button in the dialog box.

If you need outside assistance due to a program error, **Dr. Watson for Windows**, a tool that is included in Microsoft Windows XP, and Problem Reports and Solutions, a tool in Windows Vista, gather information about the computer when there is a program error. When an error occurs, these tools automatically create and save a text log. The log can then be viewed, printed or delivered electronically to any technical support professional who can then use this information to help diagnose the problem.

SYSTEM RESTORE AND BACKUP UTILITIES

Is there an undo command for the system? Say you have just installed a new software program and your computer freezes. After rebooting the computer, when you try to start the application, the system freezes once again. You uninstall the new program, but your computer continues to freeze after rebooting. What can you do now?

Windows Vista has a utility called System Restore that lets you restore your system settings back to a specific date when everything was working properly. You can find System Restore under System Tools on the Accessories menu. If the computer was running just fine before you installed software or a new hardware device, you would restore your computer back to the settings before the software or

hardware installation. System Restore does not affect your personal data files (such as Microsoft Word documents, browsing history, drawings, favorites, or e-mail), so you won't lose changes made to these files when you use System Restore.

How does the computer remember its previous settings? Every time you start your computer, or when a new application or driver is installed, Windows Vista automatically creates a snapshot of your entire system's settings. This snapshot is called a **restore point**. You also can create and name your own restore points at any time. Creating a restore point is a good idea before making changes to your computer such as installing hardware or software. If something goes wrong with the installation process, Windows Vista can reset your system to the restore point. As shown in Figure 33, Windows includes a Restore Point Wizard that walks you through the process of setting restore points.

How can I protect my data in the event something malfunctions with my system? When you use the Windows **Backup utility**, you create a duplicate copy of all the data on your hard disk and copy it to another storage device, such as a CD or external hard drive. A backup copy protects your data in the event your hard disk fails or files are accidentally erased. Although you may not need to back up *every* file on your computer, you should back up the files that are most important to you and keep the backup copy in a safe location.

BITS AND BYTES

Need a System Software Update?

Bugs, or problems, in software occur all the time. Software developers are constantly testing their products, even after releasing the software to the retail market, and as users report errors they find. Windows Update is Microsoft's service for updating operating system software. For Windows Vista users, Windows Update automatically notifies you when updates are available for download. Mac users can update their system with Software Update found under System Preferences.

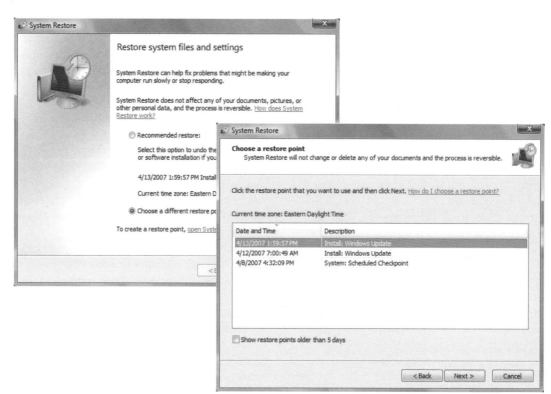

Reprinted with permission from Microsoft Corporation

Setting a restore point is good practice before installing any hardware or software.

>The Restore Point Wizard is found by clicking Start, All Programs, Accessories, System Tools. In the System Tools folder, click System Restore. The System Restore wizard displays, with Restore Point shown on the first page of the Wizard.

THE TASK SCHEDULER UTILITY

How can I remember to perform all these maintenance procedures? To keep your computer system in top shape, it is important to routinely run some of the utilities described above. Depending on your usage, you may want to defrag your hard drive or clean out temporary Internet files periodically. However, many computer users forget to initiate these tasks. Luckily, the Windows **Task Scheduler utility**, shown in Figure 34, allows you to schedule tasks to run automatically at predetermined times, with no interaction necessary on your part.

ACCESSIBILITY UTILITIES

Are there utilities designed for users with special needs? Windows Vista has created an Ease of Access Center, which is a centralized location for assistive technology and tools to adjust accessibility settings. In the Ease of Access Center, you can find tools to help you adjust the contrast of or magnify the screen image, have screen contents read to you, and display an on-screen keyboard as more fully explained in the following list. If you're not sure what where to start or what settings might help, there is a questionnaire that asks about routine tasks and

provides a personalized recommendation for settings that will help you use your computer (see Figure 35). Some of these features are described below:

- High Contrast allows you to select a color scheme setting in which you can control the contrast between text and background. Because some visually impaired individuals find it easier to see white text on a dark background, there are color schemes that invert screen colors.

- The Magnifier is a display utility that creates a separate window that displays a magnified portion of your screen. This feature makes the screen more readable for users who have impaired vision. The Narrator utility is a very basic speech program that reads what is on-screen, whether it's the contents of a window, menu options, or text you have typed. The Narrator coordinates with text utilities, such as Notepad and WordPad, as well as Internet Explorer, but may not work correctly with other programs. For this reason, Narrator is not meant for individuals who must rely solely on a text-to-speech utility to operate the computer.

ACTIVE HELPDESK

Using Utility Programs

In this Active Helpdesk call, you'll play the role of a Helpdesk staffer, fielding calls about the utility programs included in system software and what they do.

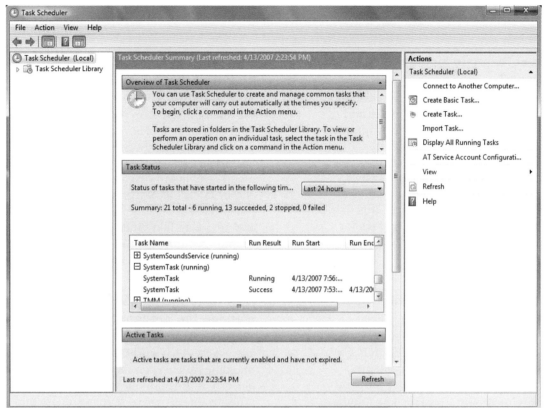

Reprinted with permission from Microsoft Corporation

- The On-Screen Keyboard displays a keyboard on the screen. You type by clicking on or hovering over the keys with a pointing device (mouse or trackball) or joystick. This utility, which is similar to the Narrator, is not meant for everyday use for individuals with severe disabilities. A separate program with more functionality is better in those circumstances.

- Windows Speech Recognition is an effective tool that allows you to dictate text and control your computer by voice. The speech recognition utility is in the Ease of Access folder, which can be found in the Control Panel.

FIGURE 34

To keep your machine running in top shape, use Task Scheduler to schedule maintenance programs to run automatically at selected times and days.

>Task Scheduler is found by clicking Start, All Programs, Accessories and then System Tools.

SOUND BYTE

Letting Your Computer Clean Up After Itself

In this Sound Byte, you'll learn how to use the various maintenance utilities within the operating system. In addition, you'll learn how to use Task Scheduler to clean up your hard disk automatically. You'll also learn the best times of the day to schedule these maintenance tasks and why they should be done on a routine basis to make your system more efficient.

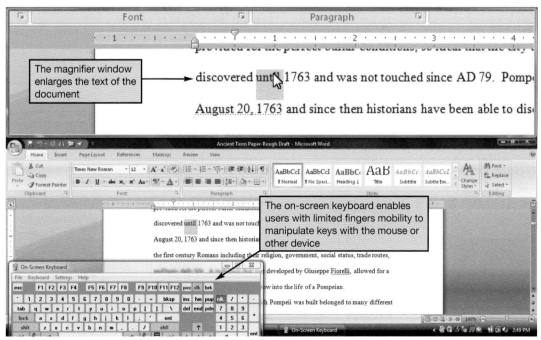

Reprinted with permission from Microsoft Corporation

FIGURE 35

Microsoft Windows includes some handy accessibility features, such as a magnifier and an on-screen keyboard, to help those with disabilities. These features are not meant to be sufficient for those users with severe disabilities. There are full-blown software applications to fill those needs.

Utility Programs

Summary

1. What software is included in system software?

System software is the set of software programs that helps run the computer and coordinates instructions between application software and hardware devices. It consists of the operating system (OS) and utility programs. The operating system controls how your computer system functions. Utility programs are programs that perform general housekeeping tasks for the computer, such as system maintenance and file compression.

2. What are the different kinds of operating systems?

Operating systems can be classified into four categories. Real-Time OSs (RTOSs) require no user intervention and are designed for systems with a specific purpose and response time (such as robotic machinery). Single-user, single-task OSs are designed for computers on which one user is performing one task at a time (such as PDAs). Single-user, multitask OSs are designed for computers on which one user is performing more than one task at a time (such as desktop computers). Multiuser OSs are designed for systems in which multiple users are working on more than one task at a time (such as networks).

3. What are the most common desktop operating systems?

Microsoft Windows is the most popular OS. It has evolved from being a single-user, single-task OS into a powerful multiuser operating system. The most recent release is Windows Vista. Another popular OS is the Mac OS, which is designed to work on Apple computers. Its most recent release, Mac OS X Leopard, is based on the UNIX operating system. You'll find various versions of UNIX on the market, although it is most often used on networks. Linux is an open-source OS based on UNIX and designed primarily for use on personal computers, although it is often found as the operating system on many other devices.

4. How does the operating system provide a means for users to interact with the computer?

The operating system provides a user interface that enables you to interact with the computer. Most OSs today use a graphical user interface (GUI). Unlike the command- and menu-driven interfaces used earlier, GUIs display graphics and use the point-and-click technology of the mouse and cursor, making the OS more user-friendly. Common features of GUIs include windows, menus, and icons.

5. How does the operating system help manage the processor?

When you use your computer, you are usually asking it to perform several tasks at the same time. When the OS allows you to perform more than one task at a time, it is multitasking. To provide for seamless multitasking, the OS controls the timing of events the processor works on.

6. How does the operating system manage memory and storage?

As the OS coordinates the activities of the processor, it uses RAM as a temporary storage area for instructions and data the processor needs. The OS is therefore responsible for coordinating the space allocations in RAM to ensure that there is enough space for the waiting instructions and data. If there isn't sufficient space in RAM for all the data and instructions, the OS allocates the least necessary files to temporary storage on the hard drive, called virtual memory. The OS manages storage by providing a file management system that keeps track of the names and locations of files and programs.

7. How does the operating system manage hardware and peripheral devices?

Programs called device drivers facilitate the communication between devices attached to the computer and the OS. Device drivers translate the specialized commands of devices to commands that the OS can understand, and vice versa, enabling the OS to communicate with every device in the computer system. Device drivers for common devices are included in the OS software, whereas other devices come with a device driver you have to install or download off the Web.

8. How does the operating system interact with application software?

All software applications need to interact with the CPU. For programs to work with the CPU, they must contain code the CPU recognizes. Rather than having the same blocks of code appear in each software application, the OS includes the blocks of code to which software applications refer. These blocks of code are called application programming interfaces (APIs).

9. How does the operating system help the computer start up?

When you start your computer, it runs through a special process, called the boot process. The boot process consists of four basic steps: (1) the basic input/output system (BIOS) is activated by powering on the CPU; (2) in the POST test, the BIOS checks that all attached devices are in place; (3) the operating system is loaded into RAM; and (4) configuration and customization settings are checked.

10. What are the main desktop and windows features?

The desktop is the first interaction you have with the OS and the first image you see on your monitor once the system has booted up. It provides you with access to your computer's files, folders, and commonly used tools and applications. Windows are the rectangular panes on your screen that display applications running on your system. Common features of windows include toolbars (or ribbons) and scrollbars, and minimize, maximize, and restore buttons.

11. How does the operating system help me keep my computer organized?

The OS allows you to organize the contents of your computer in a hierarchical structure of directories that includes files, folders, and drives. Windows Explorer helps you manage your files and folders by showing the location and contents of every drive, folder, and file on your computer. Creating folders is the key to organizing files, because folders keep related documents together. Following naming conventions and using proper file extensions are also important aspects of file management.

12. What utility programs are included in system software, and what do they do?

Some utility programs are incorporated into the OS; others are sold as stand-alone off-the-shelf programs. Common Windows utilities include those that enable you to adjust your display, add or remove programs, compress files, defrag your hard drive, clean unnecessary files off your system, check for lost files and errors, restore your system to an earlier setting, back up your files, schedule automatic tasks, and check on programs that have quit running.

Key Terms

application programming interface (API)
application software
authentication
Backup utility
basic input/output system (BIOS)
boot process
command-driven interface
desktop
device driver
Device Manager
directory
Disk Cleanup
disk defragmenter
Dr. Watson for Windows
Error-checking
event
Explorers
extension (file type)
file
File Allocation Table (FAT)
file compression utility
file management
file path
filename
Flip
Flip 3D
folder
Gadget
graphical user interface (GUI)
icon
interrupt
kernel (supervisor program)
Last Known Good Configuration
Linux
Mac OS
mainframe
menu-driven interface
menu
Microsoft Disk Operating System (MS-DOS)
Microsoft Windows

multitasking
multiuser operating system (network operating system)
open-source program
operating system (OS)
paging
path separator
platform
Plug and Play (PnP)
power-on self-test (POST)
preemptive multitasking
real-time operating system (RTOS)
Recycle Bin
registry
restore point
root directory
Safe mode
screen saver
scrollbar
sector
server
Sidebar
single-user, multitask operating system
single-user, single-task operating system
source code
spooler
swap file (page file)
system file
System Restore
system software
Task Manager utility
Task Scheduler utility
thrashing
toolbar
track
UNIX
user interface
utility program
virtual memory
window

Buzz Words

Word Bank

- defrag
- Error-checking
- Explore
- file compression
- file management
- files
- folders
- Linux
- Mac OS
- platform
- sectors
- system software
- Task Manager
- Task Scheduler
- tracks
- utility programs
- Windows
- Windows Vista

Instructions: Fill in the blanks using the words from the Word Bank above.

Veena was looking into buying a new computer and was trying to decide what (1) _____ to buy, a PC or a Mac. She had used PCs all her life, so she was more familiar with the (2) _____ operating system. Still, she liked the way the (3) _____ looked and was considering switching. Her brother didn't like either operating system, so he used (4) _____ , a free operating system instead.

After a little research, Veena decided to buy a PC. With it, she got the most recent version of Windows, (5) _____. She vowed that with this computer, she'd practice better (6) _____, because she often had a hard time finding files on her old computer. To view all of the folders on her computer, she opened (7) _____ . She made sure that she gave descriptive names to her (8) _____ and placed them in organized (9) _____ .

Veena also decided that with her new computer, she'd pay more attention to the (10) _____ , those little special-function programs that help with maintenance and repairs. These special-function programs, in addition to the OS, make up the (11) _____ . Veena looked into some of the more frequently used utilities. She thought it would be a good idea to (12) _____ her hard drive regularly so that all the files lined up in sequentially ordered (13) _____ and so that it was more efficient. She also looked into (14) _____ utilities, which would help her reduce the size of her files when she sent them to others over the Internet. Finally, she decided to use the Windows (15) _____ utility to schedule tasks automatically so that she wouldn't forget.

Becoming Computer Literate

Using key terms from the chapter, write a letter to your computer-illiterate aunt explaining the benefits of simple computer maintenance. First, explain any symptoms her computer may be experiencing (such as a sluggish Internet connection); then include a set of steps she can follow in setting up a regimen to remedy the problems. Make sure you explain some of the system utilities described in this chapter, including, but not limited to, defrag, Disk Cleanup, and Task Scheduler. Include any other utilities she might need and explain why she should have them.

Instructions: Answer the multiple-choice and true/false questions below for more practice with key terms and concepts from this chapter.

MULTIPLE CHOICE

1. Cell phones use which category of operating system?
   a. Single-user, single task
   b. Multiuser, multitask
   c. Single-user, multitask
   d. Real-time

2. Which of the following would be found in a GUI operating system?
   a. Icons   c. Scroll bars
   b. Windows   d. All of the above

3. Virtual memory is
   a. another name for hard drive storage.
   b. another name for RAM.
   c. the process of managing memory demands by borrowing space on the hard drive .
   d. smaller, faster memory used by the CPU.

4. Which is an indication that a device is Plug and Play? You can
   a. multitask by listening to a CD and surfing the Internet.
   b. install gaming software without going through Add/Remove Programs.
   c. install a hardware device without separately installing a driver.
   d. All of the above

5. Which of the following is NOT done during the boot process?
   a. Checks that all attached devices are in place and working
   b. Verifies the user's login name and password

c. Loads the OS to the hard drive
   d. Checks for customized settings put in place for the monitor and desktop

6. When an operating system allows you to do more than one task at a time, it is called
   a. thrashing.   c. caching.
   b. multitasking.   d. paging.

7. Which view option would be best to use to sort your files by date modified and type of application?
   a. Details   c. Large Icons
   b. Tiles   d. All of the above

8. Which of the following file extensions indicates a file created by a program in the Office 2007 suite?
   a. bioreport.zip   c. bioreport.ppt
   b. bioreport.xls   d. bioreport.docx

9. To regroup related pieces of files on the hard drive so that the hard drive works more efficiently, which utility would you use?
   a. System Restore
   b. Disk Defragmenter
   c. Windows Explorer
   d. Disk Cleanup

10. Which utility should you use to schedule utility programs to run automatically?
    a. Task Maintainer
    b. Task Scheduler
    c. Task Manager
    d. Task Director

TRUE/FALSE

_____ 1. Restore points cannot be set manually.

_____ 2. Linux is a single-user, multitasking operating system.

_____ 3. Open-source operating systems are proprietary and cannot be modified by users.

_____ 4. It is possible for a computer to run out of virtual memory.

_____ 5. Only files deleted from the hard drive end up in the Recycle Bin.

Making the Transition to... Next Semester

1. **Organizing Files and Folders**

   It's the beginning of a new semester, and you promise yourself that you are going to keep all files related to your schoolwork more organized this semester. Develop a plan that outlines how you'll set up folders and subfolders for each subject. Identify at least three different folders for each class. If time and schedule permit, discuss your organization scheme with your instructor.

2. **OS Compatibility Issues**

   Your school requires that you purchase a notebook to run on the school's system. The required machine runs on the Windows operating system. You have a reasonably new Apple computer at home.
   a. Research the compatibility issues between the two computers.
   b. How does a PDA running with Palm OS fit into the equation?
   c. Can you synch the PDA with either or both machines?
   d. Explore the application Virtual PC. What does it do? Would it be helpful in this situation?

3. **Understanding Safe Mode**

   It is the night before the major term paper for your philosophy class is due. Your best friend comes screaming down the hall, begging for help. His only copy of his draft paper is on his desktop computer, and it is suddenly booting up with the words Safe Mode in the corners of the screen. What would be the most useful questions to ask him? What steps would you take to debug the problem? If you cannot get the computer to come out of Safe mode, is there a way to retrieve the draft? How many times will you say, "Make backups!" that evening?

4. **Software Requirements**

   This semester you have added six new applications to your notebook. You know which courses you will be taking next semester, and you realize they will require an additional eight major software applications. A friend who is in a similar position tells you she's not worried about putting that much software on her computer because she has a really big hard drive.
   a. Is hard disk storage your only concern? Should it be your main concern, or should you worry more about having sufficient RAM? How does your use of the programs impact your answer?
   b. Does virtual memory management by your operating system allow you to ignore RAM requirements?

5. **Connecting Peripherals**

   You decide to buy a new keyboard for next semester, a very fancy one that is wireless and that features integrated volume and CD player controls, and an integrated trackball. You also are planning to upgrade your printer. Do you have to worry about having the correct device drivers for these peripherals if:

   a. you are using a Plug and Play operating system?
   b. you are upgrading to the latest version of the Windows operating system?
   c. you have an older PC and its original operating system, Windows 95?

Making the Transition to... the Workplace

1. Organizing Files and Folders

You started a new job and are given a new computer. You never kept your files and folders organized on the computer you used when in college, but now you are determined to do a better job at keeping your files organized. You know you need folders for the several clients with whom you will be working. For each client, you'll need to have folders for billing information, client documents, and account information. In addition, you need folders for the MP3 files you will listen to when you're not working, as well as a folder for the digital pictures you'll take for personal and company reasons. Finally, you're working toward an advanced degree and will be taking business finance and introduction to marketing courses at night, so you'll need folders for all the homework assignments for both courses. Determine the file structure you would need to create to accommodate your needs. Start with the C drive and assume that Documents, Pictures, and Music are the default folders for documents, pictures, and music files, respectively.

2. Using Mac Utility Programs

Your company has been having trouble with some of its Mac computers running inefficiently. Your boss asks you to research the utility programs your company could use on its Macs to make them run better. In particular, your boss would like you to determine what utilities are available in the Mac OS and then determine what utilities the company may need to purchase. Also, your boss wants to ensure the availability of a disk defrag utility, a file compression utility, and a diagnostic utility you could run to check the hard drive for errors. Using the Internet for your research, what utilities are already in the Mac OS, and what stand-alone utilities can you find? Will they run on all versions of the Mac OS?

3. Monitoring Activities with the OS

The company that you work for has just announced a new internal accounting structure. From now on, each department will be charged individually for the costs associated with computer usage, such as backup storage space, Internet usage, and so on.

a. Research how the operating system may be set up to monitor such activity by department.
b. What other activities do you think the operating system can be set up to monitor?

4. Choosing the Best OS

Your new boss is considering moving some of the department operations to UNIX-based computer systems. He asks you to research the advantages and disadvantages of moving to UNIX, Linux, or Mac OS X. How would these choices impact his department in the following areas?

a. Budget for technical support for the systems
b. Choice and budget for hardware for the systems
c. Costs of implementation
d. Possibility for future upgrades

Critical Thinking Questions

Instructions: Albert Einstein used "Gedanken experiments," or critical thinking questions, to develop his theory of relativity. Some ideas are best understood by experimenting with them in our own minds. The following critical thinking questions are designed to demand your full attention but require only a comfortable chair—no technology.

1. **Open-Source Pros and Cons**

   Open-source programming embraces a philosophy that states programmers should make their code available to everyone rather than keeping it proprietary. The Linux operating system has had much success as an open-source code. The chapter mentions some of the advantages of open-source code, such as quicker code updates in response to technological advances and changes.

   a. What are other advantages of open-source code?
   b. Can you think of disadvantages to open-source code?
   c. Why do you think that companies such as Microsoft maintain proprietary restrictions on their code?
   d. Are there disadvantages to maintaining proprietary code?

2. **The OS of the Future**

   Operating system interfaces have evolved from a text-based console format to the current graphical user interface. What direction do you think they will move toward next? How could operating systems be organized and used in a manner that is more responsive to humans and better suited to how we think? Are there alternatives to hierarchical file structures for storage? Can you think of ways in which operating systems could adapt and customize themselves based on your usage?

3. **Which OS Would You Choose?**

   Suppose you are building a computer system from scratch and have complete discretion as to your choice of operating system. Which one would you install and why?

4. **The OS: With or Without Utilities?**

   Which environment do you think is better for consumers: to have companies develop smaller, more inexpensive operating systems and then allow competing companies to develop and market utility programs, or to have very large full-featured operating systems that include most utilities as part of the operating system itself? Do you think that including utility programs with the operating system makes the cost of the operating system higher?

Problem:

You have been hired to help set up the technology requirements for a small advertising company. The company is holding off buying anything until the decision has been made as to the platform on which the computers should run. Obviously, one of the critical decisions is the operating system.

Task:

Recommend the appropriate operating system for the company.

Process:

1. Break up into three teams. Each team will represent one of the three primary operating systems today: Windows, Mac, and Linux.

2. As a team, research the pros and cons of your operating system. What features does it have that would benefit your company? What features does it not have that your company would need? Why (or why not) would your operating system be the appropriate choice? Why is your OS better (or worse) than either of the other two options?

3. Develop a presentation that states your position with regard to your operating system. Your presentation should have a recommendation, with facts to back it up.

4. As a class, decide which operating system would be the best choice for the company.

Conclusion:

Because the operating system is the critical piece of software in the computer system, the selection should not be taken lightly. The OS that is best for an advertising agency may not be best for an accounting firm. It is important to make sure you consider all aspects of the work environment and the type of work that is being done to ensure a good fit.

Multimedia

In addition to the review materials presented here, you'll find additional materials featured with the book's multimedia, including the Technology in Action Student Resource CD and the Companion Web Site (**www.prenhall.com/techinaction**), which will help reinforce your understanding of the chapter content. These materials include the following:

ACTIVE HELPDESK

In Active Helpdesk calls, you'll assume the role of Helpdesk operator, taking calls about the concepts you've learned in this chapter. You'll apply what you've learned and receive feedback from a supervisor to review and reinforce those concepts. The Active Helpdesk calls for this chapter are listed below and can be found on your Student Resource CD:

- Managing Hardware and Peripheral Devices: The OS
- Starting the Computer: The Boot Process
- Organizing Your Computer: File Management
- Using Utility Programs

SOUND BYTES

Sound Bytes are dynamic multimedia tutorials that help demystify even the most complex topics. You'll view video clips and animations that illustrate computer concepts, and then apply what you've learned by reviewing with the Sound Byte Labs, which include quizzes and activities specifically tailored to each Sound Byte. The Sound Bytes for this chapter are listed below and can be found on your Student Resource CD:

- Customizing Windows Vista
- File Management
- File Compression
- Hard Disk Anatomy Interactive
- Letting Your Computer Clean Up After Itself

COMPANION WEB SITE

The Technology in Action Companion Web Site includes a variety of additional materials to help you review and learn more about the topics in this chapter. The resources available at **www.prenhall.com/techinaction** include:

- **Online Study Guide.** Each chapter features an online true/false and multiple-choice quiz. You can take these quizzes, automatically check the results, and e-mail the results to your instructor.
- **Web Research Projects.** Each chapter features a number of Web research projects that ask you to search the Web for information on computer-related careers, milestones in computer history, important people and companies, emerging technologies, and the applications and implications of different technologies.

Computing | Alternatives

You may think that there are no viable alternatives to buying computers running Microsoft Windows and using Microsoft Office applications like Word and Excel. However, in this Technology in Focus feature, we explore software and hardware alternatives to Microsoft products that may provide you with cheaper and more flexible options. Let's get started by looking at alternatives to Microsoft Office products.

Application Software Alternatives

Commercial (or proprietary) software is developed by corporations such as Microsoft and Apple to be sold for a profit. Opponents of proprietary software contend that software should be developed without profit motive and that the source code (the actual lines of instructional code that make the program work) should be made available so that others may modify or improve the software. **Open-source software** is freely distributed (no royalties accrue to the creators), contains the source code, and can in turn be distributed to others. Therefore, you can download open-source software for free from various Web sites, install it on as many computers as you wish, make changes to the source code if you know how, and redistribute it to anyone you wish (as long as you don't charge for distributing it). In this section, we look at some open-source software that you can download and use on your computer. For a list of open-source resources available on the Web, visit **www.sourceforge.net**.

PRODUCTIVITY SOFTWARE ALTERNATIVES: OPENOFFICE

The OpenOffice.org suite (OpenOffice) is a free suite of productivity software programs that provide similar functionality to Microsoft Office. Versions of OpenOffice are available for a variety of operating systems, including Windows, Linux, and Mac OS. It currently offers support in more than 90 languages besides English, with more being added all the time by the development community. You can download the installation file you'll need to run OpenOffice at **www.openoffice.org**. The minimum system requirements for installing OpenOffice 2.3 in a Windows environment are less than those required for Microsoft Office Professional Edition 2007.

The main components of OpenOffice are word processor (Writer), spreadsheet (Calc), and presentation (Impress) programs that provide similar functionality to the Word, Excel, and PowerPoint applications you're familiar with in Microsoft Office. OpenOffice 2.3 now also includes three additional programs in the suite. Draw provides the typical tools to communicate with graphics and diagrams, Math creates equations and formulas for your documents, and Base allows you to create and manipulate database tables.

The great advantage of OpenOffice is its compatibility with most programs. This means that if your friend uses Microsoft Office 2003 and you send her an OpenOffice file, she can still read it, and you can read all of her Microsoft Office files, too. As is the case even with Microsoft Office 2003 users, however, a converter must be used to open files created in the XML format of Microsoft Office 2007. Although the individual applications in OpenOffice are not as full-featured as those in Microsoft Office, and although they do not have the new ribbon interface found in Office 2007 applications, it is still a powerful productivity software suite, and the price is right.

When you launch OpenOffice via the Quickstarter icon (see Figure 1), you are presented with a list of document types from which to choose. Once you select the appropriate document type (such as spreadsheet, presentation, or text) and click Open, the appropriate application and a new, blank document will open so that you can begin working.

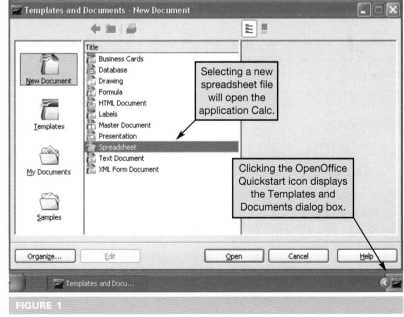

FIGURE 1

The Templates and Documents dialog box in OpenOffice 2.3 allows you to select the type of document you wish to start. The appropriate application will then open.

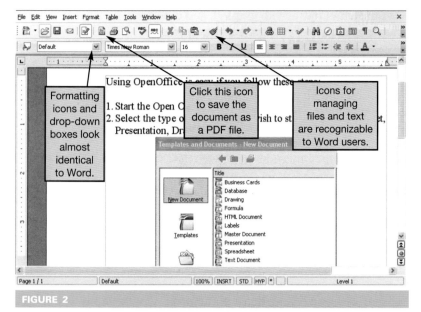

FIGURE 2

Writer provides similar functionality and icons to Microsoft Word 2003 and allows users to create versatile documents that can be saved in a variety of formats.

Writer

Writer, the OpenOffice word-processing application, is very similar in look and feel to Microsoft Word 2003. As is the case in Word, you can easily change text appearance in Writer by altering font type, style, alignment, and color. You can also easily insert graphics (pictures or clip art), tables, and hyperlinks into documents. Writer's wizards provide you with a number of templates you can use to create standard documents such as faxes, agendas, and letters.

Special tools in Writer also allow you to create bibliographic references, indexes, and tables of contents for your documents.

When saving a document in Writer, the default file format has an .odt extension. By using the Save As command, you can save files in other formats, such as various versions of Word (.doc), Pocket Word (.psw) for mobile devices, Rich Text Format (.rtf), Text (.txt), and HTML Document (.htm). The handy Export Directly as PDF icon in Writer allows you to save documents as PDF files (see Figure 2).

Calc

Opening a blank spreadsheet with Calc is just like starting one in Microsoft Excel. Once you open a spreadsheet, you enter text, numbers, and formulas into the appropriate cells. You also can apply a full range of formatting options (font size, color, style, and so on) to the cells, making it easy to create files such as the monthly budget spreadsheet shown in Figure 3. Built-in formulas and functions simplify the job of creating spreadsheets, and Calc's Function Wizard guides you through the wide range of available functions, providing suggestions as to which function to use.

When saving a document in Calc, the default file format has an .ods extension. By using the Save As command, you can save files in other formats, such as various versions of Excel (.xls), including Pocket Excel (.pxl) for use on mobile devices. The handy Export Directly as PDF icon is also available in Calc.

Impress

To start Impress, select Presentation from the OpenOffice start-up interface, and you'll be presented with a wizard that offers you the option of creating a blank presentation or building one from supplied templates. Although Microsoft PowerPoint has a vast array of stunning templates, the templates supplied with Impress are less than impressive. Still, it is easy to construct attractive slides and save them as templates yourself. Or just Google the words "OpenOffice Impress Templates" and you'll find a wide variety of templates for Impress that others have created and that you can download free of charge. To help you in the search, OpenOffice installation includes the option of installing Google search (Web or Desktop), which will appear in the taskbar, making it easily accessible while working in any of the OpenOffice applications.

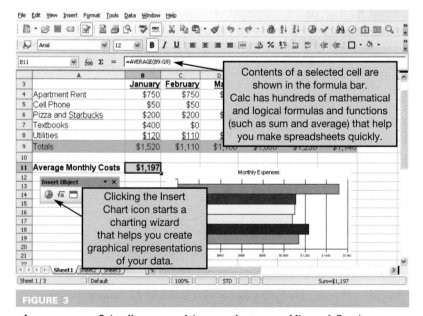

FIGURE 3

As you can see, Calc offers many of the same features as Microsoft Excel.

DATABASE SOFTWARE ALTERNATIVES: BASE AND MYSQL

OpenOffice 2.3 contains Base, a database product similar to Microsoft Access or SQL Server. Like the other OpenOffice programs, Base works seamlessly with database files created in other applications; except Access 2007 which, again, needs a separate converter. Alternatively, if you're interested in getting your hands on a free high-end SQL database application, the most popular open-source alternative is MySQL (**www.mysql.com**). Sporting many of the features contained in SQL Server and Oracle Database 10g, MySQL is a powerful database program you can use to develop serious database applications (see Figure 4). Although it is more difficult to learn and use than Microsoft Access, many books and online tutorials are available to help you get MySQL up and running.

E-MAIL CLIENT ALTERNATIVES: EUDORA AND THUNDERBIRD

If you are exploring other choices for Microsoft Office productivity applications, don't overlook exploring other e-mail clients as alternatives to Microsoft Outlook. Eudora is a popular e-mail client that is available in a free, but feature-limited, version. Although Eudora does not contain some of the components you may like in Outlook, such as a calendar and task manager, it does allow filtering, filing, and editing e-mail messages to help you keep your electronic communications organized. Mozilla Thunderbird is an open-source e-mail client and in its basic form only manages e-mail. But plenty of add-ons are available from the Mozilla Web site, including a calendar, a calculator, and search tools. Thunderbird can run on Windows, Linux, and Mac OS platforms.

DRAWING SOFTWARE ALTERNATIVES: DRAW AND DIA

Microsoft Visio is a popular program for creating flowcharts and diagrams. However, Visio is not cheap. OpenOffice includes a program called Draw that allows

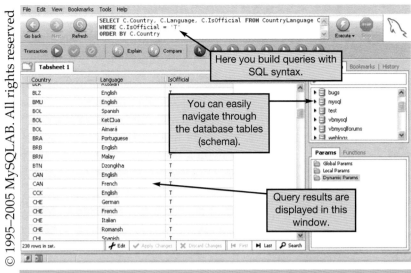

Here you build queries with SQL syntax.

You can easily navigate through the database tables (schema).

Query results are displayed in this window.

FIGURE 4

The two main components that you should download and install with MySQL are the Database Server and the Query Browser, shown here. You use the Database Server to create tables for your database and enter your data. The Query Browser provides a visual interface with the database to display the results of queries you create.

you to create simple graphs, charts, and diagrams. Another option is Dia, a free program that allows you to create Visio-like diagrams and charts (see Figure 5). You can download a Windows-compatible version of Dia from **http://live.gnome.org/Dia**. The Web site also offers a tutorial to get you up and running.

DIA created by Alexander Larsson and further developed by James Henstridge, Cyrille Chepelov, Lars Clausen, Hans Breuer, and numerous others

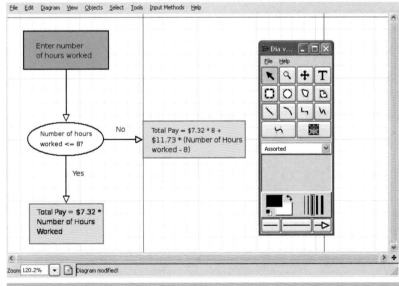

FIGURE 5

With Dia, you can create simple flowcharts, which a computer programmer might use in developing algorithms. Although not as powerful as Visio, Dia is available at no charge.

WEB PAGE AUTHORING SOFTWARE ALTERNATIVES: NVU

Although Microsoft Word and OpenOffice Writer can save documents as HTML files, sometimes you need a more versatile tool for creating Web pages, especially for larger sites with many linked pages. Adobe Dreamweaver is a popular commercial package for building Web sites. But NVU (pronounced "N-view" and available at **www.nvu.com**) is a viable open-source alternative to these commercial packages (see Figure 6). And like most open-source software, it's free. In addition to being available for the Windows operating systems, NVU also has versions that run on Mac OS X and Linux.

Another great thing about NVU is that you don't need to know HTML to generate a Web page: NVU generates the HTML code for you. However, you can reveal the HTML code with just a click of the mouse if you're familiar with HTML and want to tweak it.

IMAGE-EDITING SOFTWARE ALTERNATIVES: GIMP

Need to create or edit some digital art but can't afford a high-end package like Adobe Photoshop or even a consumer package like Adobe Photoshop Elements? Download a free copy of GIMP (short for GNU Image Manipulation Program) at **www.gimp.org** and you'll find a set of tools almost as powerful as Photoshop. In addition, GIMP is available for systems running Windows, Mac OS, Linux, or UNIX. Many good tutorials are deployed at **www.gimp.org/tutorials** to get you up to speed in no time.

Here are some handy things you can do with GIMP in five minutes or less:

- Crop or change the size of an image (see Figure 7).
- Reduce the file size of an image by decreasing its quality.
- Flip an image or rotate an image 90 degrees.

GIMP also enables you to use more advanced skills, such as applying image filters, creating textures and gradients, drawing digital art, creating animated images through layer manipulation, and changing photos into a painting or sketch.

Operating System Alternatives

Installing open-source application software like OpenOffice on a Windows machine is simple. A bit more complex is changing your operating system from Windows to an open-source OS such as Linux. Why would you want to switch to Linux if you already own Windows?

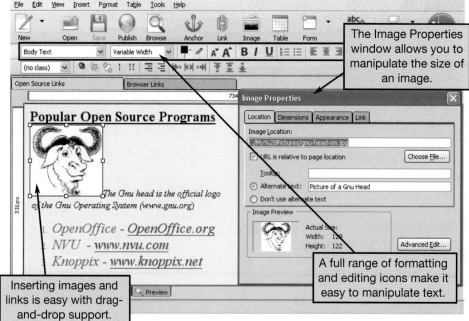

The Image Properties window allows you to manipulate the size of an image.

A full range of formatting and editing icons make it easy to manipulate text.

Inserting images and links is easy with drag-and-drop support.

Before Windows XP, many people felt Windows was not stable. Citing lockups and forced reboots, many users searched for an OS that would not crash as often. With Windows XP (especially with Service Pack 2 installed), Microsoft has done a great deal to address stability issues. Now, with Windows Vista, many fear that the instability that comes with a new operating system is back.

Stability issues aside, Windows is still plagued by security issues. A lot of spyware, computer viruses, and other hacker nuisances are designed to take advantage of security flaws in Windows. Although Windows Vista has reportedly addressed many of the security issues in Windows XP, because Windows (Vista or XP) is the most widely used OS, it's still a prime target for viruses and other annoyances. From a virus creator's or hacker's perspective, nuisances that spread through Windows will have the greatest chance of causing the most aggravation. An open-source OS alternative such as Linux that is not as widely used as Windows might be less of a target for these annoyances.

Another reason to install an open-source OS is portability. Depending on which version of Linux you use (we'll discuss various options next), you may be able to take it

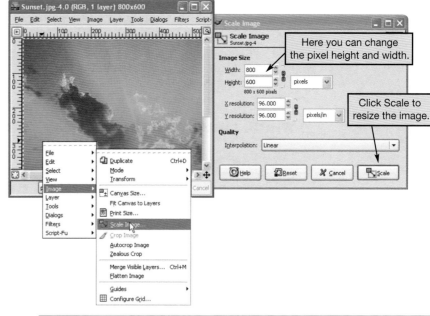

FIGURE 7

Using the Scale Image feature of GIMP, you can easily change an image (such as this image of a sunset) to the exact pixel size you need in order to fit on a Web site, for example.

with you on a CD or flash drive and use it on almost any computer. This portability feature appeals to people who use a lot of different computers (such as lab computers at school). Instead of getting used to a new

Photo Management Software Alternatives: JAlbum

If you're like many people, you have gigabytes of digital photos on your hard drive. But how can you easily organize photos for display on a Web site so that you can share them with friends and family? An open-source option is JAlbum (available at **http://jalbum.net**), a program that allows you to create Web albums of your digital images easily using simple drag-and-drop tools. JAlbum is available for the Windows, Mac OS, Linux, UNIX, and Solaris operating systems and supports 30 languages.

JAlbum provides significant advantages over some commercial photo management systems because it provides you with a high degree of control over the look and feel of the album you create. It also offers many templates if you don't have the time, energy, or artistic flair to create your own. You also can use JAlbum to create index and slide show pages, and the software will upload your album to the Internet. Best of all, your friends and family don't need any software other than a current Web browser to view your album. You can also choose to burn your albums onto a CD for sharing.

configuration every time you're away from your home computer, wouldn't it be nice to have the same environment you're used to everywhere you go? In the next section, we explore the different varieties of Linux and how to install them on your computer.

WHICH LINUX TO USE

Linux is available for download in various packages known as distributions, or distros. Think of distros as different makes and models of cars. Distros include the underlying Linux kernel (the code that provides Linux's basic functionality) and related programs. Distros also often contain special modifications or additional open-source software (such as OpenOffice). So which distro is right for you?

A good place to start researching distros is **http://distrowatch.com**. This site tracks Linux distros and provides helpful tips for beginners in choosing one. Figure 8 lists some popular Linux distros and their home pages.

Before you can decide which distro is right for you, there are a few things to consider. The general overall requirements to run Linux are relatively modest:

- A 300-MHz processor (text mode); 400-MHz processor (graphical mode)
- 128 MB of RAM (text mode); 192 MB RAM (graphical mode)
- 5 GB of hard drive space

Just like any other software program, however, Linux will perform better with a faster processor and more memory. Also, depending on how much additional software is deployed in the distro you choose to use, your system requirements may be higher and you may need more hard drive space. Check the specific recommendations for the distro you're considering on the distro's Web site.

EXPERIMENTING WITH LINUX

Some distros of Linux (such as KNOPPIX and PCLinuxOS) are designed to be run from a CD. This alleviates having to install files on the computer's hard drive. Therefore, you can boot up from a CD on an existing Windows PC and run Linux without disturbing the existing Windows installation. However, depending on the distro you use, you may not have full access to the files on your Windows hard drive.

Booting your existing computer from a CD-based version of Linux is a very low-risk way to experiment with Linux and see how well you like it. One such version of Linux is KNOPPIX, which you can download and burn onto a CD from **www.knoppix.com**. KNOPPIX uses a very Windows-like desktop. When you download KNOPPIX, you also get the Konqueror and Mozilla browsers as well as GIMP, OpenOffice, MySQL, and more than 900 other software packages, including utilities and games. The minimum system requirements to run KNOPPIX are:

- An Intel-compatible CPU (i486 or later)
- 32 MB of RAM for text mode, at least 96 MB for graphics mode (at least 128 MB of RAM is recommended to use the various office products)

FIGURE 8 Popular Linux Distros and Their Home Pages	
Distro	**Home Page**
Mandriva Linux (formerly Mandrake Linux)	**www.mandrivalinux.com**
Fedora Core (Red Hat)	**http://fedoraproject.org**
Debian GNU/Linux	**www.debian.org**
Ubuntu	**www.ubuntu.com**
Gentoo Linux	**www.gentoo.org**
Slackware Linux	**www.slackware.com**
KNOPPIX	**www.knoppix.com**
PCLinuxOS	**www.pclinuxonline.com**

- A bootable CD-ROM drive or a boot floppy and standard CD-ROM
- A standard graphics card

Figure 9 shows KNOPPIX in action. This computer is connected to the Internet via a high-speed connection as part of a home network. The computer booted from the KNOPPIX CD when it detected the CD in the drive. As part of KNOPPIX's installation sequence, it automatically detects components of the computer (such as the network card) and configures Linux to recognize them. You'll have no trouble connecting to the Internet through Mozilla, and any files you create with OpenOffice can be saved to a flash drive.

3D LINUX

Mandriva Linux (**www.mandriva.com**) offers several versions of its operating system. Free Mandriva is their most basic product, and as its name suggests, it is free and remains true to the original open-source principles. Other, more robust versions are available for varying prices. Discovery, PowerPack, and PowerPack+ are for individual users, who range in experience level from beginners to advanced Linux users. Move and Flash are Mandriva's portable OS options. Move is installed on a CD, and Flash is installed on a convenient 4 GB flash drive. Both portable versions, like Knoppix, do not make changes on the host computer, so you can bring your computer environment anywhere you go. Mandriva Flash takes up one quarter of the flash drive, allowing the remaining 3 GB for you to conveniently store and take with you all your office work, and Internet and multimedia files. All Mandriva versions run simultaneously with Windows, so you don't need to worry about partitioning your hard drive, as was the case with earlier versions. The 2007 versions of Mandriva introduce Metisse, an innovative 3D desktop environment (see Figure 10).

The Mandriva operating system also includes other open-source applications, such as OpenOffice, Mozilla Firefox browser, Mozilla Thunderbird e-mail manager, and Wengo (a VoIP application). In addition, there are several multimedia programs, including Blender (for creating interactive 3D games), and others used to create photo albums and digital music.

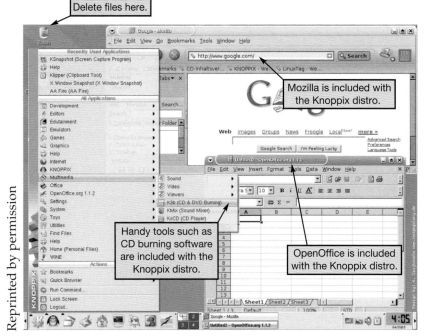

FIGURE 9

Notice how the Knoppix user interface resembles the Windows XP desktop, including the trash container (Recycle Bin).

In addition to all this, Mandriva also includes security features. The OS divides security levels into five rankings, from "Very Low" to "Paranoid." Your choice depends on how you're using the system (select "Paranoid" if you're running business

FIGURE 10

The Mandriva operating system has an innovative 3D desktop environment.

New Software Is Necessary ... Or Is It?

Switching to a new OS means buying new versions of your Windows-based software (such as Microsoft Office 2004 for Mac). Or does it? Many open-source packages are also available for the Mac OS. If you really need to run your Windows-based software on your Mac, various software products such as Guest PC (**www.lismoresystems.com**) and iEmulator (**www.iemulator.com**) allow you to install Windows on your Mac and run Windows applications. Another option when using a Mac is to not switch your operating system at all. In 2006, Apple released a beta version of software called Boot Camp, a program designed to run only on the Intel-based Macs. After installing Boot Camp and Windows on a Mac, at start-up you can choose which operating system you want to run. Virtual PC from Microsoft is another application that enables you to run Windows applications, connect to PC networks, and share files all from a Mac.

transactions through your computer). You also can set up a simple-to-configure firewall called Shorewall to prevent unauthorized Internet users from accessing your personal network.

If you don't like Mandriva Linux or Knoppix, head out to **www.distrowatch.com** and find another free Linux distro to install. With the hundreds of distros available, you're sure to find one that fits your needs.

Hardware Alternatives

Tired of your Windows-based Intel PC? Old computer too slow for your current needs and not worth upgrading? If so, you may be in the market for some new hardware. Before you head off to the store to buy another Windows-based computer, why not consider two alternatives: (1) moving to an Apple platform or (2) building your own computer.

APPLE COMPUTERS

Is a Mac right for you? The best way to decide whether a Mac is right for you is to actually get your hands on one and take it for a test drive. Chances are, someone you know has a Mac. If not, Apple has retail stores chock full of employees who are only too happy to let you test out the equipment. Be sure to check out the entry-level Macs, as shown in Figure 11.

Why make the switch? Some people are switching to Macs because they love their iPods so much. Apple is leveraging the popularity of these digital devices by designing software for their computers to work seamlessly with the iPods. In addition, many Apple fans think Macs are more user-friendly and stylish than their PC competitors. Others change to Macs because many applications (especially for digital artists and graphic designers) deliver superior features on the Apple platform.

The Mac Operating System: Mac OS X

Most Mac users, however, have switched because of the operating system, Mac OS X. Until 2005, Apple computers (Macs) used a completely different architecture than computers designed to run Windows, which use Intel and AMD processors. Apple computers originally featured PowerPC chips manufactured by Motorola and IBM; these chips required an OS other than Windows: the Mac OS. However, in 2005, Apple decided to switch to Intel chips in its computers. Fortunately, Apple had already designed its latest operating system, Mac OS X, to run on Intel platforms. So moving to an Apple computer now is really all about using OS X. If you've been using Windows for a while, you shouldn't have any problem making the transition to Mac OS X. You'll notice immediately that the Mac OS uses the same desktop metaphors that Windows does, including icons for folders and a trash can (instead of a recycle bin) to delete documents. Screen

FIGURE 11

(a) At only 6.5" wide, 6.5" long, and 2" high, the Mac mini is arguably one of the smallest system units ever made. Just add a monitor, keyboard, and mouse. (b) Apple's newest notebook—the MacBook—weighs just over five pounds and features the Intel Core 2 Duo processor and a 13-inch screen. (c) The iMac line features sleek, space-saving desktop units sporting fast Intel Core 2 Duo processors.

real estate is managed using familiar-looking windows you're already accustomed to using on Windows.

Like earlier versions of Mac OS, OS X is based on the UNIX OS, which is very stable and reliable. Aside from being stable, security and safety are great reasons to switch to Mac OS X. OS X does not seem to suffer from the exploitation of security flaws as much as Windows does. This doesn't necessarily mean that the Mac OS is better constructed than Windows; it could just be that because Windows has a lead-in market share, it is a more attractive target for hackers. Regardless of the reason, you're probably somewhat less likely to be inconvenienced by viruses, hacking, and spyware if you're running Mac OS. Of course, you won't have any better protection from spam, phishing, or other Internet scams, so you still need to stay alert. The latest version of OS X—Leopard—offers a 3D desktop environment as well as a new automated backup utility called Time Machine (see Figure 12).

When you start a Mac, a program called the Finder automatically starts. This program is like Windows Explorer and controls the desktop and the Finder windows with which you interact. It's always running when the Mac is on. Spotlight is a new desktop search feature that allows you to find

anything on your computer from one spot. Also new on the desktop is the Dashboard. With features called widgets, you have easy access to many mini-applications that allow you to perform common tasks and get quick access to real-time information such as the weather, stock prices, or sports updates. At the top of the desktop is the menu bar. The options on the menu

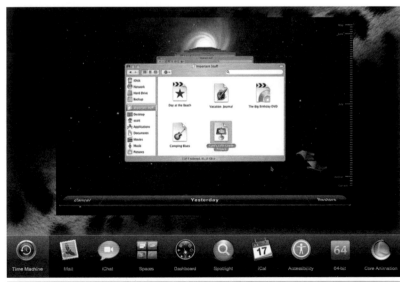

FIGURE 12

Time Machine, an automated backup utility, is one of the new features in Mac OS Leopard.

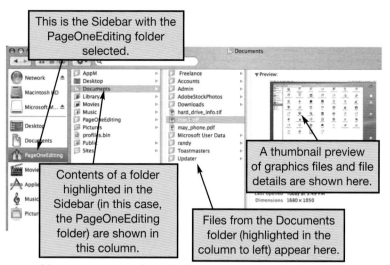

This is the Sidebar with the PageOneEditing folder selected.

Contents of a folder highlighted in the Sidebar (in this case, the PageOneEditing folder) are shown in this column.

Files from the Documents folder (highlighted in the column to left) appear here.

A thumbnail preview of graphics files and file details are shown here.

Reprinted by permission of Apple Computer, Inc.

Reprinted by permission of Apple Computer, Inc.

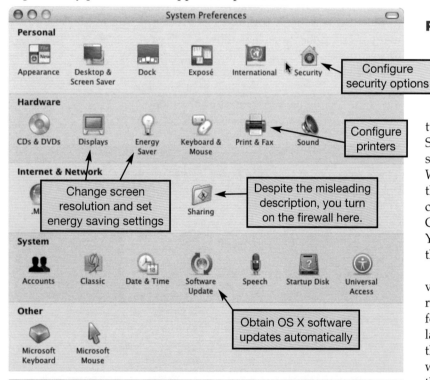

Configure security options

Configure printers

Change screen resolution and set energy saving settings

Despite the misleading description, you turn on the firewall here.

Obtain OS X software updates automatically

bar change according to which program is "active" at the moment (that is, foremost on your screen). When you click the Apple icon in the upper left corner, a drop-down menu is displayed, from which you can select a number of options. The Dock is similar to the Taskbar in Windows and is a strip of icons that runs across the bottom of the desktop.

Each Finder window has an area on the left known as the Sidebar (see Figure 13). The Sidebar holds any folders you specify (even though the icons don't look like folders) to make navigation easier and faster. Navigating around a Finder window and copying or moving files work almost exactly the same way it does in Windows.

Configuring a Mac

In Windows, you make changes to settings and preferences through the Control Panel. In OS X, you use System Preferences, which is an option on the Apple menu. Selecting System Preferences from the Apple menu displays the window shown in Figure 14.

Protecting Your Mac

Although Macs tend to be attacked less frequently by viruses and other hacker nuisances, you can still be vulnerable if you don't take precautions. OS X comes with a firewall, but by default it is turned off. To configure it, click on the Sharing icon under the Internet & Network section of the System Preferences window. When the Sharing Window opens, click on the Firewall button to display the Firewall configuration screen shown in Figure 15. Click the Start button to turn the firewall on. You should do this before going out on to the Internet for the first time.

In addition, hackers may be creating viruses and other nuisances to exploit security holes in OS X. Mac users should therefore keep their software up to date with the latest fixes and software patches by setting their system to check automatically for software updates on a periodic basis. On Macs, this feature is available through the System Preferences window by clicking the Software Update icon, which is under the System section. Figure 16 shows the options you choose to make sure the Mac OS is kept up to date.

Utility Programs

Just like Windows, OS X contains a wide variety of utility programs to help users maintain and evaluate their Macs. In Macs, utility programs are located in a folder named Utilities within the Applications folder on the hard drive.

If you're a Windows user, you know that to determine how your system is performing, you use the Windows Task Manager utility. In Macs, this utility is called the Activity Monitor, shown in Figure 17 (on page 266). It shows what programs (processes) are currently running and how much memory they're using. The CPU, System Memory, Disk Activity, Disk Usage, and Network buttons indicate the activity in each of these crucial areas.

Like the Systems Properties box in Windows, the Mac OS System Profiler shown in Figure 18, shown on pag 266, displays all the hardware (and software) installed in a Mac, including the type of processor, the amount of RAM installed, and the amount of VRAM on the video card.

As you can see, operating a Mac is fairly simple and is similar to the Windows environment. There are many books (such as the OS X books in the Peachpit Press *Visual QuickStart* series) that will help you make a smooth transition to an Apple computer.

DO IT YOURSELF!

The do-it-yourself craze has swept across America, so why not stop repainting the house and apply those do-it-yourself skills to building a computer? Of course, building a computer isn't for everyone, but for those who enjoy working with their hands and don't mind doing some up-front research, it can be a rewarding experience. The advantages and disadvantages of building your own computer are as follows:

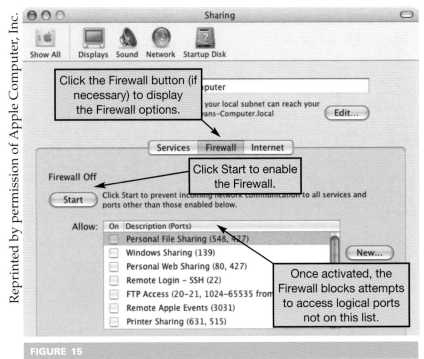

FIGURE 15

Macs have a firewall, but by default it is turned off. Make sure you turn on your Firewall before going out onto the Internet for the first time.

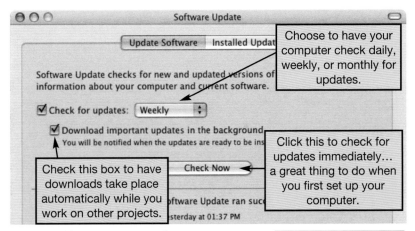

FIGURE 16

Keeping the Mac OS up to date with the latest software fixes and patches greatly decreases your chances of being the target of hackers.

>From the Apple menu, choose System Preferences and then click Software Update. In addition to these precautions, there is antivirus software (such as Norton) available for OS X.

Advantages	Disadvantages
You get exactly the configuration and features you want.	There is no technical support when things go wrong.
You have the option of using components other than those that are used in mass-produced computers.	You'll need to examine technical higher-quality specifications (such as which CPU works with the motherboard you want) which may overwhelm the average computer user.
You'll hopefully get a feeling of satisfaction from a job well done.	You won't necessarily save money.

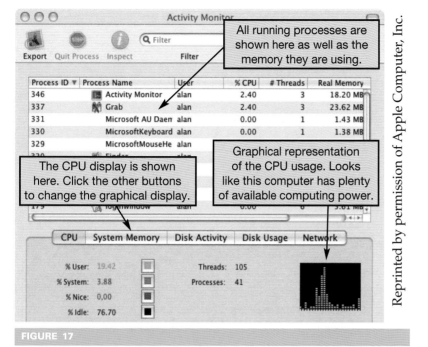

All running processes are shown here as well as the memory they are using.

Graphical representation of the CPU usage. Looks like this computer has plenty of available computing power.

The CPU display is shown here. Click the other buttons to change the graphical display.

FIGURE 17

Similar to the Task Manager in Windows, the Activity Monitor analyzes the performance of a Mac.

>Go to the Utilities folder found in the Applications folder on your hard drive and double-click Activity Monitor to open the utility.

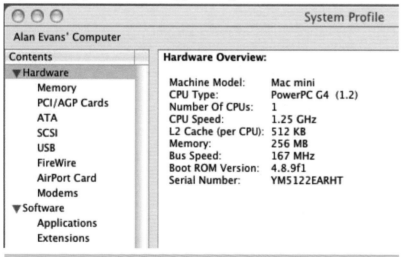

FIGURE 18

The System Profiler is similar to the Systems Properties dialog box in Windows and reveals a wealth of information about the hardware and software in your computer.

>To launch System Profiler, from the Apple menu, click About this Mac, and then click the More Info button.

Many Web sites can provide guidance for building your own computer. PC Mechanic (**www.pcmech.com/byopc**) is a good place to start. Just Google "How to build your own computer" and you'll find plenty of online help and advice. To start, you need a list of parts. Here's what you'll typically need:

1. **Case:** Make sure the case you buy is an ATX-style case, which accommodates the newest motherboards, and that it includes an adequate cooling fan. Also be sure there are enough drive bays in the case to handle the hard drive and any other peripheral drives (CD, DVD, and so on) you'll be installing.

2. **Power Supply:** A power supply provides power to the computer. Many cases come with a power supply installed. Make sure to get a power supply with adequate wattage to handle the load generated by all the computer's components.

3. **Processor (CPU):** Get the fastest one you can afford, as it will help to greatly extend the life of your computer. To cool the processor, many come with a fan installed; if not, you'll need to purchase a processor cooling fan.

4. **Motherboard:** Many motherboards come with sound, video, and network cards. These work fine for basic computing, but if you're building a PC for gaming, opt for a motherboard into which you can plug higher-end graphics and sound cards. Also make sure the motherboard you buy can accommodate the CPU you have chosen. And make sure the motherboard has expansion slots (PCI slots and a separate AGP) for a high-end graphics card.

5. **RAM:** Check your motherboard specifications before buying RAM to ensure you buy the correct type and an amount that will fit into the available slots.

6. **Video Card:** Low-end cards with 64 or 128 MB of video memory are fine for normal computer use, but for gaming or displaying high-end graphics or videos, get a card with 256 MB or more, depending on your budget.

7. **Sound Card:** Make sure to get a PCI card that is Sound Blaster-compatible (the standard for sound cards).

8. **Optical Drives (CD, DVD, and Blu-Ray Drives):** A CD or DVD drive is a must for software installation. You can install individual drives or a combination drive that have CD and DVD capabilities. For portable storage, make sure the CD/DVD drive has the capability to write CDs and DVDs. You may want to install a Blu-Ray drive to view your favorite movies using high-definition technology. Blu-Ray discs offer five times the storage capacity of a DVD, to hold up to 50 GB of data. Currently, Blu-Ray burners are very expensive, but they are available if you have the need.

9. **USB Ports:** Make sure that your motherboard has at least two to four USB ports and install a separate bay with USB and FireWire ports for flash drives and other devices. Other devices, such as your monitor and keyboard, may also have USB ports incorporated for additional flexibility.

10. **Hard Drive:** The price per gigabyte has been rapidly coming down in recent years, so get a large-volume drive. For optimal performance, choose a hard drive with the fastest RPM you can afford.

11. **Modem:** You need a modem only if you're connecting to the Internet via a dial-up connection.

12. **Network Interface Card:** Network cards are sometimes integrated in the motherboard, so check before you buy one.

In addition to these components, you'll need a keyboard, mouse or other pointing device, monitor, and operating system software.

You can buy these components at national computer superstores such as CompUSA or at reputable Web sites such as **www.tigerdirect.com** or **www.newegg.com**. Once you have the components, it is almost as simple as bolting them into the case and connecting them properly. Make sure you read all the installation instructions that come with your components before beginning installation. Don't forget to check the Web sites of component manufacturers for handy how-to videos and step-by-step installation guides. Then read through a complete installation tutorial such as the one found at Toms Hardware Web site (**www.tomshardware.com/2002/09/04/building _your_own_pc**), which provides an excellent visual guide to assembling a computer. Then grab your screwdriver and get started—you'll be up and running in no time.

So, as you can see, there are many options beyond a Windows-based computer running commercial software applications. We hope you spread your wings and try a few of them.

6

Understanding and Assessing Hardware:

Evaluating Your System

From Chapter 6 of *Technology in Action, Complete*, Fifth Edition, Alan Evans, Kendall Martin, Mary Anne Poatsy. Copyright © 2009 by Pearson Education. Published by Prentice Hall. All rights reserved.

Understanding and Assessing Hardware:

Evaluating Your System

Objectives

After reading this chapter, you should be able to answer the following questions:

1. How can I determine whether I should upgrade my existing computer or buy a new one?

2. What does the CPU do, and how can I evaluate its performance?

3. How does memory work in my computer, and how can I evaluate how much memory I need?

4. What are the computer's main storage devices, and how can I evaluate whether they match my needs?

5. What components affect the output of video on my computer, and how can I evaluate whether they match my needs?

6. What components affect my computer's sound quality, and how can I evaluate whether they match my needs?

7. What are the ports available on desktop computers, and how can I determine what ports I need?

8. How can I ensure the reliability of my system?

ACTIVE HELPDESK

- Evaluating Your CPU and RAM
- Evaluating Your Storage Subsystem and Ports

Does Your Computer Fit You?

After saving up for a computer, Natalie took the leap a few years ago and bought a new desktop PC. Now she is wondering what to do. Her friends with newer computers are burning CDs and DVDs, and they're able to hook up their digital cameras directly to their computers and create multimedia. They seem to be able to do a hundred things at once without their computers slowing down at all.

Natalie's computer can't do any of these things—or at least she doesn't think it can. And lately it seems to take longer to open files and scroll through Web pages. Making matters worse, her computer freezes three or four times a day and takes a long time to reboot. Now she's wondering whether she should buy a new computer, but the thought of spending all that money again makes her think twice. As she looks at ads for new computers, she realizes she doesn't know what such things as "CPU" and "RAM" really are, or how they affect her system. Meanwhile, she's heard it's possible to upgrade her computer, but the task seems daunting. How will she know what she needs to do to upgrade, or whether it's even worth it?

How well is your computer meeting your needs? Are you unsure whether it's best to buy a new computer or upgrade your existing system? If you don't have a computer, do you fear purchasing one because computers are changing all the time? Do you know what all the terms in computer ads mean and how the different parts affect your computer's performance?

In this chapter, you'll learn how to evaluate your computer system to determine whether it is meeting your needs. You'll start by figuring out what you want your ideal computer to be able to do. You'll then learn about important components of your computer system (its CPU, memory, storage devices, audio and video devices, and ports) and how these components affect your system. Along the way, worksheets will help you conduct a system evaluation, and multimedia Sound Bytes will show you how to install various components in your system and how to increase its reliability. You'll also learn about the various utilities available to help speed up and clean up your system. If you don't have a computer, this chapter will provide you with important information you need about computer hardware to make an informed purchasing decision.

© Corbis

SOUND BYTES

- Questions to Ask Before You Buy a Computer
- Using Windows Vista to Evaluate CPU Performance
- Memory Hierarchy Interactive
- Installing RAM
- Hard Disk Anatomy Interactive

- CD and DVD Reading and Writing Interactive
- Installing a CD-RW Drive
- Port Tour: How Do I Hook It Up?
- Letting Your Computer Clean Up After Itself

Is It the Computer or Me?

Do you ever wonder whether your computer is fine and you just need more knowledge to get it to work smoothly? Is that true, or do you really need a more sophisticated computer system? And is now a good time to buy a new one? There never seems to be a good time to buy a new computer. It seems that if you can just wait a year, computers will inevitably be faster and cost less. But is this actually true?

As it turns out, it is true. In fact, a rule of thumb often cited in the computer industry, called **Moore's Law**, describes the pace at which CPUs (the central processing units)—the small chips that can be thought of as the "brains" of the computer—improve. This mathematical rule, named after Gordon Moore, the cofounder of the CPU chip manufacturer Intel, predicts that the number of transistors inside a CPU will increase so fast that CPU capacity will double every 18 months. (The number of transistors on a CPU chip helps determine how fast it can process data.)

As you can see in Figure 1, this rule of thumb has held true since 1965, when Moore first published his theory. Imagine, what if you could find a bank that would agree to treat your money this way? If you put 10 cents in that kind of savings account in 1965, you would have a balance of more than $3.3 million today!

In addition to the CPU becoming faster, other system components also continue to improve dramatically. For example, the capacity of memory chips such as dynamic random access memory (DRAM)—the most common form of memory found on personal computers—increases about 60 percent every year. Meanwhile, hard disk drives have been growing in storage capacity by about 50 percent each year.

So, with technology advancing so quickly, how do I make sure I have a computer that matches my needs? No one wants to buy a new computer every year just to keep up with technology. Even if money weren't a consideration, the time it would take to transfer all of your files and to reinstall and reconfigure your software would make buying a new computer every year terribly inefficient. Extending the life of a computer also reduces or postpones the environmental and security concerns involved in the disposal of computers.

Of course, no one wants to keep doing costly upgrades that won't significantly extend the life of a system either. So how can you determine if your system is suitable or needs upgrading? And how can

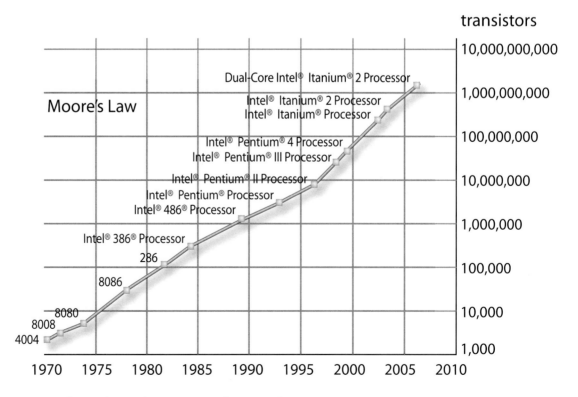

FIGURE 1

Moore's Law predicts that CPUs will continue to get faster. The number of transistors on a CPU chip helps determine how fast it can process data. With the Intel Dual-Core Itanium 2 chip, more than a billion transistors can be fabricated into one chip. Source: Adapted from the Moore's Law animated demo at **www.intel.com**.

Understanding and Assessing Hardware: Evaluating Your System

you know which is the better option: upgrading or buying a new computer? In this chapter, you'll determine how to answer these questions by learning useful information about computer systems. The first step is figuring out what you want your computer to do for you.

What Is Your Ideal Computer?

As you decide whether your computer suits you, it's important to know exactly what you want your ideal computer system to be able to do. Later, as you perform a system evaluation, you can compare your existing system to your ideal system. This will help you determine whether you should purchase hardware components to add to your system or buy a new system.

But what if I don't have a computer? Even if you're a new computer user and are looking to buy your first system, you will still need to evaluate what you want your system to do for you before you purchase a computer. Being able to understand and evaluate computer systems will make you a more informed buyer. You should be comfortable answering questions such as: What is a CPU, and how does it affect your system? How much RAM do you need, and what role does it play in your system? It's important for you to be able to answer questions such as these before you buy a computer.

How do I know what my ideal system is? To determine your ideal system, consider what you want to be able to do with your computer. For example, do you need to bring your computer with you? Do you want to be able to edit digital photos? Do you want to watch and record Digital Video Discs (DVDs or Digital Versatile Discs)? Or are you just using your computer for word processing? The worksheet in Figure 2 lists a number of ways in which you may want to use your computer. In the second column, place a check next to those computer uses that apply to you. Also, list a priority of *High*, *Medium*, or *Low* in the rightmost column so that you can determine which features are most important to you.

Next, look at the list of desired uses for your computer and determine whether your current system can perform these activities. If there are things you can't do, you may need to purchase additional hardware or a better computer. For example, if you want to play CDs or DVDs, all you need is a CD-R or DVD-R drive. However, you need a CD-RW or DVD-RW drive if you want to burn (record) CDs and DVDs. Likewise, if you plan to edit digital video files or play games that include a lot of sounds and graphics with large files, you may want to add more memory, buy a better set of speakers, get a DVD or Blu-ray burner, add a high-speed hard drive, and possibly invest in a new monitor. Depending on the costs of the individual upgrade components, you may be better off buying a new system.

Note that you also may need new software and training to use new system components. Many computer users forget to consider the training they'll need when they upgrade their computer. Missing any one of these pieces might be the difference between your computer enriching your life or it becoming another source of stress.

How do I know if I need training? Although computers are becoming increasingly user-friendly, you still need to learn how to use them to your best advantage. Say you want to edit digital photos. You know image-editing software exists, but how do you know if your computer's hardware can support the software? What will happen if you can't get it installed or don't know how to use it? If you have questions like these, you know you need training. Training shouldn't be an afterthought. Consider the time and effort involved in learning about what you want your computer to do before you buy hardware or software. If you don't, you may have a wonderful computer system but lack the skills necessary to take full advantage of it.

SOUND BYTE

Questions to Ask Before You Buy a Computer

This Sound Byte will help you consider some important questions you need to ask when you buy a computer, such as whether you should get a notebook or a desktop, or whether you should purchase a new computer or a used or refurbished one.

FIGURE 2   What Should Your Ideal Computer System Be Able to Do?

Computer Uses	Do You Want Your System to Do This?	Can Your System Do This Now?	Priority (high, medium, low)
Portability Uses			
Take Your Computer with You?			
Access the Internet Wirelessly			
Entertainment Uses			
Access the Internet/Send E-Mail			
Play CDs and DVDs			
Record (Burn) CDs and DVDs			
Produce Digital Videos			
Record and Edit Digital Music			
Edit Digital Photos			
Play Graphics-Intensive Games			
Transfer Digital Photos (or Other Files) to Your Computer Using Flash Memory Cards			
Connect All Your Peripheral Devices to Your Computer at the Same Time			
Purchase Music/Videos from the Internet			
Other			
Educational Uses			
Perform Word-Processing Tasks			
Use Other Educational Software			
Create CD or DVD Backups of All Your Files			
Access Library and Newspaper Archives			
Create Multimedia Presentations			
Other			
Business Uses			
Create Spreadsheets/Databases			
Work on Multiple Software Applications Quickly and Simultaneously			
Conduct Online Banking/Pay Bills Online/Self-Prepare Taxes			
Conduct Online Job Searches/Post Résumé			
"Synchronize" Your Mobile Device (PDA, PSP, or iPod) with Your Computer			
Other			

Assessing Your Hardware: Evaluating Your System

With a better picture of your ideal computer system in mind, you can make a more informed assessment of your current computer. To determine whether your computer system has the right hardware components to do what you ultimately want it to do, you need to conduct a **system evaluation**. To do so, you look at your computer's subsystems, what they do, and how they perform. These subsystems include the following:

- CPU subsystem
- Memory subsystem (your computer's random access memory, or RAM)
- Storage subsystem (your hard drive and other drives)
- Video subsystem (your video card and monitor)
- Audio subsystem (your sound card and speakers)
- Computer's ports

In the rest of this chapter, we examine each of these subsystems. At the end of each section, you'll find a small worksheet you can use to evaluate each subsystem on your computer. *Note:* This chapter discusses tools you can use to assess a Windows-based PC.

Evaluating a Desktop or Notebook System

The first decision in evaluating your system is whether or not you want a desktop or a notebook. To make the best decision, it's important to evaluate how and where you will use the computer. Obviously, the main distinction between desktops and notebooks is portability. If, in the chart in Figure 2, you indicated that you need to take your computer with you to work or school, or even want the flexibility to move from room to room in your house, then a notebook is the best choice. If portability is not an absolute factor, then you should consider a desktop. Review Figure 3 to better understand the advantages and disadvantages of desktops and notebooks to help you determine which type of system may best suit your needs.

FIGURE 3 Advantages and Disadvantages of Desktops and Notebook Computers

NOTEBOOK COMPUTER SYSTEMS		DESKTOP COMPUTER SYSTEMS	
Advantages	**Disadvantages**	**Advantages**	**Disadvantages**
Portable	More expensive for comparable desktop speed and capacity	Best value: more speed, memory, and storage capacity for lower price	Usually left in one place; harder to move around
Takes up little space	More easily stolen	More difficult to steal	Requires more space, although LCD monitors and smaller system units are minimizing this disadvantage
Wireless Internet Access built-in or easy to add/install	More prone to damage by dropping and mishandling Limited capability for expansion/upgrade	Easier to expand and upgrade	Difficult to ship/transport if the system needs repair

Evaluating the CPU Subsystem

Courtesy of Intel Corporation

Once you've determined whether you want a desktop or notebook computer system, the next big decision is the type of processor that best meets your needs. As mentioned earlier, your computer's **central processing unit (CPU or processor)** is very important because it processes instructions, performs calculations, manages the flow of information through a computer system, and is responsible for processing the data you input into information. The CPU, as shown in Figure 4, is located on the **motherboard**, the primary circuit board of the computer system. There are several types of processors on the market: Intel processors (such as the Pentium family, the Core Duo family, the Centrino line, and the Itanium family) and AMD processors (such as the Athlon and Sempron, both of which are used on PCs).

How does the CPU work? The CPU is composed of two units: the **control unit** and the **arithmetic logic unit (ALU)**. The control unit coordinates the activities of all the other computer components. The ALU is responsible for performing all the arithmetic calculations (addition, subtraction, multiplication, and division). In addition, the ALU makes logic and comparison decisions, such as comparing items to determine if one is greater than, less than, equal to, or not equal to another.

Every time the CPU performs a program instruction, it goes through the same series of steps. First, it fetches the required piece of data or instruction from RAM, the temporary storage location for all the data and instructions the computer needs while it is running. Next, it decodes the instruction into something the computer can understand. Once the CPU has decoded the instruction, it executes the instruction and stores the result to RAM before fetching the next instruction. This process is called a **machine cycle**.

How is CPU speed measured? The computer goes through these machine cycles at a steady and constant pace. This pace, known as **clock speed**, is controlled by the system clock, which works like a metronome in music. The system clock keeps a steady beat, regulating the speed at which the processor goes through machine cycles. Processors work incredibly fast, going through millions or billions of machine cycles *each second*. Processor speed is measured in units of Hertz (Hz). Hertz means "machine cycles per second." Older machines ran at speeds measured in **megahertz (MHz)**, or 1 million hertz, whereas current systems run at speeds measured in **gigahertz (GHz)**, or 1 billion hertz. So a 3.8-GHz processor performs work at a rate of 3.8 billion machine cycles per second. It's important to realize, however, that CPU clock speed alone doesn't determine the performance of the CPU.

What else affects CPU performance? In addition to pure processing speed, CPU performance also is affected by the speed of the **front side bus** (or **FSB**) and the amount of **cache memory**. The FSB connects the processor (CPU) in your computer to the system memory. Think of the front side bus as the highway on which data travels between the CPU and RAM. With a wider highway, traffic can move faster because more cars can travel at the same time. Consequently, the faster the FSB is, the faster you can get data to your processor. The faster you get data to the processor, the faster your processor can work on it. FSB speed is measured in megahertz (MHz).

Cache memory is another important consideration that determines CPU performance. Cache memory is a form of random access memory but is more accessible to the CPU than regular RAM. Because of its ready access to the CPU, cache memory is even faster than RAM to get data to the CPU for processing. There are several levels of cache memory, defined by its proximity to the CPU. Level 1 cache is a block of memory that is built onto the CPU chip for the storage of data or commands that have just been used. Level 2 cache is located on the CPU chip but is slightly farther away from the CPU, or it's on a separate chip next to the CPU and therefore takes somewhat longer to access. Level 2 cache contains more storage area than does Level 1 cache. Today's processors are defined by the combination of processor speed, front side bus speed, and the amount of cache memory. For example, Intel's Core 2 Duo processors come in a range of speeds, cache memory, and front side bus. The E6700 Core 2 Duo processor has 2.66 GHz processor speed, 4MB L2 cache, and 1066 MHz front side bus, while the T5600 Core 2 Duo processor has 1.83 GHz processor speed, 2 MB L2 cache, and 667 MHz front side bus.

What else might affect processor performance? As was mentioned already, the front side bus and cache memory play a part in CPU performance. In addition, CPU designers make many other choices that impact how the CPU will fit into the bigger picture of overall system performance. For example, some CPUs are optimized to process multimedia instructions and can handle audio and video processing commands much more quickly than other processors. Another design approach is to try to build a processor that can work on two separate sets of instructions at the same time, in parallel.

Both Intel and AMD have a variety of CPUs with two cores that use less power than having two CPUs running at once, and they deliver a substantial increase in performance. Figure 5 shows how commands coming from two different applications are processed at the same time with a core duo processor. So now, applications such as virus protection software and your operating system, which are always running behind the scenes, can have their own processor, freeing up the other to run your other applications such as a Web browser, Word, or iTunes more efficiently. There are some higher-end processors, such as the Intel Core 2 Quad and Core 2 Extreme processors, which have four cores for even more efficient processing power.

How fast should my CPU be? First, you need to know how fast your computer is. You can easily identify the speed of your current system's CPU by accessing the system properties. As shown in Figure 6, you can view basic information about your computer, including which CPU is installed in your system as well as its speed.

At a minimum, your CPU should meet the requirements of your system's software and hardware. If your system is older and you are buying new software and peripheral devices, your CPU may not be able to handle the load.

For example, say your computer is three years old. For the past three years, you've been using it primarily for word processing and to surf the Internet. You recently purchased a digital camera. Now you want to

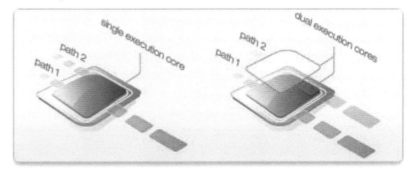

Single Path vs. the Dual Path Processors for Data

Single Core Processor   Dual Core Processor

FIGURE 5

Two is faster than one! With the dual-core processors, Intel CPUs can work in parallel, processing two separate programs at the same time instead of switching back and forth between them.

edit your digital photos, but your system doesn't seem to be able to handle this. You check the system requirements on the photo-editing software you just installed and realize that the software runs best with a more powerful processor. In this case, if everything else in your system is running properly, a faster CPU would help improve the software's performance. Pentium 4 processors or Celeron D processors running at 2 GHz or higher are good for the average user,

BITS AND BYTES

Moving to a New Computer Doesn't Have to Be Painful

Are you ready to buy a new computer, but dreading the prospect of transferring all your files and redoing all of your Windows settings? You could transfer all those files and settings manually, but Windows stores much information in the registry files, which can be tricky to update. So what do you do? PC migration software may be the thing for you. Applications such as Alohabob PC Relocator (**www.alohabob.com**) and Desktop DNA (**http://ca.miramar.com**) are designed to make transitioning to a new computer easier. Walk-through wizards in the software take you through the otherwise arduous steps of transferring your files and settings to your new computer. Some migration programs can even move applications by uninstalling them from your computer and installing them on your new one. For the latest information on such utilities, search on migration software at **www.pcmag.com**. You'll be ready to upgrade painlessly in no time. Or, if you prefer to avoid the do-it-yourself option, support technicians at retail stores, such as Best Buy's Geek Squad, will often perform the migration for a nominal charge.

The System Properties dialog box identifies which CPU you have, as well as its speed. The computer in this example contains an Intel Core 2 running at 2.0 GHz.

> Click the Start button and then click Computer from the right panel of the Start menu. On the top toolbar, click System properties.

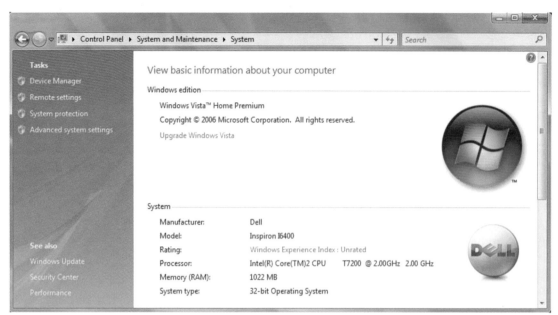

View basic information about your computer

Windows edition

Windows Vista™ Home Premium

Copyright © 2006 Microsoft Corporation. All rights reserved.

Upgrade Windows Vista

Tasks
- Device Manager
- Remote settings
- System protection
- Advanced system settings

See also

Windows Update

Security Center

Performance

System

Manufacturer:	Dell
Model:	Inspiron 16400
Rating:	Windows Experience Index : Unrated
Processor:	Intel(R) Core(TM)2 CPU T7200 @ 2.00GHz 2.00 GHz
Memory (RAM):	1022 MB
System type:	32-bit Operating System

Reprinted with permission from Microsoft Corporation

and Pentium D or Core Duo processors running at any speed are good processors for the higher-end user.

How can I tell whether my CPU is meeting my needs? Several factors determine whether your CPU is meeting your needs, as shown in Figure 7. While speed determines how fast your CPU is capable of performing operations, you need to determine whether that speed is capable of handling the tasks you need to perform. Even though your CPU meets the minimum requirements specified for a particular software application, if you're running other software (in addition to the operating system, which is always running), you'll need to check to see how well the CPU is handling the entire load. You can tell whether your CPU speed is limiting your system performance if you periodically watch how busy it is as you work

on your computer. Keep in mind, the workload your CPU experiences will vary considerably depending on what you're doing. So, while it might run Word just fine, it may not be able to handle running Word, a Web browser, iTunes, and IM at the same time. The percentage of time that your CPU is working is referred to as **CPU usage**.

A utility that can provide this kind of information is incredibly useful when considering whether you should upgrade and also when your performance suddenly seems to drop off for no apparent reason. In Windows (XP or Vista), a program called Task Manager gives you easy access to all this data. Mac OS X has a utility similar to Task Manager called Activity Monitor, which is located in the Utilities folder in your Applications folder.

To view information on your CPU usage, right-click an empty area of the taskbar, select Task Manager, and click the

FIGURE 7 Do You Need to Upgrade Your CPU?

	Current System	Upgrade
CPU Speed (in MHz or GHz)		
Cache memory (in MB)		
FSB Speed (in MHz)		
CPU Processing Style: Quad-Core? Dual-Core? Hyper-threaded?		
CPU Usage at Appropriate Level?		

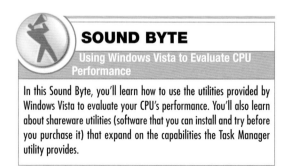

SOUND BYTE

Using Windows Vista to Evaluate CPU Performance

In this Sound Byte, you'll learn how to use the utilities provided by Windows Vista to evaluate your CPU's performance. You'll also learn about shareware utilities (software that you can install and try before you purchase it) that expand on the capabilities the Task Manager utility provides.

Performance tab, shown in Figure 8. The CPU Usage graph records your CPU usage for the past several seconds. Of course, there will be periodic peaks of high CPU usage, but if you see that your CPU usage levels are greater than 90 percent during most of your work session, a new CPU will contribute a great deal to your system performance. To see exactly how to use the Task Manager step by step, watch the Sound Byte "Using Windows Vista to Evaluate CPU Performance."

ANALYZING YOUR CPU

Is it expensive or difficult to upgrade a CPU? Replacement CPUs are expensive. In addition, although it is reasonably easy to install a CPU, it can be difficult to determine which CPU to install. Not all CPUs are interchangeable, and the replacement CPU must be compatible with the motherboard. Some people opt to upgrade the entire motherboard, but motherboards are a lot more difficult to install. As we discuss at the end of this chapter, if you plan to upgrade your computer in other ways in addition to upgrading the CPU, you may want to consider buying a new computer.

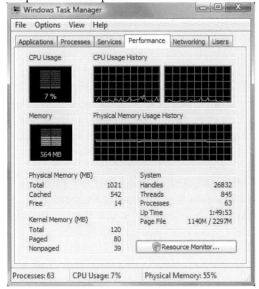

FIGURE 8

The Performance tab of the Windows Task Manager utility shows you how busy your CPU actually is when you're using your computer. In this case, current CPU usage level is at 7 percent. If CPU usage levels are above 90 percent for long periods of time, you may want to consider getting a faster, more powerful processor.

>In an empty area of the taskbar, right-click, select Task Manager, and click the Performance tab.

Are the fastest CPUs the best to use? If you decide to upgrade your CPU, consider buying one that is *not* the most recently released with the fastest speed but, rather, a slightly slower one of the same type. For example, if the Intel Pentium D dual-core family has just released a 3.8-GHz CPU, you will pay a premium to buy this newest processor. However, its release will drive

BITS AND BYTES

Feeling Hot, Hot, Hot

Heat isn't good for a computer system. However, computer chips, especially the CPU, produce heat, and if your system unit sits on the floor collecting dust, or has any vents blocked off, the temperature inside that case can climb very quickly. If the heat inside the system isn't dissipated, computer chips will have a shorter life. System cases are always designed with one internal fan, but if you're upgrading, you may want to consider a case that pays more attention to keeping your system cool. **www.highspeedpc.com** and **www.tigerdirect.com** are suppliers that offer cases featuring special venting designs and dual exhaust fans. You also can buy high-quality fans that sit directly on top of the CPU, dissipating heat directly off the chip. And if you want a more extreme solution, water cooling systems can replace the fans altogether (see Figure 9). The Corsair Hydrocool unit sits next to your computer and pumps coolant through hoses and past the CPU chip to remove heat more efficiently and quietly than airflow. Very cool indeed!

FIGURE 9

Like a radiator cools your car engine, running water past a CPU chip cools it off dramatically. The water picks up the heat and carries it away from the chip surface.

down the prices on the earlier Pentium D chips running at speeds of 3.2 GHz, 3.0 GHz, and 2.8 GHz. Buying a slightly slower CPU and investing the savings in other system components (such as additional RAM) will often result in a better-performing system. The same is true if you're buying a new computer: often, you'll save money without losing a great deal of performance by buying a computer with a CPU slightly slower than the fastest one on the market.

Will replacing the CPU be enough to improve my computer's performance? You may think that if you have the fastest processor, you will have a system with the best performance. However, upgrading your CPU will affect only the *processing* portion of the system performance, not how quickly data can move to or from the CPU. Your system's overall performance depends on many other factors, including the amount of RAM installed as well as hard disk speed. Therefore, your selection of a CPU may not offer significant improvements to your system's performance if there is a bottleneck in processing because of insufficient RAM or hard drive capacity.

Are there different choices of CPUs for a notebook and desktop? Both Intel and AMD make processors that are specific to a notebook computer. Notebook processors not only need to perform quickly and efficiently, like their desktop counterparts, but the need for better power savings to improve battery life is also important for notebooks. Intel's Centrino Duo, Celeron M, and some Pentium 4 processors; and AMD's Turion 64 Mobile and Mobile AMD Sempron processors, are used in notebooks. Desktop processors include Intel's Core 2 Duos, Pentium D, some Pentium 4, and Celeron D processors; and AMD's Athlon 64 and Sempron processors.

Evaluating RAM: The Memory Subsystem

Random access memory (RAM) is your computer's temporary storage space. Although we refer to RAM as a form of storage, RAM is really the computer's short-term memory. As such, it remembers everything that the computer needs to process the data into information, such as data that has been entered and software instructions, but only

when the computer is on. This means that RAM is an example of **volatile storage**. When the power is off, the data stored in RAM is cleared out. This is why, in addition to RAM, systems always include **nonvolatile storage** devices for permanent storage of instructions and data when the computer is powered off. Hard disks provide the greatest nonvolatile storage capacity in the computer system.

Why not use a hard drive to store the data and instructions? It's about one million times faster for the CPU to retrieve a piece of data from RAM than from a hard disk drive. The time it takes the CPU to retrieve data from RAM is measured in nanoseconds (billionths of seconds), whereas retrieving data from a fast hard drive takes an average of 10 milliseconds (or *ms*, thousandths of seconds). This difference is influential in designing a balanced computer system and can have a tremendous impact on system performance. Therefore, it's critical that your computer has more than enough RAM.

Where is RAM located? You can find RAM inside the system unit of your computer on the motherboard. **Memory modules** (or **memory cards**), the small circuit boards that hold a series of RAM chips, fit into special slots on the motherboard (see Figure 10). Most memory modules in today's systems are called dual inline memory modules (DIMMs).

Are there different types of RAM? Like most computer components, RAM has gone through a series of transitions. In current systems, the RAM memory used most often comes in the form of DDR or DDR2 memory modules, but in older systems, other types of RAM may have been used including DRAM, static RAM (SRAM), and synchronous DRAM (SDRAM).

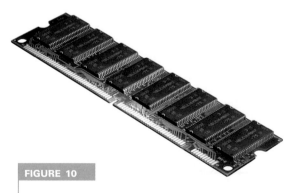

FIGURE 10

Memory modules hold a series of RAM chips and fit into special slots on the motherboard.

Understanding and Assessing Hardware: Evaluating Your System

All types of RAM are slightly different in how they function and in the speed at which memory can be accessed. While you don't have a choice as to the type of RAM you get when buying a new system, if you're adding RAM to any system, you must determine what type your system needs. Consult your user's manual or the manufacturer's Web site. In addition, many online RAM resellers (such as **www.crucial.com**) can help you determine the type of RAM your system needs based on the model number and brand of your computer.

How can I tell how much RAM I have installed in my computer? The amount of RAM that is actually sitting on memory modules in your computer is your computer's **physical memory**. The easiest way to see how much RAM you have is to look in the General tab of the System Properties dialog box. (On the Mac, choose About This Mac from the Apple menu.) This is the same tab you looked in to determine your system's CPU type and speed and is shown in Figure 6. RAM capacity is measured in megabytes (MB), or gigabytes (GB), though most machines today, especially those running Windows Vista, are sold with at least 1 GB of RAM. The computer in Figure 6 has 1021 MB (or 1GB) of RAM installed.

More detailed information on physical memory is displayed in the Physical Memory table in the Performance tab of Windows Task Manager, shown in Figure 11. The Physical Memory table shows both the total amount of physical memory you have installed as well as the available physical memory you have. If you are used to using Windows XP and have only a couple of applications running, you expect to see lots of available memory. But with even just one application running under Windows Vista, it appears you have very little available memory. This is because Windows Vista manages memory differently from previous versions of Windows by using a memory management technique known as Superfetch.

Since RAM is the fastest memory that you have in your computer and since your computer will respond faster, it would be helpful to have as much information as possible related to the programs you are currently using in RAM. Windows Vista now manages

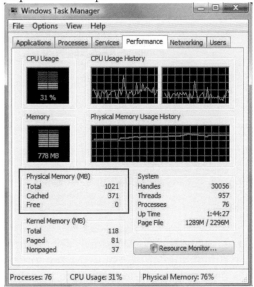

FIGURE 11

The Performance tab of the Windows Task Manager shows you how much physical memory is installed in your system, as well as how much is currently being used and how much is available. Windows Vista uses memory much more efficiently than previous versions, which is why 0 MB of Physical Memory is shown as Free.

> In the Taskbar area, right-click. Select Task Manager. Click the Performance tab.

memory this way by anticipating what information you will need next and storing it in RAM instead of in cache memory or on your hard drive. So, if you have MS Word running, Windows stores as much of the information related to Word in RAM as it can, thereby almost filling up your RAM. But don't worry, as other needs arise (you start Excel, for instance), Windows Vista reallocates the contents of RAM to account for you using multiple programs.

How much memory does the operating system need to run? The memory that your operating system uses is referred to as **kernel memory**. This memory is listed in a separate Kernel Memory table in the Performance tab. In Figure 11, the Kernel Memory table tells you that approximately 118 MB (Total Kernel Memory) of the total 1 GB of RAM is being used to run Windows Vista.

The operating system is the main software application that runs the computer. Without it, the computer would not work. At a minimum, the system needs enough RAM to run the operating system. Therefore, the amount of kernel memory that the system is using is the *absolute minimum* amount of RAM that your computer can run on. However, because you run additional applications, you need to have more RAM than the minimum.

How much RAM do I need? Because RAM is the temporary holding space for all the data and instructions that the computer uses while it's on, most computer users need quite a bit of RAM. In fact, systems running

SOUND BYTE

Memory Hierarchy Interactive

In this Sound Byte, you'll learn about the different types of memory used in a computer system.

FIGURE 12 **Sample RAM Requirements**

Application	Minimum RAM Required
Windows Vista Home Basic	512 MB
MS Office Pro 2007	256 MB
Internet Explorer 7	128 MB
iTunes	256 MB
Microsoft Picture It!	128 MB
Total RAM Required If Running All Programs Simultaneously	1,768 MB or 1.77 GB

SOUND BYTE

Installing RAM

In this Sound Byte, you'll learn how to select the appropriate type of memory to purchase, how to order memory online, and how to install it yourself. As you'll discover, the procedure is a simple one and can add great performance benefits to your system.

all the new features of Windows Vista should have a minimum of 1 GB of RAM, but for peak performance, systems are recommended to have at least 2 GB of RAM. Ultimately, the amount of RAM your system needs depends on how you use it. At a minimum, you need enough RAM to run the operating system (as explained earlier), plus whatever other software applications you're using, and then a bit of additional RAM to hold the data you're inputting.

To determine how much RAM you need, list all the software applications you might be running at one time. Figure 12 shows an example of RAM requirements. In this example, if you are running your operating system, word-processing and spreadsheet programs, a Web browser, a music player, and photo-editing software simultaneously, you will need a *minimum* of 1.3 GB RAM. It's always best to check the system requirements of any software program before you

FIGURE 13 **Do You Need to Upgrade Your RAM?**

Application	Current System
Type of RAM Your System Is Using	
Maximum Amount of RAM You Need	
Amount of RAM in Your System Now	
Amount of RAM You Want to Add	
Number of Currently Empty Memory Module Slots	
Memory Module Size	
Page File Usage Amount	
Total Amount of RAM You Can Add	

buy it to make sure your system can handle it. System requirements can be found on the software package or on the manufacturer's Web site.

However, it's a good idea to have more than the minimum amount of RAM, so you can use more programs in the future. When upgrading RAM, the rule of thumb is to buy as much as you can afford but no more than your system will handle.

VIRTUAL MEMORY

Would adding more RAM improve my system performance? As shown in Figure 13, there are several factors to consider when determining if your system needs more RAM. When there's not enough RAM installed in your system, it will become sluggish, freeze more often, or just shut down as you perform certain tasks. When this happens, the system becomes **memory bound**—that is, limited in how fast it can send data to the CPU because there is not enough memory. If this is the case, adding more RAM to your system will have an immediate impact on performance.

How do I know whether my system is memory bound? If you don't have enough RAM to hold all of the programs you're currently trying to run, the operating system will begin to store the data that doesn't fit in RAM into a space on the hard disk called **virtual memory**. When it is using virtual memory, your operating system builds a file called the **page file** on the hard drive to allow processing to continue. This enables the system to run more applications than can actually fit in your computer's RAM.

So far, this system of memory management sounds like a good idea, especially because hard drives are much cheaper than RAM per megabyte of storage. The drawback is speed. Remember that accessing data from the hard drive to send it to the CPU is more than one million times slower than accessing data from RAM. Another drawback is that some applications do not run well on virtual memory. So, using virtual memory is a method of last resort. If your system is running with a large page file (that is, if it is using a lot of virtual memory), adding more RAM will dramatically increase performance.

ADDING RAM

Is there a limit to how much RAM I can add to my computer? Every computer is designed with a maximum limit on the amount of RAM it can support. Each computer is designed with a specific number of slots on the memory board in which the memory cards fit, and each slot may have a limit on the amount of RAM it can support. In addition, the operating system running on that machine may impose its own limit. (For example, the maximum amount of RAM for Windows Vista ranges from 4 GB to 128 GB, depending on the particular version.) To determine these limits, check your owner's manual or the manufacturer's Web site.

Once you know how much RAM your computer can support, you can determine the best configuration of memory cards to achieve the greatest amount of RAM. For example, say you have a total of four memory card slots: two are already filled with 256-MB RAM cards and the other two are empty. Maximum RAM allowed for your system is 1 GB. This means you can buy two more 256-MB RAM modules for the two empty slots, for a total of 1 GB (4 X 256 MB) of RAM. If all the memory card slots are already filled, you may be able to replace the old modules with greater-capacity RAM modules, depending on your maximum allowed RAM.

Is it hard to add RAM? Adding RAM to a computer is fairly easy (see Figure 14). RAM comes with installation instructions, which you should follow carefully. RAM is also relatively inexpensive compared with other system upgrade options. Still, the cost of RAM fluctuates in the marketplace as much as 400 percent over time, so if you're considering adding RAM, you should watch the prices of memory in online or print advertisements.

Evaluating the Storage Subsystem

As you've learned, there are two ways data is saved on your computer: temporary storage and permanent storage. RAM is a form of temporary (or volatile) storage— thus, anything residing in RAM is not permanently saved. Therefore, it's critical to have the means to store data and software applications *permanently*.

iStock Photo International

Adding RAM to a personal computer is quite simple and relatively inexpensive. You simply line up the notches and push in the memory module. Just be sure that you're adding a compatible memory module to your computer.

Fortunately, several storage options exist within every computer system. Storage devices for a typical personal computer include the hard disk drive, USB flash drives, CD and DVD drives, and external hard drives. When you turn off your computer, the data stored to these devices is saved. These devices are therefore referred to as nonvolatile storage devices. Of all the nonvolatile storage devices, the hard disk drive is used the most.

THE HARD DISK DRIVE

What makes the hard disk drive the most popular storage device? With storage capacities of up to 1.5 terabytes (TB), **hard disk drives** (or just **hard drives**), shown in Figure 15, have the largest storage capacity of any storage device. The hard drive is also a much more economical device than other storage drives because it offers the most gigabytes of storage per dollar.

Second, the hard drive's **access time**, or the time it takes a storage device to locate its stored data and make it available for processing, is also the fastest of all permanent storage devices. Hard drive access times are measured in milliseconds, or thousandths of seconds. For large-capacity drives, access

SOUND BYTE

Hard Disk Anatomy Interactive

In this Sound Byte, you'll learn about the internal construction of a hard drive and see how a hard drive reads (retrieves) and writes (records) data. You'll also watch a disk being defragmented and learn how the defragmentation utility improves hard drive performance.

Hard drive inside
the system unit

FIGURE 15

Hard disk drives are
the most popular stor-
age device for per-
sonal computers. The
hard disk drive is
installed permanently
inside the system unit.

transfer is referred to as **data transfer rate** and
depending on the manufacturer is expressed
in either megabits or megabytes per second.

**How is data stored on hard
drives?** A hard disk drive is composed of
several coated **platters** (round, thin plates of
metal) stacked onto a spindle. When data is
saved to a hard disk, a pattern of magnetized
spots is created on the iron oxide coating of
each platter. Each of these spots represents a
1, whereas the spaces not "spotted" represent a 0. These 0s and 1s are bits (or binary
digits) and are the smallest pieces of data
that computers can understand. When data
stored on the hard disk is retrieved (or read),
your computer translates these patterns of
magnetized spots into the data you have
saved.

**How do I know how much storage
capacity I need?** Typically, hard drive
capacity is measured in gigabytes (GB),
with some high-end systems having a hard
drive with capacity in the terabytes (TB). To
check how much total capacity your hard
drive has, as well as how much is being
used, click the Start button and select
Computer from the right side of the Start
menu. The hard disk drives, their capacity,
and usage are shown, similar to those
shown in Figure 16.

times of approximately 9.5 milliseconds—
that's less than one-hundredth of a second—
are not unusual. This is much faster than the
access times of other popular storage
devices, such as floppy and flash drives.

Another reason hard drives are popular is
that they transfer data to other computer
components (such as RAM) much faster than
the other storage devices do. This speed of

FIGURE 16

(a) In Vista, the free and
used capacity of each
device in the computer
system is shown in the
Computer dialog box.
(b) Alternatively, you can
determine the capacity of
your hard drive using the
pie chart in the General tab
of the Properties dialog
box. The hard drive shown
has 99.7 GB of space, with
67.6 GB of free space.

>To view the computer dia-
log box, click Start, and
click Computer. To view the
pie chart from the Start
Menu, right-click the C
drive, and select
Properties.

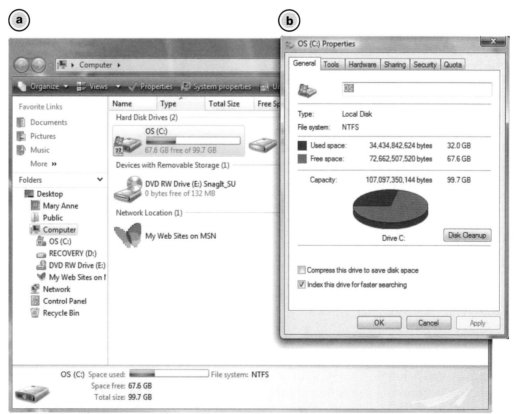

Reprinted with permission from Microsoft Corporation

How a Hard Disk Drive Works

The thin metal platters that make up a hard drive are covered with a special magnetic coating that enables the data to be recorded onto one or both sides of the platter. Hard disk manufacturers prepare the disks to hold data through a process called low-level formatting. In this process, **tracks** (concentric circles) and **sectors** (pie-shaped wedges) are created in the magnetized surface of each platter, setting up a gridlike pattern used to identify file locations on the hard drive. A separate process, called high-level formatting, establishes the catalog that the computer uses to keep track of where each file is located on the hard drive.

Hard drive platters spin at a high rate of speed, some as fast as 15,000 revolutions per minute (rpm). Sitting between each platter are special "arms" that contain **read/write heads** (see Figure 17). The read/write heads move from the outer edge of the spinning platters to the center, up to 50 times per second, to retrieve (read) and record (write) the magnetic data to and from the hard disk. As noted earlier, the average total time it takes for the read/write head to locate the data on the platter and return it to the CPU for processing is the access time. A new hard drive should have an average access time of about 10 ms.

Access time is mostly the sum of two factors: seek time and latency. The time it takes for the read/write heads to move over the surface of the disk, between tracks, to the correct track is called the **seek time** (sometimes people incorrectly refer to this as access time). Once the read/write head locates the correct track, it may need to wait for the correct sector to spin to the read/write head. This waiting time is called **latency** (or rotational delay). The faster the platters spin (or the faster the rpm), the less time you'll have to wait for your data to be accessed. Currently, you can find hard drives for your home system that spin between 5,400 and 7,200 rpm. Some people include an even faster hard drive that spins up to 10,000 rpm as a system drive and then add a slower drive with greater capacity for storage.

The read/write heads do not touch the platters of the hard drive; rather, they float above them on a thin cushion of air at a height of 0.5 microinches. As a matter of comparison, a human hair is 2,000 microinches thick and a particle of dust is larger than a human hair. Therefore, it's critical to keep your hard disk drive free from all dust and dirt, as even the smallest particle could find its way between the read/write head and the disk platter, causing a **head crash**—a stoppage of the hard disk drive that often results in data loss.

Capacities for hard disk drives in personal computers exceed 500 GB. Increasing the amount of data stored in a hard disk drive is achieved either by adding more platters or by increasing the amount of data stored on each platter. How tightly the tracks are placed next to each other, how tightly spaced the sectors are, and how closely the bits of data are placed affect the measurement of the amount of data that can be stored in a specific area of a hard disk. Modern technology continues to increase the standards on all three levels, enabling massive quantities of data to be stored in small places.

FIGURE 17

The hard drive is a stack of platters enclosed in a sealed case. Special arms fit in between each platter. The read/write heads at the end of each arm read from and save data to the platters

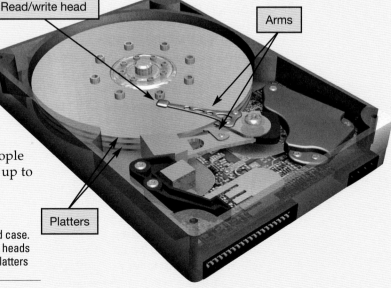

Read/write head

Arms

Platters

FIGURE 18 Sample Hard Drive Requirements

Application	Hard Disk Space Required
Windows Vista	15 GB
MS Office 2007 Professional	2 GB
Adobe Photoshop Elements	2 GB
Roxio Easy Media Creator 9	1 GB installation and up to 9 GB to copy CDs or DVDs
Total Required	20 – 29 GB

To determine the storage capacity your system needs, calculate the amount of storage capacity basic computer programs need to reside on your computer. Because the operating system is the most critical piece of software, your hard drive needs enough space to store that program. The demands on system requirements have grown with new versions of operating systems. Windows Vista, the latest Microsoft operating system, requires a 40 GB hard drive with a whopping 15 GB of available hard drive capacity. Five years ago, such software wouldn't have fit on most hard drives.

In addition to having space for the operating system, you need enough space to store software applications you use, such as Microsoft Office, a Web browser, music, and games. Figure 18 shows an example of hard drive requirements for someone storing a few programs on a hard drive.

Are some hard drives faster than others? There are several types of hard drives. Integrated Drive Electronics (IDE, also called parallel advanced technology attachment or PATA) is an older style that used wide cables to connect the hard drive to the motherboard. Serial advanced technology attachment (Serial ATA) hard drives use much thinner cables and can transfer data more quickly than IDE drives. A slower drive is fine if you use your computer primarily for word processing, spreadsheets, e-mail, and the Internet. However, "power users," such as graphic designers and software developers, will benefit from the faster Serial ATA hard drive.

Another factor affecting a hard disk's speed is access time (or the speed with which it locates data for processing). As noted earlier, access time is measured in milliseconds (ms). The faster the access time the better, although often hard drives have similar access times.

PORTABLE STORAGE OPTIONS: FLASH AND OPTICAL DRIVES

If my hard drive is so powerful, why do I need other forms of storage? Despite all the advantages that the hard drive has as a storage device, one drawback is that data stored on it is not portable. To get data from one computer to another (assuming the computers aren't networked), you'll need a portable storage device, such as a flash drive. Equally important, you need alternative storage options for backing up data on your hard drive in case it experiences a head crash or other system problems. Finally, despite the massive storage capacity of hard drives, you should remove infrequently used files from your hard drive to maintain optimal storage capacity.

What forms of portable storage are best? Several portable storage formats (or media) are popular, with varying ranges of storage capacity (see Figure 19). The **floppy disk** was once the most popular form of storage device, but the floppy disk holds the least amount of data with a storage capacity of just 1.44 MB. Floppy disks are too small to hold even one file that has been bulked up with multimedia. For this reason, floppy disks are becoming obsolete.

CD-R, CD-RW, DVD-R, and DVD-RW discs are optical media storage devices with storage capacities ranging from 700 MB to 9.4 GB. These are popular to store large files, especially audio and video files.

Flash memory cards are another form of portable storage. Flash memory is non-volatile memory that can be electrically erased and reprogrammed. These tiny removable memory cards are often used in digital cameras, MP3 players, and PDAs.

FIGURE 19 Portable Storage Capacities

Storage Media	Capacity
Floppy Disk	1.44 MB
CD	700 MB
DVD	9.4 GB
Flash Memory	512 MB–16 GB (and up)
Portable Hard Drive	20 GB and up

Note: Capacities are accurate as of publication date but are expected to continue to increase.

Understanding and Assessing Hardware: Evaluating Your System

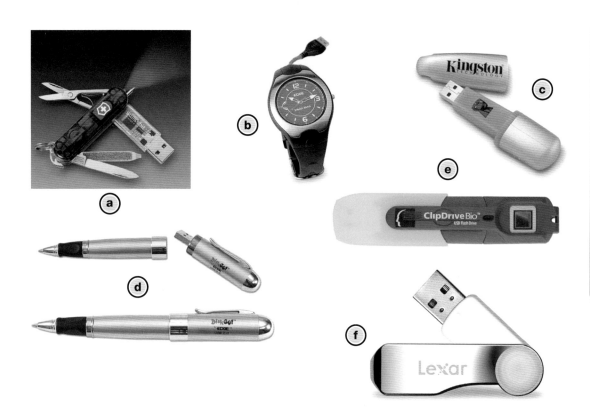

FIGURE 20

Flash drives, also known as thumb drives or jump drives, allow you to carry 8 GB or more of data in a variety of convenient packaging options. (a) Swiss Army knife with integrated flash drive, (b) watch with built-in flash drive, (c) typical flash drive, (d) pen with built-in flash drive, (e) flash drive with fingerprint recognition reader, (f) flash drive with keychain hook.

a) Courtesy of Victorinox; b) Courtesy of EdgeTech Corporation; f) Lexar Media, USA

Some flash cards can hold 8 GB or more of data. As the technology becomes more popular, capacities will continue to increase.

This same technology is also packaged as **flash drives** (sometimes called thumb drives or jump drives). Small enough to fit on a key chain, a flash drive can hold 8 GB of data (and the capacities are increasing all the time) and can be plugged into any USB port (see Figure 20). Windows Vista instantly recognizes flash drives when they are plugged into a USB port and treats them as another hard drive on the system. For less than $20 you can easily carry 1 GB with you (that's equal to almost 1,000 floppy disks) and have enough room to store a huge PowerPoint presentation, some pictures and videos, and even a bunch of MP3 songs. For these reasons, flash drives are fast becoming the most preferred means of portable storage.

Sometimes, for large amounts of portable storage, external hard drive devices are the best solution. Hard drives are now available in very small, light packages and can connect quickly to a USB 2.0 or FireWire port. Light devices such as the Apple iPod, which fits in your pocket, are another option for portable storage and can hold 80 GB of data. Larger external hard drives, still small enough to carry in a purse or backpack, can hold 500 GB or more of data. Connect them to a free USB port and they are recognized by the operating system as just another hard drive. Other larger external hard drives are perfect to use as devices to which you can back up all your important files.

So there are a number of choices available to you for portable data storage. Consider the amount of data you want to routinely transport and then select the device that meets your needs at the lowest cost.

BITS AND BYTES

Taking Care of Flash Drives

The following guidelines will help you keep your flash drives safe:

- A flash drive fits into a USB port only one way—do not force it if you feel resistance.
- When removing the drive, be sure any activity LED that may be on the drive is no longer lit. Then click the Safely Remove Hardware icon on the taskbar. Only remove the drive itself once the Safe to Remove Drive message appears. Pulling the drive out of the port earlier could corrupt your data.
- When not using the drive, keep the cap in place. Moisture and dust can damage the data stored on the drive.

BITS AND BYTES

Store It Online

Another trend in storage is letting someone else provide the space for you! With online storage, a company provides you with space on its servers, which you use to store your backup data, your photos and movies, large files—whatever you need. Companies such as Xdrive (**www.xdrive.com**) rent unlimited gigabytes of secure storage. Because your data is accessible from any Web browser, online storage is a mobile solution as well.

Web-based e-mail providers are moving in this direction also. Google Gmail (**mail.google.com**) provides users with a free account and several gigabytes of stor-

age for archiving old messages. "Don't throw anything away!" is the slogan. With Gmail, you use Google search to locate a single message, regardless of when the messages were sent or received or how many thousands of messages are archived.

Photo storage sites such as Pixagogo (**www.pixagogo.com**) and Shutterfly (**www.shutterfly.com**) provide online storage for your digital photos. You can specify who is allowed to view your images, and family and friends can order copies and merchandise with your photos directly from the site.

c) Courtesy of Kensington Corporation; d) Courtesy of EdgeTech Corporation; e) Courtesy of MXI Security; f) Courtesy of Lexar

To read information stored on a disk, a laser inside the disk drive sends a beam of light through the spinning disk.

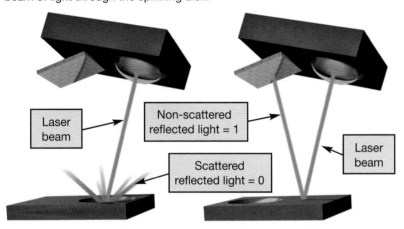

Laser beam

Non-scattered reflected light = 1

Scattered reflected light = 0

Laser beam

If the light reflected back is scattered in all directions (which happens when the laser hits a pit), the laser translates this into the binary digit 0.

If non-scattered light is reflected back to the laser (which happens when the laser hits an area in which there is no pit), the laser translates this into the binary digit 1.

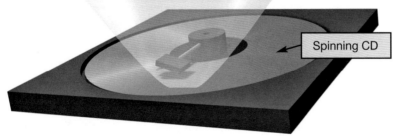

Spinning CD

In this way, the laser reads the pits and non-pits as a series of bits (0s and1s), which the computer can then process.

FIGURE 21

Data is read from a CD using focused laser light.

CDs and DVDs

How is data saved onto a CD or DVD? Like the hard drive and floppy disks, data is saved to CDs and DVDs within established tracks and sectors. However, unlike hard drives, which store their data on a magnetized platters, CDs and DVDs store data as tiny pits that are burned into a disk by a high-speed laser. These pits are extremely small, less than 1 micron in diameter, so that nearly 1,500 pits fit across the top of a pinhead. As you can see in Figure 21, data is read off the CD by a laser beam, with the pits and nonpits translating into the 1s and 0s of the binary code computers understand. Because CDs and DVDs use a laser to read and write data, they are referred to as **optical media.**

Why can I store data on some CDs but not others? CD-ROMs are read-only optical disks, meaning you can't save any data onto them. To play a CD-ROM, you use a CD-ROM (or CD-R) drive. However, most computers today are equipped with special CD drives that allow you to save, or burn, data onto specially designed CDs. **Compact Disc–Read/Writable (CD-RW) discs**, which use a CD-RW drive, can be written to hundreds of times. **Compact Disc–Recordable (CD-R) discs** can be written to once and can be used with either a CD-R drive or a CD-RW drive. If your computer isn't equipped with a CD-R or CD-RW drive, you can buy one at a reasonable cost, and they're quite simple to install.

What's the difference between CDs and DVDs? Digital Video Discs **(DVDs)** use the same optical technology to store data as CDs. The difference is that a

DVD's storage capacity is much greater than a CD's. To hold more data than CDs, DVDs have less space between tracks, as well as between bits. The size of pits on the DVD is also much smaller than those on a CD. In addition, DVD audio and video quality is superior to that of a CD. Because of their versatile nature, DVDs are the standard technology for audio and video files as well as graphics and data files.

Are there discs that can hold even more data than DVDs? DVDs can have data on just one side or both sides of the disc, with one or two layers on each side for a maximum capacity of 17 GB per disc. But with the arrival of high-definition video, even the capacity of DVDs seems small. The DVD's main competitor appears to be the HD-DVD (High-Definition DVD), which holds less data but may be cheaper to produce and may be picked up by some important manufacturers.

Blu-ray disc (BD) is the newest means to store digital media, including high-definition video (**www.Blu-ray.com**). An average two-hour standard definition movie can fit on a standard DVD, but the newer high-definition movies require a disc with about five times more storage space. A single layer Blu-ray disc can hold 25 GB of data, while a double-layer disc can hold 50 GB, enough for four hours of high-definition video. The "blue" in the name refers to the fact that a blue laser is used to write and read these discs, instead of a red laser that is used to read DVDs. Experiments are also underway using fluorescent optical discs that can store data in as many as 100 different layers, for a final capacity of 450 GB!

Do I need separate players and burners for CD/DVD and now BD formats? Although CDs and DVDs are based on the same optical technology, CD drives cannot read DVDs. If your system has only a CD drive, you need to add a DVD drive to view DVDs. However, because DVD drives can read CDs, if your system has a DVD drive, you do not need to add a CD drive to listen to CDs. Although Blu-ray discs are read with a different type of laser than CDs and DVDs, most Blu-ray players are created to play DVDs.

To record data to (burn) DVDs, you need recordable DVD discs and a read/write DVD drive. Unfortunately, technology experts have not agreed on a standard DVD format. Currently, there are two recognized

BITS AND BYTES

Taking Care of CDs and DVDs

The following guidelines will help you keep your CDs and DVDs safe:

- Exercise care in handling your CDs and DVDs. Dirt or oil on CDs/DVDs can keep data from being read properly, whereas large scratches can interrupt data completely. Hold the CD by the edge or the center ring only.
- To keep CDs/DVDs from warping, avoid placing them near heat sources and store them at room temperature.
- Clean CDs/DVDs by taking a bit of rubbing alcohol on a cotton ball and wiping them from the center to the edge of the disc in long swipes. Don't rub the CD/DVD in a circular motion, because you may cause more scratches.
- Use a felt-tip marker to label CDs/DVDs and write on the area provided for the label. Don't put stickers or labels on CDs/DVDs, unless they're specifically designed for that purpose.

formats, **DVD-R/RW** (pronounced "DVD dash") and **DVD+R/RW** (pronounced "DVD plus"). You can purchase a DVD-RW drive or a DVD+RW drive or even a "super drive" DVD-/+RW that can read and write both formats. Either the plus or dash format discs you write will be compatible in about 85 percent of all DVD players. (Web sites such as **www.videohelp.com** list the compatibility of various DVD players and the DVD plus and DVD dash formats.) However, you must make sure you purchase blank DVD discs that match the type of drive you own. Either type of DVD burner drive can burn CDs. You can also buy rewritable drives for your PC that use Blu-ray technology and let you burn CDs and DVDs.

Are some CD and DVD drives faster than others? When you buy a CD or DVD drive, knowing the drive speed is important. Speeds are listed on the device's packaging. Record (write) speed is always listed first, rewrite speed is listed second (except for CD-R drives, which cannot rewrite data), and playback speed is listed last. For example, a CD-RW drive may have speeds of 52X32X52X, meaning that the device can record data at 52X speed, rewrite data at 32X speed, and play back data at 52X speed. For CDs, the X after each number represents the transfer of 150 KB of data per second. So, for example, a CD-RW drive with a 52X32X52X rating records data at 52 X 150 KB per second, or 7,800 KB per second.

SOUND BYTE

CD and DVD Reading and Writing Interactive

In this Sound Byte, you'll learn about the process of storing and retrieving data from CD-R, CD-RW, and DVD discs. You'll be amazed to see how much precision engineering is required to burn MP3 files onto a disc.

DVD drives are much faster than CD drives. For example, a 1X DVD-ROM drive provides a data transfer rate of approximately 1.3 MB of data per second, which is roughly equivalent to a CD-ROM speed of 9X. CD and DVD drives are constantly getting faster. If you're in the market for a new CD or DVD burner, you'll want to investigate the drive speeds on the market and make sure you get the fastest one you can afford.

Blu-ray drives are the fastest. Blu-ray technology defines 1X speed as 36 MB per second. Since BD movies will require data transfer rates of at least 54 MB per second, most Blu-ray disc players will have a minimum of 2X speeds (72 MB per second).

Floppy Disks

How is data stored on floppy disks?

Only a few years ago, floppy disks were the most convenient means of portable storage. Now, they are rapidly becoming legacy technology. Inside the plastic cases of floppy disks, you'll find a round piece of plastic film covered with a magnetized coating of iron oxide. As is the case with hard drives, when data is saved to the disk, a pattern of magnetized spots is created on the iron oxide coating within established tracks and sectors. Each of these spots represents either a 0 or a 1, or a bit. When data stored on the disk is retrieved (read), your computer translates these patterns of magnetized spots into information. Because floppy disks use a magnetized film to store data, they are referred to as **magnetic media**.

UPGRADING YOUR STORAGE SUBSYSTEM

How can I upgrade my storage devices?

The table in Figure 22 will help you determine if your computer's storage subsystem needs upgrading.

If you need to upgrade, there are several ways in which you can increase your storage capacity or add extra drives to your computer.

If you find your hard drive is running out of space, or you want a place to back up or move files to create more room on your hard drive, you have several options. You can replace the hard drive installed in your system unit with a bigger one. However, replacing your internal hard drive requires backing up your entire hard drive and reloading all the data onto your new hard drive. Instead, you may want to install an *additional* hard drive in your current system, if you have an extra drive bay (the space reserved on the inside of your system unit for hard disk drives). Instead of installing a bigger hard drive, you might just choose to add an external hard drive you can plug directly into a free USB 2.0 or FireWire port. Figure 23 shows an example of such an external hard drive.

You can also upgrade your storage subsystem by adding a DVD burner or other drive to your system. If your computer did not come with an internal CD burner, or DVD burner drive, and if you have an open (unused) drive bay in your system, you can easily install an additional drive there. Many people upgrade to a CD-RW and DVD-RW not for more storage but

FIGURE 22 Do You Need to Upgrade Your Storage Subsystem?

	Current System	Upgrade Required?
Hard Disk Drive Capacity		
CD-R/CD-RW Drive		
DVD-ROM Drive		
DVD-/+RW Drive		
Blu-ray R/RW Drive		
Other Storage Devices Needed?		

FIGURE 23   Seagate Technology, Inc.

This external hard disk drive offers you up to 750 GB extra storage and includes a system to back up your files simply with the push of one button.

because they want additional multimedia capabilities (such as the ability to burn CDs or DVDs). If you don't have open bays in your system, you can still add CD/DVD drives. As is the case with hard drives, these drives are available as external units you attach to your computer through an open port.

What if I want to use flash memory? As flash memory becomes more popular, you may want your computer to be able to read flash memory cards. Many desktop computers include internal memory card readers, but if yours does not, you can purchase external memory card readers that connect to your system through an open USB port. Some flash memory comes in "sticks" that just plug directly into a USB port (shown earlier in Figure 20).

Evaluating the Video Subsystem

How video is displayed depends on two components: your video card and your monitor. It's important that your system have the correct monitor and video card to meet your needs. If you use your computer system to display files that have complex graphics, such as videos on DVD or from your camcorder, or even play graphics-rich games with a lot of fast action, you may want to consider upgrading your video subsystem.

VIDEO CARDS

What is a video card? A **video card** (or **video adapter**) is an expansion card that is installed inside your system unit to translate

ETHICS IN IT

Ethics: CD and DVD Technology: A Free Lunch—Or at Least a Free Copy

Years ago, when the electronic photocopier made its debut, book publishers and others who distributed the printed word feared they would be put out of business. They were worried that people would no longer buy books and other printed matter if they could simply copy someone else's original. Years later, when the cassette player/recorder and VCR player/recorder arrived on the market, those who felt they would be negatively affected by these new technologies expressed similar concerns. Now, with the arrival of DVD-RW and CD-RW technology, which allows users to copy DVDs and CDs in a matter of minutes, the music and entertainment industries are worried.

Although photocopiers and VCRs certainly didn't put an end to the industries they affected, some still say the music and entertainment industries will take a significant hit with CD-RW/DVD-RW technology. Already, CD and DVD sales are plummeting. Industry insiders are claiming that these new technologies are unethical, and they're pressing for increased federal legislation against such copying. And it's not just the CD-RW/DVD-RW technology that's causing problems—"copies" are not necessarily of the physical sort. Thanks to the Internet, file transferring copyrighted works—particularly music and films—is now commonplace. According to Music United (**www.musicunited.org**), more than 243 million files are downloaded illegally every month, and about one quarter of all Internet users worldwide have downloaded a movie from the Internet.

In a separate survey, the Recording Industry Association of America (RIAA), a trade organization that represents the interests of recording giants such as Sony, Capitol Records, and other major producers of musical entertainment, reported that 23 percent of music fans revealed they were buying less music because they could download it or copy a CD-ROM from a friend.

As you would expect, the music and entertainment industries want to be fairly compensated for their creative output. They blame the technology industry for the creation of means by which artists, studios, and the entertainment industry in general are being "robbed." Although the technology exists that readily allows consumers to transfer and copy music and videos, the artists who produce these works do not want to be taken advantage of. However, others claim that the technology industry should not bear the complete burden of protecting entertainment copyrights. The RIAA sums up the future of this debate nicely: "Goals for the new millennium are to work with [the recording] industry and others to enable technologies that open up new opportunities but at the same time to protect the rights of artists and copyright owners."

binary data into the images you view on your monitor. Today, almost all computers ship with a video card installed. Modern video cards, like the one shown in Figure 24, are very sophisticated. They include ports allowing you to connect to different video equipment, and they include their own RAM, called **video memory**. Several standards of video memory are available, including GDDR3 and DDR2 memory. Because displaying graphics demands a lot of the CPU, video cards also come with their own processors. Calls to the CPU for graphics processing are redirected to the processor on the video card, significantly speeding up graphics processing.

How can I tell how much memory my video card has? Information about your system's video card can be found in the Advanced Settings of the Display Settings dialog box. To get to the Display Settings dialog box, right-click on your desktop and select Personalize. Under Personalize appearance and sounds, click Display Settings, and then click the Advanced Settings button. A window will display, showing you the type of graphics card installed in your system, as well as memory information including the Total Available Graphics Memory, Dedicated Video Memory, and Shared System Memory. The documentation that came with your computer should also contain specifications for the video card, including the amount of video memory it has installed.

How much memory does my video card need? The amount of memory your video card needs depends on what you want to display on your monitor. If you work primarily in Microsoft Word and conduct general Web searches, 16 MB is a realistic minimum. For the serious gamer, no less than a 256-MB video card is essential, although cards with 640 MB are commonly found on the market and are preferred. These high-end video cards with greater amounts of memory allow games to generate smoother animations and more sophisticated shading and texture. Before purchasing new software, check the specifications to ensure your video card has enough video memory to handle the load.

What else does the video card do? The video card also controls the number of colors your monitor can display. The number of bits the video card uses to represent each pixel (or dot) on the monitor (referred to as **bit depth**) determines the color quality of the image displayed. The more bits, the better the color detail of the image. A 4-bit video card displays 16 colors, the minimum number of colors your system works with (referred to as Standard VGA). Most video cards today are 24-bit cards, displaying more than 16 million colors. This mode is called true color mode (see Figure 25).

The most recent generation of video cards can add some great features to your computer if you are a TV fan. Multimedia cards such as

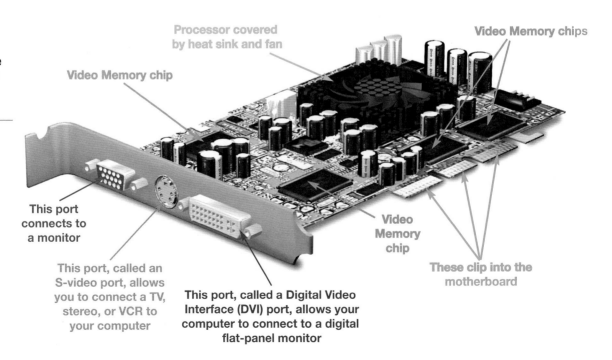

FIGURE 24

Video cards have grown to be very specialized subsystems.

Processor covered by heat sink and fan

Video Memory chips

Video Memory chip

This port connects to a monitor

This port, called an S-video port, allows you to connect a TV, stereo, or VCR to your computer

This port, called a Digital Video Interface (DVI) port, allows your computer to connect to a digital flat-panel monitor

Video Memory chip

These clip into the motherboard

Understanding and Assessing Hardware: Evaluating Your System

the ATI All-In-Wonder X1900 can open a live TV window on your screen, including features such as picture-in-picture. Using this video card, you can record programs to your hard drive or pause live TV. The card even comes with a wireless remote control.

There are also video cards that allow you to import analog video. These models have a special video-in port that you can connect to a VHS tape player or an analog video camera. The video is then digitized into a file that is stored on your hard drive. Video editing software, often included with these video cards, enables you to edit, add effects or titles to your original clips, and produce polished versions of your favorite home movies.

So how do I know if I need a new video card? If your monitor takes a while to refresh when editing photos, surfing the Web, or playing a graphics-rich game, the video card could be short on memory. You also may want to upgrade if added features such as television viewing or importing analog video are important to you. If you want to use two monitors at the same time, you may need to upgrade your video card. On a desktop computer, replacing a video card is fairly simple: you simply insert the new video card in the correct expansion slot.

MONITORS

How do I evaluate my monitor? You've evaluated your video card to ensure the best display. However, if the monitor is no good, you're still out of luck. There are two types of monitors: cathode-ray tube (CRT) and liquid crystal display (LCD). In that chapter, we discussed the factors you need to think about when deciding whether you should buy a CRT or an LCD. If you currently have a CRT monitor but would rather have an LCD, you may want to upgrade.

Another factor you need to consider in evaluating your monitor is its size. The most common monitor sizes are 17, 19, and 21 inches, although there are 30-inch monitors in use. If your monitor is 15 inches or smaller, you may want to upgrade to a larger size if you find that you need to scroll horizontally and vertically to see an entire Web page, for example. Note that monitor size listed for CRT monitors is the diagonal measurement of the tube *before* it's placed in the screen case. The actual viewing size is smaller. LCD monitors are also measured diagonally, but the

FIGURE 25 Bit Depth and Color Quality

Bit Depth	Color Quality Description	Number of Colors Displayed
4-bit	Standard VGA	16
8-bit	256-Color Mode	256
16-bit	High Color	65,536
24-bit	True Color	16,777,216
32-bit	True Color	16,777,216 plus 8 bits to help with transparency

measurement is equal to the viewing size. Therefore, the viewable area of a 17-inch LCD is approximately equal to the viewable area of a 19-inch CRT. Because the price of LCD monitors has dropped considerably and Windows Vista makes it simple to set up, if you have the desk space, you might want to consider using two monitors, especially if you like to have two separate windows open at full size at the same time. If you have a CRT monitor and want to increase the size of your monitor but can't afford giving up desktop space, you may want to consider buying the same size LCD monitor. If you can't afford to buy a larger screen but want to see more on the screen itself, you can try adjusting the resolution of your monitor. There are other factors, outlined in Figure 26 and discussed in the following sections, that will also affect your decision to upgrade your video subsystem or not.

FIGURE 26 Do You Need to Upgrade Your Video Subsystem?

	Current System	Upgrade Required?
Monitor Type (CRT or LCD)		
Monitor Size (Viewable Area)		
CRT Monitor Refresh Rate		
CRT Monitor Dot Pitch		
LCD Monitor Pixel Response Rate		
LCD Monitor Brightness		
DVI or VGA Hookup		
Video Card Memory		
TV Tuner		

How would changing my screen resolution help me see more on my screen? Most monitors can display different resolutions (the number of pixels displayed on the screen). Changing the screen resolution can make a difference in what is displayed. If you notice that you are scrolling more often to see all of a Web page, for example, increasing the screen resolution will enable you to see more of the Web page without the need for scrolling. In Figure 27, you can see the same Web page shown at increasingly greater screen resolutions. However, although increasing the screen resolution allows more to be displayed on the monitor, it also makes the images and text on the screen smaller and perhaps more difficult to read.

What other features should I look for in a CRT monitor? For a CRT monitor, several factors affect image quality, including refresh rate (the number of times per second the illumination of each pixel on the monitor is recharged) and dot pitch (the diagonal distance between pixels of the same color on the screen). For a clearer, brighter image, look for a monitor with a refresh rate of around 75 Hz and a low dot pitch (no more than 0.28 mm for a 17-inch screen or 0.31 mm for a 21-inch screen).

Are there different features to know about in choosing an LCD monitor? When choosing an LCD monitor, the main specifications and features to watch out for include aspect ratio (the standard proportion in width to height for a computer monitor) and contrast ratio (the difference in light intensity between the brightest white and the deepest black). The standard aspect ratio is 4:3, but there are monitors that display a wider format

FIGURE 27

Adjusting screen resolution will allow you to see more on your screen. In these images, the same Web page is shown at (a) 1,024 x 768 pixels, (b) 1,280 x 1,024 pixels, and (c) 1,600 x 1,200 pixels.

a-c) Google, Inc.

Understanding and Assessing Hardware: Evaluating Your System

of 16:9 or 16:10. Contrast ratios should be at least 500:1. Other features to consider when buying an LCD monitor are brightness (a measure of how much light a panel can produce) and pixel-response rate (how quickly a pixel can change colors). If you want to also watch movies on your LCD panel, choose one with a brightness measure of at least 500 for basic computing needs; a lower measure would be fine. Pixel response rates are improving all the time, but the serious gamer should have a max of 12 ms to 15 ms. Keeping these specifications in mind, you also might want to ensure that your new monitor has a digital (DVI) as well as analog (VGA) hookup, and if viewing from the side of the monitor is critical for you, make sure the monitor has a good viewing angle.

Evaluating the Audio Subsystem

Computers output sound by means of speakers (or headphones) and a sound card. For many users, the preinstalled speakers and sound card are adequate for the sounds produced by the computer itself—the beeps and so on that the computer makes. However, if you're listening to music, viewing DVDs, hooking into a household stereo system, or playing games with sophisticated sound tracks, you may want to upgrade your speakers or your sound card.

SPEAKERS

What kinds of computer speakers are available? Two types of speakers ship with most personal computers: amplified speakers (which use external power) or unamplified speakers (which use internal power). Amplified speakers are easy to identify: they come with a separate power transformer and must be plugged into an electrical outlet before they'll function. Unamplified speakers merely plug into the speaker jack on your sound card and require no extra outside power.

Which type of speaker is better? Amplified speakers generally produce better quality sound. However, they usually do not adequately reproduce the low-frequency bass sounds that make gam-

Klipsch Audio Technologies

FIGURE 28

Speaker systems that include a subwoofer have a wider dynamic range that features more bass.

ing and musical scores sound richer and fuller. For better bass sounds, consider purchasing a speaker system that includes a **subwoofer**, a special type of speaker designed to more faithfully reproduce low-frequency sounds (see Figure 28).

SOUND CARDS

What does the sound card do? Sound **cards**, like video cards, are expansion cards that attach to the motherboard inside your system unit. Like the video card that enables your computer to produce images on the monitor, sound cards enable the computer to produce sounds.

Can I hook up a surround-sound system to my computer? Most computers ship with a basic sound card, most of which are **3-D sound cards**. 3-D sound is a technology that advances sound reproduction beyond traditional stereo sound (where the human ear perceives sounds as coming from the left or the right of the performance area). 3-D sound is better at convincing the human ear that sound is omnidirectional, meaning you can't tell from which direction the sound is coming. This tends to produce a fuller, richer sound than stereo sound. However, 3-D sound is not surround sound.

What is surround sound then? The current surround-sound standard is from Dolby. There are many formats, such as Dolby Digital EX and Dolby Digital Plus, for high-definition audio. Dolby TrueHD is the newest standard featuring high-definition and lossless technology, where no data is lost in the compression process. To create surround sound, Dolby takes digital sound from a medium (such as a DVD-ROM) and reproduces it in eight channels. Seven channels cover the listening field with placement to the left front, right front, and center of the audio stage, as well as the left rear and right

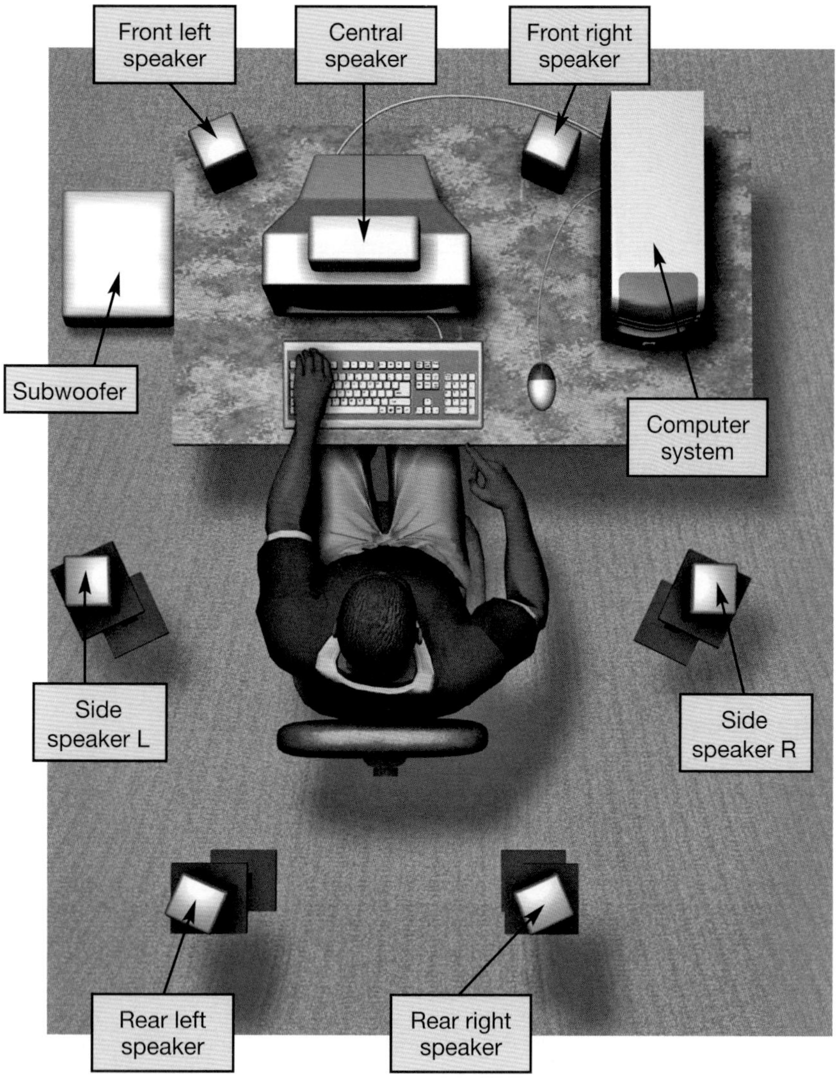

Front left speaker

Central speaker

Front right speaker

Subwoofer

Computer system

Side speaker L

Side speaker R

Rear left speaker

Rear right speaker

FIGURE 29

Dolby Digital surround sound gives you better quality audio output.

rear, and then two extra side speakers are added, as shown in Figure 29. The eighth channel holds very low-frequency sound data and is sent to a subwoofer, which can be placed anywhere in the room. To set up surround sound on your computer, you need two things: a set of surround-sound speakers and, for the greatest surround sound experience, a sound card that is Dolby digital compatible.

I don't need surround sound on my computer. Why else might I need to buy an upgraded sound card? Most basic sound cards contain the following input and output jacks (or ports): microphone in, speaker out, line in, and a gaming port. This allows you to hook up a set of stereo speakers, a microphone, and a joystick. However, what if you want to hook up a right and left speaker individually or attach other audio devices to your computer? To do so, you need more ports, which are provided on upgraded sound cards like the one shown in Figure 30.

With an upgraded sound card, you can connect portable minidisc players, MP3 players, portable jukeboxes, headphones, and CD players to your computer. Musicians also create music on their computers by connecting special devices (such as keyboards) directly to sound card ports. To determine whether your audio subsystem is meeting your needs, review the table in Figure 31.

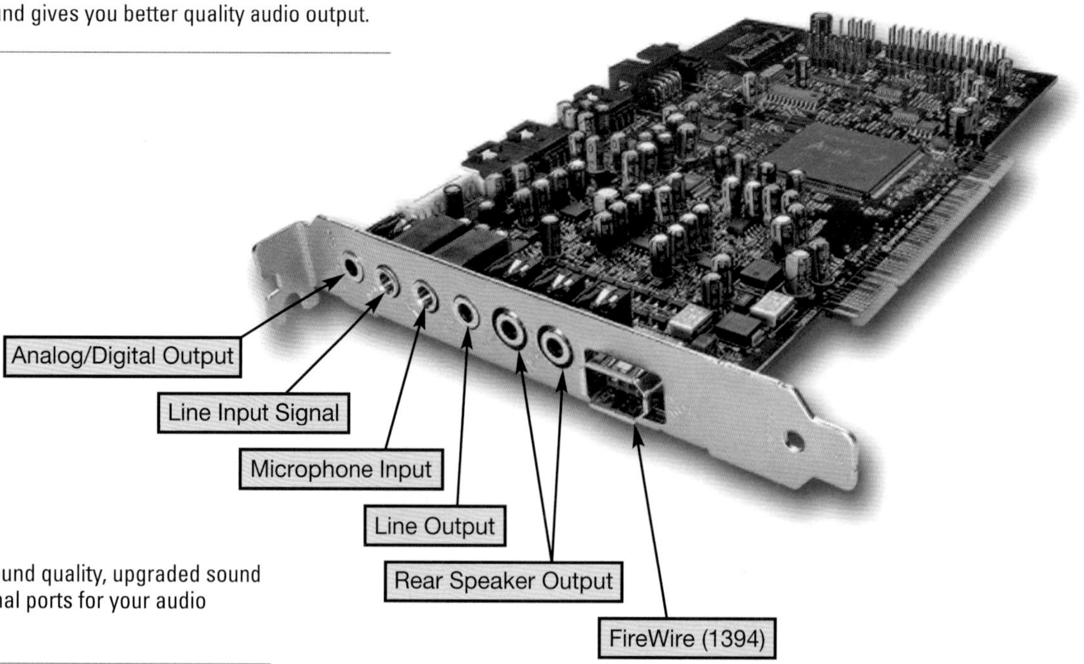

Analog/Digital Output

Line Input Signal

Microphone Input

Line Output

Rear Speaker Output

FireWire (1394)

FIGURE 30

In addition to improving sound quality, upgraded sound cards can provide additional ports for your audio equipment.

Understanding and Assessing Hardware: Evaluating Your System

Evaluating Port Connectivity

New computer devices are being introduced all the time, and the system you purchased last year may not support the hardware you're interested in today. A **port** is an interface through which external devices are connected to your computer. To evaluate your system's port connectivity, check the camera, camcorder, printer, scanner, and other devices you'd like to be able to connect to your computer and look for the type of port connection they require. Does your system have the ports necessary to connect to all of these devices?

What types of ports are there?

Although the most common types of ports on new computer systems include universal serial bus (USB), FireWire, and Ethernet, some older systems still have serial and parallel ports. Each type of port operates at a certain speed, measured in either kilobits per second (Kbps) or megabits per second (Mbps). Figure 32 lists the basic characteristics of these ports.

FIGURE 31 Do You Need to Upgrade Your Audio Subsystem?

	Current System	Upgrade Required?
Speakers (Amplified or Unamplified)		
3D Sound Card		
Dolby Digital		
Sufficient Ports?		

FIGURE 32 Ports and Their Uses

Port Name	Port Shape	Connector Shape	Data Transfer Speed	Typical Devices Attached to Port
Current Technologies				
				Game controllers Camcorders Digital cameras Maintains backward compatibility with USB 1
FireWire/FireWire 800			400 Mbps/ 800 Mbps	Digital video camcorders Digital cameras
Ethernet/Gigabit Ethernet			Up to 100 Mbps/ Up to 1,000	Network connections Cable modems
Legacy Technologies				
Serial	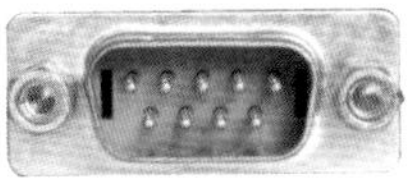		56 Kbps	Mice External modems
Parallel	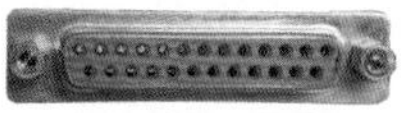	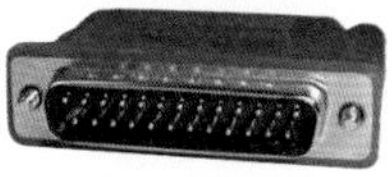	12 Mbps (12,000 Kbps)	Printers External Zip drives
USB 1.1			12 Mbps	Same devices as for 2.0 technology, but transfers at a slower speed

a-i) Courtesy of Hack In The Box, www.hackinthebox.org

The **universal serial bus (USB) port** is fast becoming the most common port on computers today. The original USB (version 1.1) port could transfer data at only 12 Mbps. However, in 2002, USB version 2 (USB 2.0) was released, increasing throughput to 480 Mbps. Printers, scanners, digital cameras, keyboards, mice, and hard disk drives can all be connected to the computer using USB ports.

The **FireWire port** (previously called the **IEEE 1394 port**) is based on a standard developed by the Institute of Electrical and Electronics Engineers (IEEE). Until the introduction of USB 2.0, FireWire was the fastest port available, with a transfer rate of 400 Mbps. The newer FireWire 800, which transfers data at 800 Mbps, is the fastest available today. FireWire is most commonly used to connect digital video devices (such as digital cameras) or hard drives to the computer.

The **Ethernet port** (technically called an RJ-45 jack) is used to connect your computer to a local network or cable modem. Because one of the most common uses of RJ-45 jacks is for connecting Ethernet networks, it is often referred to simply as an Ethernet jack. Ethernet originally offered a transfer rate of 10 Mbps. Fast Ethernet (called 100Base-T), with a transfer rate of 100 Mbps, is the standard used in most personal computers today.

If you have a network that needs to transfer lots of large files such as video files, Gigabit Ethernet networking would be useful. Gigabit Ethernet can transfer at a rate up to 1,000 Mbps.

The **serial port** allows the transfer of data, one bit at a time, over a single wire at speeds of up to 56 Kbps. Examples of devices used

to connect to serial ports once included external modems and PDA cradles. As of 2006, most computers no longer have serial ports as they are being replaced by faster ports, such as the USB port.

A **parallel port** sends data between devices in *groups* of bits and is therefore much faster than a serial port. Parallel ports have traditionally been used to connect printers and scanners to computers. Most parallel ports achieve data transfer rates of 12 Mbps, much faster than the serial port. Despite this speed increase, parallel ports are also being phased out in favor of higher-speed ports.

Are there any other kinds of ports? In addition to the more common ports, you may also need more specialized ports, such as IrDA, Bluetooth, and MIDI.

The **IrDA port** (shown in Figure 33) is based on a standard developed by the Infrared Data Association for transmitting data. IrDA ports enable you to transmit data between two devices by using infrared light waves. IrDA ports have a maximum throughput of 4 Mbps and require that a line of sight be maintained between the two ports. Many printers, notebooks, and PDAs include IrDA ports. If a printer and a notebook both have IrDA ports, the notebook can send a file to the printer without being physically connected to it.

Bluetooth technology uses radio waves to send data over short distances (see Figure 34). The maximum transfer rate of the original Bluetooth 1.0 is 1 Mbps. The newer standard Bluetooth 2.0 is three times faster, with a maximum transfer rate of 3 Mbps. Many notebooks and PDAs include a small Bluetooth chip that allows them to transfer data wirelessly to any other device with a Bluetooth chip, such as a cell phone, PDA, or Bluetooth-enabled keyboard or mouse. The advantage of Bluetooth devices is that a clear line of sight isn't needed between the two devices, although the distance between the devices is limited to about 30 feet.

Wi-Fi (Wireless Fidelity), another wireless transmission standard, differs slightly from Bluetooth. Wi-Fi is designed to cover much longer distances and to allow much faster data transfer, up to 54 Mbps. Although Wi-Fi is a great way to connect your notebook from the back porch to the PC in the upstairs bedroom, Bluetooth is a better solution for a short-distance connection, such as from a wireless keyboard to the system unit.

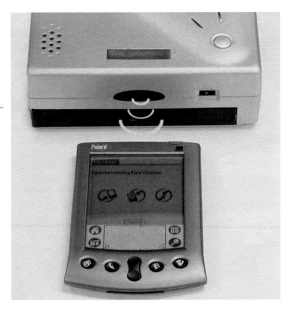

A **MIDI port** is a port that allows you to connect electronic musical instruments (such as synthesizers) to your computer. Musical Instrument Digital Interface (MIDI) is a standard adopted by the music industry that provides for capturing specific data about a sound such as pitch, duration, and volume. That data is transferred between the computer and the MIDI device at a rate of 31.5 Kbps. In addition to synthesizers, MIDI ports also work with electronic drum machines and other electronically adapted instruments. If your system does not have a MIDI port, you can get a MIDI-to-USB connector to connect your MIDI device to a USB port. Eventually, similar to the serial and parallel ports, the MIDI port will be replaced by a USB port.

ADDING PORTS: EXPANSION CARDS AND HUBS

What if I don't have all the ports I need? New port standards are developed every few years, and special expansion cards are usually the only way to add the newest ports to an older computer or to expand the number of ports on your computer. For example, your computer may have only USB 1.0 ports, but you may have several devices that would run better with USB 2.0 ports. Just as sound cards and video cards provide ports for sound and video equipment to connect to the computer, there are also expansion cards that you can install in your system unit to provide you with additional ports (such as USB 2.0 and FireWire). Like the other expansion cards, these cards clip into an open expansion slot on the motherboard. Figure 35 shows an example of such an expansion card.

Bluetooth-equipped devices communicate wirelessly with one another using radio waves.

What if there are no open slots on the motherboard for me to insert an expansion card? If there are no open slots on the motherboard and you still need extra ports, you can add an expansion hub (shown in Figure 36). An **expansion hub** is a device that connects to one port, such as a USB port, to provide four or eight new ports,

FIGURE 35

This expansion card provides your computer with additional ports.

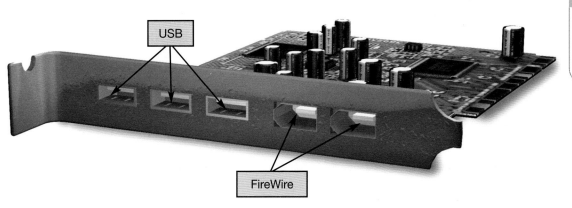

USB

FireWire

FIGURE 36

similar to a multiplug extension cord you use with electrical appliances.

You also can connect multiple USB devices through a single USB port by connecting the devices in a daisy chain. In a daisy chain, you attach one device to another through its USB port, with the last device connecting to a USB port on the computer.

Is there a limit to the number of ports I can add? Using expansion hubs, you can expand your computer so that it can handle more USB and FireWire devices. For installation of other ports, you're limited by the number of open expansion slots in your computer. Most computer users won't need more than one or two FireWire ports and four USB ports, a number that you can easily achieve using expansion hubs and cards.

You also can add ports to an empty drive bay, giving you easy-to-reach new ports. The Koutech 10-in-1, shown in Figure 37, fits into a regular drive bay and adds front-panel access to two USB 2.0 ports, two FireWire ports, three audio jacks, and a 6-in-1 digital media card reader.

Which port should I use when I have a choice? Obviously, the fastest port is preferable but may not always be possible or cost effective. For example, most currently produced inkjet printers offer the option of connecting by a parallel port or USB port. Because USB ports are faster, your printer will perform better if you connect it

ACTIVE HELPDESK

Evaluating Your Storage Subsystem and Ports

In this Active Helpdesk call, you'll play the role of a Helpdesk staffer, fielding calls about the computer's storage devices and ports.

to a USB port. However, if you don't have an available USB port and you don't want to buy an expansion hub or card, you can connect the printer to a parallel port instead.

Which devices benefit most from high-speed ports? Any device that requires the transfer of large amounts of data significantly benefits from using a high-speed port such as a FireWire or USB 2.0 port. For example, digital video cameras produce large files that need to be transferred to a computer. If your video camera has a FireWire port, but your computer doesn't, investing in a FireWire expansion port would definitely be worth the cost based on the time you'll save during downloads.

Evaluating System Reliability

Many computer users decide to buy a new system not necessarily because they need a faster CPU, more RAM, or a bigger hard drive, but because they are experiencing problems, such as slow performance, freezes, and crashes. Over time, your computer builds up excess files and becomes internally disorganized just from normal everyday use. This excess clutter and disorganization can lead to deteriorating performance, or worse, system failure. Therefore, before you buy a new system because you think yours may be unreliable, make sure the problem is not one you can fix. Proper upkeep and maintenance also may postpone an expensive system upgrade or replacement.

What can I do to ensure my system performs reliably? There are several procedures you can follow to ensure your system performs reliably:

1. **Clean out your Startup folder.** Some programs install themselves into your Startup folder and are automatically run each time the computer reboots, whether you are using them or not. This unnecessary load causes extra stress on RAM. Check your Startup folder by clicking on Start, All Programs, and then click on the Startup folder and make sure all the programs listed are important to you. Right-click on any unnecessary program and select Delete to remove it from the Startup folder. Make sure you delete *only* programs you know without a doubt are unnecessary.

2. **Clear out unnecessary files.** Temporary Internet files can accumulate very quickly on your hard drive, taking up unnecessary space. Running the Disk Cleanup utility is a quick and easy way to ensure your temporary Internet files don't take up precious hard drive space. Likewise, you should delete any unnecessary files from your hard drive regularly, because they can make your hard drive run slower.

3. **Run spyware and adware programs.** These often detect and remove different pests and should be used in addition to your regular antivirus package.

4. **Run the Disk Defragmenter utility on your hard drive.** When your hard drive becomes fragmented, its storage capacity is negatively impacted. When you defrag your hard drive, files are reorganized, making the hard drive work more efficiently.

My system crashes often during the day. What can I do? Computer systems are complex. It's not unusual to have your system stop responding occasionally. If rebooting the computer doesn't help, you'll need to begin troubleshooting:

1. Check that you have enough RAM, which you learned how to do in the section "Evaluating RAM: The Memory Subsystem" earlier in this chapter. Systems with insufficient amounts of RAM often crash.

2. Make sure you have properly installed any new software or hardware. If you're using a PC system, use the System Restore utility in Windows Vista to "roll back" to a time when the system worked more reliably.

3. If you see an error code in Windows, visit the Microsoft Knowledge Base (**http://support.microsoft.com**), an online resource for resolving problems with Microsoft products. This may help you determine what the error code indicates and how you may be able to solve the problem. If you don't find a satisfactory answer in the Knowledge Base, try copying the entire error message into Google and searching the larger community for solutions.

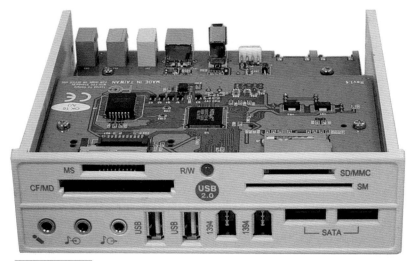

Courtesy of Koutech

You also can use an empty drive bay to add additional ports and even a flash card reader to the front panel of the system unit.

Can my software affect my system reliability? Having the latest version of software products makes your system much more reliable. You should upgrade or update your operating system, browser software, and application software as often as new patches (or fixes) are reported for resolving errors. Sometimes these errors are performance-related; sometimes they're tied to maintaining better security for your system.

How do I know whether updates are available for my software? You can configure Windows Vista so that it automatically checks for, downloads, and installs any available updates for itself and for Internet Explorer. Many applications now also include the ability to check for updates. Check under the Help menu of the product, and often you will find a Check for Updates command.

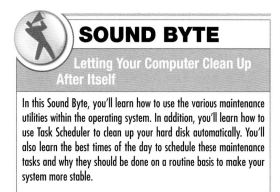

SOUND BYTE

Letting Your Computer Clean Up After Itself

In this Sound Byte, you'll learn how to use the various maintenance utilities within the operating system. In addition, you'll learn how to use Task Scheduler to clean up your hard disk automatically. You'll also learn the best times of the day to schedule these maintenance tasks and why they should be done on a routine basis to make your system more stable.

What happened to your last computer? If you threw it away hoping it would be safely recycled with your empty water bottles, think again. Mercury in screens, cadmium in batteries and circuit boards, and flame retardant in plastic housing are all toxic, as are the four to eight pounds of lead in the cathode-ray tube of nearly every monitor. An alarming trend emerging is that discarded machines are beginning to create an e-waste crisis.

Instead of throwing your computer away, you may be able to donate it to a nonprofit organization. Some manufacturers, such as Dell, offer recycling programs and have formed alliances with nonprofit organizations to help distribute your old technology to those who need it. You can also take your computer to an authorized computer recycling center in your area (find a local one at **www.usedcomputer.com**).

However, before donating or recycling a computer, make sure you carefully remove all data from your hard drive, or you may end up having your good deed turn bad, making you the victim of identity theft. Credit card numbers, bank information, social security numbers, tax records, passwords, and personal identification numbers (PINs) are just a few of the pieces of sensitive information that we casually record to our computer's hard drive. Just deleting files that contain proprietary personal information is not protection enough. Even reformatting or erasing your hard drive does not totally remove data as was proved by two MIT graduate students. In 2003, they bought more than 150 used hard drives from various sources. Although some of the hard drives were reformatted or damaged so the data was supposedly irrecoverable, the two students were able to retrieve medical records, financial information, pornography, personal e-mails, and more than 5,000 credit card numbers!

The United States Department of Defense suggests a seven-layer overwrite for a "secure erase." That is, they suggest that you fill your hard drive *seven times over* with a random series of ones and zeros. Fortunately, several software programs exist for PCs running Windows, such as Active @ KillDisk, Eraser, CyberScrub; Wipe for Linux; and Shredit X for OS X, are available that provide secure hard drive erasures, either of specific files on your hard drive or of the entire hard drive.

Keep in mind that even these data erasure software programs can't provide the ultimate level in security. Computer forensic specialists or super-cybercriminals can still manage to retrieve some data from your hard drive with the right tools. The ultimate level of protection is to destroy the hard drive altogether. Suggested methods include drilling holes in the hard drive, burning/melting the hard drive, or just taking an old-fashioned sledgehammer to it! For large companies that need to upgrade large quantities of computers and are faced with destroying or recycling their old computers, the problem becomes much worse. In these cases recycling isn't a good option, and throwing them away can become an environmental hazard. Companies like GigaBiter (**www.gigabiter.com**) eliminate security and environmental risks associated with electronic destruction by first delaminating the hard drive, and then breaking down the computer e-waste into recyclable products. The result of the final step is a sand-like substance that is 100 percent recyclable.

What if none of this helps? Is buying a new system my only option?

If your system is still unreliable after these changes, you have two options:

1. Reinstall the operating system. To do so, you'll want to back up all of your data files before the installation and be prepared to reinstall your software after the installation. Make sure you have all of the original discs for the software installed on your system, along with the product keys, serial numbers, or other activation codes so that you can reinstall them.

2. Upgrade your operating system to the latest version. There are substantial increases in reliability with each major release of a new operating system. However, upgrading the operating system may require hardware upgrades, such as additional RAM, an updated graphics processor, and an even larger hard drive. The Microsoft Windows Vista Upgrade Advisor will perform a scan of your system to determine what upgrades might be required before converting to Windows Vista. Be sure to examine the *recommended* (not required) specifications of the new operating system.

Making the Final Decision

Now that you have evaluated your computer system, you need to shift to questions of *value*. How closely does your system come to meeting your needs? How much would it cost to upgrade the system you have to match what you'd ideally like your computer to do not only today, but several years from now? How much would it cost to purchase a new system that meets these specifications?

To decide which option (upgrading or buying a new system) has better value for you, you need to price both scenarios. Figure 38 provides an upgrade worksheet you can use to evaluate both the upgrade path and the new purchase path. Be sure to consider what benefit you might obtain by having two systems, if you were to buy a new computer. Would you have a use for the older system? Would you donate it to a charitable organization? Would you be able to give it to a family member? Purchasing a new system is an important investment of your resources and you want to make a well-reasoned, well-supported decision.

FIGURE 38 Upgrade Versus New Purchase Comparison Worksheet

Needs	Hardware Upgrade Cost	Included on a New System?	Additional Expense for Item If Not Included on a New System
Portablility			
Notebook			
Wireless connectivity			
CPU and Memory Subsystems			
CPU Upgrade			
RAM Upgrade			
Storage Subsystem			
Hard Disk Upgrade			
CD-R/CD-RW Drive			
DVD-ROM Drive			
DVD-RW Drive			
Blu-ray Drive			
Flash Card Reader			
Other Storage Device			
Video And Audio Subsystems			
New Monitor			
Video Card Upgrade			
Speaker Upgrade			
Sound Card Upgrade			
Port Connectivity			
USB 2.0 Ports			
FireWire Port			
Ethernet Port			
IrDA Port			
Bluetooth Port			

Summary

1. How can I determine whether I should upgrade my existing computer or buy a new one?

To determine whether you need to upgrade or purchase a new system, you need to define your ideal system and what it can do. Then, you need to perform a system evaluation to assess the subsystems in your computer, including the CPU, memory, storage, video, audio, and ports. Last, you need to determine if it's economically practical to upgrade or whether buying a new computer would be best.

2. What does the CPU do, and how can I evaluate its performance?

Your computer's CPU processes instructions, performs calculations, manages the flow of information through a computer system, and is responsible for processing the data you input into information. It is composed of two units: the arithmetic logic unit and the control unit. CPU speed is measured in megahertz or gigahertz, or millions or billions of machine cycles a second. A machine cycle is the process the CPU goes through to fetch, decode, execute, and store data. You can tell whether your CPU is limiting your system performance by watching how busy it is as you work on your computer. The percentage of time that your CPU is working is referred to as CPU usage, which you can determine by checking the Task Manager.

3. How does memory work in my computer, and how can I evaluate how much memory I need?

RAM is your computer's short-term memory. It remembers everything that the computer needs to process data into information. However, it is an example of volatile storage. When the power is off, the data stored in RAM is cleared out. The amount of RAM sitting on memory modules in your computer is your computer's physical memory. The memory your OS uses is kernel memory. At a minimum, you need enough RAM to run the OS plus the software applications you're using, plus a bit more to hold the data you will input.

4. What are the computer's main storage devices, and how can I evaluate whether they match my needs?

Storage devices for a typical computer system include a hard disk drive, flash drives, and CD/DVD drives. When you turn off your computer, the data stored in these devices is saved. These devices are referred to as nonvolatile storage devices. Hard drives have the largest storage capacity of any storage device and the fastest access time and data transfer rate of all nonvolatile storage options. Floppy disks have a storage capacity of 1.44 MB, and CDs and DVDs have capacities from 700 MB to 9.4 GB. Portable flash drives allow easy transfer of 8 GB or more of data from machine to machine. To determine the storage capacity your system needs, calculate the amount of storage your software needs to reside on your computer. To add more storage, or to provide more functionality for your system, you can install additional drives, either internally or externally.

5. What components affect the output of video on my computer, and how can I evaluate whether they match my needs?

How video is displayed depends on two components: your video card and monitor. A video card translates binary data into the images you see. These cards include their own RAM (video memory) as well as ports that allow you to connect to video equipment. The amount of video memory you need depends on what you want to display on the monitor. If you only work in Microsoft Word and surf the Web, 16 MB is enough. More powerful cards allow you to play graphics-intense games and multimedia. Your monitor's size, resolution, refresh rate, and dot pitch all affect how well the monitor performs. For a clearer, brighter image, buy a monitor with a high refresh rate and a low dot pitch.

6. What components affect the quality of sound on my computer, and how can I evaluate whether they match my needs?

Your computer's sound depends on your speakers and sound card. Two types of speakers ship with most computers: amplified speakers and unamplified speakers. If you're listening to music, viewing DVDs, or playing games, you may want to have speakers with a subwoofer. Sound cards enable the computer to produce sounds. Users upgrade their sound cards to provide for 3-D sound, surround sound, and additional ports for audio equipment.

7. What are the ports available on desktop computers, and how can I determine what ports I need?

A port is an interface through which external devices connect to the computer. Common ports include serial, parallel, universal serial bus (USB), FireWire, and Ethernet, whereas specialized ports include IrDA, Bluetooth, and MIDI. To evaluate your port connectivity, check the devices you'd like to connect to your computer and look for the type of port they require. If your system doesn't have enough ports, you can add ports through expansion cards (which you install in your system unit) and expansion hubs (which connect to your system through a port).

8. How can I ensure the reliability of my system?

Many computer users decide to buy a new system because they are experiencing problems with their computer. However, before you buy a new system because you think yours may be unreliable, make sure the problem is not one you can fix. Make sure you have installed any new software or hardware properly, check that you have enough RAM, run system utilities such as Disk Defragmenter and Disk Cleanup, clean out your Startup folder, remove unnecessary files from your system, and keep your software updated with patches. If you continue to have troubles with your system, reinstall or upgrade your OS, and, of course, seek technical assistance.

Key Terms

3-D sound card

access time

arithmetic logic unit (ALU)

bit depth

Bluetooth

Blu-ray disc

cache memory

CD-ROM

central processing unit (CPU or processor)

clock speed

Compact Disc–Read/Writable (CD-RW) disc

Compact Disc–Recordable (CD-R) disc

control unit

CPU usage

data transfer rate

Digital Video Disc (DVD)

DVD-R/RW

DVD+R/RW

Ethernet port

expansion hub

FireWire port (IEEE 1394 port)

flash drive

flash memory card

floppy disk

front side bus (FSB)

gigahertz (GHz)

hard disk drive (hard drive)

head crash

IrDA port

kernel memory

latency

machine cycle

magnetic media

megahertz (MHz)

memory bound

memory module (memory card)

MIDI port

Moore's Law

motherboard

nonvolatile storage

optical media

page file

parallel port

physical memory

platter

port

random access memory (RAM)

read/write head

sector

seek time

serial port

sound card

subwoofer

system evaluation

track

universal serial bus (USB) port

video card (video adapter)

video memory

virtual memory

volatile storage

Buzz Words

Word Bank

- access time
- Bluetooth
- CD-RW drive
- CPU
- expansion card
- expansion hub

- FireWire
- Flash drive
- hard drive
- LCD
- monitor
- motherboard

- RAM
- sound card
- subwoofer
- system evaluation
- upgrading
- USB

Instructions: Fill in the blanks using the words from the Word Bank above.

Joe already has a PC but just heard about a great deal on a new one. He decides to perform a(n) (1) _____ on his computer to see whether he should keep it or buy the new one. First, he right-clicks Computer in the Start menu to check his System Properties. By doing so, he can check what (2) _____ is in his computer. He sees he has a Pentium 4 processor running at 2.8 GHz. Next, he checks his internal memory, or (3) _____. He then turns to the Task Manager to evaluate his CPU and RAM usage to see if he needs to add more RAM should he keep his PC.

He continues to evaluate his system by checking out what components he has and what he'll need. He notes the storage capacity of the (4) _____. Recently, he has been using a(n) (5) _____ to store files because his hard drive is nearing capacity. But the (6) _____, or the amount of time it takes for the disk to find the right data, is so slow that the larger hard drive of a new computer is appealing. Joe also notes that he is unable to download large files from the Internet and save them onto a CD like his friends do. His current system does not have a(n) (7) _____ with which to burn CDs, but the new system would. The new system would also include speakers with a(n) (8) _____ to improve the sound. He also sees that it would include a(n) (9) _____ that would allow him to connect more of his audio equipment to his PC.

Joe's 15-inch (10) _____ doesn't fit well on his desktop, and having a(n) (11) _____ monitor would conserve space. He also knows that if he wants to attach more devices to his PC in the future, he'll need more (12) _____ ports, because his current system has only a few of these faster ports. He notes, however, that it may be just as cost effective to install a(n) (13) _____ in his system to give it more ports or to buy a(n) (14) _____ he could attach to his system unit to add more ports. Finally, Joe considers the cost of buying the new computer versus (15) _____ his current system. He realizes it's more economical right now to keep his current system.

Becoming Computer Literate

Jen lives across the hall from you. She heard you worried last semester that your PC wasn't fast enough. Between the simulation program for math, the reports you did for English, and your programming class, your computer was running slowly and you were out of storage space. She's offered to help you upgrade your system, but needs you to tell her what you want upgraded and why.

Instructions: Using the preceding scenario, write a letter to Jen using key terms from the chapter. Be sure your sentences are grammatically correct and technically meaningful.

Self-Test

Instructions: Answer the multiple-choice and true/false questions below for more practice with key terms and concepts from this chapter.

MULTIPLE CHOICE

1. The amount of RAM recommended for most systems today is measured in?
  a. Gigabytes   c. Megahertz
  b. Gigahertz   d. Kilobytes

2. When evaluating CPU performance, which feature(s) do you need to consider?
  a. Amount of cache memory
  b. Speed of the processor
  c. Speed of the front side bus
  d. All of the above

3. RAM is classified as what kind of storage in a computer system?
  a. Volatile   c. Permanent
  b. Nonvolatile d. Flash

4. Physical memory is:
  a. the amount of RAM that is actually sitting on memory modules in your computer.
  b. the memory needed to run the key components of the operating system.
  c. the amount of space on the hard drive to temporarily store data when there isn't enough RAM.
  d. the memory stored on the hard drive.

5. From which location is it fastest to get data to the CPU for processing?
  a. RAM
  b. Cache memory
  c. Hard drive
  d. Virtual memory

6. Flash drives have replaced floppy disks as the preferred method of portable storage because:
  a. they hold much more data than floppy disks.
  b. data is not magnetic so it's less subject to errors.
  c. they have quicker access time than a floppy drive.
  d. All of the above

7. Flash memory cards are NOT a form of storage for what kind of device?
  a. PMPs
  b. Notebook computers
  c. Digital cameras
  d. Personal digital assistants

8. Blu-ray technology is required to store what kind of media?
  a. Standard definition video
  b. High-definition video
  c. Analog audio
  d. Digital audio

9. Which of the following is becoming the most common port on a computer system because most peripheral devices connect to it?
  a. Parallel port c. USB 2.0 port
  b. Serial port   d. Firewire port

10. Which of the following wireless connections requires a clear line of sight between two devices?
  a. Bluetooth   c. Midi
  b. WiFi   d. IrDA

TRUE/FALSE

____ 1. The Task Manager provides information about programs and processes running on your computer.

____ 2. Increasing the amount of RAM in your system will have an immediate impact on system performance if your system is memory bound.

____ 3. Data is stored in the same manner on hard drives, CDs, and flash memory cards.

____ 4. The actual viewable area for CRT and LCD monitors of similar size is the same.

____ 5. FireWire ports are used for Internet connectivity.

Making the Transition to... Next Semester

1. Evaluating Your System

A small worksheet follows the end of each section in this chapter to guide you as you evaluate your own system. These smaller worksheets have been combined into one complete worksheet that is on the book's Companion Web Site (**www.prenhall.com/techinaction**). Download the worksheet and fill it in based on the computer you are currently using when taking this class.

a. Research the costs of replacement parts for those components you feel should be upgraded.
b. Research the cost of a new system that would be roughly equivalent to your current computer after upgrades.
c. Determine whether it would be more cost effective to upgrade your computer or buy a new one.

2. Your Software Needs

What software do you need for the courses you're taking this semester? Will you need any different software for next semester? How many of these software applications do you run at one time? Examine the requirements for those software packages. Prepare a table that lists the software applications you are currently using as well as any you may need to use in the future. For each, list the minimum RAM and hard disk space requirements. How does your system measure up against those requirements?

3. Campus Computer Use

What kinds of computers do students use in college, and how do different people budget for their computer needs? To find an answer to these questions, interview several college students in different years of school. Ask them the following questions:

a. Did you need your own computing equipment, or did you use your college's equipment when you first started school? Would you recommend I do the same?
b. Did you need to upgrade your computer before you came to college? How did you do this?
c. Was the computer you used in your first year of college able to handle your workload in later years?
d. If you used one computer, what upgrades did you need to perform?
e. If you had to buy a new computer, how much money did you budget and how much did you spend? What did you do with your old computer?

4. Buying Computers Online

Visit an online seller of computer systems and components (such as **www.coolcomputing.com**, **www.pricewatch.com**, **http://shopper-zdnet.com**, and **www.tigerdirect.com**) and answer the following questions:

a. What is the current cost of RAM?
b. How much additional RAM could you add to your system?
c. What are the prices of the most popular CPU upgrades?
d. How much would you need to spend to upgrade to a new operating system?
e. How would each of these help you in your work?

5. Comparing Monitor Specs

You have many different options regarding monitors. Using the Web, research several different monitors. Make sure you have both CRT and LCD monitors on your list. Compare specifications for all monitors, including screen size, size of viewable area, refresh rate, dot pitch, and cost. From your list, identify the one monitor you would choose to add to your system and explain why.

Making the Transition to...
The Workplace

1. Using Your Computer for Education and Business

As you move from an educational environment to a business environment, how you use your computer will inevitably change. Write one or two paragraphs that describe what your computer system is like now. Then write one or two paragraphs that describe what your ideal computer system would be like after you've graduated and have entered the workforce. What different components, if any, would your system need? Could you upgrade your current system to incorporate these new components, or would you need to buy a new system? Make sure you defend either position you take with information covered in this chapter. Fill out the worksheet similar to Figure 2 that is available on the book's companion Web site (**www.prenhall.com/techinaction**) to help you in your decision.

2. Assessing Memory Use

Your home office computer is running a bit sluggish, and you want to determine which application is the memory hog so you can either avoid using it or use it without any other programs running to preserve RAM. You've been told you can do this in the Processes tab in the Task Manager utility. On your computer, open the Task Manager utility and determine which application currently running is using the most memory. Can you tell how much it is using? Note that because the names of the programs have been shortened (for example, Microsoft Word is referred to as winword.exe), you may not immediately recognize the program names.

3. IT Support at Work

When you are evaluating potential employers, one consideration will be how well they support you as an employee and provide the environment you need to do productive work. What questions would you ask in an interview to determine what kind of Information Technology (IT) support you can expect in your new position?

4. Web Programming Software at Home

You are a Web programmer and you often work from home. You need to investigate whether your home computer would be able to run three programs you use most frequently at work: Adobe Photoshop, Microsoft Visual Basic.NET, and Microsoft Word. Use the Web to research RAM and hard disk requirements for these programs. Will your computer be able to handle the load?

5. Build an Ideal System

Imagine that a client tells you she wants a system that has at least 512 MB of RAM, the fastest processor on the market, and enough storage space to edit hours of video and music files. Price three systems that would meet the client's needs by visiting manufacturer Web sites such as **www.dell.com**, **www.gateway.com**, and **www.alienware.com**. Make a final selection and justify why this is the best solution.

Understanding and Assessing Hardware: Evaluating Your System

Critical Thinking Questions

Instructions: Albert Einstein used "Gedanken experiments," or critical thinking questions, to develop his theory of relativity. Some ideas are best understood by experimenting with them in our own minds. The following critical thinking questions are designed to demand your full attention but require only a comfortable chair—no technology.

1. **Your Ideal System**

   If you could buy any new system on the market, not worrying about the price, what would you buy? What kind of monitor would you have? How much RAM and CPU? What kind of ports would you require? Which sound system would fit your needs? Would you know how to use your ideal system?

2. **Future Systems**

   Given current trends in technology, what kind of system can you imagine upgrading to or buying new in 10 years? Which components would change the most? Which components would need to stay the same, if any? What do you imagine the entire system would look like?

3. **Portable Storage Solutions**

   Many newer computers no longer include a floppy disk drive as a standard component. This is in response to many users requiring portable storage media to hold larger files that cannot fit on a floppy. What other solutions are possible? Are there reasons floppy disks are still a viable means of portable storage?

4. **Impacts of New Technology**

   We are constantly being bombarded with new technology. We hear of new tools and system improvements from our friends, relatives, and advertisements almost daily. This chapter talks about upgrading current systems so that we can take advantage of some of the newer technology. Some improvements we absolutely need (more RAM, perhaps), whereas others we may just really want (such as an LCD monitor). What do you think are the societal, economic, and environmental impacts of our wanting to have the latest and greatest computers? Do you think the push toward faster and more powerful machines is a good thing?

5. **New Technologies: Putting Industries at Risk?**

   The Trends in IT feature in this chapter discusses the impact CD and DVD technology has had on the music and entertainment industries. Can you think of other industries that might be at risk because of these new technologies?

6. **Recycling Computers**

   Mercury in screens and switches, cadmium in batteries and circuit boards, and the four to eight pounds of lead in CRT monitors are all toxic. Discarded machines are beginning to create an e-waste crisis. Who do you think should assume the cost of recycling computers? Should it be the consumer, the government, or the industry? What other options are there besides just throwing older computers away?

7. **System Longevity**

   If you purchase a computer system for business purposes, the IRS allows you to depreciate its cost over five years. The IRS considers this a reasonable estimate of the useful lifetime of a computer system. What do you think most home users expect in terms of how long their computer systems should last? How does the purchase of a computer system compare with other major household appliances in terms of cost, value, benefit, life span, and upgrade potential?

Team Time Meeting a Corporation's Computing Needs

Problem:

In a large organization, whether it is a company or a college, the IT department often has to install several different types of computing systems. There certainly would be advantages to having every computer be identical, but because different departments have different needs, and items are purchased at different times, it is typical for there to be significant differences between two computers in the same corporation.

Process:

Split your class into teams.

1. Select a department or computer lab on campus (or within your company, at the public library, and so on). Note: If you are physically unable to go to the various labs, describe the type of components that would be needed by that particular department. (For example, if you choose the computer art department, you know you will need good graphics software. You also know you will need certain levels of RAM, and so forth, to accommodate that graphics software.)

2. Following the worksheet in Figure 2, analyze the computing needs of that particular department.

3. Using the System Evaluation worksheet (found on the book's Companion Web Site at **www.prenhall.com/techinaction**), develop a complete systems evaluation of the computers at the lab.

4. Consider possible upgrades in hardware, software, and peripherals that would make this lab better able to meet the needs of its users.

5. Write a report that summarizes your findings. If purchasing a new system is more economical, recommend which system the lab should buy.

Conclusion:

The pace of technological change can make computer science an uncomfortable field for some. For others, it is precisely the pace of change that is exciting. Being able to evaluate a computer system and match it to the current needs of its users is an important skill.

Multimedia

In addition to the review materials presented here, you'll find other materials featured with the book's multimedia, including the Technology in Action Student Resource CD and the Companion Web Site (**www.prenhall.com/techinaction**), which will help reinforce your understanding of the chapter content. These materials include the following:

ACTIVE HELPDESK

In Active Helpdesk calls, you'll assume the role of a Helpdesk operator taking calls about the concepts you've learned in this chapter. You'll apply what you've learned and receive feedback from a supervisor to review and reinforce those concepts. The Active Helpdesk calls for this chapter are listed here and can be found on your Student Resource CD:

- Evaluating Your CPU and RAM
- Evaluating Your Storage Subsystem and Ports

SOUND BYTES

Sound Bytes are dynamic multimedia tutorials that help demystify even the most complex topics. You'll view video clips and animations that illustrate computer concepts, and then apply what you've learned by reviewing with the Sound Byte Labs, which include quizzes and activities specifically tailored to each Sound Byte. The Sound Bytes for this chapter are listed here and can be found on your Student Resource CD:

- Questions to Ask Before You Buy a Computer
- Using Windows Vista to Evaluate CPU Performance
- Memory Hierarchy Interactive
- Installing RAM
- Hard Disk Anatomy Interactive
- CD and DVD Reading and Writing Interactive
- Installing a CD-RW Drive
- Port Tour: How Do I Hook It Up?
- Letting Your Computer Clean Up After Itself

COMPANION WEB SITE

The Technology in Action Companion Web Site includes a variety of additional materials to help you review and learn more about the topics in this chapter. The resources available at **www.prenhall.com/techinaction** include:

- **Online Study Guide.** Each chapter features an online true/false and multiple-choice quiz. You can take these quizzes, automatically check the results, and e-mail the results to your instructor.
- **Web Research Projects.** Each chapter features a number of Web research projects that ask you to search the Web for information on computer-related careers, milestones in computer history, important people and companies, emerging technologies, and the applications and implications of different technologies.

7

Networking and Security:

Connecting Computers and Keeping Them Safe from Hackers and Viruses

Networking and Security:

Connecting Computers and Keeping Them Safe from Hackers and Viruses

Objectives

After reading this chapter, you should be able to answer the following questions:

1. What is a network, and what are the advantages of setting up one?

2. What is the difference between a client/server network and a peer-to-peer network?

3. What are the main components of every network?

4. What are the most common home networks?

5. What are wired Ethernet networks, and how are they created?

6. What are wireless Ethernet networks, and how are they created?

7. How are power-line networks created, and are they a viable alternative to Ethernet networks?

8. How can hackers attack a network, and what harm can they cause?

9. What is a firewall, and how does it keep my computer safe from hackers?

10. Why are wireless networks more vulnerable than wired networks, and what special precautions are required to ensure my wireless network is secure?

11. From which types of viruses do I need to protect my computer?

12. What can I do to protect my computer from viruses?

ACTIVE HELPDESK

- Understanding Networking
- Understanding Firewalls
- Avoiding Computer Viruses

The Problems of Sharing

The Kato family is facing computer-sharing problems. Koji and Yukari realized that they both needed computers, and they bought their children, Mari and Toshio, their own computers, too. Still, there is trouble in this "paradise."

Scarce Resources: Toshio was using his computer to scan photos for a school Web site project. Just then, his sister Mari burst into his room and demanded to use his scanner because she didn't have one and needed to scan images for an art project. Toshio wouldn't budge. The ensuing shouting match brought their mother, Yukari, to the room. Because both projects were due the next day, Yukari told Toshio he would have to let Mari use the scanner at some point. In exchange, Mari would have to let Toshio use her computer so he could print from the color printer attached to it. Neither was happy, but it was the best Yukari could do.

Internet Logjam: Koji frowned at his e-mail inbox. He was on vacation, but his boss had e-mailed him asking him to look over a marketing plan. Meanwhile, Yukari needed to get online to confirm the family's reservations at Disney World. Because they had only one phone line, they constantly had to take turns getting online, and with Mari and Toshio wanting to check their e-mail too, the phone line was almost always tied up.

Virus Attack: Later that night, Koji booted up his computer to make some changes to the marketing plan. Right away, he noticed that many of his icons had disappeared from his desktop. As he launched Microsoft Word, a message flashed on the screen that read, "The Hacker of Death Was Here!" Suddenly, his screen went black. When he rebooted his computer, it was unable to recognize the hard drive. The next day, Koji called the computer support technician at work and learned he had caught the "Death Squad" virus, which had erased the contents of his hard drive. Koji mused that he should have bought an antivirus program instead of the latest version of MechWarrior.

If this scenario doesn't reflect the situation in your home, it may in the future. As the price of computers continues to drop, more families will have multiple home computers. To avoid inconvenience and the expense of redundant equipment, computers need to be able to communicate with each other and to share peripherals (such as scanners and printers) and resources (such as Internet connections). Thus, this chapter explores how you can network computers. In addition, you'll learn strategies for keeping unauthorized outsiders from prying into your computer when you're sharing resources with the outside world, as well as how to keep your computer safe from viruses.

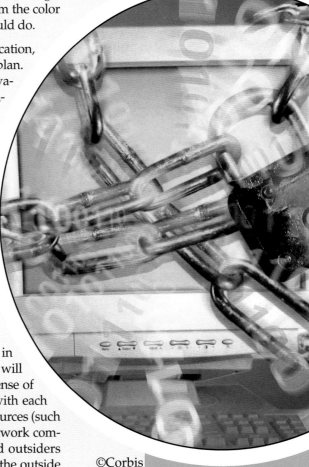
©Corbis

SOUND BYTES

- Installing a Computer Network
- Installing a Personal Firewall
- Securing Wireless Networks
- Protecting Your Computer

Networking Fundamentals

Although you may not yet have a home network, you use and interact with networks all the time. In fact, every time you use the Internet you're interacting with the world's largest network. But what exactly *is* a network? A computer **network** is simply two or more computers that are connected via software and hardware so that they can communicate with each other. Devices connected to a network are referred to as **nodes**. A node can be a computer, a peripheral (such as a printer), or a communications device (such as a modem). The main function for most networks is to facilitate information sharing, but networks provide other benefits.

What are the benefits of networks? Networks allow users to share peripherals. For example, in Figure 1a, the computers are not networked; Computer 1 is connected to the printer, but Computer 2 is not. To print files from Computer 2, users have to transfer them using a flash drive or another storage medium to Computer 1, or they have to disconnect the printer from Computer 1 and connect it to Computer 2. By networking Computer 1 and Computer 2, as shown in Figure 1b, both computers can print from the printer attached to Computer 1 without transferring files or moving the printer.

By networking computers, you can transfer files from one computer to another without using external storage media such as flash drives. And you can set up shared directories in Windows that allow the user of each computer on the network to store files that other computers on the network may need to access, as shown in Figure 2.

Can I use a network to share an Internet connection? If you install a device called a *router* on your network, you

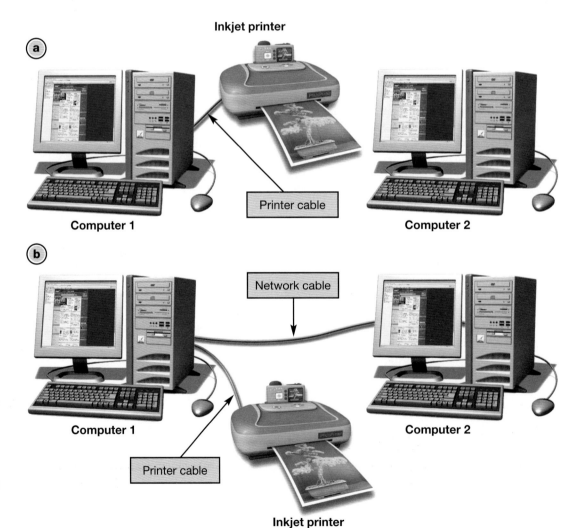

Inkjet printer

(a)

Printer cable

Computer 1   Computer 2

(b)

Network cable

Computer 1   Computer 2

Printer cable

Inkjet printer

Reprinted by permission of Cherry Blossom Bonsai

FIGURE 1

(a) Computer 1 and Computer 2 are not networked. Only Computer 1 can use the printer unless the printer is disconnected from Computer 1 and reconnected to Computer 2. (b) Computer 1 and Computer 2 are networked. Both computers can use the printer without having to move it.

Networking and Security: Connecting Computers and Keeping Them Safe from Hackers and Viruses

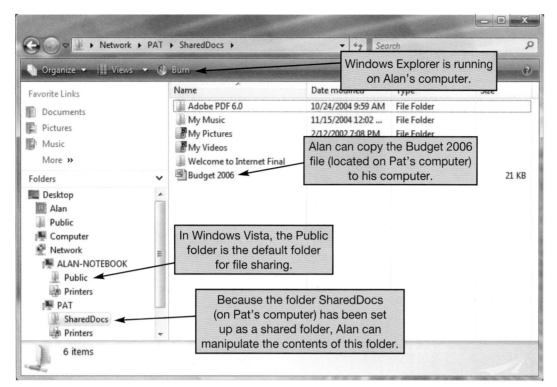

Reprinted with permission from Microsoft Corporation

FIGURE 2

This Windows network has two computers attached to it: Alan-Notebook, which is running Windows Vista, and Pat, which is running Windows XP. The Public and the SharedDocs folders have been enabled for file sharing. When Alan is working on his computer, he can easily access the files located in the shared directory on Pat's computer, such as the file called Budget 2006.

can share broadband Internet connections. Unfortunately, dial-up connections don't have sufficient bandwidth to support sharing an Internet connection. We'll discuss routers in detail later in the chapter.

Network Architectures

The term **network architecture** refers to the design of a network. Network architectures are classified according to the way in which they are controlled and the distance between their nodes.

DESCRIBING NETWORKS BASED ON NETWORK ADMINISTRATION

What do we mean by networks being "administered"? There are two main ways a network can be administered (or run): locally or centrally. A peer-to-peer network is the most common example of a locally administered network. The most common type of centrally administered network is a client/server network.

What are peer-to-peer networks? In **peer-to-peer (P2P) networks**, each node connected to the network can communicate directly with every other node on the network, instead of having a separate device exercise central control over the entire network. Thus, all nodes on this type of network are in a sense *peers*. When printing, for example, a computer on a P2P network doesn't have to go through the computer that's connected to the printer. Instead, it can communicate directly with the printer. Figure 1b shows a very small peer-to-peer network.

Because they are simple to set up, P2P networks are the most common type of home network. We discuss different types of peer-to-peer networks that are popular in homes later in this chapter.

What are client/server networks? Very small schools and offices may have P2P networks. However, most networks that have 10 or more nodes are **client/server networks**. A client/server network contains two different types of computers: clients and servers. The **client** is the computer on which users accomplish specific tasks (such as construct spreadsheets) and make specific requests (such as printing a file). The **server** is the computer that provides information or resources to the client computers on the network. The server on a client/server network also provides central administration for functions on the network (such as

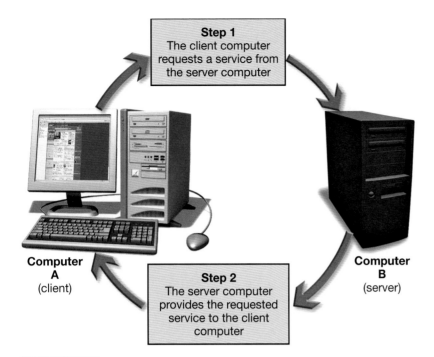

Step 1
The client computer requests a service from the server computer

Computer A
(client)

Step 2
The server computer provides the requested service to the client computer

Computer B
(server)

In a client/server network, a computer acts as a client, making requests for resources, or as a server, providing resources.

printing). Figure 3 illustrates a client/server network in action.

The Internet is an example of a client/server network. When your computer is connected to the Internet, it is functioning as a *client* computer. When connecting to the Internet through an Internet service provider (ISP), your computer connects to a *server* computer maintained by the ISP. The server "serves up" resources to your computer so that you can interact with the Internet.

Are client/server networks ever used as home networks? Although client/server networks *can* be configured for home use, P2P networks are more often used in the home because they cost less than client/server networks and are easier to configure and maintain. To set up a client/server network in your home, you have to buy an extra computer to act as the server. Although a computer could function both as a server and a client, its performance would be significantly degraded due to the complexity of the server-related functions it would have to perform. Therefore, it is impractical to use a single computer as both a client and a server. In addition, you need training to install and maintain the special software client/server networks require. Finally, the major benefits a client/server network provides (such as centralized security and administration) are not necessary in most home networks.

DESCRIBING NETWORKS BASED ON DISTANCE

How does the distance between nodes define a network? The distance between nodes on a network is another way to describe a network. **Local area networks (LANs)** are networks in which the nodes are located within a small geographic area. Examples include a network in your home or a computer lab at school. **Wide area networks (WANs)** are made up of LANs connected over long distances. Say a school has two campuses (east and west) located in different towns. Connecting the LAN at the east campus to the LAN at the west campus (by telecommunications lines) would allow the users on the two LANs to communicate. The two LANs would be described as a single WAN.

Network Components

To function, all networks include (a) a means of connecting the nodes on the network (by cables or wireless technology), (b) special devices that allow the nodes to communicate with each other and to send data, and (c) software that allows the network to run. We discuss each of these components, shown in Figure 4, next.

TRANSMISSION MEDIA

How are nodes on a network connected? All network nodes (computers and peripherals) are connected to each other and to the network by **transmission media**. A transmission medium establishes a communications channel between the nodes on a network and can take several forms:

1. Networks can use existing wiring (such as power lines) to connect nodes.
2. Networks can use additional cable to connect nodes, such as twisted pair cable, coaxial cable, or fiber-optic cable. You have probably seen twisted pair and coaxial cable. Normal telephone wire is **twisted pair cable** and is made up of copper wires that are twisted around each other and surrounded by a plastic jacket. If you have cable TV, the cable running into your TV or cable box is **coaxial cable**. Coaxial cable consists of a single copper wire surrounded by layers of plastic. **Fiber-optic cable** is made up of plastic or glass fibers that transmit data at very fast speeds.

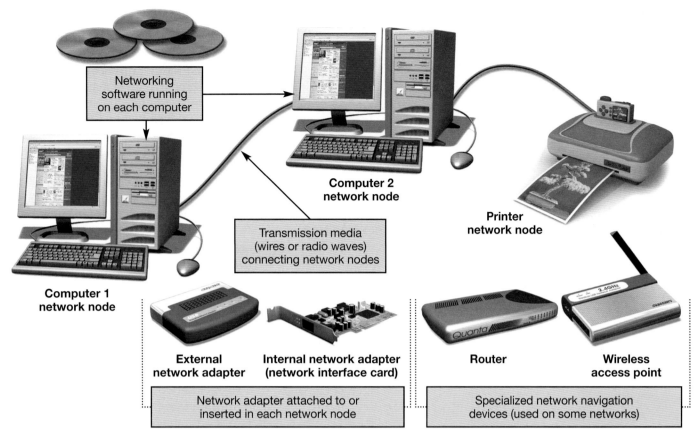

Networking software running on each computer

Computer 2 network node

Printer network node

Computer 1 network node

Transmission media (wires or radio waves) connecting network nodes

External network adapter | **Internal network adapter (network interface card)** | **Router** | **Wireless access point**

Network adapter attached to or inserted in each network node

Specialized network navigation devices (used on some networks)

Reprinted by permission of Cherry Blossom Bonsai

3. Wireless networks use radio waves instead of wires or cable to connect nodes.

Different types of transmission media transmit data at different speeds. **Data transfer rate** (also called **bandwidth**) is the *maximum* speed at which data can be transmitted between two nodes on a network. **Throughput** is the *actual* speed of data transfer that is achieved and is usually less than the data transfer rate. Data transfer rate and throughput are usually measured in megabits per second (Mbps). A megabit, when applied to data transfer rates, represents one million bits. Twisted pair cable, coaxial cable, and wireless media provide enough bandwidth for most home networks, whereas fiber-optic cable is sometimes used in client/server networks.

NETWORK ADAPTERS

How do the different nodes on the network communicate? Network

adapters are devices connected to or installed in network nodes that enable the nodes to communicate with each other and to access the network. Some network adapters take the form of external devices

that plug into an available USB port, whereas others are built right into the motherboard. Still other network adapters are installed *inside* computers and peripherals as expansion cards. These adapters are referred to as **network interface cards (NICs)**. We discuss network adapters in more detail throughout the chapter.

NETWORK NAVIGATION DEVICES

How is data sent through a network?

Data is sent over transmission media in bundles called **packets**. For computers to communicate, these packets of data must be able to flow between computers. **Network navigation devices** help to make this data flow possible. These devices, which are attached to the network, enable the transmission of data. Some simple peer-to-peer networks do not require network navigation devices because the network adapters serve that purpose. More sophisticated networks need specialized navigation devices.

The two most common specialized navigation devices are routers and switches. **Routers** transfer packets of data between two or more networks. For example, if a home network is connected to the Internet, a router is required to send data between the two networks (the home network and the Internet). **Switches** are the "traffic cops" of networks. They receive data packets and send them to the node for which they are intended *on the same network* (not between different networks). We discuss routers and switches in more detail later in the chapter.

NETWORKING SOFTWARE

What software do networks require?
Home networks need operating system (OS) software that supports peer-to-peer networking. The most common versions of Windows used in the home (Vista Home Basic or Premium, XP Home Edition, Millennium Edition, 2000 and 98) support P2P networking. You can connect computers running any of these OSs to the same network. The last several versions of the Mac OS (including all OS X versions) and the various versions of Linux also support P2P networking.

Client/server networks, on the other hand, are controlled by a central server that has specialized **network operating system (NOS)** software installed on it. This software handles requests for information, Internet access, and the use of peripherals for the rest of the network nodes. Examples of NOS software include Windows Vista Enterprise, Windows XP Professional, Windows Server 2003, and Novell NetWare.

Types of Peer-to-Peer Networks

The most common type of network you will probably encounter is a peer-to-peer network, because this is the network you would set up in your home. Therefore, we'll focus on P2P networks in this chapter. There are three main types of P2P networks:

1. Wired Ethernet networks
2. Wireless Ethernet networks
3. Power-line networks

The major differences in these networks are the transmission media by which the nodes are connected. We will now look at these networks and how each one is set up.

WIRED ETHERNET NETWORKS

What are Ethernet networks?
Ethernet networks are so named because they use the Ethernet protocol as the means (or standard) by which the nodes on the network communicate. The Ethernet protocol was developed by the Institute of Electrical and Electronics Engineers (IEEE, pronounced "I triple E"). This nonprofit group develops many standard specifications for electronic data transmission that are adopted throughout the world. Each standard the IEEE develops is numbered, with 802.3 being the standard for wired Ethernet networks.

The Ethernet protocol makes Ethernet networks extremely efficient at moving data. However, to achieve this efficiency, the algorithms for moving data through an Ethernet network are complex. Because of this complexity, Ethernet networks require additional devices (such as switches and routers).

Ethernet networks are slightly more complicated to set up than other home network options, but they're faster, more reliable, and less expensive, making them the most popular choice for home networks. Although 100-Mbps Ethernet networks are most commonly installed in homes, prices are falling quickly on 1-gigabit-per-second (1 Gbps, or 1,000 Mbps) Ethernet components. In fact, home computers now routinely ship with one-gigabit Ethernet equipment preinstalled. The potential high throughput of gigabit Ethernet is useful if you're moving large files (such as downloaded movies) around your home network.

How do I create an Ethernet network?
An Ethernet network requires that you install or attach network adapters to each computer or peripheral you want to connect to the network. Because Ethernet networks are so common, most computers sold today come with Ethernet adapters preinstalled. As noted earlier, such internal network adapters are referred to as network interface cards (NICs). Modern Ethernet NICs are usually 10/100/1000-Mbps cards (see Figure 5a). This means they can handle the old 10-Mbps and 100-Mbps data transfer rates as well as the newer 1 Gbps data transfer rate.

If your computer doesn't have a NIC, you can buy one and install it, or you can use a USB adapter, which you plug into any open

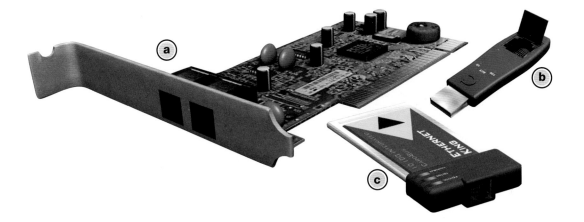

FIGURE 5

Ethernet network adapters come in a variety of versions, including (a) a 100/1000 NIC, which is installed in an expansion slot inside the system unit; (b) a USB adapter, which you plug into an open USB port; and (c) a PC Card, which you slide into a specially designed slot on a notebook.

USB port on the system unit (see Figure 5b). Although you can use USB versions in notebooks (laptops), PC Card versions of Ethernet NICs are made especially for notebooks (see Figure 5c). PC Cards are about the size of a credit card and fit into specially designed slots on a notebook. However, most new notebooks include built-in Ethernet adapters.

How are nodes connected on wired Ethernet networks? The most popular transmission media option for wired Ethernet networks is **unshielded twisted pair (UTP) cable**. UTP cable is composed of four pairs of wires that are twisted around each other to reduce electrical interference. You can buy UTP cable in varying lengths with RJ-45 connectors (Ethernet connectors) already attached. RJ-45 connectors resemble standard phone connectors (called RJ-11 connectors) but are slightly larger, as shown in Figure 6.

Do all wired Ethernet networks use the same kind of UTP cable? Figure 7 lists the three main types of UTP cable used in home-wired Ethernet networks—Cat 5, Cat 5E, and Cat 6—and their data transfer rates. In general, it's better to install Cat 5E cable than Cat 5 because they're about the same price, and installing **Cat 5E cable** enables you to take advantage of higher-bandwidth Ethernet systems when upgrading equipment. However, if you're planning on using a gigabit Ethernet network, use Cat 6 cable, which supports higher throughput. Cat 7 cable is designed for Ultra Fast Ethernet (10-gigabit Ethernet) networks that run at speeds of up to 10 Gbps. Installing a 10-gigabit Ethernet network in the home is probably unnecessary because home applications don't require this level of data transfer rate.

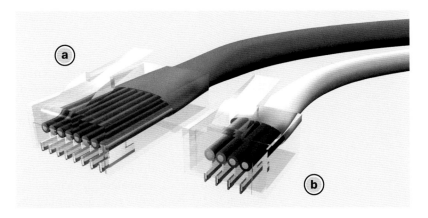

FIGURE 6

(a) An RJ-45 (Ethernet) connector, used on UTP cable, and (b) a typical RJ-11 connector, used on standard phone cord. Note that the RJ-45 is larger and has contacts for eight wires (four pairs) instead of four wires. You must use UTP cable with RJ-45 connectors on an Ethernet network because a phone cable will not work.

FIGURE 7 Data Transfer Rates for Popular Network Cable Types

UTP Cable Category	Data Transfer Rate
Category 5 (Cat 5)	Up to 100 Mbps
Category 5E (Cat 5E)	100 to 1,000 Mbps
Category 6 (Cat 6)	1,000 Mbps (1 Gbps) and higher

Is UTP cable difficult to install?

UTP cable is no more difficult to install than normal phone cable. You just need to take a few precautions: avoid putting sharp bends into the cable when running it around corners, because this can damage the copper wires inside and lead to breakage. Also, run

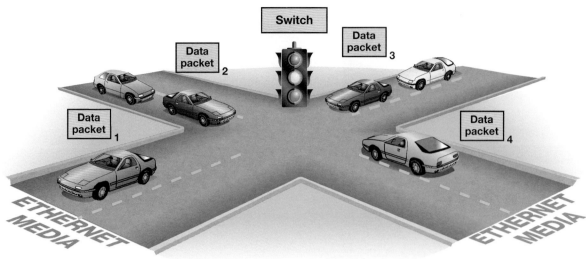

Switches (working in conjunction with NICs) act like traffic signals. They enforce the rules of the data road on an Ethernet network and help prevent data packets from crashing into each other.

the cable around the perimeter of the room (instead of under a rug, for example) to avoid damaging the wires from foot traffic.

How long can an Ethernet cable run be? Cable runs for Ethernet networks using UTP cable can't exceed 328 feet or else the signal starts to degrade. For cable runs over 328 feet, you can use **repeaters**, devices that are installed on long cable runs to amplify the signal. In effect, repeaters act as signal boosters. Repeaters can extend run lengths to 600 feet, but they do add to the cost of a network. When possible, use continuous lengths of cable. Although two cables can be sliced together with a connecting jack, this presents a source of failure for the cable, because connectors can loosen up in the connecting jack and moisture or dust can accumulate on the contacts. Usually, extending your wired network using wireless technology is a better option than using repeaters or splicing cable.

ETHERNET SWITCHES

How do Ethernet networks use switches? Data is transmitted through the wires of an Ethernet network in packets. Imagine the data packets on an Ethernet network as cars on a road. If there were no traffic signals or rules of the road (such as driving on the right-hand side), we'd see a lot more collisions between vehicles, and people wouldn't get where they were going as readily (or at all). Data packets can also suffer collisions. If data packets collide, the data in them is damaged or lost. In either case, the network doesn't function efficiently.

As shown in Figure 8, a switch in an Ethernet network acts like a traffic signal by enforcing the rules of the data road on the transmission media. The switch keeps track of the data packets and, in conjunction with network interface cards, helps the data packets find their destination without running into each other. This keeps the network running efficiently.

Switches are often referred to mistakenly as hubs. A hub is a network navigation device that merely retransmits a signal to all other nodes attached to it. Switches, on the other hand, are essentially "smart hubs," as they transmit data only to the node to which it should be sent. When Ethernet networks first came out, switches were much more expensive than hubs, so many home networks used hubs. However, today there is virtually no cost differential between hubs and switches. Therefore, most navigation devices sold for home networks are switches (even if they are mistakenly referred to as hubs).

How many computers and peripherals can be connected to a switch? Switches are differentiated by the number of ports they have for connecting network devices. Four- and eight-port switches are often used in home networks. A four-port switch can connect up to four devices to the network, whereas an eight-port switch can handle eight devices. Obviously, you should buy a switch that has enough ports for all the devices you want to connect to the network. Many people buy switches with more ports than they currently need so that they can expand their network in the future.

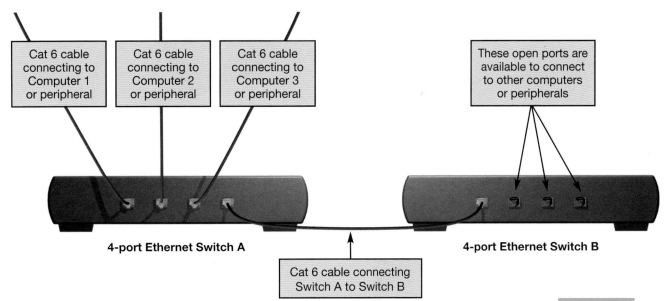

Cat 6 cable connecting to Computer 1 or peripheral

Cat 6 cable connecting to Computer 2 or peripheral

Cat 6 cable connecting to Computer 3 or peripheral

These open ports are available to connect to other computers or peripherals

4-port Ethernet Switch A

4-port Ethernet Switch B

Cat 6 cable connecting Switch A to Switch B

Adding another switch (Switch B) by chaining it to Switch A allows you to connect three more computers or peripherals to your network. Many small businesses expand their networks this way to add ports as they need them.

A wonderful feature of switches is that you can chain them together. Usually, one port on a switch is designated for plugging into a second switch. As shown in Figure 9, you can chain two four-port switches together to provide connections for a total of six devices. Most switches can be chained to provide hundreds of ports, which would far exceed the needs of most home networks, but may provide you with needed expandability in a small business network.

ETHERNET ROUTERS

How does data from an Ethernet network get shared with the Internet or another network? As mentioned earlier, routers are devices that transfer packets of data between two or more networks. If a home network is connected to the Internet, you need a router to send data between the home network and the Internet.

Because so many people are sharing Internet access in home networks, manufacturers are making devices that combine switches and routers and are specifically designed to connect to DSL or cable modems. These are often referred to as **DSL/cable routers**. If you want your Ethernet network to connect to the Internet through a DSL or cable modem, obtaining a DSL/cable router is a good idea. Because you already need a switch to connect multiple devices on an Ethernet

network, these routers (which include switching capabilities) fulfill a dual role by controlling your network traffic and allowing sharing of your Internet connection. Figure 10 shows an example of an Ethernet network configured using a DSL/cable router.

BITS AND BYTES

One Brand Equals Fewer Headaches

Networking standards set by organizations such as the IEEE make it easier for manufacturers to produce devices that work with a variety of computers and peripherals. In theory, such standards should benefit consumers as well because equipment from different manufacturers should work together when placed on the same network. The reality, however, is that devices from different manufacturers—even if they follow the same standards—don't always work together perfectly. This is because manufacturers sometimes introduce proprietary hardware and software that deviate from the standards (such as in the case of Super G wireless). This means that an Ethernet NIC from Manufacturer A might not work with a DSL/cable router from Manufacturer B. The safe course of action is to use equipment manufactured by the same company or at least save your packaging and receipt in case you need to return a component that doesn't work with the rest of your network.

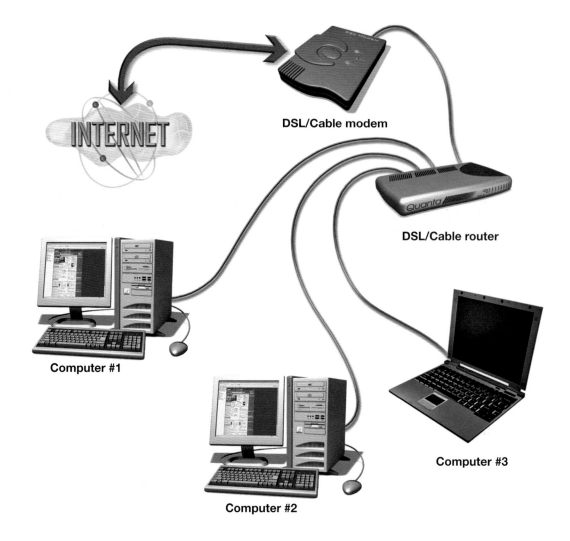

FIGURE 10

This configuration shows two desktop computers and a notebook connected to a DSL/cable router. This configuration allows all three computers to share a broadband Internet connection easily.

INTERNET

DSL/Cable modem

DSL/Cable router

Computer #1

Computer #2

Computer #3

WIRELESS ETHERNET NETWORKS

What is a wireless network? As its name implies, a **wireless network** uses radio waves instead of wires or cables as its transmission media. Just as it established the 802.3 standard for wired Ethernet networks, the IEEE has established standards for wireless Ethernet networks. Current wireless networks in the United States are based on the **802.11 standard**, established in 1997. The 802.11 standard is also known as **Wi-Fi** (short for Wireless Fidelity).

Three standards are currently defined under 802.11: 802.11a, 802.11b, and 802.11g. A fourth standard, 802.11n, is under development and is expected to be ratified in late 2008. The main difference between these standards is their maximum data transfer rate and the types of security that they support. For home networking, 802.11b and 802.11g are the standards most commonly used, although when 802.11n is ratified, its higher data transfer rate will be very attractive to home users.

The newer 802.11g standard, which supports a higher data transfer rate of 54 Mbps, is now the preferred standard for home use because it is much faster than 802.11b. Fortunately, 802.11g devices can be used together (that is, they have backward compatibility) with older 802.11b devices.

Several manufacturers also have introduced products in a new Super G (also called Extreme G or Enhanced G) category, which can be confusing to buyers. These devices are still based on the 802.11g standard but use proprietary hardware and software tweaks to increase the maximum data transfer rate to 108 Mbps. However, because Super G is not standards-based (that is, it is not based on its own IEEE standard), Super G devices from one manufacturer might not work with those of another manufacturer. Also, devices have been released in advance of the 802.11n standard ratification and are labeled as *pre-n* or *draft-n*. These devices may not necessarily work with

FIGURE 11

Wireless network adapters added to desktop computers have antennas, which they use to communicate with the other devices in the network. If your computer came with an internal wireless network card (as most notebooks now do), it probably will not have an antenna sticking out of it. Wireless network adapters are available as (a) NICs, which are inserted into an open expansion slot on the computer, or as (b) USB devices, which plug into an open USB port.

devices based on the final approved 802.11n standard. Therefore, it is safest to purchase equipment based on an approved standard such as 802.11g. To check the status of standard approvals, go to **www.ieee.org.**

What do I need to set up a wireless network? Just like other networks, each node on a wireless network requires a **wireless network adapter**. If not built into the motherboard of the computer, these adapters are available as NICs that are inserted into expansion slots on the computer (see Figure 11a) or as USB devices that plug into an open USB port (see Figure 11b). Most notebooks sold today come with an 802.11g network adapter built-in.

Wireless network adapters differ from other network adapters in that they contain transceivers. A **transceiver** is a device that translates the electronic data that needs to be sent along the network into radio waves and then broadcasts these radio waves to other network nodes. Transceivers serve a dual function because they also receive the signals from other network nodes. As shown in Figure 11, many add-on wireless network adapters have antennas poking out of them, which are necessary for the transmission and reception of these radio waves.

Do all nodes on the wireless network have to be computers? A node on a wireless network can also be a peripheral device such as a printer, storage device, or scanner. The peripheral will need to be connected to a wireless network adapter so that other nodes on the network can communicate with it.

How do I share an Internet connection on a wireless network? Just as with wired Ethernet networks, wireless Ethernet networks require installation of a router to share an Internet connection. A **wireless router** (sometimes called a **gateway**) is a device that combines the capabilities of a wired router with the ability to receive wireless signals. Note that it is important that you do not mistakenly buy a wireless access point (which we discuss later) instead of a wireless router because a wireless access point does not perform the same function.

What types of problems can I run into when installing wireless networks? The maximum range of wireless devices is about 250 feet. However, as the distance between nodes increases, throughput decreases markedly. When the 802.11n standard is ratified, equipment that adheres to this standard should provide a greater bandwidth over longer distances.

Also, 802.11b and 802.11g devices work on a bandwidth of 2.4 GHz. This is the same bandwidth that many cordless phones use, so your phone and wireless network may interfere with each other. The best solution is to buy a cordless phone that uses a bandwidth of 5.8 GHz or purchase 802.11n equipment as that is expected to use 5.8 GHz band.

Obstacles between wireless nodes also decrease throughput. Walls and large metal objects are the most common sources of interference with wireless signals. For example, placing a computer with a wireless network adapter next to a refrigerator may prevent

the signals from reaching the rest of the network. And a node that has four walls between it and the Internet connection will most likely have lower than the maximum throughput. The 802.11g devices have much better range than 802.11b devices and are less susceptible (but not immune) to interference. The 802.11n devices are expected to be even less susceptible to interference than 802.11g devices.

What if a node on the network can't communicate with other nodes or with the router? Repositioning the node or the wireless network adapter within the same room (sometimes even just a few inches from the original position) can often affect communication between the nodes. If this doesn't work, try moving the computers closer together or to other rooms in your house.

If these solutions don't work, you may need to add a wireless access point to your network. A **wireless access point (WAP)** is a device that attaches to a network and provides wireless nodes (such as a notebook with a wireless NIC installed) with a means of wirelessly connecting to the network. When you have connection problems (say the notebook on your porch can't connect to the wireless router), adding a WAP to the network will often solve the problem. Essentially, you're extending the range of the wireless network by providing a second point to which nodes can connect to the network. The WAP must be connected to the network either directly to the switch on the router or to another node that is within range of the router.

For example, as you can see in Figure 12, Notebook C on the back porch and the wireless router (connected to Computer A in the bedroom) can't make contact. However, Notebook C can connect to Computer B in the den. By connecting a WAP to Computer B, all traffic from Notebook C is relayed to the wireless router through the WAP connected to Computer B.

Can I have wired and wireless nodes on one network? Many users want to create a network in which some computers (such as desktops) connect to the network with wires, whereas other computers (such as notebooks) connect to the network wirelessly. Most wireless DSL/cable routers allow you to connect wireless and wired nodes to the same network. This type of router contains both a WAP and ports that allow you to connect wired nodes to the router. Figure 13 shows an example of a network with a wireless DSL/cable router attached. As you can see, the notebook main-

BITS AND BYTES

Surfing in Public? Beware of Social Engineering Tactics

You're at the coffee shop working on a project on your notebook, and you notice that the person sitting next to you is staring at your screen. It is just idle curiosity on their part, or do they have a more nefarious motive? As more and more users go wireless, the potential for cybercrimes increases. **Social engineering** refers to a group of activities that essentially trick users into divulging sensitive information through ordinary communication means such as conversations and e-mail.

Shoulder surfing, which involves looking over someone's shoulder while they type in access codes on notebooks—or enter calling card numbers at pay phones—can be a problem in any public place. Sometimes, less-than-honest people are more overt in obtaining your personal information. **Pretexting** is the act of creating an invented scenario (the pretext) to convince someone to divulge information. Although usually done over the telephone, this can be done in person.

Travelers at airports and people at coffee shops all around the country are often trying to connect computers to public wireless networks, and when they do, other people may be around to take advantage of them. A friendly person pretending to be an airport employee, for example, may ask you to divulge password or other sensitive information on the pretext of helping you make a wireless connection.

And now that USB drives are so inexpensive, many would-be thieves leave them around in public places loaded with software designed to capture sensitive information when a curious person picks it up and inserts it into their USB port.

So be wary of your surroundings when using electronic devices in public so you don't fall victim to these scams. Don't accept advice from strangers and never divulge any passwords or access codes to anyone even if they appear to be helpful.

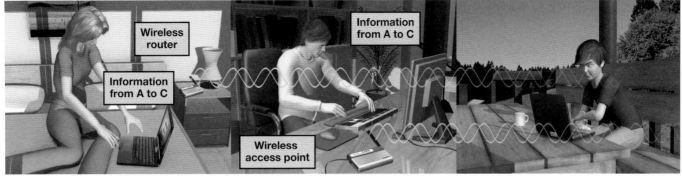

Bedroom

Wireless router

Information from A to C

Den

Information from A to C

Wireless access point

Back Porch

Computer A with wireless network adapter

Computer B with wireless access point

Notebook C with wireless network adapter

tains a wireless connection to the router, whereas the other two computers are connected by wires. Using this type of router is a cost-effective way to have some wireless connections while preserving the high-speed attributes of wired Ethernet where needed.

POWER-LINE NETWORKS

What are power-line networks? Power-line networks use the existing electrical wiring in your home to connect the nodes in the network. Thus, in a power-line network,

any electrical outlet provides a network connection. The HomePlug Power Line Alliance (**www.homeplug.org**) sets standards for home power-line networking. The original power-line networks had a maximum data transfer rate of 14 Mbps. However, the new standards recently adopted provide for power-line networks with data transfer rates approaching 200 Mbps, which can make them a viable alternative to wireless or wired Ethernet.

How do I create a power-line network? To create a power-line network, you connect a *power-line network adapter* (similar to a network adapter in an Ethernet network) to

---

FIGURE 12

With a wireless access point installed on Computer B, data can travel from Notebook C (on the back porch) to the wireless router (in the bedroom).

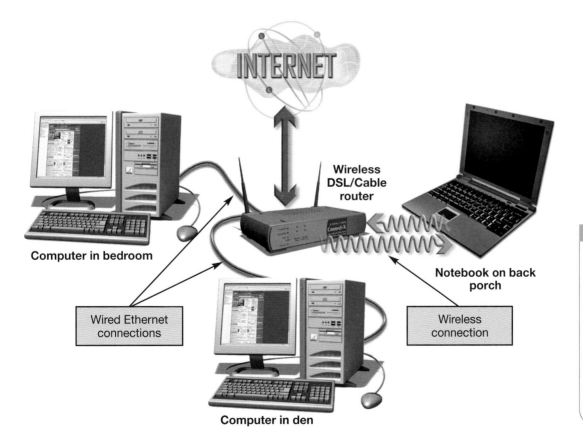

INTERNET

Wireless DSL/Cable router

Computer in bedroom

Wired Ethernet connections

Notebook on back porch

Wireless connection

Computer in den

FIGURE 13

Using a wireless DSL/cable router, the computers in the den and bedroom still maintain a high-speed wired Ethernet connection. However, the notebook can connect to the network wirelessly and be used in many areas of the home.

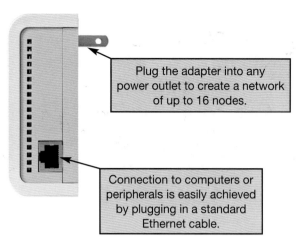

Plug the adapter into any power outlet to create a network of up to 16 nodes.

Connection to computers or peripherals is easily achieved by plugging in a standard Ethernet cable.

a-b) Netgear, Inc.

FIGURE 14

Power-line adapters, such as the Netgear HDX101, plug into any electrical outlet and are then connected to your computer (or peripheral) via an Ethernet cable. Although maximum throughput of 200 Mbps is usually unattainable, the throughput is often superior to 802.11g wireless networks.

each computer or peripheral that you're going to attach to the network (see Figure 14). You can buy power-line network adapters in either USB or Ethernet versions. After you attach a network adapter to each node on the network, you plug the adapters into an electrical outlet. Most power-line network adapters will be recognized automatically by the Windows operating system.

Why would I use a power-line network instead of an Ethernet network? Because of the low bandwidth of the original power-line networks and the lower costs of Ethernet networks, power-line networks declined in popularity. However, with the introduction of power-line equipment that supports much higher data throughput, power-line networks are becoming popular again. So if you're in a situation in which running new wires is impractical and you're experiencing too much interference to run a wireless network, you may very well want to consider installing a power-line network.

Choosing a Peer-to-Peer Network

If you're setting up a home network, the type of network you should choose depends on your particular needs. In general, consider the following factors in determining your network type:

- Whether you want wireless communications

- How fast you want your network connection to be

- Whether existing wiring is available

- How much money you can spend on your network

What if I want to use existing wiring for my home network? As noted earlier, you can use power lines (electrical wiring) as media for a home network. Obviously, you need an electrical outlet available in each room where you want to connect a node to the network. Because you have to plug most nodes (computers, printers, and so on) into an electrical outlet to operate them anyway, connecting a power-line network is usually convenient. However, these networks might be more expensive than wired or wireless Ethernet networks.

What are the pros and cons of wireless networks? Wireless networks free you from having to run wires in your home. In addition, you can use any flat surface as a workstation. However, wireless networks may not work effectively in every home. Therefore, you need to install and test the wireless network to figure out whether it will work. To avoid unnecessary expenses, make sure you can return equipment for a refund if it doesn't work properly in your home.

Which network provides the highest data transfer rate? Most routine home computing tasks (such as Web browsing and e-mailing), require minimal throughput (under 10 Mbps is sufficient). However, if high-speed data transmission is important to you (for example, if you play computer games or exchange large files), you may want a network with high throughput. With data transfer rates up to 1,000 Mbps, wired Ethernet networks are the fastest home networks. You may want to consider a gigabit network if you engage in a lot of multiplayer gaming or transfer of video. Without high throughput, streaming video can appear choppy, games can respond slowly, and files can take a long time to transfer.

Do I need to consider the type of broadband connection I have? Whether you connect to the Internet by DSL, cable, or satellite makes no difference in terms of the type of network you select. The differences occur with your particular network's hardware and software requirements.

What cost factors do I need to consider in choosing a network? You may need to consider your budget when deciding what type of network to install. Figure 15 lists the approximate costs of installing the various types of peer-to-peer networks and their various advantages and disadvantages.

FIGURE 15 Comparing the Major Types of Home Networks

| | Wired | | | Wireless | |
	100 Mbps Ethernet	Gigabit Ethernet	Powerline	802.11g	802.11n
Maximum data transfer rate (bandwidth)	100 Mbps	1,000 Mbps or 1 Gbps	200 Mbps	54 Mbps	540 Mbps
Actual Expected Throughput	50 to 60 Mbps	500 to 600 Mbps	100 Mbps	15 to 25 Mbps	150 to 200 Mbps
Operational Frequency	N/A	N/A	N/A	2.4 GHz	5 Ghz
Cost of basic access point, router or switch	$40 to $60 (switch)	$100 to $200 (switch)	$100 to $200 (adapter or router)	$40 to $70	$100 to $150
Pros	Mature, proven technology. Low cost.	Fastest practical home technology available.	No additional wiring required	Backward compatible with 802.11b devices and significantly faster.	Significantly faster than 802.11g.
Cons	Cat 5E wiring required. Can be expensive to install hidden wiring.	Cat 5E or 6 wiring required. Can be expensive to install hidden wiring.	May not have outlets in the correct locations	Interference from walls and other structures can cause signal to degrade (especially over greater distances).	Products based on final standard may not be backward compatible.

Source: Table adapted from "Pump Up Your Home Network" by Erik Rhey, *PC Magazine*, October 3, 2006.

Configuring Software for Your Home Network

Once you install the hardware for your network, you need to configure your operating system software for networking on your computers. In this section, you'll learn how to do just that using special Windows tools. Although configuration is different with Mac OS X, the setup is quick and easy. Linux, though not insurmountable, is the most complex operating system to configure for a home network.

Is configuring software difficult?
Windows Vista makes configuring software relatively simple by almost automating the entire process of setting up a network using various wizards. A wizard is a utility program included with Microsoft software that you can use to help you accomplish a spe-

cific task. You can launch the Vista wizards from the Network and Sharing Center, which can be accessed via the Control Panel. Prior to running any wizards, you should do the following:

1. Install network adapters on each node.
2. For a wired network, plug all the cables into the router, network adapters, and so on.
3. Make sure your cable/DSL modem is connected to your router and that it is connected to the Internet.
4. Turn on your equipment in the following order (allowing the modem and the router each about one minute to power up and configure):
   a. Your cable/DSL modem
   b. Your router
   c. All computers and peripherals (printers, scanners, and so on)

BITS AND BYTES

Wireless Hotspots—Convenient, But Exercise Caution

Public places (such as Starbucks) at which you can wirelessly connect to the Internet are known as *hotspots*. Sometimes the service is free; other times there is a small charge. How can you tell? Just fire up your wireless-equipped notebook or PDA, start your browser, and try to access a Web site. If the service is not free, the store's "wireless gateway sentinel" software provides you with rates and an opportunity to pay for access. Either way, you are surfing in minutes while enjoying your latte.

Some cities are installing Wi-Fi equipment to turn large areas, such as entire cities, into hotspots. One of the largest hotspots in the United States covers 700 square miles surrounding the rural town of Hermiston, Oregon. Philadelphia and San Francisco are among the major cities that have undertaken citywide Wi-Fi initiatives.

But since most hotspots are designed to be easily found and recognized by computers, they often offer little or no security. User data can be visible to anyone using the networks and is often transmitted as clear text. Hackers will often use **packet sniffers** (software designed to intercept and read the contents of data packets) on unsecured wireless networks in an attempt to gather sensitive data such as access codes and credit card numbers. Therefore, when you are surfing on a public hotspot, you should not engage in sensitive transactions that involve revealing credit card numbers or other personal information.

Going out of town and need to know where you can find a hotspot? Visit a site that offers hotspot directories, such as **www.wifinder.com**, **www.wififreespot.com**, or **www.jiwire.com**. But make sure to use common sense and surf carefully!

Completing these steps enables the wizards to make decisions about how best to configure your network. After you have completed these steps, open the Network and Sharing Center from the Control Panel (see Figure 16a). From there, select the option Set Up a Connection or Network (see Figure 16b) to access the Vista networking wizards. *Note:* If you already have a wired network set up and are connected to the Internet, plugging your Vista computer into the router is all you need to do. Vista will automatically detect an existing wired network.

What if I don't have Windows Vista on all my computers? Windows 2000, Windows XP, and Windows Vista are the most common OSs found in the home support P2P networking. Therefore, you can network these computers with other computers using Windows Vista. If you have one com-

puter with Windows Vista but your other computers run on other versions of Windows, you should set up your Windows Vista computer first. Windows Vista can automatically detect computers running other versions of Windows on your network; however, you may have to make adjustments to the non-Vista computers on your network to enable them to see the Windows Vista computers on your network (such as installing Windows XP Service Pack 2). Check the Microsoft Web site for instructions.

What if I don't have Windows Vista on *any* of my computers? Windows XP features wizards for setting up wired and wireless networks just like Windows Vista does. If you're networking all Windows 2000 machines, there is no wizard, so you have to set up your computers manually. Various resources on the Internet can assist you in setting up Windows 2000 networks. Not surprisingly, one of the best resources is the Microsoft Web site (**www.microsoft.com**).

Why does my computer have a name? When you set up your Windows Vista computer, you gave it a name. Each computer on a network needs a unique name (different from the names of all other computers on the network) so that the network can identify it. This unique name ensures that the network knows which computer is requesting services and data so that the data can be delivered to the correct computer. Also, computers on a network can be located in various workgroups. For simplicity on a home network, you should assign all your computers to the same workgroup. If you don't recall your computer's name or the workgroup to which it is assigned, open the Control Panel and click the System icon (see Figure 17). You will be able to change the name of the computer or the workgroup from here.

Is that it? Assuming you installed and configured everything properly, your home network should be up and running, allowing you to share files, Internet connections, and peripherals. Most routers will work fine right out of the box. However, with some routers you may have to alter the configuration to connect to the Internet.

How do I set up my router so that I can use it to connect to the Internet? First, contact your ISP to help you with any special settings that may be needed to configure your router to work

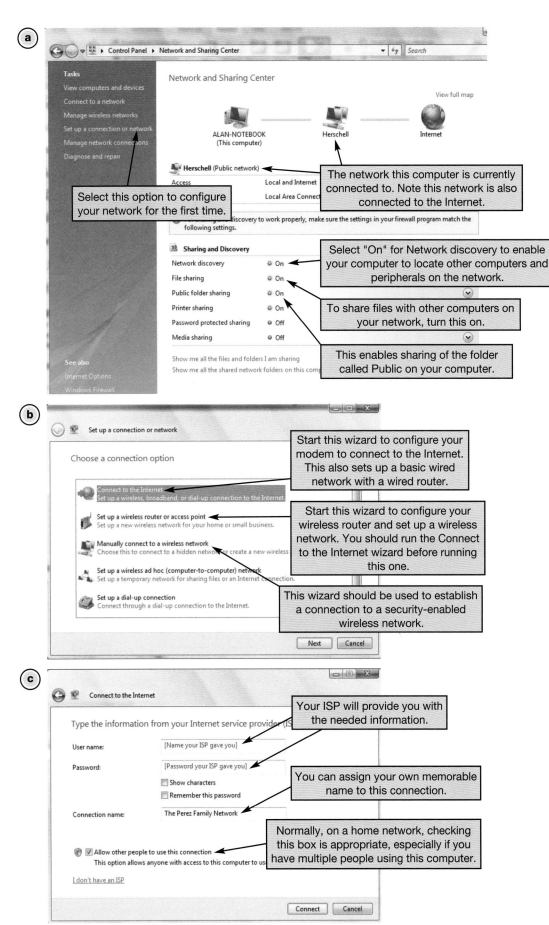

FIGURE 16

(a) The Network and Sharing Center in Windows Vista helps you configure your home network. (b) Selecting "Set Up a Connection or Network" provides you access to a number of wizards that will assist you in configuring your network. (c) Fill in the appropriate information provided by your ISP, give the connection a memorable name, and check the box to allow all users of the computer to access the connection. The wizard will then set up your connection and connect your computer to the Internet.

>The Windows Network and Sharing Center is found in the Control Panel.

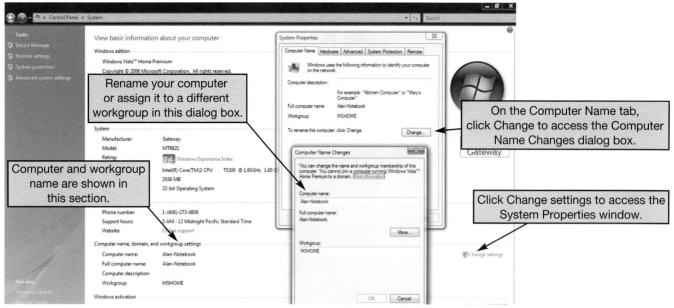

Reprinted with permission from Microsoft Corporation

FIGURE 17

Accessing the System screen from the Control Panel allows you to check your computer and work-group name, and change it if necessary.

>The Windows System screen can be accessed by clicking the System icon in the Control Panel.

with your ISP. Next, you can access your router from Internet Explorer (or another Web browser) by entering the router's IP address or default URL. You can usually find this information in the documentation that came with the router. You'll also need a user-name and password to log onto the router, both of which you'll also find in the documentation that came with the router.

Many routers feature their own wizard (which is different from the Windows Networking wizards) that takes you through unique configuration screens. A sample screen from a Netgear router is shown in Figure 18. If you're unsure of any information that needs to be entered to con-figure the router, call your ISP and ask for guidance.

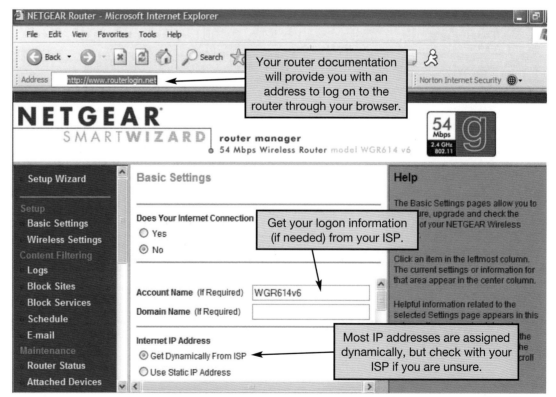

FIGURE 18

Although setups differ from router to router, basic information such as the logon informa-tion and the type of IP addressing is required to configure the router to work with your net-work and your ISP.

NetGear

Ethics: Don't Let Data Walk Out the Front Door

The weakest link in any computer security system is the users. Whether using your home network or the computer system at your workplace, you have the potential to do the most damage from practicing unsafe computing practices, such as surfing questionable sites, downloading infected files from unscrupulous file sharing sites, or accepting CD-ROMs (maybe with free music or games) from strangers and then running them on the company network, thereby causing infection.

The latest threat to add to the list is from flash drives. Now that these devices are popping up everywhere and becoming so inexpensive, they are often used (either intentionally or unintentionally) to infect computer networks. Think you won't fall victim to this security threat? Think again!

Secure Network Technologies, a security consulting firm, decided to test a client's security procedures by leaving 20 flash drives at random locations around the client's office. By the end of the day, employees had picked up 15 of the flash drives and plugged them into computers on the company network. The flash drives contained a simple program to display images as well as a Trojan horse program. While employees were viewing the images, the consultants were able to access the company network (if they wanted to do so) and steal or compromise data. It isn't hard to imagine hackers leaving flash drives around your company to act as their way into your company's network.

The other problem that flash drives pose is theft of data or intellectual property. With the devices being so portable and now coming in such large capacities, it is easy for a disgruntled employee to literally walk out the front door with stacks of valuable documents tucked right in his or her pants pocket. Industrial espionage has never been easier... no spy cameras are needed!

So what should companies do to prevent their data from being compromised or stolen via flash drives? The first step is educating employees to the dangers posed by portable media devices, and other untrusted media, and creating policies regulating the use of media in the workplace. Second, all computers in the company need to have security measures, such as personal firewalls or antivirus software, installed. The firewalls would be able to prevent malicious programs from running, if they were introduced to the computer. Last, administrators should lock down and monitor the use of USB devices. While Microsoft networking software allows network administrators to shut off access on computers to their USB ports, this prevents employees from using flash drives and other USB devices for legitimate purposes. Other software products, such as DeviceLock and Safend, can be deployed on a network to provide options such as:

- Detailed security policies
- Monitoring of USB device connections
- Tracking of users who connected devices to the network (including devices other than flash drives)

And don't forget to inform the employees that the use of these devices is being monitored. That alone is enough to scare many employees from connecting untrusted devices to the network.

In the next section, we explore how you can protect your computers and your network from intruders and hackers.

Keeping Your Home Computer Safe

The media is full of stories about computer *viruses* damaging computers, criminals stealing people's identities online, and attacks on corporate Web sites that have brought major corporations to a standstill. These are examples of **cybercrime**, which is formally defined as any criminal action perpetrated primarily through the use of a computer. The existence of cybercrime means that computer users must take precautions to protect themselves.

Who perpetrates computer crimes? **Cybercriminals** are individuals who use computers, networks, and the Internet to perpetrate crime. Anyone with a computer and the wherewithal to arm themselves with the appropriate knowledge can be a cybercriminal. In the next sections, we discuss cybercriminals and the damage they can wreak on your computer. We also discuss methods for protecting your computer from attacks.

Computer Threats: Hackers

Although there is a great deal of dissension (especially among hackers themselves) as to what a hacker actually is, a **hacker** is defined as anyone who breaks into a computer system (whether an individual computer or a network) unlawfully.

Are there different kinds of hackers? Some hackers are offended by being labeled criminals and therefore attempt to divide hackers into classes. Many hackers who break into systems just for the challenge of it (and who don't wish to steal or wreak havoc on the systems) refer to themselves as **white-hat hackers.** They tout themselves as experts who are performing a needed service for society by helping companies realize the vulnerabilities that exist in their systems.

These white-hat hackers look down on those hackers who use their knowledge to destroy information or for illegal gain. White-hat hackers refer to these other hackers as **black-hat hackers.** (The terms *white hat* and *black hat* are references to old Western movies in which the heroes wore white hats and the outlaws wore black hats.) Regardless of the hackers' opinions, the laws in the United States (and in many foreign countries) consider any unauthorized access to computer systems a crime.

What about the teenage hackers who get caught every so often? These amateur hackers are often referred to as **script kiddies.** Script kiddies don't create programs used to hack into computer systems; instead, they use tools created by skilled hackers that enable unskilled novices to wreak the same havoc as professional hackers. Unfortunately, it is easy to find these tools on the Web.

Fortunately, because the users of these programs are amateurs, they're usually not proficient at covering their electronic tracks. Therefore, it's relatively easy for law enforcement officials to track them down and prosecute them. Still, script kiddies can cause a lot of disruption and damage to computers, networks, and Web sites before they're caught.

Why would a hacker be interested in breaking into my home computer? Some hackers just like to snoop. They enjoy the challenge of breaking into systems and seeing what information they can find. Other hackers are hobbyists seek-

BITS AND BYTES

Be Careful When Joining Social Networking and Video Sites

Making contacts and meeting friends online has never been easier. Social networking services such as MySpace (**www.myspace.com**) and Facebook (**www.facebook.com**) are signing up users at a rapid pace. And YouTube (**www.youtube.com**) allows you to post videos of yourself and your friends. These services have you list personal information about yourself (interests, hobbies, photos, what school you attend, and so on) and encourage you to list connections to your friends. When your friends log on and view your profile, they can see themselves and long chains of other acquaintances. The idea is that your friends can see who else you know and get you to make appropriate introductions (or do it themselves).

Although the sites offer fairly tight protection of personal information (such as not revealing last names), you should think carefully about personal information that is visible on the site and be wary of disclosing additional information to people you meet online. Often children and young adults, who account for a large per-

centage of the users on these sites, are too trusting about revealing personal information. Cybercriminals are combing these sites with the sole purpose of using the information to perpetrate identity theft. Therefore, always avoid giving out personal information such as your full name, address, social security number, and financial information to people you have never met. Also, be careful when uploading videos of you and your friends. Identity thieves often like to steal younger people's identities because it often takes longer for the theft to be detected.

Also, be wary of accepting computer files from people you've met online because these files could contain viruses, adware, or spyware. Just because you meet someone who is a friend of a friend of your second cousin doesn't mean that person isn't a hacker or a scam artist. So, enjoy meeting new people, but exercise the appropriate amount of caution that you would elsewhere on the Internet.

BRINGING CIVILIZATION TO ITS KNEES...

ing information about a particular topic wherever they can find it. Because many people keep proprietary business information on their home computers, hackers bent on industrial espionage may break into home computers. For other hackers, hacking is a way to pass time.

WHAT HACKERS STEAL

Could a hacker steal my credit card number? If you perform financial transactions online, such as banking or buying goods and services, you probably do so using a credit card. Credit card and bank account information can thus reside on your hard drive and may be detectable by a hacker. Also, many sites that you access require you to provide a logon id and password to gain access. Even if this data is not stored on your computer, a hacker may be able to capture it when you're online by using a *packet sniffer*.

What's a packet sniffer? As you learned earlier, data travels through the Internet in small pieces called *packets*. The packets are identified with a string of numbers, in part to help identify the computer to which they are being sent. Once the packets reach their destination, they are reassembled into cohesive messages. A packet sniffer is a

program that looks at (or sniffs) each packet as it travels on the Internet—not just those that are addressed to a particular computer, but *all* packets. Some packet sniffers are configured to capture all the packets into memory, whereas others capture only certain packets that contain specific content (such as credit card numbers).

What do hackers do with the information they "sniff"? Once a hacker has your credit card information, he or she can either use it to purchase items illegally or sell the number to someone who will. Also, if a hacker steals the logon id and password to an account where you have your credit card information stored (such as eBay or Amazon), he or she can use your accounts to purchase items and have them shipped to him or herself instead of you. If hackers can gather enough information in conjunction with your credit card information, they may be able to commit **identity theft**. Identity theft is characterized by someone using personal information about you (such as your name, address, and social security number) to assume your identity for the purpose of defrauding others.

Although this sounds scary, you can protect yourself from packet sniffers by simply installing a firewall, which we discuss later in this chapter.

BITS AND BYTES

Prevention of Idenity Theft ... Don't Overlook Photocopiers!

We are constantly bombarded with identity theft warnings regarding suspicious e-mail, phishing sites, and telephone scams. But many people are unaware that photocopiers present potential danger for identity theft. This is because most photocopiers made within the last five years contain hard drives just like your computer. Documents are scanned, stored on the hard drive, and then printed by the copier. So unless the copier has been specially configured to have the hard drive overwritten to destroy data or to use encryption, copies of your tax return may be lurking on the public copier at your local library or copy shop that you used before mailing your returns to the IRS. A clever hacker could retrieve a wealth of potential information off of just one public copy machine.

So what should you do to protect yourself? Ask the local copy shop or the IT department at your office about the security measures they have set up on their copiers before you use them to copy sensitive documents. If you are buying a copier for your business, investigate security options that are available to protect your employees. And for small copying jobs (like your tax return), consider buying an all-in-one device (printer, copier, scanner, fax machine) for your home office, since you can easily keep that machine protected from wily hackers.

TROJAN HORSES

Is there anything else hackers can do if they break into my computer?
Hackers often use individuals' computers as a staging area for mischief. To perpetrate widespread computer attacks, for example, hackers need to control many computers at the same time. To this end, hackers often use Trojan horses to install other programs on computers. A **Trojan horse** is a program that appears to be something useful or desirable (like a game or a screen saver), but at the same time does something malicious in the background without your knowledge. The term *Trojan horse* derives from Greek mythology and refers to the wooden horse that the Greeks used to sneak into the city of Troy and conquer it. Therefore, computer programs that contain a hidden (and usually dreadful) "surprise" are referred to as Trojan horses.

What damage can Trojan horses do? Often, the malicious activity perpetrated by a Trojan horse program is the installation of **backdoor programs**, which

allow hackers to take almost complete control of your computer without your knowledge. Using a backdoor program, hackers can access and delete all files on your computer, send e-mail, run programs, and do just about anything else you can do with your computer. Computers that hackers control in this manner are referred to as **zombies**.

DENIAL OF SERVICE ATTACKS

What else can hackers do? Hackers can also launch an attack from your computer called a **denial of service (DoS) attack**. In a denial of service attack, legitimate users are denied access to a computer system because a hacker is repeatedly making requests of that computer system through a computer he or she has taken over as a zombie. Computers can handle only a certain number of requests for information at one time. When they are flooded with requests in a denial of service attack, they shut down and refuse to answer any requests for information, even if the requests are from legitimate users. Thus, the computer is so tied up responding to the bogus requests for information that authorized users can't gain access.

Launching a DoS attack on a computer system from one computer is easy to trace. Therefore, most savvy hackers use a **distributed denial of service (DDoS) attack**. DDoS attacks are automated attacks that are launched from more than one zombie at the same time. Figure 20 illustrates how a DDoS attack works. A hacker creates many zombies (sometimes hundreds or thousands) and coordinates them so that they begin sending bogus requests to the same computer at the same time. Administrators of the victim computer often have a great deal of difficulty stopping the attack, because it comes from hundreds of computers.

DDoS attacks are a serious problem. In February 2006, many high-profile weblogs were subjected to DDoS attacks that succeeded in locking out users who just wanted to read their favorite blogs. Problogger (**www.problogger.net**), a site that helps other bloggers learn to make money from their blogs, was one of the first victims. Among other victims was Michelle Malkin, who spearheaded a movement among bloggers related to controversial cartoons of the Prophet Mohammed, which caused a great

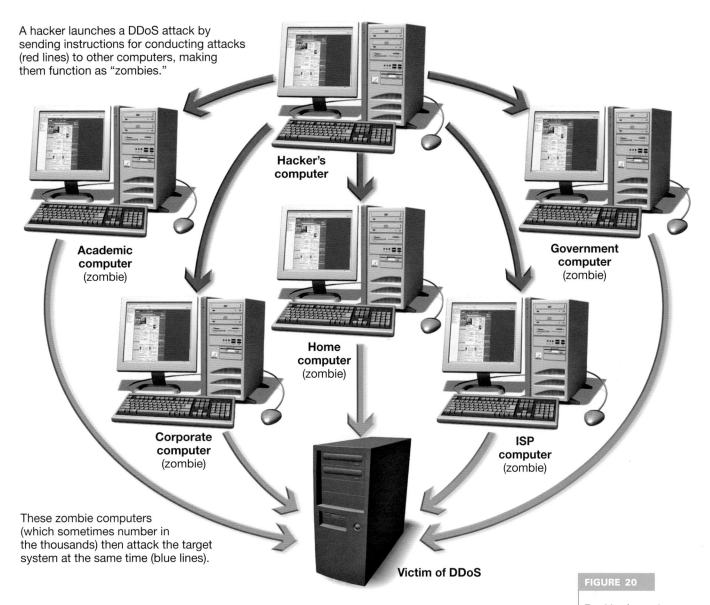

A hacker launches a DDoS attack by sending instructions for conducting attacks (red lines) to other computers, making them function as "zombies."

Hacker's computer

Academic computer (zombie)

Government computer (zombie)

Corporate computer (zombie)

Home computer (zombie)

ISP computer (zombie)

These zombie computers (which sometimes number in the thousands) then attack the target system at the same time (blue lines).

Victim of DDoS

FIGURE 20

Zombies (sometimes hundreds or thousands of them) can be used to facilitate a distributed denial of service (DDoS) attack.

deal of angst when they were published in a Danish periodical. Because many bloggers earn revenue from advertising on their sites, this can be financially distressing for the owners of the blogs and aggravating for the readers. Unfortunately, DDoS attacks are not limited to blogs but have previously been launched against such major retail sites as Amazon and eBay.

HOW HACKERS GAIN ACCESS

How exactly does a hacker gain access to a computer? Hackers can gain access to computers directly or indirectly. Direct access involves sitting down at a computer and installing hacking software. This rarely occurs in your home. However, to deter unauthorized use, you may want to

lock the room that your computer is in or remove key components (such as the power cord) when strangers (repairmen and so on) are in your house and may be unobserved for periods of time.

The most likely method a hacker will take to access a computer is indirectly through its Internet connection. When connected to the Internet, your computer is potentially open to attack by hackers. Many people forget that their Internet connection is a two-way street. Not only can you access the Internet, but people on the Internet can access your computer as well.

Think of the computer as a house. Common sense tells you to lock your doors and windows when you aren't home to deter theft. Hooking your computer up to the Internet is like leaving the front door to

Computers in Society: Identity Theft—Is There More Than One You Out There?

You've no doubt heard of identity theft: a thief steals your name, address, social security number, and bank account and credit card information and runs up debts in your name. This leaves you holding the bag as you're hounded by creditors collecting on the fraudulent debts. It sounds horrible, and it is. In fact, one of the authors of this textbook had their identity stolen and spent about 50 hours filing police reports, talking to credit agencies, closing bogus accounts, and convincing companies that the $25,000 of debt run up on six bogus credit card accounts was done by an identity thief. Many victims of identity theft spend months (or even years) trying to repair their credit and eliminate fraudulent debts.

Stories of identity theft abound in the media, such as the Long Island, New York, man accused of stealing over 30,000 identities, and should serve to make the public wary. However, many media pundits would have you believe that the only way your identity can be stolen is by a computer. This is simply not true. The U.S. Federal Trade Commission (**www.ftc.gov**) has identified the following as methods thieves use to obtain others' personal information. Identity thieves may

1. Steal purses and wallets, where people often keep unnecessary valuable personal information (such as their ATM PIN codes).
2. Steal mail or look through trash for bank statements and credit card bills, which provide valuable personal information.
3. Pose as bank or credit card company representatives and trick people into revealing sensitive information over the phone.

Although none of these methods involve using a computer, you're at risk from online attacks, too. For example, you can give personal information to crooks by responding to bogus e-mails purportedly from your bank or ISP, a practice known as phishing. Once identity thieves have obtained your personal information, they can use it in a number of different ways. Identity thieves can:

- Request a change of address for your credit card bill. By the time you realize that you aren't receiving your credit card statements, the thieves have rung up bogus charges on your account.
- Open new credit card accounts in your name.

- Open bank accounts in your name and write bad checks, ruining your credit rating.
- Counterfeit bank cards or checks for your legitimate accounts.

Although foolproof protection methods don't exist, the following precautions will help you minimize your risk:

1. Never reveal your password or PIN code to anyone or place it in an easy-to-find location.
2. Never reveal personal information unless you're sure that a legitimate reason exists for a business to know the information and you can confirm you're actually dealing with a legitimate representative. Banks and credit card companies usually request information by standard mail, not over the phone or online. If someone calls or e-mails asking you for personal information, decline and call the company where you opened your account.
3. Create hard-to-guess passwords for your accounts. Use a combination of letters and numbers and avoid using obvious passwords such as first or last names, birth dates, and so on.
4. When shopping online, be wary of unfamiliar merchants whom you can't contact through a mailing address or phone number or businesses whose prices are too good to be true. These can be an attempt to collect your personal information for use in fraudulent schemes.
5. If you have been the victim of identity theft, many states now allow you to freeze your credit history so that no new accounts can be opened until you lift the credit freeze. Even if you live in a state where you can't freeze your account, you can still place an extended fraud alert on your credit history for seven years, which also warns merchants that they should check with you (at your home address or phone number) before opening an account in your name.

Using common sense and keeping personal information in the hands of as few people as possible are the best defenses against identity theft. For additional tips on preventing identity theft or for procedures to follow if you are a victim, check out the U.S. federal government site on identity theft at **www.consumer.gov/idtheft**.

your house wide open when you're not home. Anyone passing by can access your computer and poke around for valuables. Your computer obviously doesn't have doors and windows like a house; instead, it has logical ports.

What are logical ports? Logical **ports** are virtual (that is, *not* physical) communications gateways or paths that allow a computer to organize requests for information (such as Web page downloads, e-mail routing, and so on) from other networks or computers. Unlike physical ports (USB, FireWire, and so on), you can't see or touch a logical port. It is part of a computer's internal organization.

Logical ports are numbered and assigned to specific services. For instance, logical port 80 is designated for HyperText Transfer Protocol (HTTP), the main communications protocol (or standard) for the Internet. Thus, all requests for information from your browser to the Web flow through logical port 80. E-mail messages sent by Simple Mail Transfer Protocol (SMTP), the protocol used for sending e-mail on the Internet, are routed through logical port 25. Open logical ports, like open windows in a home, invite intruders, as illustrated in Figure 21. Unless you take precautions to restrict access to your logical ports, other people on the Internet may be able to access your computer through them.

Fortunately, you can thwart most hacking problems by installing a firewall.

Computer Safeguards: Firewalls

Firewalls are software programs or hardware devices designed to keep computers safe from hackers. Firewalls specifically designed for home networks are called **personal firewalls** and are made to be easy to install. By using a personal firewall, you can close off open logical ports to invaders and potentially make your computer invisible to other computers on the Internet.

Why are they called firewalls? When houses were first being packed densely into cities (attached to each other with common walls), fire was a huge hazard because wood (the major construction component for houses) burns readily. An entire neighborhood could be lost in a sin-

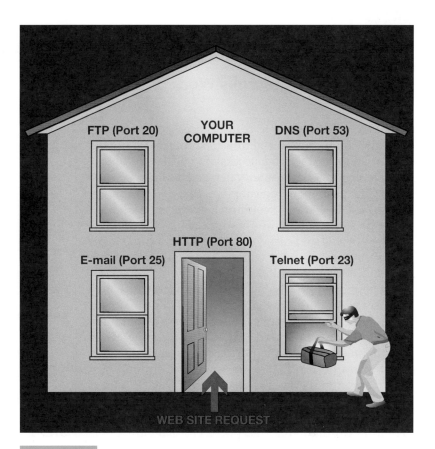

Open logical ports are an invitation to hackers.

gle fire. Thus, builders started building common walls of nonflammable or slow-burning material to stop (or at least slow) the spread of fire. These came to be known as firewalls.

TYPES OF FIREWALLS

What kinds of firewalls are there? As noted earlier, firewalls can be configured using software or hardware devices. Although installing *either* a software or a hardware firewall on your home network is probably sufficient, you should consider installing both for maximum protection.

What software firewalls are there? The most popular software firewalls for the home include Norton Personal Firewall, McAfee Firewall, ZoneAlarm, and BlackICE PC Protection. Windows Vista also comes with a reliable firewall. These products are easy to set up and include options that allow the software to make security decisions for you based on the level of security you request. These programs also come

SOUND BYTE

Installing a Personal Firewall

Firewalls provide excellent protection against hackers on a home network. In this Sound Byte, you'll learn how to install and configure software firewalls to protect your computer.

How Firewalls Work

Firewalls are designed to restrict access to a network and the computers on it. Firewalls protect you in two major ways: by blocking access to logical ports and by keeping your computer's network address secure.

To block access to logical ports, firewalls examine data packets that your computer sends and receives. Data packets contain information such as the address of the sending and receiving computers and the logical port that the packet will use. Firewalls can be configured so that they filter out packets sent to specific logical ports (a process referred to as **packet filtering**). For example, File Transfer Protocol (FTP) programs are a typical way in which hackers access a computer. If a firewall is configured to ignore *all* incoming packets that request access to port 25 (the port designated for FTP traffic), no FTP requests will get through to your computer (a process referred to as **logical port blocking**). If port 25 were a window on your home, you would have effectively locked it so that a burglar couldn't get in. If you need port 25 for a legitimate purpose, you could instruct the firewall to allow access to that port for a specified period of time or by a certain user.

For the Internet to share information seamlessly, data packets must have a way of getting to their correct location. Therefore, all computers connected to the Internet have a unique address. These addresses are called **Internet Protocol addresses** (**IP addresses** for short). As noted earlier, data packets contain the IP address of the computer to which they are being sent. Routing servers on the Internet make sure the packets get to the correct address. This is similar to the way addresses work on a conventional letter. A unique street address (such as 123 Main St., Anywhere, CA 99999) is placed on the envelope and the postal service routes it to its correct destination. Without such addressing, data packets, like letters, would not reach the intended recipients.

IP addresses are assigned when users log on to their Internet service provider (ISP) in a procedure known as **dynamic addressing**, illustrated in Figure 22. IP addresses are assigned out of a pool of available IP addresses licensed to the ISP. Because hackers use IP addresses to find victims and come back to their computers for more mischief, frequently switching IP addresses helps make users less vulnerable to attacks. However, because many broadband (cable and DSL) users leave their modems on for

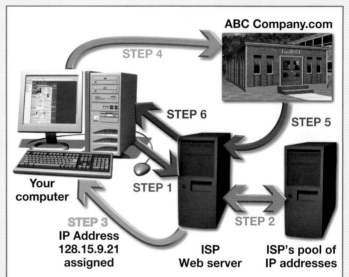

STEP 1: When you connect to your ISP, your computer requests an IP address.

STEP 2: The ISP's Web server consults its list of available IP addresses and selects one.

STEP 3: The selected IP address is communicated to your computer. The address remains in force for as long as you are connected to the ISP.

STEP 4: Once on the Internet, your Web browser requests access to ABC Company's Web site.

STEP 5: The ABC Company server consults an IP address listing and determines that the IP address of your computer is assigned to your ISP. It then forwards the requested information to the ISP's Web server.

STEP 6: The ISP's Web server knows to whom it assigned the IP address and therefore forwards the requested information on to your computer.

FIGURE 22

How Dynamic IP Addressing Works

long periods of time (consecutive days or weeks), their IP addresses tend to change less frequently than those of dial-up users. Such **static addressing** (retaining the same IP address for a period of time) makes broadband users more vulnerable to hackers because the hackers have a more permanent IP address with which to locate the computer. It also makes it easier for a hacker to go back to a computer repeatedly.

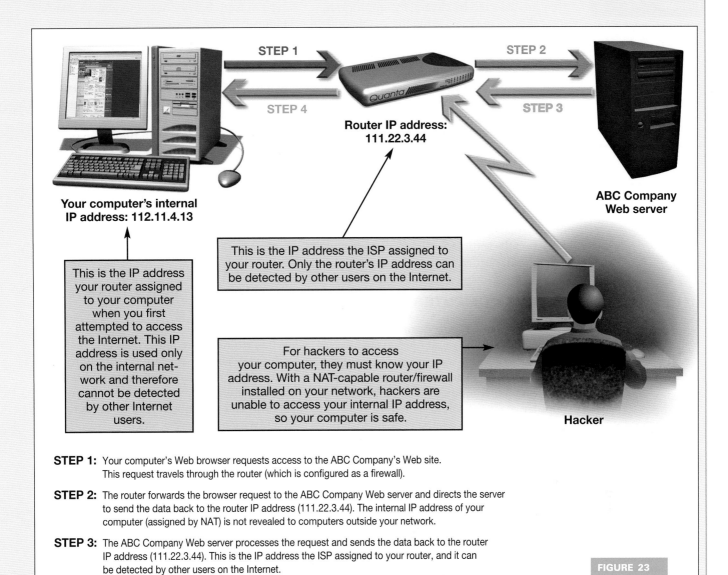

STEP 1 Your computer's Web browser requests access to the ABC Company's Web site. This request travels through the router (which is configured as a firewall).

STEP 2 The router forwards the browser request to the ABC Company Web server and directs the server to send the data back to the router IP address (111.22.3.44). The internal IP address of your computer (assigned by NAT) is not revealed to computers outside your network.

STEP 3 The ABC Company Web server processes the request and sends the data back to the router IP address (111.22.3.44). This is the IP address the ISP assigned to your router, and it can be detected by other users on the Internet.

STEP 4 The router then passes the requested data to the IP address of the computer that requested it (112.11.4.13). For hackers to access your computer, they must know your computer's IP address. With a NAT-capable router/firewall installed on your network, hackers are unable to access your internal IP address, so your computer is safe.

FIGURE 23

Network Address Translation in Action

To combat the problems associated with static addressing, firewalls use a process called **Network Address Translation (NAT)** to assign internal IP addresses on a network. These internal IP addresses are not shared with other devices that aren't part of the network, so the addresses are safe from hackers. Figure 23 shows how NAT works. You can use NAT in your home by purchasing a firewall with NAT capabilities. As noted earlier, many routers sold for home use are also configured as firewalls, and many feature NAT as well.

with monitoring systems that alert you if your computer is under attack. The newest versions of these programs have "smart agents" that automatically stop attacks as they are detected by closing the appropriate logical ports or disallowing the suspicious activity.

What are hardware firewalls? You can also buy and configure hardware firewall devices. For example, when buying a router for your network, make sure to buy one that also acts as a firewall. Manufacturers such as Linksys, D-Link, and Netgear make routers that double as firewalls. Just like software firewalls, the setup in hardware firewalls is designed for novices, and the default configuration is to keep unnecessary logical ports closed. Documentation accompanying the firewalls can assist more experienced users in adjusting the settings to allow access to specific ports if needed.

IS YOUR COMPUTER SECURE?

How can I tell if my computer is at risk? For peace of mind (and to ensure your firewall setup was successful), you can visit several Web sites that offer free services that test your computer's vulnerability. A popular site is Gibson Research (**www.grc.com**). The company's ShieldsUP

and LeakTest programs are free and easy to run and can pinpoint security vulnerabilities in a system connected to the Internet. If you get a clean report from these programs, your system is probably not vulnerable to attack. Figure 24 shows the results screen from a ShieldsUP port probe test, which checks which logical ports in your computer are vulnerable.

What if I don't get a clean report from the testing program? If the testing program detects potential vulnerabilities and you don't have a firewall, you should install one as soon as possible. If the firewall is already configured and specific ports are shown as being vulnerable, consult your firewall documentation for instructions on how to close or restrict access to those ports.

Securing Wireless Networks

When running a wireless network, installing a firewall is a key precaution. But wireless networks present special vulnerabilities that wired networks do not. Therefore, you should take additional specific steps to keep your wireless network safe.

FIGURE 24

This screen shows results from a ShieldsUP port probe test. This test was run on a computer connected to the Internet with no firewall installed. Any ports that are reported as open (such as port 1025) by this test represent vulnerabilities that could be exploited by hackers. Installation of a hardware or software firewall should close any open ports.

143	IMAP	Closed	Your computer has responded that this port exists but is currently closed to connections.
389	LDAP	Closed	Your computer has responded that this port exists but is currently closed to connections.
443	HTTPS	Closed	Your computer has responded that this port exists but is currently closed to connections.
445	MSFT DS	Stealth	There is NO EVIDENCE WHATSOEVER that a port (or even any computer) exists at this IP address!
1002	ms-ils	Closed	Your computer has responded that this port exists but is currently closed to connections.
1024	DCOM	Closed	Your computer has responded that this port exists but is currently closed to connections.
1025	Host	OPEN!	One or more unspecified Distributed COM (DCOM) services are opened by Windows. The exact port(s) opened can change, since queries to port 135 are used to determine which services are operating where. As is the rule for all exposed Internet services, you should arrange to close this port to external access so that potential current and future security or privacy exploits can not succeed against your system.
1026	Host	Closed	Your computer has responded that this port exists but is currently closed to connections.
1027	Host	Closed	Your computer has responded that this port exists but is currently closed to connections.

Ports reported as closed or in stealth mode are safe from attack

Ports reported as open are subject to exploitation by hackers

Why is a wireless network more vulnerable than a wired network? If you're keeping a wired network secure with a firewall, you're fairly safe from most hacker attacks. However, wireless networks, especially with 802.11g and 802.11n equipment, have wide ranges, including areas outside of your house. This makes it possible for a hacker to access your network without you even knowing it.

Why should I be worried about strangers using my wireless network? Some use of other people's wireless networks is unintentional. Houses are built close together. Apartments are clustered even closer together. Wireless signals can easily reach a neighbor's residence. Most wireless network adapters are set up to access the strongest wireless network signal detected. If your router is on the east side of your house and you and your notebook are on the west side, you may be getting a stronger signal from your neighbor's wireless network than from your own.

So why should you care if your neighbor is logged onto your network instead of his? Your neighbor probably isn't a hacker, but he might be using a lot of bandwidth—your bandwidth! If he's downloading a massive movie file while you're trying to do research for a term paper, he's probably slowing you down. Also, when some less than honest neighbors discover they can log onto your wireless network, they may cancel their own Internet service to save money by using yours.

In addition, because cyberattacks are traceable, criminals love to launch attacks (such as DDoS attacks) from public computers (such as in a library) so they can't be identified. If a criminal is sitting in his car outside your house and logging on to your wireless network, any cyberattacks he launches might be traced back to your IP address and you may find some law enforcement officials knocking on your door.

Won't a firewall protect me? Firewalls will protect you from a lot of cyberattacks. However, on a wireless network, because your packets of information are being broadcast through the airwaves, a savvy hacker can intercept and decode information from your transmissions that may allow him to bypass your firewall. Therefore,

to secure a wireless network, you should take the following additional precautions:

1. **Change Your Network Name (SSID):** Each wireless network has its own name to identify it. Unless you change this name when you set up your router, the router uses a default network name (also known as the service set identifier or SSID) that all routers from that manufacturer use (such as "Wireless"). Hackers know the default names and access codes for routers. If you haven't changed the SSID, it's advertising the fact that you probably haven't changed any of the other default settings for your router either.

2. **Disable SSID Broadcast:** Most routers are set up to broadcast their SSID so that other wireless devices can find them. If your router supports disabling SSID broadcasting, turn it off. This makes it more difficult for a hacker to detect your network.

3. **Change the Default Password on Your Router:** Hackers know the default passwords of most routers, and if they can access your router, they can probably break into your network. Change the password on your router to something hard to guess (use at least 8 characters with a combination of letters and numbers).

4. **Turn on Security Protocols:** Most routers ship with security protocols such as **W**ired **E**quivalent **P**rivacy (WEP) or **W**i-Fi **P**rotected **A**ccess (WPA). Both use encryption (a method of translating your data into code) to protect data in your wireless transmissions. WPA is a stronger protocol than WEP, so enable WPA if you have it; enable WEP if you don't. When you attempt to connect a node to a WEP- or WPA-enabled network for the first time, you're required to enter the encryption key. The encryption key (see Figure 25) is the code that computers on your network need to decrypt (decode) data transmissions. Without this key, it is very difficult (if not impossible) to decrypt the data transmissions from your network (see Figure 26). This prevents unauthorized access to your network as hackers won't know the correct key to use.

SOUND BYTE

Securing Wireless Networks

In this Sound Byte, you'll learn what "war drivers" are and why they could potentially be a threat to your wireless network. You'll also learn the simple steps to secure your wireless network against intruders.

FIGURE 25

By running your router configuration wizard, you can configure the security protocols available on your router and change the SSID, which helps protect your wireless network.

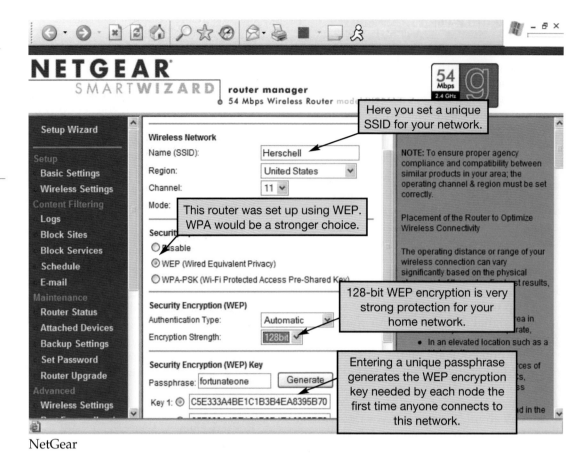

NetGear

5. **Implement Media Access Control:** Each network adapter on your network has a unique number assigned to it by the manufacturer (like a serial number). This is called a Media Access Control address (or MAC address), and it is a number printed right on the network adapter. Many routers allow you to restrict access to the network to only certain MAC addresses. This helps ensure that only authorized devices can connect to your network.

6. **Apply Firmware Upgrades:** Your router has read-only memory that has software written to it. This software is known as firmware. As bugs are found in the firmware (which hackers might exploit), manufacturers issue patches, just as the makers of operating system software do. Periodically check the manufacturer's Web site and apply any necessary upgrades to your firmware.

Computer Threats: Computer Viruses

Keeping your computer safe entails keeping it safe from more than just hackers. You must also guard against computer viruses. A computer **virus** is a computer program that attaches itself to another computer program (known as the host program) and attempts to spread itself to other computers when files are exchanged. Viruses normally attempt to hide within the code of a host program to avoid detection.

What do computer viruses do? A computer virus's main purpose is to replicate itself and copy its code into as many other files as possible. Although virus replication can slow down networks, it is not usually the main threat. The majority of viruses have secondary objectives or side effects, ranging from displaying annoying messages on the computer screen to the destruction of files or the contents of entire hard drives. Because computer viruses do cause disrup-

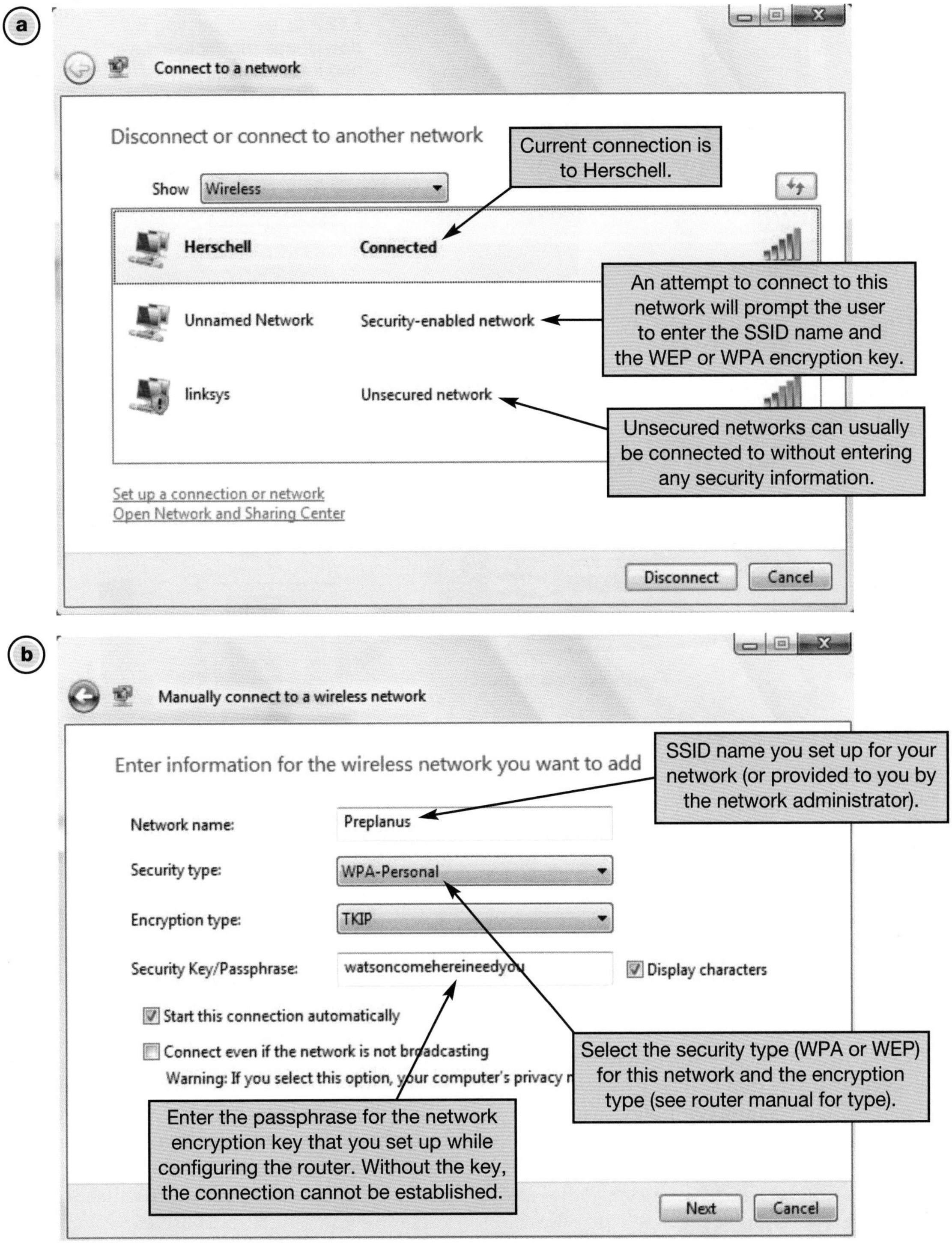

(a)

Connect to a network

Disconnect or connect to another network

Current connection is to Herschell.

Show [Wireless ▼]

Herschell	**Connected**
Unnamed Network	Security-enabled network
linksys	Unsecured network

An attempt to connect to this network will prompt the user to enter the SSID name and the WEP or WPA encryption key.

Unsecured networks can usually be connected to without entering any security information.

Set up a connection or network
Open Network and Sharing Center

[Disconnect] [Cancel]

(b)

Manually connect to a wireless network

Enter information for the wireless network you want to add

SSID name you set up for your network (or provided to you by the network administrator).

Network name: Preplanus

Security type: WPA-Personal ▼

Encryption type: TKIP ▼

Security Key/Passphrase: watsoncomehereineedyou   ☑ Display characters

☑ Start this connection automatically

☐ Connect even if the network is not broadcasting
Warning: If you select this option, your computer's privacy r

Enter the passphrase for the network encryption key that you set up while configuring the router. Without the key, the connection cannot be established.

Select the security type (WPA or WEP) for this network and the encryption type (see router manual for type).

[Next] [Cancel]

FIGURE 26

(a) The Windows Connect to a network dialog box shows all wireless networks within range. Clicking on one allows you to connect to it or prompts you for more information, such as the SSID name and security key. (b) Manually connecting to a wireless network allows you to establish a connection if you know the network encryption key and the SSID name.

>You can access the Connect to a network dialog box by right-clicking the network connection icon on the taskbar and selecting Connect to a network from the shortcut menu. You can access the Manually connect to a wireless network dialog box by accessing the Control Panel, selecting Network and Sharing Center, choosing Set up a connection or network option and then clicking on Manually connect to a wireless network.

tion to computer systems, including data destruction and information theft, virus creation is a form of cybercrime.

How does my computer catch a virus? If your computer is exposed to a file infected with a virus, the virus will try to copy itself and infect a file on your computer. If you never expose your computer to new files, it will not become infected. However, this would be the equivalent of a human being living in a bubble to avoid catching viruses from other people—quite impractical, to say the least.

Sharing disks or flash drives is a common source of virus infection, as is e-mail, although many people have misconceptions

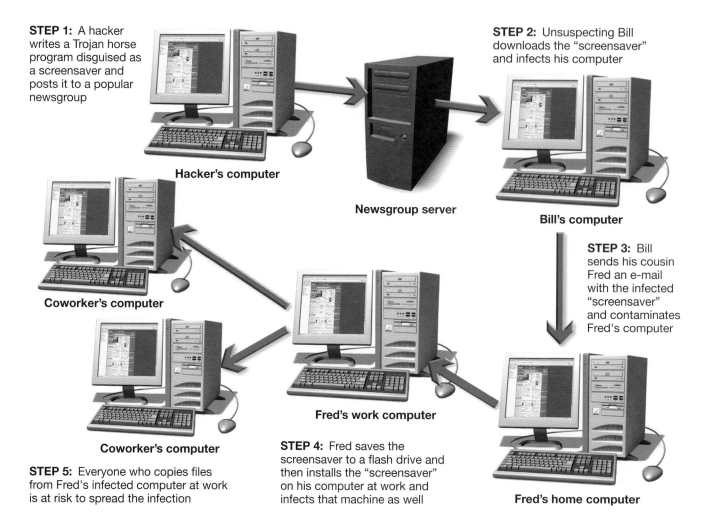

STEP 1: A hacker writes a Trojan horse program disguised as a screensaver and posts it to a popular newsgroup

Hacker's computer

Newsgroup server

STEP 2: Unsuspecting Bill downloads the "screensaver" and infects his computer

Bill's computer

STEP 3: Bill sends his cousin Fred an e-mail with the infected "screensaver" and contaminates Fred's computer

Coworker's computer

Fred's work computer

Coworker's computer

STEP 5: Everyone who copies files from Fred's infected computer at work is at risk to spread the infection

STEP 4: Fred saves the screensaver to a flash drive and then installs the "screensaver" on his computer at work and infects that machine as well

Fred's home computer

FIGURE 27

Computer viruses and other dangerous programs (such as Trojan horses) are passed from one unsuspecting user to the next.

about how e-mail infection occurs. Just opening an e-mail message will not infect your computer with a virus. Downloading or running a file that is attached to the e-mail is how your computer becomes infected. Thus, be extremely wary of e-mail attachments, especially if you don't know the sender. Figure 27 shows how computer viruses are often passed from one computer to the next.

TYPES OF VIRUSES

What are the different kinds of viruses?
Although thousands of computer viruses and variants exist, they can be grouped into six broad categories based on their behavior and method of transmission.

Boot-Sector Viruses

What are boot-sector viruses? Boot-sector viruses replicate themselves into the Master Boot Record of a hard drive. The **Master Boot Record** is a program that exe-cutes whenever a computer boots up, ensuring that the virus will be loaded into memory immediately, even before some virus protection programs. Boot-sector viruses are often transmitted by a floppy disk left in a floppy drive or a flash drive left in a USB port. When the computer boots up with the disk in the drive, it tries to launch a Master Boot Record from the floppy, which is usually the trigger for the virus to infect the hard drive. Boot-sector viruses can be very destructive: they can erase your entire hard drive.

Logic Bombs and Time Bombs

What are logic bombs? Logic bombs are viruses that are triggered when certain logical conditions are met (such as opening a file, booting your computer, or accessing certain programs). **Time bombs** are viruses that are triggered by the passage of time or on a certain date. The Michelangelo virus, first launched in 1992, is a famous time bomb that is set to trigger every year on March 6, Michelangelo's birthday. The effects of logic bombs and time bombs range from annoying messages being displayed on the screen to reformatting of the hard drive, causing complete data loss.

Worms

What are worms? Worms are slightly different from viruses in that they attempt to travel between systems through network connections to spread their infections. Viruses infect a host file and wait for that file to be executed on another computer to replicate. Worms can run independently of host file execution and are much more active in spreading themselves. The Sasser worm broke out in April 2004, infecting millions of individual computers and servers. This worm exploits a weakness in the Windows operating system, and therefore antivirus software doesn't protect against this worm. However, having a firewall installed and applying software patches (code issued by the manufacturers of software programs, such as Windows, that repairs known security problems) as they are issued can protect you from most worms.

Script and Macro Viruses

What are script and macro viruses? Some viruses are hidden on Web sites in the form of **scripts**. Scripts are a series of commands, actually mini programs, that are executed without your knowledge. Scripts are often used to perform useful, legitimate functions on Web sites, such as collecting name and address information from customers. However, some scripts are malicious. For example, say you receive an e-mail encouraging you to visit a Web site full of useful programs and information. Unbeknownst to you, clicking a link to display a video runs a script that infects your computer with a virus.

Macro viruses are attached to documents (such as Word and Excel documents) that use macros. A macro is a short series of commands that usually automates repetitive tasks. However, macro languages are now so sophisticated that viruses can be written with them. In March 1999, the Melissa virus became the first major macro virus to cause problems worldwide. It attached itself to a Word document. Anyone opening an infected document triggered the virus, which infected other Word documents on the victim's computer.

The Melissa virus was also the first practical example of an **e-mail virus**. E-mail viruses use the address book in the victim's e-mail system to distribute the virus. When executed, the Melissa virus sent itself to the first 50 people in the address book on the infected computer. This helped ensure that Melissa became one of the most widely distributed viruses ever released.

Encryption Viruses

What are encryption viruses? **Encryption viruses** are the newest form of virus. When these viruses infect your computer, they run a program that searches for common data files (such as Microsoft Word and Excel documents) and compresses them into a file using a complex encryption key. This renders your files unusable. You then receive a message asking you to send money to an account to receive the program to decrypt your files. The flaw with this type of virus, which keeps it from being widespread, is that law enforcement officials can trace the payments to an account and potentially catch the perpetrators. Still, these types of viruses are now seen from time to time.

VIRUS CLASSIFICATIONS

How else are viruses classified?

Viruses can also be classified by the methods they take to avoid detection by antivirus software:

- **Polymorphic viruses** change their own code (or periodically rewrite themselves) to avoid detection. Most polymorphic viruses infect one certain type of file (.exe files, for example).

- **Multipartite viruses** are designed to infect multiple file types in an effort to fool the antivirus software that is looking for them.

- **Stealth viruses** temporarily erase their code from the files where they reside and hide in the active memory of the computer. This helps them avoid detection if only the hard drive is being searched for viruses. Fortunately, antivirus software developers are aware of these tricks and have designed software to watch for them.

Computer Safeguards: Antivirus Software

Certain viruses merely present minor annoyances, such as randomly sending an ambulance graphic across the bottom of the screen, as is the case with the Red Cross virus. Other viruses can significantly slow down a computer or network or destroy key files or the contents of entire hard drives. The best defense against viruses is to install **antivirus software**, which is specifically designed to detect viruses and protect your computer and files from harm.

How often do I need to run antivirus software? You should run a virus check on your entire system at least once a week. By doing so, all files on your computer are checked for undetected viruses. Because these checks take time, you can configure the software to run these checks automatically when you aren't using your system, such as late at night (see Figure 28).

How does antivirus software work? Most antivirus software looks for **virus signatures** in files. Signatures are portions of the virus code that are unique to a particular computer virus. Antivirus software scans files for these signatures and thereby identifies infected files and the type of virus that is infecting them.

FIGURE 28

By setting up a schedule in the antivirus module of Norton Internet Security, complete virus scans can be set up to run automatically. This computer will be scanned every Tuesday at 10:00 p.m.

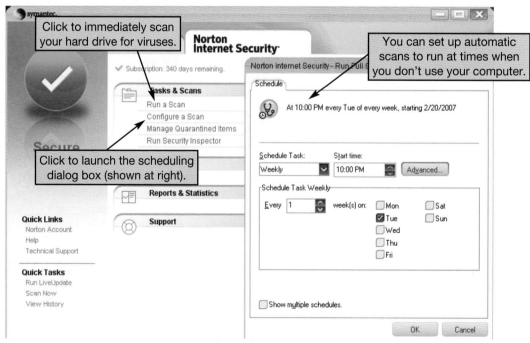

©1995–2007 Symantec Corporation

The antivirus software scans files when they're opened or executed. If it detects a virus signature or suspicious activity (such as launching an unknown macro), it stops the execution of the file and virus and notifies you that it has detected a virus. It also places the virus in a secure area on your hard drive so that it won't spread infection to other files. This procedure is known as **quarantining**. Usually the antivirus software then gives you the choice of deleting or repairing the infected file. Unfortunately, antivirus programs can't always fix infected files so that the files are usable again. You should keep backup copies of critical files so that you can restore them in case a virus damages them irreparably.

Some antivirus software will also attempt to prevent infection by inoculating key files on your computer. **Inoculation** involves the antivirus software recording key attributes about files on your computer (such as file size and date created) and keeping these statistics in a safe place on your hard drive. When scanning for viruses, the antivirus software compares the files to the attributes it previously recorded to help detect attempts by virus programs to modify your files.

Does antivirus software always stop viruses? Antivirus software catches *known* viruses effectively. Unfortunately, new viruses are written all the time. To combat unknown viruses, modern antivirus programs search for suspicious virus-like activities as well as virus signatures. However, virus authors know how antivirus software works. They take special measures to disguise their virus code and hide the effects of a virus until just the right moment. This helps ensure that the virus spreads faster and farther. Thus, your computer can still be attacked by a virus that your antivirus software doesn't recognize. To minimize this risk, you should keep your antivirus software up-to-date.

How do I make sure my antivirus software is up-to-date? Most antivirus programs have an automatic updates feature that downloads a list of upgrades you can install on your computer while you're online (see Figure 29). Automatic updates ensure that your programs are up-to-date.

FIGURE 29

Norton's LiveUpdate provides automatic updates on all virus and security products installed on the computer. It can be set to automatically update every time you connect to the Internet.

What should I do if I think my computer is infected with a virus? Boot up your computer with the antivirus CD that came with your antivirus software in your CD drive. This should prevent most virus programs from loading and will allow you to run the antivirus software directly from the CD drive. If viruses are detected, you may want to research them further to determine whether your antivirus software will eradicate them completely or if you need to take additional manual steps to eliminate the virus. Most antivirus company Web sites (such as **www.symantec.com**) contain archives of information on viruses and provide step-by-step solutions for removing viruses.

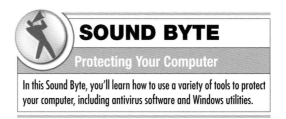

SOUND BYTE

Protecting Your Computer

In this Sound Byte, you'll learn how to use a variety of tools to protect your computer, including antivirus software and Windows utilities.

OTHER SECURITY MEASURES

Is there anything else I should do to protect my system? Many viruses exploit weaknesses in operating systems. To combat these threats, make sure your operating system is up-to-date and contains the latest security patches (or fixes). Windows Vista makes this easy by providing a utility called Windows Update. When you enable automatic updates, your computer searches for Windows updates on the Microsoft Web site every time it connects to the Internet.

How do I enable automatic updates? To enable automatic updates, click the Start button, select Control Panel, and double-click the Windows Update icon. Then click the Change Settings option to display the dialog box shown in Figure 30. It is strongly recommended that you select the Install updates automatically option.

Reprinted with permission from Microsoft Corporation

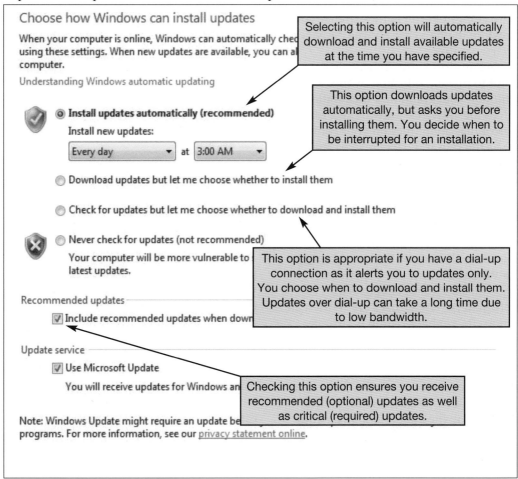

FIGURE 30

The Windows Vista Automatic Updating screen makes it easy for users to configure Windows to update itself.

>To enable automatic updates, click the Start button, select Control Panel, double-click the Windows Update icon, and click the Change Settings link.

Careers: Cybercops on the Beat—Computer Security Careers

With billions being spent on e-commerce initiatives every year, companies have a vested interest in keeping their Information Technology (IT) infrastructures humming along. The rise in terrorism has shifted the focus slightly from protecting just virtual assets and access to protecting physical assets and access points as well. The increased need for virtual and physical security measures means there should be a robust job market ahead for computer security experts.

The National Security Agency and the Office of Homeland Security are both encouraging information security professionals to be proficient in information assurance. As defined by the NSA, information assurance is "the set of measures intended to protect and defend information and information systems by ensuring their availability, integrity, authentication, confidentiality, and non-repudiation. This includes providing for restoration of information systems by incorporating protection, detection, and reaction capabilities." The five key attributes of secure information systems are as follows:

1. **Availability.** The extent to which a data-processing system is able to receive and process data. A high degree of availability is usually desirable.
2. **Integrity.** A quality that an information system has if the processing of information is logical and accurate and the data is protected against unauthorized modifications or destruction.
3. **Authentication.** Security measures designed to protect an information system against acceptance of a fraudulent transmission of data by establishing the validity of a data transmission, message, or the identity of the sender.
4. **Confidentiality.** Assurance that information is not disclosed to unauthorized persons, processes, or devices.
5. **Nonrepudiation.** A capability of security systems that guarantees that a message or data can be proven to have originated from a specific person and was processed by the recipient. The sender of the data receives a receipt for the data, and the receiver of the data gets proof of the sender's identity. The objective of nonrepudiation is to prevent either party from later denying having handled the data.

The Global Information Assurance Certification, or GIAC (**www.giac.org**), is an industry-recognized certification that provides objective evidence (through examinations) that security professionals have mastered key skills in various aspects of information assurance.

What skill sets will be most in demand for security professionals? Aside from provable information assurance technical skills (with an emphasis on network engineering and data communications), broad-based business experience is also extremely desirable. IT security professionals need to understand the key issues of e-commerce and the core areas of their company's business (such as marketing, sales, and finance). Understanding how a business works is essential to pinpointing and correcting the security risks that could be detrimental to a company's bottom line. And because of the large number of attacks by hackers, security forensic skills and related certifications are in high demand. Working closely with law enforcement officials is essential to rapidly solving and stopping cybercrime.

Another important attribute of security professionals is the ability to lead and motivate teams. Security experts need to work with diverse members of the business community, including customers, to forge relationships and understanding among diverse groups. Security professionals must conduct skillful negotiations to ensure that large project implementations are not unduly delayed by security initiatives or pushed through with inadequate security precautions. Diplomacy is therefore a sought-after skill.

Look for more colleges and universities to roll out security-based degrees and certificate programs as the demand for security professionals increases. These programs will most likely be appropriate for experienced networking professionals who are ready to make the move into the IT security field. If you're just preparing for a career, consider a degree in network engineering, followed by network security training while you're working at your first job. A degree program that is also designed to prepare you for security certification exams is particularly desirable. Networking and security degrees, combined with passing grades on certification exams, should help you ensure a smooth transition into the exciting world of cybersecurity.

Summary

1. What is a network, and what are the advantages of setting up one?

A computer network is simply two or more computers that are connected using software and hardware so that they can communicate. Networks allow users to (1) share peripherals, (2) transfer files easily, and (3) share an Internet connection.

2. What is the difference between a client/server network and a peer-to-peer network?

In peer-to-peer networks, each node connected to the network can communicate directly with every other node instead of having a separate device exercise central control over the network. P2P networks are the most common type of network installed in homes. Most networks that have 10 or more nodes are client/server networks. A client/server network contains two types of computers: a client computer on which users accomplish specific tasks, and a server computer that provides resources to the clients and central control for the network.

3. What are the main components of every network?

To function, all networks contain four components: (1) transmission media (cables or radio waves) to connect and establish communication between nodes; (2) network adapters that allow the nodes on the network to communicate; (3) network navigation devices (such as routers and hubs) that move data around the network; and (4) software that allows the network to run.

4. What are the most common home networks?

The two most common home networks are wired Ethernet and wireless Ethernet. Modern power-line networks, boasting faster data throughput, are now a viable option in certain situations. The major difference in these networks is the transmission media by which the nodes are connected.

5. What are wired Ethernet networks, and how are they created?

Ethernet networks use the Ethernet protocol as the means by which the nodes on the network communicate. This protocol makes Ethernet networks efficient but also slightly complex. Because of this complexity, additional devices (switches or routers) are required in Ethernet networks. To create a wired Ethernet network, you connect or install network adapters or NICs to each network node. Network adapters connect via cables to a central network navigation device such as a switch or a router. Data flows through the navigation device to the nodes on the network.

6. What are wireless Ethernet networks, and how are they created?

A wireless network uses radio waves instead of wires or cable as its transmission media. Current wireless protocols provide for networks with up to a maximum of 108 Mbps. To create a wireless network, you install or attach wireless network adapters to the nodes that will make up the network. If the nodes are unable to communicate because of distance, you can add a wireless access point to the network to help relay data between nodes. Wireless networks are susceptible to interference from other wireless devices such as phones.

7. How are power-line networks created, and are they viable alternatives to Ethernet networks?

Power-line networks use the electrical wiring in your home to connect the nodes in the network. To create a power-line network, you connect special network adapters to each node on the network. These adapters are then plugged into an electrical outlet, and data is transmitted through the electrical wires. Modern power-line networks can often exceed the throughput achieved in wireless Ethernet networks, making them a viable option when interference with wireless signals is present.

8. How can hackers attack a network, and what harm can they cause?

A hacker is defined as anyone who breaks into a computer system unlawfully. Hackers can use software to break into almost any computer connected to the Internet (unless proper precautions are taken). Once hackers gain access to a computer, they can potentially (1) steal personal or other important information; (2) damage and destroy data; or (3) use the computer to attack other computers.

9. What is a firewall, and how does it keep my computer safe from hackers?

Firewalls are software programs or hardware devices designed to keep computers safe from hackers. By using a personal firewall, you can close off to invaders open logical ports and potentially make your computer invisible to other computers on the Internet.

10. Why are wireless networks more vulnerable than wired networks, and what special precautions are required to ensure my wireless network is secure?

Wireless networks are even more susceptible to hacking than wired networks because the signals of most wireless networks extend beyond the walls of your home. Neighbors may unintentionally (or intentionally) connect to the Internet through your wireless connection, and hackers may try to access it. To prevent unwanted intrusions into your network, you should change the default password on your router (to make it tougher for hackers to gain access), use a hard-to-guess SSID (network name), turn off SSID broadcasting (to make it harder for outsiders to detect your network), and enable security protocols such as WPA or WEP.

11. From which types of viruses do I need to protect my computer?

A computer virus is a program that attaches itself to another program and attempts to spread itself to other computers when files are exchanged. Computer viruses can be grouped into six categories: (1) boot-sector viruses, (2) logic bombs and time bombs, (3) worms, (4) scripts and macros, (5) encryption viruses, and (6) Trojan horses. Once run, they perform their malicious duties in the background, often invisible to the user.

12. What can I do to protect my computer from viruses?

The best defense against viruses is to install antivirus software. You should update the software on a regular basis and configure it to examine all e-mail attachments for viruses. You should periodically run a complete virus scan on your computer to ensure that no viruses have made it onto your hard drive.

802.11 standard (Wi-Fi)

antivirus software

backdoor program

black-hat hacker

boot-sector virus

Cat 5E cable

client

client/server network

coaxial cable

cybercrime

cybercriminal

data transfer rate (bandwidth)

denial of service (DoS) attack

distributed denial of service (DDoS) attack

DSL/cable router

dynamic addressing

e-mail virus

encryption virus

Ethernet network

fiber-optic cable

firewall

hacker

identity theft

inoculation

Internet Protocol address (IP address)

local area network (LAN)

logic bomb

logical port blocking

logical port

macro virus

Master Boot Record

multipartite virus

network

network adapter

network architecture

Network Address Translation (NAT)

network interface card (NIC)

network navigation device

network operating system (NOS)

node

packet filtering

packet sniffer

packet

peer-to-peer (P2P) network

personal firewall

polymorphic virus

power-line network

pretexting

quarantining

repeater

router

script kiddy

script

server

shoulder surfing

social engineering

static addressing

stealth virus

switch

throughput

time bomb

transceiver

transmission media

Trojan horse

twisted-pair cable

unshielded twisted-pair (UTP) cable

virus

virus signature

white-hat hacker

wide area network (WAN)

wide area network (WAN)

Wi-Fi

wireless network

wireless network adapter

wireless routers (gateway)

worm

zombie

Buzz Words

Word Bank

- antivirus software
- Cat 5E
- Distributed Denial of Service (DDoS)
- firewall
- hacker(s)
- identity theft

- information assurance
- logical port(s)
- network adapter(s)
- peer-to-peer (P2P)
- phone cable
- repeater

- router
- throughput
- virus
- wired Ethernet
- wireless Ethernet
- zombie(s)

Instructions: Fill in the blanks using the words from the Word Bank above.

Cathi needed to network three computers for herself and her roommates (Sharon and Emily). She decided that a(n) (1) _____ network was the right type to install in their apartment because that was the most common type of home network. Because none of them were gamers or transferred large files, they didn't need high (2) _____. Still, they decided to use the fastest type of home network, a(n) (3) _____ network, because it is reliable and easy to install. To connect the computers, they needed to buy (4) _____ cable. Because Sharon already had high-speed Internet access through the cable TV company, she needed to buy a(n) (5) _____ for the network to ensure all users could share the connection. Fortunately, all their computers already had (6) _____ installed, making it easy to connect the computers to the network.

Cathi's roommate Emily was skeptical of being hooked up to the Internet because she had been the victim of (7) _____, which destroyed her credit rating. A(n) (8) _____ had obtained her credit card information by posing as an employee of her bank. Cathi assured Emily that the router could be configured as a(n) (9) _____ to repel malicious hacking mischief and assist in providing (10) _____ for the data on her computer. Turning off the unused (11) _____ would repel most attacks on their home network. With this protection, it was unlikely that a hacker would turn their PCs into (12) _____ to launch (13) _____ attacks. But after the scare with the Melissa (14) _____, Cathi was careful to warn the others not to open files from untrusted sources. She also made sure they all installed (15) _____ on their PCs to protect them from viruses.

Becoming Computer Literate

While attending college, you are working at the Snap-Tite company, a small manufacturer of specialty fasteners. Currently, the employees must copy files to flash drives to transfer them among the four PCs the company owns. Only the company president has access to the Internet. The accounts payable clerk is the only one who has a printer and is constantly being interrupted by other employees when they want to print their files. Your boss heard that you were taking a computer course and asked you to create a solution.

Instructions: Using the preceding scenario, draft a networking plan for Snap-Tite using as many of the keywords from the chapter as you can. Be sure that the company president, who is unfamiliar with many networking terms, can understand the report.

Self-Test

Instructions: Answer the multiple-choice and true/false questions below for more practice with key terms and concepts from this chapter.

MULTIPLE CHOICE

1. Which type of sharing is NOT a benefit of installing a home network?
   a. Peripheral   c. File
   b. Internet connection   d. Client/server

2. Which of the following is a reason client/server networks are generally NOT installed in homes?
   a. Client/server networks are less expandable than peer-to-peer networks.
   b. Client/server networks don't have as many security features as home networks.
   c. Client/server networks provide less security than is needed in a home network.
   d. Servers are too difficult for most home users to set up.

3. *All* networks contain the following elements except
   a. network adapters.
   b. transmission media.
   c. routers.
   d. networking software.

4. Which is an example of a network navigation device required by an Ethernet network to move data form node to node?
   a. Network adapter
   b. Switch
   c. Wireless signal sender
   d. 5E cable.

5. Wireless Ethernet networks are popular because
   a. you don't need to run wires.
   b. they provide much better security than wired Ethernet networks.
   c. they cost less than wired Ethernet networks.
   d. None of the above

6. Power-line networks are viable alternatives to Ethernet networks because
   a. they are less expensive than Ethernet networks.

   b. they don't require running any new wires to install.
   c. they provide twice the throughput of wired Ethernet networks.
   d. All of the above.

7. When hackers use a program that pretends to be useful to a user while actually allowing the hacker to gain control of the user's computer, this is called a(n)
   a. Zero-day Attack.
   b. Trojan Horse Attack.
   c. Distributed Denial of Service Attack.
   d. Boot Sector Virus Attack.

8. Which is a benefit of a firewall?
   a. They make it harder for a hacker to locate specific computers on a network.
   b. They repeatedly change the IP address of the router.
   c. They open unused logical ports to increase throughput.
   d. They filter out unwanted wireless signals.

9. Wireless Ethernet networks are attractive to hackers because
   a. The 802.11 protocol has weak security rules.
   b. You can't install a firewall on a wireless Ethernet network.
   c. The signals from the network can travel beyond the walls of your home.
   d. Wireless Ethernet networks have much greater bandwidth than wired networks.

10. Viruses that travel from computer to computer on their own (i.e., independent of host file activity) are called
    a. worms.   c. logic bombs
    b. stealth viruses.   d. macro viruses.

TRUE/FALSE

___ 1. Actual data throughput is usually lower on wireless networks.

___ 2. All home networks require each computer on the network to be equipped with its own switch.

___ 3. Installing a firewall on your network will stop most viruses from being planted on your network.

___ 4. Never downloading files from the Internet will ensure a computer never catches a virus.

___ 5. Wire Ethernet networks are NOT subject to interference from cordless phones.

Making the Transition to...
Next Semester

1. Dormitory Networking

Dave, Jerome, and Thomas were sitting in the common room of their campus suite staring at $80 piled up on the coffee table. Selling last semester's books back to the bookstore had been a good idea. As they waited for their other roommate Phil to come home, Dave said, "Wouldn't it be cool if we could network our notebooks? Then we could play Ultra Super Robot Kill-Fest in team mode!" Jerome pointed out it would be even more useful if they could all have access to Dave's laser printer because he owned the only one. "And Jerome's always bugging me to use my scanner when I'm trying to sleep," remarked Thomas. "And I can't believe the only high-speed Internet connection is out here in the lounge!" The three roommates ran down the hall and rapped on your door looking for some guidance. Consider how you would answer their questions:

a. Is $80 enough to set up a wireless network for four notebooks in four separate rooms? (Assume each computer contains a wireless network adapter already.)
b. Can the roommates share a printer and a scanner, if they set up a wireless network? Will they need any additional equipment for the printer and the scanner to share them across the network, if they are already connected to one of the notebook computers?
c. How would they share the one high-speed Internet connection wirelessly?
d. Phil just returned from the campus post office with a check from his aunt for $50. Do the roommates now have enough money to set up a wireless network to include their two friends across the hall, assuming their friends' computers do not have wireless network adapters?

To answer these questions, use the chapter text and the following resources: **www.coolcomputing.com, www.pricewatch.com, www.linksys.com, www.netgear.com, www.bestbuy.com, www.tigerdirect.com.**

2. Connecting Your Computer to Public Networks

In the course of your education, you are constantly connecting your notebook to various wireless public networks such as in the school library or the neighborhood coffee shop. As you know from reading this chapter, you are more vulnerable to hackers when connected to a wireless network. Conduct research on the Internet about surfing at public hotspots and prepare a list of sensible precautions for you and your classmates to take when surfing on an open network.

3. Identity Theft Awareness

Two students in your residence hall have recently been the victims of identity theft. You have been assigned to create a flyer telling students how they can protect themselves from identity theft in the residence hall. Using the information found in this chapter, materials you find on the U.S. federal government Web site on identity theft (**www.consumer.gov/idtheft**), as well as other Web resources, create a flyer that lists 5 to 10 ways in which students can avoid having their identities stolen.

Making the Transition to... the Workplace

1. Antivirus Protection

Your employer recently installed high-speed Internet access at the office where you work. There are 50 workstations connected to the network and the Internet. Within a week, half the computers in the office were down because of a virus that was contracted by a screen saver. In addition, network personnel from a university in England contacted the company, claiming that your employer's computer systems were being used as part of a DDoS attack on their Web site.

a. Price out antivirus software on the Internet and determine the most cost-effective package for the company to implement on 50 workstations.

b. Write a "virus prevention" memo to all employees that suggests strategies for avoiding virus infections.

c. Draft a note to the CEO to explain how a firewall could prevent distributed denial of service attacks from being launched on the company network.

2. Public Wireless Access

Many corporations are using wireless technology to enhance or drive their businesses. Assume you are opening a local coffee shop in your town. Investigate the following:

a. Starbucks (**www.starbucks.com**) currently provides wireless access (for a fee) in many of its locations. Using **www.wifinder.com** or **www.wi-fihotspotlist.com**, find the closest Starbucks to your home that features wireless access. Will this store compete with your proposed store, or is it too far away?

b. Visit your local Starbucks (or check the Starbucks Web site at **www.starbucks.com**) and find out the cost of its wireless access. Use the Internet to research whether wireless access is profitable for Starbucks and whether it drives customers to their stores (many articles have been written about this).

c. As part of your business plan, write a paragraph or two explaining why you will (or will not) offer wireless connectivity at your coffee shop and whether it will be a pay service or a free service.

d. Can you find any free alternatives for wireless access within a 10-mile radius of your proposed store location? How will this affect your decision to offer wireless connectivity at your business?

3. Testing Your Computer

Visit Gibson Research at **www.grc.com** and run the company's ShieldsUP and LeakTest programs on your computer.

a. Did your computer get a clean report? If not, what potential vulnerabilities did the testing programs detect?

b. How could you protect yourself from the vulnerabilities these programs can detect?

Critical Thinking Questions

Instructions: Albert Einstein used "Gedanken experiments," or critical thinking questions, to develop his theory of relativity. Some ideas are best understood by experimenting with them in our own minds. The following critical thinking questions are designed to demand your full attention but only require a comfortable chair—no technology.

1. Home Networking: A Profession?

Many people will be installing computer networks in their homes during the next five years.

a. Would starting a home networking installation business be a good entry-level job for a college graduate? Could it be a good part-time job for a college student?

b. Assuming the home networking business failed, what other careers would the technicians be prepared to assume?

2. Upgrading Your Wireless

You have just finished purchasing and installing a new wireless network in your home. A new wireless standard of networking will be launched next month that is 10 times as fast as the wireless network you installed.

a. What types of applications would you need to be using heavily to make it worth upgrading to the new standard?

b. Did you set up your wireless network securely so that your next door neighbor can't tap into it and save himself the cost of purchasing Internet access? Is tapping into a neighbor's wireless connection that is not secure ethical?

3. Ethical Hacking?

Hackers and virus authors cause millions of dollars worth of damage to PCs and networks annually. But hacking is a very controversial subject. Many hackers believe they are actually working for the "good of the people" or "exercising their freedom" when they engage in hacking activities. However, in most jurisdictions in the United States, hacking is punishable by stiff fines and jail terms.

a. Hackers often argue that hacking is for the good of all people because it points out flaws in computer systems. Do you agree with this? Why or why not?

b. What should the punishment be for convicted hackers and why?

c. Who should be held accountable at a corporation whose network security is breached by a hacker?

4. Keeping Networks Safe from Cyberterrorists

Many of us rely on networks every day, often without realizing it. Whether using the Internet, ordering a book from Amazon.com, or accessing your college e-mail from home, you are relying on networks to relay information. But what if terrorists destroyed key components of the Internet or other networks on which we depend?

a. What economic problems would result from DDoS attacks launched by terrorists on major e-commerce sites?

b. Research the precautions that the U.S. military and intelligence agencies (FBI, CIA) are taking to ensure that networks involving national defense remain secure from terrorist attacks. What else should they do?

5. Protection for Your Computer?

Do you have a firewall, anti-spyware, and antivirus software installed on the computer you use most often? If not, why not? What types of problems can you experience from not having this software installed? Have you ever been a victim of a hacker or a virus?

Problem:

Wireless technology is being adopted by leaps and bounds both in the home and in the workplace. Offering easy access free of physical tethers to networks seems to be a solution to many problems. However, wireless computing also has problems, ranging from poor reception to hijackers stealing your bandwidth.

Task:

Your campus has recently undertaken a wireless computing initiative. As part of the plan, your dorm has just been outfitted with wireless access points (base stations) to provide students with connectivity to the Internet and the college network. However, since the installation, students have reported poor connectivity in certain areas and extremely low bandwidth at other times. Your group has volunteered to research the potential problems and to suggest solutions to the college IT department.

Process:

Break the class into three teams. Each team will be responsible for investigating one of the following issues:

1. **Detecting Poor Connectivity:** Research methods that can be used to find areas of poor signal strength, such as signal sniffing software (**www.netstumbler.com**) and handheld scanning devices such as WiFi Finder (**http://us.kensington.com**). Investigate maximum distances between access points and network nodes (equipment manufacturers such as **www.netgear.com** and **www.linksys.com** provide guidelines) and make appropriate recommendations.

2. **Signal Boosters:** Research alternatives that can be used to increase signal strength in access points, antennas, and wireless cards. Signal boosters are available for access points. You can purchase or construct replacement antennas or antenna enhancements. Wi-Fi cards that offer higher power than conventional cards are now available.

3. **Security:** "War drivers" (people who cruise neighborhoods looking for open wireless networks from which to steal bandwidth) may be the cause of the bandwidth issues. Research appropriate measures to keep wireless network traffic secure from eavesdropping by hackers. In your investigation, look into the new Wi-Fi Protected Access (WPA) standard developed by the Wi-Fi Alliance. Check out the security section on the Wi-Fi Alliance Web site to start (**www.weca.net**).

Present your findings to your class and discuss possible causes and preventive measures for the problems encountered at your dorm. Provide your instructor with a report suitable for eventual presentation to the college IT department.

Conclusion:

As technology improves, wireless connectivity should eventually become the standard method of communication between networks and network devices. As with any other technology, security risks exist. Understanding those risks and how to mitigate them will allow you to participate in the design and deployment of network technology and provide peace of mind for your network users.

Multimedia

In addition to the review materials presented here, you'll find additional materials featured with the book's multimedia, including the Technology in Action Student Resource CD and the Companion Web Site (**www.prenhall.com/techinaction**), which will help reinforce your understanding of the chapter content. These materials include the following:

ACTIVE HELPDESK

In Active Helpdesk calls, you'll assume the role of Helpdesk operator taking calls about the concepts you've learned in this chapter. You'll apply what you've learned and receive feedback from a supervisor to review and reinforce those concepts. The Active Helpdesk calls for this chapter are listed below and can be found on your Student Resource CD:

- Understanding Networking
- Understanding Firewalls
- Avoiding Computer Viruses

SOUND BYTES

Sound Bytes are dynamic multimedia tutorials that help demystify even the most complex topics. You'll view video clips and animations that illustrate computer concepts, and then apply what you've learned by reviewing with the Sound Byte Labs, which include quizzes and activities specifically tailored to each Sound Byte. The Sound Bytes for this chapter are listed here and can be found on your Student Resource CD:

- Installing a Computer Network
- Installing a Personal Firewall
- Securing Wireless Networks
- Protecting Your Computer

COMPANION WEB SITE

The Technology in Action Companion Web Site includes a variety of additional materials to help you review and learn more about the topics in this chapter. The resources available at **www.prenhall.com/techinaction** include:

- **Online Study Guide.** Each chapter features an online true/false and multiple-choice quiz. You can take these quizzes, automatically check the results, and e-mail the results to your instructor.

- **Web Research Projects.** Each chapter features a number of Web research projects that ask you to search the Web for information on computer-related careers, milestones in computer history, important people and companies, emerging technologies, and the applications and implications of different technologies.

PROTECTING YOUR COMPUTER AND BACKING UP YOUR DATA

Just like any other valuable asset, computers and the data they contain require protection from damage, thieves, and unauthorized users. Although it's impossible to protect your computer and data completely, following the suggestions outlined in this Technology in Focus will provide you with peace of mind that you have done all you can to protect your computer from theft and to keep it in working order.

PHYSICALLY PROTECTING YOUR COMPUTER

Your computer isn't useful to you if it is damaged. Therefore, it's essential to select and ensure a safe environment for your computer. This includes protecting it from environmental factors, power surges, and power outages.

Environmental Factors

You need to consider a number of environmental factors to protect your computer.

1 Sudden movements (such as a fall) can damage your computer or mobile device's internal components. Therefore, take special care in setting up your computer. Make sure that the computer sits on a flat, level surface, and carry your notebook (laptop) in a padded case to protect it should you drop it. If you do drop your computer or notebook, have it professionally tested by a computer repair facility to uncover any hidden damage.

2 Electronic components do not like excessive heat or excessive cold. Unfortunately, computers generate a lot of heat. This is why they contain a fan to cool their internal components. Make sure that you place your computer so that the fan's input vents (usually found on the rear of the system unit) are unblocked so that air can flow inside. And don't leave computing devices in a car during very hot or cold weather, as components can be damaged by extreme temperatures.

3 Naturally, a fan drawing air into a computer also draws in dust and other particles, which can wreak havoc on your system. Therefore, keep the room in which your computer is located as clean as possible. Placing your computer in the workshop where you do woodworking and generate sawdust would obviously be a poor choice! Even in a clean room, the fan ducts on your computer can become packed with dust, so vacuum it periodically to keep a clear airflow into your computer.

4 Because food crumbs and liquid can damage keyboards and other computer components, consume food and beverages away from your computer to avoid food-related damage.

Power Surges

Power surges occur when electrical current is supplied in excess of normal voltage (120 volts in the United States). Old or faulty wiring, downed power lines, malfunctions at electric company substations, and lightning strikes can all cause power surges. **Surge protectors** are devices that protect your computer against power surges (see Figure 1). To use a surge protector, you simply plug your electrical devices into the outlets of the surge protector, which in turn plugs into the wall.

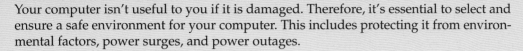

FIGURE 1
How Surge Protectors Work

During **minor** surges, the MOVs (MOV stands for metal-oxide varistor) bleed off excess current and feed it to the ground wire, where it harmlessly disappears. The MOVs can do this while still allowing normal current to pass through to the devices plugged into the surge protector. This is why it is critical to plug surge protectors into grounded power outlets.

Over time, the MOVs lose their ability to bleed off excess current, which is why you should replace your surge protector every 2 to 3 years.

During **major** surges that overwhelm the MOVs, the fuse blows, stopping all current from passing through to devices plugged into the surge protector. After a major surge, the surge protector will no longer function and must be replaced.

Surge protectors wear out over time (usually in less than five years), so buy a surge protector that includes indicator lights. Indicator lights illuminate when the surge protector is no longer functioning properly. Note that old surge protectors can still function as multiple-outlet power strips, delivering power to your equipment without protecting it. A power surge could ruin your computer and other devices if you don't protect them. At $20 to $40, a quality surge protector is an excellent investment.

It's important to protect *all* your electronic devices, not just computers, from surges. Printers and other computer peripherals all require protection. However, it can be inconvenient to use individual surge protectors on everything. A more practical method is to install a **whole-house surge protector**, shown in Figure 2. Whole-house surge protectors function like other surge protectors, but they protect *all* electrical devices in the house. Typically, you need an electrician to install a whole-house surge protector, which will cost $200 to $300 (installed).

Data lines (transmission media), such as the coaxial cable or phone wires that attach to your modem, also can carry surges. Installing a **data line surge suppressor** for each data line connected to your computer through another device (such as a modem) provides you with additional protection (see Figure 3).

A data line surge suppressor is

connected to the data line at a point before it reaches the modem or other device. In this way, it intercepts surges on the data line before they reach sensitive equipment.

Surge protectors won't necessarily guard against all surges. Lightning strikes can generate such high amounts of voltage that they can overwhelm a surge protector. As tedious as it sounds, unplugging computers and peripherals during an electrical storm is the only way to achieve absolute protection.

Power Outages

Like power surges, power outages can wreak havoc on a system. Mission-critical computers, such as Web servers, often are protected by **uninterruptible power supplies (UPSs)**, as shown in Figure 4. A UPS is a device that contains surge protection equipment and a large battery. When power is interrupted (such as during a blackout), the UPS continues to send power to the attached computer from its battery. Depending on the battery capacity, you have between about 20 minutes and 3 hours to save your work and shut down your computer properly.

FIGURE 2

A whole-house surge protector usually is installed at the breaker panel or near the electric meter. It protects all appliances in the home from electrical surges.

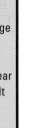

Surge protector

Image courtesy of American Power Conversion Corporation

FIGURE 3

APC, a large manufacturer of surge protection devices, makes a wide range of data line surge suppressors to accommodate almost any type of data line.

Image courtesy of American Power Conversion Corporation

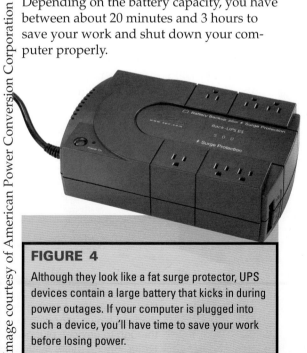

FIGURE 4

Although they look like a fat surge protector, UPS devices contain a large battery that kicks in during power outages. If your computer is plugged into such a device, you'll have time to save your work before losing power.

DETERRING THEFT

Because they are portable, notebooks are easy targets for thieves. Common sense dictates that you don't leave your notebook unattended or in places where it can be stolen easily (such as hotel rooms and coffee shops). Three additional approaches to deterring computer theft include alarming them, locking them down, or installing devices that alert you when they are stolen.

Alarms

To prevent your notebook from being stolen, you can attach a motion alarm to it, shown in Figure 5. When you leave your notebook, you use a small device called a key fob activator to activate the alarm. If your notebook is moved while the alarm is activated, it emits a wailing 85-decibel sound. The fact that the alarm is visible acts as an additional theft deterrent, just like a "beware of dog" sign in a front yard.

Locks and Surrounds

Chaining a notebook to your work surface can be an effective way to prevent theft. As shown in Figure 6, a special locking mechanism is attached to the notebook (some notebooks are even manufactured with locking ports), and a hardened steel cable is connected to the locking mechanism. The other end of the cable is looped around something large and heavy, such as a desk. The cable lock requires possessing a key or knowing the combination to free the notebook from its mooring. You should consider taking a cable lock with you when traveling to help deter theft in hotel rooms.

Many people associate computer theft only with notebooks or PDAs. But desktop computers are vulnerable to theft also, especially theft of internal components such as RAM. Cable locks are available that connect through special fasteners on the back of desktop computers, but components can still be stolen because these cables often don't prevent the system unit case from being opened. A more effective theft deterrent for desktops is a **surround** (or **cage**), shown in Figure 7. A surround is a metal box that encloses the system unit, making it impossible to remove the case while still allowing access to ports and devices such as CD players.

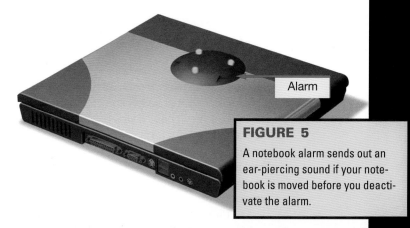

FIGURE 5

A notebook alarm sends out an ear-piercing sound if your notebook is moved before you deactivate the alarm.

FIGURE 6

Cable locks are an effective deterrent to theft. New models have combination locks that alleviate keeping track of your keys.

FIGURE 7

Computer surrounds deter theft by making access to the internal components of the computer difficult while still allowing access to ports and drives.

Computers That "Phone Home"

You've probably heard of LoJack, the theft-tracking device used in cars. Car owners install a LoJack transmitter somewhere in their vehicle. Then, if the vehicle is stolen, police activate the transmitter and use its signal to locate the car. Similar systems now exist for computers. Tracking software, such as Computrace Complete or Computrace LoJack for Laptops (**www.absolute.com**) and PC or Mac PhoneHome (**www.pcphonehome.com**), enables the computer it is installed on to alert authorities as to its location if it is stolen.

To have your computer help with its own recovery, you install the tracking software on your computer's hard drive. After you install the software, it contacts a server at the software manufacturer's Web site each time you connect to the Internet. If your computer is stolen, you notify the software manufacturer. The software manufacturer instructs your computer to transmit tracking information (such as an IP address) that will assist authorities in locating and retrieving the stolen computer.

The files and directories holding the software are not visible to thieves looking for such software. What if the thieves reformat the hard drive in an attempt to destroy all files on the computer? The tracking software is written in such a way that it detects a reformat and hides the software code in a safe place in memory or on the hard drive (some sectors of a hard drive are not rewritten during most formats). That way, it can reinstall itself after the reformatting is completed.

KEEPING HANDHELD DEVICES SAFE

PDAs and smart phones present their own unique hazards. Here are a couple of tips for keeping them secure.

Foiling Data Theft of Handheld Devices

Smart phones and PDAs can be vulnerable to unauthorized access if they are left unattended or are stolen. **Bomb software** features data and password protection for your handheld device in an attempt to combat this problem. If you have bomb software, a thief who steals your handheld device is forced to crack your password to gain access. When a thief launches a brute force attack (repetitive tries to guess a password) on your device, the software's bomb feature kicks in after a certain number of failed password attempts. The "bomb" erases all data contained on the device, thereby protecting your sensitive information. Good Mobile Defense, from Good Technology (**www.good.com**), is a popular example of bomb software.

Preventing Bluetooth Attacks

Bluetooth is a transmission medium for exchanging data wirelessly over short distances. Many smart phones and PDAs are Bluetooth-enabled. Although progress is being made, Bluetooth hardware and software still are riddled with security holes, especially on smart phones. If you have a Bluetooth-enabled device, you are susceptible to two severe types of mischief:

1 **Bluesnarfing:** Bluesnarfing involves exploiting a flaw in the Bluetooth access software for the purpose of accessing a Bluetooth device and stealing the information contained on it. Think how much valuable information is contained on your smart phone (names, contact information, and meeting notes) that might be valuable to a business competitor. Unfortunately, Bluesnarfing is relatively easy (and cheap) to do, as there is a lot of Bluesnarfing software available on the Internet.

2 **Bluebugging:** Although much more difficult and expensive to execute, Bluebugging presents much more serious dangers. Bluebugging involves a hacker actually taking over control of a Bluetooth-enabled device so that he or she can do some or all of the following:

- Make phone calls.
- Send, receive, or read SMS (Short Message Service) messages.
- Establish Internet connections.
- Write phonebook entries.
- Set call forwarding.

This is a real risk for Europeans, as Bluetooth and SMS are wildly popular there, but the rise of Bluetooth usage in the United States is making this a risk here as well. Many Europeans use their phones to make micropayments (small purchases from merchants that eventually appear on their cell phone bill) by a process known as reverse SMS. If a hacker bluebugs your phone, they could potentially send payments to fake accounts they control using reverse SMS.

So how can you protect yourself from Bluetooth attacks? Many newer devices with Bluetooth capability give you the option of making your device invisible to other Bluetooth devices. This does not affect your ability to use your devices paired to your Bluetooth device (such as a wireless headset for a phone). As vulnerabilities are discovered, smart phone and PDA manufacturers will issue software patches. You must ensure that you update the software in your phone (or PDA) just as you do for your computer operating system. Antivirus software also is beginning to appear for mobile devices, so you may wish to purchase this for your smart phone or PDA. For more information on securing your Bluetooth devices, go to **www.bluetooth.com**.

PROTECTING YOUR COMPUTER FROM UNAUTHORIZED ACCESS

To protect yourself even further, you may want to restrict access to the sensitive data on your computer. Both software and hardware solutions exist to restrict others from

accessing your computer, helping you keep its contents safe.

Password Protection and Access Privileges

Windows Vista has built-in password protection of files as well as the entire desktop. If your computer has been set up for multiple users with password protection, the Windows logon screen requires users to enter a password to gain access to the desktop. The computer can be set to default back to the Welcome screen after it is idle for a set period of time. This forces users to reenter a password to regain access to the computer. If someone attempts to log on to your computer without your password, that person won't be able to gain access. It is an especially good idea to use passwords on notebook computers or any computer that may be unattended for periods of time. Figure 8 shows the control panel screen that you use to set up a password on your user account.

There are two types of users in Windows Vista: administrators and standard users. Setting up a password on a user account prevents other standard users from being able to access that user's files. However, users with administrator privileges (perhaps your parents) could still see your files if you are a standard user. So be aware that your files may not be safe from all prying eyes!

Of course, password protection works only as well as your password does. Password cracking programs have become more sophisticated lately. In fact, some commonly available programs, such as John the Ripper, can test more than one million password combinations per second! Creating a secure password is

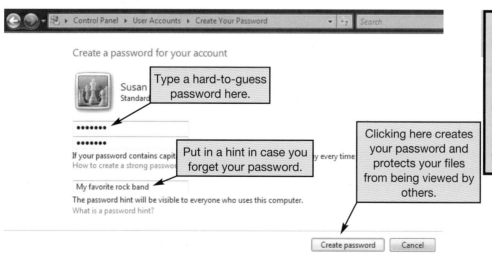

FIGURE 8

You should use this dialog box to assign a password to your user account in Windows Vista. This will provide additional security for your files by locking unauthorized users out of your account.

>Click Start, click Control Panel, and then click User Accounts.

ARE KLINGONESE PASSWORDS SAFE?

Many computer users are diehard science fiction fans. *Star Trek, Babylon 5,* and *Battlestar Galactica* have provided computer users with loads of planet names, alien races, alien vocabulary (Klingon words from the *Star Trek* series are very popular), and starship names to use as passwords. Unfortunately, hackers are on to this ploy. Recently developed hacking programs use dictionaries of "geek-speak" to attempt to break passwords. Although "Qapla" (Klingonese for "success" and also used as "good-bye") might seem like an unbreakable password, don't bet your data on it! You can still use these words if you incorporate multiple words into a password that also contains symbols and numbers.

- Use a different password for each system or Web site you need to access. This prevents access to every account you maintain, if one of your passwords is discovered.
- You should never tell anyone your password or write it down in a place where others might see it.
- You should change your password if you think someone may know it.
- Check the strength of your password by using the free password checker found on the Security at Home section of the Microsoft Web site (**www.microsoft.com**).

Figure 9 shows some possible passwords and explains why they make good or bad candidates.

Managing Your Passwords

Good security practices suggest that you have different passwords for different Web sites that you access and that you change your passwords frequently. The problem with well-constructed passwords is that they can be hard to remember. Fortunately, password management is now built into most browsers (or soon will be available). This takes the worry out of forgetting passwords because your browser does the remembering for you.

The Firefox browser from Mozilla (**www.mozilla.com**) makes it easy to keep

therefore more important than ever. To do so, follow the basic guidelines shown here:

- Your password should contain at least 14 characters and include numbers, symbols, and upper- and lowercase letters.
- Your password should not be a single word or any word found in the dictionary.
- Ideally, use a combination of several words with strategically placed uppercase characters.
- Your password should not be easily associated with you (such as your birth date, the name of your pet, or your nickname).

FIGURE 9
GOOD AND BAD PASSWORD CANDIDATES

GOOD PASSWORD	REASON
L8t2meGaNDalf351	Uses letters and numbers to come up with memorable phrase "Late to me" and adds it to a character name from *Lord of the Rings* plus a random number
IwaLR8384GdY	First initials of first line of Green Day song *I Walk a Lonely Road* plus a random number and an abbreviation for Green Day
P1zzA244WAter ShiPDowN	Easily remembered word with mix of alphanumeric characters and upper- and lowercase letters, your locker number at your gym, plus the title of a book that you like (with upper- and lowercase letters)
S0da&ICB3N&J3RRY	Mix of numbers, symbols, and letters. Stands for Soda and Ice Cream and the names of famous ice cream makers with the number 3 instead of the letter E

BAD PASSWORD	REASON
Jsmith	Combination of first initial and last name
4smithkids	Even though this has alphanumeric combination, it is too descriptive of a family
Brown5512	Last name and last four digits of phone number is easily decoded
123MainSt	Your street address is an easily decoded password

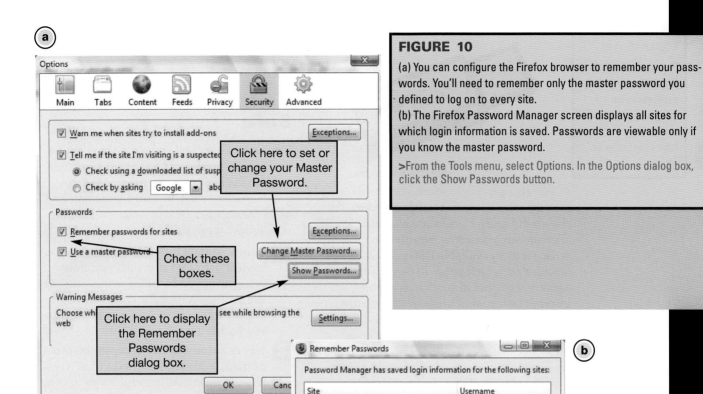

FIGURE 10
(a) You can configure the Firefox browser to remember your passwords. You'll need to remember only the master password you defined to log on to every site.
(b) The Firefox Password Manager screen displays all sites for which login information is saved. Passwords are viewable only if you know the master password.
>From the Tools menu, select Options. In the Options dialog box, click the Show Passwords button.

track of passwords. From the Tools menu, select Options, and then click the Security icon (the closed padlock) shown in Figure 10a. In the Passwords section, check *Remember passwords for sites* to have Firefox remember passwords when you log onto Web sites. Check *Use a master password*, click the Change Master Password button (which will say Set Master Password the first time you use it), and enter a well-designed, secure password. The next time you go to a Web site that requires a login, Firefox will display a dialog box prompting you to have Firefox remember the login name and password for this site. The next time you return to the site and select a login option, just enter the Master Password and the Firefox Password Manager fills in the login and password information for you.

You also can see a list of sites maintained by the Firefox Password Manager by clicking the Show Passwords button, which displays the Remember Passwords dialog box (Figure 10b). Passwords for each site are displayed after you click the Show Passwords button and enter the Master Password.

So, start using very secure passwords (following the guidelines previously explained) and let your browser relieve you of the problem of trying to remember them all!

Keep Prying Eyes from Your Web Surfing Habits

If you use shared computers in such public places as libraries, coffee shops, and college student unions, you should be concerned about a subsequent user of the computer spying on your surfing habits. You never know what nefarious tools have been installed by hackers on a public computer. And when you are surfing wirelessly with your notebook at a public hotspot, shouldn't you protect yourself from hackers trying to intercept or spy on your data? Wouldn't it be nice if protection tools for Web surfing could be carried in your pocket?

Stealth Ideas, Inc.

Portable privacy devices, such as the StealthSurfer III (**www.stealthsurfer.biz**), shown in Figure 11, now are available to alleviate such concerns. Simply plug the device into an available USB port on the machine on which you will be working. All sensitive Internet files, such as cookies, Internet history, and browser caches, are stored on the privacy device, not the computer you are using. These devices come preloaded with software, such as Anonymizer (**www.anonymizer.com**), which shields your IP address from prying eyes, making it difficult (if not impossible) for hackers to tell where you are surfing on the Internet. These privacy devices also have password management tools that store all of your logon information and encrypt it in the

event your privacy device falls into someone else's hands.

Keeping IM Sessions Safe

Virus attacks and other forms of malicious hacking are being perpetrated at an alarming rate via instant messenger (IM) programs, such as AOL Instant Messenger and MSN Messenger. To keep your IM sessions safe, follow these precautions:

1 **Allow contact only from users on your buddy list.** This prevents you from being annoyed by unknown parties. On the settings screen for your IM program (Figure 12a), select Allow only users on my Buddy List.

2 **Never automatically accept transfers of data.** Although file and video transfers are potentially useful for swapping files over IM (Figure 12b), they are a common way of receiving malicious files, which can then infect your computer with viruses. Better safe than sorry!

Whenever you have a choice, restrict your contacts to people on your buddy list. This makes it much tougher for scam artists and hackers to trick you.

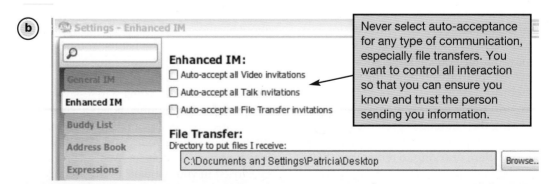

Never select auto-acceptance for any type of communication, especially file transfers. You want to control all interaction so that you can ensure you know and trust the person sending you information.

Keeping Windows Up to Date

Software patches to close security holes in Windows (or other operating systems) are issued periodically. To be sure you are protected from spreading threats, make sure these patches are installed on your computer. This can be an automatic process with Windows Vista (see Figure 13). From the Start menu in Windows, select Control Panel, and then click on the Windows Update icon to display the Windows Update window. Click the Change settings option to display the Choose how Windows can install updates dialog box shown in Figure 13. Pick the best option for your situation (the first two options are good for broadband connections; the third option is better for dial-up).

Biometric Authentication Devices

Biometric authentication devices are devices you can attach to your computer or portable computing device that read a unique personal characteristic, such as a fingerprint or the iris pattern in your eye, and convert that pattern to a digital code. When you use the device, your pattern is read and compared to the one stored on the computer. Only users having an exact fingerprint or iris pattern match are allowed to access the computer.

Because no two people have the same biometric characteristics (fingerprints and iris patterns are unique), these devices provide a high level of security. They also eliminate the human error that can occur in password protection. (You might forget your password, but you won't forget to bring your fingerprint to the computer!) Some newer Lenovo ThinkPad notebooks feature built-in fingerprint readers, and Figure 14a shows a mouse that includes a fingerprint reader. Another useful device is the APC Touch Biometric Pod Password Manager (shown in Figure 14b), which after it identifies you by your fingerprint, provides logon information to password-protected Web

sites you need to access. Other biometric devices include voice authentication and face pattern recognition systems, but these are usually too expensive for home use.

Reprinted with permission from Microsoft Corporation

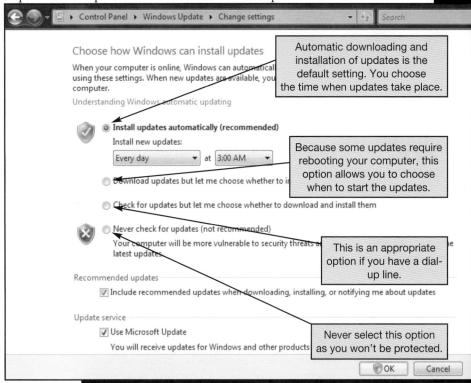

Automatic downloading and installation of updates is the default setting. You choose the time when updates take place.

Because some updates require rebooting your computer, this option allows you to choose when to start the updates.

This is an appropriate option if you have a dial-up line.

Never select this option as you won't be protected.

FIGURE 13

Turning on the Automatic Updates feature of Windows Vista is an essential part of protecting your computer.

>From the Windows Vista Control Panel, click the Windows Update icon, and then select Change settings.

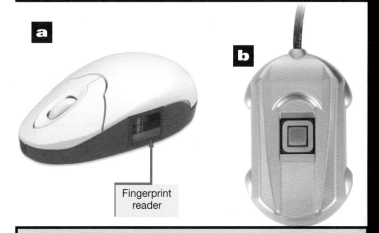

Fingerprint reader

FIGURE 14

(a) The SecuGen OptiMouse III is a two-button mouse with a scroll wheel that includes a digital fingerprint reader. (b) The APC Touch Biometric Pod Password Manager uses a fingerprint reader to recognize authorized users. The device stores all your logon names and passwords so that you don't have to keep track of them. Up to 20 users can use the same device, making it perfect for shared computers.

FIGURE 15
POPULAR PERSONAL FIREWALL SOFTWARE

FIREWALL	URL
Norton Internet Security	www.symantec.com
McAfee Internet Security Suite	www.mcafee.com
ZoneAlarm Pro	www.zonelabs.com
BlackICE PC Protection	http://blackice.iss.net

SOUND BYTE

Securing Wireless Networks

In this Sound Byte, you'll learn what "war drivers" are and why they could potentially be a threat to your wireless network. You'll also learn simple steps to take to secure your wireless network against intruders.

Firewalls

Unauthorized access often occurs when your computer is connected to the Internet. You can best prevent such cases of unauthorized access by using either hardware or software personal firewalls. Hardware firewalls are often built into a router. Many popular comprehensive security programs, such as Norton Internet Security and McAfee Internet Security Suite, include firewalls as part of their protection packages. Figure 15 lists popular security software suites and stand-alone firewall programs. Setting up either a hardware or software firewall should be an integral part of your security arsenal when connected to the Internet.

BACKING UP YOUR DATA

The data on your computer faces three major threats: unauthorized access, tampering, and destruction. A hacker can gain access to your computer and steal or alter your data. However, a more likely scenario

is that you will lose your data unintentionally. You may accidentally delete files; your hard drive may break down, resulting in complete data loss; a virus may destroy your original file; or a fire may destroy the room that houses your computer. Because many of these factors are beyond your control, you should have a strategy for backing up your files. Back-ups are especially important if you are running a small business; the back-up strategy for small businesses is very similar to the procedures recommended for individuals.

Making file **backups**—copies of files that you can use to replace the originals, if they are lost or damaged—is important. To be secure, backups must be stored away from your home or office. You wouldn't want a fire or a flood destroying the backups along with the original data. Removable storage media, such as external hard drives, DVDs, CDs, and flash drives, are popular choices for backing up files because they hold a lot of data and can be transported easily.

Two types of files need backups— program files and data files:

- **Program files** are files you use to install software and usually come on CDs or DVDs. If any programs came preinstalled in your computer, you may have received a CD or DVD that contains the original program. As long as you have the original media in a safe place, you shouldn't need to back up these files. If you have downloaded a program file from the Internet, however, you should make a copy of the program installation files on a removable storage device as a backup. If you didn't receive DVDs for installed programs with your computer, see the next section for suggested strategies for backing up your entire computer.

- **Data files** are files you create (such as spreadsheets, Word files, music files, and so on), as well as contact lists, address books, e-mail archives, and your Favorites list from your browser.

You should back up your data files frequently, depending on how much work you can afford to lose. You should always back up data files when you make changes to them, especially if those changes involve hours of work. It may not seem important to back up your history term paper file when you finish it, but do you really want to do all that work again if your computer crashes before you have a chance to turn in your paper?

FREE PROTECTION SOFTWARE

If you want to protect your computer but don't want to buy software, you're not out of luck. You can download plenty of programs for free off the Internet. Many companies offer free versions of their software that either expire after a certain time or offer fewer features than commercial versions. In many cases, these free versions are sufficient for home use. One site for downloading free software is **www.download.com**. This should be your first stop when looking for free software you can use to protect your computer.

PROTECTION FROM PHISHING SITES

Phishing attacks are attempts to lure you to Web sites that look legitimate (such as banking sites) and then trick you into revealing information that can be used in identity thefts. Since phishing has become such a problem, Internet Explorer 7 has a built-in phishing filter that examines Web sites to see if they are known or suspected fraudulent sites. Also, the major Internet security packages, such as McAfee and Norton (see Figure 16), now offer phishing protection tools. When you have the Norton Fraud Toolbar displayed in your browser, you are constantly informed about the legitimacy of the site. In fact, if you have an Internet security package installed, you can turn off the phishing filter in Internet Explorer to speed up the loading of pages in your browser.

Another way to protect yourself is to never use your credit card number when you shop online. Although it sounds impossible, credit card providers such as Citibank are offering services like "Virtual Account Numbers" for their customers. Before purchasing a product online, you visit an online site, where you are assigned a new virtual account number each time you visit. This number is tied to your real credit card account but can be used only once. That means that if the number is stolen, it's no good to thieves because they can't use the virtual account number because you've already used it once.

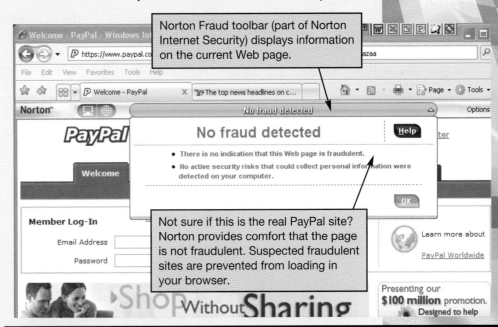

Norton Fraud toolbar (part of Norton Internet Security) displays information on the current Web page.

Not sure if this is the real PayPal site? Norton provides comfort that the page is not fraudulent. Suspected fraudulent sites are prevented from loading in your browser.

FIGURE 16

Not sure if you are on the PayPal Web site or a cleverly disguised phishing site? The Norton Fraud Toolbar reassures you that all is well.

To make backups easier, store all your data files in one folder on your hard drive. For example, on your hard drive you can create a folder called Documents. You can then create subfolders (such as History Homework, Music Files, and so on) within the Documents folder. If you store all your data files in one place, to back up your files, you simply copy the Documents folder and all of its subfolders onto an alternative storage medium.

Remembering to schedule backups is often the toughest part of file-safety procedures. Windows Vista includes a backup utility that provides a quick and easy way to schedule backups of files on a regular basis. Unfortunately, this utility lacks features that allow you to select only certain folders or directories for backup. A better choice is a free, open-source product called Cobian Backup (**www.educ.umu.se/~cobian/index.htm**), shown in Figure 17. Cobian allows you to easily configure backup tasks and select directories or individual files to back up on a regular basis.

Backup Software— Not Just for Data Files

Your operating system and software applications also need to be protected by backups. If you have the media to reinstall

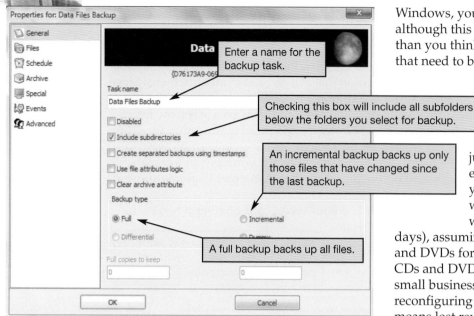

(a)

Enter a name for the backup task.

Checking this box will include all subfolders below the folders you select for backup.

An incremental backup backs up only those files that have changed since the last backup.

A full backup backs up all files.

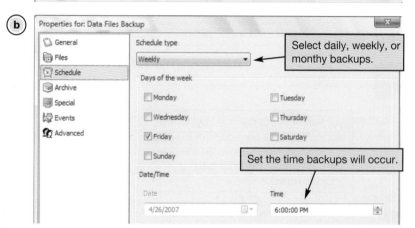

(b)

Select daily, weekly, or monthy backups.

Set the time backups will occur.

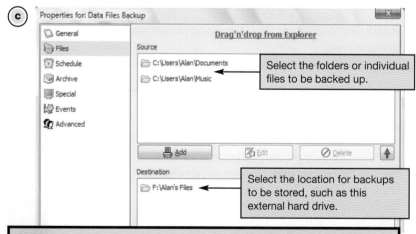

(c)

Select the folders or individual files to be backed up.

Select the location for backups to be stored, such as this external hard drive.

FIGURE 17

(a) The general tab in Cobian Backup lets you choose the type of backup and name it. (b) The schedule window makes it easy to schedule backups on a regular basis. (c) Dragging and dropping files from Windows Explorer makes it easy to define folders and files that should be backed up, as well as the destination for the backup files.

Windows, you should be in good shape—although this process may take more time than you think. Windows has many settings that need to be reinstated to get your machine functioning the way you had it set up. Working with these settings can be intimidating for the average user and just plain time consuming for experienced users. And all of your application programs would need to be reinstalled, which could take hours (or days), assuming you can locate all the CDs and DVDs for your application software CDs and DVDs. And if you are running a small business, the time you are losing reconfiguring the computers probably means lost revenue. For complete protection, you should use backup software, such as Norton Ghost (**www.norton.com**), which is designed to save an image of your entire system. Taking an image of your entire system and storing it on another hard drive provides you with the ultimate protection. With a backup of your entire hard drive, including your system image, you won't need to reinstall all of the program software from the original media. Instead, you just replace the broken hard drive with the backup hard drive (or copy the contents of the backup drive to a new drive), and you're up and running in no time!

Online Backups

A final backup solution is to store backups of your files online, which is often the most convenient solution for small businesses. For a fee, companies such as Iron Mountain (**http://onlinebackup.connected.com**) or IBackup (**www.ibackup.com**) can provide you with such online storage. If you store a backup of your entire system on the Internet, you don't need to buy an additional hard drive for backups. This method also takes the worry out of keeping your backups in a safe place because they're always stored in an area far away from your computer (such as on the backup company's server). However, if you'd like to store your backups online, make sure you have high-speed Internet access such as cable or DSL.

ADDITIONAL RESOURCES

Hackers, spammers, and advertisers constantly are developing new methods for circumventing the protection that security software provides. Although the manufacturers of such software constantly are updating and improving security, you should keep abreast of new techniques being employed that could threaten your privacy and security. *SC* magazine is a security magazine available in a free online version at **www.scmagazine.com**. Take a few minutes each month and scan the articles to make sure you have taken the appropriate protective measures on your computer to keep it safe and secure.

SOUND BYTE

Protecting Your Computer

In this Sound Byte, you'll learn how to use a variety of tools to protect your computer, including antivirus software and Windows utilities.

SHOULD YOU BACK UP YOUR FILES STORED ON THE SCHOOL NETWORK?

Most likely, if you're allowed to store files on your school's network, these files are backed up on a regular basis. However, you should check with your school's network administrators to determine how often they're backed up and how you would go about requesting files be restored from the backup media if they're damaged or deleted. But don't rely on these network backups to bail you out if your data files are lost or damaged. It may take days for the network administrators to get around to restoring your files. It is better to keep backups of your data files yourself (especially for homework and project files) so that you can immediately restore them. Buy a large-capacity flash drive and carry it with you!

8

Mobile Computing:

Keeping Your Data on Hand

From Chapter 8 of *Technology in Action, Complete*, Fifth Edition, Alan Evans, Kendall Martin, Mary Anne Poatsy. Copyright © 2009 by Pearson Education. Published by Prentice Hall. All rights reserved.

Mobile Computing:

Keeping Your Data on Hand

ACTIVE HELPDESK

- Using Portable Media Players
- Using PDAs

Using Mobile Computing Devices

Kendra wakes up at 5:00 A.M. to get an early start to what will be a long day. She's taking a business trip for her new job, and it's a long flight from Boston to Los Angeles (LA). She's packed her cell phone, her notebook (laptop), and her personal digital assistant (PDA), and she has updated the information for all her LA contacts. Despite her preparation, when she arrives at the airport, she finds her flight has been canceled. Trying not to get upset, she pulls out her PDA, accesses the Internet via a wireless Internet Service Provider, and rebooks a ticket on a competing airline while fellow passengers are racing off to the ticket counter. The airline ticket site was recently enhanced, so her booking information was automatically downloaded to her Microsoft Outlook files. With an e-mail to her business contacts in LA letting them know she'll be late, she smoothes the first wrinkle in her trip.

As Kendra waits for her new flight, she checks her work schedule on her PDA and e-mails a few clients. Because she'll be driving from the airport to the hotel on unfamiliar streets, she has purchased map software for her PDA that shows her the best route. She calls the rental car agency on her cell phone and tells them she'll be picking up the car later than planned, then checks out some LA restaurant reviews on the Internet. With an hour left before her plane takes off, she does some work on her notebook. She updates her expense report file, including the new flight information. Although canceled flights are never convenient, at least she's had a few hours to take care of some work before arriving in LA. But Kendra is getting tired of toting all three devices around. She wonders if she should consider getting a new smartphone (like her friend Jamal just bought), which might provide the same functionality as her current phone and her PDA. Or perhaps because she relies on e-mail while traveling, she is thinking about acquiring a BlackBerry (a PDA optimized for e-mail and that doubles as a cell phone). This would allow her to abandon her current cell phone and PDA.

As this scenario indicates, mobile devices can offer you a great deal of convenience and can increase your productivity, when you're away from the office. And going mobile is increasingly becoming the norm, as more people are buying cell phones and other mobile devices. In fact, the current number of subscribers to cell phone services in the United States exceeds the number of those using wired telephone service lines. With more than 200 million Americans currently owning cell phones, mobility is here to stay!

In this chapter, we discuss the advantages and disadvantages of going mobile; we also look at the range of mobile computing devices you can choose from, and discuss their components, features, and capabilities. Along the way, you'll learn how you can synchronize your mobile devices to make even better use of them. Whether you have already gone mobile or are still considering your options, this chapter will help you become a savvy consumer, taking full advantage of the world of mobile computing.

©Donna Day/Corbis

SOUND BYTES

- PDAs on the Road and at Home
- Connecting with Bluetooth
- Tablet and Notebook Tour

Mobile Computing: Is It Right for You?

Just 30 years ago, the idea of a powerful personal computer that could fit on a desktop was a dream. Today, you can carry computers around in your backpack, fit them in your pocket, and even incorporate them into your clothes. **Mobile computing devices**—portable electronic tools such as cell phones, portable media players, personal digital assistants (PDAs), and notebooks—are dramatically changing our day-to-day lives, allowing us to communicate with others, remain productive, and access a wide array of information no matter where we are.

Still, going mobile isn't for everyone. Although having instant access to your e-mail, schedule, and the Internet wherever you are during the day can be convenient and boost your productivity, there is a downside associated with mobile computing. Because mobile devices have been miniaturized, they're more expensive and less rugged than stationary desktop equipment. It's therefore important that you balance the advantages of going mobile with how well doing so fits your lifestyle.

How do I know whether mobile devices are right for me? Before you buy any mobile device, consider whether your needs match what mobile devices can offer. To do so, ask yourself these questions:

- **Do I need to communicate with others when I'm away from my home or office?** Whether it means talking on the phone or checking your e-mail, if you need to communicate no matter where you are, mobile devices may be right for you.

- **Do I need to access my electronic information when I'm away from my desk?** If you need to access and make changes to electronic information (such as an Outlook schedule or Excel report) when you're out and about, mobile devices such as PDAs and notebooks would be valuable tools. However, if it's as efficient for you to keep paper records when you're away from your computer and later enter that data into your computer, you may not need mobile devices.

- **Do I need to access the Internet when I'm away from my desk?** Mobile devices that are **Web-enabled**—that is, set up so that they can access the Internet through a wireless network—allow you to have constant access to the Internet wherever you are. Of course, you'll access the Internet at greater speeds and for less cost when you're at home or in the office. However, if you need quickly changing information when you're away from your desk, Web-enabled mobile devices may be right for you.

- **Are the convenience and productivity mobile devices offer important to me?** Mobile devices can provide you with a great deal of convenience and help you to be more productive. For example, a nursing student would have an easier time performing a diagnostic interview with a patient if the reference codes she needed were available in her PDA rather than in a huge stack of books. Likewise, students who take online classes with products such as Blackboard and WebCT can download their course and carry it on a PDA or notebook so that they can work on their assignments anywhere, with or without Internet access.

- **Is the information I need to carry already in an electronic format?** Do you currently use *personal information management (PIM)* software such as Microsoft Outlook to store your daily schedule and contact list? Or are your schedule and contact list currently in paper form? Converting information to an electronic format and learning how to use mobile devices are hidden costs of going mobile.

You also need to consider your needs when determining the type of device to select. If you are a salesperson who constantly demonstrates multimedia products to clients, perhaps you need a high-powered multimedia notebook such as the Dell XPS MS2010 see (Figure 1a)—despite its hefty price tag and weight. Or maybe you just need to keep in touch with your friends while listening to music and watching videos, so the Apple iPhone might suffice (see Figure 1b). Consider the activities you'll be pursuing while mobile before selecting a device.

Dell, Inc.

Apple/Splash News/NewsCom

FIGURE 1

The portable device that is right for you will depend on your needs. (a) With a 20.1-inch monitor, eight speakers, and a detachable wireless keyboard, the Dell XPS MS2010 is a portable computer that easily has the power of a multimedia desktop system. It also weighs 18 lbs. and costs over $3,000. (b) The Apple iPhone combines a cell phone with a media player and Internet access device, and provides an easy-to-use touch-screen interface. The revolutionary multi-point touch screen can respond to gestures with two fingers (such as spreading your fingers for a zoom command).

MOBILE DEVICE LIMITATIONS

What are the limitations of mobile devices? In addition to the questions previously discussed, it's important that you consider whether your needs match the limitations of mobile devices:

- Battery life limits the usefulness of some mobile devices.

- The screen is small on most devices (making the Internet and Microsoft Office application experiences very different).

- The speed of Internet connection available to mobile devices, though increasing, is still low compared to wired high-speed Internet access available in your home or office.

The benefits of Internet connectivity also are dependent on the wireless Internet coverage in your area. For example, if you travel in rural areas, it may be difficult to take advantage of wireless Internet connectivity. So if you are considering wireless Internet access, make sure you check the areas of coverage for the providers you are considering.

As a student, you should consider how much of your campus is covered by wireless connectivity. Is your residence hall covered? your classrooms? the library? Some schools create "wireless clouds" that enable you to be covered no matter where you are on campus. Other schools offer little coverage, making wireless connectivity to the Internet more difficult.

Finally, you must decide whether the extra cost of going mobile is worth the value and convenience. As mentioned earlier, mobile computing devices are more expensive and less rugged than desktop systems. Vibration, falls, dust, and liquids can all destroy your notebook, PDA, or cell phone. If the environment you live in or travel through is dusty or bumpy, for example, you should be prepared to spend money on equipment designed for rugged conditions, on additional warranty coverage, or on repair and replacement costs. Finally, desktop systems always boast more expandability and better performance for the same cost when compared with mobile computers.

So, is mobile computing right for me? Figure 2 presents a checklist of the factors you need to consider when deciding whether to go mobile. Do your needs to communicate and access electronic information and the Internet when you're away from your desk make mobile devices a good investment?

Mobile Computing Devices

If you do decide to go mobile, there is a wide range of mobile computing devices on the market today:

- *Paging devices* provide you with limited communication capabilities but are inexpensive options if you want some of the features of mobile computing.

FIGURE 2 **Are Mobile Devices Right for You?**

Consideration	Yes	No
I need to be able to communicate with others when I'm away from my desk.		
I need to access my electronic information wherever I am.		
I need to access the Internet when I'm away from my desk.		
The added convenience and productivity of mobile devices are important to me.		
The information I need to carry with me is already in an electronic format.		
My needs match the limitations of devices (such as short battery life, small display screen on some devices, and slower Internet connection speeds).		
Most of my living and travel locations are covered by wireless Internet access.		
It is worth the added expense for me to go mobile.		

- *Cellular phones* feature traditional phone services such as call waiting and voice mail. Many now come with calendars, contact databases, text messaging, e-mail, GPS, and Internet browsing capabilities.
- *Portable media players (PMPs)* allow you to carry music, video, and other digital files.
- *Personal digital assistants (PDAs)* are handheld devices that allow you to carry much of the same digital information as desktop systems or provide specific solutions for Web browsing or reading e-books.

- *Smartphones* are a result of the **convergence** (or combination of features) of various portable devices such as PMPs, PDAs, and cellular phones. These devices attempt to provide a single solution for your portable computing needs.
- *Tablet PCs* are larger and more powerful than PDAs and incorporate specialized handwriting-recognition software.
- *Notebook computers* are expensive and powerful tools for carrying electronic information.

Figure 3 lists the main features of these mobile devices. In the next sections, we look at each of these devices in detail.

BITS AND BYTES

Does Anyone Still Use Pagers?

People who need to be reachable but want an inexpensive and lightweight device are the primary market for pagers. Many medical professionals and volunteer firefighters still use pagers. A paging device (or a pager) is a small wireless device that allows you to receive and sometimes send numeric (and sometimes text) messages on a small display screen. Some industries still use pagers to contact key staff on call, such as doctors or critical computer technicians.

Numeric pagers display only numbers on their screens, telling you that you have received a page and providing you with the number you should call. Alphanumeric pagers are much like numeric pagers, but they also can display text messages. More useful are two-way pagers, which support both receiving and sending text messages. Given the cost of the pager and a connectivity plan, cell phones with text messaging make more sense for most users.

Cellular Phones

Cellular phones (or **cell phones**) have evolved from their early days as large, clunky, boxlike devices to become compact, full-featured communication and information storage devices. Cell phones offer all of the features available on a traditional telephone system, including auto-redial, call timers, and voice-mail capabilities. Some cell phones also feature voice-activated dialing, which is important for hands-free operation. In addition, cell phones can offer Internet access, text messaging, personal information management (PIM) features, voice recording, and digital image and video capture.

FIGURE 3 — Mobile Devices: Price, Size, Weight, and Capabilities

Device	Relative Price	Approximate Size	Approximate Weight	Standard Capabilities
Paging Device	$ (Includes cost for the pager and a monthly plan)	2″ × 2″ × 0.5″	0.2 lbs.	Provides numeric or text messaging to and from the device
Cell Phone	$$ (Includes cost for the phone, a monthly plan, and Internet access)	5″ × 2″ × 0.5″	0.25 lbs.	Provides voice, e-mail, limited access to application software, and Internet connectivity
PMP	$$–$$$	3″ × 2″ × 0.5″	0.25 lbs. or more	Provides storage of digital music, video, and other digital files
PDA	$$–$$$	5″ × 3″ × 1″	0.5 lbs.	Provides PIM capabilities, access to application software, and access to the Internet
Smartphone	$$-$$$	4.5″ × 2″ × .75″	.25 lbs	Provides a combination of features offered on cell phones, PMPs, and PDAs
Tablet PC	$$$$$	10″ × 8″ × 1″	3 lbs.	Provides PIM capabilities, access to application software, access to the Internet, and special handwriting- and speech-recognition capabilities
Notebook	$$$$–$$$$$	10″ × 13″ × 2″	5 to 8 lbs.	Provides all the capabilities of a desktop computer while also being portable

CELL PHONE HARDWARE

Is a cell phone considered a computer? Cell phones are so advanced that they have many of the same components as a computer: a processor (central processing unit, or CPU), memory, and input and output devices, as shown in Figure 4. A cell phone also requires software and has its own operating system (OS). Popular operating systems for full-featured cell phones are the **Symbian OS** and **Windows Mobile**. Because many cell phones now handle e-mail, images, and even video, complex operating systems such as Symbian OS and Windows Mobile are required to translate the user's commands into instructions for the processor. Although the Symbian OS is still popular with many cell phones, the majority of smartphones today are using the Windows Mobile operating system.

What does the processor inside a cell phone do? Although the processor inside a cell phone is obviously not as fast or as high powered as a processor in a desktop computer, it is still responsible for a great number of tasks. The processor coordinates

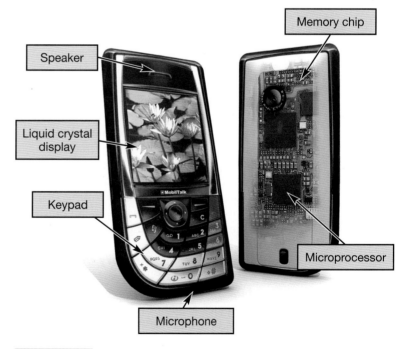

FIGURE 4

Inside your cell phone, you'll find some familiar components, including a microprocessor (CPU), a memory chip, input devices such as a microphone and a keypad, and output devices such as a display screen and a speaker.

FIGURE 5

OpenMoko, Inc./BlackPhoneFront

can store data even when the power is turned off. ROM is nonvolatile, or permanent, memory. This means that when you turn off your cell phone, the data that is stored in ROM (including the operating system) does not get lost.

Other phone data, such as ring tones, are stored in separate internal memory chips. Full-featured phones have as much as 20 megabytes (MB) of memory (smartphones generally have more) that you can use to store contact data, ring tones, images, songs, video, and even small software applications such as currency converters or a world clock.

What input and output devices do cell phones use? The input devices for a cell phone are primarily the microphone, which converts your voice into electronic signals that the processor can understand, and a keypad, which is used for numeric or text entry. Some phones, such as the Kyocera Strobe Phone (Figure 6a), feature a hidden QWERTY keyboard to make sending e-mail or text messages more efficient. Other phones feature touch-sensitive screens that allow you to input data. In addition, more and more cell phones include digital cameras. The Nokia N73 (Figure 6b) offers a high-quality 3.2 megapixel camera that can input photographs or capture live video to your phone. Picture or video messaging is quite popular now with cell phone users as a way of exchanging graphical information. Phone users can transmit photos and video files via e-mail, post the files to Web sites (such as **www.myspace.com**), or send them directly to other smartphones. The Helio Drift from Samsung (Figure 6c) is a compact phone that has a software module specifically designed to provide users with all of their MySpace functionality right from the phone.

Cell phone output devices include a speaker and a liquid crystal display (LCD). Higher-end models include full-color, high-resolution plasma displays. Such displays are becoming increasingly popular as more people are using their cell phones to send and receive the digital images included in multimedia text messages and e-mail, and even watch TV. Cell phone and cable providers are now teaming up to deliver broadcast TV programs directly to cell phones through services such as Verizon V Cast and Sprint TV live. Cell phones such as the LG VX9400 (see Figure 7) are opti-

sending all of the data between the other electronic components inside the phone. It also runs the cell phone's operating system, which provides a user interface so that you can change phone settings, store information, play games, and so on.

But each cell phone manufacturer makes its own tweaks to an operating system and designs its own user interface. This can make switching phones daunting, as you have to learn how to use a different set of commands and icons. To combat this challenge, a group of coders formed an open-source project to develop the first free phone operating system. The goal for the OpenMoko operating system (see Figure 5) is to provide a consistent operating system and interface that users can install on compatible phones when they upgrade to avoid re-learning tasks.

What does the memory chip inside a cell phone do? The operating system and the information you save into your phone (such as phone numbers and addresses) need to be stored in memory. The operating system is stored in read-only memory (ROM) because the phone would be useless without that key piece of software. As you learned earlier in this text, there are two kinds of memory used in computers: volatile memory, which requires power to save data, and nonvolatile memory, which

Mobile Computing: Keeping Your Data on Hand

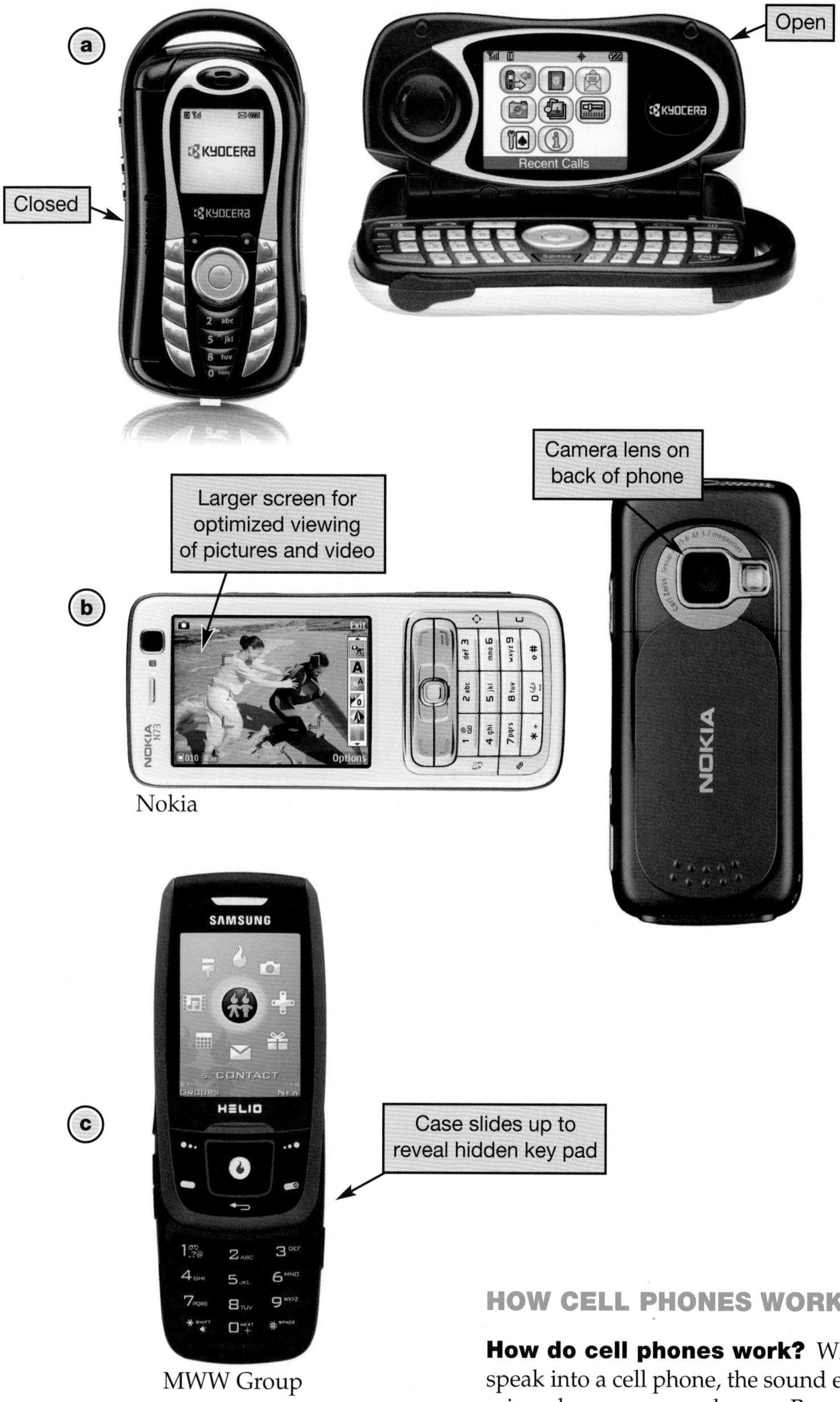
a
Closed
Open
KYOCERA
Recent Calls
b
Larger screen for optimized viewing of pictures and video
Camera lens on back of phone
NOKIA
Nokia
c
SAMSUNG
HELIO
Case slides up to reveal hidden key pad
MWW Group

FIGURE 6

(a) The Kyocera Strobe Phone includes a built-in QWERTY keyboard. (b) The Nokia N73 can input both still photographs and video to your phone. With an added memory card, you can even watch movies. (c) The Helio Drift from Samsung has a small format but delivers the full features of MySpace on the small screen. Why wait to get to a computer when you can update your page on the go!

mized for TV reception and viewing. Streaming video down to your cell phone used to be the only option, but with Verizon V Cast, programs are actually broadcast on digital channels and received in real time on your cell phone.

HOW CELL PHONES WORK

How do cell phones work? When you speak into a cell phone, the sound enters the microphone as a sound wave. Because analog sound waves need to be digitized (that is, converted into a sequence of 1s and 0s that the cell phone's processor can understand), an **analog-to-digital converter chip** converts your voice's sound waves into digital signals. Next, the digital data must be compressed, or squeezed, into the smallest possible space so

FIGURE 7

With a swiveling screen and extendable antenna, the LG VX9400 is a phone first, but a TV second!

Reuters/Steve Marcus/Landov LLC

that it will transmit more quickly to another phone. The processor cannot perform the mathematical operations required at this stage quickly enough, so a specialized chip, called the **digital signal processor**, is included in a cell phone to handle the compression work.

Finally, the digital data is transmitted as a radio wave through the cellular network to the destination phone.

When you receive an incoming call, the digital signal processor decompresses the incoming message. An amplifier boosts the signal to make it loud enough, and it is then passed on to the speaker, from which you hear the sound.

What's "cellular" about a cell phone? A set of connected "cells" makes up a cellular network. Each cell is a geographic area centered on a **base transceiver station**, which is a large communications tower with antennas, amplifiers, and receivers/transmitters. When you place a call on a cell phone, a base station picks up

the request for service. The station then passes the request to a central location, called a **mobile switching center**. (The reverse process occurs when you receive an incoming call on a cell phone.) A telecommunications company builds its network by constructing a series of cells that overlap, in an attempt to guarantee that its cell phone customers have coverage no matter where they are.

As you move during your phone call, the mobile switching center monitors the strength of the signal between your cell phone and the closest base station. When the signal is no longer strong enough between your cell phone and the base station, the mobile switching center orders the next base station to take charge of your call. When your cell phone "drops out," it sometimes does so because the distance between base stations was too great to provide an adequate signal.

CELL PHONE FEATURES: TEXT MESSAGING

What is text messaging? Short Message Service (SMS), often just called text messaging, is a technology that allows you to send short text messages (up to 160 characters) over mobile networks. To send SMS messages from your cell phone, you simply use the numeric keypad or a presaved template and type your message. You can send SMS messages to other mobile devices (such as cell phones or pagers) or to any e-mail address. You also can use SMS to send short text messages from your home computer to mobile devices, such as your friend's cell phone.

How does SMS work? SMS uses the cell phone network to transmit messages. When you send an SMS message, an SMS calling center receives the message and delivers it to the appropriate mobile device using something called "store-and-forward" technology. This technology allows users to send SMS messages to any other SMS device in the world.

Many SMS fans like text messaging because it can be cheaper than a phone call and it allows the receivers to read messages when it is convenient for them. In fact, in some countries, such as Japan, text messaging is more popular than voice messaging. However, entering text using your cell phone keypad can be time-consuming and

BITS AND BYTES

Are Cell Phones Bad for Your Health?

Cell phones work by sending electromagnetic waves into the air from an antenna. Depending on the phone's design—that is, whether there is a shield between the antenna and the user's head—up to 60 percent of the radiation emitted penetrates the area around the head. The amount of radiation a phone puts out that can be absorbed by the body is known as its Specific Absorption Rate (SAR). The Federal Communications Commission (FCC) limit for public exposure to cell phones is an SAR level of 1.6 watts per kilogram. So if you're concerned about the possible effects of radiation, buy a phone with as low an SAR as possible.

Still, it's not yet clear whether there are long-term health consequences of using cell phones because of the electromagnetic waves they emit. What is clear, however, is that using a cell phone when driving is dangerous. Studies show that motorists are four to nine times more likely to crash when talking on a cell phone while driving, a risk factor similar to the effects of driving while intoxicated. In many states, hands-free cell phone use is mandatory. For more information on laws in your state as well as links to sites with accident data, visit the Governors Highway Safety Association (GHSA) Web site (**www.ghsa.org**).

hard on your thumbs. Frequent SMS users save typing time by using a number of abbreviations, some of which are shown in Figure 8.

Besides sending messages to my friends, what else can I do with SMS? As SMS is becoming more popular worldwide, many services are becoming available that take advantage of SMS messaging to provide you with information. In some instances, you may be able to use SMS services instead of more expensive Internet services. Figure 9 provides a list of SMS services that you might find useful—and all of them are available at no charge! If you are used to sending SMS messages to your friend's cell phone numbers, some companies have SMS codes (or aliases) that take the place of a cell phone number for providing services.

Can I send and receive multimedia files over a cell phone? SMS technology allows you to send only text messages. However, an extension of SMS called **Multimedia Message Service (MMS)** allows you to send messages that include text, sound, images, and video clips to other phones or e-mail addresses. MMS messages actually arrive as a series of messages; you view the text, then the image, and then the sound, and so on. You can then choose to save just one part of the message (such as the image), all of it, or none of it. MMS users can subscribe to financial, sports, and weather services that will "push" information to them, sending it automatically to their phones in MMS format.

FIGURE 8 Popular Text Messaging Abbreviations

AFAIK	As far as I know
B4N	Bye for now
BRB	Be right back
CUL	See you later
FBM	Fine by me
F2T	Free to talk
G2G	Got to go
HRU	How are you?
IDK	I don't know
JAS	Just a sec
LOL	Laughing out loud
QPSA	¿Qué pasa?
T+	Think positive
TTYL	Talk to you later
WUWH	Wish you were here
YBS	You'll be sorry

CELL PHONE INTERNET CONNECTIVITY

How do I get Internet service for my phone? Just as you pay an Internet service provider (ISP) for Internet access for your desktop or notebook computer, connecting your cell phone to the Internet requires that you have a **wireless Internet service provider** (or **wireless ISP**). Phone companies that provide cell phone calling plans

FIGURE 9 Free Text Messaging Services

SMS Code	Service Name	Web Site	Description
46645	Google SMS	**www.google.com/sms**	Obtain information such as addresses, phone numbers, driving directions, sports scores, and movie listings from the Google search engine
6107267837	Smarter SMS	**www.smarter.com/sms**	Send product part number to find out which companies offer the product for the lowest price
44636	4INFO	**www.4info.net**	Similar to Google SMS but also handles flight information and horoscopes
8762	Upoc	**www.upoc.com**	Social network that is SMS searchable (after registering on the Web site)
3109043113	411sms	**www.411sms.com**	Offers many services, including address and phone listings, turn-by-turn directions, movie show times, stock quotes, hotspot locations, dictionary definitions, horoscopes, and foreign language translations

(such as T-Mobile, Verizon, and AT&T) usually double as wireless ISPs. Internet connectivity plans, and often text messaging plans, are usually known as **data plans**. Data charges are separate from cell phone calling charges and are provided at rates different from voice calls. You should assess your data needs and select a plan that provides an adequate amount of data usage.

At what speed can my phone connect to the Internet? As noted earlier, accessing the Internet on a mobile device comes with limitations. First, the connection often is slower than what you experience at your home. Although broadband speeds of 4,300 kilobits per second (Kbps) are achievable at home, your cell phone probably will connect at a much lower speed, which usually won't exceed 200 to 300 Kbps. This is a vast improvement over top speeds achieved just a few years ago, however, which maxed out at only 15 Kbps!

Providers have introduced a lot of new phones that support data transfer technologies based on the EDGE (short for Enhanced Data Rate for Global Evolution) and EVDO (Evolution Data Optimized) standards. EDGE and EVDO are the standards that have brought mobile devices much faster data transfer, up to 700 Kbps (or more) under ideal conditions. Using phones that support EDGE or EVDO and a phone plan that allows data transfer, both uploading information (such as e-mail messages that include photos) and downloading information (such as from a company intranet or the Internet) can take place much more quickly. These technologies are quickly replacing WiFi for Internet connectivity on mobile devices because they are more reliable and less susceptible to interference. And you don't have to hunt for a WiFi hot spot because these technologies are used to blanket major urban areas with connectivity.

What is the Internet like on a phone? Because cell phones have a very limited amount of screen space (compared to desktop computers), it is difficult to display Web pages on them without a great deal of horizontal scrolling to view content. This is because most Web sites are designed for viewing on desktop monitors, which have much wider pixel widths than mobile screens. To enhance your Internet browsing experience on mobile devices, special **microbrowser** software runs on your cell phone. Microbrowser software provides a Web browser, which is optimized to display Web content effectively on the smaller screen. Popular versions of microbrowser software include Internet Explorer Mobile (included with the Windows Mobile OS) and Opera Mobile. Opera Mobile (Figure 10) uses special Small Screen Rendering technology to reformat the Web images to fit on your cell phone screen, eliminating the need for horizontal scrolling. Although not as convenient as browsing on a desktop computer, microbrowsers allow you to experience the Web in a way that is very similar to your home computer experience (such as purchasing new ring tones or games for your phone, locating news headlines, or finding stock prices). For the best Web experience, consider a PDA or smartphone, which tend to feature larger screens than regular cell phones.

More commonly, Web sites are being created with content specifically designed for wireless devices. This specially designed content, which is text-based and contains no graphics, is written in a format called **Wireless Markup Language (WML)**. Content is designed so that it fits the tiny display screens of handheld mobile devices.

Can I keep my e-mail up to date using my cell phone? A popular feature of cell phones with Internet access is checking e-mail. BlackBerry handhelds were the original devices that were optimized to check e-mail and used to be the e-mail devices of choice. However, Windows Mobile now delivers a solid e-mail experience on a cell phone (and it syncs with your Outlook e-mail on your computer), so while BlackBerrys are still an excellent option, they aren't the only option. If checking and sending e-mail while on the go is mission critical for you, check out devices with larger displays and integrated keyboards that make it easier to manage your e-mail (which tend to be smartphones or PDAs). Most portable e-mail devices now feature special "push" technology (pioneered by BlackBerry) to automatically deliver your e-mail to your phone so that your e-mail finds you whether or not you're thinking about it.

Reprinted by permission of Opera

FIGURE 10

Microbrowser software helps you access the Internet from your cell phone or PDA.

Can I get a virus on my cell phone? Although viruses can already target cell phones, manufacturers and software engineers are bracing themselves for a tidal wave of viruses targeted to cell phones. With half of users reporting they send confidential e-mails by using their cell phones and one-third of users indicating they access bank account or credit card information, cell phones are the next most likely realm of attack by cybercriminals. The potential of cell phone viruses ranges from the mildly annoying (certain features of your phone stop working) to the expensive (your phone is used without your knowledge to make expensive calls).

How can you prevent cell phone viruses? Symantec, McAfee, and F-Secure are the leading companies currently providing antivirus software for mobile devices. Products are designed for specific phone operating systems such as Symantec Mobile Security for Symbian, which is designed for phones running the Symbian OS. While viruses plaguing cell phones have not yet reached the volume of viruses attacking PC operating systems, with the proliferation of mobile devices it is expected that cell phone virus attacks will increase. If there is not an antivirus program available for your phone's operating system, the best precautions are common sense ones. Don't download ring tones, games, or other software from unfamiliar Web sites, and check the phone manufacturer's Web site frequently to see whether your phone needs any software upgrades that could potentially patch security holes.

Portable Media Players

Portable media players have taken the electronics market by storm! Originally, these devices were known as **MP3 players** and were named after the MP3 format used for efficiently storing music as digital files (or a series of bits). **Portable media players (PMPs)** are small portable devices (such as an iPod) that enable you to carry your MP3 files around with you. But digital media isn't limited to music. Digital files (using special data formats such as AVI or MPEG-4) can hold video, audio, or images. Therefore, many companies are now manufacturing PMPs that handle video and still images, as well as music files. Many smart-

phones are capable of storing and playing media files, but for the best experience, a dedicated media player is often the optimal choice as they tend to offer more features and storage.

Depending on the player, you can carry several hours of music or video, or possibly your entire CD collection in an incredibly small device. For example, the Apple iPod (with 80 GB hard drive) is 4.1 inches by 2.4 inches (and only .55 inches thick), yet it can hold up to 20,000 songs, 25,000 images, or 100 hours of video. If you just need an MP3 player, the most compact players are slightly larger than a flash drive (although they hold far less music than the iPod). Figure 11 shows several popular models of PMPs, all of which connect to computers via USB 2.0 ports.

Are all music files MP3 files? The letters at the end of a filename (the file extension) indicate how the data in the file is organized. MP3 is the name of just one type of file format used to store digital music, but many others, such as AAC and WMA, exist. There are also many video formats, such as DivX, MPEG-4 (which usually has an *.mp4* extension), WMV, and XviD. All file formats compete on sound and video quality and compression, which relates to how small the file can be and still provide high-quality playback. If you buy a song from the iTunes Music Store, for example, you receive an .aac

FIGURE 11 **Popular Portable Media Players and Their Characteristics**

	Media Capacity	Built-In Flash Memory	Hard Disk Drive Capacity	Connection to Computer	Other Features
Creative Labs Digital MP3 Zen Nano Plus	Up to 500 songs	512 MB to 1 GB	None	USB 2.0 port	Built-in FM radio, voice recorder, and four-band equalizer
Oregon Scientific MP121	Up to 32 hours of music	512 MB	None	USB 2.0 port	Waterproof to 3 feet, built-in pedometer, built-in FM radio, and equalizer
Apple iPod Nano	Up to 2,000 songs or 25,000 images	2 GB to 8 GB	None	USB 2.0 port	Weighs only 1.5 ounces; flash memory provides for skip-free playback
Apple iPod	Up to 20,000 songs, 25,000 images, or 100 hours of video	None	30 GB to 80 GB	USB 2.0 port	Has calendar feature that syncs with Outlook; can serve as a small, portable hard drive
Zen Vision W	Up to 15,000 songs or 240 hours of movies	None	30 GB to 60 GB	USB 2.0 port	Includes 4.3"-wide screen display, integrated FM radio and a voice recorder; syncs with Outlook

a) Creative Labs/Creative Zen Vision; b) Reprinted by permission of Oregon Scientific/MP121; c) Apple Computer, Inc.; d) Photo courtesy of Apple Computers/Apple iPod; e) Creative Labs, Inc.

format file. AAC files can be played only on iPods but can be converted to the more widely seen MP3 or Windows Media Audio (WMA) formats. WMA files can be played on a wide variety of MP3 players. Most PMPs that support video playback can play a wide range of video formats.

PMP HARDWARE

How do I know how much digital media a PMP can hold? The number of songs or hours of video a portable media player can hold obviously depends on how much storage space it has. Most MP3 players use built-in **flash memory**, a type of non-volatile memory, to store files. Most PMPs that support video use a hard disk drive and can store a much larger amount of music and video. Less expensive PMPs use flash memory (ranging from 1 GB to 8 GB), whereas more expensive models use a built-in hard drive, which provides up to 80 GB of storage. Some of the PMPs that use flash memory allow you to add storage capacity by purchasing removable flash memory cards.

Another factor that determines how much music a player can hold is the quality of the MP3 music files. The size of an MP3 file depends on the digital sampling of the song. The **sampling rate** is the number of times per second the music is measured and converted to a digital value. Sampling rates are measured in kilobits per second (Kbps). The same song could be sampled at 192

Kbps or 64 Kbps. The size of the song file will be three times larger if it is sampled at 192 Kbps instead of the lower sampling rate of 64 Kbps. The higher the sampling rate, the better quality the sound, but the larger the file size.

If you are ripping, or converting, a song from a CD into a digital MP3 file, you can select the sampling rate yourself. You decide by considering what quality sound you want as well as how many songs you want to fit onto your MP3 player. For example, if your player has 1GB of storage and you have ripped songs at 192 Kbps, you can fit about 694 minutes of music onto the player. The same 1 GB could store 2,083 minutes of music if it were sampled at 64 Kbps. Whenever you are near your computer, you can connect your player and download a different set of songs, but you always are limited by the amount of storage your player has.

PMP FLASH MEMORY AND FILE TRANSFER

What if I want to store more music or video than what the memory on my PMP allows? As noted earlier, some PMPs allow you to add memory by inserting removable flash memory cards. Flash memory cards are noiseless and very light, use very little power, and slide into a special slot in the player. If you've ever played a video game on PlayStation or Nintendo and saved your progress to a memory card, you have used flash memory. Because flash memory is nonvolatile, when you store data on a flash memory card, you won't lose it when you turn off the player. In addition, flash memory can be erased and rewritten with new data.

What types of flash memory cards do PMPs use? Several different types of flash cards are used with different PMP models, as shown in Figure 12. One popular type is CompactFlash cards. These are about the size of a matchbook and can hold between 4 GB and 16 GB of data. They are very durable, so the data you store on them is very safe. Multimedia cards and SmartMedia cards are about the same size as CompactFlash cards but are thinner and less rugged. A newer type of memory card called Secure Digital is faster and offers encryption capabilities so that your data is secure even if you lose the card.

Courtesy of Sandisk

SanDisk Corporation

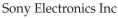
Sony Electronics Inc

PMP devices by Sony use a special format of flash memory called the Memory Stick. These tiny rectangular "sticks"—measuring just 2 inches by less than 1 inch and weighing a fraction of an ounce—are currently used only in Sony devices. Particular models of PMPs can support only certain types of flash cards, so check your manual to be sure you buy compatible memory cards.

How do I transfer media files to my portable media player? All portable media players come with software that enables you to transfer your audio and video files from your computer onto the player. As noted earlier, players that hold thousands of songs and hours of video use internal hard drives to store music. For example, devices such as Apple iPods can hold gigabytes of data. To move large volumes of data between your computer and your PMP, you want a high-speed port. Most PMPs use a USB 2.0 port, but some players may use FireWire ports, which provide comparable throughput. Using a USB 2.0 port, you can transfer two dozen MP3 files to the iPod in less than 10 seconds.

ACTIVE HELPDESK
Using Portable Media Players

In this Active Helpdesk call, you'll play the role of a helpdesk staffer, fielding calls about portable media players, what they can carry, and how they store data.

PMP ETHICAL ISSUES: NAPSTER AND BEYOND

What was Napster all about? The initial MP3 craze was fueled by sites such as MP3.com, which originally stored its song files on a public server with the permission of the original artist or recording company. Therefore, you were not infringing on a copyright by downloading songs from sites such as MP3.com (which still exists and now provides free music in streaming format).

When originally introduced, Napster was a file-exchange site created to correct some of the annoyances found by users of MP3.com and similar sites. One such annoyance was the limited availability of popular music in MP3 format. With the MP3 sites, if you found a song you wanted to download, often the links to the sites on which the file was found no longer worked. Napster differed from MP3.com because songs or locations of songs were not stored in a central public server but instead were "borrowed" directly from other users' computers. This process of users transferring files between computers is referred to as **peer-to-peer**

(P2P) sharing. Napster also provided a search engine dedicated to finding specific MP3 files. This direct search and sharing eliminated the inconvenience of searching links only to find them unavailable.

The problem with Napster was that it was so good at what it did. Napster's convenient and reliable mechanism to find and download popular songs in MP3 format became a huge success. The rapid acceptance and use of Napster—at one point, it had nearly 60 million users—led the music industry to sue the site for copyright infringement, and Napster was closed in June 2002. Napster has since reopened as a music site that sells music downloads and is sanctioned by the recording industry.

So now all music and video that is downloaded must be purchased? Although you need to pay for most music you download, artists are posting some songs for free. Business models are still evolving as artists and recording companies try to meet the audience's needs while at the same time protect their own intellectual property rights. A number of different approaches exist. One is to deliver something called tethered downloads in which you pay for the music and own it but are subject to restrictions on its use. For example, Apple currently allows you to give songs you download to anyone on audio CD but only to share the media electronically with five other computers. Other sites offer subscription services. For a monthly fee, Napster to Go allows you to download as many songs as you like to your MP3 player. These songs will be usable, however, only as long as you are paying the monthly subscription fee.

If the original Napster site was illegal, why are there still peer-to-peer (P2P) sharing sites? When Napster was going through its legal turmoil, other P2P Web sites were quick to take advantage of a huge opportunity. Napster was "easy" to shut down because it used a central index server that queried other Napster computers for requested songs. Current P2P protocols (such as Gnutella and Kazaa) differ from Napster in that they do not limit themselves to sharing only MP3 files. Video files are obtainable easily on P2P sites. More importantly, these sites don't have a central index server. Instead, they operate in a true P2P sharing environment in which computers connect directly to other computers.

BITS AND BYTES

Pimp Your iPod

Portable Music Players aren't just for playing music and videos any longer. Add-on products, such as iPodSync (**www.ipodsync.com**), are constantly being developed to provide your iPod with new features. Although this product is used mainly for synchronizing your iPod with Outlook and transferring weather forecasts, Web feeds, and pictures to your iPod, it has an additional useful feature. The product includes PowerPoint Exporter, available as a free download, which enables you to export PowerPoint presentations as images to your iPod. You can then use your iPod as a mobile presentation tool. So pass your iPod over to your customer while sipping coffee at Starbucks and close that big deal with a slick presentation!

Since Linux became popular, enthusiasts want to install it on everything—including iPods. The iPod Linux Project (**www.ipodlinux.org**) is an open-source project dedicated to developing versions of Linux to install on iPods. The current version of the OS includes a user interface called Podzilla, and many applications and modules have been written to provide functionality that the creators at Apple never dreamed of for the iPod. So if you're feeling adventurous, install it and see what else you can do with your iPod.

The argument these P2P networks make to defend their legality is that they do not run a central server like the original Napster but only facilitate connections between users. Therefore, they have no control over what the users choose to trade, and not all P2P file sharing is illegal. For example, it is perfectly legal to trade photos or movies you have created with other folks over a P2P site. Those who oppose such file-sharing sites contend that the sites know their users are distributing files illegally and breaking copyright laws. Be aware that having illegal content on your computer, deliberately or by accident, is a criminal offense in many jurisdictions.

Will PMPs eliminate radio stations? Radio stations have always had the advantages of early access to new music and the personalities and conversations they add to the listening experience. However, the Internet allows artists to release new songs to their fans immediately (on sites such as **www.mp3.com**), without relying on radio airtime. This opens up new channels for artists to reach an audience and changes the amount of power radio stations have in the promotion of music. And many radio stations have gained increased listenership by making their stations available through Internet sites. Radio stations seem to be here to stay.

Another development that competes with radio (and television) is podcasting, which allows users to download audio and video content and then to listen to those broadcasts on their PMPs whenever they want. Podcasting is paving the way for anyone to create a radio or television show at home and to distribute it easily to an audience. Using free software, such as Audacity (**http://audacity.sourceforge.net**), and a microphone, you can record voiceovers, sequence songs, and "publish" your show to the Internet. Loyal fans can use podcasting software like iPodder (**www.ipodder.org**) or iTunes (for Windows or Mac) to find their latest episode and automatically transfer it to their portable media players. Plugging your iPod into a data port on your computer causes the iPod to search iTunes for new content and automatically transfers it to your iPod. This process is known as synchronization. Podcasts are easy to subscribe to and download using iTunes (see Figure 13). And iTunes is free of charge!

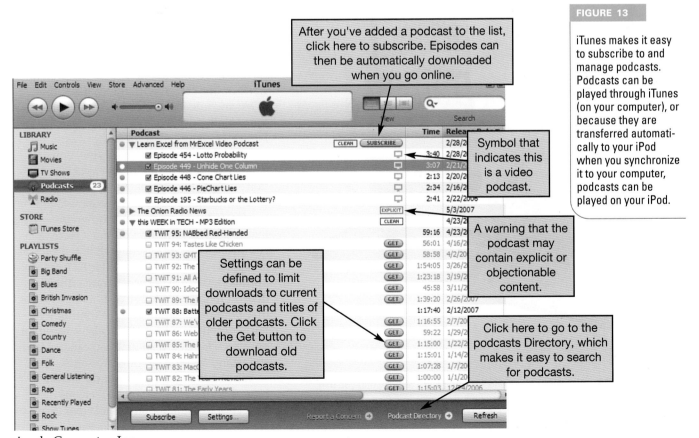

FIGURE 13

iTunes makes it easy to subscribe to and manage podcasts. Podcasts can be played through iTunes (on your computer), or because they are transferred automatically to your iPod when you synchronize it to your computer, podcasts can be played on your iPod.

Apple Computer, Inc.

Personal Digital Assistants (PDAs)

A **personal digital assistant (PDA)** is a small device that allows you to carry digital information. Often called handhelds, PDAs are about the size of your hand and usually weigh less than 5 ounces. Although small, PDAs are quite powerful and can carry all sorts of information, from calendars to contact lists to specially designed personal productivity software programs (such as Excel and Word), to songs, photos, videos, and games. And you can easily **synchronize** (the process of making sure the data on two devices is exactly the same) your PDA and your home computer so that the changes you make to your schedules and files on your PDA are made on your home or office computer files as well. Some PDAs also double as cellular phones. What makes PDAs different from cell phones (or smartphones) is that they are primarily designed for higher function business activities (such as e-mail, producing and sending documents, managing contact databases, etc.) rather than voice communication and entertainment functions (such as snapping photos).

PDA HARDWARE

What hardware is inside a PDA? Like any computing device, a PDA includes a processor (CPU), operating system software, storage capabilities, input and output devices, and ports. Generally, PDAs feature faster processors than cell phones, which tends to make them slightly larger (but more powerful) and also shortens their battery life. Because of their small size, PDAs (like cell phones) must use specially designed processors and operating system software. They store their operating system software in ROM and their data and application programs in random access memory (RAM).

What kinds of input devices do PDAs use? All PDAs feature touch-sensitive screens that allow you to enter data directly with a pen-like device called a **stylus**. To make selections, you simply tap or write on the screen with the stylus. Other PDAs include integrated keyboards or support small, portable, folding keyboards. Figure 14 shows all of these input options.

With a touch screen and stylus, you can use either handwritten text or special notation systems to enter data into your PDA. One of the more popular notation systems is the **Graffiti** text system. As shown in Figure 15, with Graffiti you must learn special strokes that represent each letter, such as an upside-down V for the letter A. Another popular system, **Microsoft Transcriber**, doesn't require special strokes and can recognize both printed and cursive writing with fairly decent accuracy. PDAs also support an on-screen keyboard so that you can use your stylus and "type" (tap out) messages.

What kinds of displays do PDAs have? PDAs come with LCD screens in a variety of resolutions. High-end color displays are the norm today and can measure almost

AP/Wide World Photos

FIGURE 14

To enter text, PDAs offer different options: (a) a text entry window that you use together with a stylus, (b) an integrated keyboard (shown here on a Sharp Zaurus SL-5500), and (c) a folding keyboard accessory.

4 inches and have resolutions as high as 640 x 480, which is sufficient for small screens.

How do I compare processors for PDAs? Popular PDA processors (CPUs) on the market today include the Samsung SC, the Texas Instruments OMP, and the Intel XScale processor. When comparing PDA processors, one consideration to keep in mind is **processor speed**. Processor speed, which is measured in hertz (Hz), is the number of operations (or cycles) the processor completes each second. Just as with computers, you should get the fastest processor your budget will allow.

If you're interested in running demanding software on your PDA, such as games, Microsoft Office applications, and image-editing applications, getting a fast processor is essential. For example, if you will be doing large sets of calculations in Excel workbooks, the speed difference between a fast processor and a slower one is very noticeable. The type of application software you plan on running should help you determine whether the additional processing power is worth the cost.

Processor speed is not the only aspect of the processor that affects performance. The internal design of the processor, both in the software commands it speaks and its internal hardware, are other factors. To measure performance, PDA reviewers often run the same task on competing PDAs and then compare the time it takes to complete the task. This process is called **benchmarking** and gives a good indication of the unit's overall system performance. When comparing PDAs, look for benchmarks in magazines (such as *PC Magazine*) in addition to online reviews (such as those found at **www.wired.com**).

As well as having different speeds, each processor uses different amounts of power, affecting how long the PDA can run on a single battery. When comparing PDAs, look for the expected operating time on one battery charge.

PDA OPERATING SYSTEMS

How do I compare PDA operating systems? The two main operating system competitors on the PDA market have traditionally been the **Palm OS** from Palm and the Windows Mobile (formerly known as **Pocket PC**) system from Microsoft. Palm OS is now found only on PDAs made by Palm.

Windows Mobile is by far the most popular and is used by Compaq, HP, Dell, and Toshiba—and now even by Palm—on their PDA models and some smartphones. As you can see in Figure 16, Windows Mobile sports a typical graphical user interface.

So which operating system is better? The Palm OS clearly ruled with market share just a few years ago. This was due primarily to the Palm OS's ability to work more efficiently on slower processors and PDAs with less memory. However, Windows Mobile is now crushing Palm in terms of market share. Today's PDAs sport fast processors with 128 MB of RAM or more, which allow Windows Mobile to deliver speedy performance. In addition, Microsoft was quicker to embrace support for new technologies such as hardware graphics acceleration and EVDO high-speed networking. Both operating systems can now handle Word, Excel, and PowerPoint files, but Windows Mobile was the first to synchronize easily with Outlook, thereby providing a significant advantage for users who use Outlook as their main e-mail software. Consequently, Windows Mobile is outselling the Palm OS now by a vast margin.

The PDA operating system affects you in another way. You may want to buy extra software for your PDA—a program to track your workouts at the gym or to provide driving directions, for example. Third-party companies, rather than the companies that built the PDAs, often develop software applications for PDAs. Before you buy a PDA, you should investigate exactly which applications you are interested in using and make sure they're available for the operating system you're considering.

Getty Images, Inc.

GPS Devices: More Than Helping You Find Your Way to the Mall

GPS devices don't just feature maps and turn-by-turn directions any longer. Full-featured GPS devices (such as the Garmin nüvi 680) include MP3 players, audio book players, the capability to display photos, and connections to the Internet. Using Internet services such as MSN Direct, your GPS can keep you informed about the weather, traffic back-ups, local movie times, and even local gas prices.

Garmin International, Inc.

Tomorrow	Sat	Sun
Clear	Clear	Rain
37°/25°	43°/32°	45°/39°
Precip 0%	Precip 10%	Precip 30%

Back

GARMIN nüvi

FIGURE 17

The Garmin nüvi 680 keeps you up to date on weather and other information via an Internet connection.

PDA MEMORY AND STORAGE

What kinds of memory does a PDA use? In PDAs, ROM is used to hold the operating system as well as the most basic programs the PDA runs, such as the calendar, to-do list, and contact list. PDAs do not contain internal hard drives. Therefore, RAM holds additional applications and any data you load into the PDA. However, because RAM is volatile storage, and you do not want your data to disappear when you shut off your PDA, a small amount of power is taken from the battery to keep the data "alive" even when the PDA is off.

The main advantage of using RAM in this way is speed. RAM is incredibly fast compared with hard drives, so programs on a PDA load and run very quickly. Because the price of RAM has decreased over the last few years, most top-of-the-line PDAs contain about 128 MB of RAM. Still, applications for PDAs (like Excel) do not have all the functions that

FIGURE 18

Different PDAs use different types of flash memory. However, all flash memory cards slide into a specialized slot on the PDA.

desktop versions include precisely because of their limited amount of RAM.

What if I need more memory on my PDA? Most PDAs cannot expand the amount of *internal* memory they contain. For memory needs beyond built-in RAM and ROM, PDAs use removable flash memory similar to that used in MP3 players. For example, if you want your PDA to hold a large MP3 collection, you might not have enough built-in RAM. But you could add the MP3s to your PDA by copying them onto flash memory and sliding the flash card into a special slot on the PDA, as shown in Figure 18. Before buying a flash card, consult your PDA manual or manufacturer's Web site to make sure it's compatible with your PDA.

PDA FILE TRANSFER AND SYNCHRONIZATION

How do I transfer data from my PDA to my computer? If you're transferring data from your PDA to another computer and it accepts the type of flash card you're using, you can simply pull the flash card out of your PDA and slip it into the flash card reader on your computer. If your desktop does not include a built-in card reader, you can connect an external memory card reader to your computer using a USB port.

You also can transfer your data from your PDA to a desktop computer by using a special device called a **cradle**. Most PDAs come with a cradle or sync cable, which connects the PDA to the desktop using a USB port (older models used a serial port), as shown in Figure 19. You also can use the PDA cradle to synchronize your PDA with your computer, and some cradles even charge the PDA's batteries at the same time.

How do I synchronize a PDA (or cell phone) with a computer? To be truly valuable as mobile computing devices, PDAs provide a means by which you can coordinate the changes you make to your to-do lists, schedules, and other files with the files on your home or office computer. This process of updating your data so that the files on your PDA and computer are the same is called **synchronizing**. To synchronize your desktop and PDA, you simply place the PDA in its cradle (or attach it to the computer via a sync cable) and touch a "hot sync" button. This begins the process of data transfer that updates both sets of files to the most current version.

Microsoft has recognized the vast increase in portable computing devices by integrating synchronization into Windows Vista. The Sync Center (see Figure 20), which is accessed from the Control Panel, allows you to set up automatic or manual synchronization. Ensure that the device for which you are trying to set up synchronization parameters is connected to your computer and then launch the Sync Center. Select the "Set up new sync partnerships" option to view available devices and configure their synchronization options.

Can I transfer files wirelessly from a PDA? Many PDAs include an infrared (IrDA) port that transmits data signals using infrared light waves. To transfer data between two PDAs, you can use the infrared port and "beam" data directly across. For example, if you missed a class, a fellow student could send you the assignment file by simply pointing her PDA at yours.

Another type of wireless connection available for PDAs is **Bluetooth**. This technology uses radio waves to transmit data signals over short distances (up to about 30 feet). Many PDAs on the market today are Bluetooth-enabled, meaning they include a small Bluetooth chip that allows them to transfer data wirelessly to any other Bluetooth-enabled device. One benefit Bluetooth has over infrared is that direct line of sight does not have to be present between the two devices for them to communicate. You also can use Bluetooth to synchronize your PDA with your computer or your Bluetooth cell phone. No cradle to connect, no buttons to push: the Bluetooth-enabled PDA and computer or phone recognize each other and automatically begin the synchronization process.

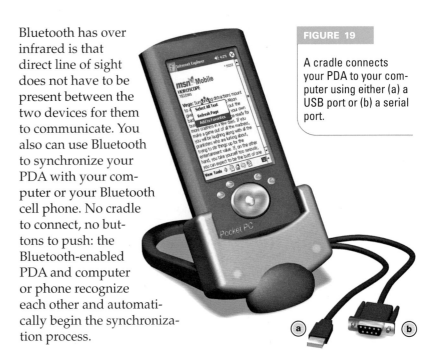

FIGURE 19

A cradle connects your PDA to your computer using either (a) a USB port or (b) a serial port.

PDA INTERNET CONNECTIVITY

How do PDAs connect to the Internet? As is the case with cell phones, connecting your PDA to the Internet requires that you have a plan with a wireless ISP, which costs an additional monthly fee. Once you're on the Internet, you can use your PDA to send and receive e-mail messages and use all the features you're familiar with from your desktop computer, including attachments, blind and carbon copies, and distribution lists.

However, you do not always need to be connected to the Internet to take advantage of its information resources. Web sites such as AvantGo (**www.avantgo.com**) allow you to download the content of many different Web sites from your computer to your PDA

FIGURE 20

The Windows Vista Sync Center makes it easy to arrange for synchronization of all your mobile devices.

>To launch Sync Center, click the Start button, select Control Panel, and double-click the Sync Center icon.

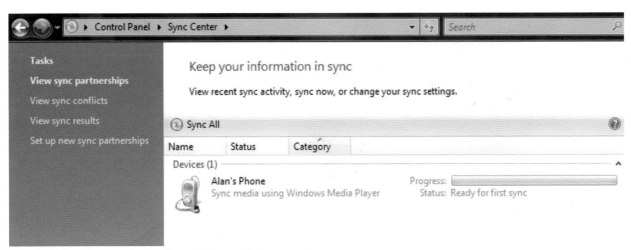

Reprinted with permission from Microsoft Corporation

(at no charge). Popular channels include CNN.com and RollingStone.com. You can then read this downloaded information any time you want without having to access the Internet. For static Web-based information, this is an ideal solution.

How are Web pages "communicated" to my PDA? Wireless **Application Protocol (WAP)** is the standard that dictates how handheld devices will access information on the Internet. WAP supports all the major PDA operating systems, including Windows Mobile and Palm OS. As mentioned earlier, mobile devices such as cell phones and PDAs run software applications called microbrowsers that allow them to surf the Internet.

PDA SOFTWARE AND ACCESSORIES

What PDA software is available? Most PDAs come with a standard collection of software such as a to-do list, contacts manager, and calendar. Modified versions of application software such as Word, Excel, Outlook, and PowerPoint also are available for PDAs. Although these programs are not as full featured as their desktop counterparts, they can read and edit files that can be transmitted to full-version applications on your computer. In addition, a variety of games, tools, and reference applications are available for PDAs from numerous software companies. A good source to locate software applications for your PDA is **www.pdastreet.com**. In addition, Web sites such as **www.download.com** and **www.tucows.com** feature plenty of shareware and freeware applications for PDA platforms.

PDA OR CELL PHONE?

Why do people use PDAs? PDAs have caught on in a variety of professions over the last few years, mostly in situations that involve time-sensitive data collection. Medical professionals (such as doctors and nurses) use PDAs loaded with patient (or case) management software. These programs provide quick access to patient records when visiting patient rooms or supervising tests (such as MRIs and CAT scans) and allow for fast updating of patient records. Package delivery companies, such as Federal Express and United Parcel Service, provide employees with specialized versions of PDAs that can record information about packages being picked up or delivered, which enhances package tracking capabilities and streamlines billing information. Scientists use PDAs to collect and summarize data observed during experiments either in the lab or in the field, which provides for much more accurate data recording than relying on notes that must be input at a later time at a desktop computer. Also, anyone who needs reference material probably would find it easier to carry an electronic version of a paper reference source that also would be instantly searchable.

For the 2010 census, the United States Census Bureau will be outfitting 500,000 census takers with specially designed PDAs made by High Tech Computer Corporation (a Taiwan-based company). The devices will run on Windows Mobile software and will transmit data wirelessly via a cellular network. It is hoped that allowing census takers to record information electronically as it is collected will reduce the number of people missed in the count (estimated to be several million in the 2000 census).

BITS AND BYTES

No Bluetooth? No Problem

Your computer doesn't have built-in Bluetooth? Devices are available now that enable you to add Bluetooth capabilities to almost any computer. One is the Linksys USB Bluetooth Adapter, shown in Figure 21. When plugged into a computer's USB port, it adds wireless capability to your computer. The adapter comes with software that supports a wide range of Bluetooth services, including PDA synchronization, headset support, dial-up networking, network access, and file transfer.

FIGURE 21

Just plug a Bluetooth adapter into any USB port on your computer and install the Bluetooth Software, and you're ready to synchronize your PDA with your computer wirelessly.

Courtesy of Linksys

So if you need to capture data, keep your appointments and calendar up to date away from the office, or refer to reference materials that would otherwise be difficult to transport, you are a good candidate for a PDA. Also, if you need to read or edit electronic documents (such as Excel files), and send and receive a significant amount of e-mail, using a PDA relieves you of having to carry a much larger notebook computer.

Do I need both a PDA and a cell phone? A number of devices are being released that attempt to combine the functionality of a cell phone, a PMP, and a PDA into one unit. These mobile devices are known as **smartphones**. For example, the Palm Treo 700wx is a PDA (note the full keyboard) that has added cell phone and PMP features (see Figure 22a). It sports high-speed EVDO Internet access capabilities, a camera for taking digital pictures, and Bluetooth capabilities to free you from wires. The T-Mobile SDA (see Figure 22b) is a phone but is customized with features to make reading your e-mail simple, including a thumbwheel for easy scrolling and a bigger screen.

Smartphones represent a step toward the ideal of convergence, or the ability to have a single compact device that features all of the capabilities you need. However, each device still makes some compromises (primarily to save weight and battery power); features available on the best cell phones and PDAs are missing from the smartphones currently on the market. But the missing feature gap is narrowing with each new generation of smartphones. So, carefully investigate the features of current smartphones, and you might be able to fulfill your needs with one device. Still, if your primary need is voice communications and small size, investigate cell phones. If your needs are more along the lines of keeping track of facts and figures or using Office application software programs, then you probably should look seriously at a high-end PDA.

Are there any other devices besides PDAs and smartphones that I could consider before purchasing a notebook computer? Specialized computing devices designed for mobility are hitting the market more regularly. Generally, they are designed for fairly specific purposes, but they may provide all the functionality you need for a specific situation. The Pepper Pad 3 (see Figure 23a) is a portable device with a large 7-inch screen that provides a significant

(a)

(b)

Courtesy of T-Mobile

Palm, Inc.

advantage over PDA or cell phone screens. It is designed primarily for surfing the Web, e-mailing, instant messaging, and downloading or streaming multimedia from the Web. It can even function as a remote control for your home entertainment system. Because it weighs only about two pounds and measures about 11 x 6 inches, it is relatively easy to transport by slipping into a backpack.

For avid readers of e-books (books stored in electronic files), the Sony Portable Reader System (see Figure 23b) could be just what you are looking for. Featuring 128 MB of internal memory, it can hold 160 e-books. And if that isn't enough, it accepts flash memory cards for even more storage. Weighing just 9 ounces certainly qualifies it as portable. And through clever technology, keeping a page displayed requires no energy, so you can get approximately 7,500 turned pages on one charge.

ACTIVE HELPDESK

Using PDAs

In this Active Helpdesk call, you'll play the role of a helpdesk staffer, fielding calls about PDAs — what you can use them for, what internal components and features they have, and how you can synchronize mobile devices with a desktop computer.

Pepper Computer, Inc.

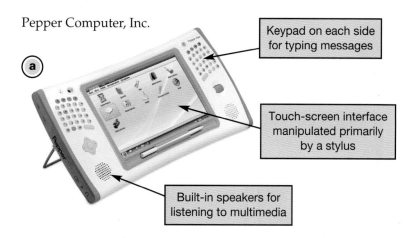

Keypad on each side for typing messages

Touch-screen interface manipulated primarily by a stylus

Built-in speakers for listening to multimedia

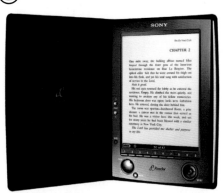

Used by permission of Sony Electronics Inc.

FIGURE 23

(a) The Pepper Pad 3 features a touch screen and keypad and is designed primarily for Web surfing and sending e-mail. (b) The Sony Portable Reader is designed to store up to 80 e-books and weighs approx. 9 ounces (without the cover). Used by permission of Sony Electronics Inc.

You can expect to see more of these types of specialty portable computing devices in the near future. While not right for every situation, they may be a good fit for your needs. Web sites such as Gizmodo, the Gadget Guide (**www.gizmodo.com**) are a great resource for keeping abreast of new developments.

Tablet PCs

A **tablet PC** is a portable computer that is lightweight, features advanced handwriting recognition, and can be rotated into a clipboard style. Tablet PCs are available from a variety of manufacturers, come in a variety of designs, and are about the same size as a clipboard. Newer models weigh just over two pounds, including the integrated keyboard, making them very thin and lightweight computing solutions.

Why are they called tablet PCs? Tablet PCs are so-named because the monitor can be used either in a traditional notebook mode or in "tablet mode," much like an electronic clipboard, as shown in Figure 24. Tablet PCs also can be connected to a full-size keyboard and monitor.

When would a tablet PC be the best mobile solution? A tablet PC can be the ideal solution when you require a lightweight, portable computer with full desktop processing power. Manufacturing employees, medical employees, educators and students, sales representatives who call

Toshiba America Information Systems, Inc.

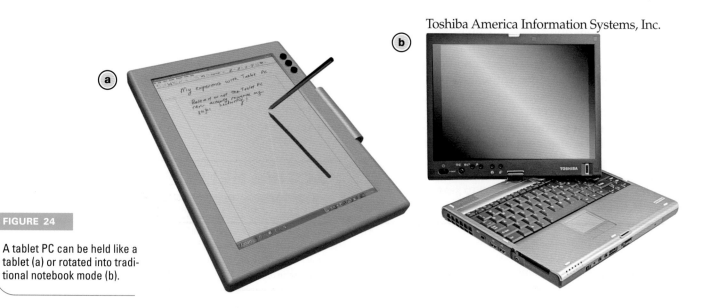

FIGURE 24

A tablet PC can be held like a tablet (a) or rotated into traditional notebook mode (b).

Mobile Computing: Keeping Your Data on Hand

on clients (and take notes during the calls), and employees who fill out electronic forms are the major purchasers of tablet PCs. They are very light and, with their handwriting-recognition capabilities, allow you to take notes silently with no distracting key-strokes. Because they generally cost more than traditional notebook computers, how-ever, they remain a niche product with less than 2 percent of the mobile computer mar-ket. Still, if they meet your needs, they are a very viable option.

TABLET PC HARDWARE

What hardware is inside a tablet PC? Like any computer, a tablet PC includes a processor (CPU), operating sys-tem software, storage capabilities, input and output devices, and ports. What makes the tablet PC unique, however, is the way in which you input data into it.

How do I input data into a tablet PC? The most innovative input technology on the tablet is its use of **digital ink**. Digital ink is an extension of the text-entry systems used on PDA devices. Supporting digital ink, the tablet PC's entire screen is pressure-sensitive and reacts to a **digital pen**, or sty-lus, allowing you to easily draw images and enter text, as shown in Figure 25. Once you enter text with the pen using your own handwriting, it is converted automatically to typewritten text. You also can select blocks of text and move them around to a different location on the page, or erase text using a scribble motion.

Windows Vista has support for digital ink built into the operating system and is cur-rently the operating system shipping with the majority of tablet PCs. When using Office 2007 products (such as Word or One Note), you can annotate (or mark up) exist-ing documents. The original document can remain unchanged, but your digital ink annotations on the document are also saved. Using this feature, you can mark up an arti-cle and send it to a coworker, add notes to a meeting agenda, or draw a route on a map.

How seamless is the use of digital ink and pens? Occasional mistakes may occur in the handwriting recognition, so the experience is not exactly like using pen on paper. Still, being able to have your notes translated into text and being able to easily enter drawings and annotations are appeal-

©Reuters New Media/Corbis

You input data into a tablet PC by writing on the touch-sensitive screen with a digi-tal pen. The tablet then uses handwriting recognition to convert your writing to typewritten text.

ing features for many users. And if you pre-fer to use a keyboard, a software keyboard can appear on the screen and you can tap in text. Tablets also accept the Graffiti notation used in PDAs.

What are the storage and transfer options on tablets? Tablets are designed to be lightweight and to minimize the use of battery power, so some models do not include a built-in DVD or CD drive. However, you can use external DVD/CD-RW (CD rewritable) drives or flash drives to transfer information from your tablet. Many tablets also include FireWire and USB 2.0 ports that enable you to attach high-speed peripherals, such as external hard disk drives, to your tablet PC. Some tablets offer flash memory slots as another option for storing and moving data, and others include built-in infrared ports that allow you to transfer data wirelessly at speeds up to 4.4 Mbps. Most tablets also feature built-in Bluetooth or WiFi connectivity, which pro-vide yet another option for transferring information.

How can I quickly connect my tablet to my peripherals? A docking station is available for most tablet PC mod-els. This piece of hardware allows you to connect printers, scanners, full-size moni-tors, mice, and other peripherals directly to the docking station (and therefore your

Ethics: The Power Of GPS...And the Threats

Most people know where the closest supermarket is in relation to their home. But if you are out of town, how can you find a local supermarket when you get a craving for potato chips? Many people aren't whizzes at geography, but knowing your current location and the location of your destination can often come in handy. Luckily for those who are "directionally impaired," **Global Positioning System (GPS)** technology enables you to carry a powerful navigational aid in your pocket.

You've probably heard of GPS, but what is it exactly and how does it work? The Global Positioning System is a system of 21 satellites (plus three working spares), built and operated by the U.S. Department of Defense, which constantly orbits the Earth. GPS devices use an antenna to pick up the signals from these satellites and special software to transform those signals into latitude and longitude. Using the information obtained from the satellites, GPS devices can tell you what your geographical location is anywhere on the planet to within 10 feet (see Figure 26). Because they provide such detailed positioning information, GPS devices are now used as navigational aids for aircraft, recreational boats, and automobiles, and they even come in handheld models for hikers.

Although this precise positioning information clearly redefines the fields of surveying and search-and-rescue operations, it also has changed other fields. Wildlife researchers now tag select animals and watch their migration patterns and how the population is distributed. Meanwhile, GPS was important to the two teams that created the Chunnel, the tunnel under the English Channel that connects England to France. One team worked from France toward England and the other from England toward France. They used GPS information along the way to make sure they were on target, and in 1990, the two sections joined to become the first physical link between England and the continent of Europe since the Ice Age.

GPS has made its way into several commercial products as well. Hertz rental cars offer in-car GPS assistance with the NeverLost system. The unit is

FIGURE 26

GPS computes your location anywhere on Earth from a system of orbiting satellites.

mounted on the front dashboard and displays your location on a map that is updated in real time as you drive. Enter your destination, and a voice warns you of lane changes and approaching turns. If you miss a turn, it automatically recalculates the required route and gives you directions to get back on course. Flip to another screen, and it shows you how far you have to drive to the next gas station, restaurant, or amusement park. Most automotive companies now offer GPS systems as installed options in their vehicles. And GPS navigation can be added to any vehicle using a portable GPS device, a PDA equipped with GPS (see Figure 27), or by adding GPS software and accessories to your notebook.

But who is watching?

Having the ability to locate and track an object anywhere on Earth does bring with it societal implications, however. The Federal Communications Commission (FCC) mandated that by the end of 2005, every cell phone had to include a GPS chip. This enabled the complete rollout of the Enhanced 911 (E911) program. E911 automatically gives dispatchers precision location information for any 911 call. It also means your cell phone records may include precise tracking information indicating where you are when you make a call. But is that information that you would want the government or other people to know? Consider if you were at a park playing baseball with your friends and you made a phone call. At the same time, in another part of the park, an organization with suspected terrorist ties was holding a rally. Would you want the government to assume because you made a phone call from the park that you are a member of that organization?

Because phones now have GPS chips, cellular phone providers offer plans (for a monthly fee) that allow you to track where a cell phone is at any given time via a Web site. This could be a real boon for tracking a lost child who wandered off into the woods during a group hike. But are other uses of the technology ethical? Did your daughter really go to the library, or is she actually at the local skate park hanging with her friends? Is your spouse really working late at the office or watching the baseball game with friends at the ballpark? Now, with a few clicks of the mouse, you can tell where a family member's phone is located. But is this an invasion of privacy? Is it ethical to track the whereabouts of your family members? This is something that you need to decide.

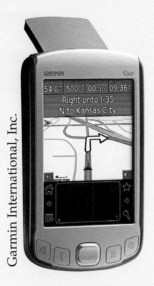

Garmin International, Inc.

FIGURE 27

As well as being a full-featured PDA, the Garmin Que is also a fully functional portable GPS unit. Just put it in your car and you'll receive turn-by-turn directions via an electronic voice and be rerouted if you make a wrong turn.

But GPS technology begs the question: What limits and supervision of the government need to be in place to ensure the ethical use of GPS technologies? In what ways could the tracking information provided by GPS devices be used unethically? If GPS tracking information is recorded in your phone data, should the criteria for allowing government agencies to subpoena phone records be changed? Should users be allowed to turn off location information from their phones? Already, location records such as these were used in determining that the *New York Times* reporter Jayson Blair had been fabricating stories, resulting in his resignation. Car rental companies, such as Acme Car Rental of New Haven, Connecticut, are using GPS records to fine customers for speeding violations. As a nation we now need to decide how we should balance the benefits and costs (to our privacy) of using this new level of tracking information.

FIGURE 28

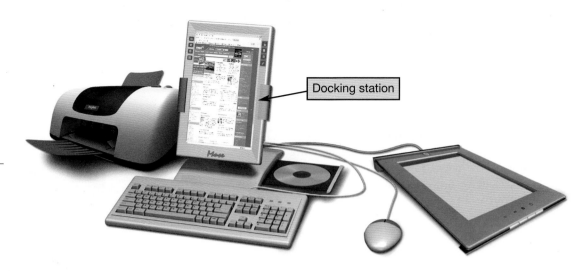

A docking station makes it easy to connect your tablet to your desktop monitor and any other peripherals. Just slide the tablet in place and you're ready to go.

Docking station

tablet) very quickly. As shown in Figure 28, you simply slide your tablet into a docking station to connect it to all peripheral devices, rather than connecting all their cables individually.

What processors are used in tablet PCs? An important criterion for any portable tool like a tablet PC is low power consumption. Another important requirement is connectivity. The Intel Core Duo processors are a popular choice and provide the tablets with the processing power of two CPUs in one chip. CPUs used in tablets are specially engineered to use less power. Consuming less power also means the battery can last much longer. On top-performing tablets, battery life can extend to almost a full workday on one charge, and batteries can be "bridged." This means the tablet can be put into standby mode, or not shut down, while you install a new battery.

How much memory can fit in a tablet? The amount of RAM designed for a specific model will vary by manufacturer. Most models on the market come with at least 512 MB of RAM but can be expanded up to 4 GB. Hard drives are offered in a range of capacities of 120 GB and up.

TABLET SOFTWARE

Do tablet PCs have a special operating system? Tablet PCs used to run the Windows XP Tablet PC Edition operating system. But since Windows Vista was designed with native support for digital ink and handwriting recognition, Vista is now the operating system you'll find on new tablet PCs.

Can tablet PCs use the same software as desktop computers? Tablets can run any applications designed for Windows Vista. Windows Vista includes the Tablet PC Input Panel, which is an accessory available on Tablet PCs that enables you to use handwriting or an on-screen keyboard to enter text (take notes). The notes you take can be sent as e-mail or converted into appointments or tasks in Outlook. Handwriting can be translated into typed text using the character-recognition feature built into the Table PC Input Panel. A more full-featured note-taking application is Microsoft Office OneNote. It allows you to easily incorporate audio recordings and clippings from Web sites and to mark material with searchable colored flags. Windows Vista recognizes digital ink,

FIGURE 29 Comparing PDAs and Tablet PCs

	Screen Size	CPU Speed	RAM	Hard Disk	Approximate Weight	Cost
PDA	3" to 4"	200 to 624 MHz	Up to 128 MB	None	5 oz.	$$–$$$
Tablet PC	8" to 14"	Dual Core up to 2.2 GHz	Up to 4 GB	Up to 120 GB	2.2 to 6 lbs.	$$$$$

and you can add handwritten notes to any of the Microsoft Office programs, including Word, Excel, Outlook, or PowerPoint. Windows Vista also provides speech-recognition capabilities, which allow you to control Microsoft Windows-based programs and dictate text to your tablet.

TABLET OR PDA?

What benefits do tablet PCs have over PDAs and vice versa? Whereas tablet PCs have faster processors, a hard drive, and more RAM than PDAs, PDAs are smaller, lighter, and much cheaper. Thus, whether a tablet PC or a PDA is best for you depends on the needs you have for processing power, note-taking capabilities and portability, as well as your budget. Figure 29 compares tablet PCs and PDAs so that you can find the one best suited to your particular needs.

Notebooks

The most powerful mobile computing solution is a **notebook computer**, sometimes called a **laptop computer**. Notebooks offer large displays and all of the computing power of a full desktop system (see Figure 31). Most notebooks weigh more than tablets. This difference is important if you're carrying the unit all day, but not if you're going to be working at a desk where the notebook can rest.

NOTEBOOK HARDWARE

What hardware comes in a notebook? Notebooks can be equipped with DVD/CD-RW drives, large hard drives (many up to 160 GB), more than 2-GHz processor speed featuring dual core CPUs, and 4 GB or more of RAM. Although the size of a notebook might prohibit it from having all of the drives you're interested in, newer models feature **hot-swappable bays**. This means that when the notebook is running, you can remove a DVD drive and exchange it with a removable hard drive, for example, allowing the notebook to be much more versatile. Input devices on notebooks include keyboards with built-in mouse functionality. In terms of output devices, many notebooks include large display screens measuring up to a whopping 20.1 inches diagonally.

BITS AND BYTES

Smart Displays

Want to be able to use your desktop computer in many different rooms of your house? "Smart displays," shown in Figure 30, are portable flat-screen monitors that allow you to access your regular desktop wirelessly from any room in your house, just like you can when you're sitting at your computer. These three-pound, touch-sensitive monitors can run for up to four hours on a single battery charge, and some come with wireless keyboards and desktop docking stations. They are already cheaper than tablet PCs, and as prices continue to drop, you'll see them appearing in more homes and offices.

FIGURE 30

Smart displays are flat-panel monitors that connect wirelessly to your desktop computer, allowing you to access your desktop from any room in your house.

Courtesy of Viewsonic

AP/Wide World Photos

(a)

(b)

Photo courtesy of Apple Computers

FIGURE 31

Notebook computers offer larger displays and more powerful processors than desktops could offer just a few years ago. Here you see (a) a PC notebook and (b) a Mac notebook.

Ubiquitous Networking: Wherever You Go, There You Are

With the rise of portable computing devices, the idea of ubiquitous networking has been generating a lot of interest. Ubiquity in computing essentially means being able to access and exchange information wherever you happen to be and having the key information that you need accessible when you need it. But how do we achieve this ultimate goal? There are two popular approaches.

The Network Is Watching You (How Orwellian)

Instead of having to move the files and programs you need onto mobile devices, how about having a network that "watches" your movements and moves the data so that it follows you? Researchers at telecommunications companies, such as the AT&T Laboratories at Cambridge University, are attempting to make this possible by creating a detection system that can track your location within a building, moving your files wherever you go. To take advantage of the network, users will carry a small device called a "bat," shown in Figure 32. This device will have a unique ID number and contain a radio transceiver and transmitter. A detection system (or central controller) installed in the building will keep track of the physical location of the bats and hence the people who carry them.

How does this system work? Suppose you go into a conference room that contains a computer and a phone. The controller is

FIGURE 32

Bats are about the size of a pager device and therefore small enough to be carried comfortably. They allow the detection system to locate the bat owners wherever they roam in the facility.

01223 343222

Laboratory for Communication Engineering.

tracking the bat you have in your pocket, so it knows you entered the conference room and therefore routes all your phone calls to the phone in the conference room. It also sends your files and desktop settings to the computer in the conference room.

What if two people are in the conference room at the same time? The controller assigns available devices to the first person who enters the room. However, using interactive buttons on your bat, you can indicate to the controller that you wish to take temporary possession of a device assigned to another person.

Take Your Computer's Soul with You

The other option for ubiquity nirvana would be to take not just your data files with you (say, on a flash drive), but instead take your entire computer with you (virtually, of course). IBM is conducting a research project called SoulPad that attempts to achieve this miracle of portability. Using a portable storage device (IBM has used 60 GB iPods in its testing), you save a suspended image of your computer, including all desktop settings and data files (essentially the "soul" of your computer), before leaving your home computer. When you arrive at another computer, you attach the portable storage device, and then your computer data and settings are loaded onto the remote computer so that you can pick up exactly where you left off. In testing, this has been piloted on computers running Windows and Linux. What is making this technology possible is the availability of tiny, high-capacity storage devices, high-speed data transfer (via FireWire or USB 2.0), and virtualization software. Eventually, it will probably be possible to deploy the SoulPad on a smartphone. This is convergence at the next level!

As we achieve ubiquity in computing, we will have to rethink our territorial approach to work and living spaces, as well as some of our ideas about privacy. In the future, because our data might follow us around (or we'll take it all with us), access to our personal information may always be right where we are.

What are popular CPUs for notebooks? CPUs available for notebooks are usually a bit slower than the latest available CPU offered for desktop units. Whereas existing desktops can currently run a 3.4-GHz processor, most notebook CPUs run at speeds less than 2.4 GHz. You won't notice the difference if you're using word-processing programs, but if you run many applications at the same time or use programs that make heavy demands on the CPU (such as video-editing software), the notebook's performance may seem slower than a desktop computer. However, many notebooks now

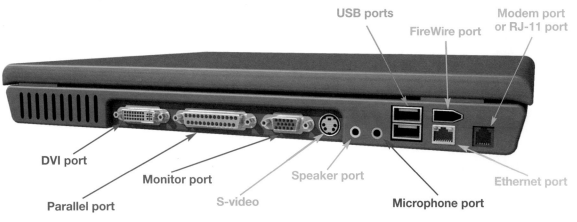

FIGURE 33

Notebooks include many of the ports you're used to seeing on desktop computers.

USB ports
FireWire port
Modem port or RJ-11 port

DVI port
Monitor port
Parallel port
S-video
Speaker port
Microphone port
Ethernet port

use dual-core CPUs, which makes the difference in processing speed much less noticeable. In addition, the new memory management schemes of Windows Vista allow the computer to use RAM more efficiently, which has also helped eliminate any noticeable performance differences between notebooks and desktops.

Many notebook systems use low-power processors designed to consume less power than other CPUs. Often CPUs in mobile computers feature integrated wireless capability as well. When combined with specially designed video chipsets, the total package consumes less power than comparable desktop units, thereby extending battery life.

NOTEBOOK OPERATING SYSTEMS AND PORTS

Are there special operating systems for notebooks? Notebooks use the same operating systems that run on desktop systems. However, notebook operating systems do have some special settings, such as power management profiles. A power management profile contains recommended power-saving settings, such as turning off your hard drive after 15 minutes of no use, shutting down the display after 20 minutes of no movement, and switching the machine to sleep or hibernation mode after a certain length of time.

Can notebooks connect to other devices easily? As you can see in Figure 33, notebooks can include a full set of ports, including FireWire, USB 2.0, parallel; RJ-11 jacks for a modem connection; and Ethernet ports for wired networking connections. Video ports often include high-quality S-video connectors as

well as digital DVI connectors, which allow a pure digital signal to run to a digital flat-panel monitor.

Windows Vista has a feature called the Windows Mobility Center that is designed to help keep track of functions on mobile computers (see Figure 34). When the Windows Mobility Center is open, you can see at a glance details on display brightness (which affects battery life), battery status, power management plant, wireless network connections, external displays, and presentation systems (projectors) connected.

Often, the size limitations of notebooks mean that they don't offer as many of each type of port as in a desktop system. Therefore, if you buy a notebook, you should consider how you will use your machine and whether you will need an

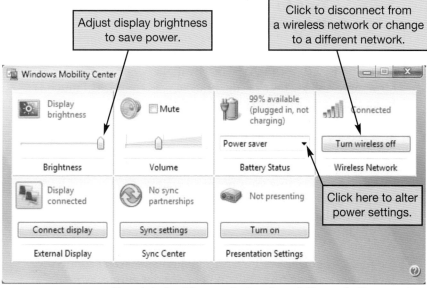

Adjust display brightness to save power.

Click to disconnect from a wireless network or change to a different network.

Click here to alter power settings.

Reprinted with permission from Microsoft Corporation

FIGURE 34

The Windows Mobility Center makes it easy to manage various operations of your mobile computing device.

Mark Leet Oqo, Inc.

FIGURE 35

The OQO is a Windows Vista computer that features a 1.5-GHz processor, 60 GB hard drive, 1 GB of RAM, integrated wireless, and Bluetooth compatibility. At only 5.6 inches by 3.3 inches and weighing in under one pound (with battery), it bridges the worlds of notebooks and PDA devices.

BITS AND BYTES

Tips to Stretch Your Notebook's Battery Life

Your notebook stores data both in RAM and on the hard disk drive. Increasing your RAM capacity makes your notebook perform more quickly because data can be read from RAM much faster than from a hard drive. Adding more RAM to your notebook also will make your battery last longer. This is because if the data needed is not in RAM, the hard drive must be powered up, requiring about 30 times as much battery power as simply reading directly from RAM.

Also, do not expose your notebook batteries to extreme heat and cold (such as leaving them in a parked car) as this will tend to shorten the battery life. Turn off all programs that are automatically loaded (check the taskbar) that you don't currently need, as this will lessen the chances the hard drive will be accessed wasting precious power. For instance, on flights you can't connect to the Internet so you probably don't need your antivirus or antispyware programs. Finally, turn off your wireless capabilities if you won't be connecting to the Internet. The wireless unit in your computer will constantly search for wireless connections and drain power in the process.

expansion hub. An expansion hub is a device that connects to a USB port, creating three or four USB ports from one. If you will be connecting a USB mouse, printer, and scanner to your notebook, you may be short one USB port, in which case a hub would come in handy.

How do notebooks connect to wireless networks? Most notebooks have integrated support for wireless connectivity. The 802.11g WiFi wireless standard is the most common standard used in wireless networks today, but 802.11n is gaining in popularity. The 802.11g standard allows wireless connections to operate at up to 54 Mbps, and 802.11n will provide even faster transfer rates and extended range. Many notebooks also offer built-in Bluetooth chips that allow you to connect to other Bluetooth-enabled devices.

NOTEBOOK BATTERIES AND ACCESSORIES

What types of batteries are there for notebooks? Rechargeable batteries today come in two main types: lithium ion (Li-Ion) and nickel metal hydride (NiMH). The new lithium and nickel-based batteries are lighter than previous generation batteries and do not show the "memory effect" that old batteries did. **Memory effect** means that the battery must be completely used up before it is recharged. If not, the battery won't hold as much charge as it originally did.

How long does a notebook battery last? The capacity of a battery is measured in ampere-hours (A-hrs). Ampere is a measure of current flow, so a battery rated at 5 A-hrs can provide 5 amps of current for an hour. Battery power depends on the device you're using and the work you're doing. A high-performance battery can operate a notebook for up to five hours if fully charged. However, using the notebook's DVD drive can consume a high-performance battery in as little as 90 minutes. Manufacturers also describe batteries as having cells (for example, 6-cell versus 9-cell). The more cells, the more capacity the battery has but also the more it weighs. Some notebook systems allow you to install two batteries at the same time, doubling the battery life but forcing you to purchase a second battery and have both fully charged.

Do I need to use my battery everywhere I go? Some environments support easy access to power for notebooks. For example, you can use an AC/DC or DC/DC converter to enable a notebook to run in a car without using battery power. In addition, many airplanes offer notebook power connections at each seat, although to use such a connection you have to buy a power converter and adapter.

What if I need notebook computing power but in a smaller, lighter configuration? The **ultraportable** (or **subnotebook**) category of computers consists of notebooks that weigh 4 pounds or less. The clear winner in the weight department is the OQO model 02 (shown in Figure 35). Ultraportables pack major computing power into a tiny package and try to extend battery life as long as possible. Although currently more expensive than many conventional notebooks, they may be just what you need if size is your biggest consideration. But be prepared to put up with a cramped keyboard and relatively small screen.

What special purchases might a notebook require? Because a notebook is so easily stolen, purchasing a security lock is a wise investment. And as is the case with regular desktops, power surges can adversely affect notebooks, so investing in a portable surge protector is also a good idea.

If you frequently make presentations to large groups, adding a lightweight projector to your notebook might prove useful. Printers have also become travel-sized. Figure 36 shows some of these special notebook accessories.

What if I need to collaborate with colleagues while I'm on the road? At the office, collaborating with your coworkers is easier because most likely everyone is connected to your office network. But there are software **collaboration tools** available to allow you to set up ad hoc networks almost anywhere. Products such as Colligo Workgroup Edition (**www.colligo.com**), shown in Figure 37, and Windows Meeting Space (included in some versions of Windows Vista) make it easy to configure secure networks of notebooks or tablets in the field (airports, client sites, and classrooms). Once the network is established, you

Brother UK, Ltd.

Boxlight Corporation

FIGURE 36

(a) The Brother MPrint micro printer is equipped with Bluetooth and USB interfaces so that you can print with or without connecting cables. It fits in your jacket pocket and can print on plain paper, address labels, and even carbon paper. The Brother MPrint is compatible with Windows-based tablets and notebooks, Windows Mobile–based PDAs, and Palm-based PDAs. (b) The Boxlight Bumblebee projector weighs only one pound, is small enough to fit in your hand (4.8 by 3.9 inches), and can project to an auditorium or conference room.

FIGURE 37

The Colligo Workgroup Edition software allows you to set up a secure wireless network wherever you are so that you can work together with your peers.

Express Cards

FIGURE 38

ExpressCards add functionality to your notebook.

can share files and printers, update Outlook calendars, and chat with other members of the network. You even have a simple whiteboard tool for sketching your ideas. Working together was never easier!

NOTEBOOK OR DESKTOP?

How does a notebook compare to a desktop? Desktop systems are invariably a better value than notebooks in terms of computing power gained for your dollar. Because of the notebook's small **footprint** (the amount of space on the desk it takes up), you pay more for each component. Each piece has had extra engineering time invested to make sure it fits in the smallest space. In addition, a desktop system offers more expandability options. It's easier to add new ports and devices because of the amount of room available in the desktop computer's design.

Desktop systems also are more reliable. Because of the amount of vibration that a

notebook experiences, as well as the added exposure to dust, water, and temperature fluctuations, notebooks do not last as long as desktop computers. Manufacturers offer extended warranty plans that cover accidental damage and unexpected drops, though at a price.

How long should I be able to keep my notebook? The answer to that question depends on how easy it is to upgrade your system. Take note of the maximum amount of memory you can install in your notebook and generally you should install as much as you can afford to extend the useful life of your notebook. Internal hard disks are not easy to upgrade in a notebook, but if you have a FireWire or USB 2.0 port, you can add an external hard drive for more storage space. Historically, notebooks have been equipped with PC Card slots, which are slots on the side of the notebook that accept special credit card–sized devices called PC Cards. A new standard has emerged called ExpressCard, and ExpressCard slots will now be the standard expansion slots on new notebooks. **ExpressCards** (shown in Figure 38) are smaller and transfer data faster than the PC Cards they are replacing. ExpressCards can add fax modems, network connections, wireless adapters, USB 2.0 and FireWire ports, and other capabilities to your notebook.

You also can add a device that allows you to read flash memory cards, such as CompactFlash, memory sticks, and Secure Digital cards. As new types of ports and devices are introduced, many will be manufactured in ExpressCard formats so that you can make sure your notebook does not become obsolete before its time.

SOUND BYTE

Tablet and Notebook Tour

In this Sound Byte, you'll take a tour of a tablet PC and a notebook computer, learning about the unique features and ports available on each.

Emerging Technologies: Nanotubes—The Next Big Thing Is Pretty Darn Small!

In the classic 1967 film *The Graduate*, Dustin Hoffman is a young man uncertain about which career he should embark on. At a cocktail party, an older gentleman provides him with some career advice, telling him, "I've got just one word for you ... plastics!" This made sense at the time because plastics were coming on strong as a replacement for metal. If *The Graduate* were remade today, the advice would be, "I've got just one word for you ... nanotubes!"

Nanoscience involves the study of molecules and structures (called nanostructures), whose size ranges from 1 to 100 nanometers (or one-billionth of a meter). Using nanotechnology, scientists are hoping to one day build resources from the molecular level by manipulating individual atoms instead of using raw materials already found in nature (such as wood or iron ore). This would allow us to create microscopic computers, the ultimate in portable devices. Imagine nano-sized robotic computers swimming through your arteries clearing them of plaque. Consider carrying with you a supercomputer the size of a pencil eraser, or even better, having the power of your desktop computer implanted in your body as a nano-sized chip.

The possibilities of miniaturization are endless, but what materials would be used to construct the computer circuits for these devices? Carbon nanotubes are poised to be the building blocks of the future. You're familiar with carbon from pencils. The graphite core in a pencil is composed of sheets of carbon atoms laid out in a honeycomb pattern. Individual sheets of graphite are very strong but don't bond well to other sheets. This makes them ideal for use in a pencil because, as you write, the graphite flakes off and leaves marks on the paper. Unfortunately, graphite doesn't conduct electricity very well. This inability, coupled with the lack of strong bonding principles, makes graphite unsuitable as a material to manufacture circuits.

Carbon nanotubes were discovered in 1991. Nanotubes are essentially a sheet of carbon atoms (much like graphite) laid out in a honeycomb pattern but rolled into a spherical tube, as shown in Figure 39. Arranging the carbon in a tube increases its strength astronomically. It is estimated that carbon nanotubes are 10 to 100 times stronger per unit of weight than steel. This should make them ideal for constructing many types of devices and building materials. Some day we may have earthquake-proof buildings constructed from nanotubes or virtually indestructible clothing woven from nanotube fibers.

But how does this help us build a computer? Aside from strength, the most interesting property of nanotubes is that they are good conductors of electricity. Nanotubes are actually classified as semimetal, meaning they can have properties that are a cross between semiconductors (such as silicon, which is used to create computer chips) and metals. In fact, depending on how a nanotube is constructed, it can change from a semiconductor to a metal along the length of the tube. These properties make it vastly superior to silicon for the construction of transistor pathways in computer chips, because they provide engineers with more versatility.

In addition, although the smallest silicon transistors that are likely to be produced in the future will be millions of atoms wide, scientists believe that transistors constructed of nanotubes would be only 100 to 1,000 atoms wide. This represents a quantum leap in miniaturization even surpassing the original invention of the transistor. Just imagine what can be done when nanotube transistors replace silicon transistors!

So, when can you buy that pencil eraser-sized computer? Not for quite a while. At this point, researchers can manufacture nanotubes only in extremely small quantities at a large cost. But the U.S. government and many multinational corporations are expected to pour billions of dollars into nanoscience research over the next decade. The ongoing research will hopefully lead to breakthroughs in manufacturing technology that will result in nano-scale computers within your lifetime.

Courtesy of Photo Researchers Inc.

FIGURE 39

Here is a highly magnified close-up of a carbon nanotube. Rolling the sheets of carbon atoms into a tube shape gives them incredible strength.

Summary

1. What are the advantages and limitations of mobile computing?

Mobile computing allows you to communicate with others, remain productive, and have access to your personal information and schedules, Internet-based information, and important software no matter where you are. However, because mobile devices have been miniaturized, they are more expensive and less rugged than desktop equipment. In addition, battery life limits the usefulness of mobile devices, the screen area is small on most devices, the speed of Internet connection is currently lower than is available in the home, and wireless Internet coverage can be limited in some areas.

2. What are the various mobile computing devices?

A range of mobile computing devices are on the market today, including paging devices (pagers), cell phones (and smartphones), portable media players (PMPs), personal digital assistants (PDAs), tablet PCs, and notebook computers.

3. How do cell phone components resemble a traditional computer, and how do cell phones work?

Just like a computer system, cell phones include a processor (CPU), memory, input and output devices, software, and an operating system. When you speak into a cell phone, the sound enters as a sound wave. Analog sound waves need to be digitized, so an analog-to-digital converter chip converts these sound waves into digital signals. The digital information is then compressed (by a digital signal processor) so that it transmits more quickly to another phone. Finally, the digital information is transmitted as a radio wave through the cellular network to the destination phone.

4. What can I carry in a portable media player, and how does it store data?

A portable media player (PMP) is a device that enables you to carry digital music, image, and video files around with you. Some PMPs also allow you to carry contact databases and calendars as well. The most inexpensive players use only flash memory to store data, whereas more expensive models use a built-in hard drive, which provides more storage.

5. What can I use a PDA for, and what internal components and features does it have?

PDAs are powerful devices that can carry calendars, contact lists, personal productivity software programs, songs, photos, games, and more. Like any computer, a PDA includes a processor, operating system software, input and output devices, and ports. All PDAs feature touch-sensitive screens that allow you to enter data with a stylus. You can use either handwritten text or special notation systems to enter data into a PDA. In terms of output devices, PDAs come with LCD screens in a variety of resolutions. The two main PDA operating systems are the Palm OS and Windows Mobile, although Windows Mobile outsells the Palm OS by a wide margin. PDAs do not come with built-in hard drives, but for memory needs beyond their built-in RAM and ROM, certain PDAs use removable flash memory.

6. How can I synchronize my PDA with my desktop computer?

The process of updating your data so that the files on your mobile device and desktop computer are the same is called synchronizing. To synchronize your desktop and PDA, you place the PDA in a cradle and touch a "hot sync" button. This begins the process of information transfer (or synchronization) that updates both sets of files to the most current version. Other options for synchronizing or transferring files include using IrDA ports and the Bluetooth wireless connectivity option.

7. What is a tablet PC, and why would I want to use one?

A tablet PC is a portable computer that includes advanced handwriting recognition and incorporates the use of digital ink. Tablet PCs are so-named because the display monitor can be used either in a traditional notebook mode or in tablet mode. The most innovative input technology on the tablet PC is digital ink. Supporting digital ink, the tablet's screen is pressure-sensitive and reacts to a digital pen. A tablet PC can be the ideal solution when you require a lightweight, portable computer with full desktop processing power.

8. How powerful are notebooks, and how do they compare to desktop computers?

The most powerful mobile computing solution is a notebook computer. Notebooks offer large displays and can be equipped with DVD/CD-RW drives, hard drives, and 4 GB or even more of RAM. Many models feature hot-swappable bays and a full set of ports. Still, desktop systems are more reliable and cost-effective than notebooks. In addition, it is easier to upgrade and add new ports and devices to a desktop than to a notebook. And though powerful, CPUs for notebooks are usually a bit slower than the latest CPU offered for desktop units. Still, many users feel that the mobility notebooks offer is worth the added expense.

Key Terms

analog-to-digital converter chip
base transceiver station
benchmarking
Bluetooth
cellular phone (cell phone)
collaboration tool
convergence
cradle
data plans
digital ink
digital pen
digital signal processor
docking station
ExpressCard
flash memory
footprint
Global Positioning System (GPS)
Graffiti
hot-swappable bay
memory effect
microbrowser
Microsoft Transcriber
mobile computing device
mobile switching center

MP3 player
Multimedia Message Service (MMS)
notebook computer (laptop computer)
numeric pagers
Palm OS
peer-to-peer (P2P) sharing
personal digital assistant (PDA)
Pocket PC
portable media player (PMP)
processor speed
sampling rate
Short Message Service (SMS)
smartphone
stylus
subnotebook computers
Symbian OS
synchronizing
tablet PC
ultraportable (or subnotebook)
Web-enabled
Windows Mobile
Wireless Application Protocol (WAP)
wireless Internet service provider (ISP)
Wireless Markup Language (WML)

Buzz Words

Word Bank

- Bluetooth
- cell phone
- cradle
- crib
- flash memory card
- GPS
- microbrowser
- MMS
- mobile computing devices
- MP3 player
- notebook
- pager
- PDA
- processor speed
- SMS
- stylus
- synchronize
- tablet PC

Instructions: Fill in the blanks using the words from the Word Bank.

Kathleen's new job as a sales rep is going to mean a lot of travel. She knows she'll need to buy one or more of the (1) _____ available today to stay productive when she's out of the office. Because she needs voice communication and not just text exchange, she'll be selecting a(n) (2) _____ rather than a(n) (3) _____. With her cell phone, she'll be able to exchange text messages with her coworkers using (4) _____. When she accesses the Internet from her phone, she'll use (5) _____ software to check the latest stock prices.

Because she travels a lot and loves music, she has been considering buying a digital (6) _____. However, she has instead decided to purchase a more expensive (7) _____ that includes MP3 capabilities. That way, she can use the device as more than just an MP3 player. She also invests in a removable (8) _____ on which she'll store her MP3 files. Because she's a hiker, she wants to use her PDA as a navigation device, so she may buy a(n) (9) _____ accessory to go with it.

To make sure she is getting the best device with the most powerful processor, Kathleen has been comparing benchmarks that measure (10) _____. In addition, she wants to make sure she can (11) _____ her PDA with her desktop computer, so that the files on both match. Thus, she bought a PDA that includes the wireless (12) _____ technology, as well as an external (13) _____ that connects her PDA to her PC through a USB port. Because she still needs to run powerful software packages when she's out of the office, she bought a(n) (14) _____ as well. It was a better choice than a full-sized (15) _____ because she carries it with her all day, taking notes while standing on the production floor.

Becoming Computer Literate

You have a job as a sales rep at a large publishing company and are on the road constantly calling on customers. Your boss is considering investing in some kind of mobile device with Internet access to help you perform your duties. However, first she requires a justification. What mobile device(s) would be best suited for your position? Would you need Internet access for it? Does it depend on which type of device you're using or your job responsibilities? What advantages would there be for the company? What hardware would be required?

Instructions: Using the preceding scenario, write a report using as many of the key terms from the chapter as you can. Be sure the sentences are grammatically and technically correct.

Self-Test

Instructions: Answer the multiple-choice and true/false questions below for more practice with key terms and concepts from this chapter.

MULTIPLE CHOICE

1. Mobile computing is useful only in professions that
   a. don't rely on Internet access.
   b. where work requires intensive graphics and large display screens.
   c. where work requires intensive computer processing power.
   d. None of the above.

2. Currently, cell phones contain ALL of the following except
   a. a CPU.   c. RAM.
   b. output devices.   d. input devices.

3. Cell phones store data
   a. on a hard drive.
   b. in RAM.
   c. in ROM.
   d. Cell phones are unable to store data.

4. To fit more songs on a personal media player you can
   a. decrease the sampling rate of digitized music files.
   b. install additional RAM in the PMP.
   c. increase the sampling rate of digitized music files.
   d. install a larger hard drive in the PMP.

5. Flash memory is
   a. nonvolatile and is not erased when power is disconnected.
   b. volatile and is erased when power is disconnected.
   c. used only in PDAs and tablet computers.
   d. the main storage medium in notebook computers.

6. The device best suited for a salesperson who has to demonstrate processor-intensive multimedia to clients is a

   a. smartphone with Internet capabilities.
   b. PDA with an external monitor.
   c. tablet PC.
   d. notebook computer.

7. GPS chips are
   a. installed in all newly manufactured automobiles.
   b. installed in all newly manufactured cell phones.
   c. reliable only when installed in tablet PCs.
   d. available only for PDAs and smartphones.

8. For Internet access, you should obtain:
   a. a tablet PC.
   b. a smartphone.
   c. a PDA.
   d. All of the above can have Internet capability.

9. When a notebook does not have enough USB ports, you
   a. can have two devices share one USB port.
   b. can add ports only if the notebook is configured with flash memory.
   c. can't add ports unless your computer uses Windows Vista.
   d. can add ports using a PC card or external hub.

10. Portable devices that can be synchronized with your home computer are
    a. PDAs and GPS units.
    b. iPods, PDAs, and cell phones.
    c. pagers and GPS units.
    d. any device with Bluetooth.

TRUE/FALSE

___ 1. Hard disk drives are found only in desktops, notebooks, and tablet PCs.

___ 2. PMPs with a hard drive are able to carry fewer songs than those with flash memory.

___ 3. PDAs and tablet PCs can exchange data wirelessly if they both have Bluetooth.

___ 4. Tablet PCs are commonly used for text messaging.

___ 5. Smartphones contain CPUs. Regular cell phones do not.

Mobile Computing: Keeping Your Data on Hand

Making the Transition to...
Next Semester

1. Choosing Devices to Fit Your Needs

As a student, which devices discussed in this chapter would have the most immediate impact on the work you do each day? Which would provide the best value (that is, the greatest increase in productivity and organization per dollar spent)?

2. Choosing the Best Notebook

Compare the Apple MacBook series of notebook computers with the Dell Inspiron series. Consider price, performance, expandability, and portability. Explain which would be the better investment for your needs next semester.

3. Choosing the Best Cell Phone Plan

Major national cellular providers include AT&T, Verizon, T-Mobile, and Sprint. Visit their Web sites and compare the prices and features of their popular cellular plans for both minimal users and power users. Based on your research, which cell phone plan would be best for your needs? Which company has the most cost-effective data plan? Would an "unlocked" phone (one not tied to a specific vendor) work best for you?

4. Choosing the Best Smartphone

Your friend wants a cell phone that doubles as an MP3 player so she can avoid carrying two devices. Visit the cellular providers' Web sites (mentioned in the preceding question) and research options. What phone would you recommend to your friend and why? Compare at least three different models of phones and list their price, music storage capacity, built-in memory, and expandability options.

a Which of the three models you compared is the best value for your friend?
b. What special features does the phone you chose have? What accessories would you recommend your friend buy to make the phone more useful?
c. Would you consider buying a used cell phone? Why or why not?

5. How Many MP3 Files Can You Fit?

Fill out the following table to determine how many minutes of MP3 files you could store depending on the sampling rate of the MP3 files. Use the following to help you fill in the table:

- Say you sample music at 192 kilobits per second. There are 8 bits in one byte, so 192 kilobits per second = 192/8 = 24 KB per second.

- There are 60 seconds in one minute, so the number of kilobytes per minute is equal to 24 KB per second times 60 seconds = 1,440 KB per minute.

- With 256 MB of space, there would be room for 256,000 KB divided by 1,440 KB per minute = approximately 177 minutes of songs that can be stored.

Sampling Rate, Kilobits per Second	Number of Kilobytes (KB) per Second (KB/sec)	Number of Kilobytes per Minute (KB/minute)	Flash Card Memory	Minutes of Songs that Can Be Stored
192 Kbps	192/8 = 24 KBps	24 KBps * 60 seconds = 1,440 KB per minute	2 GB	2,000,000 KB/ 1,440 KB per minute = 1388 minutes or 23.1 hours
128 Kbps			2 GB	
96 Kbps			2 GB	
64 Kbps			2 GB	

Making the Transition to... the Workplace

1. **Corporate Mobile Computing Needs**

   Imagine your company is boosting its sales force and looking to the future of mobile technology. Your boss has asked you to research the following issues surrounding mobile computing for the company:

   a. Do mobile computing devices present increased security risks? What would happen if you left a flash memory card at a meeting and a competitor picked it up? Are there ways to protect your data on mobile devices?

   b. Can viruses attack mobile devices? Is there any special software on the market to protect mobile devices from viruses? How much would it cost to equip 20 devices with protection?

   c. Is there a role for mobile computing devices even if employees don't leave the building? Which devices would be important for a company to consider for use within corporate offices?

   d. Should employees be allowed to use mobile devices provided by the company for personal use even though these files related to personal use might eat up potentially valuable memory and space? What restrictions should be put on personal use to protect the privacy of proprietary company information contained on the devices?

2. **3G Communications**

   The next generation of telecommunications (nicknamed "3G" for third generation) allows the speed of cellular network transmissions to rise from 144 Kbps to 2 Mbps. How does that compare to dial-up and cable modem access for wired networks? What implications does it have for information access and e-commerce?

3. **Mobile Speed Limits**

   Using the Internet, research what speed limitations are expected to exist in the future with regards to mobile devices. Also, report on the average speeds obtained during testing on two popular mobile devices. (Good sources of testing information include **www.pcmag.com** and **www.consumerreports.org**.)

4. **Too Much Mobile?**

   Imagine you are a manager of 18 employees, all of whom work in open-air cubicles (that is, there are no fixed walls or separate offices). As a manager, what concerns might you have about their personal cell phone usage? Do you think your employees would respond well to a "Quiet Zone," an area in which no personal cell phone usage is allowed? What about conduct during important meetings? Should employees be allowed to text message each other during the meeting? As a manager, are there concerns you might have if employees had a digital camera on their cell phones?

Mobile Computing: Keeping Your Data on Hand

Critical Thinking Questions

Instructions: Albert Einstein used "Gedanken experiments," or critical thinking questions, to develop his theory of relativity. Some ideas are best understood by experimenting with them in our own minds. The following critical thinking questions are designed to demand your full attention but require only a comfortable chair—no technology.

1. **Mobile Devices and Society**

   Do you think we will ever become a completely wireless society? Will there always be a need for some land lines (physical wired connections)? How will broadband wireless communication infrastructure impact a city's social and economic development? Will there be more social interaction? less? Will mobile computing promote increased understanding between people? more isolation?

2. **The Ultimate Mobile Devices**

   As devices become lighter and smaller, we are seeing a convergence of multiple functions into one device.

   a. What would the ultimate convergent mobile device be for you? Is there a limit in weight, size, or complexity?
   b. America Online Instant Messenger (AIM) service is now available on many cellular phone systems. Would the ability to be alerted to IM buddies on your cell phone be useful to you? What would you be willing to pay for this feature? What other alerts might be useful to you (eBay auctions, for instance)? Are the alerts you need available at this time?

3. **Protecting Intellectual Property**

   The recording industry, recording artists, the motion picture industry, and consumers find themselves in a complex discussion when the topic of peer-to-peer sharing systems is brought up.

   a. What solution would you propose to safeguard the business interests of industry, the intellectual property rights of artists, and the freedoms of consumers?
   b. Have you ever downloaded music or video off the Web? If so, did you download from a legal site? Do you think illegal download sites should be allowed to exist?

4. **Privacy Concerns: GPS Tracking at Work**

   You drive a delivery vehicle for your employer. How would you feel if your employer installed a GPS device in all of its delivery vehicles to monitor employee work habits? How would you feel if your employer disciplined you for speeding based on data obtained from the GPS device installed in your delivery vehicle? Should employers have the right to monitor their employees in this way? Why or why not?

5. **Privacy Concerns: GPS Tracking at Home**

   Consider the following questions related to GPS security risks:

   a. Your spouse carries a GPS-enabled cell phone. The GPS chip inside allows a private service (**www.ulocate.com**) to gather information on your spouse's last location, the path he or she took to get there, and their average speed from point to point. Would you use the service to check on your spouse's activities? What if it was your spouse monitoring you?
   b. Would you agree to insert a GPS-enabled tracking device into your pet? your child? What legislation would be required if tracking data were available on you? Would you be willing to sell that information to marketing agencies? Should that data be available to the government if you were suspected of a crime?

6. **Nanotechnology Applications**

   If you had a computer the size of a pencil eraser (built based on nanotechnology), how would your leisure time change? How would you take advantage of such a small computer in the business world?

Problem:

You have formed a consulting group that advises clients on how to move their businesses into the new mobile computing age.

Task:

Each team will be defined as an expert resource in one of the mobile devices presented in this chapter: cell phones (including smartphones), PMPs, PDAs, tablet PCs, or notebooks. For each of the scenarios described by a client, the group should assess how strong a fit their device is to that client's needs.

Process:

Divide the class into three or four teams and assign each group a different mobile device (smartphone, PMP, PDA, tablet PC, or notebook).

1. Research the current features and prices for the mobile device your team has been assigned.

2. Consider the following three clients:

   - An elementary classroom that wants to have students carry mobile devices to the nearby creek to do a science project on water quality.

   - A manufacturing plant that wants managers using a mobile device to be able to report back hourly on the production line's performance and problems.

   - A pharmaceutical company that wants to outfit its sales reps with the devices they need to be prepared to promote their products when they visit physicians.

3. Discuss the advantages and disadvantages of your device for each of these clients. Consider value, reliability, computing needs, and communication needs as well as expandability for the future.

4. As a group, prepare a final report that considers the costs, availability, and unique features of the device that led you to recommend or not recommend it for each client.

5. Bring the research materials from the individual team meetings to class. Looking at the clients' needs, make final decisions as to which mobile device is best suited for each client.

Conclusion:

There are a number of mobile computing devices on the market today. Finding the best mobile device to use in any given situation depends on factors such as value, reliability, expandability, and the computing and communication needs of the client.

Multimedia

In addition to the review materials presented here, you'll find additional materials featured with the book's multimedia, including the Technology in Action Student Resource CD and the Companion Web site (**www.prenhall.com/techinaction**), which will help reinforce your understanding of the chapter content. These materials include the following:

ACTIVE HELPDESK

In Active Helpdesk calls, you'll assume the role of a Helpdesk operator taking calls about the concepts you've learned in this chapter. You'll apply what you've learned and receive feedback from a supervisor to review and reinforce those concepts. The Active Helpdesk calls for this chapter are listed here and can be found on your Student Resource CD:

- Using Portable Media Players
- Using PDAs

SOUND BYTES

Sound Bytes are dynamic multimedia tutorials that help demystify even the most complex topics. You'll view video clips and animations that illustrate computer concepts, and then apply what you've learned by reviewing with the Sound Byte Labs, which include quizzes and activities specifically tailored to each Sound Byte. The Sound Bytes for this chapter are listed here and can be found on your Student Resource CD:

- PDAs on the Road and at Home
- Connecting with Bluetooth
- Tablet and Notebook Tour

COMPANION WEB SITE

The Technology in Action Companion Web Site includes a variety of additional materials to help you review and learn more about the topics in this chapter. The resources available at **www.prenhall.com/techinaction** include

- **Online Study Guide.** Each chapter features an online true/false and multiple-choice quiz. You can take these quizzes, automatically check the results, and e-mail the results to your instructor.
- **Web Research Projects.** Each chapter features a number of Web research projects that ask you to search the Web for information on computer-related careers, milestones in computer history, important people and companies, emerging technologies, and the applications and implications of different technologies.

Digital Entertainment

When did everything go "digital"? It used to be that you'd only find analog forms of entertainment. Today, no matter what you're interested in—music, movies, television, radio—a digital version is popular (see Figure 1). MP3 files encode digital forms of music, and digital cameras and video camcorders are now commonplace. In Hollywood, some feature films are now being shot entirely with digital equipment, and many movie theaters use digital projection equipment.

©Patrick Giardano/ Corbis

George Lucas, a great proponent of digital technology, filmed *Star Wars Episode II: Attack of the Clones* all the way back in 2002 completely in digital format. It played in special digital release at digital-ready theaters. And in January 2005, the digital film *RIZE*, by David LaChapelle, premiered at the Sundance Film Festival. It was streamed from computers in Oregon to a full-size cinema screen in Park City, Utah, beginning a new age of movie distribution. Also gaining in popularity is the MOD Films site (**www.modfilms.com**), a gathering place for people who see "remixable" films in our future. The components of these featured films—from production footage to soundtrack, dialogue, and sound effects—will be available to the audience online, and each person will be able to interact and modify the film, creating a new plotline or a different ending. Digital entertainment is here to stay.

Meanwhile, satellite radio systems such as XM Satellite Radio and HD Radio are digital formats, and Digital Television (DTV), a digital encoding of television signals, is scheduled to become the national standard sometime in 2009. In this Technology in Focus, we look at two popular forms of digital entertainment: digital photography and digital video. But first, let's consider what makes digital so unique.

What's So Special About Digital?

So what *is* so special about digital? Think about the information captured in music and film: sounds and images. Sound is carried to

FIGURE 1
Analog Versus Digital Entertainment

	ANALOG	DIGITAL
MUSIC	Vinyl record albums Cassette tapes	CDs MP3 files
PHOTOGRAPHY	35-mm single lens reflex (SLR) cameras Photos stored on film	Digital cameras, including digital SLRs Photos stored as digital files
VIDEO	8-mm, Hi8, or VHS camcorders Film stored on VHS tapes	Digital video (DV) camcorders Film stored as digital files; often distributed on DVDs
RADIO	AM/FM radio	HD Radio XM Radio
TELEVISION	Conventional broadcast analog TV	Digital Television (DTV)

your ears by sound waves, which are actually patterns of pressure changes in the air. Images are our interpretation of the changing intensity of light waves around us. These sound and light waves are called analog or continuous waves. They illustrate the loudness of the sound or the brightness of the colors in the image at a given moment in time. They are continuous signals because you would never have to lift your pencil off the page to draw them: they are just one long continuous line.

The first generation of recording devices (such as vinyl records and analog television shows) was designed to reproduce these sound and light waves. The needle in a groove of a vinyl record vibrates in the same pattern as the original sound wave. Television signals are actually waves that tell your TV how to display the same color and brightness as seen in the original studio. But it's difficult to describe a wave, even mathematically. Very simple sounds, like the C note of a piano, have a very simple shape, like that shown in Figure 2a. However, something like the word *hello* generates a very complex pattern, like that shown in Figure 2b.

Digital formats are descriptions of these signals as a long string of *numbers*. This is the main reason why digital recording has

such an advantage over analog. Digital gives us a simple way to describe sound and light waves *exactly*, so that sounds and images can be reproduced perfectly each time. We already have easy ways to distribute digital information (on CDs, DVDs, or using e-mail, for example). But how could a digital format, a sequence of numbers, act as a convenient way to express these complicated wave shapes?

The answer is provided by something called **analog-to-digital conversion**. In analog-to-digital conversion, the incoming analog signal is measured many times each second. The strength of the signal at each measurement is recorded as a simple number. The series of numbers produced by the analog-to-digital conversion process gives us the digital form of the wave. Figure 3 shows an analog and digital version of the same wave. In Figure 3a, you see the original continuous analog wave. You could draw the wave in Figure 3a without lifting your pencil from the page. In Figure 3b, the wave has been digitized and now is not a single line but rather is represented as a series of points or numbers.

So, how does this all work? Let's take music as an example. Figure 4 shows how the process of creating digital entertainment begins with the physical act of playing music,

FIGURE 2

(a) This is an analog wave showing the simple, pure sound of a piano playing middle C. (b) This is the complex wave produced when a person says "hello."

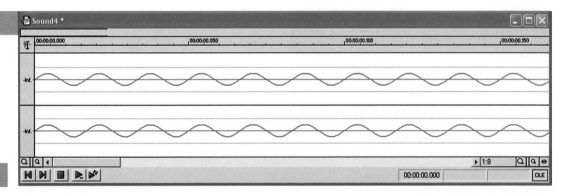

a

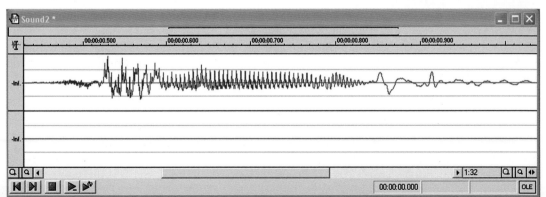

b

 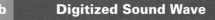

a **Analog Sound Wave**	b **Digitized Sound Wave**	**FIGURE 3**

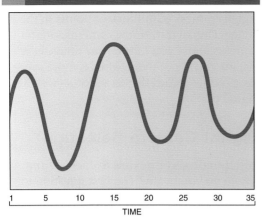

(a) Here you see a simple analog wave. (b) Here you see a digitized version of the same wave.

which creates analog waves. Next, a chip inside the recording device called an analog-to-digital converter (ADC) digitizes these waves into a series of numbers. This series of numbers can be recorded onto CDs and DVDs or sent electronically. On the receiving end, a playback device, such as a CD player or DVD player, is fed that same series of numbers. Inside the playback device, a digital-to-analog converter (DAC), a chip that converts the digital numbers to a continuous wave, reproduces the original wave exactly.

More precisely, the digital wave will be *close* to exact. How accurate it is, how close

the digitized wave is in shape to the original analog wave, depends on the **sampling rate** of the ADC. The sampling rate specifies the number of times the analog wave is measured each second. The higher the sampling rate, the more accurately the original wave can be re-created. However, higher sampling rates also produce much more data and therefore result in bigger files. For example, sound waves on CDs are sampled at a rate of 44,000 times a second. This produces a huge list of numbers—44,000 of them each second!

So, when sounds or image waves are digitized, it means that analog data is changed

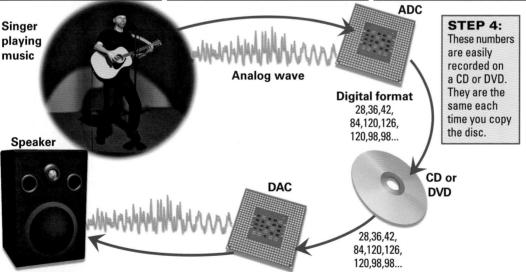

STEP 1: A singer plays music and sends complex analog sound waves into the air.

STEP 2: In the recording process, a microphone feeds these analog waves into an analog-to-digital converter (ADC).

STEP 3: The ADC digitizes the waves. They are now represented as a series of numbers.

FIGURE 4

During the complete recording process, information moves from analog form to digital data and then back again to analog sound waves.

Singer playing music

Analog wave

ADC

STEP 4: These numbers are easily recorded on a CD or DVD. They are the same each time you copy the disc.

Digital format
28,36,42,
84,120,126,
120,98,98...

Speaker

DAC

CD or DVD

28,36,42,
84,120,126,
120,98,98...

STEP 6: These analog waves tell your receiver how to move the speaker cones to duplicate the same sound waves as in the original music.

STEP 5: To play the CD, your CD player must have a digital-to-analog converter (DAC) to convert the numbers back to the analog wave.

into digital data—from a wave into a series of numbers. The digital data is perfectly reproducible and can be distributed easily on CDs and DVDs or through the airwaves. The data also can be easily processed by a computer.

These digital advantages have revolutionized photography, music, movies, television, and radio. For example, digital television has a sharper picture and superior sound quality. However, there is a cost in the shift from analog to digital technologies. The Federal Communications Commission (FCC) has set a target date of February 17, 2009, when all over-the-air broadcasters must transmit in digital format. Consumers receiving broadcast signals (i.e., not cable subscribers) will be forced to choose between upgrading to digital DTV sets or purchasing a converter for older televisions. The digital revolution in television will bring better quality and additional conveniences, but at a cost, as the older analog equipment is phased out. (Visit **www.fcc.gov/dtv** and **www.dtv.gov** for more information on when and how the FCC ruling will affect you.)

The same tension exists in the migration from analog to digital technology in photography. Let's take a look at this form of entertainment and explore the advantages and investment required in migrating to a digital format.

Digital Photography

Before digital cameras hit the market, most people used some form of 35-mm single-lens reflex (SLR) camera. When you take a picture using a traditional SLR camera, a shutter opens, creating an aperture (a small window in the camera), which allows light to hit the 35-mm film inside. Chemicals coating the film react when exposed to light. Later, additional chemicals develop the image on the film, and it is printed on special light-sensitive paper. A variety of lenses and processing techniques, special equipment, and filters are needed to create printed photos from traditional SLR cameras.

Digital cameras, on the other hand, do not use film. Instead, they capture images on electronic sensors called charge-coupled device (CCD) arrays and then convert those images to digital data, a long series of numbers that represent the color and brightness of millions of points in the image. Unlike traditional cameras, digital cameras allow you to see your images the instant you shoot them. Most camera models can now record digital video as well as digital photos.

Digital Camera Selection

With hundreds of models to choose from, where do you begin? The first question to answer is whether you want a compact "point-and-click" model camera or a more serious digital SLR. The larger digital SLR cameras allow you to switch between different lenses and offer features important to serious amateur and professional photographers (like depth of field previewing). Although having such flexibility in moving up to a larger zoom lens is a great advantage, these cameras are also larger, heavier, and use more battery power than the tiny point-and-click models. Think about how you will be using your camera and decide which will serve you best in the long run.

Next, you'll want to evaluate the quality of the camera on a number of levels. One great resource to use is Digital Photography Review (**www.dpreview.com**). Their camera reviews evaluate the camera's construction, its features, image quality, ease of use, and value for the cost.

In addition, you will find comparisons to similar camera models by other manufacturers and feedback from owners of those models. Links are provided to several resellers, making it easy to compare price as well.

Digital Camera Resolutions

Part of what determines the image quality of a digital camera is its **resolution**, or the number of data points it records for each image captured. A digital camera's resolution is measured in megapixels (MP). The prefix *mega* is short for millions. The word pixel is short for picture element, or a single dot in a digital image. Point-and-click models typically offer resolutions from 2 MB to 10 MB. Professional digital SLR cameras, such as the Canon EOS-1Ds Mark II, can take photos at resolutions up to 16.7 MP, but sell for thousands of dollars. Figure 5 shows some popular digital camera models and the

FIGURE 5

Nikon Coolpix S4 (6.1 MP)

Kodak EasyShare C64
(6.1 MP)

(Nikon Coolpix S4) Courtesy of MMW Group

(Kodak EasyShare c64) Courtesy of ©Eastman Kodak Company

Canon EOS-1 Mark II (16.7 MP)

Olympus Stylus 750 (7.1 MP)

(Canon EOS-1) "Canon" the Canon Logo. All rights reserved. Used by permission.

(Olympus Stylus 750) Courtesy of Olympus

FIGURE 6

Flash memory slides into a digital camera and is used to store images.

number of pixels they record at their maximum resolution.

If you're interested in making only 5 x 7" or 8 x 10" prints, a lower resolution camera is fine. However, low-resolution images become grainy and pixelated when pushed to make larger size prints. For example, if you tried to print an 11 x 14" enlargement from a 2-MP shot taken using your cell phone's camera, the image would look grainy—you would see individual dots of color instead of a clear, sharp image. The 5 MP–10 MP cameras on the market now have plenty of resolution to guarantee sharp, detailed images even at enlargements to 11 x 14".

Storage of Digital Images

When a digital camera takes a photo, it stores the images on a flash memory card inside the camera, as shown in Figure 6. Flash memory cards are very small and convenient, allowing you to easily transfer digital information between your camera and your computer or printer. Flash memory therefore takes the place of film used in traditional cameras.

To fit more photos on the same size flash memory card, digital cameras allow you to choose from several different file types in order to compress, or squeeze, the image data into less memory space. When you choose to compress your images, you will lose some of the detail, but in return you'll

be able to fit more images on your flash card. Figure 7 shows the most common file types supported by digital cameras: the RAW uncompressed data type and the Joint Photographic Experts Group (JPEG) type. RAW files record all of the original image information and so are larger than compressed JPEG files. JPEG files can be compressed just a bit, keeping most of the details, or compressed a great deal, losing some detail. Most cameras allow you to select from a few different JPEG compression levels.

Often cameras also support a very low-resolution storage option, creating files that you can easily attach to e-mail messages. This low-resolution setting typically provides images that are not useful for printing but that are so much smaller in size that it is easy to e-mail them. Even those with slow Internet connections are able to quickly download and view them on-screen.

FIGURE 7
File Types Commonly Used in Digital Cameras

FILE TYPE	COMPRESSED	QUALITY	SAMPLE FILE SIZE	NUMBER OF IMAGES THAT FIT ON A 512-MB FLASH CARD
RAW	No	High: Contains all the original	10.6 MB	48
JPEG (at highest camera resolution)	Yes	Medium Moderate compression; some lost quality	7.7 MB	66
JPEG (at lowest camera resolution)	Yes	Low More compression; more lost quality	1.4 MB	365

Note: The file sizes in this table refer to image storage on a Canon EOS 30D camera.

Preparing Your Camera and Taking Your Photos

Preparing your camera includes ensuring that your camera's batteries are charged and the settings are correct. Digital cameras consume a great deal of power, so you might want to carry a spare, charged battery pack. Also make sure that the flash card is installed and that it has enough space for the number of photos you plan to take.

Next, set the resolution on your camera. Most cameras offer two or three different resolution settings. For example, a 6-MP camera might be able to shoot images at 6 MP, 2.7 MP, or 1.5 MP. If you're taking a photo that will be enlarged and that needs to be at a very high quality, use the full power of your camera. Shoot the image at 6 MP and save the image as uncompressed data at the highest resolution. If you're planning to use the image for a Web page, where having a smaller file would be helpful, use a lower resolution and the space-saving compressed JPEG format. If you're unsure how you're going to use your images, record them with the maximum resolution your camera allows.

Most cameras include an autofocus feature and automatically set the aperture and correct shutter speed. Several cameras now also incorporate image stabilization algorithms to reduce the amount of vibration seen in the image if your hands are a bit shaky. This makes taking a digital photo as simple as pressing a button. The great thing about digital cameras, of course, is that they let you instantly examine your photos in a display window on the camera. If you don't like a certain photo, you can delete it immediately, freeing space on your flash card.

Transferring Your Photos to Your Computer

If you just want to print your photos, you may not need to transfer them to your computer. Many photo printers can make prints directly from your camera or from the flash memory card. However, transferring the photos to your computer allows you to store them and frees your flash card for reuse.

Transferring your photos to your computer is simple. All current model digital cameras have a built-in universal serial bus (USB) 2.0 port (some high-end models may also include a FireWire port). Using a USB 2.0 cable, you can connect the camera to your computer and copy the converted images as uncompressed files or in a compressed format as JPEG files. Another option is to transfer the flash card from your camera to the computer. Some desktops have flash card slots on the front of the system unit. However, if yours does not, you can buy an external memory card reader like the one shown in Figure 8 and attach it to your computer using an available USB port. Several newer model cameras also support wireless network connections to your computer so that you can transfer the images without the fuss of putting a cable in place!

When you connect your camera to your computer, with the Microsoft Windows Vista operating system, the rest of the transfer is automatic (see Figure 9). Assuming your sound is turned on, you'll hear an attention sound telling you the computer and camera are connected and can communicate. Next, a dialog box appears, asking you whether you want to view the images or import them to your computer. If you choose to import, you have the ability to tag the group of images. Once downloaded into Windows Photo Gallery, you can add details to each image with captions and ratings. If you're satisfied with the photos and want to share them, you can send them to your friends as e-mail attachments, or upload the images to an online Web photo album, for example. If you're not satisfied with them, you can process them further to remove red-eye, change to sepia tones, or add special effects.

Processing Your Photos and Adding Special Effects

Once you've taken your photos, you may want to process them, cropping them, for example, or adding special effects. Traditional photographers often invest in special equipment and chemicals needed to develop 35-mm film. The photographer can then resize or crop the photo, add different filtering effects, or combine photos. With digital photography, you can do all of this using inexpensive image-editing software.

There are hundreds of image-editing programs available, from freeware to very sophisticated software suites. Many times the manufacturer of your camera will include an image-editing program on a CD that comes with your camera. If you want to purchase a more powerful program, Adobe Photoshop Elements and Corel Paint Shop Pro are two well-reviewed packages suitable for home use. They allow you to remove flaws such as red-eye; crop images; correct poor color balance; apply filtering effects such as mosaics, charcoal, and impressionistic style; and merge components from multiple

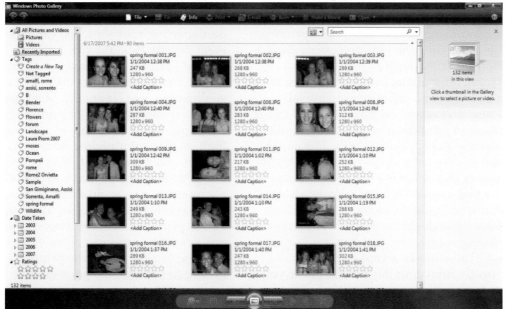

FIGURE 8

If your computer does not have a built-in flash card reader, you can buy an external reader that attaches to your computer using a USB cable and port.

Lexar

FIGURE 9

The Windows Vista operating system makes it simple to import digital images to a file on your hard drive. (a) Vista enables you to import or view images. (b) Images are imported directly to Windows Photo Gallery in which you can rate and add captions to your images.

How Do My Old Photos Become Digital?

Obviously, not every document or image you have is in an electronic form. What about all the photographs you have already taken? Or an article from a magazine or a hand-drawn sketch? How can these be converted into digital format?

Digital scanners like the one shown in Figure 10 convert paper text and images into digital formats. You can place any flat material on the glass surface of the scanner and then convert it into a digital file. Most scanner software allows you to store the converted images as RAW files or in compressed form as JPEG files. And some scanners include hardware that allows you to scan film negatives or slides as well, or even to insert a stack of photos to be scanned in sequence.

Scanner quality is measured by its resolution, which is given in dots per inch (dpi). Most modern scanners can digitize a document at resolutions up to 4,800 x 9,600 dpi, in either color or grayscale modes. You can easily connect a scanner to your computer using USB 2.0 or FireWire ports. Scanners also typically come with software supporting optical character recognition (OCR). OCR software converts pages of handwritten or typed text into electronic files. You can then open and edit these converted documents with traditional word-processing programs such as Microsoft Word. In addition, many scanners have a Copy button that allows you to scan and sometimes print documents, taking the place of a copy machine.

Courtesy of Hewlett Packard

FIGURE 10

Scanners can convert paper documents, photo prints, or strips of film negatives into digital data.

images to create collages. Figure 11 shows just a few examples of the filtering effects you can apply to an image. The exact set of filtering effects you will have depends on the software you're using.

Printing Your Photos

Once you've processed your photos, you can print them using a professional service or your own printer. Most photo printing labs, including the film-processing departments at stores such as Wal-Mart and Target, offer digital printing services, as do many high-end online processing labs. These sites accept original or edited image files and print them on professional photo paper with high-quality inks. The paper and ink used at processing labs are higher quality than what is available for home use and produce heavier, glossier prints that won't fade. In addition, Kodak and Sony have kiosks in department stores and photography stores that you can use yourself. These kiosks accept image files directly from your flash cards, allow you to do a small amount of editing such as

cropping the image or correcting red-eye, and then print the finished photos on the spot.

In addition, you can find online services, such as Flickr.com and Shutterfly.com, which let you upload your images to their Web site. On the site, you then can organize your images as an online photo album for others to view for free, and if you want hard-copy prints, mugs, t-shirts, or calendars sporting your shot, you can order them directly from the site.

Photo printers for home use are available in two technologies: inkjet and dye sublimation (see Figure 12). Most popular and inexpensive are inkjet printers. Some inkjet printers are capable of printing high-quality color photos, although they vary in speed and quality. Some include a display window so that you can review the image as you stand at the printer, whereas others are portable, allowing you to print your photos wherever you are. Some printers even allow you to crop the image right at the printer, without having to use special image-editing software.

FIGURE 11

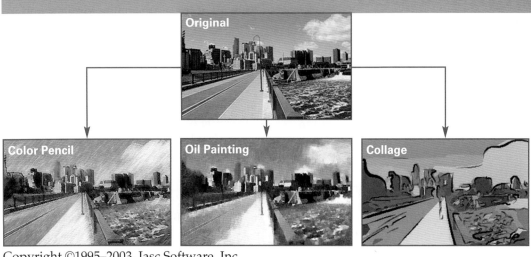

Original

Color Pencil

Oil Painting

Collage

Copyright ©1995–2003, Jasc Software, Inc.

Unlike inkjet printers, dye-sublimation printers produce images using a heating element instead of an inkjet nozzle. The heating element passes over a ribbon of translucent film that has been dyed with bands of colors. By controlling the temperature of the element, dyes are vaporized from a solid into a gas. The gas vapors penetrate the photo paper before they cool again to solid form, producing glossy, high-quality images. If you're interested in a printer to use for printing only photographs, a dye-sublimation printer is a good choice. However, some models print only specific photo sizes, such as 4 x 6 prints, so be sure the printer you buy will fit your long-term needs.

Transferring images to a printer is similar to transferring them to your computer.

If you have a direct-connection camera, you can plug the camera directly into the printer with a cable. Some printers have slots that accept different types of flash memory cards. Of course, you also can transfer your images to the printer from your computer if you have stored them there.

You may decide not to print your photos at all. As noted earlier, online albums let you share your photos without having to print them. And portable devices such as Apple's iPod and many PDAs enable you to carry and display your photos. The iPod, for example, can be connected to a TV and deliver slide shows of your photographs complete with musical soundtracks you have selected.

Photo Kodak EasyShare courtesy of Kodak

Sony Corporation

a

b

FIGURE 12

Many photo printers incorporate displays to let you see the images before you print.
(a) The Kodak EasyShare system allows you to transfer and print pictures quickly and easily.
(b) The Sony DPP-EX50 dye-sublimation printer produces professional-quality images that are fade-resistant, water-resistant, and fingerprint-resistant.

Digital Video

Digital video comes from a number of sources, not just digital camcorders. Most cell phones can record video, and most digital cameras take video as well as digital still shots. Webcams are inexpensive devices for creating digital video as well. With all these possibilities, it is useful to know what to do with digital video files once you have recorded them—how to transfer them, process them, and distribute them to an audience. We'll start by looking at video camcorders.

Digital video camcorders deliver the highest quality video. The first camcorders were analog video cameras, like the one shown in Figure 13a. These were large, heavy units that held a full-size VHS tape. The push to produce smaller, lighter models led to the introduction of compact VHS tapes and then to 8-mm and Hi8 formats. Still, all of these are analog formats, and each records to its own specific type of tape.

The newest generation of video equipment for home use is the digital video, or DV, format. Introduced in 1995, the digital video standard led to a new generation of recording equipment. Today, digital video cameras offer many advantages over their VHS counterparts. They are incredibly small and light, and most don't require any tapes at all. They store hours of video onto built-in hard disk drives. Some models even record directly to DVD discs.

Using digital video, you can easily transfer video files to your computer. Then, using video-editing software, you can edit the video at home, cutting out sections, resequencing segments, and adding titles. To do the same with analog videotape would require expensive and complex audio/video equipment usually seen only in video production studios. And with digital video, you can save (or *write*) your final product on a CD or DVD and play it in your home DVD system or on your computer. For true videophiles, cameras and burners are now available for the high-definition video formats of HD-DVD and Blu-ray video.

Preparing to Shoot Video Footage

Preparing your digital video camera involves making sure you have enough battery power and storage capacity. Batteries for digital video cameras are rechargeable and can provide between one and nine hours of shooting time. Longer-lasting batteries cost and weigh more, so you'll want to think about how you use your camera before deciding which batteries to purchase. Most videographers recommend carrying two spare batteries, though having one spare is fine if you can recharge it while you're using the second.

Digital video cameras most often record onto built-in hard disk drives, although some models use tape, memory cards, or write directly to DVDs. Make sure you have enough storage capacity to

JVC Corporation

RCA camcorder photo courtesy of Thomson.

FIGURE 13

(a) First-generation home video camcorders recorded on full-size VHS cassettes. (b) Modern digital video camcorders can record in High Definition and still be small and light.

FIGURE 14

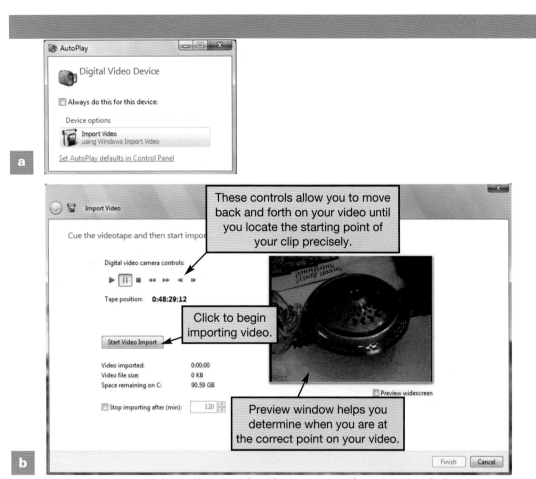

The Windows Vista operating system makes it simple to import digital video data to a file on your hard drive. (a) Windows enables you to import video with Windows Import Video, or other software if you have installed it. (b) Windows Video Import facilitates moving to any starting spot on your video. Clicking Start Video Import creates a video file on your hard drive.

Reprinted with permission from Microsoft Corporation.

cover the event you're shooting. Check the user guide for your particular camera to see how much memory you need to store video. For example, on the Sony DCR-SR42 Handycam, the 30 GB hard drive can store 20 hours of video in its lowest resolution mode, 10 hours in standard mode, and 7 hours of highest quality video.

Shooting video with a digital video camera is similar to shooting video with an analog camera. Automated programs control the exposure settings for different environments (nighttime shots, action events, and so on), while automatic focusing and telephoto zoom lens features are common as well. Many cameras include an antishake feature that stabilizes the image when you're using the camera without a tripod. Using these features, you can capture great footage by just pointing and pressing Record.

Transferring Your Video to Your Computer

Digital video cameras already hold your video as digital data, so transferring the data to your computer is simple (see Figure 14). Most cameras use a USB 2.0 port to connect the camera to your computer. Some models offer the convenience of one-button DVD transfer. With the push of just one button on the camcorder, all of the recorded video is automatically sent through your computer and written to a DVD. Data can also be transferred to your computer using a flash memory card if your camcorder supports it.

Once you connect your camera to your computer, Microsoft Vista automatically identifies it, recognizing its manufacturer and model. The operating system then scans the software on your system and presents a list of all the programs you can use to

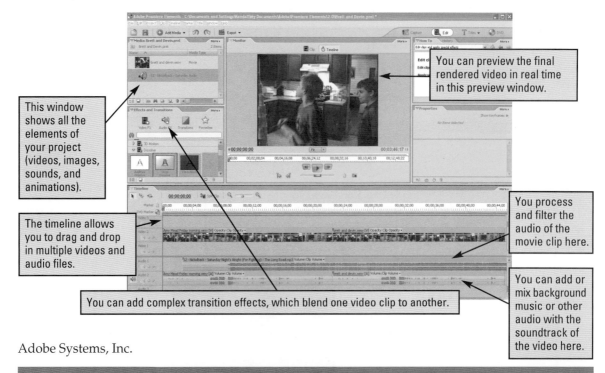

You can preview the final rendered video in real time in this preview window.

This window shows all the elements of your project (videos, images, sounds, and animations).

You process and filter the audio of the movie clip here.

The timeline allows you to drag and drop in multiple videos and audio files.

You can add or mix background music or other audio with the soundtrack of the video here.

You can add complex transition effects, which blend one video clip to another.

Adobe Systems, Inc.

FIGURE 15

Adobe Premiere allows you to build a movie from video clips and add soundtracks and special effects such as three-dimensional transitions between scenes.

import your video. You may have received a video-editing program when you purchased your digital video camera. If you installed the program, it will appear on this list (see Figure 14a). Windows Import Video is the default program for importing if you have no other software installed. Windows Movie Maker is another video-editing program and is included as part of Windows Vista. Other digital video-editing programs such as Adobe Premiere Elements and Pinnacle Studio can import video as well. These are more powerful, full-featured programs that you purchase separately.

Windows Video Import (or other software programs) allows you to fast-forward, pause, and rewind, moving to the segment you wish to transfer (or record) to your hard drive (Figure 14b). You can use the digital video camera control arrows at the top to locate the exact piece of footage you want to transfer. Click the Start Video Import button and the video file transfers to the hard drive.

Some camcorders on the market today make it even easier to get data to a DVD directly. Made by Sony, the DVD Handycam Camcorder DCR-DVD205 writes its digital data directly onto 3-inch DVDs. It can record up to 60 minutes of video per disc when using the standard quality setting. You can then drop the DVD into most DVD players and view it immediately.

Editing Your Video and Adding Special Effects

Once the digital video data is in a file on your computer's hard drive, the fun really begins. Video-editing software presents a storyboard, or *timeline*, with which you can manipulate your video file, as shown in Figure 15. Using this software, you can review your clips frame by frame or trim them at any point. You can order each segment on the timeline in whichever sequence you like and correct segments for color balance, brightness, or contrast.

In addition, you can add transitions to your video such as those you're used to seeing on TV—fades to black, dissolves, and so on. Figure 15 shows how easy it is to add transitions in Adobe Premiere. Just select the type of transition you want from the drop-down list and drag that icon into the timeline where you want the transition to occur.

Video-editing software also lets you add titles, animations, and audio tracks to your video, including background music, sound effects, and additional narration. In Figure 16 there are two audio tracks, the original voices on the video and an additional audio clip. You can adjust the volume of each audio track to switch from one to the other or have both playing together. Finally, you can preview all of these effects in real time.

There is a lot to learn about digital video editing, and it is easy to be overwhelmed with the number of choices available. Examine online tutorial resources such as Izzy's Video podcasts (**www.izzyvideo.com**) to learn how to make the most impact with the editing and effects you apply to your raw video footage.

Distributing Your Video

Once you're done editing your video file, you can save (or export) it in a variety of formats. Figure 16 shows some of the popular video file formats in use today, along with the file extensions they use. (File extensions are the letters that follow the period in a file name, such as in Movie1.*mpg*. These extensions indicate the type of data inside the file.)

Your choice of file format for your finished video will depend on what you want to do with your video. For example, the RealMedia RM streaming file format is a great choice if your file is very large and you'll be posting it on the Web. The Microsoft AVI format is a good choice if you're sending your file to a wide range of users because it's very popular and commonly accepted as the standard video format for the Windows Media Player.

When you export your video, you have control over every aspect of the file you create, including its format, window size, frame rate, audio

FIGURE 16
Typical File Formats for Digital Video

FORMAT	FILE EXTENSION	NOTES
QuickTime	.mov .qt	You can download QuickTime player without charge from **www.apple.com/quicktime**. The pro version allows you to build your own QuickTime files.
Moving Picture Experts Group (MPEG)	.mpg .mpeg	MPEG-4 video standard adopted internationally in 2000; recognized by most video player software.
Windows Media Video	.wmv	Microsoft file format recognized by Windows Media Player (included with Windows operating system).
Microsoft Video for Windows	.avi	Microsoft file format recognized by Windows Media Player (included with Windows operating system).
RealMedia	.rm	Format from RealNetworks is popular for streaming video. You can download the player for free at **www.real.com**.

a-b) Pure Digital Technologies Inc.

FIGURE 17

The Flip video camera is an inexpensive way to capture 60 minutes of video and easily post it on the YouTube service.

quality, and compression level. You can customize any of these if you have specific production goals, but most often just using the default values works well.

When would you want to customize some of the audio and video settings? If you're trying to make the file as small as possible so that it will download quickly or so that it can fit on a single CD, you would select values that trade off audio and video quality for file size. For example, you could drop the frame rate to 15 fps, shrink the window size to 320 x 240 pixels, and switch to mono audio instead of stereo.

You also can try different compression choices to see which one does a better job of compressing your particular file. **Codecs** (**co**mpression/**dec**ompression) are rules, implemented in either software or hardware, that squeeze the same audio and video information into less space. Some information will be lost using compression, and there is a variety of different codecs to choose from, each claiming better performance than its competitors. Commonly used

codecs include MPEG, Indeo, DivX, and Cinepak. There is no one codec that is always superior—a codec that works well for a simple interview may not do a good job compressing a live-action scene.

If you'd like to save your video onto a DVD, you can use special DVD authoring software, such as Ulead DVD Workshop or Adobe Encore DVD. These DVD software packages often include preset selections for producing video for mobile devices (like the Apple iPod or the Sony PSP). These programs can also create final DVDs that have animated menu systems and easy navigation controls, allowing the viewer to move quickly from one movie or scene to another. Home DVD players as well as gaming systems such as Playstation and Xbox can read these DVDs, so your potential audience is even greater!

New Options for Quick Video Delivery

Due to the popularity of videos on the Web, products and services are now available that let you quickly upload your videos. One such product is the Flip video camcorder from Pure Digital Technologies, shown in Figure 17.

The Flip camcorder, which retails at about $100, can record 60 minutes of video. After recording, the USB connector is flipped out and connected to your computer. Flip has built-in software that lets you transfer the video file directly to YouTube (**www.youtube.com**) or e-mail the file. It's a simple solution that takes advantage of the easy Web-based distribution of video.

If you don't have a camcorder, you may already have a device that records digital video and not realize it—your cell phone. Many cell phone models record low-resolution video. YouTube has a special Mobile Upload Profile that you can set up for your account. Once your unique e-mail address has been assigned, any video you have on your phone can be submitted to YouTube by merely e-mailing the file to the account address. If you have captured a breaking news story, this is the fastest way to get the word out!

Web cameras are another option for quickly pushing video up to the Web. Inexpensive Webcams (from $25 to $100) can be easily attached to your desktop or notebook. The more expensive models have motors that allow you to automatically rotate to track the sound, so you are always in the frame even if you are moving around the room. Services like YouTube offer Quick Capture buttons, so with one click, your video is shot and delivered to the Internet.

9

Behind the Scenes:

A Closer Look at System Hardware

From Chapter 9 of *Technology in Action, Complete*, Fifth Edition, Alan Evans, Kendall Martin, Mary Anne Poatsy. Copyright © 2009 by Pearson Education. Published by Prentice Hall. All rights reserved.

Behind the Scenes:

A Closer Look at System Hardware

ACTIVE HELPDESK

- Understanding the CPU
- Understanding Types of RAM

Technology in Action: Taking a Closer Look

Although Jim and Joe are twins, they are completely different in certain ways. Joe checks the oil in his car regularly, knows the air pressure in his tires, and can tell when the fan belt should be replaced. Jim, on the other hand, asks, "Oil level? What oil?" and drives from place to place relying on service departments to keep his car running. Although Jim's lack of maintenance hasn't resulted in any catastrophic problems, Joe warns his brother that by not learning a few things about cars, he'll end up paying more to keep up his car, if it even lasts that long.

Similarly, after taking a class in college, Joe has a strong but basic understanding of his computer and keeps his PC running well through periodic maintenance and upgrades. Not surprisingly, Jim is hands-off when it comes to his computer. He's happy to just turn it on and open the files he needs. He can't be bothered with all the acronyms: CPU, RAM, and all the rest. When there's a problem, Jim just calls his brother. He hates waiting and paying for technical service and is afraid he'll mess up his system if he tries to fix things himself. But after making another 2:00 a.m. call to Joe after his computer crashed, Joe told him, "Take a class or pay a technician!"

When it comes to your computer, are you most like Jim or Joe? Joe found out how easy it is to understand his computer and isn't dependent on anyone else to keep it running. But if you use a computer without understanding the hardware inside, you'll have to pay a technician to fix or upgrade it. Meanwhile, it won't be as efficient as if you were fine-tuning it yourself, and you may find yourself buying a new computer earlier than necessary.

There are other advantages to having a deeper understanding of computer hardware. If you're preparing for a career in programming, for example, understanding computer hardware will affect the speed and efficiency of the programs you design. In addition, if you're interested in computers, you're no doubt excited by advances you hear about. How do you evaluate the impact of a new type of memory or a new processor? A basic appreciation of how a computer system is built and designed is a good start.

In this chapter, we'll build on what you've learned about computer hardware and go behind the scenes, looking at the components of your system unit in more detail. First, we examine how computers translate the commands you input into the digits they can understand: 1s and 0s. Next, we analyze the internal workings of the central processing unit (CPU) and memory. We then look at buses—the highways that transport data between the CPU, memory, and other devices connected to the computer. But first, let's look at the building blocks of computers: switches.

© Bryan Allen/Corbis

SOUND BYTES

- Binary Numbers Interactive
- Where Does Binary Show Up?

- Memory Hierarchy Interactive
- Computer Architecture

Digital Data: Switches and Bits

The **system unit** is the box that contains the central electronic components of the computer, including the central processing unit (CPU), memory, motherboard, and many other circuit boards that help the computer to function. But how exactly does the computer perform all of its tasks? How does it process the data you input? In this section, we discuss how the CPU performs its functions—adding, subtracting, moving data around the system, and so on—using nothing but a large number of on/off switches. In fact, as you'll learn, a computer system can be viewed as just an enormous collection of on/off switches.

ELECTRICAL SWITCHES

What are switches, and what do they do? You learned earlier that, unlike humans, computers work exclusively with numbers (not words). To process data into information, computers need to work in a language they understand. This language, called **binary language,** consists of just two numbers: 0 and 1. Everything a computer does (such as process data or print a report) is broken down into a series of 0s and 1s. **Electrical switches** are devices inside the computer that can be flipped between these two states: 1 or 0, on or off.

Why do computers use 0s and 1s to process data? Because modern computers are electronic, digital machines, they understand only two states of existence: on and off. Computers represent these two possibilities, or states, using the binary switches (or digits) 1 and 0.

Although the notion of switches may seem complex, you use various forms of switches every day. For example, the on/off button on your DVD player is a mechanical switch: pushed in, it could represent the value 1 (on), whereas popped out, it could represent the value 0 (off). Another switch you use each day is a water faucet. As shown in Figure 1, shutting off the faucet so that no water flows could represent the value 0, whereas turning it on could represent the value 1.

Because computers are built from a huge collection of switches, using buttons or water faucets obviously would limit the

FIGURE 1

Water faucets can be used to represent binary switches. Turning on the faucet could represent the value 1, whereas shutting off the faucet so that no water flows could represent the value 0.

amount of data computers could store. It would also make computers very large and cause them to run at very slow speeds. Thus, the history of computers is really a story about creating smaller and faster sets of electrical switches so that more data can be stored and manipulated quickly.

What were the first switches used in computers? The earliest generation of electronic computers used devices called **vacuum tubes** as switches, as shown in Figure 2. Vacuum tubes act as computer switches by allowing or blocking the flow of electrical current. The problem with vacuum tubes is that they take up a lot of space. The first high-speed digital computer, the Electronic Numerical Integrator and Computer (ENIAC), was deployed in 1945 and used nearly 18,000 vacuum tubes as switches, which filled approximately 1,800 square feet of floor space. That's about one-half of a standard high school basketball court! In addition to being very large, the vacuum tubes produced a lot of heat and burned out frequently. A tube failed about every other day, and it took more than 15 minutes to locate and replace the problem tube each time. Thus, although they are still used as switches in some high-end audio equipment, vacuum tubes make for impractical switching devices in personal computers because of their size and reliability.

What do personal computers use as switching devices? Since the introduction of ENIAC's vacuum tubes, two major revolutions have occurred in the design of switches, and consequently computers, to make them smaller and faster: the invention of the transistor and the fabrication of integrated circuits.

What are transistors? Transistors are electrical switches that are built out of layers of a special type of material called a **semiconductor.** A semiconductor is any material that can be controlled to either conduct electricity or act as an insulator (to prohibit electricity from passing through). Silicon, which is found in common sand, is the semiconductor material used to make transistors.

By itself, silicon does not conduct electricity particularly well, but if specific chemicals are added in a controlled way to the silicon, it begins to behave like a switch. The silicon allows electrical current to flow easily when a certain voltage is applied, and it prevents electrical current from flowing otherwise, thus behaving as an on/off switch. This

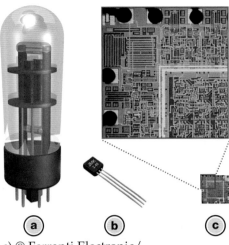

(a) (b) (c)

c) © Ferranti Electronic/
A. Sternberg/Photo Researchers

FIGURE 2

Electrical switches have become smaller and faster over time, from (a) vacuum tubes to (b) discrete single transistors to (c) integrated circuits that can hold more than 1.7 billion transistors.

kind of behavior is exactly what is needed to store digital information, the 0s (off) and 1s (on) in binary language.

Early transistors were built in separate units as small metal rods (as shown in Figure 2b), with each rod acting as a single on/off switch. These first transistors were much smaller than vacuum tubes, produced very little heat, and could be switched from on to off (allowing or blocking electrical current) very quickly. They also were less expensive than vacuum tubes.

It wasn't long, however, before transistors reached their limits. Continuing advances in technology began to require more transistors than circuit boards could reasonably handle at the time. Something was needed to pack more transistor capacity into a smaller space. Thus, integrated circuits, the next technical revolution in switches, developed.

What are integrated circuits?
Integrated circuits (or chips) are very small regions of semiconductor material, such as silicon, that support a huge number of transistors, as shown in Figure 2c. Along with all the many transistors, other components critical to a circuit board (such as resistors, capacitors, and diodes) are also located on the integrated circuit. Most integrated circuits are no more than a quarter inch in size.

Why are integrated circuits important? Because so many transistors can fit

into such a small area, integrated circuits have enabled computer designers to create small yet powerful **microprocessors,** which are chips that contain a CPU. In 1971, the Intel 4004 was the first complete microprocessor to be located on a single integrated circuit, marking the beginning of true miniaturization of computers. The Intel 4004 contained slightly more than 2,300 transistors. Today, more than 500 *million* transistors can be manufactured in a space as tiny as the nail of your smallest finger!

This incredible feat has fueled an industry like none other. In 1951, the Univac I computer was the size of a large room—the processor/memory unit itself was 14 feet by 8 feet by 8.5 feet high and could perform about 1,905 operations per second. Thanks to advances in integrated circuits, the IBM PC released just 30 years later took up just 1 cubic foot of space, cost $3,000, and performed 155,000 times more quickly.

But how can computers store information in a set of on/off switches? So computers use on/off switches to perform their functions. But how can these simple switches be organized so that they enable you to use a computer to pay your bills online or write an essay? How could a set of switches describe a number or a word or give a computer the command to perform addition? Recall that to manipulate the on/off switches, the computer works in binary language, which uses only two digits, 0 and 1. Therefore, to understand how a computer works, it's necessary to first look at how the computer uses a special numbering system called the binary number system to represent all of its programs and data.

THE BINARY NUMBER SYSTEM

What is a number system? A number system is an organized plan for representing a number. Although you may not realize it, you are already familiar with one number system. The **base 10 number system,** also known as **decimal notation,** is the system you use to represent all of the numeric values you use each day. It's called base 10 because it uses 10 digits, 0 through 9, to represent any value.

To represent a number in base 10, you break the number down into groups of ones, tens, hundreds, thousands, and so on. Each digit has a place value depending on where it shows up in the number. For example, using base 10, in the whole number 6,954, there are 6 sets of thousands, 9 sets of hundreds, 5 sets of tens, and 4 sets of ones. Working from right to left, each place in a number represents an increasing power of 10, as shown here:

$$6,954 = 6 * (1,000) + 9 * (100) + 5 * (10) + 4 * (1)$$
$$= 6 * 10^3 + 9 * 10^2 + 5 * 10^1 + 4 * 10^0$$

Note that in this equation, the final number 1 is represented as 10^0 because any number raised to the zero power is equal to 1.

Anthropologists theorize that humans developed a base 10 number system because we have 10 fingers. But computer systems, with their huge collections of on/off switches, are not well suited to thinking about numbers in groups of 10. Instead, computers describe a number as powers of 2 because each switch can be in one of two positions: on or off. This numbering system is referred to as the **binary number system.** It is the number system used by computers to represent all data.

How does the binary number system work? Because it only includes two digits (0 and 1), the binary number system is also referred to as the **base 2 number system.** However, even with just two digits, the binary number system can still represent all the same values that a base 10 number system can. Instead of breaking the number down into sets of ones, tens, hundreds, and thousands, as is done in base 10 notation, the binary number system describes a number as the sum of powers of 2. Binary numbers are used to represent *every* piece of data stored in a computer: all of the numbers, all of the letters, and all of the instructions that the computer uses to execute work.

Representing Numbers in the Binary Number System

How does the binary number system represent a whole number? As noted earlier, in the base 10 number system, a whole number is represented as the sum of ones, tens, hundreds, and thousands—sums of powers of 10. The binary system works in the same way but describes a value as the sum of groups of 64s, 32s, 16s, 8s, 4s, 2s, and 1s—that is, powers of 2: 1, 2, 4, 8, 16, 32, 64, and so on.

Let's look at the number 67. In base 10, the number 67 would be 6 sets of 10s and 7 sets of 1s, as follows:

$$\text{Base 10: } 67 = 6 * 10^1 + 7 * 10^0$$

DIG DEEPER

Advanced Binary and Hexadecimal Notations

You understand how the binary number system represents a positive number, but how can it represent a negative number? In the decimal (base 10) system, a negative value is represented by a special symbol, the minus sign (–). In the binary (base 2) system, a negative number is represented using a **sign bit.** The sign bit is usually the left-most bit. There are several methods to determine the sign bit. In each method, when the sign bit is 1, the binary number has a negative (or nonpositive) value, and when it is 0, the binary number has a positive value.

The binary pattern 11101 can represent both a positive number and a negative number. So how does the computer know that what it is looking at is a negative number and not a positive binary number? If we know the number is a binary number using a sign bit, we read the first bit (the sign bit) as 1 and therefore know that the number is a negative number. Following the sign bit are the digits that represent the value of the number itself. Because 1101 in binary (base 2) has the value 13 in the decimal (base 10) system, the final interpretation of the bits 11101 would be –13.

But what if we were told in advance that 11101 is definitely a positive number? We would then read this number differently and compute 1 * 16 + 1 * 8 + 1 * 4 + 0 * 2 + 1 * 1 and get the base 10 value of 29. The bits themselves are exactly the same. The only thing that has changed is our agreement on what the same five digits mean: the first time they represented a negative number, and the second time they represented a positive number. In a program's code, the computer is told ahead of time whether to expect a sign bit.

The binary number system also can represent a decimal number. How can a string of 1s and 0s capture the information in a value such as 99.368? Because every computer must store such numbers in the same way, the Institute of Electrical and Electronics Engineers (IEEE) has established a standard called the floating-point standard that describes how numbers with fractional parts should be represented in the binary number system. Using a 32-bit system, we can represent an incredibly wide range of numbers. The method dictated by the

One way to figure out how 67 is represented in base 2 is to find the largest possible power of 2 that could be in the number 67. Two to the eighth power is 256, and there are no groups of 256 in the number 67. Two to the seventh power is 128, but that is bigger than 67. Two to the sixth power is 64, and there is a group of 64 inside a group of 67. So,

67 has	1 group of	64	That leaves 3 and
3 has	0 groups of	32	
	0 groups of	16	
	0 groups of	8	
	0 groups of	4	
	1 group of	2	That leaves 1 and
1 has	1 group of	1	And now nothing is left

Therefore, the binary number for 67 is written as 1000011 in base 2:

$$\text{Base 2: } 67 = 64 + 0 + 0 + 0 + 0 + 2 + 1$$
$$= (1 * 2^6) + (0 * 2^5) + (0 * 2^4) + (0 * 2^3) + (0 * 2^2) + (1 * 2^1) + (1 * 2^0)$$
$$= (1000011) \text{ base 2}$$

You can also convert base 10 numbers to binary manually by repeatedly dividing the number by 2 and examining the remainder at each stage. An example will make this clearer. Let's convert the base 10 number 67 into binary:

$$67 \div 2 = 33 \text{ remainder } 1$$
$$33 \div 2 = 16 \text{ remainder } 1$$
$$16 \div 2 = 8 \text{ remainder } 0$$
$$8 \div 2 = 4 \text{ remainder } 0$$
$$4 \div 2 = 2 \text{ remainder } 0$$
$$2 \div 2 = 1 \text{ remainder } 0$$
$$1 \div 2 = 0 \text{ remainder } 1$$
$$1000011$$

The binary number is then read from the bottom up. Therefore, 1000011 is the binary (base 2) equivalent of the base 10 number 67. In computer memory, bytes store data as a set of eight bits, so the same value would be stored inside a byte of RAM with a leading 0 as **01000011**.

IEEE standard works the same for any number with a decimal point, such as the number –0.75. The first digit, or bit (the sign bit), is used to indicate whether the number is positive or negative. The next eight bits store the magnitude of the number, indicating whether the number is in the hundreds or millions, for example. The standard says to use the next 23 bits to store the value of the number.

As you can imagine, some numbers in binary result in quite a long string of 0s and 1s. For example, the number 123,456 is a 17-digit sequence of 1s and 0s in binary code: 11110001001000000. When working with these long strings of 0s and 1s, it is easy for a human to make a mistake. Thus, many computer scientists use hexadecimal notation, another commonly used number system, as a form of shorthand.

Hexadecimal notation is a base 16 number system, meaning it uses 16 digits to represent numbers instead of the 10 digits used in base 10 or the 2 digits used in base 2. The 16 digits it uses are the 10 numeric digits, 0 to 9, plus six extra symbols: A, B, C, D, E, and F. Each of the letters, A through F, correspond to a numeric value, so that A equals 10, B equals 11, and so on. Looking back at the number we started with, 123,456 is represented as 1E240 in hexadecimal notation. This is much easier for computer scientists to use than the long string of binary code. The Scientific Calculator in Windows also can perform conversions to hexadecimal notation. (You can watch a video showing you how to perform conversions between bases using the Windows Calculator in the Sound Byte "Where Does Binary Show Up?")

When will you ever use hexadecimal notation? Unless you become a professional programmer, computer hardware designer, or you write your own Web pages (where hexadecimal notation is used to represent colors), you will likely encounter hexadecimal notation only when you see an error code on your computer. Generally, the location of the error will be represented in hexadecimal notation.

Why Doesn't My 60 GB Drive Have 60 GB?

If you look at the properties of your hard drive (right-click Computer and then click Properties), you'll see one number reporting the size of the hard drive in bytes—say 60,003,381—and a different value listed in gigabytes—say, 55.8 GB. But isn't 60 billion bytes equal to 60 GB?

Well, not exactly. Historically the sizes of computer storage devices were measured in bytes using the standard international (SI) prefixes: kilo for one thousand, mega for one million, and giga for one billion. Notice that the numbers 1,000, 1,000,000, and 1,000,000,000 are all powers of ten. In computer memory devices, though, the capacity is most often a power of 2. A gigabyte has been used to mean the power of 2 that is nearest to a billion. That number is 2^{30}, or 1,073,741,824 bytes, which is a difference of 7 percent.

So 60 billion bytes and 55.8 GB are the same, but the situation is confusing. That is why a special set of binary prefixes has been introduced. The new prefixes are *kibi, mebi,* and *gibi.* One kibibyte is exactly 1,024 = 2^{10} bytes, one mebibyte is exactly 2^{20} bytes, and one gibibyte is exactly 2^{30} bytes. This notation has been adopted by governing bodies (like the IEEE), but most manufacturers are still using the traditional SI prefixes.

Is there a faster way to convert between base 10 (decimal) and binary? Programmers and engineers who work with binary codes daily learn to convert between decimal and binary mentally. However, if you use binary notation less often, it is easier to use a calculator. Some calculators identify this operation with a button labeled *DEC* (for decimal) and one labeled *BIN* (for binary). In Windows, you can access a scientific calculator that supports conversion between decimal (base 10) and binary (base 2) by choosing Start, All Programs, Accessories, then clicking Calculator, and then clicking the View menu to select Scientific.

Representing Letters and Symbols: ASCII and Unicode

How can the binary number system represent letters and punctuation symbols? We have just been converting numbers from base 10, which we understand, to base 2 (binary state), which the computer understands. Similarly, we need a system that converts letters and other symbols that we understand to a binary state

that the computer understands. To provide a consistent means for representing letters and other characters, there are codes that dictate how to represent characters in binary format. Older mainframe computers use Extended Binary-Coded Decimal Interchange Code (EBCDIC, pronounced "Eb sih dik"). However, most of today's personal computers use the American National Standards Institute (ANSI, pronounced "An-see") standard code, called the **American Standard Code for Information Interchange** (**ASCII,** pronounced "As-key"), to represent each letter or character as an 8-bit (or 1-byte) binary code.

As you know by now, binary digits correspond to the on and off states of your computer's switches. Each of these digits is called a **binary digit**, or **bit** for short. Eight binary digits (or bits) combine to create one **byte.** In the previous discussions, we have been converting base 10 numbers to a binary format. In such cases, the binary format has no standard length. For example, the binary format for the number 2 is two digits (10), whereas the binary format for the number 10 is four digits (1010). Although binary numbers can have more or less than 8 bits, each single alphabetic or special character is 1 byte (or 8 bits) of data and consists of a unique combination of a total of eight 0s and 1s.

The ASCII code represents the 26 uppercase letters and 26 lowercase letters used in the English language, along with a number of punctuation symbols and other special characters, using 8 bits. Figure 3 shows a number of examples of ASCII code representation of printable letters and characters.

Can ASCII represent the alphabets of different languages? Because it represents letters and characters using only 8 bits, the ASCII code can assign only 256 (or 2^8) different codes for unique characters and letters. Although this is enough to represent English and many other characters found in the world's languages, ASCII code cannot represent *all* languages and symbols because some languages require more than 256 characters and letters. Thus, a new encoding scheme, called **Unicode**, was created. By using 16 bits instead of the 8 bits used in ASCII, Unicode can represent nearly 1,115,000 code points and currently assigns more than 96,000 unique character symbols. The first 128 characters of Unicode

SOUND BYTE

Where Does Binary Show Up?

In this Sound Byte, you'll learn how to use tools to work with binary, decimal, and hexadecimal numbers. (These tools come with the Windows operating system.) You'll also learn where you might see binary and hexadecimal values showing up as you use a computer.

are identical to ASCII, but because of its depth, Unicode is also able to represent the alphabets of all modern and historic languages and notational systems, including such languages as Tibetan, Tagalog, Japanese, and Canadian-Aboriginal syllabics. As we continue to become a more global society, it is anticipated that Unicode will replace ASCII as the standard character formatting code.

So *all* data inside the computer is stored as bits? Yes! As noted in the Dig Deeper feature, both positive and negative numbers can be stored using signed integer notation, with the first bit (the sign bit) indicating the sign and the rest of the bits indicating the value of the number. Decimal numbers are stored according to the IEEE floating-point standard, whereas letters and symbols are stored according to the ASCII code or Unicode. All of these different number systems and codes exist so that computers can store different types of information in their on/off switches. No matter what kind of data you input in a computer—a color, a musical note, or a street address—that data will be stored as a string of 1s and 0s. The important lesson is that the interpretation of 0s and 1s is what matters. The same binary pattern could represent a positive number, a negative number, a fraction, or a letter.

How does the computer know which interpretation to use for the 1s and 0s? When your brain processes language, it takes sounds you hear and uses the rules of English along with other clues to build an interpretation of the sound as a word. If you are in New York City and hear someone shout, "Hey, Lori!" you expect someone is saying hello to a friend. If you are in London and hear the same sound—"Hey! Lorry!"—you jump out of the way because a truck is coming at you! You knew which interpretation to apply to the same sound because you had some other information—that you were in England.

Likewise, the CPU is designed to understand a specific language, a set of instructions. But certain instructions tell the CPU to expect a negative number next or to interpret the following bit pattern as a character. Because of this extra information, the CPU always knows which interpretation to use for a series of bits.

FIGURE 3 ASCII Standard Code for a Sample of Letters and Characters

ASCII Code	Represents This Symbol	ASCII Code	Represents This Symbol
01000001	A	01100001	a
01000010	B	01100010	b
01000011	C	01100011	c
01011010	Z	00100011	#
00100001	!	00100100	$
00100010	"	00100101	%

Note: For the full ASCII table, see **www.asciitable.com**.

The CPU: Processing Digital Information

The **central processing unit** (**CPU**, or **processor**), the "brains" of the computer, executes every instruction given to your computer. As you learned earlier, the entire CPU fits on a tiny chip, called the microprocessor. The microprocessor contains all of the hardware (including millions of transistors—the switches we discussed earlier) that is responsible for processing information.

The CPU is located in the system unit on the computer's **motherboard,** the main circuit board that connects all of the electronic components of the system: the CPU,

BITS AND BYTES

Work with Several Languages?

Windows supports multinational environments in several different ways. If you want to change the language used by Windows to a language other than English, you can change the display language. The display language is the language used for dialog boxes, wizards, and so on and can be selected from 33 choices. You can also change the keyboard input language, the language used to enter text, and switch between different keyboard layouts with just a click of the taskbar. What does all this mean? You can read and type in your native language, and work in multilanguage documents—whether it's Tibetan stacked symbols, Chinese characters, or standard English—with just a few simple clicks! For more information, visit **http://windowshelp.microsoft.com**.

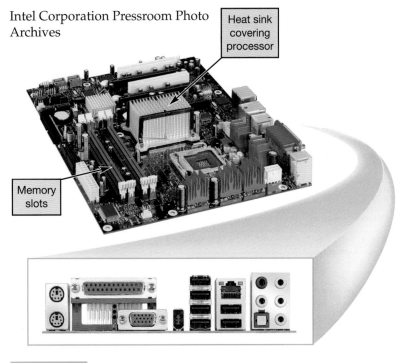

Intel Corporation Pressroom Photo Archives

Heat sink covering processor

Memory slots

FIGURE 4

The motherboard is the home of all the most essential computer hardware, including the CPU socket, memory card slots, and expansion slots where you can insert expansion (or adapter) cards.

memory, the expansion slots where you can insert expansion (or adapter) cards, and all of the electrical paths that connect these components. Figure 4 shows a typical motherboard and the location of each of these components.

Looking at a CPU chip gives you very little information about how exactly it accomplishes its work. However, understanding more about how the CPU is designed and how it operates will give you greater insight into how computers work, what their limitations are, and what technological advances may be possible in the future.

What CPUs are used in desktop and notebook computers? Only a few major companies manufacture CPUs for desktop computers. Intel manufactures the Xeon, Core 2 Extreme (shown in Figure 5a), Celeron, Itanium 2, and Pentium processors. Advanced Micro Devices (AMD) produces the AMD-K6, the Athlon, Sempron, and Turion processors. Intel and AMD chips are used in the majority of Windows-based PCs.

ETHICS IN IT

Ethics: Which Strategy Makes More Money—To Share or To Hide?

In system design, both in hardware and software, corporations need to make a decision about how they will work with the world: will they provide an open system or be "closed"? It speaks to an ethical view of the world and how it operates by the company leadership. Is it better for businesses to be open about their design specifications, even though others may copy their system? Or will it lead to more profit if they hide the details of what has been done and protect their investment?

Different companies have taken widely different approaches to this question. One example in hardware is the system design of the original IBM PC. It was not a closed system, and the specifications on how to build a system and how to interface were available to other companies. This led to a huge number of similar "clone" systems, manufactured by competitors but able to run the same software and operating system, and basically do the same work. The availability of cheap clones fueled the market for home PCs tremen-

dously. While IBM did not profit from clone systems directly, it benefited from the larger market. Many users found the lack of quality in knockoff systems a problem and eventually bought IBM hardware. IBM was able to push ahead with its deep R&D pockets and produce new systems with more advanced features, keeping a continual performance edge over clone systems. Third-party companies popped up like crazy, creating a huge number of peripheral devices, boards, and add-ons, because they knew the hardware details for the system and could design to them.

The main competitor, Apple Computers, took the opposite approach. The Apple Macintosh was a "closed" design, and no other company was able to manufacture a similar system. This meant every person who wanted a Macintosh had to purchase it from Apple, at their selling price, with no competition. It kept the price higher than the plunging PC cost, driven down by the proliferation of clone manufacturers. Apple systems won some niche markets in graphics

Apple computer systems (such as the iMac and the PowerBook series of notebooks) used a different CPU design in the past. The G4 and PowerPC G5 chips were used by Apple machines for more than 10 years. But in 2005, Apple shook up the CPU playing field when it announced that all of its systems would be redesigned to use Intel CPUs. Versions of the PowerPC chip (shown in Figure 5b) still live on in some version in video gaming system consoles such as the Nintendo Wii and the Xbox 360.

The processor used on a computer also determines what operating system is used. The combination of operating system and processor is referred to as a computer's platform.

What makes CPUs different from each other? The primary distinction between CPUs is processing power, which is determined by the number of cores on each CPU. A core is a complete processing section from a CPU embedded into the same physical chip. In addition to multi-core design, as you'll learn in the next section, other factors

a) Intel Corporation Pressroom Photo Archives; b) Reprinted by permission of International Business Machines Corporation. Unauthorized use not permitted.

FIGURE 5

(a) The Core 2 Extreme chip is used in many Windows-based PCs. (b) The Microsoft Xbox 360 gaming console uses a custom PowerPC–based CPU to perform 1,000 billion calculations per second.

differentiate CPUs, but the greatest differentiators are how quickly the processor can work (called its clock speed) and the amount of immediate access memory the CPU has (called its cache memory).

Until recently, the latest advancement in processors was hyperthreading, which provides quicker processing of information by

design and education, but today the market is about 95 percent Windows-based PCs.

Neither strategy is without advantages. Steve Jobs recently announced the iPhone will be a closed system. "You don't want your phone to be an open platform," say Jobs, meaning that anyone can write applications for it and potentially gum up the provider's network. "You need it to work when you need it to work. Cingular [now AT&T] doesn't want to see its West Coast network go down because some application messed up." This continues to be Apple's position on other products—you can't even change the battery in your iPod without sending it back to Apple for a $99 battery replacement, but that allows them to have a unique design and shape to the iPod. In Nick Carr's blog site *Rough Type*, he says, "In Jobs's world, users are users, creators are creators, and never the twain shall meet."

The advantage of product stability can be more easily guaranteed with a closed system. Others argue that the collective energy of allowing any company to design for your system results in better choices, lower prices to the consumer, and widespread market penetration of your product. External developers and content providers have already worked with AT&T and their network to provide applications for devices like Windows Mobile and Palm OS smartphones.

The Web 2.0 ideology, where every user is a creator, and user-generated content is an essential component of products, provides challenges for hardware/software systems designers. Consider the following:

- How much do you as a consumer value product stability versus the ability to have choice from a number of third-party vendors?
- Do you think more innovative product design comes from a closed-system approach or an open system?
- Do you think one system would always lead to more profit for a company?
- How will the push toward more user-generated content impact the design of computer systems and mobile devices?

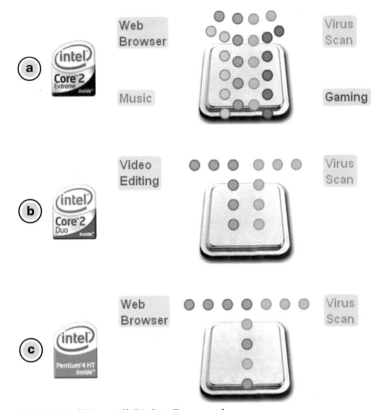

FIGURE 6

(a) The Intel Core 2 Extreme is a four-core processor, running four programs simultaneously. (b) The Intel Core 2 Duo is a two-core processor. (c) The Intel Pentium 4 Hyperthreading operates with only one core but hyperthreads, trying to simulate working on two processes at once.

enabling a new set of instructions to start before the previous set has finished. The most recent design innovation for PC processors, an improvement upon hyperthreading, is known as **multi-core technology.** With multi-core technology, there are two or more processors on the same chip, enabling the execution of two sets of instructions at the *exact* same time. Figure 6 shows these different approaches.

In Figure 6c, hyperthreading allows two different programs to be processed at one time, but they are sharing the computing resources of the chip. With multi-cores (Figures 6a and 6b) each has the full attention of its own processing core. This results in faster processing and smoother multitasking. Figure 7 shows the basic specifications of several of the major processors on the market today.

FIGURE 7 Processors on the Market Today

Processor	Manufacturer	Number of Transistors	Typical Clock Speed	Multi-Core Modules	Description
Athlon 64 x2	AMD	233 million	2.4 GHz	2	64-bit processor for heavy computation and demanding video gaming needs.
Core 2 Extreme QX6700	Intel	582 million	2.7 GHz	4	First quad-core processor introduced; four independent processors on one chip.
Core 2 Duo	Intel	291 million	1.6–2.16 GHz	2	Designed specifically for mobile computers; transfers power only to those areas of the processor that need it, improving battery life.
Itanium 2	Intel	592 million	1.3–1.66 GHz	1	Seen in high-end server computers.
Pentium 4 Extreme Edition 955	Intel	225 million	3.46 GHz	2	Uses a dual-core design and hyperthreading to process four tasks at once.
Pentium D Dual-Core	Intel	230 million	2.8–3.4 GHz	2	Includes dual-core processor for more efficient multitasking. No hyperthreading capabilities.
PowerPC G4	Freescale Semiconductor (once part of Motorola)	57 million	1.5–1.67 GHz	1	Until 2006, powered the Apple line of computers.

THE CPU MACHINE CYCLE

What exactly does the CPU do? Any program you run on your computer is actually a long series of binary code, 1s and 0s, describing a specific set of commands the CPU must perform. Each CPU is somewhat different in the exact steps it follows to perform its tasks, but all CPUs must perform a series of similar general steps. These steps, referred to as a CPU **machine cycle** (or **processing cycle**), are shown in Figure 8 and are described here:

1. When any program begins to run, the 1s and 0s that make up the program's binary code must be "fetched" from their temporary storage location in random access memory (RAM) and moved to the CPU before they can be executed.

2. Once the program's binary code is in the CPU, it is decoded into the commands the CPU understands.

3. Next, the CPU actually performs the work described in the commands. Specialized hardware on the CPU performs addition, subtraction, multiplication, division, and other mathematical and logical operations at incredible speeds.

4. The result is stored in **registers**, special memory storage areas built into the CPU, which are the most expensive, fastest memory in your computer. The CPU is then ready to fetch the next set of bits encoding the next instruction.

No matter what program you are running, be it a Web browser or a word-processing program, and no matter how many programs you are using at one time, the CPU performs these four steps over and over at incredibly high speeds. Shortly, we'll look at each stage in more detail so that you can understand the complexity of the CPU's design, how to compare different CPUs on the market, and what enhancements to expect in CPU designs of the future. But first, let's examine a few other components of the CPU that help it perform its tasks.

The System Clock

How does the CPU know when to begin the next stage in the machine cycle? To move from one stage of the machine cycle to the next, the motherboard contains a built-in **system clock.** This internal clock is actually a special crystal that acts like a metronome, keeping a steady beat and thereby controlling when the CPU moves to the next stage of processing.

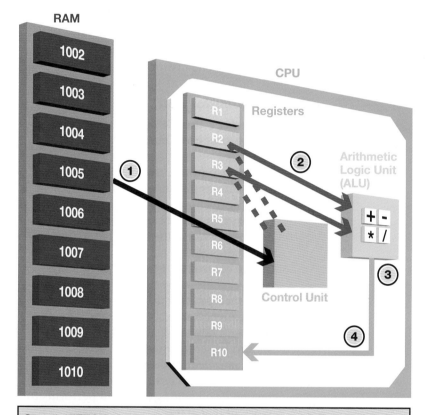

Step 1: FETCH: When a program begins to run, the program's binary code must be "fetched" from RAM and moved to the CPU's control unit before it can be executed.

Step 2: DECODE: Once the program's binary code is in the CPU, it is "decoded" into the commands the CPU understands. The control unit then tells the registers which data to feed to the arithmetic logic unit (ALU), the part of the CPU designed to perform mathematical operations.

Step 3: EXECUTE: The ALU performs the work described in the command.

Step 4: STORE: The result is stored in the registers. The CPU is then ready to fetch the next set of bits encoding the next instruction.

FIGURE 8

The CPU Machine Cycle

These steady beats or "ticks" of the system clock, known as the **clock cycle,** set the pace by which the computer moves from process to process. The pace, known as **clock speed,** is measured in hertz (Hz), a unit of measure that describes how many times something happens per second. Today's system clocks are measured in gigahertz (GHz), or one billion clock ticks per second. Therefore, in a 3-GHz system, there are three billion clock ticks each second. Computers with older processors would sometimes need one or more cycles to process one instruction. Today, however, CPUs are designed to handle more instructions more efficiently, therefore executing more than one instruction per cycle.

The Control Unit

How does the CPU know which stage in the machine cycle is next? The CPU, like any part of the computer system, is designed from a collection of switches. How can simple on/off switches "remember" the fetch-decode-execute-store sequence of the CPU machine cycle? How can they perform the work required in each of these stages?

The **control unit** of the CPU manages the switches inside the CPU. It is programmed by CPU designers to remember the sequence of processing stages for that CPU and how each switch in the CPU should be set, on or off, for each stage. With each beat of the system clock, the control unit moves each switch to the correct on or off setting and then performs the work of that stage.

Let's now look at each of the stages in the machine cycle in a bit more depth.

STAGE 1: THE FETCH STAGE

Where does the CPU find the necessary information? The data and program instructions the CPU needs are stored in different areas in the computer system. Data and program instructions move between these areas as needed or not needed by the CPU for processing. Programs (such as Microsoft Word) are permanently stored on the hard disk because the hard disk offers nonvolatile storage, meaning the programs remain stored there even when you turn the power off. However, when you launch a program (that is, when you double-click an icon to execute the program), the program, or sometimes only the essential parts of a program, is transferred from the hard disk into RAM.

The program moves to RAM because the CPU can access the data and program instructions stored in RAM more than one million times faster than if they are left on the hard disk drive. This is because RAM is much closer to the CPU than is the hard disk drive. Another reason for the delay in access of data and program instructions from the hard disk drive to the CPU has to do with the fact that the hard disk drive is a physical device. The hard disk drive has read/write heads that have to sweep over the platters, which takes longer. RAM is faster because it's electrical, not physical.

As specific instructions from the program are needed, they are moved from RAM into registers (the special storage areas located on the CPU itself), where they wait to be executed.

Why doesn't the CPU chip just contain enough memory to store an entire program? The CPU's storage area is not big enough to hold everything it needs to process at the same time. If enough memory were located on the CPU chip itself, an entire program could be copied to the CPU from RAM before it was executed. This certainly would add to the computer's speed and efficiency because there would not be any delay to stop and fetch instructions from RAM to the CPU. However, including so much memory on a CPU chip would make these chips very expensive. Also, CPU design is so complex that only a limited amount of storage space is available on the CPU itself.

Cache Memory

So, the CPU needs to fetch every instruction from RAM each time it goes through a cycle? Actually, there is another layer of storage that has even faster access than RAM, called **cache memory.** The word *cache* is derived from the French word *cacher,* meaning "to hide." Cache memory consists of small blocks of memory located directly on and next to the CPU chip. These memory blocks are holding places for recently or frequently used instructions or data that the CPU needs the most. When these instructions or data are stored in cache memory, the CPU can retrieve them more quickly than would be

Behind the Scenes: A Closer Look at System Hardware

the case if it had to access the instructions or data in RAM.

Taking data you think you'll be using soon and storing it nearby is a simple idea but a powerful one. This is a strategy that shows up in other places in your computer system. For example, when you are browsing Web pages, it takes longer to download images than text. Your browser software automatically stores images on your hard disk drive so that you don't have to wait to download them again if you want to go back and view a page you've already visited. Although this cache of files is not related to the cache storage space designed into the CPU chip, the idea is the same.

How does cache memory work? Modern CPU designs include a number of types of cache memory. If the next instruction to be fetched is not already located in a CPU register, instead of looking directly to RAM to find it, the CPU first searches Level 1 cache. **Level 1 cache** is a block of memory that is built onto the CPU chip for the storage of data or commands that have just been used.

If the command is not located in Level 1 cache, the CPU searches Level 2 cache. Depending on the design of the CPU, **Level 2 cache** is located on the CPU chip, but is slightly farther away from the CPU, or it's on a separate chip next to the CPU and therefore takes somewhat longer to access. Level 2 cache contains more storage area than does Level 1 cache. For the Intel Core 2 Duo, for example, the Level 1 cache is 32 kilobytes (KB), and the Level 2 cache is 2 megabytes (MB).

Only if the CPU doesn't find the next instruction to be fetched in either Level 1 or Level 2 cache will it make the long journey to RAM to access it.

Are there any other types of cache memory? The current direction of processor design is toward larger and larger multi-level CPU cache structures. Therefore, some newer CPUs, such as Intel's Xeon processor for workstations and servers, have an additional third level of cache memory storage, called **Level 3 cache.** On computers with Level 3 cache, the CPU checks this area for instructions and data after it looks in Level 1 and Level 2 cache, but before it makes the longer trip to RAM (see Figure 9). The Level 3 cache holds between 2 and 8 megabytes (MB) of data. With 8 MB of Level 3 cache,

there is virtually enough storage for an entire program to be transferred to the CPU for its execution.

How do I use cache memory? As an end user of computer programs, you do nothing special to use cache memory. In fact, you will not even be able to notice that caching is being used—nothing special

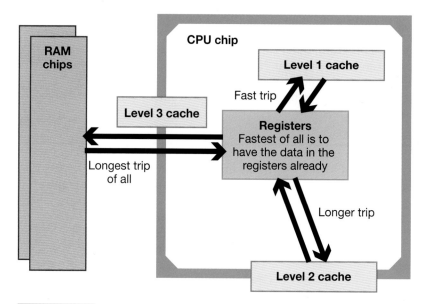

FIGURE 9

Modern CPUs have two or more levels of cache memory, which leads to faster CPU processing.

BITS AND BYTES

The Future of RAM

As the demand for portable computing devices accelerates, researchers are constantly looking for ways to save space and power consumption (to increase battery life). Magnetoresistive Random Access Memory (MRAM) may soon provide solutions to these common challenges.

Most RAM used today is DRAM (dynamic RAM). DRAM uses electrical charges to store data, whereas MRAM uses magnetic plates to store data. A significant advantage of MRAM over DRAM is that it uses almost 99 percent less power, making it ideal for portable computing devices.

Currently, DRAM can be manufactured with more transistors per square inch, but it is anticipated that MRAM will eventually be created with a higher density of transistors than the current DRAM. When this happens, MRAM should replace DRAM in most devices.

Why Does Caching Work?

Did you know that 80 percent of the time your CPU spends processing it is working on the same 20 percent of code? Software monitoring programs have been built to test this conjecture for specific systems, and it generally holds up well. This is the concept that cache memory exploits. It would be much too expensive to design a system with enough memory on the CPU to store an entire program. But if careful management of a cache of fast memory can make sure that the majority of the 20 percent of the program used the most often is already sitting in the cache (and is therefore closer to the CPU), the improvement in overall performance is great.

lights up on your system unit or keyboard. However, the advantage of having more cache memory is that you'll experience better performance because the CPU won't have to make the longer trip to RAM to get data and instructions as often. Unfortunately, because it is built into the CPU chip or motherboard, you can't upgrade cache: it is part of the original design of the computer system. Therefore, like RAM, it's important when buying a computer to consider buying the one, everything else being equal, with the most cache memory.

STAGE 2: THE DECODE STAGE

What happens during the decode stage? The main goal of the decode stage is for the CPU's control unit to translate (or **decode**) the program's instructions into commands the CPU can understand. A CPU can understand only a very small set of commands. The collection of commands a specific CPU can execute is called the **instruction set** for that system. Each CPU has its own unique instruction set. For example, the AMD Athlon 64 X2 Dual-Core processor used in an Alienware Aurora gaming computer has a different instruction set than does the Intel Core 2 Duo used in a Dell Inspiron notebook. The control unit interprets the code's bits according to the instruction set the CPU designers laid out for that particular CPU. Based on this process of translation, the control unit then knows how to set up all the switches on the CPU so that the proper operation will occur.

What does the instruction set look like? Because humans are the ones to write the instructions initially, all of the commands in an instruction set are written in a language that is easier for humans to work with, called **assembly language**. However, because the CPU knows and recognizes only patterns of 0s and 1s, it cannot understand assembly language, so these human-readable instructions are translated into long strings of binary code. The control unit uses these long strings of binary code, called **machine language**, to set up the hardware in the CPU for the rest of the operations it needs to perform. Machine language is a binary code for computer instructions, much like the ASCII code is a binary code for letters and characters. Similar to each letter or character having its own unique combination of 0s and 1s assigned to it, a CPU has a table of codes consisting of combinations of 0s and 1s for each of its commands. If the CPU sees that pattern of bits arrive, it knows the work it must do. Figure 10 shows a few commands in both assembly language and machine language.

Many CPUs have similar commands in their instruction sets, including the commands listed here:

ADD	Add
SUB	Subtract
MUL	Multiply
DIV	Divide
MOVE	Move data to RAM
STORE	Move data to a CPU register
EQU	Check if equal

CPUs differ in the choice of additional assembly language commands selected for the instruction set. Each CPU design team works to develop an instruction set that is both powerful and speedy.

FIGURE 10 Representations of Sample CPU Commands

Human Language for Command	CPU Command in Assembly Language (Language Used by Programmers)	CPU Command in Machine Language (Language Used in the CPU's Instruction Set)
Add	ADD	1110 1010
Subtract	SUB	0001 0101
Multiply	MUL	1111 0000
Divide	DIV	0000 1111

STAGE 3: THE EXECUTE STAGE

Where are the calculations performed in the CPU? The **arithmetic logic unit (ALU)** is the part of the CPU designed to perform mathematical operations such as addition, subtraction, multiplication, and division and to test the comparison of values such as greater than, less than, or equal to. For example, in performing its calculations, the ALU would decide whether the grade point average of 3.9 was greater than, less than, or equal to the grade point average of 3.5. The ALU also performs logical OR, AND, and NOT operations. For example, in determining whether a student can graduate, the ALU would need to ascertain whether the student had taken all required courses AND obtained a passing grade in each of them. The ALU is specially designed to execute such calculations flawlessly and with incredible speed.

The ALU is fed data from the CPU's registers. The amount of data a CPU can process at a time is based in part on the amount of data each register can hold. The number of bits a computer can work with at a time is referred to as its **word size**. Therefore, a 64-bit processor can process more information faster than a 32-bit processor.

STAGE 4: THE STORE STAGE

What happens in the last stage of CPU processing? In the final stage, the result produced by the ALU is stored back in the registers. The instruction itself will explain

ACTIVE HELPDESK
Understanding the CPU

In this Active Helpdesk call, you'll play the role of a Helpdesk staffer, fielding calls about what is inside the CPU and how these components operate, as well as how a CPU processes data and instructions and how cache memory works.

which register should be used to store the answer. Now the entire instruction has been completed. The next instruction will be fetched, and the fetch-decode-execute-store sequence will begin again.

RAM: The Next Level of Temporary Storage

By now you are aware of **random access memory (RAM)** and the role it plays in your computer system. As you'll recall, RAM is volatile, meaning that when you turn off your computer, the data stored in RAM is erased. RAM is located as a set of chips on the system unit's motherboard, and its capacity is measured in megabytes and gigabytes, with most modern systems containing 1 GB to 4 GB of RAM. The type of memory chips your computer uses is tied to the type and speed of your CPU.

Figure 11 shows a hierarchy of the different types of memory found in your computer system in addition to the more permanent storage devices. You've already read about the top two tiers: CPU registers

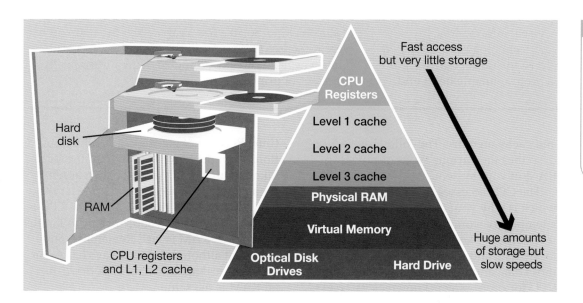

FIGURE 11

There are many different levels of memory in a computer system, ranging from the very small amounts in the CPU to the much slower but more plentiful storage of a hard disk drive.

Emerging Technologies: Printable Processors—The Ultimate in Flexibility

You know that the CPU is the "brains" of the computer. Without this important little chip, the computer couldn't process information. The innovations of the transistor and the integrated circuit have shrunk the processor so much that even a pen-sized instrument can house computer processing capabilities. Miniaturization has made technology very much a part of our lives.

Manufacturing tiny bits of electronic circuitry on silicon is a time-consuming and costly process. But imagine if making microprocessors were as easy as printing them out on your inkjet printer. Or for larger projects, imagine printing out computer components on rolls similar to those that are fed through newspaper presses. Sound crazy? At FASwitch, this technology is under development. Their visions of what will one day be possible with computer technology make even the *Jetsons* seem old-fashioned.

According to FASwitch, if computer processors could be printed on common materials, such as flexible plastic or even paper, rather than manufactured on silicon, computers could be cheaper, smaller, and more completely incorporated into objects we use every day. In fact, the computer would be nearly invisible. You might, for example, download a processor from the Internet and print this processor directly onto a plastic-type substance using your desktop printer. You could then incorporate these plastic-based processors into everything— even wallpaper that could change images or provide lighting for a room.

Printable processors might even have uses you would expect to see in a James Bond movie, such as wearable computers. Your jacket might have a processor with a built-in thermostat that "reads" your body temperature, and your sunglasses could include processors in the lenses that display visual information.

The printable processor technology is anticipated to lead to other innovations, including lightweight medical devices such as programmable heart and blood pressure monitors, food cans that could tell you when they are out of date, high-capacity memory devices, ultrathin batteries that are safe and inexpensive, and flexible information devices (like today's personal digital assistants) that could roll up and fit inside your purse or pocket. They also anticipate that printable processors will become extremely cheap, lowering the price as well as the size of most computing devices and helping to close the so-called *digital divide*.

Realistically, flexible processors are several years out from actual production. The use of flexible electronic technology, however, is already being seen in other applications. Ultrathin, flexible displays are being developed with the intention of integrating the technology in a wide variety of applications, military being at the top of the list. The flexible display technology would enable the production of rollable maps and display-embedded uniforms. Anticipated commerce uses include improving on current automotive displays as well as other mobile displays for phones, Tablet PCs, personal digital assistants (PDAs), and so on. Similar strides are being made in developing memory chips on plastic that are then printed using roll-to-roll technology.

Possibilities like these represent only the tip of the iceberg in terms of printable electronics. Another company, Plastic Logic, is also working on printing electronic circuitry onto plastic. In addition to the new and creative applications that plastic microprocessors would produce, Plastic Logic touts an added environmental benefit of printable processors. The technology to make them doesn't use toxic or environmentally damaging materials that are currently used in the manufacturing of silicon chips. So, in a few years, when the coat you're wearing senses that you're still cold and turns on a built-in heater, you may be able to thank the innovative processes of printable processors!

---

and cache memory. The following section describes the various types of physical RAM in your system.

The CPU accesses RAM very rapidly, which is why your computer uses RAM as a temporary storage location for data and instructions. The time it takes a device to locate data and instructions and make those data and instructions available to the CPU for processing is known as its **access**

time. Recall that getting data and instructions from the hard disk drive to the CPU takes about 10 milliseconds (ms), or ten-thousandths of a second. The time it takes to get instructions from RAM to the CPU is expressed in nanoseconds (ns), or billionths of seconds. RAM is fast! Remember, however, that although RAM always has faster access times than the hard disk drive, not all RAM is the same.

TYPES OF RAM

Why are there different types of RAM? Like all other components of your computer, over time, improvements have been made to the design of RAM. Today, there are several kinds of RAM. Each type of RAM has a very different internal design, allowing some types to work at much faster speeds and to transfer data much more quickly than others.

Therefore, not all systems need or use the same type of RAM. Low-end computer systems may have one type of RAM, whereas more expensive computer systems that are designed for heavy multimedia use may have another type. If you compare ads for computer systems, you'll see a number of different acronyms describing the various types of memory, including DRAM, DDR SDRAM, GDDR-4, and DDR2 RAM. Despite their differences in design, all of these forms of RAM share the same purpose in a computer system: to store data and allow it to be quickly accessed by the CPU. Understanding the different types of RAM will make you a more knowledgeable consumer and will prepare you to evaluate future memory technologies.

What is the most basic type of RAM? The cheapest and most basic type of RAM is **dynamic RAM (DRAM)**. It is used now only in older systems or in systems in which cost is an important factor. DRAM offers access speed on the order of 60 ns. This means that when the CPU requests a piece of information, it experiences a delay of 60 billionths of a second while the data is retrieved from DRAM.

How does DRAM work? In storing 1 bit of data inside DRAM, a transistor and a capacitor are used. As you learned earlier, a transistor is a switch that can be turned on (allowing electrical current to flow) or off (blocking current). A capacitor is an electronic device that is easily fabricated from silicon and that acts like a huge bathtub, or storage space, for the charged electrons coming from the transistors. To store a 1 (or an "on" bit), the transistor is turned to the "on" position, and it fills the capacitor with charge. When a capacitor is full of charge, it will be read as a 1, whereas when the capacitor is empty, or without charge, it will be read as a 0.

Why is DRAM referred to as "dynamic" RAM? Like a leaky bathtub, capacitors leak charge all the time. If the

capacitor is just filled with charge once, it eventually loses all its charge. The data being stored in memory is read by looking at a specific capacitor for each bit. If the capacitor at that location is filled with enough charge to be called "on" (that is, if the "bathtub" has been filled with "water"), that bit is read as a 1. If that capacitor *should* be holding a 1 value, but has been sitting there for a while, it may have lost all its charge (that is, the charge may have leaked away over time). The bit would now be read as a 0, and the data stored there would be corrupted.

To make sure each capacitor holding a 1 value is filled with enough charge to be read as a 1 at any time, a refresh signal is applied. The refresh will flood current through the open transistors to refill the capacitors so that they continue to store a valid 1. This is the dynamic factor in DRAM: the fact that capacitors leak charge and therefore must be recharged as they are used so that the data they hold keeps its true value. This process is illustrated in Figure 12.

Are there different kinds of DRAM? Yes. The design of DRAM has greatly evolved over the years. A variety of types of DRAM are currently on the market, each with different performance levels and prices. For example, synchronous DRAM (SDRAM) is much faster than basic DRAM. The typical type of DRAM in many home systems is double data rate synchronous DRAM (DDR SDRAM). DDR SDRAM is faster than regular SDRAM but not as fast as DDR2 SDRAM, which can push data through twice as fast. In high-end multimedia machines and on gaming systems, where the speed is necessary to handle the demands of graphics and audio/video processing efficiently, you will see dual-channel DDR2 SDRAM. This type of memory has a factor of two and is faster than even DDR2! Each of these types of

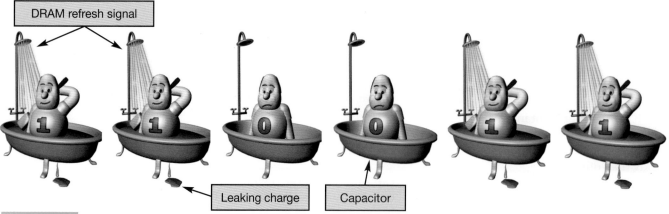

placement reference for labels: DRAM refresh signal, Leaking charge, Capacitor

FIGURE 12

The binary data 110011 is stored in DRAM using capacitors. However, like a bathtub with a leak, these capacitors leak charge, so the DRAM must be refreshed (the bathtub refilled) with charge every clock cycle.

DRAM increases not only the speed with which the CPU can access data but also the cost of the memory modules.

Is there a faster RAM than DRAM? All of the refresh signals required to keep the data "fresh" in DRAM take time. A faster type of RAM is **static RAM (SRAM).** In SRAM, more transistors are used to store a single bit, but no capacitor is needed. This eliminates the need for a refresh signal (thereby avoiding recharging), thus making SRAM much faster than DRAM. However, because it is more expensive than DRAM, it is used only in locations such as the CPU's cache, where the system demands the fastest possible storage.

What kind of memory should I buy for my system? You really do not have a choice in the type of RAM that comes with your system. As described earlier, the system manufacturer installs the specific type of RAM, and it will vary depending on the system's processor and performance requirements. If you decide to purchase additional memory for your system, you'll need to be sure to match the kind of RAM already installed. A system with SDRAM will not be compatible with DDR SDRAM technology, for example.

Most RAM chips reside on small circuit boards called memory modules. Newer computers generally use DIMMs (dual

inline memory modules). DIMMs replaced SIMMs (single inline memory module) when Pentium processors became so prevalent in the market. Pentium processors have a 64-bit bus width, which matches the 64-bit data path of the DIMMs. SIMMs with a 32-bit data path could be used but would need to be installed in matched pairs.

Does ROM help the CPU work? As you've learned, read-only memory (ROM) is a set of memory chips located on the motherboard that stores data and instructions that cannot be changed or erased. ROM chips can be found on most digital devices and usually contain the start-up instructions the computer needs. ROM chips do not provide any other form of data storage.

Buses: The CPU's Data Highway

A **bus** is an electrical wire in the computer's circuitry—the highway that data (or bits) travels on between the computer's various components. Computers have two different kinds of buses. **Local buses** (or **front side buses** or **FSB**) are on the motherboard and run between the CPU and the main system memory. Most systems also have another type of bus, called an **expansion bus,** which expands the capabilities of your computer by allowing a range of different expansion cards (such as video cards and sound cards) to communicate with the motherboard.

Do buses affect a computer's performance? Some buses can move data along more quickly than others, whereas others can move more data at one time. The rate of speed that data moves

ACTIVE HELPDESK

Understanding Types of RAM

In this Active Helpdesk call, you'll play the role of a Helpdesk staffer, fielding calls about the different types of RAM on the market.

from one location to another, known as bus clock speed, affects the overall performance of the computer. Bus clock speed is measured in units of megahertz (MHz), or millions of clock cycles per second. Systems on the market now have FSB speeds ranging from 667 MHz to 1066 MHz. The width of the bus (or the **bus width**) determines how many bits of data can be sent along a given bus at any one time. The wider the bus, the more data that can be sent at one time.

Bus width is measured in terms of bits, so a 32-bit bus can carry more data at one time than a 16-bit bus. Together, *bus clock speed* and *bus width* determine how quickly any given amount of data can be transferred on a bus (see Figure 13). This data transfer rate (measured in units of megabytes per second) is calculated by multiplying the speed of the bus by the bus width.

The bus width also affects the processor's word size, or the number of bits a processor can manipulate at one time. Even if a processor can manipulate 64 bits at a time, if the bus width allows only 32 bits of data to be sent at one time, the processor's performance will be affected.

What kinds of expansion buses do I need to know about? As noted earlier, the motherboard contains expansion slots in which you insert expansion cards. These expansion cards (such as a graphics card) enable you to connect peripheral devices (such as a monitor) to your computer. For the peripherals to be able to communicate (send and receive data) with your CPU, the motherboard includes expansion buses. The expansion buses provide the pathways that enable the CPU to communicate with the peripheral devices attached through the cards.

Expansion buses have evolved to provide faster transfer speeds and wider bit widths

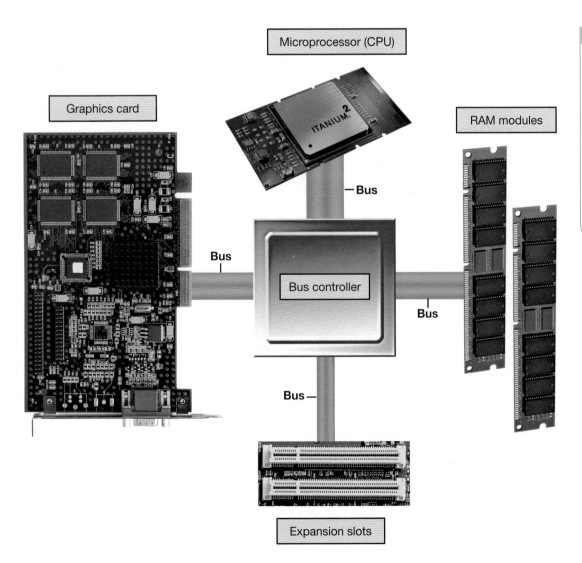

Microprocessor (CPU)

Graphics card

ITANIUM 2

RAM modules

— Bus

Bus

Bus controller

Bus

Bus —

Expansion slots

FIGURE 13

Buses connect components in your computer so that data can move between them. The width of the bus (bus width) determines how many bits of data can be sent along a given bus at any one time. The wider the bus, the more data that can be sent at one time.

to deliver higher data transfer rates to the many peripheral devices you may connect to your computer. There are several types of expansion buses. Older computers include buses such as the **Industry Standard Architecture (ISA) bus** and the **Extended Industry Standard Architecture (EISA) bus** to connect devices such as the mouse, modem, and sound cards. These are being replaced by faster, more efficient connections.

The **Accelerated Graphics Port (AGP) bus** design was specialized to help move three-dimensional graphics data quickly. In a modern computer system, you'll find **Peripheral Component Interconnect Express (PCIe) buses**. PCIe expansion buses connect directly to the CPU and support such devices as network cards, sound, and video cards. They extend the speeds of the

original PCI bus design, which has been used for much of the past decade. There are PCIe x8 and PCIe x16 buses, which are 8 times and 16 times faster than the original PCIe specification.

Figure 14 lists the many bus architectures and their respective features.

Making Computers Even Faster: Advanced CPU Designs

Knowing how to build a CPU that can run faster than the competition can make a company rich. However, building a faster CPU is not easy. When a company decides to design a faster processor, it must take into consideration the time it will take to design, manufacture, and test that processor. When the processor finally hits the market, it must be faster than the competition to even hope to make a profit. To create a CPU that will be released 36 months from now, it must be built to perform at least twice as fast as anything currently available.

Gordon Moore, the cofounder of processor manufacturer Intel, predicted more than 40

FIGURE 9.14 Bus Design Evolution

Bus Architecture	Introduced	Bus Width	Bus Clock Speed	Data Transfer Rate	Notes
ISA (Industry Standard Architecture)	1982	8 or 16 bits	4.77 MHz to 8 MHz	16 MB/sec	Increased performance from the original PC bus design
EISA (Extended Industry Standard Architecture)	Late 1980s	32 bits	8 MHz	32 MB/sec	Next evolution of ISA standard
PCI (Peripheral Component Interconnect)	Early 1990s	32 or 64 bits	33 to 133 MHz	133 to 1,024 MB/sec	Made popular with Windows 95 Long-lived with continued evolution
AGP (Accelerated Graphics Port)	1997	32 bits	66 to 533 MHz	266 to 2,133 MB/sec	Especially for 3-D graphics Uses pipelining to increase speed
PCIe (Peripheral Component Interconnect Express)	2004/5	1X = 8 bits; 16X = 128 bits	325 to 500 MHz	250 MB/sec for 1X; 4 GB/sec for 16X	Has better reliability and power management and can outperform AGP

years ago that the number of transistors on a processor would double every 18 months. Known as Moore's Law, this prediction has been remarkably accurate—but only with tremendous engineering ingenuity. The first 8086 chip had only 29,000 transistors and ran at 5 MHz. Advances in the number of transistors on processors through the 1970s, 1980s, and 1990s continued to align with Moore's prediction.

However, there was a time near the turn of the 21st century when skeptics questioned how much longer Moore's Law would hold true. These skeptics were proved wrong with the microprocessor's continued growth in power. Today's Itanium 2 chip has 592 million transistors and runs at 3.6 GHz—nearly 300 times faster than its original counterpart. And Intel's Itanium 2 chip is flaunting a whopping 1.72 billion transistors! How much longer can Moore's prediction hold true? Only time will tell. One thing is for certain, though: CPU design is an area where companies can make great profits, but they risk great fortunes at the same time.

How can processors be designed so they are faster? Processor manufacturers can increase CPU performance in many different ways. One approach is to use a technique called pipelining to boost performance. Another approach is to design the CPU's instruction set so that it contains specialized, faster instructions for handling multimedia and graphics. In addition, some CPUs, such as Intel's Core 2 Extreme processors, now have four independent processing paths inside, with one CPU chip doing the work of four separate CPU units. Some heavy computational problems are attacked by actually clustering together large numbers of computers working at the same time.

PIPELINING

Earlier in the chapter you learned that as an instruction is processed, the CPU runs through the four stages of processing in a sequential order: fetch, decode, execute, store. **Pipelining** is a technique that allows the CPU to work on more than one instruction (or stage of processing) at a time, thereby boosting CPU performance.

For example, without pipelining, it may take four clock cycles to complete one instruction (one clock cycle for four processing stages). However, four-stage pipeline, the computer can process four instructions *at the same time*. Like a car assembly line, instead of waiting for one car to go completely through each process of assembly, painting, and so on, you can have four cars going through the assembly line at the same time. When every component of the assembly line is done with its process, the cars all move on to the next stage.

Pipelined architectures allow several instructions to be processed at the same time. The computer allows several instructions to be processed at the same time. The ticks of the system clock (the clock cycle) indicate when all instructions move to the next process. The secret of pipelining is that the CPU is allowed to be fetching one instruction while it is simultaneously decoding another, executing a third, storing a fourth, and so on. Using pipelining, a four-stage processor can therefore potentially run up to four times faster because some instruction is finishing every clock cycle rather than waiting four cycles for each instruction to finish, as shown in Figure 15.

BITS AND BYTES

Does Your Computer Need More Power? Team It Up!

If one computer is powerful, two are twice as powerful—but only if you can get them to work together. A *computing cluster* is a group of computers, connected by specialized clustering software, that work together to solve complex equations. Most clusters work on something called the *load balancing principle,* which means that computational work is transferred from overloaded (busy) computers in the cluster to computers with more available computing resources. Computing clusters, although not as fast as supercomputers (single computers with extremely high processing capabilities), can perform computations faster than one computer working alone and are used for complex calculations such as weather forecasting and graphics rendering. You can even set up a computing cluster at home, as long as you have at least two computers. Using the Linux operating system and clustering software based on openMosix (**http://openmosix.sourceforge.net**), you can build your own computing cluster for free.

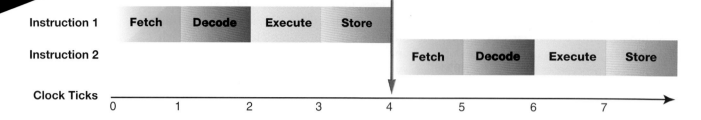

e, Non-Pipelined: At the end of four clock cycles, Instruction 1 has completed a cycle and Instruction 2 is about to be fetched from RAM.

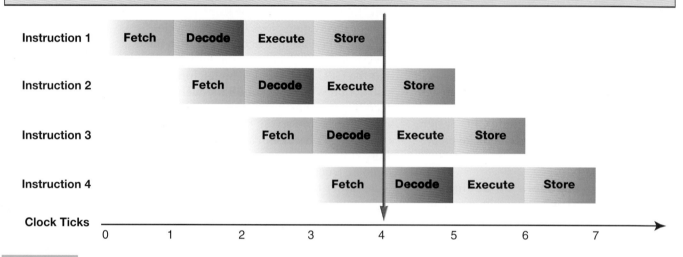

(b) Instruction Cycle, Pipelined: At the end of four clock cycles, Instruction 1 has completed a cycle, Instruction 2 has just finished executing, Instruction 3 has finished decoding, and Instruction 4 has been fetched from RAM.

FIGURE 15

The Effects of Pipelining

How many stages can a pipeline have? This depends entirely on design decisions. In this chapter we discussed a CPU that went through four stages in the execution of an instruction. The Intel Pentium 4 with hyperthreading features a 31-stage pipeline, and the PowerPC G5 processor uses a 10-stage pipeline. Thus, similar to an assembly line, in a 31-stage pipeline, up to 31 different instructions can be processed at any given time, making the processing of information much faster. However, because so many aspects of the CPU design interact, you cannot predict performance based solely on the number of stages in a pipeline.

How does pipelining impact the design of the CPU chip? There is a cost to pipelining a CPU. The CPU must be designed so that each stage (fetch, decode, execute, store) is independent. This means that each stage must be able to run at the same time that the other three stages are running. This requires more transistors and a more complicated hardware design.

SPECIALIZED MULTIMEDIA INSTRUCTIONS

How are some processors designed to process multimedia more quickly than others? Each design team developing a new CPU tries to imagine what users' greatest needs will be in four or five years. Currently, several processors on the market reflect this consideration in the incorporation of specialized multimedia instructions into the basic instruction set. The hardware engineers have redesigned the chip so that the instruction set contains new commands that are specially designed to speed up the work needed for video and audio processing. For example, Intel has integrated the Streaming Single Instruction Multiple Data (SIMD)

Extensions 3 set of commands into the newer Pentium 4 processor design, adding a special group of 157 commands to the base instruction set. These multimedia-specific instructions work to accelerate video, speech, and image processing in the CPU.

MULTIPLE PROCESSING EFFORTS

Can I have more than one CPU in my desktop computer? Many high-end server systems employ **dual processors,** two completely separate CPU chips on one motherboard. Often, these server systems can later be scaled so that they can accommodate four, six, or even eight processors. Some of the most powerful mainframes support up to 32 processors!

Meanwhile, Intel is promoting a technology called **multi-core processing** in its Core 2 Duo line of chips. Chips with dual-core processing capabilities have two separate parallel processing paths inside them, so they are almost as fast as two separate CPUs. Combining this with another Intel approach called hyper-threading (or HT), these chips can run up to four tasks (fetch, decode, execute, store) at one time. Dual-core processing is especially helpful because antivirus software and other security programs are often running in the background as you use your system. A dual-core processor enables these multiple applications to execute much more quickly than with traditional CPUs. Quad-core processors are appearing in high-performance home-based systems now as well.

When do I need all that processing power? Dual- or multi-core processor systems are often used when intensive computational problems need to be solved in such areas as computer simulations, video production, and graphics processing. Having two processors allows the work to be done *almost* twice as quickly, but not quite. It is not quite twice as fast because the system must do some extra work to decide which processor will work on which part of the problem and to recombine the results each CPU produces.

Could I have more than one machine working on a single task? Certain types of problems are well suited to a parallel-processing environ-

ment. In **parallel processing,** there is a large network of computers, with each computer working on a portion of the same problem simultaneously. To be a good candidate for parallel processing, a problem must be one that can be divided into a set of tasks that can be run simultaneously. If the next step of an algorithm can be started only after the results of the previous step have been computed, parallel processing will present no advantages.

A simple analogy of parallel processing is a laundromat. Instead of taking all day to do five loads of laundry with one machine, you can bring all your laundry to a laundromat, load it in five separate machines, and finish it all in approximately the same time it would have taken you to do just one load on a single machine. In real life, parallel processing is used for complex weather forecasting to run calculations over many different regions around the globe, in the airline industry to analyze customer information in an effort to forecast demand, and by the government in census data compilation.

BITS AND BYTES

Today's Supercomputers: The Fastest of the Fast

Supercomputers are the biggest and most powerful type of computer. Scientists and engineers use these computers to solve complex problems or to perform massive computations. Some supercomputers are single computers with multiple processors, whereas others consist of multiple computers that work together.

The fastest supercomputer today is the IBM-developed Blue Gene/L, which is used for computing the safety of the nation's nuclear-weapons stockpile. It operates at more than 280.6 teraflops (or 280 trillion operations per second). That's almost 140,000 times faster than the average personal computer! Of course, the Blue Gene/L does use more than 131,000 separate processors at the same time. The supercomputer Columbia, which as of 2007 is the eighth fastest supercomputer, operates at 52 teraflops and supports NASA space exploration projects like the International Space Station. Its 10,000 processors can compute the impact of space shuttle damage on the craft's orbit in 24 hours, instead of the three months required by older systems. Check out the world's fastest supercomputers at **www.top500.org**.

TRENDS IN IT

Emerging Technologies: Computer Technology—Changing the Face of Medicine

As you know by now, computers are no longer just for gaming and spreadsheets. Microprocessors, nanotechnology, and other technologies developed during the personal computing explosion of the last two decades are rapidly being adapted to the medical field. You can look forward to the appearance of the following medical advancements within the next decade:

1. **Mechanisms delivering drugs.** Although drugs such as insulin are self-administered by patients, the current injection delivery method can be uncomfortable or difficult to handle, especially for young and elderly patients. Many physicians view inhalation of insulin as the answer (because most people do not find this unpleasant), but the difficulty is in developing an efficient aerosol delivery method. Aradigm, a California manufacturer, is developing an inhaler called AerX that uses the same technology as inkjet printer nozzles to process liquid medication into an aerosol (required for appropriate absorption of the medication through the membranes in the lungs). For many, this may mean saying good-bye to syringes.

2. **Chips that let you forget to take your pills.** Many drugs must be delivered in precise doses on a regular basis to be effective in treating disease. Although you may be able to remember to take a pill three times a day, not everyone is capable of adhering to this schedule, especially the elderly, young children, or individuals with mental challenges. Therefore, researchers are developing new technologies to deliver medication automatically without any patient intervention. One such promising technology is a dime-sized silicon wafer implant being developed by MicroCHIPS, a Massachusetts-based company. The implants, which are produced using the same methods used to produce silicon microchips for CPUs, contain hundreds of storage areas (called *reservoir arrays*)

that store individual doses of medication. The chips are implanted beneath the skin in your abdominal area. Preprogrammed microprocessors on the chip tell the wafer when to administer the doses of medication. No human interaction needed!

3. **Invasive medical procedures** If you need to have an endoscopy (an examination of your gastrointestinal tract), doctors today normally insert a rather large hose that holds a camera into your body. The Food and Drug Administration has approved a camera that uses small-scale (not yet nano-scale) computer technologies to shrink the camera to the size of a small pill. A patient swallows the camera, which then beams images of the small intestine to a recording device worn on a belt. Now that's an easier pill to swallow.

4. **Computers monitoring your body functions.** Israeli scientists have devised a computer that runs on DNA molecules and enzymes, as opposed to silicon chips. The computer, though having no practical applications just yet, is extremely fast—in fact, it can perform 330 trillion operations per second, approximately 100,000 times as fast as any personal computer on the market today. Also, where silicon chips are reaching their limit of miniaturization, DNA computers can be constructed using only a few molecules—you don't get much smaller than that! As shown in Figure 15, DNA computers are combinations of DNA and specially constructed enzymes. Within a single drop of this special fluid, chemical reactions are taking place in billions of DNA computers that generate data and perform rudimentary calculations.

DNA computers use chemical reactions caused by mixing enzymes and DNA molecules. The reactions are designed to provide data and the energy for any

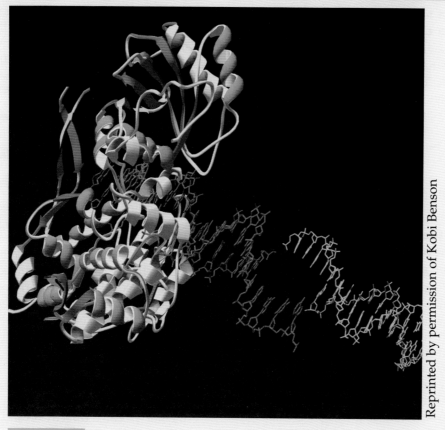

FIGURE 16

Here you see a representation of what it is like inside a DNA-based computer. The double-stranded DNA is combined with enzymes, and together they become the CPU for this biological computing device.

calculations needed. Because chemical reactions can be measured precisely and their outcomes predicted reliably, there is no need for conventional hardware and software. All information can be passed at the molecular level. Although DNA computing is today in its infancy, in the future, doctors envision devices constructed from DNA computers that will patrol our bodies and make repairs (such as clearing plaque from arteries) as soon as a problem is detected.

So, as you can see, computing technology can be used not only to improve the quality of your life, but also some day to improve the quality of your health.

Summary

1. What is a switch, and how does it work in a computer?

Electrical switches are devices inside the computer that flip between two states: 1 or 0, on or off. Transistors are switches built out of layers of semiconductor material. Integrated circuits (or chips) are very small regions of semiconductor material that support a huge number of transistors. Integrated circuits enable computer designers to fit millions of transistors into a very small area.

2. What is the binary number system, and what role does it play in a computer system?

The binary number system uses only two digits, 0 and 1. It is also referred to as the base 2 number system. It is used instead of the base 10 number system to manipulate the on/off switches that control the computer's actions. Even with just two digits, the binary number system can still represent all the same values that a base 10 number system can. To provide a consistent means for representing letters and other characters, codes dictate how to represent characters in binary format. The ASCII code uses 8 bits (0s and 1s) to represent 255 characters. Unicode uses 16 bits of data for each character and can represent more than 65,000 character symbols.

3. What is inside the CPU, and how do these components operate?

The CPU executes every instruction given to your computer. CPUs are differentiated by their processing power (how many transistors are on the microprocessor chip), how quickly the processor can work (called clock speed), and the amount of immediate access memory the CPU has (called cache memory). The CPU consists of two primary units: the control unit controls the switches inside the CPU, and the arithmetic logic unit (ALU) performs logical and arithmetic calculations.

4. How does a CPU process data and instructions?

All CPUs must perform a series of similar general steps. These steps, referred to as a CPU machine cycle (or processing cycle), include: fetch (loading program and data binary code into the CPU), decode (translating the binary code into commands the CPU can understand), execute (carrying out the commands), and store (placing the results in special memory storage areas, called registers, before the process starts again).

5. What is cache memory?

Cache memory consists of small blocks of memory, located directly on and next to the CPU chip, that hold recently or frequently used instructions or data that the CPU needs the most. The CPU can more quickly retrieve data and instructions from cache memory than from RAM.

6. What types of RAM are there?

RAM is volatile storage, meaning that when you turn off your computer, the data stored there is erased. The cheapest and most basic type of RAM is DRAM (dynamic RAM). There are many types of RAM, including SDRAM, DDR SRAM, and DDR2s DRAM. All of these forms of RAM store data that the CPU can access quickly.

7. What is a bus, and how does it function in a computer system?

A bus is an electrical wire in the computer's circuitry through which data (or bits) travels between the computer's various components. Local buses are on the motherboard and run between the CPU and the main system memory. Expansion buses expand the capabilities of your computer by allowing a range of different expansion cards to connect to the motherboard. The width of the bus (or the bus width) determines how many bits of data can be sent along a given bus at any one time.

8. How do manufacturers make CPUs so that they run faster?

Pipelining is a technique that allows the CPU to work on more than one instruction (or stage of processing) at a time, thereby boosting CPU performance. A dual-processor design has two separate CPU chips installed on the same system. Multi-core systems are often used when intensive computational problems need to be solved. In parallel processing, computers in a large network each work on a portion of the same problem at the same time.

Key Terms

Accelerated Graphics Port (AGP) bus

access time

American Standard Code for Information
   Interchange (ASCII)

arithmetic logic unit (ALU)

assembly language

base 2 number system

base 10 number system (decimal notation)

binary digit (bit)

binary language

binary number system

bus

bus width

byte

cache memory

central processing unit (CPU, or processor)

clock cycle

clock speed

control unit

decode

dual processor

dynamic RAM (DRAM)

electrical switch

expansion bus

Extended Industry Standard Architecture
   (EISA) bus

hexadecimal notation

Industry Standard Architecture
   (ISA) bus

instruction set

integrated circuit

Level 1 cache

Level 2 cache

Level 3 cache

local bus (front side bus or FSB)

machine cycle (processing cycle)

machine language

microprocessor

motherboard

multi-core technology

multi-core processing

number system

parallel processing

Peripheral Component Interconnect
   (PCI) bus

pipelining

random access memory (RAM)

register

semiconductor

sign bit

static RAM (SRAM)

system clock

system unit

transistor

Unicode

vacuum tube

word size

Buzz Words

Word Bank

- AGP
- ALU
- ASCII
- binary
- buses
- byte
- cache
- control unit
- decoded
- DRAM
- fetch
- instruction set
- Level 1 cache
- Level 2 cache
- Level 3 cache
- number system
- PCI
- registers

Instructions: Fill in the blanks using the words from the Word Bank.

Computers are based on a system of switches, which can be either on or off. The
(1) _____ number system, which has only two digits, models this well. A(n)
(2) _____ is a set of rules for the representation of numbers. Eight binary digits are
combined to create one (3) _____, so they are easier to work with. The (4) _____
code organizes bytes in unique combinations of 0s and 1s to represent characters, letters,
and numerals.

The CPU organizes switches to execute the basic commands of the system. No matter what
command is being executed, the CPU steps through the same four processing stages. First it
needs to (5) _____ the instruction from RAM. Next the instruction is (6) _____,
and the (7) _____ sets up all of the CPU hardware to perform that particular command. The actual execution takes place in the (8) _____. The result is then saved by
storing it in the (9) _____ on the CPU. Another form of memory the CPU uses is
(10) _____ memory. (11) _____ is the form of this type of memory located closest
to the CPU. (12) _____ is located a bit farther from the CPU.

RAM comes in several different types. (13) _____ must be refreshed each cycle to keep
the data it stores valid. The pathways connecting the CPU to memory are known as
(14) _____. The speeds at which they can move data, or the data transfer rates, vary.
(15) _____ is a bus designed primarily to move three-dimensional graphics data
quickly.

Becoming Computer Literate

Your new boss is unsure what the differences between high-end systems are and would like
you to compile a report on two high-end systems, a Macintosh desktop and a Windows-
based PC. She has asked you to compare the price/performance ratio, the hardware features including CPU design, and memory capacities.

Instructions: Using the preceding scenario, write a report using as many of the key
words from the chapter as you can. Be sure the sentences are grammatically correct and
technically meaningful.

Self-Test

Instructions: Answer the multiple-choice and true/false questions below for more practice with key terms and concepts from this chapter.

MULTIPLE CHOICE

1. Switching can be done
   a. using transistors built of semiconductors.
   b. turning on and off the flow of water.
   c. using vacuum tubes to allow electricity to flow or not flow.
   d. All of the above

2. Hexadecimal notation is based on
   a. powers of 10.   c. powers of 2.
   b. powers of 8.   d. powers of 16.

3. Bits can be encoded in different ways to represent
   a. numeric values.
   b. the letters and symbols of the ASCII table.
   c. the alphabets of all modern languages.
   d. All of the above

4. A CPU's clock speed
   a. is the only important factor in system performance.
   b. is measured in units of billions per second.
   c. depends on which time zone the machine is in.
   d. is a measure of the number of transistors on the chip.

5. The decode stage of the CPU cycle is used to
   a. gather data from the registers.
   b. execute an instruction in the ALU.
   c. pull data from the Level 1 cache.
   d. translate the program's binary code into instructions the CPU understands.

6. Dynamic RAM is called "dynamic" because
   a. it is faster than static RAM (SRAM).
   b. it must be refreshed to keep the data valid.

   c. it has a great personality.
   d. it changes its value every clock cycle.

7. Which of the following is a computer bus standard?
   a. PCIe   c. HTT
   b. Core Extreme   d. All of the above

8. Intel processors are found
   a. are used in both Windows and Apple computer systems.
   b. are used only in Windows-based computer systems.
   c. are used only in Apple computer systems.
   d. are used in some Windows-based systems and all Apple computer systems.

9. Multi-core CPU design means
   a. more than one processing path can run at the same time in the CPU.
   b. only one CPU is used in the system but there are several different types of RAM.
   c. there are multiple, separate CPU chips on the motherboard.
   d. multiple CPUs, but only if each has its own operating system.

10. There are different types of memory in a computer system because
   a. RAM is more economical and better for larger temporary storage needs.
   b. cache memory is used only for most needed instructions.
   c. there is a need for both volatile and nonvolatile storage.
   d. All of the above

TRUE/FALSE

___ 1. A binary number can be only two digits long.

___ 2. SDRAM is standard in most new home desktop systems.

___ 3. The system clock runs at different speeds depending on the workload.

___ 4. Bus designers use pipelining to change the speed of the front side bus.

___ 5. All of the different types of buses inside a computer system run at the same speed.

Behind the Scenes: A Closer Look at System Hardware

Making the Transition to... Next Semester

1. Upgrading RAM

As your college career continues, are you finding your computer needs increasing? Upgrading the RAM in your machine can greatly improve performance. What kind of RAM is installed in the computer you use for schoolwork (your own or the lab system you use)? How much would an upgrade to 2 GB of RAM cost for that type of RAM? An upgrade to 4 GB of RAM? Use the supplier Crucial Technology (**www.crucial.com**) to get information about the type of RAM in your system.

2. Lab Processors

It is always challenging for administrators to keep computer laboratories up-to-date. Investigate the type of processor installed in the computer systems you use in your lab. Visit the manufacturer's Web site to get detailed specifications about the design of that processor—the number of cores in its design, how many levels of cache it has, how much total cache memory it has, its speed, and the number of pipeline stages in the CPU. How does that processor compare with the latest model available from the manufacturer?

3. Comparison Shopping for Systems

Do some comparison shopping. Pick three relatively comparable, moderately priced computer systems—one Macintosh desktop computer, one Windows-based desktop computer, and a notebook that use either the Windows or Macintosh OS. Create a spreadsheet that outlines all the specific features of each machine. What kind of processor does each machine include? How fast is it? How many levels of cache and how much storage capacity does each cache level have? Look at the RAM: what kind and how much RAM does each machine have? What is the bus architecture of each machine?

4. Game Time

The next generation of video gaming consoles is on the market, and you want to reward yourself for having worked hard all semester. Consider the three main entries in the market: Microsoft Xbox 360, Sony PlayStation 3, and Nintendo Wii. For each of these gaming consoles, find out what CPU is being used and what features it has that support high-end gaming. What overall processing power can the system achieve (measured in units of FLOPS, or floating-point operations per second)? What kind of graphics card is used? What kind of ports are included? How does the system handle Internet connectivity? Consider research sources like **www.extremetech.com**, **www.gameinformer.com**, and the Sony, Microsoft, and Nintendo Web sites.

5. Which Processor?

Word gets out that you know a lot about CPUs, and you are suddenly the one everyone is coming to with questions. Some of your friends want to buy notebooks, some want high-end video gaming systems, and some need inexpensive solutions. To prepare yourself to be the "CPU guru," look at the table in Figure 7 and find out what setting or application is most common for each processor. Use manufacturer Web sites as well as **www.pcmag.com** and **www.tomshardware.com** for information.

Making the Transition to... the Workplace

1. Finding Your Network Adapter Address

Almost every business today uses networks to connect the computer systems they own. Each machine is assigned its own identifying number, called a network adapter address. This value is a long binary number that uniquely labels each adapter card in the business. On the networked machine, click Start, click Run, and then type "command" in the Open text box of the Run dialog box. Then type "ipconfig" in the console window to find your own network adapter address. Is it presented in binary? hexadecimal? decimal? Why?

2. CPUs: The Next Generation

In an effort to stay technologically current, you have been asked to research the most recently released CPUs to determine whether it's worth buying new machines with the new CPUs or waiting for perhaps the next generation. Investigate the newest CPUs released by Intel and AMD. Compare these new CPUs with the current "best" CPUs. What technological advancements are present in the latest CPUs? From a cost perspective, does it make sense to replace the old systems with these new CPUs? What is the buzz on the next-generation CPUs? Would it be better to wait for these future CPUs to come out?

3. Using Pipelining

You work in a car assembly plant, so production lines are a familiar concept to your boss. However, he still doesn't understand the concept of pipelining and how it expedites a computer's processing cycle. Create a presentation for your boss that describes pipelining in enough detail so that your boss will understand it. In doing so, compare it with the automobile assembly process.

4. Super Power

Your team at work is exploring a sophisticated stock price prediction model. But the algorithm requires a supercomputer or a computing cluster (multiple computers joined by software working together) to achieve maximum efficiency. Your boss is not interested in spending department funds on this, but if you can find a way to explore this cheaply, using open-source software that runs on Linux, he'll support it. Research low-cost cluster computing solutions (like Beowulf clusters) at sites such as **www.beowulf.org**, **http://openmosix.sourceforge.net**, and **http://bofh.be/clusterknoppix**. Would it be feasible to use existing Windows computers to run the cluster? Describe how to set up a small cluster and the benefits of doing so, including cost estimates for a 16-node cluster (using cheap PCs that can run Linux).

5. Error Handling Using Binary Numbers

At work you have been bothered by an error message that occasionally pops up from one of your programs. It displays the following message:

```
Error code Number 0011 1010 1111 0011 Please call tech support
help line.
```

Before you call in, take each group of four binary digits and write down the equivalent hexadecimal digit. You can do this by computing the base 10 equivalent of the four binary digits first, then figuring out the base 16 representation of that number.

Critical Thinking Questions

Instructions: Albert Einstein used "Gedanken experiments," or critical thinking questions, to develop his theory of relativity. Some ideas are best understood by experimenting with them in our own minds. The following critical thinking questions are designed to demand your full attention but require only a comfortable chair—no technology.

1. **Processors of the Future**

   Consider the current limitations of the design of memory, how it is organized, and how a CPU operates. Think radically—what extreme ideas can you propose for the future of processor design? What do you think the limit of clock speed for a processor will be? How could a CPU communicate more quickly with memory? What could future cache designs look like?

2. **Increasing Processor Speed**

   SIMD and 3DNow! (used by AMD in its processors) are two approaches to modifying the instruction set to speed up graphics operations. What do you think will be the next important type of processing users will expect from computers? How could you customize the commands the CPU understands so that processing occurs faster on the CPU you are designing?

3. **The Impact of Registers**

   How would computer systems be different if we could place 1 GB of registers on a single CPU? How would that impact the design of video cards? Would it change the way RAM is used in the system?

4. **The CPU Processing Cycle**

   The four stages of the CPU processing cycle are fetch, decode, execute, and store. Think of some real-world tasks you perform that could be described the same way. For each example, describe how it would be changed if it were pipelined. What additional resources would the pipelined task require?

5. **Binary Events**

   Binary events, things that can be in one of only two positions, happen around you all the time. A common example is a light switch that is toggled on or off. How about a coin? It must always be either heads up or heads down. What other events or objects behave in a binary style?

6. **Lots of Ways to Remember**

   Why does there need to be a memory hierarchy within a computer system, such as the one drawn in Figure 11? How would you design a system if it were very inexpensive to produce lots of CPU registers and very expensive to build hard disk drives? What if someone discovered a way to make hard disk drives a million times faster than they are today? How would you design a system then?

Problem:

For a system to be effective, it must be balanced—that is, the performance of each subsystem must be well matched so that there are no bottlenecks in the overall performance. In this exercise, teams will develop balanced hardware designs for specific systems within several different price ranges.

Task:

Each group will select one part of a computer—either the CPU, the memory, or the bus architecture. The group will be responsible for researching the available options and collecting information on both price and performance specifications. The group will write a report that recommends a specific product for each of three price ranges—entry level, midrange, and high performance. Finally, the three groups will combine their reports so that the team has developed a specification for the entire system.

Process:

1. Divide into three groups: processor, memory, and bus design.

2. Consider the following three price ranges:
   - $500 to $1,000
   - $1,001 to $2,500
   - Unlimited

   For each price range, try to specify at least two components that would keep the system cost in range and would provide the best performance. Keep track of all performance information so that you can later meet with the other groups and make sure each subsystem is well matched.

3. Bring the research materials from the group meetings to one final team meeting. Looking at the system level, make final decisions on the system design for each of the three price ranges. Each range is the sum of total cost that can be expended for hardware for the system unit (monitor and other peripherals not included). The system case, power supply, motherboard, RAM, video card, and storage must be included. Research vendors that supply parts to home developers, such as TigerDirect.com (**www.tigerdirect.com**).

4. Produce a report that documents the decisions and trade-offs evaluated en route to your final selections.

Conclusion:

A performance increase in one subsystem contributes to the overall performance, but only in proportion to how often it is used. This affects system design and how limited financial resources can be spent to provide the most balanced, best-performing system.

Multimedia

In addition to the review materials presented here, you'll find additional materials featured with the book's multimedia, including the Technology in Action Student Resource CD and the Companion Web Site (**www.prenhall.com/techinaction**), which will help reinforce your understanding of the chapter content. These materials include the following:

ACTIVE HELPDESK

In Active Helpdesk calls, you'll assume the role of a Helpdesk operator taking calls about the concepts you've learned in this chapter. You'll apply what you've learned and receive feedback from a supervisor to review and reinforce those concepts. The Active Helpdesk calls for this chapter are listed here and can be found on your Student Resource CD:

- Understanding the CPU
- Understanding Types of RAM

SOUND BYTES

Sound Bytes are dynamic multimedia tutorials that help demystify even the most complex topics. You'll view video clips and animations that illustrate computer concepts, and then apply what you've learned by reviewing with the Sound Byte Labs, which include quizzes and activities specifically tailored to each Sound Byte. The Sound Bytes for this chapter are listed here and can be found on your Student Resource CD:

- Binary Numbers Interactive
- Where Does Binary Show Up?
- Memory Hierarchy Interactive
- Computer Architecture

COMPANION WEB SITE

The Technology in Action Companion Web Site includes a variety of additional materials to help you review and learn more about the topics in this chapter. The resources available at **www.prenhall.com/techinaction** include:

- **Online Study Guide.** Each chapter features an online true/false and multiple-choice quiz. You can take these quizzes, automatically check the results, and e-mail the results to your instructor.
- **Web Research Projects.** Each chapter features a number of Web research projects that ask you to search the Web for information on computer-related careers, milestones in computer history, important people and companies, emerging technologies, and the applications and implications of different technologies.

Careers in IT

It's hard to imagine an occupation in which computers are not used in some fashion. Even such previously low-tech industries as junkyards and fast food use computers for inventory management and commodity ordering. In this Technology in Focus feature, we explore various information technology (IT) career paths open to you.

What to Consider First: Job Outlook

If you want to investigate a career with computers, the first question you probably have is: "Will I be able to get a job?" With all the media hoopla surrounding the loss of IT jobs, many people think the boom in computer-related jobs is over. However, current projections of the U.S. Department of Labor's Bureau of Labor Statistics show that 5 out of the top 20 fastest-growing occupations through 2014 are still in a computer field (Figure 1). Recently, *Money* magazine rated the top 10 best jobs in America; computer IT analysts came in at number 7, and software engineers were number 1! *Money* projects growth rates for these jobs over the next 10 years at 36.1 percent and 46.07 percent, respectively.

Despite this forecast, recent surveys by the Higher Education Research Institute at the University of California at Los Angeles (HERI/UCLA) of incoming college freshmen who declared they would major in computer science has fallen 60 percent since the fall of 2000! This trend developed mainly because of the media furor surrounding the demise of Internet start-ups in the early 2000s. Because of declining enrollment, critical shortages of computing professionals in the United States are projected over the next 5 to 10 years. In terms of job outlook, this is a perfect time to consider an IT career.

Regardless of whether you choose to pursue a career in IT, you should visit the Bureau of Labor Statistics site at **www.bls.gov**. One of the site's most useful features is the *Occupational Outlook Handbook*. Aside from projecting job growth in a career field, it describes typical tasks that workers perform, the amount of training and education needed, and salary estimates.

In the global economy in which we now operate, job outlook also includes the risk of jobs being outsourced, possibly to other countries (known as *offshoring*). **Outsourcing** is a process whereby a business hires a third-party firm to provide business services (such as customer support call centers) that were previously handled by in-house employees. **Offshoring** occurs when the outsourcing firm is located (or uses employees) outside the United States. India was the first country where offshoring occurred, and countries

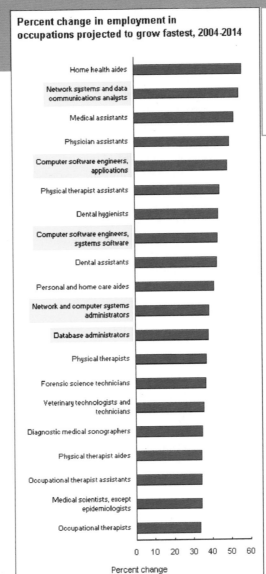

Percent change in employment in occupations projected to grow fastest, 2004-2014

- Home health aides
- Network systems and data communications analysts
- Medical assistants
- Physician assistants
- Computer software engineers, applications
- Physical therapist assistants
- Dental hygienists
- Computer software engineers, systems software
- Dental assistants
- Personal and home care aides
- Network and computer systems administrators
- Database administrators
- Physical therapists
- Forensic science technicians
- Veterinary technologists and technicians
- Diagnostic medical sonographers
- Physical therapist aides
- Occupational therapist assistants
- Medical scientists, except epidemiologists
- Occupational therapists

Percent change (0 10 20 30 40 50 60)

Figure 1

The Bureau of Labor Statistics is projecting huge growth in five different computer occupations, as highlighted in this chart.

such as China, Romania, and other former Eastern Bloc countries now are vying for a piece of the action. The big lure of outsourcing and offshoring is cost savings; that is, the outsourcing firm can do the work cheaper than you can by hiring in-house employees. Considering that the standard of living (and hence salaries) are much lower in many countries than in the United States, offshoring is an attractive option for many employers.

But outsourcing and offshoring do not always deliver the vast cost savings that chief executive officers (CEOs) envision. TPI, a global sourcing advisory firm, conducted a survey that showed the average cost savings from outsourcing was only 15 percent. Often, however, other less tangible factors can outweigh the cost savings of outsourcing. Communications problems can arise between

internal and external employees, for example, and cultural differences between the home country and the country doing the offshoring can result in product design rework. Data also can be less secure in an external environment or during the transfer between the company and an external vendor. A study by Deloitte Consulting found that 70 percent of survey participants had "negative experiences" with overseas outsourcing, and 44 percent of participants saw no cost savings due to outsourcing. Although outsourcing and offshoring won't be going away, companies are approaching it with more caution.

So, what IT jobs will be staying in the United States? According to the January 2006 issue of *InformationWeek* magazine, most of the jobs in these three categories (Figure 2) will stay put:

1. **Customer facing:** Jobs that require direct input from customers or that involve systems with which customers interface daily.

2. **Enablers:** Jobs that involve getting key business projects accomplished, often requiring technical skills beyond the realm of IT and good people skills.

3. **Infrastructure jobs:** Jobs that are the nuts and bolts of moving and storing information that U.S.-based employees need to do their jobs.

Common Myths about IT Careers

Many people have misconceptions about pursuing a career in IT that scare them away from considering a career in computing or convince them to pursue a computing career for the wrong reasons. Do you have any of the misconceptions shown on the next page?

Is an IT Career Right for You?

A career in IT can be a difficult path. Before preparing yourself for an IT career, consider the following:

1. **Salary range.** What affects your salary in an IT position? Your skill set and experience level are obvious answers. However, the size of your employer and geographic location also are factors. Large companies tend to pay more, so if you're pursuing a high salary, set your sights on a large corporation. But remember that making a lot of money isn't everything—be sure to consider other quality-of-life issues, such as job satisfaction.

FIGURE 2

Jobs Least Likely to Be Offshored

Customer Facing	Enablers	Infrastructure Jobs
Application developers	IT or business architects	Security
Web application programmers	Business analysts	Data modelers
Data-warehouse and business intelligence specialists	Business technologists	Network managers and engineers
Enterprise Resource Planning (ERP) and Customer Relationship Management (CRM) professionals	Business-process modelers	Wireless engineers and administrators
Database developers and analysts	Project managers	Software engineers
Helpdesk specialists		Disaster-recovery specialists System auditors and integrators Storage administrators

Source: Information Week, January 30, 2006, p. 78.

COMMON MYTHS ABOUT IT CAREERS

Myth #1 Getting a computer science degree means you're going to be rich. Computer-related careers often offer high salaries, but choosing a computer career isn't a guarantee you'll get a high-paying job. Just as in other professions, you probably will need years of training and on-the-job experience to earn a high salary. However, starting salaries in certain IT professions are very robust.

Myth #2 All the jobs are going offshore. Although many IT jobs have been lost to international competition over the past few years, most networking, analyst (business, systems, and database), and creative jobs (digital media creation and game development) have stayed in the United States. As demand for IT professionals has increased overseas, this has driven up foreign wages, making "offshoring" jobs less attractive. Bottom line—there are still plenty of IT jobs in the United States!

Myth #3 You have three professional certifications ... you're ready to work. Many freshly minted technical school graduates sporting IT certifications feel ready to jump into a job. But employers routinely cite experience as being more desirable than certification. Experience earned through an internship or a part-time job will make you much more marketable when your certification program is complete.

Myth #4 Women are at a disadvantage in an IT career. Currently, women make up less than 20 percent of the IT workforce, and the percentage is not showing signs of increasing. This presents a huge opportunity for women with IT skills, because many IT departments are actively seeking to diversify their workforce. Also, although a salary gender gap (difference between what men and women earn for the same job) exists in IT careers, it's smaller than in many other professions.

Myth #5 People skills don't matter in IT jobs. Despite what many people think, IT professionals are not locked in lightless cubicles, basking in the glow of their monitors. Most IT jobs require constant interaction with others, often in team settings. People skills are important, even when you work with computers.

Myth #6 Mathematically impaired people need not apply. It is true that a career in programming involves a fair bit of math, but even if you're not mathematically inclined, you can explore other IT careers. IT positions also value such attributes as teamwork, creativity, leadership ability, and artistic style.

Myth #7 Working in IT means working for a computer company or in an IT department. Computers and information systems are used across all industries and in most job functions. As an accounting major, if you minor in IT, employers may be more willing to consider hiring you because working in accounting today means constantly interfacing with management information systems and manipulating data.

Resolving myths is an important step toward considering a job in IT. But you need to consider other issues related to IT careers before you decide to pursue a particular path.

---

2. **Gender bias.** Many women view IT departments as Dilbert-like microcosms of antisocial geeks and don't feel they would fit in. Unfortunately, some mostly male IT departments do suffer from varying degrees of gender bias. Although some women may thrive on the challenge of enlightening these "male enclaves" and bringing them forward to the 21st century, others find such environments difficult to work in.

3. **Location.** Location in this case refers to the setting in which you work. IT jobs can be office-based, field-based, project-based, or home-based. Not every situation is perfect for every individual. Figure 4 summarizes the major job types and their locations.

4. **Changing workplace.** In IT, the playing field is always changing. New software and hardware are constantly being developed. It's almost a full-time job to keep your skills up-to-date. You can expect to spend a lot of time in training and self-study trying to learn new systems and techniques.

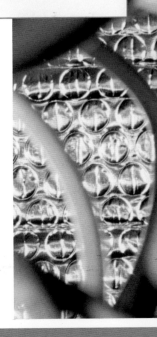

HOW MUCH WILL I EARN?

Like many other professional jobs, IT employees can earn a very good living. Although starting salaries for some IT positions (computer desktop support and help desk analysts) are in the modest $32,000 to $37,000 range, starting salaries for students with Bachelor's degrees in computer science are fairly robust. A recent article in *Money* magazine showed that the highest starting salaries belong to engineers (chemical, electrical, and mechanical). But coming in at a respectable fourth place is computer science, at just over $50,000. And the recent *Money* magazine survey of the best jobs in America ranked several IT positions as very desirable for young employees.

IT salaries vary widely depending on experience level and the geographic location of the job. To obtain the most accurate information, research salaries yourself. Job posting sites such as Monster.com can provide guidance, but a better site is Salary.com. As shown in Figure 3, you can use the salary wizard on this site to determine what IT professionals in your area are making compared with national averages. Hundreds of IT job titles are listed so that you can fine-tune your search to the specific job in which you're interested.

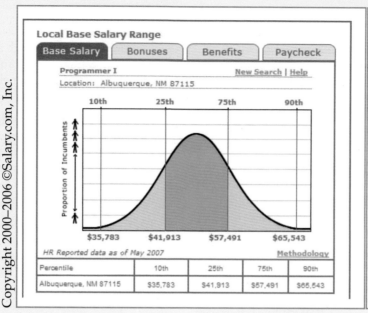

Copyright 2000–2006 ©Salary.com, Inc.

Local Base Salary Range

| Base Salary | Bonuses | Benefits | Paycheck |

Programmer I · New Search | Help
Location: Albuquerque, NM 87115

HR Reported data as of May 2007 · Methodology

Percentile	10th	25th	75th	90th
Albuquerque, NM 87115	$35,783	$41,913	$57,491	$65,543

Figure 3

The salary wizard at Salary.com shows that for an entry-level programming position (programmer I) in Albuquerque, New Mexico, you could expect to earn a median salary of approximately $49,702 (midway between the 25th and 75th percentiles). The wizard is easy to tailor to your location and job preferences.

©Paul Alan/Corbis

FIGURE 4

Where Do You Want to Work?

Type of Job	Location/Hours	Special Considerations
Office-based	Report for work to the same location each day and interact with the same people on a regular basis Requires regular core hours of attendance (such as 9 to 5)	May require working beyond "normal" working hours Some positions require workers to be on call 24/7
Field-based	Travel from place to place, as needed, and perform short-term jobs at each location	Involves a great deal of travel and working independently
Project-based	Work at client sites on specific projects for extended periods of time (weeks or months) Contractors and consultants fall into this area	Can be very attractive to individuals who like workplace situations that vary on a regular basis
Home-based (Telecommuting)	Work from home	Involves very little day-to-day supervision and requires an individual who is self-disciplined

5. **Stress.** Whereas the average American works 42 hours a week, a survey by *InformationWeek* shows that the average IT staff person works 45 hours a week and is on call for another 24 hours. On-call time (hours an employee must be available to work in the event of a problem) has been increasing in recent years because more IT systems (such as e-commerce systems) require 24/7 availability. See Figure 5.

The good news is that despite the stress and changing nature of the IT environment, most computing skills are portable from industry to industry. A networking job in the clothing manufacturing industry uses the same primary skill set as a networking job for a supermarket chain. So, if something disastrous happens to the industry you're in, you should be able to transition to another industry with little trouble.

What Realm of IT Should You Work In?

Figure 7, on the next page, provides an organizational chart for a modern IT department that should help you understand the careers currently available. The chief information officer (CIO) has overall responsibility for the development, implementation, and maintenance of information systems and infrastructure. Usually the CIO reports to the chief operating officer (COO).

The responsibilities below the CIO are generally grouped into two units: development and integration (responsible for the development of systems and Web sites) and technical services (responsible for the day-to-day operations of the company's information infrastructure and network, including all hardware and software deployed).

Figure 5

Stress comes from multiple directions in IT jobs.

©John Feingersh/ Corbis/stressed worker; ©LWA-JDC/ Corbis/marketing dept; ©Mark A. Johnson/Corbis/golfer; ©Gabe Palmer/ Corbis/supervisor; ©Larry Williams/ Corbis/customer

MATCHING A CAREER TO YOUR SKILLS

Totally unsure about what career you would like to pursue? Online tools such as the ISEEK Skills Assessment (**www.iseek.org**) can help you identify careers based on your skills. This tool has you fill out a skills matrix (see Figure 6), rating your skills in various categories. The program then evaluates the skills matrix and suggests job titles for you to explore.

Assessments - ISEEK Skills Assessment

Click on the skill name to display a detailed description of the skill you are rating.

Rate your skills as follows:

+2 It is very important to me that this skill is part of my career.
+1 It is somewhat important to me that this skill is part of my career.
 0 I don't care if this skill is part of my career.
-1 It is somewhat important to me that this skill is NOT part of my career.
-2 It is very important to me that this skill is NOT part of my career.

When you have completed rating skills in this category, click the "Continue" button.

Interpersonal Skills	+2	+1	0	-1	-2
Adjusting to Others' Actions	○	○	◉	○	○
Awareness of Others	○	○	◉	○	○
Helping or Serving Others	○	○	◉	○	○
Instructing	○	○	◉	○	○
Negotiating	○	○	◉	○	○
Persuading	○	○	◉	○	○

Continue

Figure 6

Here you see one of 10 categories on the ISEEK skills matrix that you can complete to help you assess which career paths match your talents.

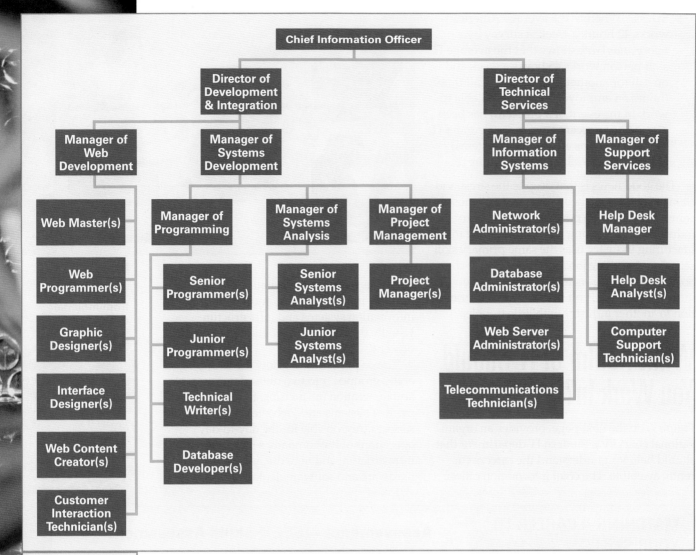

Chief Information Officer

Under **Director of Development & Integration**:
- **Manager of Web Development**
  - Web Master(s)
  - Web Programmer(s)
  - Graphic Designer(s)
  - Interface Designer(s)
  - Web Content Creator(s)
  - Customer Interaction Technician(s)
- **Manager of Systems Development**
  - **Manager of Programming**
    - Senior Programmer(s)
    - Junior Programmer(s)
    - Technical Writer(s)
    - Database Developer(s)
  - **Manager of Systems Analysis**
    - Senior Systems Analyst(s)
    - Junior Systems Analyst(s)
  - **Manager of Project Management**
    - Project Manager(s)

Under **Director of Technical Services**:
- **Manager of Information Systems**
  - Network Administrator(s)
  - Database Administrator(s)
  - Web Server Administrator(s)
  - Telecommunications Technician(s)
- **Manager of Support Services**
  - **Help Desk Manager**
    - Help Desk Analyst(s)
    - Computer Support Technician(s)

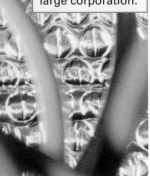

Figure 7

This is a typical structure for an IT department at a large corporation.

In large organizations, responsibilities are distinct and jobs are defined more narrowly. In medium-sized organizations, there can be overlap between position responsibilities. At a small shop, you might be the network administrator, database administrator, computer support technician, and helpdesk analyst all at the same time. Let's look at each department and explore typical jobs found in them.

Working in Development and Integration

Two distinct paths exist in this division: Web development and systems development. Because everything involves the Web today, there is often a great deal of overlap between these departments.

Web Development

When most people think of Web development careers, they usually equate them to being a *Web master*. However, today's Web masters usually are supervisors with responsibility for certain aspects of Web development. At smaller companies, they may be responsible for tasks that the other folks in a Web development group usually do:

- **Web content creators** generate the words and images on the Web. Journalists, writers and editors, and marketing personnel prepare an enormous amount of Web content, while **video producers, graphic designers,** and **animators** create Web-based multimedia. **Interface designers** work with graphic designers and animators to create a look and feel for the site and make the site easy to navigate. Content creators have a thorough understanding of their own fields as well as HTML/XHTML and JavaScript. They also need to be familiar with the capabilities and limitations of modern Web development tools so that they know what the Web publishers can accomplish.

- **Web publishers** build Web pages to deploy the materials that the content creators develop. They wield the Web tools (such as Adobe Dreamweaver and Microsoft Expression) that develop the Web pages and create links to databases (using products such as Oracle and SQL Server) to keep information flowing between users and the Web page. They must possess a solid understanding of client- and server-side Web languages (HTML/XHTML, XML, Java, JavaScript, ASP, and PERL) and development environments such as the Microsoft .NET Framework.

- **Customer interaction technicians** provide feedback to a Web site's customers. Answering e-mail, sending requested information, funneling questions to appropriate personnel (technical support, sales, and so on), and providing suggestions to Web publishers for site improvements are major job responsibilities. Extensive customer service training is essential to work effectively in this area.

As you can see in Figure 8, many different people can work on the same Web site. The education required varies widely for these jobs. Web programming jobs often require a four-year college degree in computer science, whereas graphic designers with two-year art degrees often are hired.

Systems Development

Ask most people what systems developers do and they will say "programming," but this is only one aspect of systems development. Because large projects involve many people, there are many job opportunities in systems development. An explanation of each key area follows:

- **Systems analysts** spend most of their time in the beginning stages of the sys-

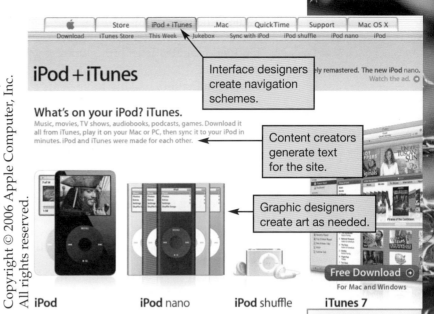

Figure 8

As you can see, it takes a team to create and maintain a Web site.

tems development life cycle (SDLC). They talk with end users to gather information about problems and existing information systems. They document systems and propose solutions to problems. Having good people skills is essential to success as a systems analyst. In addition, analysts work with programmers during the development phase to design appropriate programs to solve the problem at hand. Therefore, many organizations insist on hiring systems analysts who have both a solid business background and prior programming experience (at least at a basic level). For entry-level jobs, a four-year degree is usually required. Many colleges and universities offer degrees in Management Information Systems (MIS) that include a mixture of systems development, programming, and business courses.

- **Programmers** participate in the SDLC, attending meetings to document user needs and working closely with systems analysts during the design phase. Programmers need excellent written communication skills because they often generate detailed systems documentation for end-user training purposes. Because programming languages are mathematically based, it is essential for programmers to have strong math skills and an ability to think logically. Programmers should also be proficient at more than one programming language. A four-year degree is usually required for entry-level programming positions.

- **Project managers** usually have years of experience as programmers or systems analysts. This job is part of a career path upward from entry-level programming and systems analyst jobs. Project managers manage the overall systems development process, including assignment of staff, budgeting, reporting to management, coaching team members, and ensuring deadlines are met. Project managers need excellent time-management skills because they are pulled in several directions at once. Many project managers obtain master's degrees to supplement their undergraduate degrees in computer science or MIS.

In addition to these key players, the following people are also involved in the systems development process:

- **Technical writers** generate systems documentation for end users and for programmers who may make modifications to the system in the future.

- **Network engineers** help the programmers and analysts design compatible systems, because many systems are required to run in certain environments (UNIX or Windows, for instance) and must work well in conjunction with other programs.

- **Database developers** design and build databases to support the software systems being developed.

Large development projects may have all of these team members on the project. Smaller projects may require an overlap of positions (such as a programmer also acting as a systems analyst). The majority of these jobs require four-year college degrees in computer science or Management Information Systems (MIS). As shown in Figure 9, team members work together to build a system.

It is important to emphasize that all systems development careers are stressful. Deadlines are tight for development projects, especially if they involve getting a new product to market ahead of the competition. But if you enjoy challenges and can endure a fast-paced, dynamic environment, there should be plenty of opportunities for good systems developers in the decade ahead.

Working in Technical Services

Technical services jobs are vital to keeping IT systems running. The people in these jobs install and maintain the infrastructure

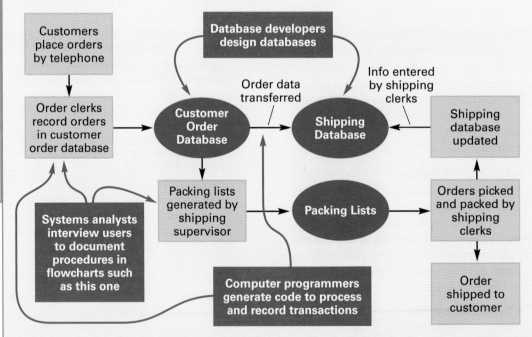

Figure 9

Here you see a flowchart of an order-processing system. Each member of the systems development team performs functions critical to the development process (as shown in the red boxes).

behind the IT systems and work with end users to make sure they can effectively interact with the systems. These also are the least likely IT jobs to be outsourced because hands-on work with equipment and users is required on a regular basis. The two major categories of technical services careers are information systems and support services.

GET IN THE GAME: CAREERS IN GAME DEVELOPMENT

The video gaming industry in the United States is gaining rapidly on the earning power of the Hollywood movie industry ($9.3 billion in 2006) to become a $7.4 billion (2006) per year behemoth. Although some aspects of game development such as scenery design and certain aspects of programming are being sent offshore, the majority of game development requires a creative team that needs to work in close proximity to each other. Therefore, it is anticipated that most game development jobs will stay in the United States. And with the release of the Xbox 360 and PlayStation 3 consoles, development budgets for games have doubled because the new consoles support more sophisticated games. As the majority of development costs are personnel-related, this translates into more job opportunities.

Game development jobs usually are split along two paths: designers and programmers. Game designers tend to be artistic and are responsible for creating 2-D and 3-D art, game interfaces, video sequences, special effects, game levels, and scenarios. Game designers must master software packages such as Autodesk 3ds Max, Autodesk Maya, NewTek LightWave 3D, Adobe Photoshop, and Adobe Flash (see Figure 10). Programmers are then responsible for coding the scenarios developed by these designers. Using languages such as C, C++, Assembly, and Java, programmers build the game and ensure that it plays accurately.

Aside from programmers and designers, playtesters and quality assurance professionals play the games with the intent of breaking them or discovering bugs within the game interfaces or worlds. *Playtesting* is an essential part of the game development process because it assists designers in determining which aspects of the game are most intriguing to players and which parts of the game need to be repaired or enhanced.

No matter what job you may pursue in the realm of gaming, you will need to have a two- or four-year college degree. If you're interested in gaming, look for a school with a solid animation/ 3-D art program or computer game programming curriculum.

So, how can you get started on a game development career? One key task that is often performed by high school and college students is beta testing. Just before a game is ready to go to market, the beta version (the last version tested before release) is distributed to volunteers for testing. The objective is to play the game and report any problems in game play or design. Although beta testing is an unpaid job, playtesters (who are compensated) often are recruited from the beta testers who provide good feedback. For more information on gaming careers, check out **www.igda.org** and **www.gamecareerguide.com**.

Figure 10

LightWave is a popular package that is used to create realistic graphics for games such as the one shown here.

Information Systems

The information systems department keeps the networks and telecommunications up and running at all times. Within the department, you'll find a variety of positions:

- **Network administrators** (sometimes called network engineers) install and configure servers, design and plan networks, and test new networking equipment (see Figure 11).

- **Database administrators (DBAs)** install and configure database servers and ensure that the servers provide an adequate level of access to all users.

- **Web server administrators** install, configure, and maintain Web servers and ensure that the company maintains Internet connectivity at all times.

- **Telecommunications technicians** oversee the communications infrastructure, including training employees to use telecommunications equipment. They are often on call 24 hours a day.

Support Services

As a member of the support services team, you interface with users (external customers or employees) and troubleshoot their computer problems. These positions include the following:

- **Helpdesk analysts** staff the phone (or e-mail) and solve problems for customers or employees, either remotely or in person. Often, helpdesk personnel are called on to train users on the latest software and hardware.

- **Computer support technicians** go to a user's physical location and fix software

©Corbis/Royalty Free

and hardware problems. They also often have to chase down and repair faults in the network infrastructure.

As important as these people are, they often receive a great deal of abuse by angry users whose computers are not working. When working in support services, you need to be patient and have a "thick skin."

Technical services jobs often require two-year college degrees or training at trade schools or technical institutes. At smaller companies, job duties tend to overlap between the help desk and technician jobs. And these jobs are in demand. A survey of 1,400 chief information officers sponsored by Robert Half Technology identified Windows administration, wireless network management, and database management (SQL) as the top skills needed by U.S. IT departments.

How Should You Prepare for a Job in IT?

A job in IT requires a robust skill set and formal training and preparation. Most employers today have an entry-level requirement of a college degree, a technical institute diploma, appropriate professional certifications, and/or experience in the field. How can you prepare for a job in IT?

1. **Get educated.** Two- and four-year colleges and universities normally offer three degrees to prepare students for IT careers: computer science, MIS, and computer engineering (although titles vary). Alternatives to colleges and universities are privately licensed technical (or trade) schools. Generally, these programs focus on building skill sets rapidly and obtaining a job in a specific field. The main advantage of trade schools is that their programs usually take less time to complete than college degrees. However, to have a realistic chance of employment in IT fields other than networking or Web development, you should attend a degree-granting college or university.

2. **Investigate professional certifications.** Certifications attempt to provide a consistent method of measuring skill levels in specific areas of IT. Hundreds of IT certifications are available, most of which you get by passing a written exam. Software and hardware vendors (such as

SO YOU WANT TO BE A NETWORK ADMINISTRATOR?

You know that network administrators are the people who design, install, and maintain the network equipment and infrastructure. But what *exactly* do they do?

Network administrators are involved in every stage of network planning and deployment. They decide what equipment to buy and what type of media to use, and they determine the correct topology for the network. They also often develop policies regarding network usage, security measures, and hardware and software standards.

After the planning is complete, network administrators help install the network (either by supervising third-party contractors or by doing the work themselves). Typical installation tasks include configuring and installing client computers and peripherals, running cable, and installing wireless media devices.

Installing and configuring security devices and software are also critical jobs.

When equipment and cables break, network administrators must locate the source of the trouble and fix the problem. They also obtain and install updates to network software, and evaluate new equipment to determine whether the network should be upgraded. In addition, they monitor the network performance to ensure that users' needs are met.

Given the importance of the Internet to most organizations, network administrators also ensure that the Internet connection is maintained at all times, which usually is a high priority on their to-do list. Finally, network administrators plan disaster recovery strategies (such as what to do if a fire destroys the server room).

Microsoft and Cisco) and professional organizations (such as the Computing Technology Industry Association) often establish certification standards. (Visit **www.microsoft.com**, **www.cisco.com**, **www.comptia.org**, and **www.sun.com** for more information on certifications.)

Employees with certifications generally earn more than employees who aren't certified. However, most employers don't view a certification as a substitute for a college degree or a trade school program. You should think of certifications as an extra edge beyond your formal education that will make you more attractive to employers. To ensure you're pursuing the right certifications, ask employers which certifications they respect or explore online job sites to see which certifications are listed as desirable or required.

3. **Get experience.** Aside from education, employers want you to have experience, even for entry-level jobs. As you're completing your education, consider getting an internship or part-time job in your field of study. Many colleges will help you find internships and allow you to earn credit toward your degree through internship programs.

4. **Do research.** Find out as much about the company and the industry it is in before going on an interview. Start with the company's Web site and then expand your search to business and trade publications (such as *BusinessWeek* and *CIO* magazines).

How Do You Find a Job in IT?

Training for a career is not useful unless you can find a job at the end of your training. Here are some tips on getting a job:

1. **Visit your school's placement office.** Many employers recruit at schools, and most schools maintain a placement office to help students find jobs. Employees in the placement office can help you with résumé preparation and job interviewing skills as well as provide you with leads for internships and jobs.

2. **Visit online employment sites.** Most IT jobs are advertised online at sites such as Monster.com and CareerBuilder.com (see Figures 12 and 13). Begin searching

---

Figure 12

Online IT Career Resources

_____

_____

_____

_____

_____

_____

_____

www.gamasutra.com

Figure 13

Employment sites, such as CareerBuilder.com, enable you to search for specific jobs within a defined geographic area. These sites also allow you to store your résumé at the site and apply for positions with one click.

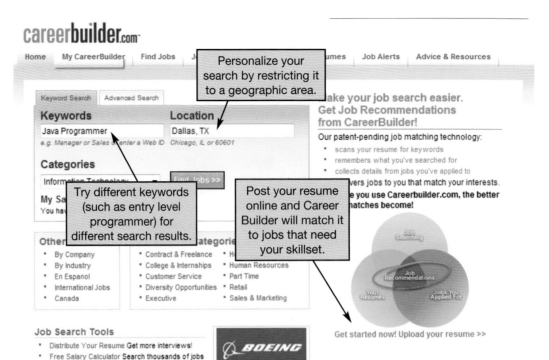

Personalize your search by restricting it to a geographic area.

Try different keywords (such as entry level programmer) for different search results.

Post your resume online and Career Builder will match it to jobs that need your skillset.

for jobs on these sites early in your education because the job listings detail the skill sets employers require. Focusing on coursework that will provide you with desirable skill sets will make you more marketable.

3. **Start networking.** Many jobs are never advertised but instead are filled by word of mouth. Seek out contacts in your field and discuss job prospects with them. Find out what skills are needed and ask them to recommend others in the industry with whom you can speak. Professional organizations such as the Association for Computing Machinery (ACM) are one way to network. These organizations often have chapters on college campuses and offer reduced membership rates for students. The contacts you make there could lead to your next job. Figure 14 lists major

FIGURE 14

Professional Organizations

Organization Name	Purpose	Web Site
Association for Computing Machinery (ACM)	Oldest scientific computing society. Maintains a strong focus on programming and systems development.	**www.acm.org**
Association for Information Systems (AIS)	Organization of professionals who work in academia and specialize in information systems.	**www.aisnet.org**
Association of Information Technology Professionals (AITP)	Heavy focus on IT education and development of seminars and learning materials.	**www.aitp.org**
Institute of Electrical and Electronics Engineers (IEEE)	Provides leadership and sets engineering standards for all types of network computing devices and protocols.	**www.ieee.org**
Information Systems Security Association (ISSA)	Not-for-profit, international organization of information security professionals and practitioners.	**www.issa.org**

FIGURE 15

Resources for Women in IT

Organization Name	Purpose	Web Site
Anita Borg Institute for Women and Technology	Organization whose aim is to "increase the impact of women on all aspects of technology."	**www.anitaborg.org**
Association for Women in Computing (AWC)	A not-for-profit organization dedicated to promoting the advancement of women in computing professions.	**www.awc-hq.org**
Center for Women and Information Technology (CWIT)	Established at the University of Maryland Baltimore County (UMBC), the organization is dedicated to providing global leadership in achieving women's full participation in all aspects of IT.	**www.umbc.edu/cwit**
Diversity/Careers in Engineering & Information Technology	An online magazine whose articles cover career issues focused on technical professionals who are members of minority groups, women, or people with disabilities.	**www.diversitycareers.com**
Women in Technology International (WITI)	A global trade association for tech-savvy, professional women.	**www.witi.com**

professional organizations you should consider investigating.

If you are a woman considering pursuing an IT career, there are many resources and groups that cater to female IT professionals and students. The oldest and best known organization is the Association for Women in Computing, founded in 1978. Figure 15 provides a list of resources to investigate.

4. **Check corporate Web sites for jobs.** Many corporate Web sites list current job opportunities. For example, Apple features a searchable site (see Figure 16) you can tailor to a specific job type. Check the sites of companies in which you are interested and then do a search on the site for job openings or, if provided, click the Employment link.

The outlook for IT jobs should continue to be positive in the future. We wish you luck with your education and job search.

Job Opportunities

Apple Pro

Are you an experienced pro? New college grad? We're looking for the best. Explore the groups below for more information.

Mac Hardware Engineering
Join the team of ingenious engineering minds that design and develop Apple's revolutionary products. Mac hardware engineering looks for people with disciplines in electrical, mechanical, and specialized engineering, industrial design, and quality assurance.

Software Engineering
Employing UNIX experts, programmers, QA engineers, and user interface designers, software engineering invents and fuels the powerhouse Mac OS-including the breakthrough features included in the latest version, Tiger.

Applications
Each Apple application is managed by a dedicated team of programmers, marketers, and project managers. Their passion for music, photography, and film is showcased in innovative applications such as iTunes, iPhoto, and Final Cut Pro.

iPod Engineering
This is team that delivers many of Apple's cutting-edge consumer electronics. The talented iPod engineers, project managers, and designers are driving the digital music revolution with products such as the new iPod and iPod nano.

Marketing
This team creates the imaginative strategies-in product marketing, marketing communications, and public relations-that represent our products to the world. Their innovative point-of-view is an integral part of the product development

Sales
The Sales team-including field and education sales, enterprise sales, the online store, and more-manages relationships with our resellers and customers. Our sales reps have the right combination of passion and product knowledge to

Figure 16

Corporate Web sites often list available jobs. The Apple site arranges jobs into broad categories and then provides easy search tools to zero in on the right job for you.

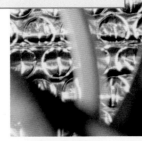

10

Behind the Scenes:

Networking and Security

From Chapter 12 of *Technology in Action, Complete*, Fifth Edition, Alan Evans, Kendall Martin, Mary Anne Poatsy. Copyright © 2009 by Pearson Education. Published by Prentice Hall. All rights reserved.

Behind the Scenes:

Networking and Security

ACTIVE HELPDESK

Understanding How Networks Work

Computer networks are everywhere. In fact, the Internet is a large (actually, the largest) network of networks. Most people interact with other, smaller computer networks on a daily basis, whether or not they are aware of it. Even something as simple as buying gas involves interacting with a network. The "pay-at-the-pump" convenience of purchasing gas with a credit card is made possible because the gas pump can connect to a network. When you swipe your card at the pump, the network interface in the pump connects to the network at the oil company that owns the gas station. That network connects with the network at your credit card company and checks to ensure you're not over your credit limit. Assuming you have sufficient credit, the oil company network sends an authorization back to the pump to enable you to buy gas.

When your transaction is complete, the pump sends the purchase information to the corporate network. The amount of gas you purchased is then recorded in an inventory control database and is used to help determine when a gas delivery needs to be made to the gas station. Without networks, you couldn't use your credit card to buy gas conveniently at the pump because there would be no way to check your credit. Also, without the corporate network tracking gas purchases, your neighborhood station might run out of gas more frequently. As you can see, networks assist in making your life easier.

Why is it important to understand networks and their capabilities? For one, it will help you interact with the information technology professionals responsible for configuring and maintaining the networks where you work or go to school. In addition, a fundamental grasp of network principles can help you decide whether you want to pursue additional coursework or even a career in networking. Finally, it can enhance your productivity by keeping you connected with today's fast-moving world.

This chapter builds on the information you learned about networks and takes you behind the scenes of networking principles. We look at how client/server networks work and examine exactly how these networks are designed and built. Along the way, we discuss the various kinds of servers used in such networks as well as the layout and equipment used to create them. Finally, we discuss how large networks are kept secure.

©Cameron Beck/Corbis

SOUND BYTES

- Network Topology and Navigation Devices
- What's My IP Address? (and Other Interesting Facts about Networks)
- A Day in the Life of a Network Technician

Networking Advantages

A **network** is a group of two or more computers (or nodes) that are configured to share information and resources such as printers, files, and databases. Essentially, a network enables computers and other devices to communicate with each other. But why do we network computers? Home networks enable users to share peripherals (such as printers), transfer files simply, and share Internet connections. Large business networks provide similar and additional advantages over individual stand-alone computers:

- **Networks increase productivity.** Computers are powerful stand-alone resources. However, to increase productivity, people need to be able to share data and peripherals with coworkers and communicate with them efficiently. Without a network, only one person at a time can access information because it would reside on a single computer. Information sharing is therefore the largest benefit a company gains by installing a network.

- **Networks enable expensive resources to be shared.** Networks enable people to share peripherals such as printers, eliminating the need for duplicate devices. You probably have a printer hooked up to your home computer. Think about how often it sits idle. Compound that by having an office of 20 employees, each with his or her own printer. Having 20 printers sitting idle 90 percent of the time is a tremendous waste of money. Installing a network enables two printers (working most of the time) to serve all 20 employees, generating cost savings.

- **Networks facilitate knowledge sharing.** Networked databases can serve the needs of many people at one time and increase the availability of data. Your company's databases are much more useful when you and your coworkers can look up customer records at the same time.

- **Networks enable software sharing.** Installing a new version of software on everyone's desktop in a company with 1,000 employees can be time-consuming. However, if the computers are networked, all employees can access the same copy of a program from the server. Although companies must still purchase a software license for each employee, with a network they avoid having to install the program on every desktop. This also saves space on individual desktops, because the software doesn't reside on every computer.

- **Networks facilitate Internet connectivity.** Most employees need to connect to the Internet to perform their jobs. Providing each employee's computer with its own dedicated connection to the Internet (using a modem) is costly. Through a network, large groups of employees can share one Internet connection, reducing Internet connectivity expenses.

- **Networks enable enhanced communication.** E-mail and text messaging are extremely powerful applications when deployed on a network (especially one connected to the Internet). You can easily exchange information with your coworkers, and valuable data can be easily shared by transferring files between users.

Are there disadvantages to businesses using networks? Because business networks are often complex, additional personnel are usually required to maintain them. These people, called **network administrators**, have training in computer and peripheral maintenance and repair, networking design, and the installation of networking software. In addition, networks require additional equipment and software to operate. However, most companies feel that the cost savings of peripheral sharing and the ability to have employees access information simultaneously outweigh the costs associated with network administrators and equipment.

Aside from very small networks (such as peer-to-peer networks, which are typically used in homes and small businesses), the majority of computer networks are based on the client/server model of computing.

Client/Server Networks

As you've learned, a **server** is a computer that both stores and shares resources on a network, whereas a **client** is a computer that requests those resources. A **client/server network** (also called a **server-based network**) contains servers as well as client computers. The inclusion of servers is what differentiates a client/server network from a typical peer-to-peer (P2P) network. (As you'll recall, each node connected to the P2P network can communicate directly with every other node on the network, instead of having a separate device exercise control over the network.) Figure 1 illustrates the client/server relationship.

The main advantage of a client/server relationship is that it makes data flow more efficiently than in peer-to-peer networks. Servers can respond to requests from a large number of clients at the same time. Also, servers are configured to perform specific tasks (such as handling e-mail or database requests) efficiently.

For instance, say you are hungry and go to a fast-food restaurant. As the customer ordering food, you are the *client* making a request. The cook, in the role of the *server*, responds to the request and prepares the meal. Certainly, you could go to the restaurant and cook your own meal, but this would hardly be efficient. You would be floundering around in the kitchen with other customers trying to cook their meals. By assigning specialized tasks to a fast-food cook (the server), many customers (clients) can be served efficiently at the same time. This is how servers work. One server can provide services efficiently to a large number of clients at one time.

Does my home network have a server? Peer-to-peer networks, which are typically set up in homes or very small businesses, do not require servers. In these networks, computers act as both clients and servers when appropriate.

Why don't businesses use peer-to-peer networks? P2P networks become difficult to administer when they are expanded beyond 10 users. Each individual computer may require updating for changes to the network, which is not efficient. Also, security can't be implemented centrally on a P2P network but instead must be handled by

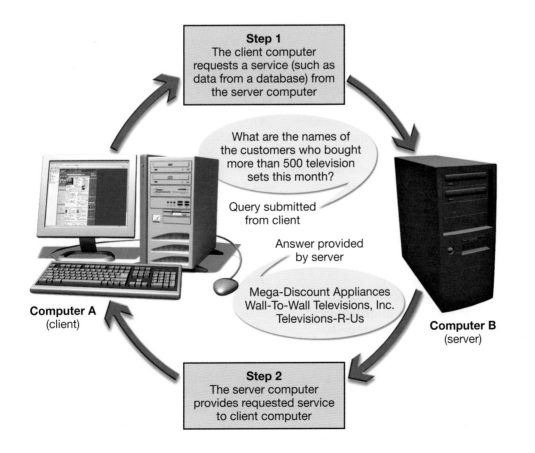

Step 1
The client computer requests a service (such as data from a database) from the server computer

What are the names of the customers who bought more than 500 television sets this month?

Query submitted from client

Answer provided by server

Mega-Discount Appliances
Wall-To-Wall Televisions, Inc.
Televisions-R-Us

Computer A
(client)

Computer B
(server)

Step 2
The server computer provides requested service to client computer

FIGURE 1

Basic Client/Server Interaction

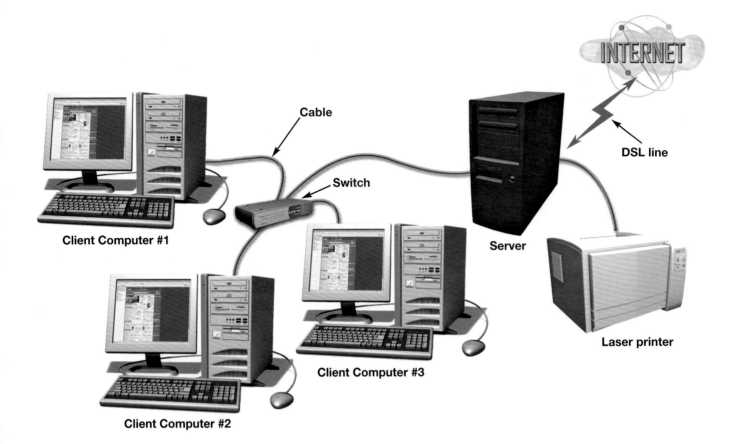

Cable

Switch

Client Computer #1

Client Computer #2

Client Computer #3

INTERNET

DSL line

Server

Laser printer

This small client/server network enables users to share a printer and an Internet connection.

each individual user. As noted earlier, client/server networks contain at least one server that provides shared resources and services (including security) to the client computers that request them.

In addition, client/server networks move data more efficiently than P2P networks, making them appropriate for large numbers of users. For example, Figure 2 shows a very small client/server arrangement. The server in this figure provides printing and Internet connection services for all the client computers connected to the network.

Besides having a centralized server, what makes a client/server network different from a peer-to-peer network? The main difference is that client/server networks have increased scalability. With a **scalable network**, more users can be added easily without affecting the performance of the other network nodes (computers or peripherals). Because servers

handle the bulk of tasks performed on the network (printing, Internet access, and so on), it is easy to accommodate more users by installing additional servers to help with the increased workload. Installing additional servers on a network is relatively simple and can usually be done without disrupting services for existing users.

In addition, peer-to-peer networks are **decentralized**. This means that users are responsible for creating their own data backups and for providing security for their computers. In client/server networks, all clients connect to a server that performs tasks for them. Therefore, client/server networks are said to be **centralized**. Many tasks that individual users must handle on a P2P network can be handled centrally at the server.

For instance, data files are normally stored on the server. Therefore, backups for all users on a network can be performed by merely backing up all the files on the server. Also, security can be exercised over the server instead of on each user's computer; this way, the server, rather than the individual user, coordinates file security.

Classifications of Client/Server Networks: LANs, WANs, and MANs

Networks are generally classified according to their size and the distance between the physical parts of the network. The three main classifications are LANs, WANs, and MANs.

Local area networks (LANs) are generally small groups of computers and peripherals linked together over a relatively small geographic area. The computer lab at your school or the network on the floor of the office where you work is probably a LAN.

For large companies that operate at diverse geographic locations, a LAN is not sufficient for meeting their computing needs. **Wide area networks (WANs)** comprise large numbers of users or separate LANs that are miles apart and linked together. A large college campus would have a WAN that spans all of its lecture halls, residence halls, and administrative offices.

Similarly, corporations often use WANs to connect two or more geographically diverse branches. For example, ABC Shoe Company has manufacturing plants and administrative offices all over the globe. The LAN at each ABC Shoe Company office is connected to other ABC Shoe Company LANs, forming a global ABC Shoe Company WAN. Figure 3 shows an example of what part of the ABC Shoe Company WAN might look like.

The Internet is the largest WAN in existence, comprising hundreds of thousands of internetworked computers around the world.

Sometimes government organizations or civic groups establish WANs to link users in a specific geographic area (such as within a city or county). These special types of WANs are known as **metropolitan area networks (MANs)**.

What sort of network connects personal digital assistants (PDAs) and cell phones? Personal area networks (PANs) are used to connect wireless devices (such as Bluetooth-enabled devices) in close proximity to each other. (Bluetooth technology uses radio waves to transmit data over short distances.) PANs are wireless and

BITS AND BYTES

Smoothing Traffic Patterns with MANs!

How are metropolitan area networks (MANs) used? One common way is to collect traffic information on so-called smart highways. When IKEA announced it was locating a store in Dublin, California, civic planners were concerned about the traffic that would be generated by a popular retail outlet such as IKEA. To solve this problem, an "intelligent transportation system" plan was developed and then implemented. This system, which includes both video cameras (mounted on poles) and sensors embedded in the road, monitors the intersections leading to and from the new IKEA site. This MAN feeds its data into central computers at the Dublin Traffic Operations Center, which is critical to maintaining a smooth traffic flow when things go wrong. By monitoring traffic flow, traffic engineers can respond to incidents (such as car accidents), and by analyzing traffic patterns, they can change the timing of traffic lights to affect traffic flow in real time.

The San Diego Traffic Management Center (TMC) also uses a MAN to analyze traffic patterns. Real-time information is gathered from a variety of sources such as electronic sensors in the roadways, video cameras, phone calls from motorists, and traffic reporters. The system is used to make a variety of decisions such as setting up detours, dispatching road repair crews, alerting motorists to problems using changeable road signs, and closing highways because of disasters (such as earthquakes). The general public can view traffic maps created by the TMC on the Web at **www.dot.ca.gov/sdtraffic.**

So, when will all this happen on a roadway near you? Currently, only 5 percent of U.S. highways are "smart" (most of them being in California) and able to collect real-time data on traffic. But as traffic increases, municipalities will be more willing to find funding for computerized solutions to smooth out the rough spots in the road. So if you have a traffic problem near you, attend your next local planning commission meeting and suggest planners investigate adding a smart highway!

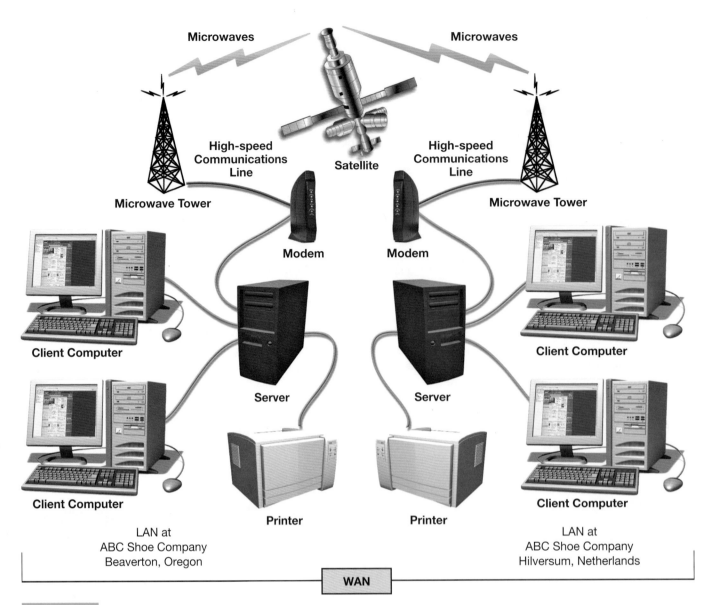

Microwaves

Microwaves

Satellite

High-speed
Communications
Line

High-speed
Communications
Line

Microwave Tower

Microwave Tower

Modem

Modem

Client Computer

Client Computer

Server

Server

Client Computer

Client Computer

Printer

Printer

LAN at
ABC Shoe Company
Beaverton, Oregon

LAN at
ABC Shoe Company
Hilversum, Netherlands

WAN

WANs are several LANs in different geographic locations connected by telecommunications media. Satellite communication is often used to transmit data over long distances.

operate in the personal operating space of an individual, which is generally defined to be within 30 feet (or 10 meters) of your body. Today, PANs free you from having wires running to and from the devices you're using. One day, PANs may use the human body to transmit and receive signals.

What other sort of networks do businesses use? An **intranet** is a private corporate network that is used exclusively by company employees to facilitate information sharing, database access, group scheduling, videoconferencing, or other employee collaboration. Intranets are deployed using Transmission Control Protocol/Internet Protocol (TCP/IP) networks and generally include links to the Internet. The intranet is not accessible to nonemployees; a firewall

(software or hardware used to prevent unauthorized entry) protects it from unauthorized access through the Internet.

One of the main uses of intranets is groupware, which is software that enables users to share and collaborate on documents. Software such as Lotus Notes, a type of groupware, facilitates sharing of employee information and brainstorming to solve problems. Most groupware programs also support messaging and group calendaring.

Constructing Client/ Server Networks

Client/server networks share many of the same components of P2P networks as well as some components specific to client/server networks:

- **Server.** Unlike peer-to-peer networks, client/server networks contain at least one computer that functions solely as a server.

- **Network topology.** Because client/server networks are more complex than peer-to-peer networks, the layout and structure of the network, which is called the network topology, must be carefully planned.

- **Transmission media.** Data needs a way to flow between clients and servers on networks. Therefore, an appropriate type of transmission media (cable or wireless communications technology) based on the network topology is needed. Client/server networks use a wider variety of cable types than do simpler P2P networks.

- **Network operating system (NOS) software.** All client/server networks require network operating system (NOS) software, which is specialized software that

is installed on servers and client computers that enables the network to function. Most modern operating systems (such as Windows Vista and OS X) include the software needed for computers to function as clients on a network.

- **Network adapters.** As is the case with peer-to-peer networks, network adapters (or network interface cards) must be attached or installed to each device on the network. These adapters enable the computer (or peripheral) to communicate with the network using a common data communication language, or protocol.

- **Network navigation devices.** Because of the complexity of a client/server network, specialized network navigation devices (such as routers, switches, and bridges) are needed to move data signals around the network.

Figure 4 shows the components of a simple client/server network. In the following sections, we explore each component in more detail.

FIGURE 4

The basic components of a typical client/server network are shown in this small network. The method of connecting the computers to the server defines a network's topology.

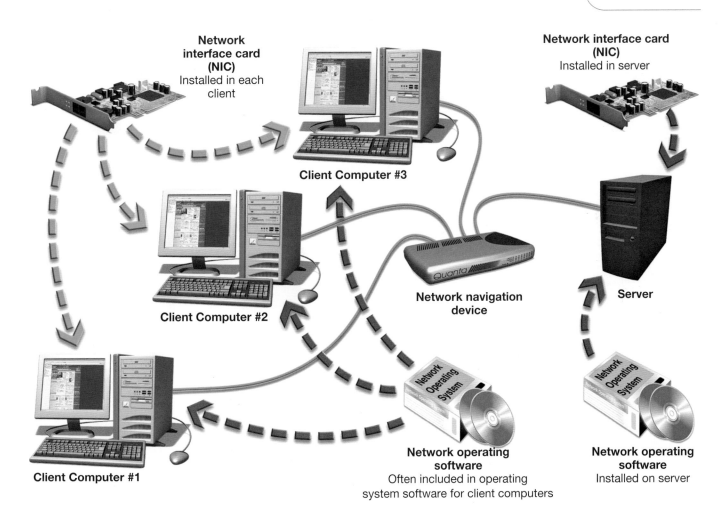

Network interface card (NIC)
Installed in each client

Network interface card (NIC)
Installed in server

Client Computer #3

Client Computer #2

Network navigation device

Server

Client Computer #1

Network operating software
Often included in operating system software for client computers

Network operating software
Installed on server

Servers

Servers are the workhorses of the client/server network. They serve many different network users and assist them with accomplishing a variety of tasks. The number and types of servers on a client/server network depend on the network's size and workload. Small networks (such as the one pictured in Figure 2) would have just one server to handle all server functions such as file storage, delivery of applications to the clients, printing, and so on.

As more users are added to a network, dedicated servers are also added to take the load off of the main server. **Dedicated servers** are used to fulfill one specific function (such as handling e-mail). When dedicated servers are deployed, the main server then becomes merely an authentication server and/or a file server.

What are authentication and file servers? **Authentication servers** keep track of who is logging on to the network and which services on the network are available to each user. Authentication servers also act as overseers for the network. They manage and coordinate the services provided by any other dedicated servers located on the network. **File servers** store and manage files for network users. On the network at your workplace or school, you may be provided with space on a file server to store files you create.

What functions do dedicated servers handle? Any task that is repetitive or demands a lot of time from the server's processor (CPU) is a good candidate to relegate to a dedicated server. Common types of dedicated servers are print servers, application servers, database servers, e-mail servers, communications servers, and Web servers. Servers are connected to a client/server network so that all client computers that need to use their services can access them, as shown in Figure 5.

PRINT SERVERS

How does a print server function? Printing is a function that takes a large quantity of central processing unit (CPU) time

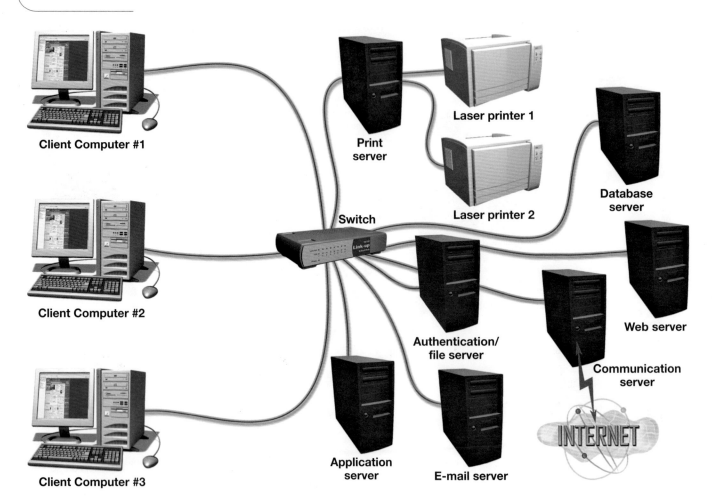

Client Computer #1

Client Computer #2

Client Computer #3

Switch

Print server

Laser printer 1

Laser printer 2

Database server

Web server

Communication server

Authentication/file server

Application server

E-mail server

INTERNET

and that most people do quite often. Setting up a **print server** to manage all client-requested printing jobs for all printers on the network helps enable client computers to complete more productive work than printing. When you tell your computer to print a document, it passes off the task to the print server. This frees the CPU on your computer to do other jobs.

When the print server receives a printing request (or job) from a client computer, it puts the job into a print queue on the print server. A print queue is a software holding area for printing jobs. Normally, each printer on a network has its own uniquely named print queue. Jobs receive a number when entering the queue and are sent to the printer in the order in which they are received. Print queues thus function like the "take a number" machines at a supermarket deli. Thus print servers organize print jobs into an orderly sequence to make printing more efficient on a shared printer. Another useful aspect of print servers is that they can prioritize print jobs. Different users and types of print jobs can be assigned different priorities, and higher-priority jobs are printed first. For instance, in a company where documents are printed on demand for clients, you would want these print jobs to take precedence over an employee printing routine correspondence.

APPLICATION SERVERS

What function does an application server perform? In many networks, all users run the same application software (such as Microsoft Office) on their computers. In a network of thousands of personal computers, installing application software on each individual computer is time consuming. An **application server** acts as a repository for application software.

When a client computer connects to the network and requests an application, the application server delivers the software to the client computer. Because the software does not reside on the client computer itself, this eases the task of installation and upgrading: the application needs to be installed or upgraded only on the application server, not on each network client.

BITS AND BYTES

Too Much Data? Here Comes the SAN

Databases can become so large that conventional database servers can't handle the information flowing in and out of them. A **storage area network (SAN)** is specifically designed to store and distribute large amounts of data to client computers or servers. SANs are made up of several **network attached storage (NAS) devices**, which are specialized devices attached to a network whose sole function is to store and disseminate data. Picture a computer with nothing but hard drives in it, and you have a pretty good idea of what a NAS device looks like. NAS devices are the filing cabinets of the new millennium and exist merely to store the huge amounts of data network users generate. Although they behave like dedicated servers, NAS devices have their own operating systems and file storage algorithms. Because they don't perform any network services other than storage and retrieval, they can do so quickly and efficiently. Any large database that will be searched by many users simultaneously, such as Amazon or eBay, is a good candidate for a SAN.

DATABASE SERVERS

What does a database server do? As its name implies, a **database server** provides client computers with access to information stored in a database. Often, many people need to access databases at the same time. For example, airline ticketing clerks can serve multiple people at the same time because they all have access to the ticket reservation database. This is achieved by storing the database on a database server, which each clerk's computer can access through the network. If the database were not on a network but instead on a stand-alone computer, only one clerk could use it at a time, making the ticketing system very inefficient.

E-MAIL SERVERS

When is an e-mail server necessary? The volume of e-mail on a large corporate network could quickly overwhelm a server that was attempting to handle other functions as well. Therefore, the sole function of an **e-mail server** attached to the network is to process and deliver incoming and outgoing e-mail. On a network with an e-mail server, when you send an e-mail from your computer, it

ACTIVE HELPDESK

Using Servers

In this Active Helpdesk call, you'll play the role of a Helpdesk staffer, fielding calls about various types of servers and client/server software.

goes to the e-mail server, which then handles the routing and delivery of your message. The e-mail server functions much like a postal carrier, who picks up your mail and sees that it finds its way to the correct destination.

COMMUNICATIONS SERVERS

What types of communications does a communications server handle?
A **communications server** handles all communications between the network and other networks, including managing Internet connectivity. All requests for information from the Internet and all messages being sent through the Internet pass through the communications server. Because Internet traffic is substantial at most organizations, the communications server has a heavy workload.

Often, the communications server is the only device on the network connected to the Internet. E-mail servers, Web servers, and other devices needing to communicate with the Internet usually route all their traffic through the communications server. Providing a single point of contact with the outside world makes it easier to secure the network from hackers.

WEB SERVERS

What function does a Web server perform?
A **Web server** is used to host a Web site available through the Internet. Web servers run specialized software, such as Apache (open-source server software) or Microsoft Internet Information Server (IIS), which enables them to host Web pages. Not every large network has a Web server. Many companies use an Internet service provider (ISP) to host their corporate Web sites instead.

SOUND BYTE

Network Topology and Navigation Devices

In this Sound Byte, you'll learn about common network topologies, the types of networks they are used with, and various network navigation devices.

Network Topologies

Just as buildings have different floor plans depending on their uses, networks have different blueprints denoting their layout. **Network topology** refers to the physical or logical arrangement of computers, transmission media (cable), and other network components. Because networks have different uses, not all networks have the same topology.

In this section, we explore the most common network topologies (bus, ring, and star) and discuss when each topology is used. As you'll see, the type of network topology used is important because it can affect the network's performance and scalability. Knowing how the basic topologies work and the strengths and weaknesses of each will help you understand why particular network topologies were chosen on the networks you use.

BUS TOPOLOGY

What does a bus topology look like?
In a **bus (or linear bus) topology**, all computers are connected in sequence on a single cable, as shown in Figure 6. This topology is deployed most often in peer-to-peer networks (not client/server networks). Each computer on the bus network can communicate with every other computer on the network directly. A limitation of bus networks is that data collisions can occur very easily if two computers transmit data at the same time because a bus network is essentially composed of one main communication medium (single cable).

Think of a data collision as having a group of three people (e.g., Emily, Reesa, and Luis) sitting in a room having a conversation. For the conversation to be effective, only one person can speak at a time; otherwise, they would not be able to hear and understand each other. Therefore, if Emily is speaking, Reesa and Luis must wait until she finishes before presenting their ideas, and so on.

Because two signals transmitted at the same time on a bus network may cause a data collision, an **access method** has to be established to control which computer is allowed to use the transmission media at a certain time. Computers on a bus network behave the same way as a group of people having a conversation. The computers "listen" to the network data traffic on the media.

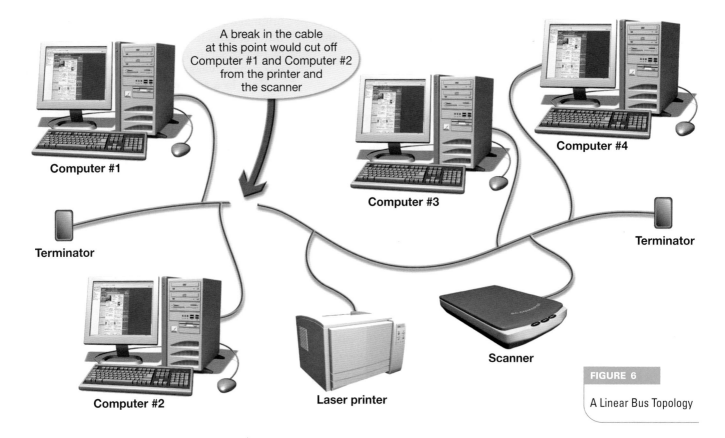

A break in the cable at this point would cut off Computer #1 and Computer #2 from the printer and the scanner

Computer #1

Computer #3

Computer #4

Terminator

Terminator

Computer #2

Laser printer

Scanner

FIGURE 6

A Linear Bus Topology

When no other computer is transmitting data (that is, when "conversation" stops), the computer knows it is allowed to transmit data on the media. This means of taking turns "talking" avoids **data collisions**, which happen when two computers send data at the same time and the sets of data collide somewhere in the media. When data collides, it is often lost or irreparably damaged.

How does data get from point to point on a bus network? When it is safe to send data (that is, when no other computers are transmitting data), the sending computer broadcasts the data onto the media. The data is broadcast throughout the network to *all* devices connected to the network. The data is broken into small segments called **packets**. Each packet contains the address of the computer or peripheral device to which it is being sent. Each computer or device connected to the network listens for data that contains its address. When it "hears" data addressed to it, it takes the data off the media and processes it.

For example, say your computer needs to print something on the printer attached to the network. Your computer "listens" to the network to ensure no other nodes are transmitting. It then sends the print job out onto the network. When the printer "hears" a job

addressed to it (the print job your computer just sent), it pulls the data off the network and executes the job.

The devices (nodes) attached to a bus network do nothing to move data along the network. This makes a bus network a **passive topology**. The data merely travels the entire length of the medium and is received by all network devices. The ends of the cable in a bus network are capped off by terminators (as shown in Figure 6). A **terminator** is a device that absorbs the signal so that it is not reflected back onto parts of the network that have already received it.

What are the advantages and disadvantages of bus networks? The simplicity and low cost of configuring a bus network are the major reasons this topology is deployed most often in P2P networks. The major disadvantage is that if there is a break in the cable, the bus network is effectively disrupted, because some computers are cut off from others on the network.

Also, because transmission signals degrade as the distance of the cable increases, a bus network is difficult to expand to a large number of users. And because only one computer can communicate at a time, adding a large number of nodes to a bus network limits performance and causes delays in sending data. Therefore, you rarely see a bus network deployed except in very small networks that are not expected to grow.

RING TOPOLOGY

What does a ring topology look like?
Not surprisingly, given its name, the computers and peripherals in a **ring** (or **loop**) **topology** are laid out in a configuration resembling a circle, as shown in Figure 7. Data flows around the circle from device to device in one direction only. Because data is passed using a special data packet called a **token**, this type of topology is commonly referred to as a **token-ring topology**. The

original token-ring networks achieved **data transfer rates** (bandwidth) of either 4 Mbps or 16 Mbps, but more recent token technologies can deliver speeds of up to 100 Mbps.

How is a token used to move data around a ring? A token is passed from computer to computer around the ring until it is grabbed by a computer that needs to transmit data. The computer holds onto the token until it is done transmitting data. Only one computer on the ring can "hold" the token at a time, and usually only one token exists on each ring.

If a computer (or node) has data to send, it waits for the token to be passed to it. It then takes the token out of circulation and sends data to its destination. When the

FIGURE 7

A Token-Ring Topology

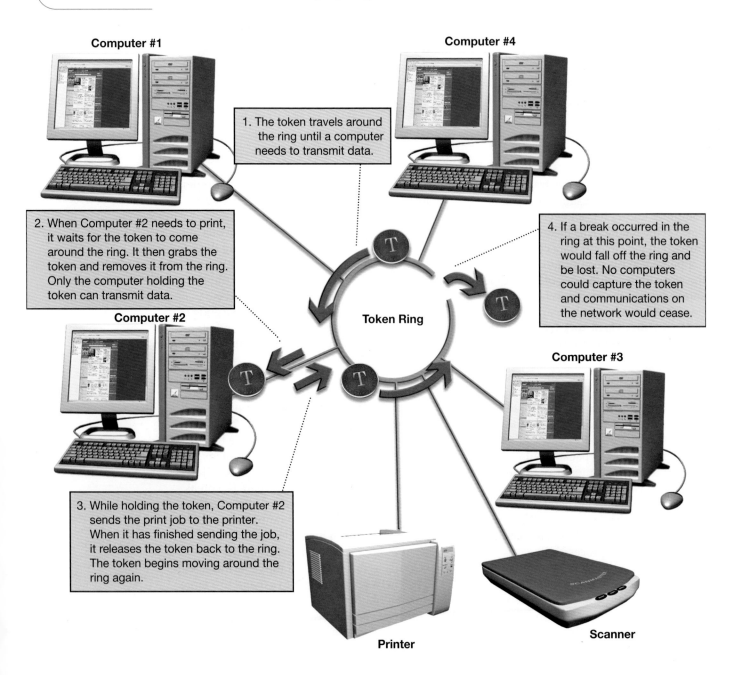

Computer #1

1. The token travels around the ring until a computer needs to transmit data.

Computer #4

2. When Computer #2 needs to print, it waits for the token to come around the ring. It then grabs the token and removes it from the ring. Only the computer holding the token can transmit data.

4. If a break occurred in the ring at this point, the token would fall off the ring and be lost. No computers could capture the token and communications on the network would cease.

Computer #2

Token Ring

Computer #3

3. While holding the token, Computer #2 sends the print job to the printer. When it has finished sending the job, it releases the token back to the ring. The token begins moving around the ring again.

Printer

Scanner

receiving node receives a complete transmission of the data, it sends an acknowledgment to the sending node. The sending node then generates a new token and starts it going around the ring again. This **token method** is the access method that ring networks use to avoid data collisions.

A ring topology is an **active topology** because each node on the network is responsible for retransmitting the token or the data to the next node on the ring. Large ring networks have the capability to use multiple tokens, which help move more data faster.

Is a ring topology better than a bus topology? A ring topology provides a fairer allocation of network resources than does a bus topology. By using a token, a ring network enables all nodes on the network to have an equal chance to send data. One "chatty" node cannot as easily monopolize the network bandwidth because after sending a batch of data, it must pass the token on.

In addition, the ring topology's performance remains acceptable even with large numbers of users. However, if one computer fails on a ring network, it can bring the entire network to a halt because that computer is unavailable to retransmit tokens and data. Problems in the ring can also be hard for network administrators to find. It's easier to expand a ring topology than a bus topology, but adding a node to a ring does cause the ring to cease to function while the node is installed.

STAR TOPOLOGY

What is the layout for a star topology?
A **star topology** is the most widely deployed client/server network layout in businesses today because it offers the most flexibility. In a star topology, the nodes connect to a central communications device called a switch, thus resembling a star, as shown in Figure 8. The switch receives a signal from the sending node

FIGURE 8

In a star topology, network nodes are connected through a central switch, forming a star. The only drawback is that if the switch fails, the network no longer functions. However, it is relatively easy to replace a switch.

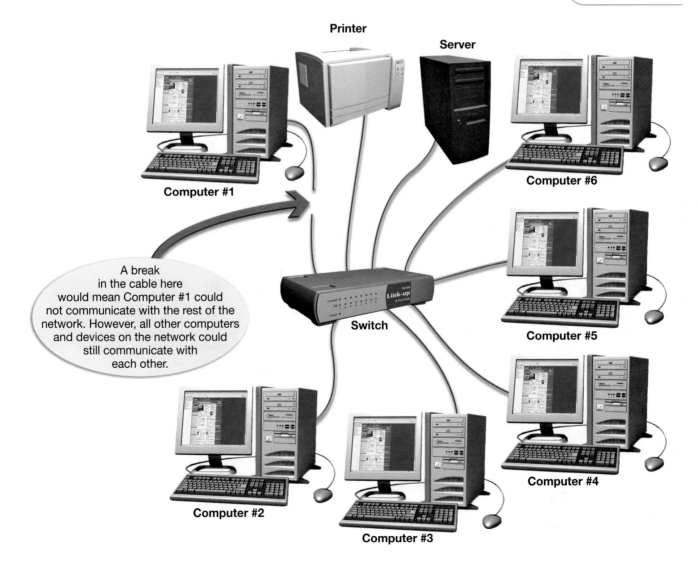

Printer

Server

Computer #1

A break in the cable here would mean Computer #1 could not communicate with the rest of the network. However, all other computers and devices on the network could still communicate with each other.

Switch

Computer #6

Computer #5

Computer #4

Computer #2

Computer #3

and retransmits it to all other nodes on the network. The network nodes examine data and only pick up the transmissions addressed to them. Because the switch retransmits data signals, a star topology is an active topology. (We discuss switches in more detail later in this chapter.)

Many star networks use the Ethernet protocol. Networks using the Ethernet protocol are by far the most common type of network in use today. Although many students think that Ethernet is a type of network topology, it is actually a communications protocol. A topology is a physical design of a network, whereas a **protocol** is a set of rules for exchanging communication. Therefore, an Ethernet network can be set up using a bus, a ring, or a star topology. The original Ethernet networks achieved maximum data transfer rates of 10 Mbps. However, newer equipment delivers 100 Mbps and even 1-Gigabit transfer rates at very affordable prices. For businesses that need even more speed, the new 10-Gigabit standard sup-

ports a transfer rate of up to 10 Gbps, but the equipment supporting this standard is still expensive and therefore is not seen in small businesses unless very high bandwidth is required.

For example, assume that your class has to send a message to the class next door. You decide to arrange your class in a straight line from your classroom to the other classroom. Each student will whisper the message to the next student in the line until the message is eventually passed to a student in the other classroom. The arrangement of the students in a straight line is your topology. The passing of the message from student to student using the English language is your protocol.

How do computers on a star network avoid data collisions? Because most star networks are Ethernet networks, they use the method used on all Ethernet networks to avoid data collisions: **CSMA/CD** (short for Carrier Sense Multiple Access with Collision Detection). With CSMA/CD, a node connected to the network listens (that is, has

FIGURE 9

Avoiding Data
Collisions on an
Ethernet Network

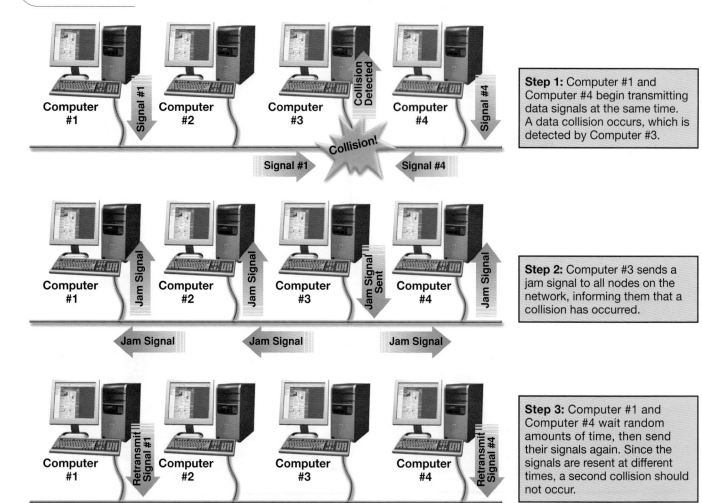

Step 1: Computer #1 and Computer #4 begin transmitting data signals at the same time. A data collision occurs, which is detected by Computer #3.

Step 2: Computer #3 sends a jam signal to all nodes on the network, informing them that a collision has occurred.

Step 3: Computer #1 and Computer #4 wait random amounts of time, then send their signals again. Since the signals are resent at different times, a second collision should not occur.

14 nanoseconds later   18 nanoseconds later

carrier sense) to determine that no other nodes are currently transmitting data signals. If the node doesn't hear any other signals, it assumes it is safe to transmit data. All devices on the network have the same right (that is, they have multiple access) to transmit data when they deem it safe. It is therefore possible for two devices to begin transmitting data signals at the same time. If this happens, the two signals collide.

What happens when the signals collide? As shown in Figure 9, when signals collide, a node on the network detects the collision. It then sends a special signal called a **jam signal** to all network nodes, alerting them that a collision has occurred. The nodes then stop transmitting and wait a random amount of time before retransmitting their data signals. The wait time needs to be random; otherwise, both nodes would start transmitting at the same time and another collision would occur.

What are the advantages and disadvantages of a star topology? Because of the complexity of the layout of star networks, they require more cable and are often more expensive than bus or ring networks. However, a star topology generally is considered to be superior to a ring topology because if one computer fails it doesn't affect the rest of the network. This is extremely important in a large network, in which one disabled computer affecting the operations of several hundred other computers would be totally unacceptable.

It is also easy to add nodes to star networks, and performance remains acceptable even with large numbers of users. In addition, the centralization of communications (through a switch) makes troubleshooting and repairs on star networks easier for network technicians. Technicians can usually pinpoint a communications problem just by examining the switch, as opposed to searching for a particular length of cable that broke in a ring network.

COMPARING TOPOLOGIES

So which topology is the best one? Figure 10 lists the advantages and disadvantages of bus, ring, and star topologies. In all but the smallest networks, star topologies are the most common. Because networks are constantly adding new users, the ability to add new users simply (that is, by installing a new switch) without affecting users already on the network is the deciding factor. The networks you'll encounter at school and in the workplace will almost certainly be laid out in a star topology. However, bus topologies are still the most common layout for simple home networks, and ring topologies are popular when fair allocation of network access is a major requirement of the network.

ACTIVE HELPDESK

Selecting a Network Topology and Cable

In this Active Helpdesk call, you'll play the role of a Helpdesk staffer, fielding calls about how a client/server network differs from a peer-to-peer network, the different classifications of client/server networks, various network topologies, and the types of transmission media used in client/server networks.

FIGURE 10 Advantages and Disadvantages of Bus, Ring, and Star Topologies

Topology	Advantages	Disadvantages
Bus	Uses a minimal amount of cabling. Easy, reliable, and inexpensive to install.	Breaks in the cable can disable the network. Large numbers of users will greatly decrease performance because of high volumes of data traffic.
Ring	Allocates access to the network fairly. Performance remains acceptable even with large numbers of users.	Adding or removing nodes disables the network. Failure of one computer can bring down the entire network. Problems in data transmission can sometimes be difficult to find.
Star	Failure of one computer does not affect other computers on the network. Centralized design simplifies troubleshooting and repairs. Easy to add more computers or groups of computers as needed (high scalability). Performance remains acceptable even with large numbers of users.	Requires more cable and is often more expensive than a bus or ring topology. The switch is a central point of failure. If it fails, all computers connected to that switch are affected.

Can topologies be combined within a single network? Because each topology has its own unique advantages, topologies are often combined to construct business networks. Combining multiple topologies into one network is known as constructing a **hybrid topology**. For instance, fair allocation of resources may be critical for reservation clerks at an airline (requiring a token ring network), whereas a purchasing department's network may require a star topology. One disadvantage of hybrid topologies is that hardware changes must usually be made to switch a node from one topology to another.

Transmission Media

When constructing a house, a variety of building material is available, depending on the needs of the builder. Similarly, when building a network, network engineers can use different types of media. **Transmission media**, whether it is cable or wireless communications technology, comprise the routes data takes to flow between devices on the network. Without transmission media, network devices would be unable to communicate.

WIRED TRANSMISSION MEDIA

What types of cable are commonly used for networks? Most home networks use either twisted pair cable (phone wire or Ethernet) or electrical wires as transmission media. For business networks, the three main cable types that are used today are twisted pair, coaxial, and fiber optic. Although each type is different, they share many common factors that need to be considered when choosing a cable type:

- **Maximum run length.** Each type of cable has a maximum run length over which signals sent across it can be "heard" by devices connected to it. Therefore, when designing a network, network engineers must accurately measure the distances between devices to ensure that appropriate cable is selected.

- **Bandwidth.** Bandwidth is the amount of data that can be transmitted across a transmission medium in a certain amount of time. Each cable is different and is rated by the maximum bandwidth it can support. Bandwidth is measured in bits per second, which represents how many bits of data can be transmitted along the cable each second.

- **Bend radius (flexibility).** When installing cable, it is often necessary to bend the cable around corners, surfaces, and so on. The bend radius of the cable defines how many degrees a cable can be bent in a one-foot segment before it is damaged. If many corners need to be navigated when installing a network, network engineers use cabling with a high bend radius.

- **Cable cost.** The cost per foot of different types and grades of cable varies widely. Cable selection may have to be made on the basis of cost if adequate funds are not available for the optimal type of cabling.

- **Installation costs.** Certain cable (such as twisted pair, which is used in home networks) is easy and inexpensive to install. Fiber-optic cable requires special training and equipment to install, which increases the installation costs.

- **Susceptibility to interference.** Signals traveling down a cable are subject to two types of interference. Electromagnetic interference (EMI), caused by the cable being exposed to strong electromagnetic fields, can distort or degrade signals on

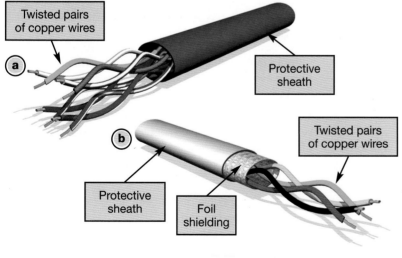

FIGURE 11

Anatomy of (a) unshielded twisted pair (UTP) cable and (b) shielded twisted pair (STP) cable.

the cable. Fluorescent lights and machinery with motors or transformers are the most common sources of EMI emissions. Cable signals also can be disrupted by radio frequency interference (RFI), which is usually caused by broadcast sources (television and radio signals) being located near the network. Cable types are rated as to how well they resist interference.

- **Signal transmission methods.** Both coaxial cable and twisted pair cable send electrical impulses down conductive material to transmit data signals. Fiber-optic cable transmits data signals as pulses of light.

In the sections that follow, we discuss the characteristics of each of the three major types of cable. We also discuss the use of wireless media as an alternative to cable.

Twisted Pair Cable

What does twisted pair cable look like? Twisted pair cable should be familiar to you because the telephone cable (or wire) in your home is one type of twisted pair cable. **Twisted pair cable** consists of pairs of copper wires twisted around each other and covered by a protective jacket (or sheath). The twists are important because they cause the magnetic fields that form around the copper wires to intermingle, which makes them less susceptible to outside interference. It also reduces the amount of crosstalk interference, or the tendency of signals on one wire to interfere with signals on a wire next to it.

If the twisted pair cable contains a layer of foil shielding to reduce interference, it is known as **shielded twisted pair (STP) cable**. If it does not contain a layer of foil shielding, it is known as **unshielded twisted pair (UTP) cable**, which is more susceptible to interference. Figure 11 shows illustrations of both types of twisted pair cable. Because of its lower price, UTP is more widely used, unless significant sources of interference must be overcome (such as in a production environment where machines create magnetic fields). However, there are different standard categories of UTP cable from which to choose.

What types of UTP cable are available? The two most common types of UTP cable in use today are Category 5E (Cat 5E) and Category 6 (Cat 6). Cat 6 cable can handle a bandwidth of 1 gigabit per second (Gbps),

whereas Cat 5E can handle a bandwidth of just 200 megabits per second (Mbps).

Unless severe budget constraints are in place, network engineers usually install the highest-bandwidth cable possible because reinstalling cable later (and the subsequent tearing up of walls and ceilings) can be very expensive. Therefore, since the fall of 2002, when the standard for Cat 6 cable was approved, new cable runs in businesses have been made with Cat 6 cable. Home networks that use twisted pair cable generally use Cat 5E cable because it's less expensive and most home networks don't need gigabit networks.

Coaxial Cable

What does coaxial cable look like? **Coaxial cable** should be familiar to you if you have cable television, because most cable television installers use coaxial cable. Coaxial cable (as shown in Figure 12) consists of four main components:

1. The core (usually copper) is in the very center and is used for transmitting the signal.

2. A solid layer of nonconductive insulating material (usually a hard, thick plastic) surrounds the core.

3. A layer of braided metal comes next to reduce interference with signals traveling in the core.

4. Finally, an external jacket of lightweight plastic covers the internal cable components to protect them from damage.

Although coaxial cable used to be the most widely used cable in business networks, advances in twisted pair cable shielding and

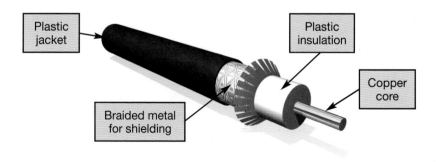

Coaxial cable consists of four main components: the core, an insulated covering, a braided metal shielding, and a plastic jacket.

FIGURE 13

Fiber-optic cable is made up of a glass (or plastic) fiber (or a bundle of fibers), a glass or plastic cladding, and a protective sheath.

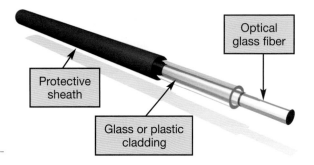

Optical glass fiber

Protective sheath

Glass or plastic cladding

ThinNet is used in homes because it is cheaper and because most houses do not have significant sources of interference (such as industrial machinery).

Fiber-Optic Cable

What does fiber-optic cable look like? As shown in Figure 13, **fiber-optic cable** is composed of a glass (or plastic) fiber (or a bundle of fibers) that comprises the core of the cable (where the data is transmitted). Cladding, a protective layer made of glass or plastic, is wrapped around the core to protect it. Finally, for additional protection, an outer jacket (sheath) is added, often made of durable materials such as Kevlar (the substance used to make bullet-proof vests). Data transmissions can pass through fiber-optic cable in only one direction. Therefore, usually at least two cores are located in each fiber-optic cable to enable transmission of data in both directions.

transmission speeds, as well as twisted pair's lower cost, have reduced the popularity of coaxial cable.

Are there different types of coaxial cable? The two main coaxial cable types are ThinNet and ThickNet. ThinNet is the cable used by the cable TV company to wire your home and is usually covered by a black plastic jacket. ThickNet, usually distinguished by a yellow jacket, is similar to ThinNet but is more rigid and better shielded to protect against interference. ThickNet, because it is better shielded, is used in industrial settings where there is a lot of electrical interference.

How does fiber-optic cable differ from twisted pair and coaxial cable? As noted earlier, the main difference between fiber-optic cable and other types of cable is the method of signal transmission. Twisted pair and coaxial cable use copper wire to conduct electrical impulses. In a fiber-optic cable, electrical data signals from network devices (client computers, peripherals, and so on) are converted to light pulses before they are transmitted. Because EMI and RFI do not affect light waves, fiber-optic cable is virtually immune to interference.

BITS AND BYTES

A Network on the Move!

When you think of cutting-edge technology, do you think of city buses? If you visited Portsmouth, England, you would. Portsmouth is a small city visited by more than 6.5 million tourists each year. Because the city is always full of people, 320 buses are deployed in it, each one equipped with a very sophisticated wireless network, including an onboard computer and wireless network card. And each bus stop is equipped with an Internet terminal that enables patrons to check e-mail, buy bus tickets, and find out exactly where the bus they are waiting for is located and when it will arrive.

The network keeps track of the exact location of all the network nodes (the computers on the buses) by sending test signals (pings) to them and measuring the time communications take to travel back and forth. The network doesn't use 802.11 technology; instead, it uses a competing standard developed for the military called QDMA (quad-division multiple access). The main advantage of QDMA is that it can network devices moving as fast at 250 miles an hour without losing the link. However, there are plans to add 802.11-compatible wireless access points at bus kiosks and on the buses to allow riders to use their own computers, PDAs, and cell phones to surf the net.

WIRELESS MEDIA OPTIONS

What wireless media options are there? Although the word *wireless* implies no wires, in businesses, **wireless media** are usually add-ons to extend or improve access to a wired network. In the corporate environment, wireless access is often provided to give employees a wider range to their working area. For instance, if conference rooms offer wireless access, employees can bring their notebooks (laptops) to meetings and gain access to the network during the meeting. However, when they go back to their offices, they may connect to the regular wired network through a wired connection. So, today's corporate networks are often a combination of wired and wireless media.

Wireless devices must use the same communications standard to communicate with each other. Wireless networks in the United

States are currently based on the **802.11 standard**, also known as **Wi-Fi** (short for Wireless Fidelity), established by the Institute of Electrical and Electronics Engineers (IEEE). Wireless devices attached to networks using the 802.11 standard communicate with each other using radio waves.

The 802.11 standard is actually divided into a number of separate standards. The 802.11g standard is the most common standard in use now. With a maximum **throughput** (bandwidth) of 54 Mbps, 802.11g standard is widely deployed in corporate and personal networks. 802.11g devices include Super G (also called Extreme G or Enhanced G) devices, which use proprietary algorithms and hardware to increase maximum throughput to 108 Mbps. However, 802.11g devices are being replaced by 802.11n devices. The 802.11n standard supports much higher throughput and greatly increased range (often by using multiple antennas to send and receive signals), which makes it an ideal choice for providing wireless coverage over an entire office, or in environments where large data files (such as video) are being transmitted.

COMPARING TRANSMISSION MEDIA

So which medium is best for client/server networks? Network engineers specialize in the design and deployment of networks and are responsible for selecting network topology and media types. Their decision as to which transmission medium the network will use is based on the topology selected, the length of the cable runs needed, the amount of interference present, and the need for wireless connectivity.

Figure 14 compares the attributes of the major cable types. Most large networks have a mix of media. For example, coaxial cable may be appropriate for the portion of the network that traverses the factory floor where interference from magnetic fields is significant. However, unshielded twisted pair cable may work fine in the general office area. And wireless media may be required in conference rooms and other areas where employees are likely to connect their notebooks or where it is impractical or expensive to run cable.

Network Operating Systems

Merely connecting computers and peripherals with media does not create a client/server network. Special software, known as a **network operating system (NOS)**, needs to be installed on each client computer and server connected to the network to provide the services necessary for them to communicate. Many modern operating systems (such as Windows Vista and Mac OS X) include NOS client software as part of the basic installation. However, if

FIGURE 14 Comparison of Characteristics of Major Cable Types

Cable Characteristics	Twisted Pair (Cat 6)	Coaxial (ThinNet)	Coaxial (ThickNet)	Fiber Optic
Maximum Run Length	328 feet (100 m)	607 feet (185 m)	1,640 feet (500 m)	Up to 62 miles (100 km)
Bandwidth	1,000 Mbps	10 Mbps	10 Mbps	100 Mbps to 2 Gbps
Bend Radius (Flexibility)	No limit	360 degrees/foot	30 degrees/foot	30 degrees/foot
Cable Cost	Very low	Low	Moderate	High
Installation Cost	Very low	Low	Slightly higher than ThinNet	Most expensive because of installation training required
Susceptibility to Interference	High	Low	Very low	None (not susceptible to EMI and RFI)

The OSI Model: Defining Protocol Standards

The Institute of Electrical and Electronics Engineers (IEEE) has taken the lead in establishing recognized worldwide networking protocols, including a standard of communications called the Open Systems Interconnection (OSI) reference model. The OSI model, which was quickly adopted as a standard throughout the computing world, provides the protocol guidelines for all modern networks. All modern network operating system (NOS) protocols are designed to interact in accordance with the standards set out by the OSI model.

The OSI model divides communications tasks into seven distinct processes called layers. Each layer of an OSI network has a specific function. Figure 15 shows the layers of the OSI model and their functions. Each layer knows how to communicate with the layer above and below it.

This layering approach makes communications more efficient because specialized pieces of the NOS perform specific tasks. The layering approach is akin to assembly-line manufacturing. For example, producing thousands of cars per day would be difficult if one person had to build a car on his or her own. However, by splitting up the work of assembling a car into specialized tasks (such as installing the engine, bolting on the bumpers, and so on) and assigning them to people who perform exceptionally well at certain tasks, greater efficiency is achieved. This is how the OSI layers work. By handling specialized tasks and communicating only with the layers above and below them, the layering approach makes communications more efficient.

FIGURE 15 The Layers of the OSI Model and Their Functions

Application Layer	Handles all interfaces between the application software and the network Translates user information into a format the presentation layer can understand
Presentation Layer	Reformats data so that the session layer can understand it Compresses and encrypts data
Session Layer	Sets up a virtual (not physical) connection between the sending and receiving devices Manages communications sessions
Transport Layer	Creates packets Handles packet acknowledgment
Network Layer	Determines where to send the packets on the network
Data Link Layer	Assembles the data into frames, addresses them, and sends them to the physical layer for delivery
Physical Layer	Transmits (delivers) data on the network so it can reach its intended address

your operating system does not include NOS client software, it must be installed on each client. The NOS provides a set of common rules (a protocol) that controls communication between devices on the network. The major NOSs on the market today include Windows Server 2003, UNIX, and Novell NetWare.

Do peer-to-peer networks need special NOS software? The software that P2P networks require is built into the Windows and Macintosh operating systems. Therefore, there is no need to purchase specialized NOS software.

How does NOS software differ from operating system software? Operating system (OS) software is designed to facilitate communication between the software and hardware components of your computer. NOS software is specifically designed to provide server services, network communications, management of network peripherals, and storage. To provide network communications, the client computer must run a small part of the NOS in addition to the OS. Windows Vista is an OS and is installed on home computers. As noted above, because it also has some NOS

Let's look at how each OSI layer functions by following an e-mail you create and send to your friend:

- **Application layer:** Handles all interaction between the application software and the network. It translates the data from the application into a format that the presentation layer can understand. For example, when you send an e-mail, the application layer takes the e-mail message you created in Microsoft Outlook, translates it into a format your network can understand, and passes it to the presentation layer.
- **Presentation layer:** Reformats the data so that the session layer can understand it. It also handles data encryption (changing the data into a format that makes it harder to intercept and read the message) and compression, if required. In our e-mail example, the presentation layer notices that you selected an encryption option for the e-mail message and encrypts the data before sending it to the session layer.
- **Session layer:** Sets up a virtual (not physical) connection between the sending and receiving devices. It then manages the communication between the two. In our e-mail example, the session layer would set up the parameters for the communications session between your computer and the Internet service provider (ISP) where your friend has her e-mail account. The session layer then tracks the transmission of the e-mail until it is satisfied that all the data in the e-mail was received at your friend's ISP.
- **Transport layer:** Breaks up the data into packets and sequences them appropriately. It also handles acknowledgment of packets (that is, it determines whether the packets were received at their destina-

tion) and decides whether packets need to be sent again. In our e-mail example, the transport layer breaks up your e-mail message into packets and sends them to the network layer, making sure that all the packets reach their destination.
- **Network layer:** Determines where to send the packets on the network and the best way to route them there. In our e-mail example, the network layer examines the address on the packets (the address of your friend's ISP) and determines how to route the packets so they get to your ISP and can ultimately get to the receiving computer.
- **Data link layer:** Responsible for assembling the data packets into frames (a type of data packet that holds more data), addressing the frames, and delivering them to the physical layer so they can be sent on their way. It is the equivalent of a postal worker who reads the address on a piece of mail and makes sure it gets sent to the proper recipient. In our e-mail example, the data link layer assembles the e-mail data packets into frames, which are addressed with appropriate routing information received from the network layer.
- **Physical layer:** Takes care of delivering the data. It converts the data into a signal and transmits it onto the network so that it can reach its intended address. In our e-mail example, the physical layer sends out the data over the Internet to its ultimate destination (your friend's ISP).

By following standardized protocols set forth by the OSI model, NOS software can communicate happily with the computers and peripherals attached to the network as well as with other networks.

functionality, client computers (in a client/server network) that have Windows Vista installed as the OS do not need an additional NOS. Windows Server 2003 is an NOS that is deployed on servers in a client/server network.

How does the NOS control network communications? Each NOS has its own proprietary communications language, file management structure, and device management structure. The NOS also sets and controls the protocols (rules) for all devices wishing to communicate on the network. Many different proprietary networking pro-

tocols exist, such as Novell Internetwork Packet Exchange (IPX), Microsoft NetBIOS Extended User Interface (NetBEUI), and the Apple File Protocol (AFP). These protocols were developed for a specific vendor's operating system. For example, IPX was developed for networks running the Novell NOS. Proprietary protocols such as these do not work with another vendor's NOS.

However, because the Internet uses an open protocol (called TCP/IP) for communications, many corporate networks use TCP/IP as their standard networking protocol regardless of the manufacturer of their NOS. All modern NOSs support TCP/IP.

Can a network use two different NOSs? Many large corporate networks use several different NOSs at the same time. This is because different NOSs provide different features, some of which are more useful in certain situations than others. For instance, although the employees of a corporation may be using a Microsoft Windows environment for their desktops and e-mail, the file servers and print servers may be running a Novell NOS.

Because NOSs use different internal software languages to communicate, they can't communicate directly with each other. However, if both NOSs are using the same protocol (such as TCP/IP), they can pass information between the networks and it can be interpreted by the other network.

Network Adapters

Client computers and peripherals need an interface to connect with and communicate on the network. **Network adapters** are devices that perform specific tasks to enable computers to communicate on a network. Certain network adapters are installed *inside* computers and peripherals as expansion cards. These adapters are referred to as network interface cards (NICs).

Although you could use network adapters that plug into universal serial bus (USB) ports on a client/server network,

most network adapters are NICs. That's because external devices are more susceptible to damage.

What do network adapters do? Network adapters perform three critical functions:

1. **They generate high-powered signals to enable network transmissions.** Digital signals generated inside the computer are fairly low-powered and would not travel well on network media (cable or wireless technology) without network adapters. Network adapters convert the signals from inside the computer to higher-powered signals that have no trouble traversing the network media.

2. **They are responsible for breaking the data into packets and preparing them for transmission across the network.** They also are responsible for receiving incoming data packets and, in accordance with networking protocols (rules), reconstructing them, as shown in Figure 16.

3. **They act as gatekeepers for information flowing to and from the client computer.** Much like a security guard in a gated community, network adapters are responsible for permitting or denying access to the client computer (the community) and controlling the flow of visitors (data).

Are there different types of network adapters? Although there are different types of network adapters, almost

FIGURE 16

A network interface card (NIC) is responsible for breaking down data into packets and preparing the packets for transmission across the network. It also is responsible for receiving incoming data packets and reconstructing them.

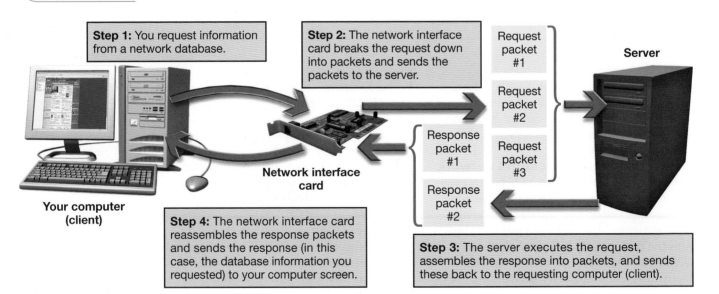

Step 1: You request information from a network database.

Step 2: The network interface card breaks the request down into packets and sends the packets to the server.

Request packet #1

Request packet #2

Request packet #3

Response packet #1

Response packet #2

Server

Network interface card

Your computer (client)

Step 4: The network interface card reassembles the response packets and sends the response (in this case, the database information you requested) to your computer screen.

Step 3: The server executes the request, assembles the response into packets, and sends these back to the requesting computer (client).

without exception, Ethernet (either wired or wireless) is the standard communications protocol used on most current networks. Therefore, the adapter cards shipping with computers today are always Ethernet compliant. The majority of Ethernet adapters provide connection ports that accept RJ-45 (Ethernet) connector plugs for connection to twisted pair cable. However, adapters that provide other types of connectors for direct connections to other types of network media (such as fiber-optic cables) are available.

Do wireless networks require network adapters? Most corporate networks are not entirely wireless, but they do provide wireless connectivity to some computers. Computers that connect to the network using wireless access need special network adapter cards, called **wireless network interface cards (wireless NICs)**, installed in the system unit. Unlike wired NICs, wireless NICs don't connect to the network with cables. Instead, the network must be fitted with devices called **wireless access points** that give wireless devices a sending and receiving connection point to the network.

Figure 17 shows an example of a typical corporate network with a wireless access point. The access point is connected to the wired network through a conventional cable. When a notebook (or other device with a wireless NIC) is powered on near a wireless access point, it establishes a connection with the access point using radio waves. Many computers can communicate with the network through a single wireless access point.

Do network adapters require software? Because the network adapter is responsible for communications between the client computer and the network, it needs to speak the same language as the network's special operating system software. Therefore, special communications software called a device driver is installed on all client computers in the client/server network. **Device drivers** enable the network adapter to communicate with the server's operating system and with the operating system of the computer in which the adapter is installed.

What are my options if I'm not located in range of a wireless network? You can bring your own wireless network with you! Most cellular telephone companies, like AT&T and Sprint, offer broadband PC modem cards for your

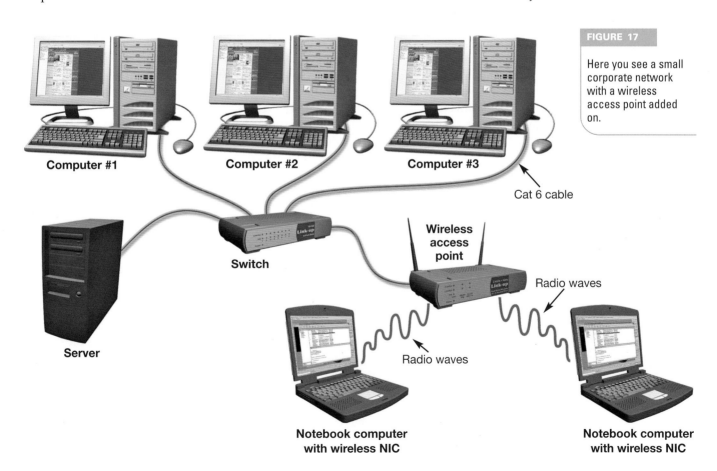

FIGURE 17

Here you see a small corporate network with a wireless access point added on.

Computer #1

Computer #2

Computer #3

Cat 6 cable

Switch

Wireless access point

Radio waves

Server

Radio waves

Notebook computer with wireless NIC

Notebook computer with wireless NIC

Ethics: RFID—Friend or Foe?

Bought anything at Wal-Mart or Best Buy lately? If so, there is a good chance that you brought home a **radio frequency identification tag (RFID tag)** with your purchase. Originally, RFID tags were used to keep track of cattle, but now they've moved into the retail sector to keep track of products. So what are RFID tags, how did they end up in retail stores, and why should you care about them?

RFID tags can look like stickers or labels, or in some cases they look like the thin plastic wristbands you get when you check into a hospital. The tags are attached to batches of merchandise (usually cases or pallets), and all tags contain a microchip that holds a unique sequence of numbers used to identify the product to which it is attached. The tags also contain a tiny antenna that broadcasts information about the merchandise, such as its date of manufacture or price. Think of RFID tags as the next generation of UPC codes.

Two types of tags are in use: active and passive. Active tags are equipped with a battery and constantly transmit information. Passive tags don't have their own power source but instead get their energy from tag readers. Passive tags are more common because they are cheaper. Tag readers are devices that scan the information on the tags as the tags are passed by the reader. They do this through antennas that generate magnetic fields, which the passive tags sense. In response, the passive tags transmit their product code to the tag reader. The reader then sends the digital information to a computer system, most likely a database.

So how do RFID tags help retailers? Inventory for large retailers can be daunting to manage. Retailers, such as Wal-Mart, have tens of thousands of suppliers sending hundreds of thousands of products to its warehouses and stores. The use of RFID tagging allows the recording of inventory receipts and shipments to stores to be largely automated, resulting in fewer mistakes, fewer instances of merchandise getting lost and forgotten in the warehouse, and tighter control over stock levels. This helps retailers and their suppliers ensure that the correct inventory levels are maintained at all times, resulting in fewer shortages of merchandise and, ultimately, increased sales because the product is on the shelf when you go to buy it. Retailers also can use the product serial number information that can be embedded in tags to speed repair or return service. This process is shown in Figure 18.

Someday, RFID could be a huge benefit for consumers. Imagine if all products in your local grocery store had RFID tags. When you entered the store and grabbed a shopping cart, you could swipe your credit card in a reader on the cart. Then, after you finished shopping, you could walk out the door, at which time an RFID reader would take an inventory of the contents of your cart and charge your credit card for what you purchased. No more waiting in checkout lines! And the streamlining of payment could result in lower costs for consumers. After you got home, if your refrigerator was equipped with RFID equipment, it could scan your purchases and keep track of your groceries, including expiration dates. Your refrigerator might contact your PDA (via the Internet) and let you know that your milk was out of date so you could buy more on the way home. Now that's a smart fridge!

But convenience could come with a price. There is concern that people might gather information about consumers' buying habits without their knowledge, similar to the concerns people have about spyware on computers today, because the RFID tags would be operational outside of the retail store. For example, someone could sit in the parking lot with a tag reader and detect exactly what you purchased as you unknowingly pushed your shopping cart by the car. If this person were from a competing retailer, this com-

---

notebook that will keep you connected (for a fee, of course). PC cards fit into expansion slots on your notebook and enable it to send and receive data using your cellular provider's wireless network. Broadband download speeds now can reach a respectable 700 Kbps, making this a very viable option if you need to ensure you have connectivity wherever you go— or virtually everywhere. Check with the cellular provider to ensure they have coverage most places you will travel.

Network Navigation Devices

Earlier in this chapter, you learned that to flow through the network, data is broken into small segments called packets. Data packets are like postal letters. They don't get to their destinations without some help. In this section, we explore the various conventions and devices that help speed data packets on their way through the network.

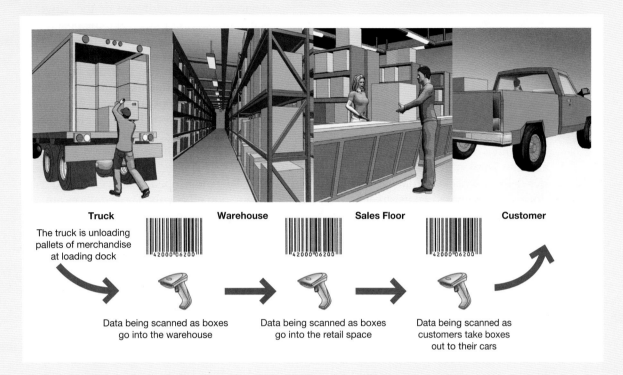

Truck

The truck is unloading pallets of merchandise at loading dock

Warehouse

Sales Floor

Customer

Data being scanned as boxes go into the warehouse

Data being scanned as boxes go into the retail space

Data being scanned as customers take boxes out to their cars

FIGURE 18

As merchandise equipped with RFID tags enters the warehouse, the tags are scanned and the inventory database is updated. When merchandise is moved to the sales floor, tags are scanned once more, and another inventory database is updated so that management can easily locate the stock. The tags are scanned one last time as customers purchase the items, which will trigger the stock ordering system to place another order with a supplier if inventory is too low.

petitive information could be very valuable. Or this person could be from a government enforcement agency that was trying to determine whether underage consumers were purchasing alcoholic beverages. And depending on the range of the tags, some pundits have speculated that thieves could drive by houses and scan for desirable items to steal, such as large-screen TVs. However, this is unlikely with the state of the current RFID technology.

Many consumers resent any potential invasion of their privacy. Therefore, retailers will need to educate consumers about RFID tags and their benefits. Retailers also will need to ensure that consumers have the option to deactivate or remove tags to protect their privacy if so desired.

MAC ADDRESSES

How do data packets know where to go on the network? Each network adapter has a physical address similar to a serial number on an appliance. This is called a **Media Access Control (MAC) address,** and it is made up of six two-position characters such as 01:40:87:44:79:A5. The first three numbers (in this case, 01:40:87) specify the manufacturer of the network adapter, whereas the second set of numbers (in this case, 44:79:A5) comprises a unique address. Because all MAC addresses must be unique, the IEEE runs a committee that is responsible for allocating blocks of numbers to network adapter manufacturers. MAC should not be confused with Apple computers of the same name.

Are MAC addresses the same as IP addresses? MAC addresses and Internet Protocol (IP) addresses are not the same thing. A MAC address is used for identification purposes *internally* on a network, similar to giving people different names to differentiate them. An IP address is the address *external* entities use to communicate with your network and is similar to your home street address. Think of it this way: the postal carrier delivers a package (data packet) to your dorm building based on its street address (IP address). The dorm's mail clerk delivers the package to your room because it has your name on it (MAC address) and not that of your neighbor. Both pieces of information are necessary to ensure that the package (or data) reaches its destination.

How does a data packet get a MAC address? Data packets are not necessarily sent alone. Sometimes groups of data packets are sent together in a group called a frame. **Frames** are containers that can hold multiple data packets. This is similar to placing several letters going to the same postal address in a big envelope. When the data packets are being assembled into frames, the NOS software assigns the appropriate MAC address to the frame. The NOS keeps track of all devices and their addresses on the network. Much like a letter placed into the postal service, the frame is delivered to the MAC address that the NOS assigned to the frame.

What delivers the frames to the correct device on the network? In a small bus network, frames just bounce along the wire until the correct client computer notices the frame is addressed to it and pulls the signal off the wire. This is inefficient in a larger network. Therefore, many types of devices have been developed to deliver data to its destination efficiently. These devices are designed to amplify signals, route signals, and exchange data with other networks.

Are MAC addresses useful for anything besides identifying a particular network device? On networks with wireless capabilities, MAC addresses can be used to enhance network security. Most wireless routers and access points can be used to filter MAC addresses to eliminate ones from unauthorized devices. Because each MAC address is unique, you can input a list of authorized MAC addresses into the router. If someone who is using an unauthorized network adapter (i.e., one with an unauthorized MAC address) attempts to connect to the network, they will be unable to make a connection. Although impractical for a large organization with many employees being hired and leaving constantly, MAC address filtering is a very useful security tool on home networks and small business networks.

REPEATERS AND HUBS

What types of devices amplify signals on a single network? Repeaters are relatively simple devices whose sole function is to amplify a signal and retransmit it. Repeaters are used to extend cable runs beyond the maximum run length (over which a signal would degrade and be unreadable).

Hubs are devices that also transmit signals. In addition, they have multiple ports to which devices are connected. As shown in Figure 19, the hub receives the signal from a device, reconstructs it, and transmits it to all other ports on the hub.

FIGURE 19

A hub broadcasts messages to all devices attached to it regardless of the intended recipient.

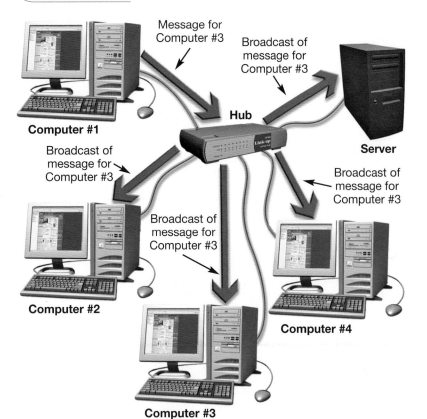

Message for Computer #3

Broadcast of message for Computer #3

Hub

Computer #1

Broadcast of message for Computer #3

Server

Broadcast of message for Computer #3

Broadcast of message for Computer #3

Computer #2

Computer #4

Computer #3

Ethics: Network Technicians' Access to Networks—Who Is Watching the Watchers?

According to Salary.com, the majority of employers report that they are monitoring their employees in some fashion. The monitoring of phone calls, e-mail, and Web usage by employers is legal in almost all jurisdictions in the United States. Employers that suspect employees are "goofing off" can install spyware to monitor employee computer keystrokes and keep track of Web sites visited down to the individual computer level. Naturally, network administrators are often involved in employee monitoring. Consider the case of Vernon Blake, the network administrator at the Alabama Department of Transportation. His boss was constantly playing computer games at work. This was common knowledge, yet no action was taken. Vernon installed software on his boss's computer and captured screen images that verified the boss was playing solitaire about 70 percent of the time. When Blake reported the results to management, the boss was reprimanded and Blake was fired! The company cited Blake's lack of authority or permission to install the monitoring software.

In addition, businesses are constantly receiving from their customers sensitive information such as social security numbers, birth dates, and credit card numbers—all valuable information for identify thieves. The job of protecting this data ultimately falls on the network administrators who are in charge of network and data security. Another example involves the American Institute of Certified Public Accountants (AICPA), a professional organization of CPAs. The AICPA maintains membership lists that include names, addresses, birth dates, and social security numbers. The AICPA has

clearly defined written policies that forbid equipment containing member information (such as a hard drive on a computer) from being sent out to external vendors for repair. Yet in early 2006, an IT staff member violated this policy and sent a hard drive containing membership information on 330,000 members to an external vendor. The hard drive was lost in transit when being returned to the AICPA. The AICPA quickly notified members of the security breach and offered them a free year of credit monitoring service to head off any problems—most likely at considerable expense to the AICPA. Although the AICPA has not indicated the disciplinary action taken against staff involved, it would seem likely that the penalties were severe.

So who is in charge of monitoring the network administrators so that they don't abuse their access to sensitive information or fail to exercise proper safeguards over sensitive data? Savvy companies put written policies in place for employees regarding computer usage. These policies need to include guidelines for network administrators who have higher levels of access than normal employees. Procedures for safeguarding data and guidelines for investigating employee misuse of computers must be clearly explained, and management needs to periodically review the activities of the network administrators to ensure compliance with polices. Although all employees need to follow approved company procedures regarding computer usage, it is especially important to ensure employees with high levels of access and high-level security responsibilities are adhering to company guidelines.

SWITCHES AND BRIDGES

Which devices are used to route signals through a single network?

Switches and bridges are used to send data on a specific route through the network. A **switch** can be viewed as a "smart" hub. It makes decisions, based on the MAC address of the data, as to where the data is to be sent. Therefore, only the intended recipient of the data receives the signal as opposed to a hub, which sends out data to all devices connected to it. This improves network efficiency by helping ensure that devices receive data intended only for them.

Switches are generally not needed on small networks (such as home networks) because there is not a large amount of data

traffic, making increasing efficiency unnecessary. Figure 20 shows a switch being used to rebroadcast a message.

As a corporate network grows in size, performance can decline as many devices compete for transmission time on the net-

ACTIVE HELPDESK

Selecting Network Navigation Devices

In this Active Helpdesk call, you'll play the role of a Helpdesk staffer, fielding calls about how network adapters enable computers to participate in a client/server network and what devices assist in moving data around a client/server network.

FIGURE 20

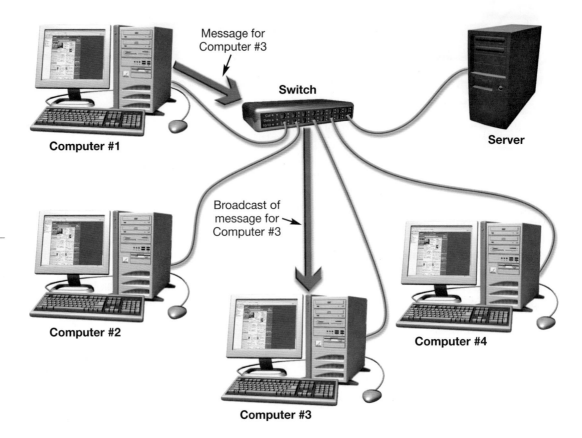

Message for Computer #3

Switch

Server

Computer #1

Broadcast of message for Computer #3

Computer #2

Computer #4

Computer #3

work media. To solve this problem, a network can be broken into multiple segments known as collision domains. **Bridges** are devices that are used to send data between these different collision domains. A bridge sends data between collision domains depending on where the recipient device is located, as indicated in Figure 21. Most home networks contain only one segment and therefore do not require bridges.

ROUTERS

What device is designed to move data to another network? Whereas repeaters, hubs, switches, and bridges perform their functions within a single

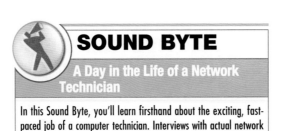

SOUND BYTE

A Day in the Life of a Network Technician

In this Sound Byte, you'll learn firsthand about the exciting, fast-paced job of a computer technician. Interviews with actual network technicians and tours of networking facilities will provide you with a deeper appreciation for the complexities of the job.

network, **routers** are designed to send information between two networks. To accomplish this, routers must look at higher-level network addresses (such as IP addresses), not MAC addresses. When the router notices data with an address that does not belong to a device on the network from which it originated, it sends the data to another network to which it is attached (or out onto the Internet).

Network Security

A major advantage that client/server networks have over peer-to-peer networks is that they contain a higher level of security. With client/server networks, users can be required to use a user ID and a password to gain access to the network. Also, the security can be centrally administered by network administrators, freeing individual users of the responsibility of maintaining their own data security (as they must do on a peer-to-peer network).

In the next section, we explore the challenges network administrators face to keep a client/server network secure. We use a college network as our example, but note that the same principles apply to all client/server networks.

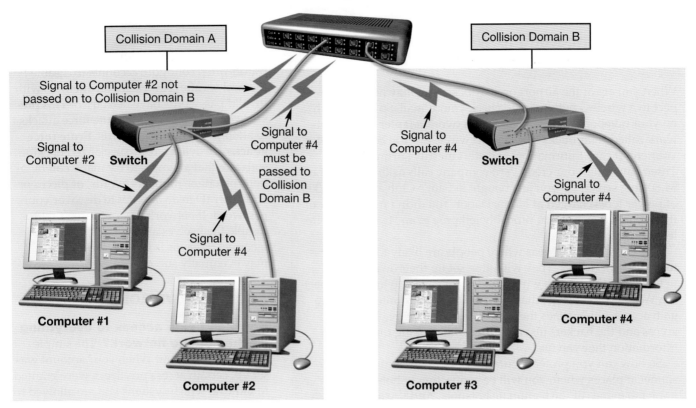

Bridge

Collision Domain A

Collision Domain B

Signal to Computer #2 not passed on to Collision Domain B

Signal to Computer #2   **Switch**

Signal to Computer #4 must be passed to Collision Domain B

Signal to Computer #4

Signal to Computer #4   **Switch**

Signal to Computer #4

Signal to Computer #4

Computer #1

Computer #4

Computer #2

Computer #3

FIGURE 21

Bridges are devices that are used to send data between different network collision domains. Here, signals received by the bridge from collision domain A are forwarded only to collision domain B if the destination computer is located in that domain.

What sources of security threats do all network administrators need to watch for? Threats can be classified into three main groups as shown here:

- **Human Errors and Mistakes:** Everyone makes mistakes. For example, the clerk processing your tuition payment could accidentally delete your records. A member of the computer support staff could mistakenly install an old database on top of the current one. Even physical accidents fall into this category, such as losing control of a car and driving it through the wall of the main server room.

- **Malicious Human Activity:** Malicious actions can be perpetrated by current employees, former employees, or third parties. For example, a disgruntled employee could introduce a virus to the network. A hacker could break into the student database server to steal credit card records. A former employee who feels he or she was unjustly fired could deliberately destroy data.

- **Natural Events and Disasters:** Some events—such as broken water pipes or fire, or disasters such as hurricanes, floods, earthquakes, and other acts of nature—are beyond human control. All can lead to the inadvertent destruction of data.

Who does a college network need to be secure from? A college network, like any network, is vulnerable to unauthorized users and manipulation or misuse of the data contained on it. The person who sat next to you last semester in English class who failed may be interested in changing his grade to an A. Hackers may be interested in the financial and personal information (such as social security numbers and credit card numbers) stored in college financial office databases on the network. Thus, one of the network administrator's key functions is to keep network data secure.

AUTHENTICATION

How does a college ensure that only authorized users access its network?
Authentication is the process whereby users prove they have authorization to use a

BITS AND BYTES

Connecting to Wireless Networks on the Road? Beware of "Evil Twins"!

When you are at the airport or Starbucks, you may need to connect to a wireless network and check your e-mail. So you switch on your notebook, and the wireless network adapter finds a network called "star bucks" or "airport wireless." You connect, enter your credit card information, and start merrily surfing away. Three days later your credit card company calls asking about the $4,800 big screen TV you just bought at Sam's Club and the $6,300 of power tools charged at Home Depot. You didn't make either of these purchases, but you probably fell prey to an "evil twin" wireless hotspot.

Hackers know the areas where people are likely to seek access to wireless networks. They will often set up their own wireless networks in these areas with sound-alike names to lure unsuspecting Web surfers and get them to enter credit card information to gain access. Other times these "evil twins" offer free Internet access and the hackers just monitor traffic looking for sensitive information they can use.

So how can you protect yourself? Check with authorized personnel at places where you will be connecting to hotspots to determine the names of the legitimate hotspots. And if you run across "free" access to a hotspot that isn't provided by a legitimate merchant, you are better off not connecting at all because you can't be sure your information won't be used against you.

computer network. The type of authentication most people are familiar with is providing a password. However, authentication can also be achieved through the use of biometric devices (discussed later in this chapter) and through **possessed objects**. A possessed object is any object that a user carries to identify himself and that grants him access to a computer system or computer facility. Examples include identification badges, magnetic key cards, and smart keys (similar to flash drives).

How do most colleges handle authentication on their networks? As mentioned earlier, to gain access to a typical college client/server network, you have to enter a user ID and a password. This is a process known as authentication. By correctly inputting your ID and password, you prove to the network who you are and show that you have authorized access (because the ID was generated by the network administrator when you became a student).

Can hackers use my account to log on to the network? If a hacker knows your user ID and password, he or she can log on and impersonate you. Sometimes network user IDs are easy to figure out because they have a certain pattern (such as your last name and first initial of your first name). Because of this potential vulnerability, network administrators often configure accounts to disable themselves after several logon attempts with invalid passwords have been tried. This prevents hackers from using brute force attacks to attempt to crack passwords. **Brute force attacks** are delivered by specialized hacking software that attempts to try many combinations of letters, numbers, words, or pieces of your user ID in an attempt to discover your password. If network accounts aren't set to disable themselves after a small number of incorrect passwords is tried, these attacks may eventually succeed.

ACCESS PRIVILEGES

How can I gain access to everything on the college network? The simple answer is you can't! When your account was set up, certain access privileges were granted to indicate which systems you are allowed to use. For example, your access privileges probably include the ability to access the Internet. You also might have access privileges to view your transcript and grades online, depending on the sophistication of your college network. However, you definitely were not granted access to the grade reporting system, which would enable you to change your grades. Likewise, you do not have access to the financial systems; otherwise, you might be able to change your account, indicating that your bill was paid when it had not been.

Because network access accounts are centrally administered on the authentication server, it is easy for the network administrator to set up accounts for new students and grant them access only to the systems and software they need. The centralized nature of the creation of access accounts and the ability to restrict access to certain areas of the client/server network make it more secure than a peer-to-peer network.

PHYSICAL PROTECTION MEASURES

Are any physical measures taken to protect the network? Restricting physical access to servers and other sensitive equipment is critical to protecting the net-

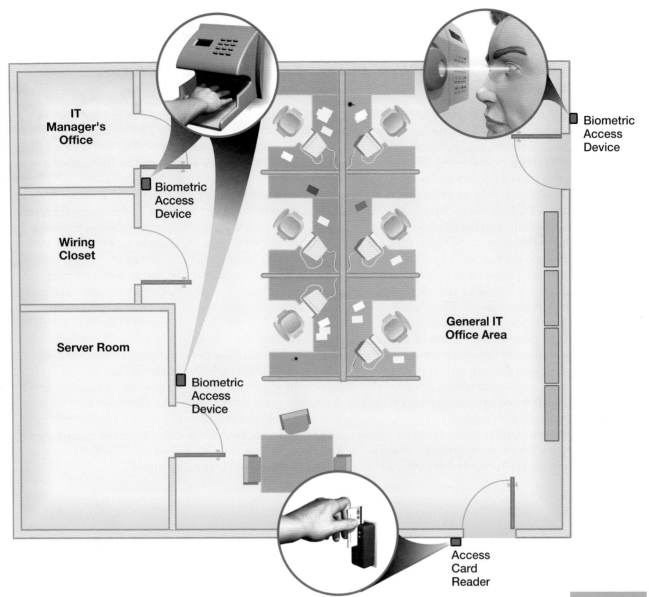

IT Manager's Office

Biometric Access Device

Wiring Closet

Server Room

Biometric Access Device

General IT Office Area

Biometric Access Device

Access Card Reader

FIGURE 22

Access card readers can be used to limit access to semisensitive areas such as the IT office. Higher-security areas, such as the server room, may deserve the additional protection biometric access devices offer.

work. Where are the servers that power your college network? They are most likely behind locked doors to which only authorized personnel have access. Do you see any routers or hubs lying about in computer labs? Of course you don't. These devices are securely tucked away in ceilings, walls, or closets, safe from anyone who might tamper with them in an attempt to sabotage the network or breach its security.

As shown in Figure 22, access to sensitive areas must be controlled. Many different devices can be used to control access. **Access card readers** are relatively cheap devices that read information from a magnetic strip on the back of a credit card-like access card (such as your student ID card). The card reader, which can control the lock on a door, is programmed to admit only authorized

personnel to the area. Card readers are easily programmed by adding authorized ID card numbers, social security numbers, and so on.

Biometric access devices are becoming more popular, although they are still cost prohibitive to many organizations, especially colleges. Biometric devices use some unique characteristic of human biology to identify authorized users. Some devices read fingerprints or palm prints when you place your hand on a scanning pad. Other devices shine a beam of laser light into your eye and read the unique patterns of your retina to identify you. Facial recognition systems store unique characteristics of an individual's face for later comparison and identification. All of these devices are preprogrammed when authorized individuals

Emerging Technologies: Wi-Fi Phones Keep Doctors and Nurses Connected

Have you ever noticed that you can't make cell phone calls when you're in a hospital? Cell phone signals can interfere with sensitive electronic equipment such as heart monitors and IV monitors, rendering them ineffective. Unfortunately, this means doctors and nurses can't communicate quickly with cell phones in the hospital either. However, using a Wi-Fi network, they can.

A number of U.S. hospitals, such as Mission Community Hospital in Panorama City, California, are providing their nurses and doctors with SpectralLink's NetLink Wi-Fi-enabled cell phones that enable communications over the hospital's wireless network (instead of by conventional cell phone signals). These phones cause no interference with medical equipment, and, unlike conventional cell phones, the phones offer a special feature that allows users to broadcast a message to multiple phones throughout the hospital. This is especially useful for emergency situations (like a "code blue" cardiac arrest alert) when various personnel must be gathered quickly to deal with a crisis.

How does this all work? Unlike traditional cell phone calls that flow through a telephone company's switching or microwave system, Wi-Fi-enabled cell phones route calls through the Internet either to land lines or out to other cell phones (see Figure 23), avoiding the interference associated with traditional cell phone calls. In addition, the NetLink system can be integrated with conventional phone systems.

Any business or college with a physical campus could potentially benefit from the connectivity achieved by such a network. And with concerns about responding to emergencies growing since 9/11, being able to alert an entire organization at once by pushing a button and talking makes this type of network communications very attractive. And especially with sensitive medical data, appropriate security measures need to be implemented on the wireless network. There is a need to prevent hackers from cruising around the hospital, connecting to wireless networks, and then scanning them for medical and billing information. And in addition to the expense of beefing up wireless security, this does require all participants in the network to have a Wi-Fi-enabled phone. Time will tell whether more organizations decide that it is worth the cost of equipping key personnel (such as security guards) when the time comes to replace their existing phones.

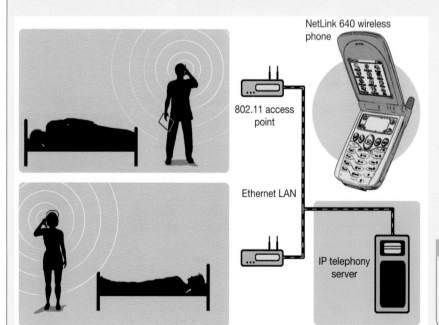

NetLink 640 wireless phone

802.11 access point

Ethernet LAN

IP telephony server

FIGURE 23

Keeping connected, especially in emergencies, is safe and easy when doctors and nurses can use special Wi-Fi-enabled cell phones to communicate.

use them for the first time and then their fingerprints, face patterns, or retinal patterns are scanned and stored in a database.

Financial institutions and retail stores are considering using such devices to attempt to eliminate the growing fraud problem from theft and counterfeiting of credit and debit cards. If fingerprint authorization were required at Wal-Mart to make a purchase, a thief who stole your wallet and attempted to use your credit card would be unsuccessful.

Biometric devices currently on the market, however, don't always function as intended. Facial recognition and retinal systems can sometimes be fooled using pictures or videos of an authorized user. Fingerprint readers have been fooled by researchers using fingers made out of Play-Doh, using the fingers of cadavers, or by having unauthorized persons breathing on the sensor, which makes the previous user's fingerprint visible (fingers leave an oily residue behind when they touch a surface). Research institutions, such as Clarkson University, are designing next-generation fingerprint readers that are much more difficult to fool. These will use specially designed algorithms that will detect moisture patterns on a person's fingers. Another approach may involve readers that will detect an electrical current when a finger touches the reader, which is possible because the human body conducts electrical current. Future retinal readers will check to see whether the person blinks or if a person's eyes contract when a bright light is shone on them. Suffice it to say, these devices have a ways to go before they are foolproof.

FIREWALLS

Is the college Internet connection vulnerable to hackers? Just like a home network, when a college network is connected to the Internet, this creates an attractive nuisance. A college network will most likely have a high-bandwidth connection to the Internet that will attract hackers. A well-defended college network, just like a home network, includes a firewall. Firewalls can be composed of software or hardware, and many sophisticated firewalls include both. Routers are often equipped to act as hardware firewalls.

Does the firewall on my college network work the same way as a personal firewall installed on a home network? Although the firewall at your school

may contain a few extra security options, making it even harder to breach than a personal firewall, the school's firewall works on the same basic principles as a home network. At a minimum, most firewalls work as packet screeners. **Packet screening** involves examining incoming data packets to ensure they originated from or are authorized by valid users on

BITS AND BYTES

Building a Business-Class Firewall for Free!

Corporate networks, such as the one shown in Figure 24, have very sophisticated firewalls designed to keep even the most persistent intruders at bay. Most home networks probably don't need this level of protection (the firewall included with Windows Vista is probably sufficient for most users), but malware (software that carries out malicious activities on a computer) and hacker attacks are becoming more prevalent every day. Wouldn't it be nice to beef up your protection at your home office without spending a fortune?

If you're upgrading your current computer, why not use your old computer (or another old computer you may already have lying around) as a bastion host (a heavily secured server). Even old computers can run the Linux operating system very adequately. Once Linux is installed, download Linux firewall software such as Firestarter (**www.fs-security.com**), which is available at no charge. Step-by-step configuration instructions make it relatively easy to install. You'll have high-level protection for your home network (or small business) in no time!

Firestarter is Copyrighted © 1998–2004 by Tomas Junnonen

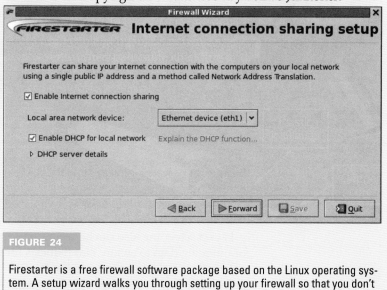

FIGURE 24

Firestarter is a free firewall software package based on the Linux operating system. A setup wizard walks you through setting up your firewall so that you don't need to be familiar with Linux.

Computers in Society: California Maintains a Reliable Network to Respond to Earthquake Emergencies

Californians often worry about earthquakes and when "the big one" will strike. We all hope that another major earthquake, like the 9.0 boomer that hit the Indian Ocean in 2004, will never take place. However, given the fault lines that run under California, most seismologists agree that another large earthquake is inevitable. Getting emergency response crews where they are most needed after an earthquake can have a critical impact on saving lives.

Many separate agencies and monitoring stations have been recording information on earthquakes for decades, but efforts to coordinate data collection and analysis were lacking. In 2002, the California Integrated Seismic Network (CISN) was formed. The founding partners include the California Geological Survey, the Seismological Laboratory of Caltech, U.S. Geological Survey (USGS) sites at Menlo Park and Pasadena, and the Berkeley Seismological Laboratory. CISN's mission is to maintain a statewide network of computers to supply scientists and emergency response teams with up-to-date quake information, even if the Internet goes down. The USGS hosts the main server, but various backup servers are maintained at different locations in case a quake or other natural disaster disables the main server.

Within minutes of an earthquake (greater than magnitude 3.5), CISN generates a ShakeMap (see Figure 25). Through color coding, these maps show the areas most affected by the quake. Emergency response teams, state and local police, and the National Guard can use the ShakeMaps to determine how to deploy labor and resources to assist victims of a quake.

In addition to ShakeMaps, CISN maintains an archive of seismological data and ground motion records for all earthquakes recorded in California. This data is available through the Internet to scientists and the general public for the purpose of conducting further research into the causes and behaviors of earthquakes.

Computer networks and the Internet make achieving the CISN's mission possible. Without a robust network, it would be impossible to accumulate and disseminate quickly the data needed to respond to these natural disasters.

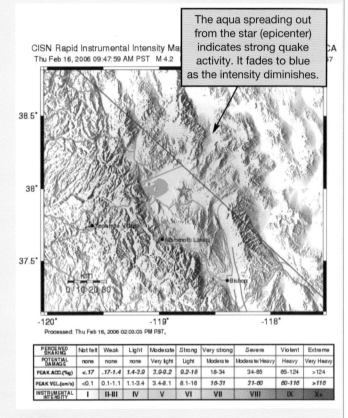

The aqua spreading out from the star (epicenter) indicates strong quake activity. It fades to blue as the intensity diminishes.

FIGURE 25

This color-coded ShakeMap was generated by the California Integrated Seismic Network (CISN).

the internal network. The router is the device that performs the packet screening. Unauthorized or suspect packets are discarded by the firewall before reaching the network.

Packet screening also can be configured for outgoing data to ensure that requests for information to the Internet are from legitimate users. This helps detect Trojan horse programs that may have been installed by hackers. Trojan horses masquerade as harmless programs but have a more sinister pur-

pose. They often try to disguise where they are sending data from by using bogus IP addresses on the packets the programs send instead of an authorized IP address belonging to the network.

If packet screening is working, packets going in and out of the network are checked to ensure they are either from or addressed to a legitimate IP address on the network. If the addresses are not valid addresses for the network, the firewall discards them.

What other security measures does the firewall on a client/server network use? To increase security even further, most large networks add a **bastion host**—a heavily secured server located on a special perimeter network between the company's secure internal network and the firewall. A bastion host gets its name from the fortified towers (called bastions), located along the outer walls of medieval castles, which were specifically designed to defend the castles against attackers.

To external computers, the bastion host gives the appearance of being the internal network server. Hackers can waste a lot of time and energy attacking the bastion host. However, even if a hacker breaches the bastion host server, the internal network is not vulnerable because the bastion host is not on the internal network. And during the time the hackers spend trying to penetrate the bastion host, network administrators can detect and thwart their attacks.

Bastion hosts are often configured as **proxy servers.** A proxy server acts as a go-between for computers on the internal network and the external network (the Internet). All requests from the internal network for Internet services are directed through the proxy server. Similarly, all incoming requests from the Internet must pass through the proxy server. It is much easier for network administrators to maintain adequate security on one server than it is to ensure that security is maintained on hundreds or thousands of computers in a college network. Figure 26 shows a network secured by a firewall, a bastion host, and a screening router.

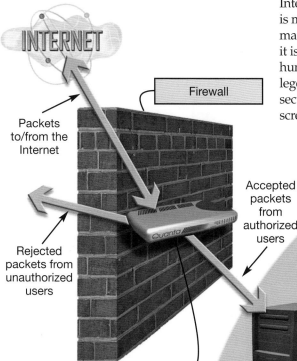

Packets to/from the Internet

Rejected packets from unauthorized users

Firewall

Accepted packets from authorized users

External screening router
External screening routers examine all incoming and outgoing packets to/from the Internet. Only packets to/from authorized internal users are permitted into the perimeter network. Packets from unauthorized users are rejected.

Perimeter Network

Authorized requests for Internet services

Valid Internet services

Secure Internal Network

Bastion host & proxy server
The bastion host/proxy server acts as the single point of contact for all incoming and outgoing Internet traffic. Even if this server is breached, because it is not located on the internal network, the computers on the internal network are still secure.

Internal screening router
Internal screening routers can be set to only allow certain types of Internet services (such as e-mail and Web browsing) and to reject all other requests.

Computer #1

Computer #2

FIGURE 26

This illustration shows a typical college network firewall layout. Although it may seem complicated, such protection measures are necessary to keep hackers at bay.

1. What are the advantages of a business network?

A network enables employees to communicate with each other more easily even over large distances. Networks also enable expensive resources, such as printers, to be shared, saving the cost of providing these resources to individual employees. Software can be deployed from a network server, thereby reducing the costs of installation on each user's computer. And networks enable employees to share an Internet connection, avoiding the cost of providing each employee with a dedicated Internet connection.

2. How does a client/server network differ from a peer-to-peer network?

A client/server network requires that at least one server be attached to the network. The server coordinates functions such as data transmission and printing. In a peer-to-peer network, each node connected to the network can communicate directly with every other node on the network, instead of having a separate device exercise control over the network. Data flows more efficiently in client/server networks than in peer-to-peer networks. In addition, client/server networks have increased scalability, meaning users can be added to the network easily.

3. What are the different classifications of client/server networks?

Local area networks (LANs) are small groups of computers (as few as two) and peripherals linked together over a small geographic area. A group of computers on the floor of the office where you work is most likely a LAN. Wide area networks (WANs) are comprised of large numbers of users or of separate LANs that are miles apart and linked together. Corporations often use WANs to connect two or more branches (such as an office in California and one in Ohio). Sometimes government organizations or civic groups establish WANs to link users in a specific geo-graphic area (such as within a city or county). These special WANs are known as metropolitan area networks (MANs).

4. What components are needed to construct a client/server network?

Client/server networks have many of the same components of peer-to-peer networks as well as some components specific to client/server networks, including servers, a network topology, transmission media, network operating system (NOS) software, network adapters, and network navigation devices.

5. What do the various types of servers do?

Dedicated servers are used on large networks to increase efficiency. Authentication servers control access to the network and ensure that only authorized users can log on. File servers provide storage and management of user files. Print servers manage and control all printing jobs initiated on a network. Application servers provide access to application software (such as Microsoft Office). Database servers store database files and provide access to users who need the information in the databases. E-mail servers control all incoming and outgoing e-mail traffic. Communications servers are used to control the flow of information from the internal network to outside networks (such as the Internet). Web servers are used to host a Web site.

6. What are the various network topologies (layouts), and why is network topology important in planning a network?

In a bus topology, all nodes are connected to a single linear cable. Ring topologies are comprised of nodes arranged roughly in a circle in which the data flows from node to node in a specific order. In a star topology, nodes are connected to a central communication device (a switch) and branch out like points of a star. A hybrid topology is a blending of other types of topologies in one network. Each topology has its own advantages and disadvantages. Topology selection depends mainly on two factors: (1) the network budget and (2) the specific needs of network users (speed, fair allocation of resources, and so on).

7. What types of transmission media are used in client/server networks?

In addition to wireless media, three main cable types are used: twisted pair cable, coaxial cable, and fiber-optic cable. Twisted pair cable consists of four pairs of wires twisted around each other to reduce interference. Coaxial cable is the same type of cable used by your cable TV company to run a signal into your house. It provides better shielding from interference than twisted pair cable but is more expensive. Fiber-optic cable uses glass or plastic bundles of fiber to send signals using light waves. It provides the largest bandwidth, but is expensive and difficult to install. Wireless media utilizes radio waves to send data between nodes on a network.

8. What software needs to be running on computers attached to a client/server network, and how does this software control network communications?

Network operating system (NOS) software needs to be installed on each computer and server connected to a client/server network to provide the services necessary for the devices to communicate. The NOS provides a set of common rules (called a protocol) that controls communication between devices on the network.

9. How do network adapters enable computers to participate in a client/server network?

Network adapters provide three critical functions: (1) They take low-power data signals generated by the computer and convert them into higher-powered signals that can traverse network media easily. (2) They break the data generated by the computer into packets and package them for transmission across the network media. (3) They act as gatekeepers to control the flow of data to and from the computer. Without a network adapter, a computer could not communicate on a network.

10. What devices assist in moving data around a client/server network?

Repeaters are used to amplify signals on a network ensuring that signals are received even at the end of a long cable run. Hubs receive and retransmit signals to all devices attached to them. Switches are "smart" hubs in that they can read the address of data packets and retransmit a signal to its destination instead of to every device connected to the switch. Routers are used to route data between two different networks such as between a corporate network and the Internet.

11. What measures are employed to keep large networks secure?

Access to most networks requires authentication procedures (such as entering a user ID and password) to ensure that only authorized users access the network. The system administrator defines access privileges for users so that they can access only specific files. Network equipment is physically secured behind locked doors, which are often protected by biometric access devices. Biometric devices, such as fingerprint and palm readers, use unique physical characteristics of individuals for identification purposes. Firewalls are also employed to keep hackers from attacking networks through Internet connections. Packet screeners review traffic going to and from the network to ascertain whether it was generated by a legitimate user.

Key Terms

802.11 standard (Wi-Fi)
access card reader
access method
active topology
application server
authentication
authentication server
bandwidth
bastion host
biometric access device
bridge
brute force attack
bus (linear bus) topology
centralized
client
client/server network (server-based
   network)
coaxial cable
communications server
CSMA/CD
data collision
data transfer rate
database server
decentralized
dedicated server
device driver
e-mail server
fiber-optic cable
file server
frames
hubs
hybrid topology
intranet
jam signal
local area network (LAN)
Media Access Control (MAC) address
metropolitan area network (MAN)
network

network adapter
network administrator
network attached storage (NAS)
   device
network operating system (NOS)
network topology
packet
packet screening
passive topology
personal area network (PAN)
possessed object
print server
protocol
proxy server
radio frequency identification tag
   (RFID tag)
repeater
ring (loop) topology
router
scalable network
server
shielded twisted pair (STP) cable
star topology
storage area network (SAN)
switch
terminator
throughput
token
token method
token-ring topology
transmission media
twisted pair cable
unshielded twisted pair (UTP) cable
Web server
wide area network (WAN)
wireless access point
wireless media
wireless network interface card
   (wireless NIC)

Buzz Words

Word Bank

- application server
- bastion host
- bridges
- bus
- database server
- fiber-optic
- LAN
- network administrator
- packet screener
- packets
- repeaters
- routers
- scalable
- star
- switches
- twisted pair
- WAN
- wireless access points

Instructions: Fill in the blanks using the words from the Word Bank.

As a(n) (1) _____ , Susan's first task was to configure her company's new network. Because the company had branch offices in three different states, she knew it would be necessary to configure the network as a(n) (2) _____ . However, to handle all the wireless devices the sales representatives carried, (3) _____ would need to be installed throughout the building. Software would need to be shared among 50 employees, so a robust (4) _____ would be a necessity. And because the company was experiencing rapid growth, the network would have to be highly (5) _____ , which would require the selection of a(n) (6) _____ topology as opposed to a(n) (7) _____ topology, which would only work for a small network.

Powerful electrical fields on the factory floor would make using (8) _____ cabling an absolute necessity in the manufacturing plant, whereas (9) _____ cabling would be sufficient for the office areas. Because the company had experienced hacking on its old network, Susan insisted that a(n) (10) _____ be installed to further bolster the network defenses by filtering unauthorized transmissions of data. Combined with a(n) (11) _____ installed as part of the perimeter network, she felt they would be adequately protected from wily hackers.

(12) _____ would be necessary to shift data (13) _____ between collision domains on the network. For the farthest reaches of the building, (14) _____ would need to be installed to amplify the network data signals. If a star topology was to be used, several (15) _____ would need to be deployed to handle all 50 network users.

Becoming Computer Literate

Chemco Brothers, Inc., a manufacturer of specialty chemicals, has decided that to increase the accuracy of its production records, the network used for management and clerical workers should extend onto the manufacturing floor. Although most employees do not travel more than a few feet from their main work areas during their shift, the three supervisors roam the entire plant and need access to computers wherever they go.

Instructions: Draft a memo (with supporting diagrams, if necessary) detailing how to deploy 15 computers (12 for workers, 3 for supervisors) in the factory areas. Justify the network topology you select, explain your choice of transmission media, and indicate the device(s) needed to connect the computers to the existing network.

Self-Test

Instructions: Answer the multiple-choice and true/false questions below for more practice with key terms and concepts from this chapter.

MULTIPLE CHOICE

1. Which of the following is NOT an advantage of installing a network in a business?
a. Decreased productivity
b. Facilitation of Internet connectivity
c. Sharing of peripherals
d. Reduced cost to buy peripherals

2. Why are client/server networks often installed in businesses instead of peer-to-peer networks?
a. Cheaper to install.
b. Eliminate the need for dedicated servers.
c. Less scalable than peer-to-peer networks.
d. Security is much easier to implement.

3. If a city deploys a network to assist in monitoring traffic flow or to provide wireless access to visitors, this network would be classified as a
a. WAN.   c. PAN.
b. MAN.   d. LAN.

4. Which of the following is necessary in all client/server networks?
a. Router
b. Authentication server
c. Transmission media
d. E-mail server

5. To efficiently manage software distributed to employees at their client computers, a corporate network would include which server?
a. Internet   c. Communications
b. E-mail   d. Application

6. Which type of network topology is most commonly used today?
a. Ring   c. Star
b. Ethernet   d. Linear

7. Twisted pair cable most likely would be used in a corporate network when
a. Cost is more important than speed.
b. Electrical or magnetic interference is present.
c. Very long cable runs are required.
d. Speed is more important than cost.

8. NOS software is
a. not absolutely essential for running a client/server network.
b. needed only on the servers in a client/server network.
c. needed on all computers in a client/server network.
d. needed only when configuring a network in a ring topology.

9. Network adapters are
a. necessary to connect computers to any type of network.
b. only needed for connecting computers wirelessly to networks.
c. only used in peer-to-peer networks.
d. necessary only in networks using the star topology.

10. Providing adequate security on a corporate network involves all of these issues except
a. limiting network access by requiring passwords.
b. authentication.
c. proprietary software lockout.
d. restricting access to servers.

TRUE/FALSE

____ 1. Bridges are used to route data between two or more network collision domains.

____ 2. Two different types of network operating software cannot be deployed on the same network.

____ 3. Twisted pair cable is less susceptible to interference than fiber-optic cable.

____ 4. Client/server networks are easier to administer than peer-to-peer networks.

____ 5. An authentication server is used to control access to a client/server network.

Making the Transition to...
Next Semester

1. Internet Usage Policy

Schools face many potential liability issues when they connect students to the Internet. Your school most likely has a written policy (perhaps posted on the school's Web site) on appropriate usage of the network and the Internet by students. Other issues that network usage policies typically address include guidelines on student file storage, antivirus protection, and backups. Obtain a copy of your school's policy (or speak with the appropriate IT personnel) and answer the following questions:

a. What types of sites are students not permitted to access?
b. Are there restrictions in effect on usage of peer-to-peer file-sharing sites? What are those restrictions?
c. How much storage space is provided for student files (if any)?
d. How often are student files backed up (if ever)? Are these incremental backups (only new files or files that have changed are backed up) or full backups (all files are backed up)?
e. Are files deleted after each semester?
f. Are students prohibited from commenting about the school and professors on blogs, wikis, or other Web sites? If so, how do you feel about that?

2. Wireless Connections at School

Wireless networks are growing in popularity as more and more students are bringing notebooks and other portable devices onto campus. Investigate the following:

a. Does your school offer wireless connectivity to students? If so, what areas of the campus are currently covered by wireless access?
b. What technologies are being deployed for connectivity (802.11b, 802.11g, or 802.11n)? If 802.11b currently is deployed, is there a plan to upgrade to a faster standard in the future?
c. Is access to the wireless network restricted (i.e., is authentication required to log on)? If not, is this under consideration to prevent poaching of bandwidth by neighbors and visitors?

3. Internet Security Measures at School

Visit your IT services department and investigate the current security measures in place for the following:

1. **Firewall protection of the Internet connection.** What hardware/software is installed? Have there been any recent hacking attempts? If so, were they successful?
2. **Antivirus protection.** Is antivirus software installed on all computers deployed on campus? If so, what package is being used, and how often is it updated? What measures (if any) are in place to prevent users who bring their own computers onto campus (such as notebooks connected wirelessly) and connect to the network from infecting the network with a virus? Are products (other than antivirus software) installed to detect and prevent the installation of other malware products, such as adware and spyware?

Making the Transition to... the Workplace

1. Security Issues at Work

You have been interning in the IT department of an insurance company, and you have applied for a full-time job at the company. One morning, you come to work and are told to clean out your desk and that your internship is ended effective immediately and that you will not be considered for a full-time position. Your boss explained that the human resources director was checking your references when she located your profile on MySpace.com. She noted that you had made derogatory comments about certain company personnel and that you described your current work assignments as boring. Although this was not covered by the computer usage policy at your workplace, company management feels you are disgruntled.

a. Using the Internet, research employment laws in your state. Can you be fired for what you wrote on your MySpace page? Do you have any legal recourse against the company?

b. Would the company be more justified in firing you if you had been warned (in the company's computer usage policy) that the types of activities for which you were fired were not permitted? Would the company be in a better legal position had it included these infractions in its written policies?

2. Client/Server Networks

The owner of the company for which you work announces that the company will be hiring another 25 workers over the next six months. Currently, your peer-to-peer network is adequately handling the needs of the 10 employees who now work at the company. However, you know that adding 25 more employees to the network would overload it.

a. Write a memo explaining why a switch to a client/server network would be appropriate. Be sure to explain which topology you think would be best to install.

b. In the memo, estimate the costs of constructing a 35-person client/server network, including the costs of one server, cabling, workstations for the 25 new employees, and switches. Use resources such as **www.dell.com** and **www.compaq.com** for designing and pricing network components.

3. Antivirus Solutions at Work

Recently, the company you work for had its network brought to a halt by an employee who inadvertently infected the server after opening an e-mail attachment containing a worm. Your boss has charged you with the task of locating a cost-effective antivirus solution to protect the corporate network. Complete the following tasks:

a. Compare the costs of installing antivirus products from the two industry leaders, McAfee (**www.mcafee.com**) and Norton (**www.symantec.com**), on each of the 20 computers and the one server in your corporate network.

b. Write a draft memo to employees explaining the types of e-mail messages and attachments they should avoid opening and passing on to others. Make sure to include warnings about phishing, attachments containing viruses, and hoaxes.

Critical Thinking Questions

Instructions: Albert Einstein used "Gedanken experiments," or critical thinking questions, to develop his theory of relativity. Some ideas are best understood by experimenting with them in our own minds. The following critical thinking questions are designed to demand your full attention but require only a comfortable chair—no technology.

1. **Internet Risks at School**

   Internet access is deemed essential to enable students to research projects and papers adequately. But granted that access potentially invites people to engage in dangerous or unacceptable behaviors.

   a. Do you think your school should restrict access to certain Internet sites (such as peer-to-peer file-sharing services) to prevent students from violating laws by illegally sharing copyrighted material?

   b. Plagiarism is thought to be spreading because of the easy exchange of information on the Internet. What should the penalty be for a student who plagiarizes material from a Web site and why? Should a student who plagiarizes have his or her Internet access privileges revoked? Why or why not?

   c. Should schools prohibit students from writing negative comments about faculty and administrators on their blogs and MySpace pages? Why or why not?

2. **Ethical Hackers?**

   Some hackers argue that hacking should not be a crime because they are performing a service to the companies that they are hacking by pointing out weaknesses in network security.

   a. Should hackers be punished for gaining unapproved access to computer systems?

   b. Are there any instances in which hacking is a "necessary evil" and the law enforcement officials should just look the other way?

   c. Is it unethical for software companies not to share with users known security risks in their software?

3. **Acceptable Use Internet Policies**

   Many companies are drafting acceptable use policies for computers and Internet access to inform employees of the approved uses for corporate computing assets. Consider these areas of a potential company policy:

   a. Should employees be allowed to use their computers and Internet access for personal use (such as checking noncompany e-mail, shopping online, or playing games)? If so, how much time per day is reasonable for employees to spend on personal tasks? Should employees be permitted to use their computers for personal tasks only during personal time (such as breaks and lunch hours)?

   b. Should employee computer and Internet usage be monitored to ensure compliance with the personal use policies? Should employers inform employees that they are being monitored? What should the penalties be for violating these policies? Should your productivity (and pay raises) be determined based on what activities you perform during the day as monitored by the company (via computers, cameras, tracking devices, etc.)?

   c. Many corporations block access to Internet Web sites that would enable employees to participate in potentially illegal activities (such as downloading music, gambling, or viewing pornography). Should corporations have the right to block users from Web sites when they are at work? Why or why not?

4. **Network Layout Designs**

   Assume you are designing the network layout for a potato chip company. Which employees would you suggest be provided with notebook computers? In which areas of the main office would you provide wireless network access? What level of access would be needed on the manufacturing floor? Would special durable equipment (like Panasonic Toughbook computers) be needed in the factory? Would you provide all employees with Internet access? If not, whom would you exclude?

Problem:

As wireless devices become more prevalent, increased demands for wireless access will be placed on networks. Although many schools already deploy adequate wireless access, there is room for improvement of coverage in numerous areas.

Task:

The network manager at your school has requested that you assist in developing a plan for deploying/expanding wireless coverage for the campus. Your group has been selected to assist with the research. Before presenting your findings to the network manager, your group needs to fine-tune its recommendations.

Process:

Divide the class into small teams.

1. Explore the areas of your campus where students congregate to socialize or engage in research. Determine if these areas are covered by wireless Internet access (this may require interviewing your school's network manager). For areas of the school that are covered by wireless technology (such as the library), test the signal strength of the connection by attempting to connect to the Internet in various locations.

2. Present your findings to your class. Lead a discussion with the other students and solicit feedback as to their experiences with wireless connectivity on the campus. In which other areas of the campus do you feel wireless technology should be deployed?

3. Prepare a report for the network manager that includes your suggestions for improvements/upgrades to the wireless network on your campus. If possible, address options for wireless connectivity when students are off campus for field trips, seminars, and so on.

Conclusion:

Being tied down to a wired computer terminal just doesn't cut it in the 21st century. Although wireless technology can be difficult and expensive to deploy in some instances, today's students will continue to demand the portable connections that they need to function effectively. Some day, your children may visit the Smithsonian Institution to view wired computers and see what hardships Mom and Dad had to endure in the "good old days."

Multimedia

In addition to the review materials presented here, you'll find additional materials featured with the book's multimedia, including the Technology in Action Student Resource CD and the Companion Web Site **www.prenhall.com/techinaction**), which will help reinforce your understanding of the chapter content. These materials include the following:

ACTIVE HELPDESK

In Active Helpdesk calls, you'll assume the role of a Helpdesk operator taking calls about the concepts you've learned in this chapter. You'll apply what you've learned and receive feedback from a supervisor to review and reinforce those concepts. The Active Helpdesk calls for this chapter are listed here and can be found on your Student Resource CD:

- Using Servers
- Selecting a Network Topology and Cable
- Selecting Network Navigation Devices

SOUND BYTES

Sound Bytes are dynamic multimedia tutorials that help demystify even the most complex topics. You'll view video clips and animations that illustrate computer concepts, and then apply what you've learned by reviewing with the Sound Byte Labs, which include quizzes and activities specifically tailored to each Sound Byte. The Sound Bytes for this chapter are listed here and can be found on your Student Resource CD:

- Network Topology and Navigation Devices
- What's My IP Address? (and Other Interesting Facts about Networks)
- A Day in the Life of a Network Technician

COMPANION WEB SITE

The Technology in Action Companion Web Site includes a variety of additional materials to help you review and learn more about the topics in this chapter. The resources available at **www.prenhall.com/techinaction** include:

- **Online Study Guide.** Each chapter features an online true/false and multiple-choice quiz. You can take these quizzes, automatically check the results, and e-mail the results to your instructor.
- **Web Research Projects.** Each chapter features a number of Web research projects that ask you to search the Web for information on computer-related careers, milestones in computer history, important people and companies, emerging technologies, and the applications and implications of different technologies.

Glossary

3D sound cards An expansion card that enables a computer to produce sounds that are omnidirectional or three-dimensional.

802.11 standard A wireless standard established in 1997 by the Institute of Electrical and Electronics Engineers; also known as Wi-Fi (short for Wireless Fidelity), it enables wireless network devices to work seamlessly with other networks and devices.

A

academic fair use A provision that gives teachers and students special consideration regarding copyright violations. As long as the material is being used for educational purposes, limited copying and distribution are allowed.

Accelerated Graphics Port (AGP) bus The AGP bus design was designed to help move three-dimensional graphics data quickly. It establishes a direct pathway between the graphics card and main memory so that data does not have to travel on the Peripheral Component Interconnect (PCI) bus, which already handles transferring a great deal of system data being moved through the computer.

access card reader A device that reads information from a magnetic strip on the back of a credit card-like access card (such as a student ID card); card readers are easily programmed by adding authorized ID card numbers, social security numbers, and so on.

access method A program or hardware mechanism that controls which computer is allowed to use the transmission media in a network at a certain time.

access time The time it takes a storage device to locate its stored data.

accounting software An application program that helps business owners manage their finances more efficiently by providing tools for tracking accounting transactions such as sales, accounts receivable, inventory purchases, and accounts payable.

active-matrix displays With an LCD monitor using active-matrix technology, each pixel is charged individually, as needed. The result is that an active-matrix display produces a clearer, brighter image than a passive-matrix display.

Active Server Pages (ASP) A scripting environment in which users combine HyperText Markup Language (HTML), scripts and reusable Microsoft ActiveX server components to create dynamically generated Web pages.

active topology A network topology in which each node on the network is responsible for retransmitting the token, or the data, to other nodes.

Adobe Flash A software product from Adobe for developing Web-based multimedia.

adware Programs that download on your computer when you install a freeware program, game, or utility. Generally, adware enables sponsored advertisements to appear in a section of your browser window or as a pop-up ad box.

affective computing Computing that relates to emotion or deliberately tries to influence emotion.

aggregator Software programs that go out and grab the latest update of Web material (usually podcasts) according to your specifications.

algorithm A set of specific, sequential steps that describe in natural language exactly what a computer program must do to complete its task.

alphabetic check Confirms that only textual characters are entered in a database field.

Alt key One of the keys on a standard PC computer keyboard used in conjunction with other keys for shortcuts and special tasks.

American Standard Code for Information Interchange (ASCII) A format for representing each letter or character as an 8-bit (or 1-byte) binary code.

analog-to-digital converter chip Converts analog signals into digital signals.

antivirus software Software that is specifically designed to detect viruses and protect a computer and files from harm.

APIs *See application programming interfaces (APIs)*

applet A small program designed to be run from within another application. Java applets are often run on your computer by your browser through the Java Virtual Machine (an application built into current browsers).

application programming interfaces (APIs) Blocks of code in the operating system that software applications need to interact with.

application server A server that acts as a repository for application software.

application software The set of programs on a computer that helps a user carry out tasks such as word processing, sending e-mail, balancing a budget, creating presentations, editing photos, taking an online course, and playing games.

arithmetic logic unit (ALU) Part of the central processing unit (CPU) that is designed to perform mathematical operations, such as addition, subtraction, multiplication, and division, and comparison operations, such as greater than, less than, and equal to.

artificial intelligence (AI) The science that attempts to produce computers that display the same type of reasoning and intelligence that humans do.

ASCII *See American Standard Code for Information Interchange (ASCII)*

ASP *See Active Server Pages (ASP)*

assembly languages Languages that enable programmers to write their programs using a set of short, English-like commands that speak directly to the central processing unit (CPU) and give the programmer very direct control of hardware resources.

audio editing software Tools that perform basic editing tasks on audio files, such as cutting dead-air space from the beginning or end of the song or cutting a portion from the middle.

authentication The process of identifying a computer user, based on a login or username and password. The computer system determines whether the computer user is authorized and what level of access is to be granted on the network.

authentication servers Servers that keep track of who is logging on to the network and which services on the network are available to each user.

B

backdoor program A program that enables a hacker to take complete control of a computer without the legitimate user's knowledge or permission.

backup utility A software application that creates a duplicate copy of selected data on the hard disk and copies it to another storage device.

back up To create a duplicate copy of all the data on the hard disk (or other data storage device) and copy it to another storage device, such as a CD or external hard drive.

bandwidth (or data transfer rate) The maximum speed at which data can be transmitted between two nodes on a network, usually measured in megabits per second (Mbps).

base class The original object class from which other classes are derived.

base 2 number system (or binary system) A number system that uses only two digits, 0 and 1, to represent any value. Also called the binary number system.

base 10 number system (or decimal notation) A number system that uses 10 digits, 0 through 9, to represent any value.

base transceiver station A large communications tower with antennas, amplifiers, and receivers/transmitters.

basic input/output system (BIOS) A program that manages the data between the operating system and all the input and output devices attached to the computer system. BIOS is also responsible for loading the operating system (OS) from its permanent location on the hard drive to random access memory (RAM).

bastion host A heavily secured server located on a special perimeter network between the company's secure internal network and the firewall.

batch processing Accumulating transaction data until a certain point is reached, then processing those transactions all at once.

benchmarking A process used to measure performance in which two devices or systems run the same task and the times are compared.

beta versions Early versions of software programs that are still under development. Beta versions are usually provided free of charge in return for user feedback.

binary decisions Decision points that can be answered in one of only two ways: yes (true) or no (false).

binary digit (or bit) A digit that corresponds to the on and off states of a computer's switches. A bit contains a value of either 0 or 1.

binary language The language computers use to process information, consisting of only the values 0 and 1.

binary large object (BLOB) In databases, a type of object that holds extremely large chunks of data in binary form, which are usually video clips, pictures, or audio clips.

binary number system The number system used by computers to represent all data. Because it includes only two digits (0 and 1), the binary number system is also referred to as the base 2 number system.

biometric access devices Devices that use some unique characteristic of human biology to identify authorized users.

BIOS *See basic input/output system (BIOS)*

bit depth The number of bits the video card uses to store data about each pixel on the monitor.

black-hat hackers Hackers who use their knowledge to destroy information or for illegal gain.

blog *See Weblog (blog)*

Bluetooth technology A type of wireless technology that uses radio waves to transmit data over short distances.

Blu-ray disc An optical storage device, similar in size and shape to a DVD, that can hold up to 50 GB of data, or 4.5 hours of high-definition video.

Bookmark A feature in some browsers that places a marker of a Web site's Uniform Resource Locator (URL) in an easily retrievable list (called Favorites in Microsoft Internet Explorer).

Boolean operators Words used to refine logical searches. For Internet searches these words—AND, NOT, and OR—describe the relationships between keywords in the search.

boot process (or start-up process) Process for loading the operating system into random access memory (RAM) when the computer is turned on.

boot-sector viruses Viruses that replicate themselves into the master boot record of a floppy or hard drive.

breadcrumb list A list that shows the hierarchy of previously viewed Web pages within the Web site that you are currently visiting. Shown at the top of some Web pages, it provides an aid to Web site navigation.

bridges Network devices that are used to send data between two different local area networks (LANs) or two segments of the same LAN.

brightness A measure of the greatest amount of light showing when the monitor is displaying pure white; measured as candelas per square meter (cd/m2) or nits.

broadband connections High-speed Internet connections, including cable, satellite, and Digital Subscriber Line (DSL).

browsing (1) Viewing database records. (2) "Surfing" the Web.

brute force attacks Attacks delivered by specialized hacking software that try many combinations of letters, numbers, and pieces of a user ID in an attempt to discover a user password.

buddy list A list of contacts set up in an instant messaging program.

bus A group of electrical pathways inside a computer that provide communications between various parts of a computer and the central processing unit (CPU) and main memory.

bus (or linear bus) topology A system of networking connections in which all devices are connected to a central cable called the bus (or backbone).

bus width The number of bits of data that can be transferred along a data pathway at one time.

business-to-business (B2B) E-commerce transactions between businesses.

business-to-consumer (B2C) E-commerce transactions between businesses and consumers.

byte Eight binary digits (or bits).

C

C The predecessor language of C++, developed originally for system programmers by Brian Kernighan and Dennis Ritchie of AT&T Bell Laboratories in 1978. It provides higher-level programming language features (such as if statements and for loops) but still allows programmers to manipulate the system memory and central processing unit (CPU) registers directly.

C++ The successor language to C, developed by Bjarne Stroustrup. It uses all of the same symbols and keywords as C but extends the language with additional keywords, better security, and more support for the reuse of existing code through object-oriented design.

cable Internet connection A data transmission line that transmits data at high speeds along coaxial or fiber-optic cable.

cable modem A device that enables a computer to send data over cable lines. A modem modulates and demodulates the signal into digital data and back again.

cache memory Small blocks of memory located directly on and next to the central processing unit (CPU) chip that act as holding places for recently or frequently used instructions or data that the CPU accesses the most. When these instructions or data are stored in cache memory, the CPU can more quickly retrieve them than if it had to access the instructions or data from random access memory (RAM).

CAD *See computer-aided design (CAD)*

Carrier Sense Multiple Access with Collision Detection (CSMA/CD) A protocol that nodes on a network can use. With CSMA/CD, a node connected to the network listens (that is, has carrier sense) to determine that no other nodes are currently transmitting data signals. If the node doesn't hear any other signals, it assumes it is safe to transmit data. All devices on the network have the same right (that is, they have multiple access) to transmit data when they deem it safe. It is therefore possible for two devices to begin transmitting data signals at the same time. If this happens, the two signals collide. When signals collide, a node on the network alerts the other nodes.

Cat 5E cable A type of UTP cable used in home-wired Ethernet networks.

cathode-ray tube (CRT) A picture tube device in a computer monitor; very similar to the picture tube in a conventional television set. A CRT screen is a grid made up of millions of pixels, or tiny dots. The pixels are illuminated by an electron beam that passes back and forth across the back of

the screen very quickly so that the pixels appear to glow continuously.

CD-R (Compact Disc-Recordable) disc A portable, optical storage device that can be written to once and can be used with either a CD-R drive or a CD-RW drive.

CD-R drive An optical drive that can read and write CD-R media.

CD-ROM disc A portable, read-only optical storage device.

CD-ROM drive A drive for reading compact discs (CDs).

CD-RW (Compact Disc-ReWritable) disc A portable, optical storage device that can be written and rewritten to many times.

CD-RW drive A drive that can both read and write data to CDs.

cellular phones (cell phones) Telephones that operate over a wireless network. Cell phones can also offer Internet access, text messaging, personal information management (PIM) features, and more.

cells Individual boxes formed by the columns and rows in a spreadsheet. Each cell can be uniquely identified according to its column and row position.

central processing unit (CPU) The part of the system unit of a computer that is responsible for data processing (or the "brains" of the computer); it is the largest and most important chip in the computer. It controls all the functions performed by the computer's other components and processes all the commands issued to it by software instructions.

centralized A type of network design in which users are responsible neither for creating their own data backups nor for providing security for their computers; instead, those tasks are handled by a centralized server, software, and a system administrator.

cgi-bin A directory where Common Gateway Interface (CGI) scripts are normally placed.

CGI scripts Computer programs that conform to the Common Gateway Interface (CGI) specification, which provides a method for sending data between end users (using browsers) and Web servers.

circuit switching A method of communication in which a dedicated connection is

formed between two points (such as two people on telephones) and the connection remains active for the duration of the transmission.

classes A collection of descriptive variables and active functions that together define a set of common properties. Actual examples of the class are known as objects.

Classless Inter-Domain Routing (CIDR) An addressing scheme that allows a single IP address to represent several unique IP addresses by adding a network prefix to the end of the last octet.

click-and-brick businesses Traditional stores that have an online presence.

clickstream data Information captured about each click that users make as they navigate a Web site.

client A computer that requests information from a server in a client/server network (such as your computer when you are connected to the Internet).

client-based e-mail E-mail that is dependent on an e-mail account provided by an Internet service provider (ISP) and a client software program, such as Microsoft Outlook or Eudora.

client/server model A way of describing typical network functions. Client computers (your desktop PC) request services, and servers provide (or serve up) those services to the clients.

client/server network A network that consists of client and server computers, in which the clients make requests of the server and the server returns the response.

client-side program A computer program that runs on the client computer and requires no interaction with a Web server.

clock cycle The "ticks," or base time unit, of the system clock. One cycle equals one "tick."

clock speed The steady and constant pace at which a computer goes through machine cycles, measured in hertz (Hz).

coaxial cable A single copper wire surrounded by layers of plastic insulation and sheathing used mainly in cable television and cable Internet service.

code editing The step in which programmers actually type the code into the computer.

coding Translating an algorithm into a programming language.

cold boot Starting a computer from a powered down or off state.

collaboration tools Products that allow you to connect easily with other individuals, often in remote locations, for the purposes of communicating or working together on a project.

command-driven interface The interface between user and computer in which the user enters commands to communicate with the computer system.

comments (or remarks) Plain English notations inserted into program code for documentation. The comments are not ever seen by the compiler.

commerce servers Computers that host software that enables consumers to purchase goods and services over the Web. These servers generally use special security protocols to protect sensitive information (such as credit card numbers) from being intercepted.

Common Gateway Interface (CGI) Provides a methodology by which a browser can request that a program file be executed (or run) instead of just being delivered to the browser.

communications server A server that handles all communications between the network and other networks, including managing Internet connectivity.

compilation The process by which code is converted into machine language, the language the central processing unit (CPU) can understand.

compiler The program that understands both the syntax of the programming language and the exact structure of the central processing unit (CPU) and its machine language. It can "read" the source code and translate the source code directly into machine language.

completeness check Ensures that all database fields defined as "required" have data entered into them.

computed field (or computational field) A numeric field in a database that is filled as the result of a computation.

computer A data processing device that gathers, processes, outputs, and stores data and information.

computer-aided design (CAD) 3D modeling programs used to create automated designs, technical drawings, and model visualizations.

computer fluent Describes a person who understands the capabilities and limitations of computers and knows how to use them to accomplish tasks efficiently.

computer forensics The application of computer systems and techniques to gather potential legal evidence; a law enforcement specialty used to fight high-tech crime.

computer literate Being familiar enough with computers that you understand their capabilities and limitations, and know how to use them.

computer network *See network*

computer protocol A set of rules for accomplishing electronic information exchange. If the Internet is the information superhighway, protocols are the driving rules.

connectionless protocol A protocol that a host computer can use to send data over the network without establishing a direct connection with any specific recipient computer.

connection-oriented protocol A protocol that requires two computers to exchange control packets, which set up the parameters of the data exchange session, before sending packets that contain data.

connectivity port A port that enables the computer (or other device) to be connected to other devices or systems such as networks, modems, and the Internet.

consistency check Comparing the value of data in a database field against established parameters to determine whether the value is reasonable.

consumer-to-consumer (C2C) E-commerce transactions between consumers through online sites such as eBay.com.

contrast ratio A measure of the difference in light intensity between the brightest white and the darkest black colors that a monitor can produce; if the contrast ratio is too low, colors tend to fade when the brightness is adjusted to a high or low setting.

Control (Ctrl) key One of the keys on a PC computer keyboard that is used in combination with other keys to perform shortcuts and special tasks.

control structure The general term used for keywords in a programming language that allow the programmer to control, or redirect, the flow of the program based on a decision.

control unit A component that controls the switches inside the central processing unit (CPU).

convergence The bringing together of a combination of features into one device.

cookies Small text files that some Web sites automatically store on a client computer's hard drive when a user visits the site.

course management software Programs that provide traditional classroom tools such as calendars and grade books over the Internet, as well as areas for students to exchange ideas and information in chat rooms, discussion forums, and using e-mail.

CPU *See central processing unit (CPU)*

CPU usage The percentage of time a central processing unit (CPU) is working.

cradle Connects a personal digital assistant (PDA) to a computer using either a universal serial bus (USB) port or a serial port.

CRT *See cathode-ray tube (CRT)*

CSMA/CD A method of data collision detection in which a node connected to the network listens (that is, has carrier sense) to determine that no other nodes are currently transmitting data signals; short for Carrier Sense Multiple Access with Collision Detection.

cursor The flashing | symbol on a computer monitor that indicates where the next character will be inserted.

cursor control keys The set of special keys on a keyboard, generally marked by arrows, that move the cursor one space at a time, either up, down, left, or right. Other cursor control keys move the cursor up or down one full page or to the beginning or end of a line.

custom installation Installing only those features of a software program that a user wants on the hard drive, thereby saving space on the hard drive.

customer relationship management (CRM) software A business program used for storing sales and client contact information in one central database.

cybercrime Any criminal action perpetrated primarily through the use of a computer.

cybercriminals Individuals who use computers, networks, and the Internet to perpetrate crime.

D

data Numbers, words, pictures, or sounds that represent facts or ideas.

data centralization Having all data in one central location (usually a database). Data centralization helps ensure data integrity by requiring data to be updated only in one place if the data changes.

data collisions When two computers send data at the same time and the sets of data collide somewhere in the media.

data dictionary (or database schema) A file which defines the name, data type, and length of each field in the database.

data inconsistency Differences in data in lists caused when data exists in multiple lists and not all lists are updated when a piece of data changes.

data integrity When data contained in a database is accurate and reliable.

data marts Small slices of a data warehouse.

data mining The process by which great amounts of data are analyzed and investigated to spot significant patterns or trends within the data that would otherwise not be obvious.

data plans Connectivity plans or text messaging plans in which data charges are separate from cell phone calling charges and are provided at rates different from voice calls.

data projectors Devices that are used to project images from a computer onto a wall or viewing screen.

data redundancy When the same data exists in more than one place in a database.

data staging A three-step process: extracting data from source databases, transforming (reformatting) the data, and storing the data in a data warehouse.

data transfer rate The maximum speed at which data can be transmitted between two nodes on a network, usually measured in megabits per second (Mbps).

data type (or field type) Indicates what type of data can be stored in the database field or memory location.

data warehouse A large-scale electronic repository of data that contains and organizes in one place all the data related to an organization.

database Electronic collections of related data that are organized and searchable.

database administrator (or database designer) An individual trained in the design, construction, and maintenance of databases.

database management system (DBMS) Specially designed application software (such as Oracle or Microsoft Access) that interacts with the user, other applications, and the database to capture and analyze data.

database query An inquiry the user poses to the database to extract a meaningful subset of data.

database server A server that provides client computers with access to information stored in a database.

database software An electronic filing system best used for larger and more complicated groups of data that require more than one table, and where it's necessary to group, sort, and retrieve data, and to generate reports.

date fields Fields in a database that hold date data such as birthdays, due dates, and so on.

debugger A tool that helps programmers step through a program as it runs to locate errors.

debugging The process of running the program over and over to find errors and to make sure the program behaves in the way it should.

decentralized A type of network in which users are responsible for creating their own data backups and for providing security for their computers.

decision points Points at which a computer program must choose from a set of different actions based on the value of its current inputs.

decision support system (DSS) A system designed to help managers develop solutions for specific problems.

decode To translate the program's instructions into commands the CPU can understand.

dedicated servers Servers used to fulfill one specific function (such as handling e-mail).

default values The values a database will use for fields unless the user enters another value.

denial of service (DoS) attack An attack that occurs when legitimate users are denied access to a computer system because a hacker is repeatedly making requests of that computer system to tie up its resources and deny legitimate users access.

deployed A computer or another piece of equipment on a network that has been installed is said to have been deployed. Various types of servers are deployed (installed) on the networks that make up an Intranet from which clients can request services.

derived class A class created on the basis of a previously existing class (i.e., base class). Derived classes inherit all of the member variables and methods of the base class from which they are derived.

desktop As its name implies, your computer's desktop puts at your fingertips all of the elements necessary for a productive work session that are typically found on or near the top of a traditional desk, such as files and folders.

desktop box A style of system unit for desktop computers that sits horizontally on top of a desk.

desktop publishing (DTP) software Programs for incorporating and arranging graphics and text to produce creative documents.

detail report A report generated with data from a database that shows the individual transactions that occurred during a certain time period.

device driver Software that facilitates the communication between a device and the operating system.

Device Manager A feature in the operating system that lets individuals view and change the properties of all devices attached to the computer.

dial-up connection A connection to the Internet using a standard telephone line.

dial-up modem A device that converts (modulates) the digital signals the computer understands to the analog signals that can travel over phone lines. In turn, the computer on the other end also must have a modem to translate (demodulate) the received analog signal back to a digital signal that the receiving computer can understand.

digital divide The discrepancy between those who have access to the opportunities and knowledge computers and the Internet offers and those who do not.

digital home A home that has a computer(s) and other digital devices that are all connected to a home network.

digital ink An extension of the text-entry systems used on personal digital assistant (PDA) devices.

digital pen A device for drawing images and entering text in a tablet PC.

digital signal processor A specialized chip that processes digital information and transmits signals very quickly.

Digital Subscriber Line (DSL) A type of connection that uses telephone lines to connect to the Internet and that allows both phone and data transmissons to share the same line.

Digital Subscriber Line (DSL) modem A device that connects the computer data to the DSL line and then separates the types of signals into voice and data signals.

digital video-editing software Programs for editing digital video.

directories Hierarchical structures that include files, folders, and drives used to create a more organized and efficient computer.

Disk Cleanup A Windows utility that removes unnecessary files from the hard drive.

disk defragmenter Utilities that regroup related pieces of files together on the hard disk, enabling faster retrieval of the data.

distributed denial of service (DDoS) attacks Automated attacks that are launched from more than one zombie computer at the same time.

docking station Hardware for connecting a portable computing device to printers, scanners, full-size monitors, mice, and other peripherals.

documentation A description of the development and technical details of a computer program, including how the code works and how the user interacts with the program.

domain name Part of a Uniform Resource Locator (URL). Domain names consist of two parts: the site's host and a three-letter suffix that indicates the type of organization. (Example: popsci.com)

Domain Name System (DNS) server A server that contains location information for domains on the Internet and functions like a phone book for the Internet.

DoS attack *See denial of service (DoS) attack*

dot-matrix printer The first type of computer printer, which has tiny hammer-like keys that strike the paper through an inked ribbon.

dot pitch The diagonal distance, measured in millimeters, between pixels on the screen. A smaller dot pitch means that there is less blank space between pixels, and thus the image is sharper and clearer.

dotted decimal numbers The numbers in an Internet Protocol (IP) address.

double data rate synchronous DRAM (DDR SDRAM) Memory chips that are faster than SDRAM but not as fast as RDRAM.

drawing software (or illustration software) Programs for creating or editing two-dimensional line-based drawings.

drive bays Special shelves inside computers designed to hold storage devices.

Dr. Watson for Windows A tool that is included in Microsoft Windows XP for assistance with program errors.

DSL *See Digital Subscriber Line (DSL)*

DSL/cable routers Routers that are specifically designed to connect to Digital Subscriber Line (DSL) or cable modems.

DSL modem *See Digital Subscriber Line (DSL) modem*

dual-processor A design that has two separate central processing unit (CPU) chips installed on the same system.

DVD disc A method of storage that uses similar optical technology to that which is used to store data on CDs. The difference is that a DVD's storage capacity is much greater than a CD's.

DVD drive A drive that enables the computer to read digital video discs (DVDs). A DVD±R/RW drive can write DVDs as well as read them.

DVD-R/RW One of two recognized DVD formats that enables you to both read and rewrite data on the disc.

DVD+R/RW One of two recognized DVD formats that enables you to both read and rewrite data on the disc.

DVD-RW drive A drive that enables the computer to read and write to DVDs.

Dvorak keyboard A leading alternative keyboard that puts the most commonly used letters in the English language on "home keys," the keys in the middle row of the keyboard. It is designed to reduce the distance your fingers travel for most keystrokes, increasing typing speed.

dynamic addressing The process of assigning Internet Protocol (IP) addresses when users log on using their Internet service provider (ISP). The computer is assigned an address from an available pool of IP addresses.

dynamic decision making Means that a Web page can decide how to display itself, based on the choices the reader makes as she looks at the page.

Dynamic Host Configuration Protocol (DHCP) Handles dynamic addressing. Part of the Transmission Control Protocol/Internet Protocol (TCP/IP) protocol suite, DHCP takes a pool of IP addresses and shares them with hosts on the network on an as-needed basis.

dynamic RAM (DRAM) The most basic type of random access memory (RAM); used in older systems or in systems for which cost is an important factor. DRAM offers access times on the order of 60 nanoseconds.

E

editor A tool that helps programmers as they enter code, highlighting keywords and alerting the programmers to typos.

edutainment software Software that both educates and entertains the user.

electrical switches Devices inside the computer that can be flipped between two states: 1 or 0, on or off.

electronic commerce (e-commerce) Conducting business online for purposes ranging from fund-raising to advertising to selling products.

elements In HyperText Markup Language (HTML), elements are the tags and the text between the tags.

e-mail (electronic mail) Internet-based communication in which senders and recipients correspond.

e-mail clients Software programs that run on the computer and that are used to send and receive e-mail through the ISP's server.

e-mail server A server that processes and delivers incoming and outgoing e-mail.

e-mail virus A virus transmitted by e-mail that often uses the address book in the victim's e-mail system to distribute itself.

embedded computers Specially designed computer chips that reside inside other devices such as your car. These are self-contained computer devices that have their own programming and typically do not receive input from you, nor do they interact with other systems.

encryption The process of encoding data (ciphering) so that only the person with a corresponding decryption key (the intended recipient) can decode (or decipher) and read the message.

encryption virus A malicious program that searches for common data files and compresses them into a file using a complex encryption key, rendering the files unusable.

Enterprise Resource Planning (ERP) systems Software used to control "back-office" operations and processing functions such as billing and inventory management. ERP systems are implemented by third-party vendors and matched directly to the specific needs of a company.

entertainment software Programs designed to provide users with entertainment; computer games make up the vast majority of entertainment software.

Entertainment Software Rating Board (ESRB) A self-regulatory body established in 1994 by the Entertainment Software Association that rates computer and video games according to the age appropriateness of content.

ergonomics Refers to how a user sets up his or her computer and other equipment to minimize risk of injury or discomfort.

Error-Checking A Windows utility that checks for lost files and fragments as well as physical errors on a hard drive.

error handling In programming, the instructions that the program runs if the input data is incorrect or another error is encountered.

Ethernet networks Networks that use the Ethernet protocol as the means (or standard) by which the nodes on the network communicate.

Ethernet port A port that is slightly larger than a standard phone jack and transfers data at speeds of up to 10,000 megabits per second (Mbps). It is used to connect a computer to a cable modem or a network.

event Every keystroke, every mouse click, and each signal to the printer create an action, or event, in the respective device (keyboard, mouse, or printer) to which the operating system responds.

exception reports Reports that show conditions that are unusual or that need attention by users of a system.

executable program The binary sequence (code) that instructs the central processing unit (CPU) to perform certain calculations.

expansion bus An electrical pathway that expands the capabilities of a computer by enabling a range of different expansion cards (such as video cards and sound cards) to communicate with the motherboard.

expansion cards (or adapter cards) Circuit boards with specific functions that augment the computer's basic functions as well as provide connections to other devices.

expansion hub A device that connects to one port, such as a universal serial bus (USB) port, to provide additional new ports, similar to a multiplug extension cord for electrical appliances.

expert system A system designed to replicate the decision-making processes of human experts to solve specific problems.

export Putting data into an electronic file in a format that another application can understand.

ExpressCards Electronic cards that when plugged into notebook computers provide functionality such as wireless network connections, USB ports, or FireWire ports.

Extended Industry Standard Architecture (EISA) bus An older expansion bus for connecting devices such as the mouse, modem, and sound cards.

Extensible HyperText Markup Language (XHTML) A standard established by the World Wide Web Consortium (W3C) that combines elements from both Extensible Markup Language (XML) and HyperText Markup Language (HTML). XHTML has much more stringent rules than HTML does regarding tagging (for instance, all elements require an end tag in XHTML).

Extensible Markup Language (XML) A language that enables designers to define their own tags, making it much easier to transfer data between Web sites and Web servers.

extension (or file type) In a filename, the three letters that follow the user-supplied filename after the dot (.); the extension identifies what kind of family of files the file belongs to or which application should be used to read the file.

external data sources Any source not owned by the company that owns a decision support system, such as customer demographic data purchased from third parties.

external hard drives Internal hard drives that are enclosed in a protective case to make them portable. They are connected to the computer with a data transfer cable and often used to back up data.

extranets Pieces of intranets that only certain corporations or individuals can access. The owner of the extranet decides who will be permitted to access it.

F

Favorites A feature in Microsoft Internet Explorer that places a marker of a Web site's Uniform Resource Locator (URL) in an easily retrievable list in the browser's toolbar. (Called Bookmarks in some browsers.)

fetch The action of a computer program that involves retrieving binary code from a temporary storage location in random access memory (RAM) and moving it to the CPU for execution.

fiber-optic line (or cable) Lines that transmit data at close to the speed of light along glass or plastic fibers.

field Where a category of information in a database is stored. Fields are displayed in columns.

field constraints Properties that must be satisfied for an entry to be accepted into the database field.

field name An identifying name assigned to each field in a database.

field size The maximum number of characters (or numbers) that a field in a database can contain.

fifth-generation languages (5GLs) Considered the most "natural" of languages. With 5GLs, instructions closely resemble human speech or are visual in nature so that little programming knowledge is necessary.

file A collection of related pieces of information stored together for easy reference.

file allocation table (FAT) An index of all sector numbers that the hard drive stores in a table to keep track of which sectors hold which files.

file compression utility A program that takes out redundancies in a file to reduce the file size.

file management Provides organizational structure to the computer's contents.

file path Identifies the exact location of a file, starting with the drive in which the file is located, and including all folders, subfolders (if any), the filename, and extension. (Example: C:\My Documents\Spring 2009\ English Comp\Term Paper\ Illustrations\EBronte.jpg)

file servers Computers deployed to provide remote storage space or to act as a repository for files that users can access.

File Transfer Protocol (FTP) A protocol used to upload and download files from one computer to another over the Internet.

filename The first part of the label applied to a file, similar to our first names; it is generally the name a user assigns to the file when saving it.

financial planning software Programs for managing finances, such as Intuit's Quicken and Microsoft Money, which include electronic checkbook registers and automatic bill payment tools.

firewalls Software programs or hardware devices designed to prevent unauthorized access to computers or networks.

FireWire 400 (IEEE 1394) An interface port that transfers data at 400 Mbps.

FireWire 800 One of the fastest ports available, moving data at 800 megabits per second (Mbps).

FireWire port (previously called the IEEE 1394 port) A port based on a standard developed by the Institute of Electrical and Electronics Engineers (IEEE), with a transfer rate of 400 megabits per second (Mbps). Today, it is most commonly used to connect digital video devices such as digital cameras to the computer.

first-generation languages (1GLs) The actual machine languages of a central processing unit (CPU); the sequence of bits— 1s and 0s—that the CPU understands.

flash drives Drives that plug into a universal serial bus (USB) port on a computer and store data digitally. Also called USB drives.

flash memory Portable, nonvolatile memory.

flash memory card A form of portable storage. This removable memory card is often used in digital cameras, MP3 players, and personal digital assistants (PDAs).

flat-panel monitors (LCD) Monitors that are lighter and more energy-efficient than CRT monitors; often used with portable computers such as notebooks.

floppy disk A portable 3.5-inch storage format, with a storage capacity of 1.44 megabytes (MB).

floppy disk drive A drive that reads and writes floppy disks.

flowcharts Visual representations of the patterns an algorithm comprises.

folder A collection of files stored on a computer.

footprint The amount of physical space on the desk a computer takes up.

For and Next Keywords in Visual Basic to implement a loop.

foreign key The primary key of another database table that is included for purposes of establishing relationships with another table.

frames Containers designed to hold multiple data packets.

freeware Any copyrighted software that can be used for free.

frequently asked questions (FAQs) A list of answers to the most common questions.

front side bus (FSB) The electronic pathway by which data travels between the CPU and RAM.

full installation Installing all the files and programs from the distribution CD to the computer's hard drive.

function keys Shortcut keys that perform special tasks; they are sometimes referred to as the "F" keys because they start with the letter F followed by a number.

fuzzy logic Allows the interjection of experiential learning into the equation by considering probabilities.

G

gadgets Mini-applications that run on the desktop, offering easy access to frequently used tools such as weather or calendar items.

gaming keyboards Keyboards that are optimized for playing specific video games and that contain special keys that perform special functions.

gigabyte (GB) About a billion bytes.

gigahertz (GHz) One billion hertz.

Global Positioning System (GPS) A system of 21 satellites (plus three working spares), built and operated by the U.S. military, that constantly orbit the earth. They provide information to GPS-capable devices to pinpoint locations on the earth.

Graffiti One of the more popular notation systems for entering data into a personal digital assistant (PDA).

graphical user interface (or GUI) Unlike the command- and menu-driven interfaces used earlier, GUIs display graphics and use the point-and-click technology of the mouse and cursor, making them much more user-friendly.

grid computing A form of networking that enables linked computers to use idle processors of other networked computers for complex calculations.

groupware Software that helps people who are in different locations work together using tools such as e-mail, threaded messaging, and online scheduling.

H

hacker (or cracker) Anyone who breaks into a computer system (whether an individual computer or a network) unlawfully.

handshaking The process of two computers exchanging control packets that set up the parameters of a data exchange.

hard disk drive (or hard drive) Holds all permanently stored programs and data; is located inside the system unit.

hardware Any part of the computer you can physically touch.

head crash Impact of read/write head with magnetic platter of the hard disk drive that often results in data loss.

hertz The unit of measure for processor speed, or machine cycles per second.

hexadecimal notation A number system that uses 16 digits to represent numbers; also called a base 16 number system.

hibernation When a computer is in a state of deep sleep. Pushing the power button awakens the computer from hibernation, at which time the computer reloads everything to the desktop exactly as it was before it went into hibernation.

historical data Data that illustrates trends over time.

History list A feature on a browser's toolbar that shows all the Web sites and pages visited over a certain period of time.

hits A list of sites (or results) that match an Internet search.

home page The main or opening page of a Web site.

home phoneline network adapter (or HPNA adapter) A device that attaches to computers and peripherals on a phoneline

network to enable them to communicate using phone lines.

host Organization that maintains the Web server on which a particular Web site is stored.

hot-swappable bays Bays that provide the ability to remove one drive and exchange it with another drive while the computer is running.

HTML *See HyperText Markup Language (HTML)*

HTML embedded scripting language A language used to embed programming language code directly within the HyperText Markup Language (HTML) code of a Web page.

HTML/XHTML embedded scripting language A client-side method of embedding programming language code directly within the HTML/XHTML code of a Web page.

HyperText Transfer Protocol (HTTP) The protocol allows files to be transferred from a Web server so that you can see them on your computer by using a browser.

hubs Simple amplification devices that receive data packets and retransmit them to all nodes on the same network (not between different networks).

hybrid topologies Multiple topologies combined into one network.

hyperlink fields Fields in a database that store hyperlinks to Web pages.

hyperlinks Specially coded text that, when clicked, enables a user to jump from one location, or Web page, to another within a Web site or to another Web site altogether.

hypertext Text that is linked to other documents or media (such as video clips, pictures, and so on).

HyperText Markup Language (HTML) A set of rules for marking up blocks of text so that a Web browser knows how to display them. It uses a series of tags that define the display of text on a Web page.

I

icons Pictures on computer displays that represent an object such as a software application or a file or folder.

identity theft Occurs when someone uses personal information about someone else

(such as the victim's name, address, and social security number) to assume the victim's identity for the purpose of defrauding others.

if else Keywords in the programming language C++; used for binary decisions.

image-editing software (sometimes called photo-editing software) Programs for editing photographs and other images.

impact printers Printers that have tiny hammer-like keys that strike the paper through an inked ribbon, thus making a mark on the paper. The most common impact printer is the dot-matrix printer.

import To bring data into an application from another source.

imported Data that is brought into one program from another program or data source.

Industry Standard Architecture (ISA) bus An older expansion bus used for connecting devices such as the mouse, modem, and sound cards.

information Data that has been organized or presented in a meaningful fashion.

information system A system that includes data, people, procedures, hardware, and software and is used to gather and analyze information.

information technology The set of techniques used in information handling and retrieval of information automatically.

inheritance The ability of a new class of objects to automatically pick up all of the data and methods of an existing class, and then extend and customize those to fit its own specific needs.

initial value A beginning point in a loop.

inkjet printer A nonimpact printer that sprays tiny drops of ink onto paper.

inoculation The process by which the antivirus software records key attributes about files on the computer (such as file size and date created) and keeps these statistics in a safe place on the hard drive so that the software program can compare the files to the attributes it previously recorded to help detect attempts by virus programs to modify the files.

input device Hardware device used to enter, or input, data (text, images, and sounds) and instructions (user responses and commands) into a computer; input devices include keyboards, mice, scanners, microphones, and digital cameras.

input form Provides a view of the data fields to be filled in a database, with appropriate labels to assist database users in populating the database.

instant messaging (IM) services Programs that enable users to communicate in real time with others who are also online.

instruction set The collection of commands a specific central processing unit (CPU) can run.

instructions The steps and tasks the computer needs to process data into usable information.

integrated circuits (or chips) Very small regions of semiconductor material, such as silicon, that support a huge number of transistors.

integrated development environment (IDE) A development tool that helps programmers write, compile, and test their programs.

integrated help Documentation for a software product that is built directly into the software.

integrated software application A single software program that incorporates the most commonly used tools of many productivity software programs into one integrated stand-alone program.

Internet A network of networks and the largest network in the world, connecting millions of computers from more than 100 countries.

Internet 2 An ongoing project sponsored by hundreds of universities (supported by government and industry partners) to develop new Internet technologies and disseminate them as rapidly as possible to the rest of the Internet community. The Internet2 backbone supports extremely high-speed communications.

Internet backbone The main pathway of high-speed communications lines over which all Internet traffic flows.

Internet cache A section of your hard drive that stores information that you may need again for surfing (such as IP addresses and frequently accessed Web pages).

Internet Corporation for Assigned Names and Numbers (ICANN) The organization responsible for allocating IP addresses to network administrators, to ensure they are unique and have not been assigned to other users.

Internet Exchange Points Devices that allow different Internet Service Providers to exchange information between networks.

Internet Explorer (IE) A popular graphical browser from Microsoft Corporation for displaying different Web sites, or locations, on the Web; it can display pictures (graphics) in addition to text, as well as other forms of multimedia, such as sound and video.

Internet hoaxes E-mail messages or Web sites that contain information that is untrue.

Internet Protocol (IP) A protocol for sending data between computers on the Internet.

Internet Protocol address (IP address) The means by which all computers connected to the Internet identify each other. It consists of a unique set of four numbers separated by dots, such as 123.45.178.91.

Internet Protocol version 4 (IPv4) The original IP addressing scheme.

Internet Protocol version 6 (IPv6) A proposed IP addressing scheme that makes IP addresses longer, thereby providing more available IP addresses. It uses eight groups of 16-bit numbers.

Internet service providers (ISPs) Companies that connect individuals, groups, and other companies to the Internet.

Internet telephony Hardware and software that enables people to use the Internet to transmit telephone calls.

interpreter Translates source code into an intermediate form, line by line. Each line is then executed as it is translated.

interrupt A signal that tells the operating system that it is in need of immediate attention.

interrupt table A place in the computer's primary memory (or random access memory, RAM) where interrupt requests are placed.

intranet A private corporate network that is used exclusively by company employees and other authorized users (such as customers) to facilitate information sharing, database access, group scheduling, videoconferencing, or other employee/customer collaboration.

IP *See Internet Protocol (IP)*

IP address *See Internet Protocol address (IP address)*

IrDA port A port based on a standard developed by the Infrared Data Association for transmitting data. IrDA ports transmit data between two devices using infrared light waves, similar to a TV remote control. IrDA ports require that a line of sight be maintained between the two ports.

J

jam signal A special signal sent to all network nodes, alerting them that a data collision has occurred.

Java A platform-independent programming language that Sun Microsystems introduced in the early 1990s. It quickly became popular because its object-oriented model enables Java programmers to benefit from its set of existing classes.

Java applets Small Java-based programs.

JavaScript A programming language often used to add interactivity to Web pages. JavaScript is not as full featured as Java, but its syntax, keywords, data types, and operators are a subset of Java's.

Java Server Pages (JSP) An extension of the Java servlet technology with dynamic scripting capability.

join query A database query that links (or joins) two database tables using a common field in both tables and extracts the relevant data from each.

K

kernel (or supervisor program) The essential component of the operating system, responsible for managing the processor and all other components of the computer system. Because it stays in random access memory (RAM) the entire time the computer is powered on, the kernel is called memory resident.

kernel memory The memory that the computer's operating system uses.

key pair A public and a private key used for coding and decoding encrypted messages.

keyboard A hardware device used to enter typed data and commands into a computer.

keywords (1) Specific words a user wishes to query (or look for) in an Internet search. (2) The set of specific words that have predefined meanings for a particular programming language.

kilobyte (KB) A unit of computer storage equal to approximately 1,000 bytes.

knowledge-based system A support system that provides additional intelligence that supplements the user's own intellect and makes a decision support system (DSS) more effective.

L

label Descriptive text that identifies the components of a spreadsheet.

LANs *See local area networks (LANs)*

laptop computer *See notebook computer*

Large Scale Networking (LSN) A program created by the U.S. government, the objective of which is to fund the research and development of cutting-edge networking technologies. Major goals of the program are the development of enhanced wireless technologies and increased network throughput.

laser printer A nonimpact printer known for quick and quiet production and high-quality printouts.

Last Known Good Configuration A Windows feature that starts the computer by using the registry information that was saved during the last shutdown.

latency (or rotational delay) Occurs after the read/write head of the hard drive locates the correct track, then waits for the correct sector to spin to the read/write head.

legacy technology Comprised of computing devices, software, or peripherals that use techniques, parts, and methods from an earlier time that are no longer popular.

Level 1 cache A block of memory that is built onto the central processing unit

(CPU) chip for the storage of data or commands that have just been used.

Level 2 cache A block of memory that is located either on the central processing unit (CPU) chip or on a separate chip near the CPU. It takes somewhat longer to access than the CPU registers. Level 2 cache contains more storage area than Level 1 cache.

Level 3 cache On computers with Level 3 cache, the central processing unit (CPU) checks this area for instructions and data after it looks in Level 1 and Level 2 cache, but before it looks in random access memory (RAM). The Level 3 cache is often designed to hold between 2 megabytes (MB) and 4 MB of data.

Linux An open-source operating system based on UNIX. Because of the stable nature of this operating system, it is often used on Web servers.

liquid crystal display (LCD) Technology used in flat-panel computer monitors.

listservs Electronic mailing lists of e-mail addresses of people who are interested in a certain topic or area of interest.

Live bookmark A bookmark that delivers updates to you as soon as they become available, using Really Simple Syndication (RSS).

local area networks (LANs) Networks in which the nodes are located within a small geographic area.

local buses Located on the motherboard, these buses run between the central processing unit (CPU) and the main system memory.

logic bombs Computer viruses that run when a certain set of conditions is met, such as specific dates keyed off of the computer's internal clock.

logical port A virtual communications gateway or path that enables a computer to organize requests for information (such as Web page downloads and e-mail routing) from other networks or computers.

logical port blocking When a firewall is configured to ignore all incoming packets that request access to a certain port so that no unwanted requests will get through to the computer.

loop An algorithm that performs a repeating set of actions. A logical yes/no expression is evaluated. As long as the expres-

sion evaluates to TRUE (yes), the algorithm will perform the same set of actions and continue to loop around. When the answer to the question is no, the algorithm breaks free of the looping structure and moves on to the next step.

M

Mac OS Apple Inc.'s operating system. In 1984, Mac OS became the first operating system to incorporate the user-friendly point-and-click technology in a commercially affordable computer. The most recent version of the Mac operating system, Mac OS X, is based on the UNIX operating system. Previous Mac operating systems had been based on Apple's own proprietary program.

machine cycle (or processing cycle) The time it takes to fetch and execute a single machine-level instruction by the central processing unit (CPU).

machine language A set of instructions executed directly by the central processing unit (CPU).

macro viruses Viruses that are distributed by hiding them inside a macro.

macros Small programs that group a series of commands to run as a single command.

magnetic card readers Devices that read information from a magnetic strip on the back of a credit card-like access card (such as a student ID card). The card reader, which can control the lock on a door, is programmed to admit only authorized personnel to the area.

magnetic media Portable storage devices, such as floppy disks and Zip disks, that use a magnetized film to store data.

magnetically shielded microphones Computer microphones that are designed to reduce interference from external sources and that usually plug into a port on the sound card of the computer.

mainframes Large, expensive computers that support hundreds or thousands of users simultaneously.

malware Software that is intended to render a system temporarily or permanently useless or to penetrate a computer system completely for purposes of information gathering. Examples include spyware, viruses, worms, and Trojan horses.

management information system (MIS) A system that provides timely and accurate information that enables managers to make critical business decisions.

mapping programs Software that provides street maps and written directions to locations.

master boot record A small program that runs whenever a computer boots up.

Media Access Control (MAC) address A physical address similar to a serial number on an appliance that is assigned to each network adapter; it is made up of six 2-digit numbers such as 01:40:87:44:79:A5.

megabyte (MB) A unit of computer storage equal to approximately a million bytes.

megahertz (MHz) A measure of processing speed equal to one million hertz.

memo fields Text fields in a database that are used to hold long pieces of text.

memory A component inside the system unit that holds (or stores) the instructions or data that the central processing unit (CPU) processes.

memory bound A system that is limited in how fast it can send data to the central processing unit (CPU) because there's not enough random access memory (RAM) installed.

memory effect The result of a notebook battery needing to be completely used up before it is recharged or it won't hold as much charge as it originally did.

memory modules (or memory cards) Small circuit boards that hold a series of random access memory (RAM) chips.

menu-driven interface A user interface in which the user chooses a command from menus displayed on the screen.

menus Lists of commands that display on the screen.

meta search engine A search engine that searches other search engines rather than individual Web sites.

metadata Data that describes other data.

methods (or behaviors) Actions associated with a class of objects.

metropolitan area networks (MANs) Wide area networks (WANs) that link users in a specific geographic area (such as within a city or county).

microbrowser Software that makes it possible to access the Internet from a cell phone or personal digital assistant (PDA).

microphone A device for capturing sound waves (such as voice) and converting them to an electrical signal.

microprocessors Chips that contain a central processing unit (CPU).

Microsoft Disk Operating System (MS-DOS) A single-user, single-task operating system created by Microsoft. MS-DOS was the first widely installed operating system in personal computers.

Microsoft Transcriber Notation software that doesn't require special strokes and can recognize both printed and cursive writing with fairly decent accuracy.

Microsoft Visual Basic (VB) A powerful programming language used to build a wide range of Windows applications. VB's strengths include a simple, quick interface that is easy for a programmer to learn and use. It has grown from its roots in the language BASIC to become a sophisticated and full-featured object-oriented language.

Microsoft Windows The most popular operating system for desktop computers.

MIDI port *See Musical Instrument Digital Interface (MIDI) port*

MIME *See Multipurpose Internet Mail Extensions (MIME)*

mobile computing devices Portable electronic tools such as cell phones, personal digital assistants (PDAs), and notebooks.

mobile switching center A central location that receives cell phone requests for service from a base station.

model management system Software that assists in building management models in decision support systems (DSSs).

modem card A device that provides the computer with a connection to the Internet via conventional phone lines.

modem port A port that uses a traditional telephone signal to connect a computer to the Internet.

monitor (or display screen) A common output device that displays text, graphics, and video as "soft copies" (copies that can be seen only on-screen).

Moore's Law A mathematical rule, named after Gordon Moore, the cofounder of the central processing unit (CPU) chip manufacturer Intel; the rule predicts that the number of transistors inside a CPU will increase so fast that CPU capacity will double every 18 months.

motherboard A special circuit board in the system unit that contains the central processing unit (CPU), the memory (RAM) chips, and the slots available for expansion cards. It is the largest printed circuit board; all of the other boards (video cards, sound cards, and so on) connect to it to receive power and to communicate.

mouse A device used to enter user responses and commands into a computer.

MP3 player A small portable device for storing MP3 files (digital sound files).

multi-core processing Technology in which two or more processors have been attached to an integrated circuit board for more enhanced computing performance.

multidimensional database A database that stores data in multiple dimensions and is organized in a cube format.

multifunction printer A device that combines the functions of a printer, scanner, fax machine, and copier into one machine.

multimedia Anything that involves one or more forms of media plus text.

Multimedia Message Service (MMS) An extension of Short Message Service (SMS) that enables messages that include text, sound, images, and video clips to be sent from a cell phone or PDA to other phones or e-mail addresses.

multimedia software Programs that include image, video, and audio editing software, animation software, and other specialty software required to produce computer games, animations, and movies.

multipartite viruses Literally meaning "multipart" viruses; a type of computer virus that attempts to infect both the boot sector and executable files at the same time.

Multipurpose Internet Mail Extensions (MIME) A specification that was introduced in 1991 to simplify attachments to e-mail messages. All e-mail client software now uses this protocol for attaching files.

multitasking When the operating system allows a user to perform more than one task at a time.

multiuser operating system (or network operating system) Enables more than one user to access the computer system at one time by efficiently juggling all the requests from multiple users.

Musical Instrument Digital Interface (MIDI) port A port for connecting electronic musical instruments (such as synthesizers) to a computer.

N

nanoscience The study of molecules and nanostructures whose size ranges from 1 to 100 nanometers (one billionth of a meter).

nanotechnology The science revolving around the use of nanostructures to build devices on an extremely small scale.

natural language processing (NLP) system A system that enables users to communicate with computer systems using a natural spoken or written language as opposed to using computer programming languages.

negative acknowledgment (NAK) What computer Y sends to computer X if a packet is unreadable, indicating the packet was not received in understandable form.

netiquette General rules of etiquette for Internet chat rooms and other online communication.

network A group of two or more computers (or nodes) that are configured to share information and resources such as printers, files, and databases.

network adapters Adapters that enable the computer (or peripheral) to communicate with the network using a common data communication language, or protocol.

Network Address Translation (NAT) A process that firewalls use to assign internal Internet Protocol (IP) addresses on a network.

network administrator Someone who has training in computer and peripheral maintenance and repair, network design, and the installation of network software.

network architecture The design of a computer network, which includes both physical and logical design.

network attached storage (NAS) devices Specialized devices attached to a network whose sole function is to store and disseminate data.

network interface card (NIC) An expansion (or adapter) card that enables a computer to connect with a network.

network navigation devices Devices on a network such as routers, hubs, and switches that move data signals around the network.

network operating system (NOS) Software that handles requests for information, Internet access, and the use of peripherals for the rest of the network nodes.

network prefix Part of a network address under the CIDR IP addressing scheme. It consists of a slash and a number added to the end of the last octet in an IP address.

network topology The layout and structure of the network.

NIC *See network interface card (NIC)*

nodes Devices connected to a network, such as a computer, a peripheral (such as a printer), or a communications device (such as a modem).

nonimpact printers Printers that spray ink or use laser beams to make marks on the paper. The most common nonimpact printers are inkjet and laser printers.

nonvolatile storage Permanent storage, as in read-only memory (ROM).

normalization The process of recording data only once in a database to reduce data redundancy.

notebook computer (laptop computer) A powerful mobile computing solution that offers a large display and all of the computing power of a full desktop system.

number system An organized plan for representing a number.

numeric check Confirms that only numbers are entered in a database field.

numeric fields Fields in a database that store numbers.

numeric keypad Section of a keyboard that enables a user to enter numbers quickly.

numeric pagers Paging devices that display only numbers on their screens, telling the user that he or she has received a page and providing the number to call.

Numeric pagers do not allow the user to send a response.

O

object A variable in a program that is an example of a class. Each object in a specific class is constructed from similar data and methods.

object fields Fields in a database that hold objects such as pictures, video clips, or entire documents.

object-oriented analysis An approach to software design that differs from the traditional "top-down" design. In OO analysis, programmers first identify all of the classes (collections of data and methods) that are required to completely describe the problem the program is trying to solve.

object-oriented database A database that stores data in objects, not in tables.

object query language (OQL) A query language that is used to extract information from an object-oriented database.

object-relational database A hybrid between a relational and an object-oriented database. It is based primarily on the relational database model, but it is better able to store and manipulate unstructured data such as audio and video clips.

octet Eight bits. For example, each of the four numbers in the dotted decimal notation of an Internet Protocol (IP) address is represented with an octet.

office support system (OSS) A system (such as Microsoft Office) designed to assist employees in accomplishing their day-to-day tasks and to improve communications.

omnidirectional microphones Microphones that pick up sounds from all directions at once; best for recording more than one voice.

online transaction processing (OLTP) The immediate processing of user requests or transactions.

open-source software Program code made publicly available for free; it can be copied, distributed, or changed without the stringent copyright protections of proprietary software products.

open systems Systems whose designs are public, enabling access by any interested party.

operating system (OS) System software that controls the way in which a computer system functions, including the management of hardware, peripherals, and software.

operators The coding symbols that represent the fundamental actions of a computer language.

optical media Portable storage devices that use a laser to read and write data, such as CDs, DVDs, and Blu-ray discs.

optical mouse A mouse that uses an internal sensor or laser to control the mouse's movement. The sensor sends signals to the computer, telling it where to move the pointer on the screen.

output device A device that sends processed data and information out of a computer in the form of text, pictures (graphics), sounds (audio), or video.

outsource To have work performed by outside vendors of a corporation, which could include sourcing work in other countries (offshoring).

P

packet A small segment of data that is bundled to be sent over transmission media. Each packet contains the address of the computer or peripheral device to which it is being sent.

packet filtering A process that firewalls perform to filter out packets sent to specific logical ports.

packet screening Involves examining incoming data packets to ensure they originated from or are authorized by valid users on the internal network.

packet sniffer A program that looks at (or sniffs) each data packet as it travels on the Internet.

packet switching A communications methodology in which data is broken into small chunks (called packets) and sent over various routes at the same time. When the packets reach their destination, they are reassembled by the receiving computer.

page file The file the operating system builds on the hard drive when it is using virtual memory to enable processing to continue.

paging If the data or instructions that have been placed in the swap file are needed later, the operating system swaps them back into active random access memory (RAM) and replaces them in the hard drive's swap file with less active data or instructions.

Palm OS One of the two main operating systems for personal digital assistants (PDAs).

parallel port A port that sends data between devices in groups of bits at speeds of 92 kilobits per second (Kbps). Parallel ports were commonly used to connect printers to computers.

parallel processing A network computer environment in which each computer works on a portion of the same problem simultaneously.

Pascal The only modern computer language that was specifically designed as a teaching language; it is seldom taught at the college level any longer.

passive-matrix displays Computer monitor technology in which electrical current passes through a liquid crystal solution and charges groups of pixels, either in a row or a column. This causes the screen to brighten with each pass of electrical current and subsequently to fade.

passive topology When data merely travels the entire length of the communications medium and is received by all network devices.

path (or subdirectory) The information following the slash or colon in a Uniform Resource Locator (URL).

path separators The backslash marks (\) used by Microsoft Windows and DOS in file names. Mac files use a colon (:), and UNIX and Linux use the forward slash (/) as the path separator.

patient simulator A computer-controlled mannequin that simulates human body functions and reactions. Patient simulators are used in training doctors, nurses, and emergency services personnel by simulating dangerous situations that would normally put live patients at risk.

PC cards (or PCMCIA, short for Personal Computer Memory Card International Association) Credit card–sized cards that enable users to add fax modems, network connections, wireless adapters, USB 2.0 and FireWire ports, and other capabilities primarily to notebook computers.

PDA *See personal digital assistant (PDA)*

peer-to-peer (P2P) network A network in which each node connected to the network can communicate directly with every other node on the network.

peer-to-peer (P2P) sharing The process of users transferring files between computers.

Peripheral Component Interconnect (PCI) buses Expansion buses that connect directly to the central processing unit (CPU) and support such devices as network cards and sound cards. They have been the standard bus for much of the past decade and continue to be redesigned to increase their performance.

peripheral devices Devices such as monitors, printers, and keyboards that connect to the system unit through ports.

personal area networks (PANs) Networks used to connect wireless devices (such as Bluetooth-enabled devices) in close proximity to each other.

personal digital assistant (PDA) A small device that enables a user to carry digital information. Often called palm computers or handhelds, PDAs are about the size of a hand and usually weigh less than 5 ounces.

personal firewalls Firewalls specifically designed for home networks.

personal information manager (PIM) software Programs such as Microsoft Outlook or Lotus Organizer that strive to replace the various management tools found on a traditional desk, such as a calendar, address book, notepad, and to-do lists.

Personal Shopper System (PSS) A small handheld computer that enables individuals to scan products, get information about products, and check out in one easy step.

phishing The process of sending e-mail messages to lure Internet users into revealing personal information such as credit card or social security numbers or other sensitive information that could lead to identity theft.

PHP Hypertext Preprocessor A programming language for creating dynamic content that interacts efficiently with databases.

physical memory The amount of random access memory (RAM) that is installed in a computer.

pipelining A technique that enables the central processing unit (CPU) to work on more than one instruction (or stage of processing) at a time, thereby boosting CPU performance.

pixels Single points that create the images on a computer monitor. Pixels are illuminated by an electron beam that passes back and forth across the back of the screen very quickly so that the pixels appear to glow continuously.

platform The combination of a computer's operating system and processor. The two most common platform types are the PC and the Apple Macintosh.

platters Thin, round metallic plates stacked onto the hard disk drive spindle.

plotters Large printers that use a computer-controlled pen to produce oversize pictures that require precise continuous lines to be drawn, such as in maps or architectural plans.

Plug and Play (PnP) Technology that enables the operating system, once the system is booted up, to recognize automatically any new peripherals and configure them to work with the system.

plug-in (or player) A small software program that "plugs in" to a Web browser to enable a specific function; for example, to view and hear certain multimedia files on the Web.

Pocket PC (formerly Windows CE) One of the two main operating systems for personal digital assistants (PDAs), made by Microsoft.

podcast A clip of audio or video content that is broadcast over the Internet using compressed audio or video files in formats such as MP3s.

point of presence (POP) A bank of modems through which many users can connect to an Internet service provider (ISP) simultaneously.

polymorphic viruses A virus that changes its virus signature (the binary pattern that makes the virus identifiable) every time it infects a new file. This makes it more difficult for antivirus programs to detect the virus.

pop-up windows Windows that pop up when you install freeware programs or enter Web sites. They often offer "useful" information or tout products.

port An interface through which external devices are connected to the computer.

portability The capability to move a completed solution easily from one type of computer to another.

portable media player (PMP) A small portable device (such as an iPod) that enables you to carry your MP3 files around with you.

portal A subject directory on the Internet that is part of a larger Web site that focuses on offering its visitors a variety of information, such as the weather, news, sports, and shopping guides.

positive acknowledgment (ACK) What computer Y sends when it receives a data packet that it can read from computer X.

possessed object Any object that a user carries to identify himself and that grants him access to a computer system or computer facility.

powerline network Network that uses the electrical wiring in a home to connect the nodes in the network.

power-on self-test (POST) The first job the basic input/output system (BIOS) performs, ensuring that essential peripheral devices are attached and operational. This process consists of a test on the video card and video memory, a BIOS identification process (during which the BIOS version, manufacturer, and data are displayed on the monitor), and a memory test to ensure memory chips are working properly.

power supply Used to regulate the wall voltage to the voltages required by computer chips; it is housed inside the system unit.

preemptive multitasking When the operating system processes the task assigned a higher priority before processing a task that has been assigned a lower priority.

presentation software An application program for creating dynamic slide shows, such as Microsoft PowerPoint or Corel Presentations.

pretexting The act of creating an invented scenario (the pretext) to convince someone to divulge information.

Pretty Good Privacy (PGP) A public-key encryption package.

primary key (or key field) The unique field that each database record in a table must have.

print server A server that manages all client-requested printing jobs for all printers on the network.

printer A common output device that creates tangible or hard copies of text and graphics.

private key One-half of a pair of binary files that is needed to decrypt an encrypted message. The private key is kept only by the individual who created the key pair and is never distributed to anyone else. The private key is used to decrypt messages created with the corresponding public key.

private-key encryption A procedure in which only the two parties involved in sending a message have the code. This could be a simple shift code where letters of the alphabet are shifted to a new position.

problem statement A very clear description of which tasks the computer program must accomplish and how the program will execute these tasks and respond to unusual situations. It is the starting point of programming work.

processing Manipulating data into information.

processor speed The number of operations (or cycles) the processor completes each second, measured in hertz (Hz).

productivity software Programs that enable a user to perform various tasks generally required in home, school, and business. This category includes word processing, spreadsheet, presentation, personal information management (PIM), and database programs.

program A series of instructions to be followed by a computer to accomplish a task.

program development life cycle (PDLC) A number of stages, from conception to final deployment, a programming project follows.

programming The process of translating a task into a series of commands a computer will use to perform that task.

programming language A kind of "code" for the set of instructions the central processing unit (CPU) knows how to perform.

project management software An application program such as Microsoft Project that helps project managers easily create and modify project management scheduling charts.

proprietary software A program that is owned and controlled by the company it is created by or for.

proprietary (or private) systems Systems whose design is not made available for public access.

protocol (1) A set of rules for exchanging data and communication. (2) The first part of the Uniform Resource Locator (URL) indicating the set of rules used to retrieve the specified document. The protocol is generally followed by a colon, two forward slashes, www (indicating World Wide Web), and then the domain name.

prototype A small model of a computer program, often built at the beginning of a large project.

proxy server Acts as a go-between for computers on the internal network and the external network (the Internet).

pseudocode A text-based approach to documenting an algorithm.

public domain The status of software (or other created works) which are not protected by copyright.

public key One-half of a pair of binary files that is needed to decrypt an encrypted message. After creating the keys, the user distributes the public key to anyone he wishes to send him encrypted messages. A message encrypted with a public key can be unencrypted only using the corresponding private key.

public-key encryption A procedure in which the key for coding is generally distributed as a public key that may be placed on a Web site. Anyone wishing to send a message codes it using the public key. The recipient decodes the message with a private key.

Q

quarantining The placing of a computer virus by antivirus software in a secure area

on the hard drive so that it won't spread infection to other files.

query The process of requesting information from a database.

query language Language used to retrieve and display records. A query language consists of its own vocabulary and sentence structure, used to frame the requests.

queue The organization of printer requests so that the printer can process the requests in order.

QWERTY keyboard A keyboard that gets its name from the first six letters on the top-left row of alphabetic keys on the keyboard.

R

radio frequency identification tags (RFID tags) Tags that look like stickers or labels, are attached to batches of merchandise, and contain a microchip that holds a unique sequence of numbers used to identify the product to which it is attached.

random access memory (RAM) The computer's temporary storage space or short-term memory. It is located as a set of chips on the system unit's motherboard, and its capacity is measured in megabytes and gigabytes.

range checks A type of data validation used in databases to ensure that a value entered falls within a specified range (such as requiring a person's age to fall in a range of between 1 and 120).

rapid application development (RAD) A method of system development in which developers create a prototype first and generate system documents as they use and remodel the product.

read-only memory (ROM) A set of memory chips located on the motherboard that stores data and instructions that cannot be changed or erased; it holds all the instructions the computer needs to start up.

read/write heads The read/write heads are mechanisms that retrieve (read) and record (write) the magnetic data to and from the data disk. They move from the outer edge of the spinning platters to the center, up to 50 times per second.

real-time operating system (RTOS) A program with a specific purpose that must

guarantee certain response times for particular computing tasks, or the machine's application is useless. Real-time operating systems are found in many types of robotic equipment.

real-time processing The process of updating a database (or information system) immediately as changes are made.

record A collection of related fields in a database.

Recycle Bin A folder on a Windows desktop where deleted files from the hard drive reside until permanently purged from the system.

referential integrity For each value in the foreign key of one table, there is a corresponding value in the primary key of the related table.

refresh rate (or vertical refresh rate) The number of times per second an electron beam scans the monitor and recharges the illumination of each pixel.

registers Special memory storage areas built into the central processing unit (CPU).

registry Contains all the different configurations (settings) used by the operating system (OS) as well as by other applications.

relational algebra The use of English-like expressions that have variables and operations, much like algebraic equations.

relational database Organizes data in table format by logically grouping similar data into relations (or tables) that contain related data.

relations Database tables that contain related data.

relationships In relational databases, the links between tables that define how the data are related.

repeaters Devices that are installed on long cable runs to amplify a signal.

resolution The clearness or sharpness of an image, which is controlled by the number of pixels displayed on the screen.

response rate The measurement (in milliseconds) of the time it takes for a pixel to change color; the lower the response time, the smoother moving images will appear on the monitor.

restore point The snapshot of the entire system's settings that Windows creates every time the computer is started, or when a new application or driver is installed.

reusability The ability to reuse existing classes of objects from other projects, enabling programmers to produce new code quickly.

ring (or loop) topology Networked computers and peripherals that are laid out in a logical circle. Data flows around the circle from device to device in one direction only.

ROM *See read-only memory (ROM)*

root directory The top level of the filing structure in a computer system. In Windows computers, the root directory of the hard drive is represented as C:\.

root DNS servers A group of servers maintained throughout the Internet that ISP Web servers contact to locate the master listings for an entire top-level domain.

routers Devices that route packets of data between two or more networks.

runtime (or logic) errors The kinds of errors in the problem logic that are only caught when the program executes.

S

safe mode A special diagnostic mode designed for troubleshooting errors that occur during the boot process.

sampling rate The number of times per second a signal is measured and converted to a digital value. Sampling rates are measured in kilobits per second.

SANs *See storage area networks (SANs)*

satellite Internet A way to connect to the Internet using a small satellite dish, which is placed outside the home and connects to a computer with coaxial cable. The satellite company then sends the data to a satellite orbiting the earth. The satellite, in turn, sends the data back to the satellite dish and to the computer.

scalable network A type of network that enables the easy addition of users without affecting the performance of the other network nodes (computers or peripherals).

screen savers Animated images that appear on a computer monitor when no

user activity has been sensed for a certain time.

script kiddies Amateur hackers without sophisticated computer skills; typically teenagers, who don't create programs used to hack into computer systems but instead use tools created by skilled hackers that enable unskilled novices to wreak the same havoc as professional hackers.

scripting languages Simple programming languages that are limited to performing a specific set of specialized tasks.

scripts Lists of commands (mini-programs or macros) that can be executed on a computer without user interaction.

scrollbars On the desktop, bars that appear at the side or bottom of the window that control which part of the information is displayed on the screen.

search engine A set of programs that searches the Web for specific words (or keywords) you wish to query (or look for) and then returns a list of the Web sites on which those keywords are found.

second-generation languages (2GLs) Also known as assembly languages. 2GLs deal directly with system hardware but provide acronyms that are easier for human programmers to work with.

second-level domains Domains that fall within top-level domains of the Internet. Each second-level domain needs to be unique within that particular domain, but not necessarily unique to all top-level domains.

sectors A section of a hard disk drive platter, wedge-shaped from the center of the platter to the edge.

Secure HyperText Transfer Protocol (S-HTTP) An extension to the HTTP protocol that supports sending data securely over the Web.

Secure Sockets Layer (SSL) A protocol that provides for the encryption of data transmitted using the Internet. The current versions of all major Web browsers support SSL.

seek time The time it takes for the hard drive's read/write heads to move over the surface of the disk, between tracks, to the correct track.

select query A query that displays a subset of data from a table based on the criteria the user specifies.

semiconductor Any material that can be controlled to either conduct electricity or act as an insulator (not allowing electricity to pass through).

serial port A port that enables the transfer of data, one bit at a time, over a single wire at speeds of up to 56 kilobits per second (Kbps); it is often used to connect external modems to the computer.

server A computer that provides resources to other computers on a network.

server-side application A program that runs on the Web server as opposed to running inside a browser on a client computer.

server-side program Programs that are run on a Web server as opposed to inside a Web browser.

shareware Software that enables users to "test" the software by running it for a limited time free of charge.

shielded twisted pair (STP) cable Twisted pair cable that contains a layer of foil shielding to reduce interference.

Short Message Service (SMS) (or text messaging) Technology that enables short text messages (up to 160 characters) to be sent over mobile networks.

shoulder surfing The process of looking over someone's shoulder while the person types in an effort to obtain passwords or other access codes.

sidebar In Windows Vista, the pane on the right side of the desktop that organizes gadgets for easy access.

sign bit In the binary (base 2) system, the representation of a negative number; usually the left-most bit.

Simple Mail Transfer Protocol (SMTP) A protocol for sending e-mail along the Internet to its destination.

single-user, multitask operating system An operating system that allows only one person to work on a computer at a time, but the system can perform a variety of tasks simultaneously.

single-user, single-task operating system An operating system that allows only one user to work on a computer at a time to perform just one task at a time.

smartphone A device that combines the functionality of a cell phone, a PMP, and a PDA into one unit.

SMTP *See Simple Mail Transfer Protocol (SMTP)*

social engineering A group of hacking techniques that rely on weaknesses in people rather than in information systems. Activities normally include tricking people into divulging sensitive information through ordinary communication means such as conversations and e-mail.

social networking A system of connections between people, supported by electronic tools such as e-mail, instant messaging, and file transfer.

software The set of computer programs or instructions that tells the computer what to do and enables it to perform different tasks.

software license An agreement between the user and the software developer that must be accepted prior to installing the software on a computer.

software piracy Violating a software license agreement by copying an application onto more computers than the license agreement permits.

software suite A collection of software programs that have been bundled together as a package.

software updates (or service packs) Small downloadable software modules that repair errors identified in commercial program code.

sort (or index) The process of organizing a database into a particular order.

sound card An expansion card that attaches to the motherboard inside the system unit and that enables the computer to produce sounds.

source code The instructions programmers write in a higher-level language.

spam Unwanted or junk e-mail.

spam filter An option you can select in your e-mail account that places known or suspected spam messages into a folder other than your inbox.

speech-recognition software (or voice-recognition software) Software that translates spoken words into typed text.

spider (or crawler or bot) A program that constantly collects information on the Web, following links in Web sites and reading Web pages. Spiders get their name because they crawl over the Web using multiple "legs" to visit many sites simultaneously.

spooler A program that helps coordinate all print jobs being sent to the printer at the same time.

spreadsheet software An application program such as Microsoft Excel or Lotus 1-2-3 that enables a user to do calculations and numerical analyses easily.

speakers An output device used for sound; included with most computers.

speech-recognition systems Software that enables a computer to operate via directions given verbally through a microphone, telling it to perform specific commands (such as to open a file) or to translate spoken words into data input.

spyware An unwanted piggyback program that downloads with the software you want to install from the Internet and then runs in the background of your system.

SSL *See Secure Sockets Layer (SSL)*

Stand By mode When a computer's more power-hungry components, such as the monitor and hard drive, are powered down to save energy.

star topology The most widely deployed client/server network layout in businesses. In a star topology, the nodes connect to a central communications device called a switch. The switch receives a signal from the sending node and retransmits it to the node that should receive it. Because the switch retransmits data signals, a star topology is an active topology.

statements Sentences in programming code.

static addressing Assigning an Internet Protocol (IP) address for a computer that never changes and is most likely assigned manually by a network administrator.

static RAM (SRAM) A type of random access memory that is faster than DRAM. In SRAM, more transistors are used to store a single bit, but no capacitor is needed.

stealth viruses Viruses that temporarily erase their code from the files where they reside and hide in the active memory of the computer.

storage area networks (SANs) A network specifically designed to store and disseminate large amounts of data to client computers or servers.

storage devices Devices such as hard disk drives, floppy disk drives, and CD drives used for storing data and information.

streaming audio Technology that enables audio files to be fed to a browser continuously. This lets users avoid having to download the entire file before listening.

streaming video Technology that enables video files to be fed to a browser continuously. This lets users avoid having to download the entire file before viewing.

structured (analytical) data Data that can be identified and classified as discrete bits of information (such as a name or phone number). Unstructured data includes non-traditional data such as audio clips (including MP3 files), video clips, and pictures that must be viewed in their entirety as opposed to discrete segments.

Structured Query Language (SQL) The most popular database query language today.

stylus A device used to tap or write on touch-sensitive screens.

subject directory A structured outline of Web sites organized by topics and subtopics.

subnotebook computers A category of computers that consists of notebooks that weigh 4 pounds or less.

subwoofer A special type of speaker designed to more faithfully reproduce low-frequency sounds.

summary data report *See summary report*

summary report A report that summarizes data in some fashion (such as a total of the day's concession sales at an amusement park).

supercomputers Specially designed computers that can perform complex calculations extremely rapidly. They are used in situations in which complex models requiring intensive mathematical calculations are needed (such as weather forecasting or atomic energy research).

Surround sound Speaker systems set up in such a way that they surround an entire area (and the people in it) with sound.

swap file (or page file) A temporary storage area on the hard drive where the operating system "swaps out" or moves the data or instructions from random access memory (RAM) that have not recently been used. This process takes place when more RAM space is needed.

switch A device for transmitting data on a network. A switch makes decisions, based on the Media Access Control (MAC) address of the data, as to where the data is to be sent.

Symbian OS A popular operating system for full-featured cell phones.

Symmetrical Digital Subscriber Line (SDSL) A Digital Subscriber Line (DSL) transmission that uploads and downloads data at the same speed.

synchronizing The process of updating data so that the files on different systems are the same.

syntax An agreed-upon set of rules defining how a programming language must be structured.

syntax errors Violations of the strict, precise set of rules that define a programming language.

system clock A computer's internal clock.

system development life cycle (SDLC) An organized process (or set of steps) for developing an information processing system.

system evaluation The process of looking at a computer's subsystems, what they do, and how they perform to determine whether the computer system has the right hardware components to do what the user ultimately wants it to do.

system files The main files of the operating system.

system requirements Minimum storage, memory capacity, and processing standards recommended by the software manufacturer to ensure proper operation of a software application.

System Restore A utility in Windows that restores system settings to a specific previous date when everything was working properly.

system software The set of programs that enables a computer's hardware devices and application software to work together; it includes the operating system and utility programs.

system unit The metal or plastic case that holds all the physical parts of the computer together, including the computer's processor (its brains), its memory, and the many circuit boards that help the computer function.

T

T lines High-speed fiber-optic communications lines that are designed to provide much higher throughput than conventional voice (telephone) and data (DSL) lines.

T-1 lines High-speed fiber-optic communications lines that can support 24 simultaneous voice or data channels and achieve a maximum throughput of 1.544 megabits per second (Mbps).

T-2 lines High-speed fiber-optic communications lines composed of four T-1 lines that deliver a throughput of approximately 6.3 megabits per second (Mbps).

table In database terminology, a group of related records.

Tablet PC A portable computer designed specifically to work with handwriting recognition technology.

tags In HyperText Markup Language (HTML), a way to indicate how the text should look (such as < b > and < /b > to indicate boldface text).

Task Manager utility A Windows utility that shows programs currently running and permits you to exit nonresponsive programs when you click End Task.

Task Scheduler utility A Windows utility that enables you to schedule tasks to run automatically at predetermined times, with no interaction necessary on your part.

tax-preparation software An application program such as Intuit's TurboTax and H&R Block's TaxCut for preparing state and federal taxes. Each program offers a complete set of tax forms and instructions as well as expert advice on how to complete each form.

TCP/IP *See Transmission Control Protocol/Internet Protocol (TCP/IP)*

Telnet Both a protocol for connecting to a remote computer and a Transmission Control Protocol/Internet Protocol (TCP/IP) service that runs on a remote computer to make it accessible to other computers.

templates Forms included in many productivity applications that provide the basic structure for a particular kind of document, spreadsheet, or presentation.

terminator A device that absorbs a signal so that it is not reflected back onto parts of the network that have already received it.

test condition A check to see whether a loop is completed.

testing plan In the problem statement, a plan that lists specific input numbers that the program would typically expect the user to enter. It then lists the precise output values that a perfect program would return for those input values.

text fields Fields in a database that can hold any combination of alphanumeric data (letters or numbers) and are most often used to hold text.

thermal printer A printer that works by either melting wax-based ink onto ordinary paper (in a process called thermal wax transfer printing) or by burning dots onto specially coated paper (in a process called direct thermal printing).

third-generation languages (3GLs, or high-level languages) Computer languages that use symbols and commands to help programmers tell the computer what to do, making 3GL languages easier to read and remember. Programmers are relieved of the burden of having to understand everything about the hardware of the computer to give it directions. In addition, 3GLs enable programmers to name storage locations in memory with their own names so they are more meaningful to them.

thrashing A condition of excessive paging in which the operating system becomes sluggish.

three-way handshake A process the Transmission Control Protocol (TCP) uses to establish a connection.

throughput The actual speed of data transfer that is achieved. It is usually less than the data transfer rate and is measured in megabits per second (Mbps).

time bombs Viruses that are triggered by the passage of time or on a certain date.

time-variant data Data that doesn't all pertain to one period in time, such as data in a data warehouse.

toggle key A keyboard key whose function changes each time it's pressed; it "toggles" between two or more functions.

token A special data packet used to pass data in a token-ring network.

token method The access method that ring networks use to avoid data collisions.

token-ring topology A network layout in which data is passed using a special data packet called a token.

toolbars On the desktop, groups of icons collected together in a small box.

top-down design A systematic approach in which a programming problem is broken down into a series of high-level tasks.

top-level domain (TLD) The three-letter suffix in the domain name (such as .com or .edu) that indicates the kind of organization the host is.

touch-screen monitors A monitor (or display in a notebook or PDA) that accepts input from a user touching the screen.

touchpad A small, touch-sensitive screen at the base of the keyboard. To use the touchpad, you simply move your finger across the pad to direct the cursor.

trackball mouse A mouse with a rollerball on top instead of on the bottom. Because you move the trackball with your fingers, it doesn't require much wrist motion, so it's considered healthier for your wrists than a traditional mouse.

trackpoint device A small, joystick-like nub that enables you to move the cursor with the tip of your finger.

tracks Concentric circles on a hard disk drive platter.

transaction processing system (TPS) A system used to keep track of everyday business activities (such as sales of products).

transceiver In a wireless network, a device that translates the electronic data that needs to be sent along the network into radio waves and then broadcasts these radio waves to other network nodes.

transistors Electrical switches that are built out of layers of a special type of material called a semiconductor.

Transmission Control Protocol/Internet Protocol (TCP/IP) The main suite of protocols used on the Internet.

transmission media The radio waves or cable that transport data on a network.

Trojan horse A computer program that appears to be something useful or desirable (such as a game or a screen saver), but at the same time does something malicious in the background without the user's knowledge.

twisted pair wiring (or twisted pair cable) Cables made of copper wires that are twisted around each other and are surrounded by a plastic jacket (such as traditional home phone wire).

U

ultraportable (subnotebook) computers A category of computers consisting of notebooks that weigh 4 pounds or less.

Unicode An encoding scheme that uses 16 bits instead of the 8 bits used in ASCII. Unicode can represent more than 65,000 unique character symbols, enabling it to represent the alphabets of all modern languages and all historic languages and notational systems.

unidirectional microphones Microphones that pick up sound from only one direction. These are best used for recording podcasts with a single voice or making phone calls over the Internet.

Uniform Resource Locator (URL) A Web site's unique address, such as www.microsoft.com.

universal serial bus (USB) port A port that can connect a wide variety of peripherals to the computer, including keyboards, printers, flash drives, and digital cameras. USB 2.0 transfers data at 480 megabits per second (Mbps) and is approximately 40 times faster than the original USB port.

UNIX An operating system originally conceived in 1969 by Ken Thompson and Dennis Ritchie of AT&T's Bell Labs. In 1974, the UNIX code was rewritten in the standard programming language C. Today there are various commercial versions of UNIX.

unshielded twisted pair (UTP) cable The most popular transmission media option for Ethernet networks. UTP cable is composed of four pairs of wires that are twisted around each other to reduce electrical interference.

unstructured data Nontraditional database data such as audio clips (including MP3 files), video clips, pictures, and extremely large documents. Data of this type is known as a binary large object (BLOB) because it is actually encoded in binary form.

URL *See Uniform Resource Locator (URL)*

USB *See universal serial bus (USB) port*

USB 2.0 External bus that supports a data throughput of 480 megabits per second (Mbps). These buses are backward compatible with buses using the original universal serial bus (USB) standard.

User Datagram Protocol (UDP) A protocol that prepares data for transmission but has no re-sending capabilities.

user interface Part of the operating system that enables individuals to interact with the computer.

Utility Manager A utility in the Accessories folder of Windows XP that enables you to magnify the screen image; you can also have screen contents read out loud or you can display an on-screen keyboard.

utility programs Small programs that perform many of the general housekeeping tasks for the computer, such as system maintenance and file compression.

V

vacuum tubes Used in early computers, vacuum tubes act as computer switches by allowing or blocking the flow of electrical current.

validation The process of ensuring that data entered into a database is correct (or at least reasonable) and complete.

validation rules Rules that are set up in a database to alert the user to possible wrong entries.

variable declaration Alerts the operating system that the program needs to allocate storage space in random access memory (RAM) for the variable.

variables A name or symbol that stands for a value.

VBScript A subset of Visual Basic; also used to introduce interactivity to Web pages.

vertical market software Software that is developed for and customized to a specific industry's needs (such as a wood inventory system for a sawmill) as opposed to software that is useful across a range of industries (such as word-processing software).

video card (or video adapter) An expansion card that is installed inside a system unit to translate binary data (the 1s and 0s the computer uses) into the images viewed on the monitor.

video logs (vlogs or video blogs) Personal online journals that use video as the primary content in addition to text, images, and audio.

video memory RAM that is included as part of a video card.

videoconferencing Technology that enables a person sitting at a computer and equipped with a personal video camera and a microphone to transmit video and audio across the Internet (or other communications medium). All computers participating in a videoconference need to have a microphone and speakers installed so that participants can speak to and hear one another.

viewing angle The distance you can move to the side of (or above or below) the monitor before the image quality degrades to unacceptable levels.

virtual memory The space on the hard drive where the operating system stores data if there isn't enough random access memory (RAM) to hold all of the programs you're currently trying to run.

virtual private network (VPN) Utilizes the public Internet communications infrastructure to build a secure, private network between various locations.

virtual reality programs Software that turns an artificial environment into a realistic experience.

virus A computer program that attaches itself to another computer program (known as the host program) and attempts

to spread itself to other computers when files are exchanged.

virus signatures Portions of the virus code that are unique to a particular computer virus and make it identifiable by antivirus software.

visual programming A technique for automatically writing code when the programmer says the layout is complete. It helps programmers produce a final application much more quickly.

Voice over IP (VoIP) The transmission of phone calls over the same data lines and networks that make up the Internet. Also called Internet telephony.

volatile storage Temporary storage, such as in random access memory (RAM); when the power is off, the data in volatile storage is cleared out.

VPN *See virtual private network (VPN)*

WAN *See wide area network (WAN)*

WAP *See Wireless Application Protocol (WAP)*

warm boot The process of restarting the system while it's powered on.

Web 2.0 Tools and Web-based services that emphasize online collaboration and sharing among users.

Web-based application software A program that is hosted on a Web site and does not require installation on the computer.

Web browser Software that enables a user to access the Web and display Web pages.

Webcast The broadcast of audio or video content over the Internet. Unlike podcasts, Webcasts are not updated automatically.

Web-enabled The capability of a device, such as a desktop computer, notebook, or mobile device, to access the Internet.

Weblog (or blog) Personal logs, or journal entries, that are posted on the Web.

Web browser (browser) Software installed on a computer system that allows individuals to locate, view, and navigate the Web.

webcams Small cameras that usually sit on top of a computer monitor (connected to the computer by a cable) or are built

into a notebook computer; usually used to transfer live video.

Web page authoring software Programs you can use to design interactive Web pages without knowing any HyperText Markup Language (HTML) code.

Web server A computer running a specialized operating system that enables it to host Web pages (and other information) and provide requested Web pages to clients.

Web services Programs that a Web site uses to make information available to other Web sites.

Web site A location on the Web.

white-hat hackers Hackers who break into systems just for the challenge of it (and who don't wish to steal or wreak havoc on the systems). They tout themselves as experts who are performing a needed service for society by helping companies realize the vulnerabilities that exist in their systems.

wide area network (WAN) A network made up of local area networks (LANs) connected over long distances.

Wi-Fi (Wireless Fidelity) The 802.11 standard for wireless data transmissions established by the Institute of Electrical and Electronics Engineers (IEEE).

wiki A type of Web site that allows anyone visiting the site to change its content by adding, removing, or editing the content.

wildcards Symbols used in an Internet search when the user is unsure of the keyword's spelling or when a word can be spelled in different ways or can contain different endings. The asterisk (*) is used to replace a series of letters and the percent sign (%) to replace a single letter in a word.

windows In a graphical user interface, rectangular boxes that contain programs displayed on the screen.

Windows Explorer The program in Microsoft Windows that helps a user manage files and folders by showing the location and contents of every drive, folder, and file on the computer.

Windows key A function key specific to the Windows operating system. Used alone, it brings up the Start menu; however, it's used most often in combination with other keys as shortcuts.

Windows Mobile An operating system for smartphones.

wireless access point A device similar to a switch in an Ethernet network. It takes the place of a wireless network adapter and helps to relay data between network nodes.

Wireless Application Protocol (WAP) The standard that dictates how handheld devices will access information on the Internet.

wireless Internet service provider Providers such as Verizon or T-Mobile that offer their subscribers wireless access to the Internet.

Wireless Markup Language (WML) A format for writing content viewed on a cellular phone or personal digital assistant (PDA) that is text-based and contains no graphics.

wireless media Communications media that do not use cables but instead rely on radio waves to communicate.

wireless network A network that uses radio waves instead of wires or cable as its transmission medium.

wireless network adapter Devices that are required for each node on a wireless network for the node to be able to communicate with other nodes on the network.

wireless network interface cards (wireless NICs) Cards installed in a system that connect with wireless access points on the network.

wireless router (gateway) A device that combines the capabilities of a wired router with the ability to receive wireless signals.

wizards Step-by-step guides that walk you through the necessary steps to complete a complicated task.

WML *See Wireless Markup Language (WML)*

word-processing software Programs used to create and edit written documents such as papers, letters, and résumés.

word size The number of bits a computer can work with at a time.

World Wide Web (WWW or Web) The part of the Internet used the most. What distinguishes the Web from the rest of the Internet is (1) its use of common communication protocols (such as Transmission Control Protocol/Internet Protocol, or TCP/IP) and special languages (such as the HyperText Markup Language, or HTML) that enable different computers to talk to each other and display information in compatible formats, and (2) its use of special links (called hyperlinks) that enable users to jump from one place to another in the Web.

worm A program that attempts to travel between systems through network connections to spread infections. Worms can run independently of host file execution and are active in spreading themselves.

WWW *See World Wide Web (WWW or Web)*

XML *See Extensible Markup Language (XML)*

Zip disk drive A drive that resembles a floppy disk drive but has a slightly wider opening; these drives are becoming legacy technology.

zombies Computers that are controlled by hackers who use them to launch attacks on other computer systems.